W9-BMQ-042

ISSUES FOR DEBATE IN
AMERICAN PUBLIC POLICY

ISSUES FOR DEBATE IN AMERICAN PUBLIC POLICY

SELECTIONS FROM CQ RESEARCHER

14TH EDITION

Los Angeles | London | New Delhi
Singapore | Washington DC

Los Angeles | London | New Delhi
Singapore | Washington DC

FOR INFORMATION:

CQ Press

An Imprint of SAGE Publications, Inc.

2455 Teller Road

Thousand Oaks, California 91320

E-mail: order@sagepub.com

SAGE Publications Ltd.

1 Oliver's Yard

55 City Road

London EC1Y 1SP

United Kingdom

SAGE Publications India Pvt. Ltd.

B 1/I 1 Mohan Cooperative Industrial Area

Mathura Road, New Delhi 110 044

India

SAGE Publications Asia-Pacific Pte. Ltd.

3 Church Street

#10-04 Samsung Hub

Singapore 049483

Printed in the United States of America

Library of Congress Control Number: 2013937364

ISBN: 978-1-4522-8725-6

This book is printed on acid-free paper.

Acquisitions Editor: Charisse Kiino
Editorial Assistant: Davia Grant
Production Editor: Stephanie Palermini
Copy Editor: Brenda White
Typesetter: C&M Digitals (P) Ltd.
Cover Designer: Candice Harman
Marketing Manager: Erica DeLuca
Permissions Editor: Jennifer Barron

SUSTAINABLE FORESTRY INITIATIVE
Label applies to the text stock
Certified Sourcing
www.sfiprogram.org
SFI-00341

13 14 15 16 17 10 9 8 7 6 5 4 3 2 1

Contents

Annotated Contents

NATIONAL POLITICS

Changing Demographics

The nation is undergoing one of the most important demographic transitions in its history. For the first time, minority babies outnumbered white newborns in 2011, and Census estimates predict that by 2042 non-Hispanic whites will no longer be in the majority. Already, more than a third of Americans are minorities, and non-whites accounted for 92 percent of population growth between 2000 and 2010, a trend driven by rising Hispanic immigration. Meanwhile, as millions of baby boomers retire, the nation is growing older. More than a fifth of Americans will be 65 or older by 2030, compared with one in eight today. Seismic changes also are occurring on the religious front: Protestants are no longer in the majority, and millions have abandoned religion altogether. And, in a striking trend of reverse migration, millions of blacks are moving back to the South.

Social Media Politics

Social media, including Facebook, Twitter, and YouTube, have become major battlegrounds in this year's elections. Candidates are using the platforms to identify and organize supporters and raise funds. They bypass traditional news media to send their messages unfiltered to the public. They target niche audiences with growing precision, contact hard-to-reach voters, extend their influence as online supporters forward their messages, and carry out many campaign tasks at much lower cost than before. The increasing ability of campaign strategists to collect and analyze information about individual voters has raised privacy concerns, and many worry that the social networks' insular nature contributes to political polarization. But social media's low cost, ease of use, and wide reach also raise hopes that they can level the campaign-spending playing field.

Farm Policy

Congress is debating a new farm bill, a sprawling measure typically enacted every five to seven years that sets broad directions for U.S. agriculture policy. Current proposals would eliminate some hotly debated subsidies that mainly benefit large farmers. But the proposed bills would still provide nearly $1 trillion over the next decade for programs including crop insurance, land and water conservation programs, disaster relief, and food aid for the poor. Conservatives say the federal government spends too much on agriculture and advocate major cuts to food aid programs, which they see as runaway entitlements. Liberals oppose cutting food aid, which they say provides crucial help for needy Americans during a slow economic recovery. And many public health advocates want more support for production of healthy crops, such as fruits and vegetables, and for local outlets such as farmers markets that connect people directly to food producers.

THE ENVIRONMENT
U.S. Oil Dependence

The United States is producing more oil today than it has since 1998, but gasoline prices are still high, averaging more than $3.50 per gallon nationally in early June 2012. New technology is making it possible to extract oil from tar sands and shale rock, but that oil is expensive, and its production causes major environmental impacts. President Obama advocates expanding production of all energy sources, including oil, gas, nuclear power, wind, and solar, while warning that the United States can never pump enough oil to sway world prices. Republicans counter that the Obama administration has restricted oil production and that drilling should expand in Western states, the Arctic, and coastal waters. Environmentalists want more support for technologies to replace oil, such as electric cars

and biofuels. But until those sources become economically competitive with oil, the United States will be subject to price swings in a world oil market that it cannot control.

Genetically Modified Food

California voters will decided in November 2012 whether foods produced with genetically modified ingredients—so-called GM foods—should bear special labels. The controversial measure reflects the uneven acceptance of genetically engineered crops since their rise in the 1990s. Organic farmers and other opponents of GM foods contend they may pose health or environmental risks, despite widespread scientific consensus that they are not inherently more risky than other crops. Foes of the labeling referendum, including GM farmers and seed producers, such as Monsanto, say that GM crops are more productive, pest-resistant, and environmentally friendly than conventional crops and that the fast-growing organic industry and misguided consumer groups are to blame for confusion about the science behind them. Even as GM crops have been embraced by U.S. commodity growers, Europe remains skeptical. However, eight of the 10 countries with the most acreage in biotech crops are now in the developing world.

BUSINESS AND THE ECONOMY
Internet Regulation

Lawmakers are struggling with tough questions about how to regulate digital media and the Internet. With digitized versions of feature films and recorded music playable on personal computers and cell phones, the film, television, and music industries have repeatedly complained that global "pirates" use cheap, widely available computer technology and the Internet to steal their intellectual property and profits. A bill to require Internet service providers (ISPs) to shut down websites suspected of posting or distributing copyrighted material stalled in Congress. Meanwhile, ISPs are fighting government attempts to bar them from discriminating against certain websites. Advocates say such "net neutrality" rules are needed to prevent situations in which, for example, a cable TV-owned ISP that also sells video content might slow the flow of video that customers buy from other companies. But ISPs argue that it wouldn't be in their financial interest to conduct business that way.

Youth Unemployment

Across the globe, the economic crisis has led to soaring youth unemployment—above 50 percent in Spain, nearly that high in Greece, and above 30 percent in many other countries. The crisis also has exacerbated already-high levels of youth unemployment in the Middle East and North Africa, where frustrated, unemployed college graduates were at the forefront of last year's Arab Spring revolutions. Angry, jobless youths have taken to the streets in other countries, as well, including the U.K. Countries are grappling with the problem, but solutions remain elusive. Youth unemployment is seen both as a matter of demographics—disproportionately higher numbers of young people in many countries—and structural problems in labor markets, such as laws protecting older workers' jobs. Many observers believe if the issue isn't addressed, further upheavals will occur, while others worry that the world could be facing a "lost generation" of discouraged workers whose earnings will be diminished for decades.

Financial Misconduct

The United States is slowly coming out of the worst financial crisis since the Great Depression, but many Americans want tougher law enforcement against the companies and executives they say created the mess. Four years after the crisis began, no prominent financial executives have been prosecuted. Civil charges were brought against major banks for misleading investors by packaging subprime mortgages with insufficient disclosure, but a federal judge recently rejected a proposed settlement as too lenient. Meanwhile, major mortgage lenders are negotiating a potential multibillion-dollar settlement over allegations of improper home foreclosures. Some states, however, are balking at banks' request for protection from subsequent lawsuits. Many experts say the government has failed to devote adequate resources to prosecuting wrongdoers. But some also acknowledge that certain activities that triggered the crisis were not necessarily illegal.

EDUCATION
Future of Public Universities

Massive changes are buffeting America's public colleges and universities, spurring experts to predict a radically different higher-education environment in coming years. A weakened economy has forced drastic cuts in state higher-education funding, leading many schools to raise tuition to record levels and put the brakes on expansion after years of pell-mell growth fueled by government spending. Meanwhile, colleges and universities are under pressure to rethink their traditional modes of operation as they try to compete with an explosion of new educational models, including for-profit institutions, distance learning and so-called MOOCs—massive online open courses that offer free, high-quality instruction to thousands of digitally connected students simultaneously.

RIGHTS AND LIBERTIES
Gun Control

The debate over gun control has been inescapable since last December, when Adam Lanza killed 20 first-graders and six adults at Sandy Hook Elementary School in Newtown, Conn., before taking his own life in one of the nation's most horrific mass shootings. There have been marches and protests, Super Bowl advertisements, emotional and contentious congressional and state hearings, and a new, tough gun-control law in New York State. Polls show broad bipartisan public support for expanding background checks to include private gun purchases, although support is weaker and more polarized for a ban on assault-style weapons and large-capacity ammunition magazines. Yet momentum may be fading in Congress for passage of any new gun-control legislation as members grapple with the federal government's looming debt limit and this month's automatic budget cuts.

SOCIAL POLICY
Immigration Conflict

Americans are very concerned about illegal immigration but ambivalent about what to do about it—especially the 11 million aliens currently in the United States illegally. Frustrated with the federal government's failure to secure the borders, several states passed laws allowing state and local police to check the immigration status of suspected unlawful aliens. Civil rights organizations warn the laws will result in ethnic profiling of Latinos. The Obama administration is suing to block several of the laws for infringing on federal prerogatives. Advocates of tougher enforcement say undocumented workers are taking jobs from U.S. citizens, but many business and agricultural groups say migrant workers are needed to fill jobs unattractive to U.S. workers. Two years ago, the U.S. Supreme Court upheld an Arizona law providing stiff penalties for employers that knowingly hire illegal aliens. Now, the justices are preparing to hear arguments on the controversial, new Arizona law that inspired other states to crack down on illegal immigration.

Gay Marriage Showdowns

The California Supreme Court gave gay rights advocates a major victory in May, ruling the state's constitution guarantees same-sex couples the same marriage rights as opposite-sex pairs. Thousands of same-sex couples from California and around the country have already taken advantage of the decision to obtain legal recognition from California for their unions. Opponents, however, have placed on the state's Nov. 4 ballot a constitutional amendment that would deny marriage rights to same-sex couples by defining marriage as the union of one man and one woman. Similar proposals are on the ballot in Arizona and Florida. The ballot-box showdowns come as nationwide polls indicate support for some legal protection for same-sex couples, but not necessarily marriage equality. In California, one early poll showed support for the ballot measure, but more recently it has been trailing. Opposing groups expect to spend about $20 million each before the campaign ends.

HEALTHCARE
Assessing the New Health Care Law

In June 2012, the Supreme Court upheld most of the Obama administration's 2010 health care law, allowing the government to fine people who decline to buy medical insurance. But the court barred cutting off Medicaid funds for states that refuse to participate in a new program expanding health care for the poor. Some

Republican governors have balked at the expanded coverage, undermining the administration's goal of adding 30 million people to the health insurance rolls. Meanwhile, GOP presidential nominee Mitt Romney, along with many congressional Republicans, vows to repeal the entire Affordable Care Act, arguing it is too costly and abridges individual freedoms. The law's supporters, however, say its benefits already are evident, as children with pre-existing illnesses can no longer lose coverage and young adults can enroll in their parents' health plans.

Preventing Disease

The U.S. health care system faces spiraling costs from chronic, or noncommunicable, illnesses such as diabetes, heart disease, and preventable cancers. But public health experts are discovering that just pushing people to change bad habits isn't working. Instead, they are placing more focus on "making the healthy choice the easy choice" through such efforts as reformulating processed foods and making streets safe for walkers and bikers. Some in Congress and the Obama administration made a big push for community-based disease prevention approaches, but concerns over the budget deficit could result in major cuts to the Prevention and Public Health Fund enacted as part of the 2010 health reform act. However, some say the government is overreaching in its war on obesity, and studies show that some prevention efforts add to health care costs. The fight against preventable disease is not a U.S. problem alone. In poor countries, the biggest threats are the same ones afflicting Americans: lack of exercise, smoking, and unhealthy diets.

FOREIGN AFFAIRS AND NATIONAL SECURITY POLICY
Unrest in the Arab World

The wave of popular uprisings that toppled dictators in Tunisia, Egypt, and Libya is still roiling the Arab world, but other governments have held on by cracking down on protests or instituting modest reforms. Meanwhile, Syria is engulfed in a bloody civil war that many experts predict will force President Bashar Assad from office but leave the country devastated and politically unstable. Some experts say the events have transformed political attitudes in Arab nations. Others stress that a majority of those countries still have authoritarian regimes. The political dramas are playing out against the backdrop of pressing economic problems, including high unemployment among Arab youths. In addition, the growing power of Islamist parties and groups is raising concerns among advocates of secular government and creating risks of sectarian disputes among different Muslim sects.

Privatizing the Military

The United States and other nations increasingly rely on private contractors, many of them armed, to guard military bases, protect diplomatic personnel, conduct surveillance of potential military targets, and carry out other such duties. Over the past decade, security companies have greatly increased in number and size, becoming a major industry that attracts private-sector clients as well. Multinational corporations hire the same armed contractors that governments use to guard remote mining operations, and shipping companies hire them to fight pirates. Governments and other clients say private guards save money and provide strategic flexibility. Critics argue, however, that using soldiers-for-hire gives governments too much leeway to take armed actions without citizens' or lawmakers' consent. Furthermore, they contend, no system of law—national or international—holds armed contractors or those who hire them fully accountable for human-rights violations.

Preface

Should lawmakers tighten firearm restrictions? Do Facebook and Twitter influence voters? Should states crack down on unlawful aliens? These questions—and many more—are at the heart of American public policy. How can instructors best engage students with these crucial issues? We feel that students need objective, yet provocative examinations of these issues to understand how they affect citizens today and will for years to come. This annual collection aims to promote in-depth discussion, facilitate further research, and help readers formulate their own positions on crucial issues. Get your students talking both inside and outside the classroom about *Issues for Debate in American Public Policy.*

This fourteenth edition includes sixteen up-to-date reports by *CQ Researcher,* an award-winning weekly policy brief that brings complicated issues down to earth. Each report chronicles and analyzes executive, legislative, and judicial activities at all levels of government. This collection is divided into eight diverse policy areas: national politics; the environment; business and the economy; education; rights and liberties; social policy; healthcare; and foreign affairs and national security policy—to cover a range of issues found in most American government and public policy courses.

CQ RESEARCHER

CQ Researcher was founded in 1923 as *Editorial Research Reports* and was sold primarily to newspapers as a research tool. The magazine was renamed and redesigned in 1991 as *CQ Researcher.* Today, students are its primary audience. While still used by hundreds of journalists and newspapers, many of which reprint portions of the reports, the

Researcher's main subscribers are now high schools, colleges, and public libraries. In 2002, *Researcher* won the American Bar Association's coveted Silver Gavel award for magazine excellence for a series of nine reports on civil liberties and other legal issues.

Researcher staff writers—all highly experienced journalists—sometimes compare the experience of writing a Researcher report to drafting a college term paper. Indeed, there are many similarities. Each report is as long as many term papers—about 11,000 words—and is written by one person without any significant outside help. One of the key differences is that writers interview leading experts, scholars, and government officials for each issue.

Like students, staff writers begin the creative process by choosing a topic. Working with the *Researcher's* editors, the writer identifies a controversial subject that has important public policy implications. After a topic is selected, the writer embarks on one to two weeks of intense research. Newspaper and magazine articles are clipped or downloaded, books are ordered, and information is gathered from a wide variety of sources, including interest groups, universities, and the government. Once the writers are well informed, they develop a detailed outline, and begin the interview process. Each report requires a minimum of 10 to 15 interviews with academics, officials, lobbyists, and people working in the field. Only after all interviews are completed does the writing begin.

CHAPTER FORMAT

Each issue of *CQ Researcher,* and therefore each selection in this book, is structured in the same way. Each begins with an overview, which briefly summarizes the areas that will be explored in greater detail in the rest of the chapter. The next section chronicles important and current debates on the topic under discussion and is structured around a number of key questions, such as "Should same-sex couples be allowed to marry?" and "Was illegal conduct a major cause of the financial crisis?" These questions are usually the subject of much debate among practitioners and scholars in the field. Hence, the answers presented are never conclusive but detail the range of opinion on the topic.

Next, the Background section provides a history of the issue being examined. This retrospective covers important legislative measures, executive actions, and court decisions that illustrate how current policy has evolved. Then, the Current Situation section examines contemporary policy issues, legislation under consideration, and legal action being taken. Each selection concludes with an Outlook section, which addresses possible regulation, court rulings, and initiatives from Capitol Hill and the White House over the next five to ten years.

Each report contains features that augment the main text: two to three sidebars that examine issues related to the topic at hand, a pro versus con debate between two experts, a chronology of key dates and events, and an annotated bibliography detailing major sources used by the writer.

CUSTOM OPTIONS

Interested in building your ideal CQ Press Issues book, customized to your personal teaching needs and interests? Browse by course or date, or search for specific topics or issues from our online catalog of over 150 *CQ Researcher* issues at http://custom.cqpress.com.

ACKNOWLEDGMENTS

We wish to thank many people for helping to make this collection a reality. Thomas J. Billitteri, managing editor of *CQ Researcher,* gave us his enthusiastic support and cooperation as we developed this fourteenth edition. He and his talented staff of editors and writers have amassed a first-class library of *Researcher* reports, and we are fortunate to have access to that rich cache. We also thankfully acknowledge the advice and feedback from current readers and are gratified by their satisfaction with the book.

Some readers may be learning about *CQ Researcher* for the first time. We expect that many readers will want regular access to this excellent weekly research tool. For subscription information or a no-obligation free trial of *Researcher,* please contact CQ Press at www.cqpress.com or toll-free at 1–866–4CQ-PRESS (1–866–427–7737).

We hope that you will be pleased by the fourteenth edition of *Issues for Debate in American Public Policy.* We welcome your feedback and suggestions for future editions. Please direct comments to Charisse Kiino, Publisher, College Publishing Group, CQ Press, 2300 N Street, NW, Suite 800, Washington, D.C. 20037, or ckiino@cqpress.com.

—The Editors of CQ Press

About the Contributors

Nellie Bristol is a veteran Capitol Hill reporter who has covered health policy in Washington for more than 20 years. She now writes for *The Lancet, Health Affairs,* and *Global Health* magazine. She recently earned a master's degree in public health/global health from The George Washington University, where she earned an undergraduate degree in American studies.

Staff writer **Marcia Clemmitt** is a veteran social-policy reporter who previously served as editor in chief of *Medicine & Health* and staff writer for *The Scientist.* She has also been a high school math and physics teacher. She holds a liberal arts and sciences degree from St. John's College, Annapolis, and a master's degree in English from Georgetown University. Her recent reports include "Digital Education" and "Computer Hacking."

Associate Editor **Kenneth Jost** graduated from Harvard College and Georgetown University Law Center. He is the author of the *Supreme Court Yearbook* and editor of *The Supreme Court from A to Z* (both *CQ Press*). He was a member of the *CQ Researcher* team that won the American Bar Association's 2002 Silver Gavel Award. His previous reports include "Financial Crisis" and "Corporate Crime." He is also author of the blog *Jost on Justice* (http://jostonjustice.blogspot.com).

Reed Karaim, a freelance writer living in Tucson, Arizona, has written for *The Washington Post, U.S. News & World Report, Smithsonian, American Scholar, USA Weekend,* and other publications. He is the author of the novel, *If Men Were Angels,* which was selected for the Barnes & Noble Discover Great New Writers series. He is also the winner of the Robin Goldstein Award for Outstanding Regional Reporting and other journalism honors. Karaim is a graduate of North Dakota State University in Fargo.

Robert Kiener is an award-winning writer based in Vermont whose work has appeared in *The London Sunday Times, The Christian Science Monitor, The Washington Post, Reader's Digest,* Time Life Books, and other publications. For more than two decades he worked as an editor and correspondent in Guam, Hong Kong, Canada, and England. He holds an M.A. in Asian studies from Hong Kong University and an M.Phil. in international relations from England's Cambridge University.

Barbara Mantel is a freelance writer in New York City. She is a 2012 Kiplinger Fellow and has won several journalism awards, including the National Press Club's Best Consumer Journalism Award and the Front Page Award from the Newswomen's Club of New York for her November 1, 2009, CQ Global Researcher report "Terrorism and the Internet." She holds a B.A. in history and economics from the University of Virginia and an M.A. in economics from Northwestern University.

Jason McLure is a New Hampshire-based correspondent for Thomson Reuters. Previously he was an Africa correspondent for Bloomberg News and *Newsweek* and worked for *Legal Times* in Washington, D.C. His writing has appeared in publications such as *The Economist, The New York Times,* and *Business Week.* His last *CQ Global Researcher* was "Russia in Turmoil." His work has been

honored by the Washington, D.C., chapter of the Society for Professional Journalists, the Maryland-Delaware-District of Columbia Press Association, and the Overseas Press Club of America Foundation. He is also coordinator of the Committee to Free Eskinder Nega, a jailed Ethiopian journalist.

Tom Price, a Washington-based freelance journalist and *CQ Researcher* contributing writer, has written about the Internet's impact on public affairs since the mid-1990s. Last year the Foundation for Public Affairs published his report, "Beyond Control: How Social Media and Mobile Communication Are Changing Public Affairs." Before he began freelancing, Price was a correspondent in the Cox Newspapers Washington Bureau and chief politics writer for the *Dayton Daily News* and *The* (Dayton) *Journal Herald.* He is author or coauthor of five books, including *Changing the Face of Hunger* and, most recently, *Washington, DC, Free & Dirt Cheap* with his wife Susan Crites Price.

Bill Wanlund is a freelance writer in the Washington, D.C., area. He is a former foreign service officer, with service in Europe, Asia, Africa, and South America. He holds a journalism degree from The George Washington University and has written for *CQ Researcher* on drone warfare and downtown development.

Jennifer Weeks is a Massachusetts freelance writer who specializes in energy, the environment, and science. She has written for *The Washington Post, Audubon, Popular Mechanics,* and other magazines and previously was a policy analyst, congressional staffer, and lobbyist. She has an A.B. degree from Williams College and master's degrees from the University of North Carolina and Harvard. Her recent *CQ Researcher* reports include "Gulf Coast Restoration" and "Energy Policy."

Issues for Debate in American Public Policy, 14th Edition

1

Changing Demographics

Bill Wanlund

Hundreds of older Americans rally in Chicago on Nov. 7, 2011, against cuts in programs that benefit the elderly. Each day for the next 19 years, 10,000 baby boomers will reach the traditional retirement age of 65. By 2030, more than one in five Americans will be 65 or older, compared with about one in eight today. The number of older Americans is expected to more than double between now and 2050, to about 84 million.

From *The CQ Researcher*,
November 16, 2012.

Getty Images/Scott Olson

The nation is undergoing a profound population makeover, a transformation so sweeping that just about every aspect of American life will be affected in coming years, from economic growth and electoral politics to social-welfare policies and religious affiliation.

Growing ethnic and racial diversity is the most striking sign of change. For the first time in U.S. history, minority babies outnumbered white newborns last year, a trend driven by rising Hispanic immigration.[1] By 2042, non-Hispanic whites will cease to be in the majority. Already, more than a third of Americans are minorities, and non-whites accounted for 92 percent of population growth between 2000 and 2010.[2]

The pace of demographic change in the nation, whose population has grown to about 315 million, has stunned even the experts. "It was always predicted that we would be diverse, but it's happened faster than anyone predicted," said Cheryl Russell, former editor in chief of *American Demographics* magazine and now editorial director of New Strategist Publications. "Diversity and the rapid growth in diversity is one of the reasons we have a black president today. That's one thing that would never have been predicted."[3]

Nowhere have the effects of diversity been more evident than in this month's presidential election. In his Nov. 6 victory over GOP contender Mitt Romney, President Obama garnered an estimated 71 percent of the Hispanic vote, according to election day polling by the Pew Hispanic Center.[4] Asian-Americans, who supported Obama by about 47 percentage points, made up 3 percent of the 2012 electorate, up a full point from 2008.[5] "The nonwhite vote has been growing — tick,

More Americans Religiously Unaffiliated

The percentage of Americans who classify themselves as religiously unaffiliated has steadily increased since 2007, to nearly 20 percent, and Protestants comprise less than half the population for the first time in U.S. history. Experts say fewer and fewer young adults are embracing the religious traditions of their elders and that more Americans are choosing to remain unaffiliated with any faith group.

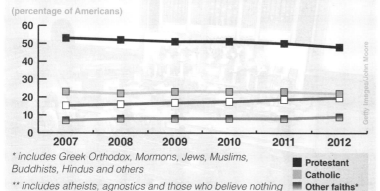

Religious Affiliation Among Americans, 2007-2012

(percentage of Americans)

* includes Greek Orthodox, Mormons, Jews, Muslims, Buddhists, Hindus and others

** includes atheists, agnostics and those who believe nothing in particular

- Protestant
- Catholic
- Other faiths*
- Unaffiliated**

Source: " 'Nones' on the Rise: One-in-Five Adults Have No Religious Affiliation," Pew Research Center, October 2012, p. 13, www.pewforum.org/uploadedFiles/Topics/Religious_Affiliation/Unaffiliated/ NonesOnTheRise-full.pdf

tick, tick — slowly, steadily," said Paul Taylor, executive vice president of the nonpartisan Pew Research Center. "Every four-year cycle the electorate gets a little bit more diverse. And it's going to continue."[6]

That diversity extends to Capitol Hill. Next year's 113th Congress will include 28 Latinos in the House of Representatives, the largest Latino class in U.S. history, and a third Latino will join the U.S. Senate.[7]

The nation's demographic evolution goes far beyond ethnicity, race and politics, however. For example:

- By 2030, more than one in five Americans will be age 65 or older, compared with about one in eight today. (See chart, p. 6.)
- More than one-fourth of Americans have left the religious denomination of their childhood and either joined a different faith or abandoned organized religion altogether.

- For the first time, Protestants are a minority in the United States: Only 48 percent of Americans identify themselves as Protestants — down from 53 percent in 2007.[8] (See chart, p. 2.)

The nation's shifting demographic profile has huge implications for many facets of American life, noted Laura B. Shrestha and Elayne J. Heisler, researchers for the Congressional Research Service, which advises Congress on policy issues. "There is ample reason to believe that the United States will be able to cope with the current and projected demographic changes if policy makers accelerate efforts to address and adapt to the changing population profile as it relates to . . . work, retirement and pensions, private wealth and income security — and the health and well-being of the aging population," they wrote.[9]

Indeed, the rise in the average age of the U.S. population is among the benchmarks demographers and economists are watching most closely. The number of Americans 65 or older is expected to more than double between now and 2050 — from 40 million to 84.5 million. On Jan. 1, 2011, the first of the 78 million Americans born between 1946 and 1964 — the baby boomers — reached the traditional retirement age of 65. For the next 19 years, 10,000 more will cross that threshold every day, according to the Pew Research Center.[10]

Experts note that as a nation's citizens age out of the workforce, its tax base declines, reducing the amount of money available for pensions and publicly supported medical and residential needs. What's more, older people generally spend less on consumer goods, putting less money into the economy.

Yet, while an aging U.S. population poses challenges for social-welfare programs targeted at the elderly, including Medicare and Social Security, experts say the nation retains an economic advantage over Europe, Japan and China, all of which are aging faster than the United States.[11] The reason for the U.S. edge, they say, is immigration. The Census Bureau estimates that 14 million immigrants came legally or illegally to the U.S. between 2000 and 2010 — the largest decennial influx in history. Some 40 million Americans — about one in eight — are foreign-born.[12]

"If the U.S. depended on white births alone, we'd be dead," said Dowell Myers, a professor of policy, planning and demography at the University of Southern California. "Without the contributions from all these other groups, we would become too top-heavy with old people."[13]

Myers noted that countries with low immigration rates, such as Japan, can end up with young, working-age populations too small to support the larger group of aging citizens.

Along with immigration, birth rates also are keeping America younger than other industrialized countries. Between 2000 and 2010, the Hispanic population — now the nation's largest minority — grew 43 percent, to more than 50 million, partly because the birth rate among Hispanics is 60 percent higher than among whites. The Asian-American population grew at about the same rate, reaching 17 million, while the black population rose 15.4 percent, to 42 million.

For some whites, predictions that minorities will grow to more than half of the U.S. population come as a jolt. They feel as though they had gone "from being a privileged group to all of a sudden becoming whites, the new victims," said Charles Gallagher, a sociologist at La Salle University in Pennsylvania who researches racial attitudes among whites.[14] In fact, a 2011 joint survey by the Brookings Institution and the Public Religion Research Institute, both in Washington, found that nearly half of whites believe discrimination against them is now as big a problem as discrimination against minorities.[15]

Religion and the 2012 Election

White evangelicals and white Catholics largely backed GOP contender Mitt Romney in this year's presidential election, as did most members of his Mormon faith. Black Protestants and Hispanic Catholics largely supported President Obama's re-election. Experts say the ethnic identity of minority voters, who traditionally support Democratic candidates, often trumps religious affiliation at the polls. Religiously unaffiliated voters overwhelmingly backed Obama.

Presidential Vote by Religious Affiliation and Race, 2012
(by percentage of voters)

Religion	Barack Obama	Mitt Romney
Total Percentage	50%	48%
Protestant/other Christian	42	57
White Protestant/other Christian	30	69
Born-again/evangelical	20	79
Non-evangelical	44	54
Black Protestant/other Christian	95	5
Catholic	50	48
White Catholic	40	59
Hispanic Catholic	75	21
Jewish	69	30
Mormon	21	78
Other faiths	74	23
Religiously unaffiliated	70	26

Source: "How the Faithful Voted: 2012 Preliminary Analysis," Pew Forum on Religion and Public Life, November 2012.

Meanwhile, "non-affiliated" is now the fastest-growing category in the nation's religious profile. Twenty percent of Americans say they have no church affiliation — up from 15 percent five years ago, according to a study by the Pew Forum on Religion and Public Life released in October. "Young people today are coming of age at a time when they are less religious than at any time before in our polling," says Greg Smith, a lead researcher on the study. (*See graphs, pp. 2, 3.*)

In what Smith calls a "churn" taking place in American religion, 28 percent of adults have left the faith in which they were raised to join another religion — or to practice no religion at all. Roughly 44 percent have either switched religious affiliation, rejoined a church after being unaffiliated or dropped out of organized religion altogether.[16]

AFP/Getty Images/Nicholas Kamm

Worshippers at the First Church of Seventh-day Adventists in Washington, D.C., on March 31, 2012, pray for the families of slain Florida teenager Trayvon Martin and the neighborhood watch volunteer who killed him. More than a fourth of Americans have left the religious denomination of their childhood and either joined a different faith or abandoned organized religion.

The Protestant decline marks an important transition point, says Randall Balmer, chairman of the religion department at Dartmouth College. But he adds, "The U.S. has always been a pluralistic country in terms of religion, and this is simply another indication that we are a religiously diverse people."

The Catholic Church has lost the most followers of any major denomination in the United States: Four Catholics leave the Church for every individual who converts to the faith.[17]

Nevertheless, about 25 percent identify themselves as Catholic, a proportion that has remained steady for decades, Smith notes. "Immigration from Latin America is boosting the size of the Catholic population, and it's mostly responsible for the Catholic share of the population holding steady," he says.

As demographic changes bring sweeping changes to American society, here are some of the questions being debated:

Will changing demographics affect American values?

The late Harvard University political scientist Samuel P. Huntington feared that America was losing its way. He was particularly concerned about the influx of Hispanic immigrants, specifically from Mexico. Huntington feared that their sheer numbers and the rise of multiculturalism in the United States would be a challenge to America's "core culture."[18]

But Joel Kotkin, distinguished presidential fellow in urban futures at Chapman University in Orange, Calif., took a different view of immigrants. "America's ability to absorb newcomers represents . . . a new paradigm, where race itself begins to matter less than culture, class and other factors," he wrote. "Rather than a source of national decline, the new Americans represent the critical force that can provide the new markets, the manpower, and, perhaps most important, the youthful energy to keep our country vital and growing."[19]

Attitudes toward abortion and gay marriage are often seen as a yardstick of religious values. Hispanics — many of whom are Catholic — are more conservative than the U.S. population overall on abortion, according to a 2012 survey by the Pew Hispanic Center. Slightly more than half of Hispanics believe abortion should be illegal in all or most cases, compared to 41 percent of the general population.

Americans' support for same-sex marriage has been gradually increasing, and in 2011, according to the Pew Research Center, the public was evenly divided on whether gay and lesbian couples should be allowed to marry. A slim majority of Hispanics believes same-sex marriage should be legal.[20]

Pew also found that Asian-Americans' views on abortion and homosexuality largely mirror those of the nation at large. Like Hispanics, Asians are more likely to call themselves liberal — 31 percent do so — and less likely than the overall population to describe themselves as conservative.[21]

"Another measure of Americans' acceptance of diversity is the increase in interracial marriage, which demographers typically interpret to mean that race relations are improving, says Cornell University sociology professor Daniel Lichter. "It means the things that promote intimacy between racial and ethnic groups — for example, residential proximity or economic equality or similar levels of education — have taken place," Lichter says.

A 2012 study by the Pew Research Center showed that about 15 percent of all new marriages in the United States in 2010 were between spouses of different races or ethnicity, more than double the 6.7 percent share in 1980.[22]

However, "This doesn't mean that we're in a post-racial society," Lichter says. "We've made great strides, but we have an awfully long way to go before race doesn't matter in this culture."[23]

Twenty-eight percent of Asians married people of another race, the highest percentage of all ethnic groups. "The rate of intermarriage in the Asian-American, especially the Japanese-American, community is definitely having a cultural impact," says Lane Hirabayashi, a professor of Asian-American studies at the University of California, Los Angeles.

However, Hirabayashi also notes that the rate of increase of Asian interracial marriage has slowed. "Increasing immigration from Asia gives immigrants a larger pool of potential partners from the same ethnic group," he says.

John Nieto-Phillips, a history professor at Indiana University who specializes in Latino studies, says, "Latinos are comfortable with marrying a person of another heritage or background. Latinos are less comfortable, however, defining their own identity by existing racial categories. The 'browning of America' by way of intermarriage portends the blurring of conventional racial boundaries, though it may not mitigate the social or structural inequalities that tend to sustain boundaries."

Pew found that 43 percent of Americans feel that having more interracial marriages has been a change for the better, and nearly two-thirds say it "would be fine" with them if a member of their own family were to marry someone outside their own racial or ethnic group. In 1986, only one-third viewed intermarriage as acceptable.[24]

Pew Research Center researcher Kim Parker, who worked on the intermarriage study, says increased immigration over the past 40 years has helped spur the attitudinal change. "With greater diversity, there's more opportunity for people of different ethnic backgrounds to interact," Parker says. "As people get to know each other, the pool of 'candidates' becomes larger. And as an individual gains familiarity with people from different backgrounds, the degree of acceptance may rise."

It's difficult to generalize about baby boomers' impact on values. Some formed their political consciousness during the turbulent anti-Vietnam War movement, while many others were influenced by the conservative "Reagan Rebellion" of the early 1980s.

In general, however, according to a 2011 Pew survey, boomers appear to be nudging the values needle leftward. On issues such as abortion and same-sex marriage, they are somewhat less conservative than their parents' generation but less liberal than their children. Still, Pew found, in recent years "more boomers have come to call themselves conservatives [and] many . . . express reservations about the changing face of America. . . . Boomers' current attitudes bear little imprint from coming of age in an era of great social change."[25] (*See sidebar, p. 14.*)

American University communications professor Leonard Steinhorn, author of *The Greater Generation: In Defense of the Baby Boom Legacy*, believes embracing diversity may be the boomers' chief lasting contribution to America. "It used to be that the white men who ran our businesses could exclude women and minorities with a wink and a nod," he says. "That's no longer acceptable. [Boomers] have made diversity a moral value. And they have created a cultural norm that says prejudice and discrimination are immoral; they have created new norms, and the children they have raised under those norms have internalized them."

Still, says Brookings Institution demographer William Frey, "Demography marches on. It's the younger population that [will] be living, working and building communities with each other in a very different kind of America. They are developing a different set of values, in terms of their acceptance of diversity — from having more mixed race and racially diverse friends, dating partners, spouses — and are generally more accepting of new social trends including same-sex couples, alternative religions, etc. They will also be more globally conscious due to their associations with more new Americans and their greater ability to "network" across the country and globally through social media. . . . [A]s we move into the next decade or two we're going to be much more about the people who are under age 30 than the people who are over age 50."

Will the nation's demographic changes benefit the U.S. economy?

As the U.S. population ages, economists see both trouble and opportunity ahead.

The number of Americans 65 or older is expected to more than double by 2050, to about 84 million, and today's 65-year-old can expect to live another 20 years, up from 13 years in 1950.[26]

Increased longevity and a desire to remain active are spurring many older workers to remain in the labor

Older Population on Rise

The number of Americans age 65 or older is projected to surpass 70 million by 2030. Experts cite two key reasons for the rise: the aging of the post-World War II baby boom generation and medical advances that have increased average life expectancy.

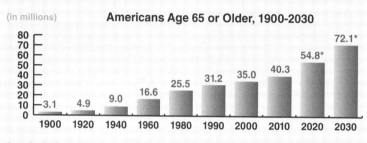

(in millions)

Americans Age 65 or Older, 1900-2030

	1900	1920	1940	1960	1980	1990	2000	2010	2020	2030
	3.1	4.9	9.0	16.6	25.5	31.2	35.0	40.3	54.8*	72.1*

* projected

Source: "A Profile of Older Americans: 2011," Administration on Aging, U.S. Department of Health and Human Services, 2011, p. 3, www.aoa.gov/aoaroot/aging_statistics/Profile/2011/docs/2011profile.pdf

force. But so too are economic pressures, stemming in part from the loss of trillions of dollars in retirement assets during the recent recession.

Researchers Frank W. Heiland and Zhe Li of Boston College's Center for Retirement Research found that nearly 23 percent of men over age 65 were working in 2010, compared to 16.8 percent in 1994. The participation rate for women over 65 nearly doubled, from 7.4 percent in 1988 to 13.8 percent.[27]

As more older workers remain on the job, some experts believe they may be preventing younger workers from finding employment. One of the reasons [that young people can't find jobs is] because older people are not leaving the workforce," said Sung Won Sohn, an economist at California State University-Channel Islands.[28] But others disagree with the view that older workers are hurting the prospects of younger ones. There is "no evidence that increasing the employment of older persons reduces the job opportunities or wage rates of younger persons," said Alicia Munnell, director of the Center for Retirement Research. In fact, she said, "greater employment of older persons leads to better outcomes for the young in the form of reduced unemployment, increased employment and a higher wage."[29]

"Younger workers come into the labor force with a different vintage of education, and they don't have

work experience. So, you don't often find old and young workers clamoring for the same low-wage McDonald's job," said Jeffrey Zax, a professor at the University of Colorado who specializes in labor economics. Moreover, Zax said, "A senior worker with experience might allow a company to hire more junior employees because you have someone who can manage them."[30]

Inevitably, aging Americans will require medical care and specialized living and transportation accommodations — which will open up job opportunities for younger workers, says Sara Rix, senior strategic policy adviser at the AARP Public Policy Institute.

"The proportion of older people living in nursing homes is declining, but we are going to see a substantial increase in the 'very, very old' — people in their upper 90s and 100s — many of whom . . . will need assisted-living facilities." As a result, Rix says, construction workers will be needed to build and upgrade assisted-living facilities, and doctors, nurses and home health care workers will be needed to care for the elderly.

Even so, America's aging population poses deep challenges for the health care system. For example, a projected nursing shortage is expected to grow worse as baby boomers grow older and care needs grow.[31]

As policy makers debate the implications of America's aging population, they also are studying the impact of immigration — particularly the influx of undocumented workers — on the economy.

The Federation for American Immigration Reform (FAIR), a group in Washington that promotes reduced immigration, argues that by curbing illegal immigration, "there would be many more jobs available to native workers — jobs that paid higher wages and offered better working conditions."[32]

Pia Orrenius, an assistant vice president and senior economist with the Federal Reserve Bank of Dallas, says illegal immigration might have some adverse effects on employment among specific groups — native-born teenagers, for example. "It looks like if employers have the choice of an undocumented, somewhat higher-skilled 23- or 24-year-old, they'll take that person over a 16- to 19-year-old." But, she adds, "the effects are modest."

Julie Hotchkiss, a research economist and policy adviser at the Federal Reserve Bank of Atlanta, researched undocumented workers in Georgia. "Our research shows that newly arriving undocumented workers appear to displace only earlier-arriving undocumented workers," she said. "This makes sense since undocumented workers are going to be the closest substitutes for each other."[33]

Many economists say that immigrant workers have a positive effect on the economy. "There is no evidence that immigrants crowd out U.S.-born workers in either the short or long run," wrote Giovanni Peri, an economics professor at the University of California-Davis. "The economy absorbs immigrants by expanding opportunities rather than by displacing U.S.-born workers. Data show that, on net, immigrants expand the U.S. economy's productive capacity, stimulate investment and promote specialization that in the long run boosts productivity."[34]

Moreover, Peri says in an interview, in the short run the loss of immigrant workers would cause an economic contraction. And while the economy might recover, the loss of immigrant labor could turn out to be "quite costly.

"If we don't have people picking vegetables and fruit in California, for example, we'll end up importing [those products]. Other jobs can't be outsourced — such as construction workers or waiters. We have seen very few natives taking these jobs, especially at the low end . . . a lot of businesses will have to slim down or substitute with imports or pay more wages."

Will changing demographics affect future U.S. elections?

Obama's victory in this year's presidential election was due, in the words of *The Hill*, a Washington newspaper that covers national politics, to "at least three concrete, demographic reasons" — the president's "broad advantage among female voters," his negation of the erroneous view "that black enthusiasm for Obama would taper off this year" and the fact that "Latinos went for Obama by even bigger margins than they did in 2008."[35]

While Obama may be particularly popular among female, black and Latino voters, many experts view the influence of those demographic groups in the 2012

Pedestrians pass an American flag mural in San Francisco's Chinatown on June 19, 2012. In 2011, the number of Asian immigrants who came to the United States outnumbered Hispanics for the first time: 438,000 came from East and South Asia and the Middle East, compared with 404,000 who arrived from Central or South America or the Caribbean.

election as a harbinger of how demographics might shape political destiny in campaigns of the future.

Ruy Teixeira, a senior fellow at the Center for American Progress, a liberal think tank in Washington, says a growing minority population and a shrinking white working class — a traditionally Republican-voting demographic — point to growing minority influence in future elections, a force he said would favor liberal candidates. However, he cautioned, "There is no guarantee that demographic trends will automatically lead to [electoral] dividends. . . . Parties always have to deliver."[36]

While the expected majority-minority tipping point for the general population is still 30 years off, it will come by 2023 for the younger sector of the population, primarily because of the rapid growth in the Hispanic population, according to Census Bureau estimates. Among children under age 17, about 17 million, or 23 percent, were Latinos, a rise of 39 percent in a decade, according to the Pew Hispanic Center.[37]

Brookings Institution demographer Frey said minorities' electoral influence is just becoming apparent. He pointed to the relative youth of the minority population: Currently, only 44 percent of Hispanics, 69 percent of African-Americans and 53 percent of Asians are eligible to vote, compared with 78 percent of whites. "It's because they are disproportionately below age 18, and among Hispanics and Asians, are less likely to be citizens," he says.

Whites still comprise 71 percent of the electorate, Frey pointed out, and will outnumber minority voters "well beyond" the 2012 election. Nevertheless, he added, "the handwriting is on the wall." In coming elections, as today's minority children reach the voting age of 18, "minority votes will matter, and both parties need to pay attention," Frey observed.[38]

Alan Abramowitz, a political science professor at Emory University in Atlanta, predicts that the minority electorate, which stood at 13 percent in 1992, will comprise more than a third of voters by the 2020 election.[39]

Cornell University's Lichter, who also directs the Cornell Population Center, believes the divide between older and younger voters is an issue to watch. He says, "In the 2012 elections, we saw a large, aging, mostly white population voting in one direction, and a mostly minority population voting differently. The question is, how will an older, aging, white population vote and what will it support? When older people vote, are they going to vote to support children of people who might not share the same culture?

"In 15 or 20 years, today's minorities are going to be America's taxpayers and leaders," Lichter points out. "They're going to be replacing the white baby boom generation. Will they vote to support pension and health care programs for older, American, white baby boomers? And will boomers support the kind of education, employment and social programs that help make these groups good citizens?"

Raw numbers aren't the only measure of minority voters' influence; another is location. Teixeira and Frey wrote that minorities are strongly influencing election outcomes in "swing states," where races are particularly hotly contested. Between 2008 and 2012, the minority share of eligible voters rose 9 percent in Nevada, 4 percent in Florida and North Carolina, 3 percent in Colorado and Wisconsin, 2 percent in Pennsylvania and Michigan, and 1 percent in Virginia. At the same time, the share of white voters in those states declined by between 1 and 3 percent.[40] And of those states, all but North Carolina voted for Obama in 2012. As for the electorate's changing religious makeup, some scholars say that just because Hispanic immigrants are predominantly Catholic does not

mean they constitute a Catholic voting bloc. Indeed, said presidential scholar John Kenneth White, a professor of politics at Catholic University (CU) in Washington, the "Catholic vote" has effectively vanished. "For Hispanics, ethnic identity trumps Catholic identity," he said at a Sept. 27, 2012, forum at the university.

In 2004 more Catholics voted for George W. Bush, an evangelical Christian, than for Catholic John Kerry. William Dinges, a CU professor of religion and culture, agrees there is no such thing as a Catholic vote any more. "People are becoming more independent," he said at the CU forum. "They can support a candidate or party who supports ideas not consistent with teachings of the faith. And, the church hierarchy can't force votes the way it once could."

For example, the tide appears to be changing with regard to gay marriage, which Catholic leaders and evangelical Protestants have strongly opposed. After voters rejected same-sex marriage in 32 state referendums since the late 1990s, a measure to legalize it passed on Nov. 6 in three states (Maine, Maryland and Washington), and a constitutional amendment to define marriage as between a man and a woman failed in Minnesota.[41]

According to a Pew Forum on Religion & Public Life analysis of exit polls, traditionally Republican groups such as white evangelicals and weekly churchgoers strongly backed Republican Mitt Romney, while traditionally Democratic groups such as black Protestants, Hispanic Catholics, Jews and the religiously unaffiliated backed Obama by large margins. Obama's support among white Catholics fell 7 percentage points from 2008 but gained 3 points among Hispanic Catholics. Meanwhile, his support among white evangelicals fell by 6 percentage points.[42]

The apparent growing electoral support for same-sex marriage indicates to some analysts that the political power of white evangelicals may be on the wane. Dartmouth's Balmer, an evangelical himself, says that while the religious right will continue to be a force in U.S. politics, its influence may be less apparent in coming elections.

"I think it's going to be a bit less forceful, less dramatic than it was in the 1980s and '90s and the first decade of the 21st century," Balmer says.

BACKGROUND

Race, Religion, Age, Children

Pioneering Blacks

The first blacks who came to North America hundreds of years ago were not slaves — far from it.

In 1613, João Rodrigues — son of a Portuguese sailor and an African woman — served as a translator on a Dutch trading ship that had sailed to the North American island known as Manhatta. When the ship returned to Europe, Rodrigues stayed behind to start a trading post selling hatchets and knives provided by the ship's captain. He also served as an interpreter and facilitator for Dutch merchants who came to the island to trade with the Indians. That's how a black man became the first non-native American to live and do business in what was to become New York City.

A little over 150 years later, Jean Baptiste Point Sable — son of a French father and African mother and probably born in the Caribbean in what is now the Dominican Republic — established himself in North America as a trader at the mouth of a river in an area called Eschecagou. Point Sable, a black man, is regarded as the first non-Indian to set up permanent residence in present-day Chicago.

And in 1781, 26 full or mixed-race blacks were among the 44 Mexicans who settled the little pueblo that would become Los Angeles.

Far better known, of course, is the tragic history of the blacks who came to North America under extreme duress. England began taking captured Africans to serve as slaves in its Carolina colony in 1670. During the colonial period, an estimated 600,000 African slaves were brought to America. In 1808, Congress banned the importation of slaves, but the law was not seamlessly enforced. It did effectively end the transatlantic slave trade — though not the practice of slavery in the colonies. By 1860, the slave population in the United States was about 4 million.

With the end of the Civil War and ratification in 1865 of the 13th amendment abolishing slavery, blacks were granted citizenship. Black males gained the right to vote with ratification of the 15th Amendment in 1870. The postwar Reconstruction period saw improved educational and economic opportunities for Southern blacks, and many even were elected to public office. In the Carolinas alone, nearly 100 black legislators were elected during Reconstruction, including 22 who were elected to Congress between 1870 and 1901.[43] Tens of thousands of African-Americans living in the North moved south to become teachers or farmers or just to reunite with families.

By 1876, however, the federal government's commitment to protect the rights of black citizens was wavering. States enacted harsh "Jim Crow" laws that institutionalized racial segregation in schools and other public places, and black voting was blocked by fraud, intimidation or worse. In 1896, a nearly unanimous U.S. Supreme Court, in the infamous *Plessy v. Ferguson* decision, upheld the concept that state laws could require separate facilities for blacks and whites, as long as the facilities were equivalent. But equivalence was left undefined. The ruling in effect conferred constitutionality to the South's Jim Crow caste system.

Early Immigrants

In the first years of the democracy, immigration to the United States was relatively slight; even so, one of the early legislative acts of the cautious Founding Fathers was the Naturalization Act of 1790, which limited naturalized citizenship to "free white persons" of "good moral character."

Immigration gathered momentum in the early 19th century. During the 1820s, 143,000 immigrants were reported; in the following decade, immigration — mostly by Irish and Germans — more than quadrupled. The 1840s recorded 1,713,000 immigrants, nearly half of them from Ireland escaping the 1845-49 potato famine. Politics also helped swell the immigrant tide, as unsuccessful European revolutions in 1848 spurred large numbers of intellectuals and political activists to flee their homelands. By 1850 foreign-born residents made up 9.7 percent of America's 23 million population.

While early post-colonial America was largely a Protestant nation, large numbers of Catholics were absorbed with the acquisition of the Louisiana Purchase from France in 1803, Florida from Spain in 1819, and territory in what is now New Mexico and California in 1847 as a result of the Mexican-American War.

The second half of the century saw the Catholic population triple, in large part the result of immigration from Europe — notably Ireland, Italy, and Poland. By 1906, there were 14 million Catholics in America, 17 percent of the total population.[44]

Asian immigrants were rare in North America until 1849, when Chinese workers were recruited to work in the California gold fields, and later to help build the transcontinental railway system and work in other, mostly menial, jobs. As the Chinese population grew, racial prejudice and distrust increased among whites, and in 1882 Congress passed the Chinese Exclusion Act, which ended immigration by Chinese laborers. The law also made Chinese immigrants already in the country ineligible for citizenship.

Expanding Equality

The 20th century saw the United States experience major demographic changes. The start of World War I (1914-1918) helped spark the mass South-to-North movement of African-Americans, and the end of World War II (1939-1945) led to the birth of the baby boom generation — the largest population bulge in the nation's history. In addition, after the United States loosened immigration restrictions, a flood of new citizens dramatically altered the country's ethnic mixture. All these forces began to come together around the middle of the 20th century, ultimately changing the way Americans perceived each other and their own values.

Meanwhile, the black population, which had reached 8.8 million by 1900 — 90 percent of whom lived in the South — began to change rapidly in the early to mid-1900s. Jobs were being created in the rapidly industrializing North, while the South's oppressive Jim Crow laws were spurring a mass exodus known as the Great Migration. Over six decades, an estimated 6 million blacks left the South for new lives in the North and West. (*See sidebar, p. 12.*)

Mexican migration also began to accelerate in the early to mid-20th century. It had begun in the late 1800s with the building of the railroads across the American Southwest. By 1900, half a million Mexicans were living in the United States. Though they weren't treated as well as Northern European immigrants, Mexicans didn't experience the same exclusion as Asians. All Mexicans living in territories acquired from Mexico were granted citizenship. In 1897, a U.S. district court ruled that the skin color of Mexicans should not be a factor in determining eligibility for citizenship.

The vast majority, however, had no interest in citizenship. "Why bother to become an American citizen when the land one loved, the land of family, language and *la*

raza (the people or race), was so close by?," wrote historian Lawrence H. Fuchs.[45]

But eligibility for citizenship didn't stop discrimination, of course. "The Mexican-American has been the black man of the Southwest," wrote Ronnie Lopez, executive assistant to former Arizona Democratic Gov. Bruce Babbitt. "There have been rapings and lynchings. . . . People's land was taken from them."[46]

The immigrant waves of the first quarter of the century brought another 750,000 legal immigrants from Mexico. The flow ebbed during the Great Depression, when many recent Mexican arrivals voluntarily returned to their homeland, and the United States tightened its immigration policy. Some 400,000 Mexicans — including many born in the United States — were deported. Mexican immigration to the United States picked up again — though slightly — in the 1940s, spurred by wartime labor shortages. In 1942, the nation initiated the "Bracero" guestworker program, under which large numbers of temporary workers were transported north. The program was supposed to end with the war but lasted until Congress refused to renew it in 1964. The Mexican guestworkers — 4.8 million over the life of the program — worked in at least 38 states, mostly picking fruit and vegetables in the Southwest.[47]

By the 1960s, public sympathy for the Civil Rights Movement was spreading across the country, giving President Lyndon B. Johnson (1963-1969) the support he needed to push through the 1964 Civil Rights Act, which outlawed segregation in public places. A year later, Johnson signed the Voting Rights Act of 1965, significantly improving blacks' access to the polls.

The new laws were the crowning legislative achievements of the Civil Rights Movement and reflected its successful effort to mobilize public support for its cause. The movement's success also inspired other groups that felt they were treated unfairly. Feminist scholar Jo Freeman wrote, "During the fifties and early sixties, the Civil Rights Movement captured the public imagination and educated it on the immorality of discrimination and the legitimacy of mass protest . . . . For women, it provided not only a model for action but a very different world view from that of the 'separate spheres' [for women and men], which had been the reigning ideology for the previous century."[48]

C H R O N O L O G Y

1600s-1700s *Slavery is introduced to North America.*

1670-1783 England begins importing African slaves to its Carolina colony. Some 600,000 African slaves are brought to America during the colonial period.

1790 Congress restricts naturalized citizenship to "free white persons" of "good moral character."

1800s *Slavery is abolished, and new rights are granted to African-Americans.*

1808 Congress bans the transatlantic slave trade but not slavery.

1849 Chinese laborers recruited for California gold fields.

1863 President Abraham Lincoln issues the Emancipation Proclamation, declaring slaves in the Confederate states to be free.

1865 Thirteenth Amendment to Constitution is ratified Dec. 1, freeing all slaves.

1866 Congress enacts legislation giving blacks full citizenship.

1870 Fifteenth Amendment gives black men the right to vote.

1876 First "Jim Crow" laws in South mandate segregated public facilities.

1882 Chinese Exclusion Act forbids immigration by Chinese laborers.

1896 Supreme Court upholds "separate but equal" doctrine for whites and blacks in *Plessy v. Ferguson.*

1900s-1945 *Congress seeks "homogeneity" by favoring immigrants from northern and western Europe while severely restricting everyone else. U.S. blacks migrate northward for jobs and rights.*

1915 Blacks begin "Great Migration" from the South to the North.

1924 Immigration Act of 1924 essentially limits citizenship to immigrants from northern and western Europe.

1943 Congress repeals Chinese Exclusion Act (but 1924 Immigration Act is still in force).

1946-2000 *Post-war baby boom creates huge population "bulge." Immigrant pool expands. Civil Rights Movement makes major advances.*

1946 First of 78 million post-World War II baby boomers are born.

1963 March for Jobs and Freedom attracts up to 300,000 demonstrators to Washington in pivotal moment for the Civil Rights Movement.

1964 President Lyndon B. Johnson signs Civil Rights Act, outlawing segregation in public places.

1965 Immigration and Nationality Act opens citizenship to Asians, Hispanics, Africans and others largely excluded by the 1924 Immigration Act. The Supreme Court, in *Loving v. Virginia,* unanimously rules that restrictions on interracial marriage are unconstitutional."

1970s Rev. Jerry Falwell and other leaders call on conservative Christians to become politically active; the Religious Right becomes political force.

2000s *America contemplates "majority-minority" status. Baby boomers enter old age.*

2001 U.S. Hispanic population reaches 37 million, making Latinos the largest ethnic minority.

2008 Census Bureau projects that by 2042 whites will no longer be majority in the United States.

2011 Minority births outnumber white newborns. . . . Net Mexican immigration to United States falls to zero, mostly in response to Great Recession that began in 2007. First baby boomers reach retirement age of 65.

2012 Religion survey indicates that for the first time Protestants comprise less than half of Americans.

Black Migration Makes a U-Turn

Millions fled the South, but many are returning.

Demographers and historians call it the "Great Migration," an extraordinary exodus of blacks from the South to the urban North throughout much of the 20th century. Now that epic shift is reversing, bringing millions of African-Americans back to a region that once shunned or tormented them and their ancestors.

Between 1916 and 1975, an estimated 6 million African-Americans left the South in search of greater economic opportunity and social freedom in cities such as Chicago, Detroit, Cleveland and New York. But in the 1990s demographers began to notice something remarkable: Millions of black Americans were leaving their homes and jobs in the North and returning to their roots in the South.

Census data released in 2011 show that 57 percent of American blacks now live in the South, the highest percentage since 1960. Michigan and Illinois, home to large concentrations of African-Americans, both lost black population for the first time, according to the 2010 census, and Atlanta replaced Chicago as the city with the second-largest African-American population, after New York. More than one million blacks now living in the South were born in the Northeast, a 10-fold increase since 1970.[1]

"This is the decade of black flight," Brookings Institution demographer William Frey told *The New York Times* last year.[2]

Frey credited the return of many blacks to the South to an improved racial and economic climate there, along with "the strong cultural and economic ties that the South holds for blacks." Even so, he noted that "blacks, by and large, are not settling in the Deep South states that registered the greatest out-migration of blacks in the 1960s" and where discriminatory "Jim Crow" laws restricted blacks' freedom.[3]

That out-migration began in earnest in the second decade of the 20th century, driven by the demand for workers in Northern munitions factories during World War 1.

Between 1916 and 1919, half a million African-Americans came North.

Yet, jobs were far from the only lure for Southern blacks. Isabel Wilkerson, author of the Pulitzer Prize-winning portrait of the Great Migration, *The Warmth of Other Suns*, frames the migration as a flight from racial hatred and abuse.

"This was . . . a defection from a system that had held [black] Americans in an artificial hierarchy that restricted their every move . . .," Wilkerson told *CQ Researcher* in an e-mail interview. "They were, in effect, seeking political asylum from a caste system that limited every aspect of their lives and [that] was enforced with such brutality that, in the two decades leading up to the Migration, an African-American was lynched in a public spectacle every four days for some perceived breach of that caste system."

The economic impact the South faced from the exodus of blacks wasn't apparent at first. Some Southerners gloated: "As the North grows blacker, the South grows whiter," the New Orleans *Times-Picayune* wrote.[4]

Then, as the implications of the loss of so much of the South's agricultural workforce became clear, worry set in. Southern authorities tried to stem the hemorrhaging of cheap farm labor by invoking "anti-enticement" laws to discourage agents from northern companies from recruiting blacks.[5] But it was too late: The Great Migration was on. And it kept going long after the lure of Northern jobs ended following World War I.

"Those in the World War I-era wave of the Great Migration didn't see their move as permanent — they thought when the war was over, they'd go back home," says Lorenzo Morris, a political science professor at Howard University in Washington. "But when the war ended, although it was difficult to stay [in the North], to return was intolerable."

Lessons from the Civil Rights Movement also helped to frame the push for gay rights. Bayard Rustin, a civil rights leader and a key organizer of the landmark 1963 March on Washington, later turned the lessons he had learned to promoting gay rights. "Today, blacks are no longer the litmus paper or the barometer of social change," he said in 1986. "The new 'niggers' are gays. . . . It is in this sense that gay people are the new barometer for social change."[49]

The New Newcomers

The Exclusion Act, which prohibited Chinese and most other Asians from immigrating to the United States,

During the post-war 1920s, the industrial economy kept booming, and so did the migration: Nearly a million more blacks headed North during the decade, and nearly half a million more left the South during the Depression era of the 1930s. The exodus continued — 1.6 million in the 1940s, 1.4 million in the '50s, another million in the '60s. When the Great Migration began, one in 10 American blacks lived outside the South; by the 1970s, nearly one in two did.[6] Within the migration statistics is evidence of an evolution in American society, culture and politics. "Many leading figures in American culture — from [writers] Toni Morrison and August Wilson to [performers] Miles Davis and Aretha Franklin to [sports figures] Jesse Owens and Jackie Robinson — are people whose names we likely would never have known had there been no Great Migration," Wilkerson said in the e-mail interview. "Each one of them was a child of this Migration, whose life chances were altered because their parents or grandparents chose to escape the restrictions of the South."

The Great Migration came to a close in the 1970s after its over-arching catalyst — a caste system sanctioned by law — ended with passage of landmark civil rights legislation during the previous decade. By the 1990s, the Great Migration had turned around. But its legacy lives on.

"Perhaps one of the least recognized effects of the migration was its role, unintended though it was, in helping bring the South into mainstream culture and ultimately helping it open up to the rest of the country," Wilkerson said in the e-mail interview. "The upending of the caste system brought the South more in line with the rest of the country and made it a more welcoming place for white Northerners and for immigrants who might never have considered living there under the old regime, as well as for the children and grandchildren of black Southerners who had fled in previous generations.

"The return migration of many of the children and grandchildren of the Great Migration is, in my view, one of the legacies of the Great Migration itself," Wilkerson continued. "The people who left, by their heartbreaking decision

Schomburg Center for Research in Black Culture

An estimated 6 million African-Americans left the South between 1916 and 1975 in search of greater economic opportunity and social freedom, settling in such cities as Chicago, Detroit, Cleveland and New York. Today, many blacks are leaving the North and returning to their Southern roots.

to leave, helped to change the region they had been forced to flee and make it a more welcoming place for everyone, including immigrants from other parts of the world, for white Northerners who might never have considered living in the South and for the migrants' own descendants."

— *Bill Wanlund*

[1] Sabrina Tavernise and Robert Gebeloff, "Many U.S. Blacks Moving to South, Reversing Trend," *The New York Times*, March 24, 2011, www.nytimes.com/2011/03/25/us/25south.html?pagewanted=all.

[2] Quoted in *ibid.*

[3] William Frey, "The New Great Migration: Black Americans' Return to the South, 1965-2000", The Brookings Institution, May 2004, www.brookings.edu/~/media/research/files/reports/2004/5/demographics%20frey/20040524_frey.

[4] Isabel Wilkerson, *The Warmth of Other Suns: The Epic Story of America's Great Migration* (2010), p. 162.

[5] *Ibid.*

[6] *Ibid.*, p. 8.

was repealed in 1943, when China was an American ally in World War II. However, another strict law — the Immigration Act of 1924, which put annual quotas on the number of immigrants from each country who could be accepted into the United States — was still in effect.

In a later analysis, the State Department historian's office wrote, "The most basic purpose of the 1924 Immigration Act was to preserve the ideal of American homogeneity."[50] To do so, the act tied the quotas to numbers from the 1890 census, in a thinly disguised attempt to limit a new flood of immigrants — many of

Boomers More Conservative but Still Feisty

Mistrust of government still spurs '60s generation.

Forty years ago, the anti-establishment protests of the baby boom generation helped end the Vietnam War. Today, many of those same boomers form the core of the conservative Tea Party movement.

The Tea Party phenomenon reflects a general move to the right by many of the 78 million Americans born between 1946 and 1964, pollsters and demographers say. In 2008, 12 percent of boomers identified themselves as liberal, compared with 30 percent in 1972, according to the American National Election Survey. Meanwhile, the percentage calling themselves conservative more than doubled, from 21 percent to 46 percent.[1]

Still, many experts say the ideological transformation of the boomer generation is not inconsistent with its formative ideals in the 1960s.

"Tea Partiers are mistrustful of authority," says Leonard Steinhorn, a communications professor at American University in Washington who has studied the boomers. "In many ways that distrust of any sort of power or authority is not so dissimilar to what so many boomers throughout the years have expressed against either unchecked power or illegitimate authority, which many felt was exercised during the Vietnam War."

The Pew Research Center, which tracks Americans' social and political attitudes, says many boomers who pushed for sweeping societal change in the '60s are feeling uncomfortable with demographic and cultural shifts occurring in society today.

"Many boomers express reservations about the changing face of America," the Pew Research Center said in a report outlining the results of a survey on political views. "Boomers' current attitudes bear little imprint from coming of age in an era of great social change."[2]

Citing the Pew report, William Frey, a demographer at the Brookings Institution, a Washington think tank, noted boomers' attitudes on immigration. "[Twenty-three] percent of baby boomers regard the country's growing population of immigrants as a change for the better," he wrote. "Forty-three percent saw it as a change for the worse. Almost half of white boomers said the growing number of newcomers from other countries represented a threat to traditional U.S. customs and values."[3]

The conservative shift belies boomers' popular image — honed by the counterculture of the 1960s — as left-wing idealists whose motto was "don't trust anyone over 30."

Under that banner, boomers challenged the "establishment" over issues such as the Vietnam War, racial and sexual equality and matters of faith. More than 60 percent left organized religion, most while in their teens or early 20s, though about a third of those eventually returned.[4]

---

them poor and uneducated — from Eastern and Southern Europe. So, while the law allowed immigration by about 51,000 Germans and 62,000 people from Great Britain and Ireland, it permitted fewer than 4,000 Italians and around 2,000 Russians to enter. In fact, 86.5 percent of the yearly immigrant quota of 164,667 was to come from northwest Europe and Scandinavia.[51]

With only minor modifications, the act remained in force for 40 years. Then, reflecting the growing atmosphere of tolerance in the 1960s, Congress passed the Immigration and Nationality Act of 1965, which abolished the national origins quota system. The new law limited to 170,000 the total number of immigrants allowed into the country but eliminated regional quotas and tied immigration to immigrants' skills and family relationships with citizens or U.S. residents.

"This is not a revolutionary bill," President Johnson said at the time. "It does not affect the lives of millions. . . . It will not reshape the structure of our daily lives or add importantly to either our wealth or our power."[52]

Johnson may have underestimated the impact of the law, or he may have been understating the case to ease the fears of nervous nationalists. In any event, 30 years after the law went into effect, the United States had admitted more than 18 million new immigrants, more than three times the number who had entered over the previous three decades.

This time, instead of northern Europeans, immigrants from Latin America topped the list. While European immigrants made up nearly 60 percent of the United States' total foreign population in 1970,

A 2009 survey by pollster John Zogby found that 36 percent of boomers thought their generation would be remembered for its self-indulgence, compared with 31 percent who said its legacy would be social change.[5]

Still, in gauging the boomer generations' legacy, it's important to see the nation's transformation in the past four decades in a positive light, Steinhorn says.

"We are a far better, more inclusive, more equal, more free, more environmentally conscious and less bigoted and prejudiced society than we have ever been in our nation's history," he says. "And given that our nation's original sin was built on bigotry and discrimination . . ., we have come a very long way in just a few decades."

— *Bill Wanlund*

[1]Survey cited by Karlyn Bowman and Andrew Rugg, "As the Baby Boomers Turn," *Los Angeles Times*, Sept. 12, 2011, www.latimes/news/opinion/commentary/la-oe-bowman-baby-boomers-more-conservative-20010912,0,4867587.story.

[2]"The Generation Gap and the 2012 Election," Pew Research Center for the People and the Press, Nov. 3, 2011, p. 11, www.people-press.org/2011/11/03/the-generation-gap-and-the-2012-election/3.

[3]William Frey, "Baby Boomers Had Better Embrace Change," *The Washington Post*, June 8, 2012, www.brookings.edu/research/opinions/2012/06/08-baby-boomers-frey.

[4]Research by Prof. Wade Clark Roof, cited in Leonard Steinhorn, *The Greater Generation* (2006).

[5]John Zogby, "The Baby Boomers' Legacy," *Forbes.com*, July 23, 2009, www.forbes.com/2009/07/22/baby-boomer-legacy-change-consumer-opinions-columnists-john-zogby.html.

AFP/Getty Images/Kimihiro Hoshino

Some 78 million Americans, known as the baby boom generation, were born between 1946 and 1964. In 2008, 12 percent of boomers identified themselves as liberal, compared with 46 percent who said they were conservative.

they accounted for only 15 percent by the end of the century. The percentage of immigrants from Latin America, however, grew from less than 19 percent to more than 50 percent in the same period.[53]

In recent years the United States has admitted more than a million new immigrants annually. Today, Hispanics make up the lion's share of the immigrant population. Nearly 22 million, or around 55 percent of foreign-born Americans, came from Central or South America or the Caribbean; about 404,000 arrived in 2011 alone, or about 37 percent of the total.

However, in 2011, for the first time, Asian immigrants outnumbered Hispanics: Some 438,000 came from East and South Asia and the Middle East, representing 41 percent of new immigrants. About 8.4 percent of American immigrants came from Europe, another 9.1 percent from Africa and the remainder, around 5.1 percent, from "other regions" — principally, Canada and Oceania.[54]

Overall, the U.S. population is aging. In 1950, when the baby boom was just getting under way, 8.2 percent of Americans were 65 or older; now, with the boomers reaching that age, 13.3 percent are in that age bracket.[55] Meanwhile, the birth rate is declining: The United States recorded 4 million births in 2010, down 3 percent from the previous year, continuing a recent trend.[56]

These factors, along with increasing longevity (expected life span in the United States now is about 78.5 years), pushed the median age of Americans to 37.2 in 2010 — up from 35.3 in 2000. "The aging of the baby boom population, along with stabilizing birth rates and longer life expectancy, have contributed to the increase in median age," according to the Census Bureau.[57]

CURRENT SITUATION

Immigration Standstill

Once a flood, the flow of immigrants from Mexico into the United States has come to a halt.

In April, the Pew Hispanic Center reported that since 2007 net immigration from Mexico — the single largest source of immigrants to the United States — had dropped to zero. Mexicans are still emigrating to the United States, the center said, but just as many, and maybe more, are returning home.

"The standstill appears to be the result of many factors, including the weakened U.S. job and housing construction markets, heightened border enforcement, a rise in deportations, the growing dangers associated with illegal border crossings, the long-term decline in Mexico's birth rates and broader economic conditions in Mexico," Pew said.[58]

Audrey Singer, a senior fellow at the Metropolitan Policy Program at the Brookings Institution, believes the decline is due largely to developments in Mexico. "They've been sending labor to the U.S. for one or two generations, but now they have a shrinking supply themselves. Fertility rates are dropping, and they have a birthrate close to ours. Moreover, Mexican education levels are rising, and people are deciding not to come who may have taken a chance before."

The immigration pause is not likely to continue, however, she says. "We can probably assume that when our economy begins to pick up, immigration from Mexico will resume."

Even with the recent slowdown, America has about 12 million Mexican immigrants — more immigrants than from all other countries combined. Roughly 10 percent of people born in Mexico currently reside in the United States.[59]

However, more than half of the Mexicans in the United States are undocumented, according to the Department of Homeland Security, a fact that stirs heated debate, especially in the Border States.[60] Cities and states have adopted a variety of measures to deal with illegal immigration, including a controversial law adopted by Arizona in 2010 aimed at driving illegal immigrants away. Known as SB 1070, the measure requires law enforcement officials to check the immigration papers of suspected undocumented workers.[61]

Under challenge in the courts, SB 1070 is regarded as at least partly responsible, along with high unemployment rates, for a sharp decline in the number of undocumented immigrants in Arizona, from 560,000 in 2008 to 360,000 in 2011.[62]

"The greatest effect of the bill is its deterrent effect," said Republican state Rep. John Kavanagh, a sponsor of SB 1070. "It probably scared a lot of illegal immigrants from coming here in the first place or staying if they were here." Kavanagh said the loss of illegal immigrants opened up job opportunities for U.S. citizens and legal immigrants at a time when the state's unemployment rate is 9.5 percent. "So losing 100,000 or 200,000 workers who were undercutting legal workers and depressing wages is a big plus, as far as I am concerned," he said. "Good riddance."[63]

But the Center for American Progress, a liberal Washington, D.C., research organization that opposes the legislation, estimates that if all undocumented workers were expelled from Arizona, the state would lose $29.5 billion in pre-tax salary and wage earnings, $4.2 billion in tax revenue and more than 500,000 jobs for both legal and undocumented workers.[64]

Dayton Model

In some places, especially cities far removed from the Border States, public officials are encouraging immigration instead of discouraging it.

For instance, the once-thriving manufacturing center of Dayton, Ohio, started losing population in the 1970s after businesses began relocating to Sun Belt states with cheaper, non-union labor. General Motors closed a large assembly plant in 2008, eliminating 2,400 jobs; NCR, born in Dayton in 1884 as the National Cash Register Co., moved to Atlanta in 2009, eliminating another 1,000 jobs. Dayton's population plunged 42 percent between 1970 and 2010, sinking to 141,000. Unemployment is currently over 10 percent.

Hoping to end the downward spiral, civic leaders in 2011 introduced the "Welcome Dayton" initiative to attract immigrant entrepreneurs and workers. Welcome Dayton serves as a catalyst for public institutions such as police, libraries and community-service organizations to help brand the city as immigrant-friendly. For instance, the city's teachers are offered classes in Spanish, Arabic, Turkish and Swahili to make it easier for them to work with immigrant students.

Dayton also helped to establish a center to provide education, recreation and other services to immigrants for the region's Ahiska Turkish community. Officials plan to authorize grants to help immigrants establish businesses, and the city's First Annual World Soccer Tournament, held in September, featured local adult and youth teams representing the international community.

Tom Wahlrab, who retired in January as director of the city's Office of Human Rights, says, "Two things are fueling Welcome Dayton: The need for economic development and the human factor. Many of those who are coming are refugees with a lot of needs. Unless we recognize those needs and do what we can to help them gain a foothold in our community, they're going to be a burden. They won't be productive, and they're going to cost the community in terms of the social services we'll need to provide."

It's too early to measure concrete results, although Dayton in 2011 added 600 new residents, Wahlrab says — a small gain, but the first population increase after 40 years of steady decline. Still, other localities are taking notice. Financially strapped Detroit, which launched "Global Detroit" in 2010 with the slogan, "Welcoming and Connecting the World to Our City," invited Wahlrab to come and discuss Dayton's experiences. "There is a certain elegance and opportunity in the plan that Dayton has put together," said Steve Tobocman, director of Global Detroit. "They've done certain things so profoundly right that I think we have a lot to learn from it."[65]

Aging in Place

As cities and states try to adjust to immigration trends, they also are beginning to taking steps — albeit haltingly in some cases — to accommodate the transportation, housing, health and other needs of the aging population. In eight years, one-fourth of residents in half of Ohio's counties will be at least 60 years old, and Arizona and Pennsylvania are projecting that a quarter of their residents will top age 60 by 2020.[66]

Some cities are stepping up to the challenge. For example:

• New York City, where more than one in eight residents are over 60, established Age-Friendly New York City, which officials describe as "promoting an 'age-in-everything' lens across all aspects of city life. The initiative asks the city's public agencies, businesses, cultural, educational and religious institutions, community

Young people at the Coalition for Humane Immigrant Rights of Los Angeles on Aug. 15, 2012, hear about a new federal program under which eligible undocumented young people can avoid deportation and obtain work permits. Many economists argue that immigrant workers have a positive effect on the economy, but others contend that curbing immigration would leave more jobs for U.S.-born workers.

groups and individuals to consider how changes to policy and practice can create a city more inclusive of older adults and more sensitive to their needs." The effort, formed in 2009, is part of a broader Age-friendly Cities project sponsored by the World Health Organization.[67]

• In Atlanta, where one-fifth of residents will be over age 60 by 2030, the Atlanta Regional Commission created a Lifelong Communities Initiative aimed at promoting housing and transportation options, encouraging healthy lifestyles and expanding information and access to services tailored to older residents.[68]

Still, many localities are ill-prepared to accommodate the coming wave of older residents, experts say. A 2005 survey of communities by the National Association of Area Agencies on Aging found that while many communities had some programs for older people, "few had undertaken a comprehensive assessment to create a 'livable community' for all ages." A 2011 follow-up survey found "only limited progress" toward that goal, the group said. Indeed, as a result of the recent recession, "most communities have been able only to 'hold the line' — maintaining policies, programs and services already established," the association said. "They have not been able to move

Is large-scale immigration good for the U.S. economy?

YES
Audrey Singer
Senior Fellow,
The Brookings Institution

Written for *CQ Global Researcher*, November 2012

The typical way of viewing immigration's impact on the economy is through costs and benefits derived from their presence in the labor market.

While economists debate how best to address this issue, there is some agreement that immigrants are a net benefit as measured by national GDP.

A benefit of a steady flow of immigrant workers to the United States is that they are responsive to labor-market changes and can go where workers are needed. This is especially so for newcomers, who tend to be most flexible on where to locate. The plateauing of immigration to the United States in response to declining jobs following the recession is an important illustration at the national level; many local areas mirror this trend.

It is not surprising, then, that the greatest economic impact of immigrants is at the state and local levels, where the brunt of costs to schools, health care systems and law enforcement is borne.

In the past two decades, immigrant settlement patterns have shifted significantly. Between 1930 and 1990, half of all immigrants in the United States lived in just five metropolitan areas, primarily in the Northeast and Midwest. Since then, the share in the top five places has declined to 40 percent, as immigrants have found opportunities in new places, particularly in the South and West.

Areas with new immigrant streams are more focused on the costs of immigration because, at least in the pre-recession economy, these areas attracted low-wage undocumented workers at a fast pace.

Estimates summarized by the Congressional Budget Office in 2007 show that in the aggregate and over the long term, tax revenues paid by immigrants are greater than the services they use. However, unauthorized immigrants use more state and local services than they pay for because of the types of services provided and because of the eligibility rules.

For example, while the percentage of school-age children of unauthorized immigrants is small nationally, this population tends to be concentrated at the very local level, and thus its impact can be swift.

The long-term view brings an important economic benefit into focus. Most of the future growth of the U.S. labor force will come from immigrants and their offspring. This next generation of workers will support the large cohort of baby boom retirees that now looms large. This is a reward that the United States should reap — with proper investments — as the next economy and workforce take shape.

NO
Madeleine Sumption
Senior Policy Analyst,
Migration Policy Institute

Written for *CQ Global Researcher*, March 2012

The assertion that large-scale immigration is good for the U.S. economy implies that more immigration is inherently better than less. This is not necessarily true. The types of immigrants a country has — and whether their skills meet U.S. labor market needs — arguably matters much more than raw numbers.

Most economists believe that immigration to the United States has raised average incomes (albeit recognizing the gains are not universal), and that immigrants — through their tax contributions — make it easier to provide public services without raising tax rates. Other research suggests immigrants have contributed disproportionately to innovation and productivity. But these findings come with caveats.

First, not all immigration is the same, and the benefits of some types of immigration are more clear-cut than others. The greatest economic gains come from highly skilled immigrants, many of whom compete for the tiny share of permanent visas available for employment-based immigration. (Most U.S. green cards are issued on the basis of family ties, not prospective economic value.)

Low-skilled immigrants bring some economic benefits, such as lower prices for goods and services like food and child care. But these overwhelmingly low-paid workers also draw on public services such as education. More selective policies to admit and retain the low-skilled workers best able to support themselves might help shift this calculus. Balancing current costs and benefits, the overall economic impact of low-skilled workers today is probably close to zero.

The green card lottery, known as the diversity visa, is also likely to have a low economic return, since its annual 50,000 beneficiaries fare relatively poorly in the U.S. labor market. A similar argument applies to some refugees and to the parents and adult siblings of U.S. citizens. These types of immigration are almost certainly not economically detrimental, and there are plenty of noneconomic arguments in their favor (like the value of family unity and the moral obligation to protect people fleeing persecution). The economic arguments, however, are not particularly compelling.

Immigration policies are adopted with more than economic benefit in mind — and for good reason. But if the goal is purely economic gain, simply opening the immigration spigot is not the best strategy. Rather than a bottom-line focus on numbers, a more reliable approach for making immigration an engine for economic growth would be to create more thoughtful, predictable and transparent policies to select the immigrant workers who will succeed here.

forward to the degree needed to address the nation's current 'age wave.' "[69]

"The bottom line is, the baby boomers are hitting," Charles Gehring, president and CEO of LifeCare Alliance, an agency that serves seniors in central Ohio, told the *Columbus Dispatch*. "Are communities prepared for this? No."[70]

OUTLOOK

Political Changes

The 2012 presidential election underscored in dramatic fashion the crucial role that demographic changes are having in political and policy circles. Experts expect that role to grow even stronger in coming years as the profile of the electorate continues to evolve.

Many analysts believe the Republican Party fared poorly in this year's election in part because it did not do enough to address the interests of the nation's burgeoning Hispanic population. "The Hispanic population will grow faster than any other demographic, meaning this political problem is growing for Republicans," GOP strategist Matt Mackowiak told *The Hill* after the Nov. 6 elections. "We need more Hispanic candidates, more Hispanic outreach and less bellicose language on immigration."[71]

Former Secretary of State Condoleezza Rice, who served in the administration of Republican George W. Bush, said Republicans had sent "mixed messages" on immigration and women's issues and must do a better job of adapting to changing U.S. demographics.

"Right now for me, the most powerful argument is that the changing demographics in the country really necessitate an even bigger tent for the Republican Party," she said. "But when you look at the composition of the electorate, clearly we are losing important segments of that electorate, and what we have to do is to appeal to those people not as identity groups but understanding that if you can get the identity issues out of the way, then you can appeal on the broader issues that all Americans share concerns for."[72]

The demographic challenges facing policy makers in coming years cross party lines, however. Dealing with the burgeoning ranks of seniors and adequately funding Social Security, Medicare and Medicaid — which pays for nursing home care for low-income elderly people — are among the biggest challenges.

More than 56 million Americans now receive Social Security benefits, and 23 percent of married couples and about 46 percent of unmarried persons who are 65 years old or older rely on Social Security for 90 percent or more of their income.[73]

In 2010, for the first time, Social Security collected less in taxes than it paid out in benefits. The Social Security Board of Trustees told Congress that the combined assets of the two trust funds from which Social Security benefits are paid will be exhausted in 2033.[74]

Meanwhile, some question whether Obama's re-election, along with the growing prominence of minorities in the nation's demographic profile, means that policy makers no longer need to pay the same degree of attention to race and ethnicity as in the past.

Brian Smedley, vice president of the Joint Center for Political and Economic Studies, a Washington-based research organization dealing with minority public policy issues, doesn't think so.

"One of the most significant challenges for the Civil Rights Movement today is to somehow tackle the notion that the United States is now color-blind or post-racial," he says. He fears the nation is in danger of leaving behind the ideals of racial equality.

"There are many who believe that because we have [elected] an African-American president, and people of color are leading *Fortune* 500 companies, etc., race no longer matters in our society. Of course, we've made tremendous progress in race relations in the United States over the past 50-plus years, and that should be celebrated," he says. "It's remarkable that we have created a society that is much more egalitarian, and we're moving closer to our ideal as a nation where people truly are judged by the content of their character and not by the color of their skin.

"However," he continues, "many people of color still face profound inequities across a host of dimensions . . . such as health, wealth, educational status, income, home ownership, you name it. It's more critical than ever that we focus the nation's attention on these problems because the demographic shifts that are coming suggest that we need to be very mindful of what our nation will look like and how the inequities will hurt everyone in this country unless we solve them."

NOTES

1. "Most Children Younger Than Age 1 are Minorities, Census Bureau Reports", U.S. Census Bureau news release, May 17, 2012, www.census.gov/newsroom/releases/archives/population/cb12-90.html.

2. "An Older and More Diverse Nation by Midcentury", U.S. Census Bureau news release, Aug. 14, 2008, www.census.gov/newsroom/releases/archives/population/cb08-123.html.

3. Haya El Nasser and Paul Overberg, "Census tracks 20 years of sweeping change," *USA Today*, Aug. 10, 2011, http://usatoday30.usatoday.com/news/nation/census/2011-08-10-census-20-years-change_n.htm.

4. Mark Hugo Lopez and Paul Taylor, "Latino Voters in the 2012 Election," Pew Hispanic Center, Nov. 7, 2012, www.pewhispanic.org/2012/11/07/latino-voters-in-the-2012-election/.

5. Michael D. Shear, "Demographic Shift Brings New Worry for Republicans," *The New York Times*, Nov. 7, 2012, www.nytimes.com/2012/11/08/us/politics/obamas-victory-presents-gop-with-demographic-test.html?ref=politics.

6. "Obama Win Shows Demographic Shifts," *op. cit.*

7. Press release, "Latino Candidates Make History on Election Night," National Association of Latino Elected and Appointed Officials Education Fund, Nov. 7, 2012, www.prnewswire.com/news-releases/latino-candidates-make-history-on-election-night-177729141.html.

8. " 'Nones' on the Rise: One-in-Five Adults Have No Religious Affiliation", Report by the Pew Research Center Forum on Religion & Public Life, Oct. 9, 2012, www.pewforum.org/Unaffiliated/nones-on-the-rise.aspx.

9. Laura B. Shrestha and Elayne J. Heisler, "The Changing Demographic Profile of the United States", Congressional Research Service, March 31, 2011, www.fas.org/sgp/crs/misc/RL32701.pdf.

10. D'Vera Cohn and Paul Taylor, "Baby Boomers Approach Age 65 — Glumly," Pew Research Center, Dec. 20, 2010, http://pewresearch.org/pubs/1834/baby-boomers-old-age-downbeat-pessimism.

11. For background see Alan Greenblatt, "The Graying Planet," *CQ Global Researcher*, March 15, 2011, pp. 133-156.

12. 2010 Census Data, U.S. Census Bureau, http://2010.census.gov/2010census/data/.

13. Sabrina Tavernise, "Whites Account for Under Half of Births in U.S.," *The New York Times*, May 17, 2012, www.nytimes.com/2012/05/17/us/whites-account-for-under-half-of-births-in-us.html?pagewanted=all.

14. John Blake, "Are Whites Racially Oppressed?", CNN, March 4, 2011, www.cnn.com/2010/US/12/21/white.persecution/index.html.

15. Daniel Cox; E.J. Dionne, Jr.; William A. Galston; Robert P. Jones, "What it Means to be an American," Brookings Institution, Sept. 6, 2011, www.brookings.edu/research/reports/2011/09/06-american-attitudes.

16. "U.S. Religious Landscape Survey", Pew Forum on Religion and Public Life, February 2008, http://religions.pewforum.org/pdf/report-religious-landscape-study-full.pdf.

17. *Ibid.*

18. Samuel P. Huntington, *Who Are We? The Challenges to America's National Identity* (2004), p. 18.

19. Joel Kotkin, "Minority America," Newgeography.com, Aug. 20, 2008, www.newgeography.com/content/00175-minority-america.

20. Paul Taylor, Mark Hugo Lopez, Jessica Hamar Martinez and Gabriel Velasco, "When Labels Don't Fit: Hispanics and Their Views of Identity," Pew Hispanic Center, April 4, 2012, "Two-Thirds of Democrats Now Support Gay Marriage," Poll, Pew Forum on Religion and Public Life, July 31, 2012, www.pewforum.org/Politics-and-Elections/2012-opinions-on-for-gay-marriage-unchanged-after-obamas-announcement.aspx.

21. "The Rise of Asian Americans," Pew Research Center, June 19, 2012, www.pewsocialtrends.org/2012/06/19/the-rise-of-asian-americans/.

22. Wendy Wang, "The Rise of Intermarriage," Pew Research Center, Feb. 16, 2012, www.pewsocialtrends.org/2012/02/16/the-rise-of-intermarriage/?src=prc-headline.

23. For background, see Haya El Nasser, "Black-white marriages on the rise," *USA Today*, Sept. 20, 2011, http://usatoday30.usatoday.com/news/nation/story/2011-09-19/interracial-marriages/50469776/1.

24. Wang, *op. cit.*

25. "The Generation Gap and the 2012 Election," The Pew Research Center, Nov. 3, 2011, www.people-press.org/2011/11/03/the-generation-gap-and-the-2012-election-3/.

26. Linda A. Jacobsen, *et al.*, "America's Aging Population," *Population Bulletin 66*, no. 1 (2011), Population Reference Bureau.

27. Frank W. Heiland and Zhe Li, "Changes in Labor Force Participation of Older Americans and Their Pension Structures: A Policy Perspective," Boston College Center for Retirement Research, August 2012, http://crr.bc.edu/working-papers/changes-in-labor-force-participation-of-older-americans-and-their-pension-structures-a-policy-perspective-2.

28. Don Lee, "More older workers making up labor force," *Los Angeles Times*, Sept. 4, 2012, http://articles.latimes.com/2012/sep/04/business/la-fi-labor-seniors-20120903.

29. Alicia H. Munnell and April Yanyuan Wu, "Will Delayed Retirement by the Baby Boomers Lead to Higher Unemployment Among Younger Workers?", Center for Retirement Research at Boston College, October 2012, http://crr.bc.edu/working-papers/will-delayed-retirement-by-the-baby-boomers-lead-to-higher-unemployment-among-younger-workers/.

30. Mark Miller, "Are Older Workers Getting in the Way of the Young?," Reuters, Jan. 6, 2012, www.reuters.com/article/2012/01/06/retirement-jobs-idUSN1E80507520120106.

31. Press release, American Association of Colleges of Nursing, "Nursing Shortage," www.aacn.nche.edu/media-relations/fact-sheets/nursing-shortage.

32. "Immigration, Poverty and Low-Wage Earners: The Harmful Effects of Unskilled Immigrants on American Workers," Federation for American Immigration Reform, July 2010 (revised Feb. 2011), www.fairus.org/publications/immigration-poverty-and-low-wage-earners-the-harmful-effects-of-unskilled-immigrants-on-american-wor.

33. "Georgia Data Quantify Impact of Undocumented Workers," Southwest Economy, Federal Reserve Bank of Dallas, second quarter 2012, www.dallasfed.org/assets/documents/research/swe/2012/swe1202e.pdf.

34. Giovanni Peri, "The Effect of Immigrants on U.S. Employment and Productivity," Federal Reserve Bank of San Francisco Economic Letter, August 30, 2010, www.frbsf.org/publications/economics/letter/2010/el2010-26.html.

35. Niall Stanage, "Women, minorities propel Obama victory," *The Hill*, Nov. 7, 2012, http://thehill.com/homenews/campaign/266485-women-minorities-propel-obama-victory.

36. Quoted in Dylan Scott, "Political Demographic Trends Brighter for Democrats," *Governing*, April 11, 2012, www.governing.com/blogs/politics/gov-political-demographic-trends-brighter-for-democrats.html.

37. Jeffrey Passell, D'Vera Cohn and Mark Hugo Lopez, "Hispanics Account for More than Half of Nation's Growth in Past Decade," Pew Hispanic Center, March 24, 2011, www.pewhispanic.org/2011/03/24/hispanics-account-for-more-than-half-of-nations-growth-in-past-decade/.

38. William H. Frey, "Will 2012 be the Last Hurrah for Whites?," *National Journal*, "The Next America," June 13, 2012, http://nationaljournal.com/thenextamerica/demographics/will-2012-be-the-last-hurrah-for-whites—20120613.

39. Alan I. Abramowitz, "Beyond 2010: Demographic Change and the Future of the Republican Party," University of Virginia Center for Politics, "Larry J. Sabato's Crystal Ball," March 11, 2010, www.centerforpolitics.org/crystalball/articles/aia2010031101/.

40. Ruy Teixeira and William Frey, "New Data on Obama's Massive Demographic Advantage," *The New Republic*, July 9, 2012, www.tnr.com/blog/plank/104746/how-much-will-demographic-changes-help-obama-in-swing-states.

41. Lila Shapiro, "Gay Marriage Victory In Maine, Maryland; Minnesota Votes Down 'Traditional' Amendment (UPDATE)," *The Huffington Post*, Nov. 7, 2012, www.huffingtonpost.com/2012/11/07/gay-marriage-victory_n_2085900.html.

42. "How the Faithful Voted: 2012 Preliminary Analysis," Pew Forum on Religion & Public Life, Nov. 7, 2012, www.pewforum.org/Politics-and-Elections/How-the-Faithful-Voted-2012-Preliminary-Exit-Poll-Analysis.aspx.

43. "Black Americans in Congress," Office of the Clerk, U.S. House of Representatives, http://baic.house.gov/historical-essays/essay.html?intID=1&intSectionID=11.

44. Roger Finke and Rodney Starke, *The Churching of America, 1776-2005: Winners and Losers in Our Religious Economy* (2002), p. 123.

45. Lawrence H. Fuchs, *The American Kaleidoscope: Race, Ethnicity, and the Civic Culture* (1990), p. 134.

46. Rodman D. Griffin, "Hispanic Americans," *CQ Researcher*, Oct. 30, 1992.

47. For background, see Congressional Quarterly, *Congress and the Nation Vol. I* (1965), pp. 762-767.

48. Jo Freeman, "From Suffrage to Women's Liberation: Feminism in Twentieth Century America," published in Jo Freeman, ed., *Women: A Feminist Perspective* (5th ed., 1995), excerpted at www.uic.edu/orgs/cwluherstory/jofreeman/feminism/suffrage.htm.

49. Rev. Osagyefo Uhuru Sekou, "Killing the Buddha" blog, http://killingthebuddha.com/mag/damnation/gays-are-the-new-niggers/.

50. U.S. State Department, Office of the Historian, Milestones 1921-1936, http://history.state.gov/milestones/1921-1936/ImmigrationAct.

51. "Who Was Shut Out?: Immigration Quotas, 1925-1927," History Matters, http://historymatters.gmu.edu/d/5078/.

52. Remarks by President Lyndon B. Johnson at the Signing of the Immigration Bill, Liberty Island, New York, Oct. 3, 1965, www.lbjlib.utexas.edu/johnson/archives.hom/speeches.hom/651003.asp.

53. "U.S. Historical Immigration Trends," Migration Policy Institute, www.migrationinformation.org/datahub/historicaltrends.cfm#source.

54. "The Newly Arrived Foreign-Born Population of the United States: 2010," American Community Survey Brief, U.S. Census Bureau, November 2011, www.census.gov/prod/2011pubs/acsbr10-16.pdf.

55. "USA Quick Facts", US Bureau of the Census, http://quickfacts.census.gov/qfd/states/00000.html.

56. "Births: Final Data for 2010", Joyce Martin, M.P.H., *et al.*, National Center for Health Statistics, August 2012, www.cdc.gov/nchs/births.htm.

57. "2010 Census Shows Nation's Population is Aging ", News Release, US Census Bureau, May 26, 2011, http://2010.census.gov/news/releases/operations/cb11-cn147.html.

58. Jeffrey Passel, D'Vera Cohn and Ana Gonzalez-Barrera, "Net Migration from Mexico Falls to Zero-and Perhaps Less," Pew Hispanic Center, April 23, 2012, www.pewhispanic.org/2012/04/23/net-migration-from-mexico-falls-to-zero-and-perhaps-less/.

59. Jeffrey Passel, *et al.*, "Net Migration from Mexico Falls to Zero-and Perhaps Less", Pew Hispanic Center, April 23, 2012, www.pewhispanic.org/2012/04/23/net-migration-from-mexico-falls-to-zero-and-perhaps-less/.

60. Michael Hoefer, Nancy Rytina and Bryan Baker, "Estimates of the Unauthorized Immigrant Population Residing in the United States: January 2011," Report of the Department of Homeland Security, March 2012, www.dhs.gov/files/statistics/publications/estimates-unauthorized-immigrant-population.shtm.

61. For background, see Kenneth Jost, "Immigration Conflict," *CQ Researcher*, March 9, 2012, pp. 229-252.

62. Daniel González, "Arizona's illegal-immigration population plunges," *The Arizona Republic*, March 23, 2012, www.azcentral.com/arizonarepublic/news/articles/2012/03/23/20120323arizona-illegal-migrant-population-plunges.html.

63. Daniel Gonzalez, "Arizona immigration law: A look at bill's impact 1 year later," *The Arizona Republic*, April 23, 2011, www.azcentral.com/news/election/azelections/articles/2011/04/23/20110423arizona-immigration-law-impact-year-later.html.

64. Raul Hinojsa-Ojeda and Marshall Fritz, "A Rising Tide or a Shrinking Pie: The Economic Impact of Legalization Versus Deportation in Arizona," Center for American Progress, March 2011, www.americanprogress.org/wp-content/uploads/issues/2011/03/pdf/rising_tide.pdf.

65. Andrew O'Reilly, "Dayton's Immigration Strategy for Growth is Drawing Notice", Fox News Latino, May 10, 2012, http://latino.foxnews.com/latino/news/2012/05/10/dayton-immigration-strategy-for-growth-is-drawing-notice/.

66. "Few U.S. cities are ready for aging Baby Boomer population," Associated Press, March 25, 2012, http://usatoday30.usatoday.com/news/health/story/health/story/2012-03-25/Few-US-cities-are-ready-for-aging-baby-boomer-population/53765292/1.

67. "Age-Friendly NYC," Nov. 9, 2012 www.nyam.org/agefriendlynyc/.

68. "Lifelong Communities," Atlanta Regional Commission, Nov. 9, 2012, www.atlantaregional.com/aging-resources/lifelong-communities-llc.

69. "The Maturing of America: Communities Moving Forward for an Aging Population," National Association of Area Agencies on Aging, June 2011, pp. i, ii, www.n4a.org/files/MOA_FINAL_Rpt.pdf.

70. Quoted in "Few cities are ready . . .," *op. cit.*

71. Stanage, *op. cit.*

72. "Condoleezza Rice: GOP Sent 'Mixed Messages' On Immigration And Women's Issues," The Associated Press/ *The Huffington Post*, Nov. 9, 2012, www.huffingtonpost.com/2012/11/09/condoleezza-rice_n_2099505.html.

73. "Social Security Basic Facts," Social Security Administration fact sheet, July 30, 2012, www.ssa.gov/pressoffice/basicfact.htm.

74. "The 2012 Annual Report of the Board Of Trustees of the Federal Old-Age and Survivors Insurance and Federal Disability Insurance Trust Funds", April 25, 2012, U.S. Government Printing Office 73-947, Washington, DC.

BIBLIOGRAPHY

Selected Sources

Books

Ehrenhalt, Alan, *The Great Inversion and the Future of the American City*, Alfred A. Knopf, 2012.
The executive editor of Stateline news service and former executive editor of *Governing* magazine explores how American cities are changing and the implications for the future.

Huntington, Samuel P., *Who Are We? The Challenges to America's National Identity*, Simon & Shuster, 2004.
The late Harvard University political scientist (1927-2008) examines the impact of immigrants and their cultural values on American society.

Putnam, Robert D., and David E. Campbell, *American Grace: How Religion Divides and Unites Us*, Simon & Schuster, 2010.
A professor of public policy at Harvard (Putnam) and a political science professor at the University of Notre Dame (Campbell) examine how religion, politics and culture intersect.

Steinhorn, Leonard, *The Greater Generation: In Defense of the Baby Boom Legacy*, Thomas Dunne Books, 2006.
A professor of communications at American University argues that the postwar generation shaped America for the better.

Wilkerson, Isabel, *The Warmth of Other Suns: The Epic Story of America's Great Migration*, Random House, 2010.
A journalist and Boston University professor provides a Pulitzer Prize-winning account of the exodus of 6 million African-Americans from the South to the urban North and West between 1915 and 1970.

Articles

Brownstein, Ron, "Do Immigrants Threaten American Values?" *National Journal*, June 14, 2012, www.nationaljournal.com/thenextamerica/immigration/do-immigrants-threaten-american-values—20120614.
A journalist dissects a decade of Pew research polling that reveals consistent divides among whites over the impact of immigrants on American society.

Castañeda, Jorge G., and Douglas S. Massey, "Do-it-Yourself Immigration Reform," *The New York Times*, June 1, 2012, www.nytimes.com/2012/06/02/opinion/do-it-yourself-immigration-reform.html?_r=1&ref=jorgegcastaneda.
A former Mexican foreign minister (Castañeda) and a Princeton sociology and public affairs professor (Massey) discuss the causes and effects of the current stasis in immigration from Mexico.

"A Contentious Flock," *The Economist*, July 7, 2012, pp. 33-34.
The reporter examines polarization and diversity among American Catholics.

Frey, William, "Baby Boomers Had Better Embrace Change," *The Washington Post*, June 8, 2012, www

.brookings.edu/research/opinions/2012/06/08-baby-boomers-frey.

A demographer at the Washington, D.C.-based think tank discusses population and attitudinal trends.

Howe, Neal, "What Makes Boomers the Boomers?" *Governing.com*, September 2012, www.governing.com/generations/government-management/gov-what-makes-boomers.html.

A demographer, historian, author and consultant on generational transitions investigates the myths about and realities of the baby boom generation.

Reports and Studies

"Immigration, Poverty and Low-Wage Earners: The Harmful Effect of Unskilled Immigrants on American Workers (2011)," Federation for American Immigration Reform, 2011, www.fairus.org/issue/immigration-poverty-and-low-wage-earners-the-harmful-effect-of-unskilled-immigrants-on-american-work.

A national nonprofit organization that seeks stricter limits on immigration argues that unskilled immigrant labor harms native-born Americans.

"State of Metropolitan America: On the Front Lines of Demographic Transformation," Metropolitan Policy Program, Brookings Institution, 2010.

The Washington-based public policy think tank analyzes the impact of recent demographic changes on U.S. metropolitan areas.

Funk, Cary, and Greg Smith, " 'Nones' on the Rise: One-in-Five Adults Have No Religious Affiliation," Pew Forum on Religion and Public Life, Oct. 9, 2012, www.pewforum.org/Unaffiliated/nones-on-the-rise.aspx.

A nonpartisan research organization examines trends in American religious belief and practice.

Jacobsen, Linda A., *et al.*, "America's Aging Population," Population Reference Bureau, 2011, www.prb.org/pdf11/aging-in-america.pdf.

The think tank report examines the costs and implications of an aging population.

Myers, Dowell, and John Pitkin, "Assimilation Tomorrow: How America's Immigrants will Assimilate by 2030," Center for American Progress, November 2011, www.americanprogress.org/issues/immigration/report/2011/11/14/10583/assimilation-tomorrow/.

A demographer/urban planner (Myers) and a demographer/economist from the University of Southern California (Pitkin) examine the outlook for American immigrants.

For More Information

American Association of Retired Persons, 601 E St., N.W., Washington, DC 20009; 888-687-2277; www.aarp.org. Membership organization that advocates for people 50 years of age and older.

Brookings Institution, 1775 Massachusetts Ave., N.W., Washington, DC 20036; 202-797-6000; www.brookings.edu. Research organization focusing on wide range of issues, including economics, social policy, urban affairs and politics.

Center for Immigration Studies, 1629 K St., N.W., Suite 600, Washington, DC 20006; 202-466-8185; www.cis.org. Research organization that supports lower levels of immigration.

Center for Retirement Research at Boston College, Hovey House, 258 Hammond St., Chestnut Hill, MA 02467;

617-552-1762; www.crr.bu.edu. Research institution focusing on retirement issues.

Pew Research Center, 901 E St., N.W., Washington, DC 20004-2008; 202-552-2000; www.pew.org. Arm of the Pew Charitable Trusts that conducts research on such topics as Hispanics in America and the role of religion in public life.

Urban Institute, 2100 M St., N.W., Washington, DC 20037; 202-833-7200; www.urban.org. Non-partisan research organization focusing on social and economic issues.

U.S. Social Security Administration, Windsor Park Building, 6401 Security Blvd., Baltimore, MD 21235; 800-772-1213; www.ssa.gov. Federal agency that administers the Social Security retirement, disability and survivors' benefits programs.

2

Social Media and Politics

Tom Price

Mitt Romney

Republican presidential candidate Mitt Romney sleds with one of his grandsons in a family photo posted on Pinterest by his wife, Ann. Mrs. Romney and Michelle Obama, as well as the candidates themselves, have posted recipes, family photographs and other personal information on the site in an effort to humanize the candidates and forge closer links to voters.

From *The CQ Researcher*, October 12, 2012.

As Republicans sought to boost Mitt Romney's then-flagging presidential campaign during their August nominating convention in Tampa, this message popped up on the social media website reddit on Aug. 29:

"I am Barack Obama, President of the United States — AMA" (reddit shorthand for "ask me anything").[1]

For the next half hour, Obama fielded questions from reddit participants, generating 5,266 queries and comments. By the morning of Aug. 31, the discussion had logged nearly 5.3 million page views. He wrapped up the unprecedented online session — complete with a photo of him at his computer, shirtsleeves rolled up, tie loosened, to prove he was really answering questions — with a pitch for voting and a link to an online voter-registration form.[2]

In the process, the president asserted his affinity for the rapidly growing world of social media and enrolled more than 10,000 reddit users as potential campaign volunteers, Obama chief digital strategist Joe Rospars said. The president also served notice that he would not allow Romney a solo moment in the sun, even during the GOP convention.

Obama's command of the Internet proved a key to his victory over Arizona Sen. John McCain in 2008. This year, all candidates are striving to emulate Obama's 2008 online success, but there are differences:

- The president's 2012 campaign is doing much more online than it did four years ago.
- The buzz now is about social media such as Facebook, Twitter, YouTube and the many less-prominent platforms such as

Many Voters Ignore Internet Comments

Two-thirds of voters say they are taking little or no account of comments posted on social media and Internet forums before voting for president in November. More consideration is given to conversations with family and friends and opinions voiced by experts on major news outlets.

How much do you consider the following in deciding whom to vote for in the November presidential election?

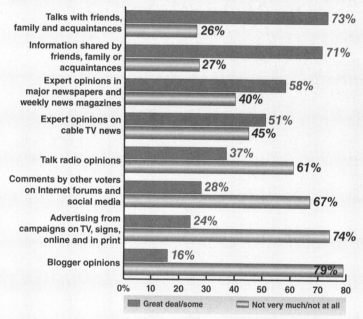

Source: "Heartland Monitor Poll," *National Journal*, June 9, 2012, p. 24, www.allstate.com/Allstate/content/refresh-attachments/Heartland_monitor_XIII_topline.pdf

One proof of social media's growing importance, says Vincent Harris, who ran GOP presidential hopeful Newt Gingrich's online activities in some of this year's primaries, is its incorporation as an integral component of many campaigns' operations. No longer is the "new-media guy" sent to a corner to manage the Internet in isolation from the rest of the staff, Harris explains.

Other proof is in the numbers. Twitter users posted 1.8 million tweets on Election Day in 2008, the kind of event that spurs social media activity. Now tweets average 340 million a day — nearly 200 times as much.[4] This year's Republican National Convention generated more tweets the day before it opened than the 2008 convention did during its full run, according to Adam Sharp, head of Twitter's government, news and social innovation operations.

"More tweets are sent every two days today than had had been sent in total from Twitter's creation in 2006 to the 2008 election," he told a panel at the Democratic National Convention in early September. Registered voters who use Facebook today outnumber those who actually voted in the 2008 general election, says Katie Harbath, a Facebook manager who helps Republicans use the platform.

Overall, nearly two-thirds of U.S. adults say they use social media regularly.[5] And "they don't skew as young as you may think," says Michael Reilly, a partner in the Democratic campaign consulting firm Murphy Vogel Askew Reilly in Alexandria, Va.

While younger people are more likely to use social media, the contingent of older adults is growing most rapidly. Eighty-six percent of 18- to 29-year-olds use social media, compared with about a third of those 65 and older. But participation nearly quintupled among those 50 and older between 2008 and 2012. Nearly

reddit, all of which had far less impact — or didn't even exist — in 2008.

- And Romney's camp is determined to keep up.

"The tools people can use to get messages to their friends are much more powerful than they were in 2008," says Joe Trippi, architect of former New Hampshire Gov. Howard Dean's 2004 campaign for the Democratic presidential nomination, which tapped the powers of the Internet more than any candidate had done before.[3] "The sheer size of the networks has exploded. [Prominent Democratic strategist James] Carville used to say: 'It's the economy, stupid.' Now 'It's the networks, stupid.'"

three times as many 30- to 49-year-olds use social media now as in 2008. Among 18- to 29-year-olds, the increase was just 19 percent, with the same proportion using social media this year as two years ago.[6] (*See graph, p. 30.*)

That growing participation increases social media's attractiveness to politicians, who use the platforms to identify and organize supporters, raise funds and spread their messages. Candidates bypass traditional news media to send unfiltered communication to the public. They target recipients of their messages with growing precision. They contact hard-to-reach voters — especially the young — who record television programs and fast-forward through the commercials. They use online communication to organize phone banks, door-to-door canvassing and other offline activities. And they tap into what is believed to be the most effective form of persuasion: friend-to-friend conversation.

Social media's interactive nature allows candidates to engage in what can be — or can appear to be — conversations with individual voters. Those voters can forward the candidates' posts to their friends, extending the candidates' reach and adding the endorsement of the people who pass the messages on.

But the increasing ability of online campaign strategists to collect and analyze detailed personal information about individual voters has raised privacy concerns.

Polled in May about information sources they tap when deciding how to vote, Americans put family, friends and acquaintances at the top. Bloggers ranked at the bottom, just below advertisements and online comments by people voters don't know.[7] (*See graph, p. 26.*)

Each social medium offers its own political tools. Trying to label one more valuable than the other is "sort of like asking which is your favorite child," says Phil Noble, a Democratic online political consultant since the 1990s. "Advantage," says George Washington University political scientist Michael Cornfield, "goes to people who can use all of them."

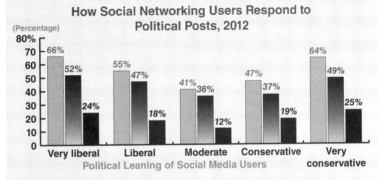

Strongest Views Dominate Political Posts

Social media users who identify themselves as "very liberal" or "very conservative" are more likely than those who identify themselves as less partisan to "like" political posts, write positive comments or "friend" those who share their political views.

How Social Networking Users Respond to Political Posts, 2012

(Percentage)

Source: "Social Networking Sites and Politics," Pew Research Center, March 2012, p. 8, www.pewinternet.org/~/media//Files/ Reports/2012/PIP_SNS_and_politics.pdf

- Hit "like" button for political post
- Posted positive comment
- "Friended" someone with shared views

But one network clearly dominates. "Facebook is the 800-pound gorilla," with its large number of users and friend-to-friend networks, Harris says. Politicians communicate with journalists through Twitter and use its brief messages for rapid response to political attacks. Television news media often pick up YouTube videos and give them wider distribution.

These interactive media's greatest value comes from how they interact with each other, says Ken Deutsch, who manages the digital practice at the Jones Public Affairs communications firm's Boston office. "If YouTube wasn't shared on Facebook and Twitter and blogs and those other places, it would have no [political] value," Deutsch explains. "If you couldn't link newspaper articles to Twitter, Twitter would have no value."

Social media enable individuals to enter the public political debate in ways previously reserved to politicians and the traditional news outlets. That poses a challenge to candidates, who can't control their messages once social media users start passing them around and commenting on them. But candidates also benefit when supporters rise to the candidates' defense after a social media attack.

Indeed, the millions of citizen postings create an unending barrage of attacks, defenses and counterattacks that demand rapid responses from campaigns. That heightens the likelihood of gaffes, which in turn get amplified in online repostings, adding to the cacophony, and the allure, of social media.

Smart phones and other mobile devices increase the speed and ubiquity of the debate, which individuals can enter whenever they want from wherever they happen to be. The devices' cameras also enable individuals to record candidates' gaffes and post them online instantly.

As campaign 2012 races to its conclusion on Nov. 6, here are some questions being raised about social media's impact on the American political process:

Does online data mining threaten voters' privacy?

Political operatives and political scientists are talking about "Big Data" a lot this year.

The phrase refers to political organizations' ability to collect enormous amounts of information about individual voters — through social media and traditional means — then crunch it and use the results to send finely tuned messages to narrowly targeted audiences. Some critics worry that it's also a highly intrusive invasion of privacy. (*See "At Issue," p. 41.*)

By gathering material from social media, other websites and offline sources, campaigns can identify individuals' browsing habits, online purchases, social media discussions, data about friends and friends' interests and other information.[8]

When people signed up for a smart phone app that was to notify them of Romney's vice presidential pick, the campaign gathered their email addresses and other data.[9] Those who joined Obama's campaign by clicking "I'm in" on Facebook gave the campaign their Facebook data plus information on their Facebook friends, according to Trippi, the architect of Howard Dean's Internet-dependent 2004 campaign. "People would want to turn their machines off if they knew everything these campaigns know about them," he says, only partly in jest.

When campaigns target voters now, Democratic online consultant Noble says, "it's not [an anonymous] white male voter in this precinct. It's James Q. Smith on Grand Street."

That so-called "microtargeting" is quite valuable, according to Mike Zaneis, senior vice president of the Interactive Advertising Bureau, a New York-based trade group for companies that sell online advertising. In the commercial sector, he says, targeted ads are 2.5 times as effective as nontargeted ones.

Directly addressing a voter's precise interests through social media allows a campaign to "engage people in detail on issues you might not otherwise have had the time or resources to talk about through traditional media," says Reilly, the Democratic campaign consultant.

"If you want to reach people who are interested in a particular topic, there are groups and sub-groups for everything in social media with their own thought leaders that you can identify and either advertise to or reach out to directly," Deutsch of Jones Public Affairs notes.

The practice carries "great potential for abuses of privacy," according to John Allen Hendricks, chair of the mass communication department at Stephen F. Austin State University in Nacogdoches, Texas, and co-editor of a book about the 2008 Obama campaign. "I don't know that there are prominent enough disclaimers on the politicians' websites to inform the electorate that they are giving up a lot of information that they may not want revealed in the future," he explains. "We do not know what the campaigns will do with that data after the election is over."

Jeffrey Chester, executive director of the Center for Digital Democracy, a consumer-protection and privacy advocacy group in Washington, D.C., argues that the privacy threat is especially serious because it involves voting. "It's not about selling books and music and T-shirts," he says. "It's about the heart of the democratic process. Do we really want giant political parties and well-funded special interest groups like the Super PACs compiling millions of dossiers on voters and becoming a series of private National Security Agencies or FBIs?"

Chester wants the federal government to adopt "new rules that enable the voters to make the decisions about how their data can be collected and used." Voters should have to give permission before organizations could gather information about them online, he says. "Retention limits" should allow data to be used only for a short time and not be archived or sold, he adds.

He also worries that microtargeting will enable politicians to distribute false campaign pitches "under the radar, without being accountable to the public fact-checking process."

Zaneis calls Chester's under-the-radar warning "a bit of a red herring. It's no more of a potential problem in the digital world than it is in the offline world," he says, pointing out that direct-mailers have targeted individuals with postal mail for decades.

Gingrich online director Harris notes that "there's a reason people who subscribe to *Guns* magazine get direct-mail pieces about the Second Amendment."

"If somebody wants to deceive," Zaneis says, "they're going to be able to do that in any medium."

The Interactive Advertising Bureau's code allows consumers to opt out of being tracked and targeted online, he says, although that doesn't apply to political organizations that don't belong to the organization. An opt-in requirement would hinder the operations of the $35-billion online advertising industry, which supports 3 million jobs, he says. Most consumers wouldn't bother to opt in, even though most also don't bother to opt out, he says.

"I'm not sure why the Internet should be the redheaded stepchild of the media," he adds. "You can collect data about people all over the place" offline.

Jim Harper, director of information policy studies at the libertarian Cato Institute, says federal legislation would be too blunt an instrument.

"Legislation is going to produce privacy protection that is too high for many people and too low for many people," he says. "My argument is that privacy is a product of personal responsibility. You don't share what information you don't want others to have. That way you get custom privacy protection, because you've done it yourself."

Douglas Pinkham, president of the Public Affairs Council, an association of public affairs professionals that studies online political activity, observes that many younger Americans are comfortable revealing information on the Internet because they "just don't care about privacy as much as middle-aged and older people do."

Do social media cause political polarization?

"It's constitutional. B----es," Democratic National Committee Executive Director Patrick Gaspard tweeted crudely when the Supreme Court upheld Barack Obama's signature health-care legislation in June.[10]

After Republicans attacked him for the intemperate remark, Gaspard tweeted an apology, explaining that "I

AP Photo/Evan Vucci

Republican presidential candidate Mitt Romney works online aboard his bus after a campaign stop in Council Bluffs, Iowa, on June 8. In an effort to enhance his social media presence, Romney urged his Facebook friends on Aug. 21: "We're almost to 5 million likes — help us get there! 'Like' and share this with your friends and family to show you stand with Mitt!" By the second week of October, Romney had 8.6 million "likes."

let my excitement [at the Supreme Court's ruling] get the better of me." Then he let his Twitter feed go silent for six weeks.[11]

Gaspard's gaffe is just one example of the polarization and hostility that seem to characterize some online political communication. And the ill feelings are not restricted to political leaders.

A woman in the Houston, Texas, area became so disturbed about the tone of political debate that she declared her Facebook page to be a "Politics-Free zone." "Let's all take a deep breath, step back and remember that we are friends — in spite of our political views," Sandy Mansfield posted.[12]

More than a third of social media users in a Pew Research Center study this year reported receiving a "strong negative reaction" after they posted a political comment.[13]

Explanations for the phenomenon range from the overall polarized political climate to the nature of social media themselves.

The brevity of social media messages tends to "tweak people's impulses rather than cause them to think," said Bill Shireman, president of Future 500, a San Francisco consulting firm that helps businesses work with activist

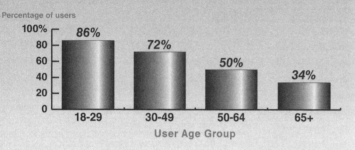

Social Media Use Declines With Age

More than 70 percent of adults under age 50 say they use social networking sites, with usage highest among those 18 to 29. Only about a third of those 65 and older use social media. Experts say a lower level of technological literacy among seniors is the reason for less social media use, but their participation is increasing rapidly.

Social Networking Use by Age Group, 2012

Source: "Older Adults and Internet Use," Pew Research Center, June 2012, p. 9, www.pewinternet.org/~/media//Files/Reports/2012/PIP_Older_adults_and_internet_use.pdf

groups. "So prejudice and group-think can appear very quickly with few restraints."[14]

Social media worsen polarization that already exists in American politics, says Deutsch, the online communications manager at Jones Public Affairs. "People follow people they agree with. On Facebook, you're seeing news put up by friends who are reinforcing your own views."

ComScore Inc., which measures online activity, this year released a study that found people tend to visit Internet sites that share their political leanings. Some Republicans visit the liberal TalkingPointsMemo.com, for instance, but Democrats account for 70 percent of the time spent at the site. Conversely, Democrats account for just 9 percent of the time spent at the conservative DailyCaller.com site.[15]

Aaron Smith, who studies politics and the Internet at the Pew Research Center, says most political posts in social media are made by activists with strong views. In one Pew survey, for instance, 66 percent of "very liberal" people said they had "liked" a political post, as did 64 percent of "very conservative" people. Only 41 percent of self-described "moderates" did so. Pew found the same pattern when asking if people had posted political comments.[16]

"They come to this [online] world with a certain set of attitudes and a team mentality, and social networking sites provide a way for them to support their team," Smith says of the activists. "While you can see ways social networking sites can exacerbate [polarization], in a way they're only reflecting that broader political culture."

Social media promote nationalization of politics, just as cable TV news and the Internet in general do, Democratic campaign consultant Reilly says. Nationalization then promotes polarization, as ideological activists from around the country jump into local political debates, he explains.

"No matter where you're running," he says, "the challenge to make it about [often-less-polarized] local issues and local candidates is tremendous," Reilly says.

Former House Speaker Thomas P. "Tip" O'Neill, D-Mass., famously proclaimed that "all politics is local," Reilly noted, but the media now are making it more accurate to say that "all politics is national."

Social media amplify the heated, negative campaigning that often appears in polarized debates, Reilly says. But well-funded independent organizations tend to drive the negativity through the offline advertisements that they purchase, he adds.

Other aspects of social media can combat polarization and negativity.

While Twitter requires micro-comments and Facebook encourages brevity, tweets and Facebook postings can link to longer documents, and long videos can be posted on YouTube, for example.

"On television, you're limited to the sound bite you can get on the news and the 30-second ad," Reilly notes. "On social media, you can be posting as much as you want every day. It's an avenue for getting more information to people that wasn't available before social media came about."

Although people tend to associate with others who have similar beliefs, few people's networks are devoid of diversity.

Asked in a May survey about the political orientation of their social media contacts, 24 percent of those polled said most were the same as their own, 9 percent said most were different, and 60 percent said there was an even mix. The rest didn't know or didn't answer.[17]

"There are plenty of echo chambers, but there also are lots of tunnels among the echo chambers," the Cato Institute's Harper says.

"People are on social media to interact with the drama of their lives," not to form political organizations, Harris says. Their networks tend to be comprised of family and friends. And "not everyone in a family or at a high school or in college agrees on all the same political points." As a result, he says, "the average person on Facebook is friends with people of diverse political views, religions and backgrounds."

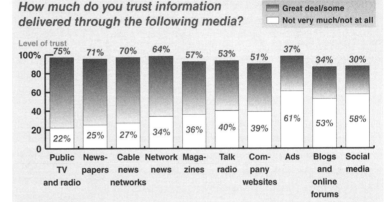

Social Media Lag in Trustworthiness

Americans find traditional news outlets such as public television and newspapers as the most trustworthy sources of news. More than half of those surveyed say social media platforms as well as blog and online forums — which allow anybody to post content — are not very trustworthy.

How much do you trust information delivered through the following media?

Source: "Heartland Monitor Poll," National Journal, June 9, 2012, p. 24, www .allstate.com/Allstate/content/refresh-attachments/Heartland_monitor_XIII_ topline.pdf

Do social media level the campaign-spending playing field?

Mark McKinnon, chief media adviser for George W. Bush's presidential campaigns, has become an Internet evangelist.

"Americans are leveraging technology to more fully engage in the political process," McKinnon proclaimed earlier this year. "Voters have become more than just passive consumers of these digital messages. . . . 'We the people' can now compete against the near-deafening influence of unlimited campaign contributions."[18]

McKinnon is not alone in his optimism. Low cost and ease of use have led many to view social media as weapons that underfunded candidates and common citizens can use to combat the enormous campaign spending of millionaires and billionaires that was unleashed by the Supreme Court's *Citizens United* decision in 2010.[19] They also view social media as an inexpensive tool for solving problems that defy traditional media.

Social media are "good for niche issues," Democratic online consultant Noble says, noting that television is too expensive for addressing topics of interest to small groups. Social media offer effective access to young people, who watch less television than their elders, Democratic campaign consultant Reilly says. Because the young are less likely to vote, as well, their cost-per-vote in television advertising can be prohibitive, he adds.

Social media also open an avenue of influence that can't be tapped by traditional, geographically bound media, according to Deutsch of Jones Public Affairs.

Presidential campaigns concentrate their television spending in the handful of states where the race is close. But "most of us are influenced by people who live outside the media market we live in — our friends, our classmates, our colleagues," as well as by advertising and by people who live nearby, Deutsch points out. Social media enable those people to be in touch with each other and allow campaigns to try to influence them no matter where they live, he says.

Social media also have become a leveling tool as television advertising becomes less effective.

Zac Moffatt, digital director of the Romney campaign, has identified "off-the-gridders" — people who avoid television commercials by not watching programs when

Getty Images/Justin Sullivan

President Obama talks with Facebook CEO Mark Zuckerberg during a town hall meeting at the social media company's headquarters in Palo Alto, Calif., on April 20, 2011. A majority of young adults 18 to 29 say Facebook is their top news source, and a fifth name Comedy Central's Jon Stewart and Stephen Colbert, according to a recent survey.

they're broadcast. Instead, they record shows and fast-forward through the ads later, or they get their commercial-free entertainment from such sources as Netflix.

Surveys found that a third of the residents of Ohio and Virginia — key swing states — fall into that category, watching only sporting events at their scheduled broadcast time, Moffatt said in a panel discussion during the Republican Convention. Advertising that runs next to online search results or in social media offers ways to reach these potential voters, Moffatt said. In addition, he noted, recipients of online advertising can share it with friends, thus extending its reach.

Social media will not replace traditional news sources anytime soon, however. One important reason: Other than information they receive from friends and relatives, people — including young people — don't trust what they're told on social media as much as they trust what traditional news outlets tell them.

In a May *National Journal* survey, three-quarters of Americans polled said they have some or a great deal of trust in public television and public radio. Newspapers and cable news followed close behind with 71 and 70 percent. Next came network news (64 percent), magazines (57) and talk radio (53). Social media finished dead last, with just 30 percent.[20] (*See graph, p. 31.*)

Television also topped a 2011 Public Affairs Council survey that asked Americans where they get most of their news. Print newspapers or magazines stood second at 12 percent, well below TV's 70 percent. Just 1 percent picked social media.[21]

In an August survey for the *Los Angeles Times* and the University of Southern California's Annenberg communication school, a majority of young adults ages 18 to 29 said Facebook is their top news source, and a fifth listed Jon Stewart and Stephen Colbert, the Comedy Central cable station's fake news anchor and commentator. But those sources finished below traditional news media in trust.[22]

"An insurgent candidate with little money can use the Web to catch fire," former Gingrich online coordinator Harris says. "But every survey continues to show that television is where people are spending most of their time. So, until those numbers change, television will continue to take the lion's share of the media money."

The candidates with the lion's share of the money will be able to buy the lion's share of television time, which limits social media's ability to level the field, Deutsch says.

"In a world where there was some regulation of size of donations, social media may have leveled it," he says. "But, at this point, with the number of individual donors you have to have to make up for the wealthiest donors who support PACs, I don't think it can be."

Hendricks of Stephen F. Austin State University agrees that "the wealthy's ability to spend unlimited amounts on campaigns may overcome the Internet's people power." But Cornfield of George Washington University suggests that the enormous amount of cash being poured into this year's campaigns may, ironically, limit money's impact in the closing weeks before the election.

"I'm hearing that we're going to see, because of the rise of Super PACs, much less advertising space available, especially in broadcast and cable TV and radio," he says. "All the time's been bought up. That's forcing campaigns to rely more on Web ads. And there are starting to be anticipated shortages on the favorite Web ad spaces."

BACKGROUND

Nascent Revolution

Today's global Internet can trace its birth to the transmission of one word — "log" — from a computer at the University of California, Los Angeles to a computer at

CHRONOLOGY

1990s *The Internet becomes a political instrument.*

1991 Commercial activities are allowed on the Internet. . . . Point-and-click navigation invented. . . . World Wide Web name coined.

1992 Clinton-Gore campaign uses Internet to reach out to prospective voters.

1994 First graphical browser invented. . . . White House website introduced.

1995 Library of Congress creates www.thomas.gov site, named after President Thomas Jefferson, to put legislative information online.

1996 More campaigns go online. . . . Center for Responsive Politics puts campaign finance information on the Web.

1998 Professional wrestler Jesse Ventura demonstrates Internet's value to the underdog by winning Minnesota governorship as a third-party candidate.

1999 Federal Election Commission allows matching federal campaign funds for online credit-card donations. . . . Napster music-sharing network founded. . . . New Jersey Sen. Bill Bradley raises more than $600,000 online in unsuccessful campaign for 2000 Democratic presidential nomination.

2000s *Online campaigning expands, and social media enter politics.*

2000 After upset victory in New Hampshire primary, Republican presidential candidate John McCain raises $2.7 million online in three days.

2001 Accused of violating copyrights, Napster goes offline and is later reborn as a legal online music store.

2002 LinkedIn business networking site and Friendster, a prototypical social networking platform, launched; Friendster later morphs into a gaming website.

2003 Exploiting Internet's fundraising and voter outreach capabilities, former New Hampshire Gov. Howard Dean becomes frontrunner for 2004 Democratic presidential nomination but ultimately loses to Sen. John Kerry.

2004 TheFacebook (later just Facebook) begins business as a networking platform for Harvard undergraduates. . . . Flickr photo-sharing platform created. . . . Dean's 2004 campaign taps power of Internet fund-raising as never before.

2005 YouTube video-sharing platform founded. Facebook expands on college campuses and allows some high school students to participate.

2006 After expanding to more college campuses, Facebook is opened to anyone 13 and older. . . . Twitter established.

2007 CNN and YouTube sponsor Democratic and Republican debates during which viewers submit video questions.

2008 Barack Obama wins presidency after raising $500 million online and conducting most-ever campaign activities online. . . . Twitter records 1.8 million tweets on Election Day.

2009 White House begins posting photos to Flickr. . . . Grassroots conservatives tap social media to find like-minded activists and grow the decentralized Tea Party movement.

2010 Social media contribute to conservative election victories at all levels of government.

2011 In run-up to 2012 election, all major political candidates campaign on social media; GOP presidential candidates debate on Twitter; Obama hosts "Twitter Town Hall" from White House.

2012 Social media play larger campaign role than ever; Twitter averages 340 million tweets a day; U.S. Facebook users outnumber 2008 total voters; Obama leads Romney in most measures of social media activity, but some think Romney's social media supporters may be more engaged; online data-mining raises privacy concerns; researchers study social media activity to evaluate political campaigns' effectiveness. . . . Candidates use social media for on-the-fly tests of campaign tactics' effectiveness. . . . Companies create fake social media followers to inflate apparent size of campaigns' online support.

Twitter: A New Political Weathervane

"We have never had a way to peer into discussions before."

Can social media conversations predict election results? A growing number of organizations are trying to find out.

Twitter launched the Twitter Political Index — or Twindex — on Aug. 1.[1] It's an attempt to measure Twitter users' opinions about the leading presidential candidates by evaluating their tweets.

The index was developed in partnership with two prominent political pollsters — Democrat Mark Mellman and Republican Jon McHenry — and a firm that analyzes social media activity, Topsy.

Topsy uses software to evaluate the sentiments expressed about people or things in tweets by Americans each day. It then compares the results with tweets about Barack Obama and Mitt Romney. Finally, it creates a 0-100 ranking that resembles an SAT percentile. An 80 score means tweets about the candidate were more positive than tweets about 80 percent of all people and things that were tweeted about that day. A score of 20 means the candidate's tweets were more negative than 80 percent of the others.

Computing Obama's Twindex scores for the previous two years, Topsy said they often paralleled his approval ratings in Gallup polls.[2]

Adam Sharp, Twitter's head of government, news and social innovation, said the index offers a peek into "conversations that just an election cycle ago were limited to coffee shops, dinner tables and water coolers."[3]

The most influential conversations are among friends, relatives and colleagues, Mellman said, but "we have never really had a way to peer into those discussions before."

The index can't claim the precision of scientific surveys, both pollsters said. But the way the index has paralleled Obama's Gallup ratings suggests that "what we're seeing in these conversations is not radically divorced from what we're seeing in the country as a whole," Mellman said.[4]

Mining the conversations reveals nuances that aren't captured in yes-or-no or multiple-choice questions in a poll, Sharp said.[5] A campaign could find the Twindex data helpful if the data could show which topics link a candidate to more positive conversations, McHenry said.[6]

Twindex might offer a "leading indicator" of opinion, Sharp said during the Democratic National Convention. In the days following the spike of American good feeling caused by Osama bin Laden's death in May 2011, for instance, Obama's Twindex score dropped more quickly than his approval ratings in polls, "as the Twitter conversation returned to being more focused on economic issues," Sharp said at the index's launch.[7]

Twindex has obvious weaknesses, says Brad Fay, chief operating officer of the Keller Fay Group, a research and consulting firm that specializes in word-of-mouth marketing. For one thing, three-quarters of conversations occur face-to-face and 15 percent by phone, he says. Only about 10 percent occur online, and just a fraction of those on Twitter, he says.

"We know that the Twitter universe skews young whereas the voting universe skews a little older," he says. "Some people participate at a much higher frequency rate than other people. You could tweet once a month or 10 times a day, but on Election Day everyone gets just one vote."

Fay's firm has teamed with *National Journal* to evaluate conversations offline as well as online by conducting weekly surveys of people who match the demographics of the total U.S. adult population. They are asked the topics of conversations they had face-to-face, over the phone and online and whether the tone was positive or negative.

Stanford University about 360 miles up the California coast.[23] The UCLA computer was logging into the Stanford computer on Oct. 29, 1969, to create the first link in a network that now serves about 2 billion users.[24]

The $19,800 contract that funded the first Internet research was paid for by the federal government's Defense Advanced Research Projects Agency (ARPA) to facilitate information exchange among military research facilities.

As more computers joined the network, it became known as ARPANET.

To facilitate civilian research, the federal government's National Science Foundation (NSF) created the Computer Science Network (CSNET) in 1981. Five years later, the foundation established the faster NSFNET. As these early networks began to link to each other, they created a network of networks that became known as the Internet.

An interesting finding of "Conversation Nation," as the project is called: Political polling results tend to be stable while "we find the conversation changes quite a bit," Fay says.[8]

The project does not pretend to be predictive, Fay says. But when Keller Fay did the same surveying as an R&D project four years ago, Obama "was running away with the conversation, both in the amount of conversation and the positive nature of the conversation. It was very clear in that data who was leading on Election Day."

For the week ending Sept. 30, Fay's survey found 52 percent of conversations about Romney were mostly negative, 23 percent mostly positive and the rest neutral or mixed. It was the Republican's most negative score since the surveying began in late May. Obama recorded his highest positive score, 47 percent, to 30 percent negative.[9]

The Twitter index showed tweets about the candidates were much more negative than all tweets on Sept. 30. Obama scored higher than Romney, 20-19, and led for most of the entire preceding week.

Others attempting to measure online sentiment include CNN, in a collaboration with Facebook, and NBC News.

CNN's "Election Insights" simply reports the number of Facebook posts about the presidential and vice presidential candidates, broken down by state and various demographics.[10] Obama and Romney ran close together through most of the week ending Sept. 30, with each spiking occasionally. GOP vice presidential nominee Paul Ryan inspired many more posts than Vice President Joe Biden.

NBC analyzes social media posts using a tool developed by Crimson Hexagon, a Boston firm that monitors and analyzes social media activity. The analysis appears on the network's "Politics" page.[11] On Sept. 29, Romney received more expressions of support than Obama in all tweets and a sample of Facebook posts.

— *Tom Price*

Mitt Romney's Twitter site registers more than 1.3 million followers. The new Twitter Political Index attempts to measure Twitter users' opinions about the presidential candidates by evaluating their tweets.

[1]"The Twitter Political Index," https://election.twitter.com.

[2]"Topsy Analytics for Twitter Political Index," Topsy, http://about .topsy.com/election.

[3]Adam Sharp, "A new barometer for the election," Twitter Blog, Aug. 1, 2012, http://blog.twitter.com/2012/08/a-new-barometer-for-election.html.

[4]Ariel Edwards-Levy and Mark Blumenthal, "Twindex, New Twitter Polling System, Tracks Opinions On Presidential Candidates," *The Huffington Post*, Aug. 1, 2012, www.huffingtonpost.com/2012/08/01/ twindex-twitter-polling-candidates_n_1730488.html.

[6]*Ibid.*

[5]*Ibid.*

[7]Sharp, *op. cit.*

[8]"Conversation Nation," http://nationaljournal.com/conversation-nation.

[9]"Conversation Nation," *National Journal*, Oct. 3, 2012, http://national journal.com/conversation-nation.

[10]www.cnn.com/election/2012/facebook-insights.

[11]"NBC Politics," www.msnbc.msn.com/id/3032553/#.UGoWZVGruSq.

The general public didn't acquire Internet access until the late 1980s, when MCI Mail and CompuServe began selling email services. Earlier in the '80s, companies offered slow phone-line connections to private networks. In 1989, a service called "The World" offered the public its first full-service access to the Internet.

Hints at the Internet's eventual wide popularity appeared in the early '90s, when companies were allowed to conduct commercial operations online and scientists invented the point-and-click navigation system and the graphical browser — a web browser that allows interaction with both graphics and text.

The Internet found an early congressional advocate in Tennessee Sen. Al Gore, who helped turn the Web into a campaign tool when he joined presidential nominee Bill Clinton on the Democratic ticket in 1992.

Shortly after they took office in 1993, Clinton and Gore launched the first White House website. Two years later, the Library of Congress created an online legislative information system named "Thomas," after President Thomas Jefferson, who sold his personal book collection to the library after British troops burned it during the War of 1812. Following the White House lead, members of Congress began to create websites and use email.

Political use of the Web was spreading by the time Clinton and Gore ran for re-election in 1996. Candidates' websites now contained graphic elements, links to other sites and capabilities for exchanging email with voters. The Republican presidential nominee, Sen. Bob Dole of Kansas, became the first candidate to promote a website on television, doing so during a debate with Clinton.

Two years later, professional wrestler Jesse Ventura demonstrated the Internet's political value when he used it in running a successful upstart campaign for Minnesota governor. To help overcome doubts about his qualifications, he posted detailed position papers online. He raised $50,000 in cyberspace — nearly 10 percent of his treasury — and used email to help manage far-flung volunteers.

"We didn't win the election because of the Internet," Phil Madsen, Ventura's webmaster, said. But Ventura "could not have won the election without the Internet."[25]

The Federal Election Commission (FEC) greatly boosted the Internet's political value in 1999 when it ruled that campaign contributions charged to credit cards online would be eligible for matching federal funds. Sen. Bill Bradley of New Jersey raised more than $600,000 online that year as he prepared to challenge Gore in the 2000 Democratic presidential primaries, and Arizona Sen. John McCain raised $260,000 in the runup to the GOP contest. McCain then raised $2.7 million online in three days following his upset win over George W. Bush in the Feb. 2 New Hampshire primary.

Gore and Bush won the nomination, but the losers demonstrated the Web's political potential, which Howard Dean exploited dramatically in 2004.

Dean made the Internet central to his campaign, using its ever-strengthening capabilities to organize, motivate and manage his paid and volunteer workers. His supporters organized meetings at Meetup.com. He used the Internet to become the most prolific Democratic fundraiser in history up to that point.

Massachusetts Sen. John Kerry won the nomination but learned from Dean's Internet prowess. He and Bush both developed sophisticated websites with video and audio files, search capabilities and interactive features. In addition to raising funds online, they recruited volunteers, encouraged supporters to bring their friends and neighbors into the campaign, distributed good news about themselves and attacked their opponent.

Kerry and Bush also:

• Used their Senate and White House websites to supplement their campaigns' online activities;
• Placed targeted advertising on others' websites;
• Used email to deploy workers shortly before and on Election Day; and
• Guided their canvassers with information about individual voters that was gleaned from analyzing huge computer databases.

By voting day, they — along with nearly every other serious effort to influence the election — campaigned online.

Empowering the People

Steve Murphy — managing partner at Murphy Vogel Askew Reilly, the Democratic campaign consulting firm — described online campaigning as a new, more effective way to conduct old-style grassroots campaigning.

"You can't call them on the phone any more because nobody wants to talk on the phone because they've been inundated by telemarketers," he said. "You can't knock on the door anymore because nobody's ever home. But everybody's always home on the Internet."[26]

Bush press secretary Scott Stanzel agreed. "Our Internet effort empowers people to go to their neighbors and distribute information on their email lists," he said. "So we are bringing the campaign back to a very grassroots, neighbor-to-neighbor effort."[27]

Four years later, then-Sen. Barack Obama of Illinois took Internet campaigning to heights not dreamed of by the 2004 activists. McKinnon, the Bush media adviser, called Obama's 2008 campaign a "seminal, transformative race" and "the year campaigns leveraged the Internet in ways never imagined."[28]

Obama turned down public financing, which, according to FEC rules, would have limited his spending to $126 million in the primary and general elections, and raised $745 million, including $500 million online — unheard-of figures.[29]

Obama collected more than 13 million email addresses and compiled a million-member audience for text messages. He hired 90 people to run his online operations — Web developers, bloggers, videographers and others — and put them to work on communication, fundraising, grassroots organizing and other tasks. (GOP nominee John McCain hired four.)[30] Obama spent tens of millions of dollars on Internet ads. He campaigned on Facebook, Twitter and YouTube, as well as on lesser-known sites such as AsianAvenue and BlackPlanet. He even bought ads in video games, such as billboards along the highways of the Xbox racing game "Need for Speed: Carbon."[31] He also "killed public financing for all time," in the words of Steve Schmidt, McCain's chief campaign strategist.[32]

Although social media had far less reach in 2008 than 2012, they offered hints of their potential. Black Eyed Peas singer will.i.am's "Yes We Can" video and "I've Got a Crush on Obama" composed and sung by Leah Kauffman and lip-synched by actress Amber Lee Ettinger (better known as "Obama Girl") went spectacularly viral. On a more serious note, Hollywood film producer Robert Greenwald created several videos showing McCain contradicting himself. Dean's online manager Trippi says the songs showed, importantly, that social media enable private citizens to become a notable part of the campaign discussion with no assist from the candidates.

Conservative Victories

In the 2010 elections, social media contributed to many conservative victories at all levels of government. ComScore said Twitter "played a key role, providing a broadcast channel for candidates to voice their thoughts, ideas and opinions directly to their constituents and public at large."[33]

According to Facebook's Harbath, social media helped unhappy, unorganized conservatives locate each other and make the Tea Party a political force. "There wasn't a single group that said: 'Let's create the Tea Party,'" she said. "It was a lot of people finding themselves through social media."[34]

YouTube and Facebook had cosponsored debates with CNN and ABC during the 2008 presidential campaign, and the YouTube sessions included viewer questions submitted through the platform. They cosponsored debates again during the 2012 GOP presidential campaign, with Facebook also enabling viewer-submitted questions. In addition, an entire GOP debate took place on Twitter. The candidates made two or three 140-character Twitter posts in response to the questions.[35]

The GOP candidates made extensive use of social media, and some political analysts say that probably helped keep this year's Republican primary contest going for an unusually long time.

"Chunks of the Republican base, including Tea Partiers, anti-abortion activists and evangelicals, are using social media to form self-reinforcing factions within the larger party that are less and less susceptible to what nominal party leaders may want them to do," according to Micah Sifry, a networking consultant who studies how the Internet and other technologies are changing politics.[36] As a result, the various conservative factions were less likely to heed pleas to unite around frontrunner Romney, Sifry said.

That's not the sole reason the primary race lasted so long, Harbath says, but "it allowed [less-established] candidates like Herman Cain a lot of momentum because of something they said that was spread on social media."

According to Deutsch of Jones Public Affairs, social media enabled underdogs to continue raising money, finding supporters and engaging with them.

Rep. Michele Bachmann, R-Minn., for instance, credited Facebook with playing an important role in her surprise victory in the Iowa straw poll. Former Republican Pennsylvania Sen. Rick Santorum created a Facebook page for every state and used the pages to organize supporters. He also used Fundly, a social media fundraising site, to collect more than $230,000 through nearly 3,000 supporters who created Fundly pages of their own to seek contributions from friends.[37] And Gingrich created the #250 Twitter category to promote his promise to lower gasoline prices to $2.50 a gallon.

But candidates don't get to campaign by themselves in social media. Obama bought advertising that sent an Obama tweet on energy policy to everyone who searched for #250 gas.[38] Similarly, Romney bought Google

Social Media Give a Dark Horse the Edge

"The Internet allowed him to compete with someone with deep pockets."

Lt. Gov. David Dewhurst was supposed to be the next U.S. senator from Texas, succeeding the retiring Kay Bailey Hutchison. He had money. He had experience. He had name recognition and the support of Gov. Rick Perry and the rest of the state's Republican establishment.

Paul Burka, longtime columnist for *Texas Monthly* magazine, questioned if the race would be worth covering.

"Dewhurst has the money and the name I.D. Dewhurst has already driven most of the hopefuls out of the race," Burka wrote in mid-2011 as candidates jockeyed for positions in the 2012 campaign. "He will win in November. . . . The only way Dewhurst loses is if someone with more money and better conservative credentials than he has gets into the race. And that would be . . . who?"[1]

It turns out that would be Ted Cruz, a 40-year-old lawyer who had never held elected office, was not well known to the public, who might have had better conservative credentials but who certainly didn't have more money. Cruz won the GOP nomination for many reasons, one of the most important being his mastery of social media.

"For Ted Cruz to be outspent in the huge state of Texas, people thought he could never win," says Vincent Harris, digital consultant to Cruz's campaign. "But the Internet allowed him to raise money in small-dollar donations and to compete with someone with deep pockets."

Katie Harbath, an associate manager for policy in Facebook's Washington office, says Cruz's GOP primary victory demonstrates that "just having a ton of money doesn't matter. He used Facebook and other social media to help build up his ID and to talk to voters, and he ended up winning."

Cruz understood the power of social media from the beginning and integrated them throughout his campaign, says Harris, a Texas-based consultant who ran online operations for Perry and then Newt Gingrich in this year's Republican presidential primaries. Eventually the campaign dedicated three staff members to digital operations and received frequent help from Harris' consulting firm.

The campaign tapped social media and other online resources to raise money, recruit and engage supporters, organize campaign activities, distribute Cruz's messages and respond to opponents' attacks, Harris says. Cruz was especially effective in connecting with Tea Party members, who tend to be quite active online, Harris says.

Cruz announced his candidacy during a conference call with conservative Texas bloggers at the beginning of 2011, then tweeted the announcement.[2] He maintained an active relationship with the bloggers throughout the campaign, meeting with them individually and encouraging them to keep in touch with his staff.[3]

---

advertising that displayed criticism of Gingrich to anyone who searched for information on the former House speaker.[39]

CURRENT SITUATION

Courting 'Likes'

As the Nov. 6 election draws near, Obama and Romney are locked in battle to rack up as many YouTube subscribers, Facebook "likes" and Twitter retweets as possible. But political analysts view the importance of such metrics in different ways, and some say the data can be unreliable or even bogus.

Trying to enhance his social media presence, Romney sent a plea to his Facebook friends on Aug. 21: "We're

almost to 5 million likes — help us get there! 'Like' and share this with your friends and family to show you stand with Mitt!"[40]

That same day, Obama's Facebook page boasted more than 27 million likes — more than five times Romney's and just one piece of evidence that the president is running far ahead of his Republican challenger in online popularity.[41]

By the second week of October, Obama had 29.4 million Facebook "likes" to Romney's 8.6 million, 20.7 million Twitter followers to Romney's 1.3 million and 237,000 YouTube subscribers to Romney's 23,000.[42]

Moffatt, the digital director of Romney's campaign, dismisses those statistics as "vanity metrics" that don't tell how much effect the candidate's online efforts are having. "List size has no bearing," he said during the GOP

To engage supporters from the beginning, Cruz conducted an online poll to choose the campaign bumper sticker. As Cruz began to collect endorsements from prominent conservatives and conservative organizations — such as former vice presidential candidate Sarah Palin, U.S. Sen. Jim DeMint of South Carolina, the Club for Growth and FreedomWorks — the campaign would place search engine ads around their names and Facebook ads directed at users who liked them. The ads promoted Cruz's candidacy and solicited donations.

The campaign used advertising on search engines to respond to attacks. The ads — containing Cruz's answer to an attack — appeared with results that would likely be found by someone searching for information about the attack.

In addition, Cruz's supporters used social media on their own to respond to attacks.

Online advertising tends to raise more money than it costs — a key advantage, Harris says. "When was the last time a television advertisement raised money back?" he asks.

On election days — the initial primary and a two-candidate runoff — the campaign used social media posts and ads to encourage supporters to vote. Supporters were invited to virtually join Cruz's victory celebration when he wrapped up the nomination by watching live streaming of his election-night party on his Facebook page.[4]

Cruz had to use social media effectively, Harris says, because he didn't have the money to compete with Dewhurst in television advertising early in the race. Eventually Cruz "caught fire" and raised enough funds to compete on TV as well, Harris says. Substantial contributions from conservative organizations added to the small donations the campaign received online.

Cruz finished second in the May primary with 34 percent of the vote to Dewhurst's 45 percent in a field of nine.[5] Cruz won the runoff with 57 percent.[6] He's favored in the general election against Democrat Paul Sadler, a former state legislator.

"Ted Cruz is the Barack Obama of 2012," University of Texas political scientist Sean Theriault said, referring to Obama's groundbreaking use of the Internet in 2008. "It is a great case study of using these tools in politics."[7]

— *Tom Price*

---

[1]Paul Burka, "The Senate race," *Texas Monthly*, July 5, 2011, www .texasmonthly.com/blogs/burkablog/?p=10803.

[2]Steve Friess, "Ted Cruz's secret: Mastering social media," *Politico*, July 31, 2012, http://dyn.politico.com/printstory.cfm?uuid=0BC 9A312-8A76-4517-B003-7BBF5AA4613D.

[3]Rick Dunham, "Q&A with Vincent Harris, the mastermind behind Ted Cruz's social media success," *The Houston Chronicle*, Aug. 6, 2012, http://blog.chron.com/txpotomac/2012/08/qa-with-vincent-harris-the-mastermind-behind-ted-cruzs-social-media-success.

[4]Alicia M. Cohn, "Ted Cruz wins social media victory," *The Hill*, Aug. 1, 2012, http://thehill.com/blogs/twitter-room/other-news/241643-ted-cruz-wins-social-media-victory.

[5]Friess, *op. cit.*

[6]Anna M. Tinsley, "A Texas stunner: Cruz beats Dewhurst in Senate runoff," *Fort Worth Star-Telegram*, Aug. 1, 2012, www.star-telegram .com/2012/08/01/4145441/a-texas-stunner-cruz-beats-dewhurst.html.

[7]Friess, *op. cit.*

convention. "It really doesn't matter how many people you have following you if you don't have people really engaged with your campaign."

Moffatt prefers measures such as Facebook's "talking about" metric, which is the weekly total of the number of unique visitors who interact with a Facebook page by taking such actions as "liking," commenting or sharing, plus the viral effect of their friends doing such things as resharing.[43] At the beginning of October, Romney's "talking about" number was 1.7 million, Obama's 1.4 million. But on Oct. 8 Obama had pulled ahead, 3.2 million to 2.9 million.

Moffatt also likes to compare those kinds of statistics with the candidate's fan base. Those 2.9 million interacting with Romney's site represented 34 percent of his likes, compared with Obama's 11 percent.[44]

Complicating assessments of the campaigns' relative standing in social media are companies that will create fake Twitter followers for as little as a penny apiece.[45] Two companies say they have developed methods for detecting fake followers.

Barracuda Labs, a threat-assessment firm, said most of a 117,000 jump in Romney followers in one day in July were fake.[46] StatusPeople, which develops tools for managing use of social networks, alleged that 30 percent of Obama's followers are fake and 40 percent are inactive. For Romney it's 15 percent fake and 31 percent inactive, StatusPeople said.[47]

Both campaigns deny buying followers, and others have questioned the accuracy of the analysis. Barracuda research scientist Jason Ding said it is impossible to determine who is responsible for buying the fake

President Obama's Facebook page has more than 29 million "likes." Candidates this year are using social media sites such as Facebook, Twitter and YouTube to identify and organize supporters and raise funds. Using such platforms also allows them to bypass traditional news media and send their messages unfiltered to the public.

followers — the campaigns, campaign supporters or opponents trying to embarrass the campaigns.[48]

As hazy as social media metrics may sometimes seem, both Obama and Romney have made huge strides in building online support, though Obama is widely perceived as still having the edge.

It appears Republicans have made "a great amount of progress in closing the technology gap," says Hendricks of Stephen F. Austin State University. "But I do not believe Romney and the Republicans have quite caught up with the Obama campaign."

Costas Panagopoulos, an assistant professor of political science at Fordham University and editor of the book *Politicking Online*, says counting Obama's social media contacts may overstate the president's current Internet strength. "Much of Obama's online following is a result of the 2008 election cycle," and some may no longer be in his camp, Panagopoulos notes.

But having the older operation can give Obama a head start on activities that matter now, Hendricks points out, saying that Obama released a smart-phone app to promote his campaign in 2010, something Romney's organization didn't do until 2012. This year, Obama distributed an app that gives door-to-door canvassers access to voter registration lists, neighborhood maps, talking points and the ability to process contributions.[49]

Incumbency Edge

And Obama benefits from incumbency online as well as off. His weekly radio addresses also appear as videos on YouTube, where they can be viewed at any time. Press briefings and other White House events also are posted to YouTube. Videos are made available at the White House Facebook site as well.

Obama also leads in other recent statistical measures.

His convention acceptance speech generated 52,756 tweets in the minute following its conclusion, the highest per-minute rate ever recorded for a political event, while Romney's acceptance speech generated 14,289. The figures were 28,003 when the president joined Michelle Obama on stage in the first minute following her speech, 6,195 when Romney joined his wife Ann.[50]

As of Sept. 24, Obama's acceptance speech had been viewed 4.9 million times on YouTube, compared with Romney's 1.1 million. Michelle Obama's convention speech had outdrawn Ann Romney's YouTube audience, 3.2 million to 560,000. Perhaps even more troubling for Romney: Clint Eastwood's lecture to an empty chair drew three times the YouTube viewers as Romney's speech, as did the surreptitiously recorded video that shows Romney saying 47 percent of Americans don't "take personal responsibility" for their own lives.[51]

One of the most interesting developments in this election, according to George Washington University's Cornfield, is the campaigns' ability to use social media and powerful computers to conduct on-the-fly experiments that can lead to rapid changes in campaign tactics.

Likening it to medical research, Cornfield describes a campaign delivering a message to a "treatment group" while a "control group" doesn't get the message. The campaign then measures how well the message worked. Or the campaign tries variations on a message with more than one group and determines which works better. "It's hard to know, when a campaign switches from message to message, whether they're undisciplined or experimenting," Cornfield says.

Moffatt, Romney's digital director, termed Facebook "a way for us to test messages for online advertising and other platforms, because it's instant feedback."[52] Twitter, also, "helps us keep our finger on the pulse of the fast-moving pace of new media," Romney spokesman Ryan Williams said.[53]

Should government restrict online data collection to protect voters' privacy?

YES
Jeffrey Chester
Executive Director, Center for Digital Democracy

Written for *CQ Global Researcher*, October 2012

A political campaign sends a striking digital ad personalized to your age, gender, race, spending habits, location and favorite musician or TV show. That interactive ad later appears on your mobile device, gaming platform and computer screen as you surf the Web. Its message and visual content keep changing, as if it learned about you — including what you had most recently done online. Your best friend gets an ad from the same candidate, but with a different message. It seems you care about the economy, your friend about the Middle East.

Such scenarios are no longer fantasy. Campaigns, candidates and special-interest groups, tapping into the personalized data-mining capabilities of digital marketing, now can "shadow" or track voters wherever they go or whatever they do online — including using their mobile phones. Political groups can buy individual profiles that contain information culled from both online and offline data brokers, producing a "road map" to the specific issues likely to sway a particular voter.

Our digital dossier can include our race and ethnicity, gender, relationships, events that have affected us (a loan application or a medical treatment, for example), favorite websites and even our past actions (products purchased or videos viewed). It can access the torrent of social media information that tells not only about us but also about our relations with friends. New, interactive multimedia tools perfected for selling cars, computers and entertainment on websites and mobile phones make data-enabled voter ads even more effective.

We shouldn't allow voter decisions to be influenced by digital micro-targeting tactics that invade our privacy and set the stage for potential manipulation. As campaigns increasingly have the ability to tell each of us what they think we want to hear, the truth can easily become a victim. As tens of millions of finely tuned, personalized interactive ads are delivered to mobile phone screens, how will news organizations and other watchdogs effectively monitor the information to say what's right or misleading?

We are allowing powerful special interests — campaigns, candidates, super Pacs and the like — to build a vast data mining and targeting apparatus that is transforming our political process without public debate. Congress must step in to both protect the rights of voters and enact fair ground rules for digital political campaigns. Voters — not the K Street complex — should have the power to decide what online information can be collected and used.

NO
Jim Harper
Director, Information Policy Studies, Cato Institute

Written for *CQ Global Researcher*, October 2012

Just like marketers do year in and year out, political campaigns are doing everything they can at election time to learn the interests of voters and how to reach them. Is democracy better served by campaigns that know less about voters or by campaigns that know more?

Nobody loves the tawdry tone of electoral politics, and some of the obscure techniques campaigns use to gather voter information leave us squirming. But this is hardly a justification for laws that could blinder our political system.

Political privacy is an interesting beast. Some people are reticent to speak even with family members about their politics and their votes. Others put on garish costumes and post signs on their lawns and cars to advertise what they think. No law regulating how campaigns can collect and use information would hit the right notes for communities this diverse.

Instead of taking privacy off the table as a campaign issue, why not push it forward? This problem should be put to the politicians vying for votes. Their tact and skill in handling voter information is a signal of how they might handle things they oversee, such as government agencies' collection and use of citizen data.

It's not likely to be a top issue, but the use of data in campaigns might sway privacy-sensitive voters. A campaign data law would prevent this competition. Voters couldn't learn which candidates demonstrate sensitivity toward personal information. These are skills elected officials should have.

The best way to learn voters' preferences, just like consumers' preferences, is to hash things out through real-world experience. Rather than having lawmakers decide for all of us how data can be used in society, let voters and consumers render their judgments, casting their ballots and dollars with the candidate or marketer who satisfies them the most.

Privacy regulation is impossible to write well, easy to sidestep and, in the campaign area, contrary to free-speech principles, if not the actual First Amendment. The long-term solution for privacy problems has always been consumer empowerment and awareness, so that sensitive voters can hide their politics online as well as off.

Over time, people will learn how their electronic devices work to protect or expose them. Social practices will catch up with the rapid advance of personal information technology. And people will have political privacy to the extent they want it.

The campaigns use the experiments' findings to guide advertising in all media. Both have sophisticated strategies for advertising beside the results of online searches.[54] Keeping an ear to what people were talking about earlier this year, for instance, Obama bought advertising beside Google results for "Warren Buffett," "Obama singing," "Obama birthday" and "Obama [NCAA basketball tournament] bracket."[55]

That strategy isn't restricted to presidential campaigns, notes Deutsch of Jones Public Affairs. After Rep. Todd Akin, R-Mo., sparked a nationwide furor by saying victims of "legitimate rape" don't get pregnant, Sen. Claire McCaskill, his Democratic opponent in the Missouri U.S. Senate race, put fundraising solicitations next to searches on Akins' name, Deutsch says.

Obama even repeated his 2008 tactic of advertising on video games — this year in the "Madden NFL 13" football game, the free online game site Pogo.com and mobile phone games such as "Tetris."[56]

Close and Personal

Candidates are tapping new social media to connect with voters on a personal level.

At Pinterest — which resembles a scrapbook or a refrigerator door and appeals primarily to women — Ann Romney and Michelle Obama emphasize their roles as wife and mother. Romney identifies herself as "Mom of five boys, Grandmother of 18." Among her posts are recipes, crafts and family photographs.[57] Michelle Obama also posts recipes and family photos as well as pictures of "people who inspire me."[58]

The candidates also created Pinterest pages. Romney's includes lists of his favorite movies, television shows and books — including the science fiction novel *Battlefield Earth* by Scientology founder L. Ron Hubbard. Obama's includes family photos but focuses primarily on the campaign.

Gingrich online director Harris called Pinterest "a great way to humanize a candidate. The Romney campaign has done a very good job of using Pinterest to showcase that Ann Romney's interests are very similar to the interests of average female voters in this country."

Both candidates also post favorite songs on the music site Spotify and participate on other social media, Hendricks of Stephen F. Austin State University says. "Both the Democrats and the Republicans realize that

they need to adopt those platforms and reach the demographic groups who are using them," he says.

During the presidential campaign's last big events — the October debates — social media provided platforms for users to watch, evaluate and discuss the clashes while they were in progress. The first debate, on Oct. 3, for instance, generated more than 10 million tweets during its 90-minute run, making it the most-tweeted-about event in U.S. politics.[59]

The debates illustrate one challenge to traditional news media that Twitter's Adam Sharp noticed during the conventions. Tweets would spike at points during a speech, peak in the first minute after the speech ended, then decline rapidly over 10 or 15 minutes, he said in a panel discussion during the Democratic convention.

During the first debate, tweeting peaked when Obama and Romney clashed with moderator Jim Lehrer over control of the proceedings and when they discussed Medicare.[60]

"By the time the pundits have actually gotten on the air and are sitting around the round table talking about it, the audience's conversation has already moved on," Sharp said. "Viewers are no longer waiting for that post-game analysis. They are participating in it in real time."

OUTLOOK
Creative Approaches

Candidates are poised to end this election year with a big bang as they deploy social media to get voters to the polls.

"I expect we're going to see a social-media-based campaign geared toward turnout that is like something we've never seen before," says Pinkham of the Public Affairs Council. "There probably will be a lot of creative approaches to how social media can be used to get people to show up to vote. They'll be saving some of their best ideas for last."

"It's not just connecting people online," says Trippi, the architect of Democrat Howard Dean's 2004 presidential campaign. "It's connecting the online army to do the hard work of getting out in the community, knocking on doors and making phone calls."

The effort will be especially important for Democrats, Trippi says, because of recently enacted voter-ID laws and cutbacks in early voting that are expected to make voting more difficult for Democrat-leaning young people, minorities and the elderly.[61]

"I suspect this is going to be a very close election," Trippi says, "and the ability of Obama to activate his network could very well be the difference in Ohio or Florida," which are viewed as key swing states. "If Romney's beating Obama by 10 points" — which polls indicate is unlikely — "no social network makes that up."

Experts say it's difficult to foresee what's likely to occur in future elections.

"One thing we know for sure is that the social media landscape is continually changing and evolving," Panagopoulos of Fordham University points out, "and campaigns and political parties will have to adapt to the changing circumstances."

Trippi envisions "a lot of kids in their garages who are working on really compelling technology. We're going to wake up in two months and there will be something that will totally change and empower people in a completely different way from what Twitter has. These networks, as big as they are, are going to be dwarfed four years from now."

Because of the technology they've developed, Obama, Romney and their social media experts will remain influential by helping candidates in future campaigns, Hendricks of Stephen F. Austin State University says.

"The Obama camp has been constantly building on and improving their platform," he notes. "They'll continue to do that beyond the 2012 campaign, and the Republicans will continue to build on what they started this year. This does not end after 2012."

Trippi also sees a "lasting impact" from this year's campaigns. "The Dean campaign had a lasting impact, and I think it laid the foundation for Obama," he says. "They took that and went far higher in orbit than we ever did. We were like the Wright brothers, and they landed a guy on the moon."

Technological developments will continue to make nuts-and-bolts campaigning more effective and efficient, says Harris, the Gingrich campaign's online director. For example, he says, "Campaign advertising is going to get to a degree of accuracy that was almost unimaginable when direct mail was started in the '80s."

"Big Data" will grow even bigger, Trippi says. Panagopoulos sees online fundraising becoming more dominant.

Rapid improvement in mobile devices will continue, and their popularity will continue to grow, Pew's Smith says. As a result, campaigns will acquire continually improving capabilities for "getting out political messages and encouraging people to take action where they are."

At some point, Trippi says, "an independent candidacy or a new party is going to happen, [because] there are only two reasons left to be in a party from a tactical point of view: money and organization." Both increasingly can be addressed outside the old institutions, he notes.

Television's influence will diminish gradually, and the Internet's importance will increase, Harris says. But Smith warns against predicting television's demise any time soon.

"People layer the new things on top of their existing communication," Smith says. "Just because we have text messaging doesn't mean people don't talk on the phone anymore. All of these things fit into the same big basket, and people pick the tool that's right for them based on their needs of the moment."

Hendricks says that won't happen until social media "are perceived by the citizens as being a reliable source of information," which they aren't now.

All of this will make old-fashioned campaigning more important, Pinkham says. "More and more money is going to be allocated toward the ground game to encourage turnout and to get volunteers who will try to help persuade undecided voters." But much of that will occur through social media.

"Personal contact still matters," Pinkham adds. "There's still no substitute for the candidate making personal appearances. What Obama did on reddit was the social media equivalent of making a personal appearance."

NOTES

1. "President Obama," reddit, undated, www.reddit.com/user/PresidentObama.

2. "POTUS IAMA Stats," reddit, Aug. 31, 2012, http://blog.reddit.com/2012/08/potus-iama-stats.html; www.reddit.com/user/PresidentObama.

3. See Tom Price, "Cyberpolitics," *CQ Researcher*, Sept. 17, 2004, pp. 757-780.

4. Jake Tapper, Richard Coolidge and Sherisse Pham, "#Campaign: How Twitter is Playing Politics

in 2012," *Yahoo News*, May 7, 2012, http://news.yahoo
.com/blogs/power-players-abc-news/campaign-
twitter-playing-politics-2012-101813518.html;_
ylt=A0LkuK2N6adPPD0AyACs0NUE;_ylu=
X3oDMTNtdDY0NGs2BG1pdANKdW1ib3Ryb2
4gRlAEcGtnA2Q3YzBkNDE1LTU0YzUtM2Jh
Ni1hNGU5LWU1MzFiZWJlNWM4NgRwb
3MDMQRzZWMDanVtYm90cm9uBHZlcgNm
NTQ2OTc2MC05ODJkLTExZTEtOWU3Zi00
YmJiODJmODVmZjA-;_ylg=X3oDMTFlam
ZvM2ZlBGludGwDdXMEbGFuZwNlbi11cw
Rwc3RhYQDBHBzdGNhdAMEcHQDc2Vjd
GlvbnM-;_ylv=3.

5. Ronald Brownstein, "Communications is changing
the relationship between business, government, and
individuals," *National Journal*, June 7, 2012, http://
nationaljournal.com/magazine/how-the-internet-is-
reshaping-us-and-our-government-20120607?
page=1. Jenna Wortham, "Winning Social Media
Votes," *The New York Times*, Oct. 8, 2012, p. B1,
www.nytimes.com/2012/10/08/technology/
campaigns-use-social-media-to-lure-younger-voters
.html?_r=1.

6. Pew Research Center Internet & American Life surveys, www.pewinternet.org/~/media/Files/Reports/
2011/PIP-SNS-Update-2011.pdf and www.pewinter
net.org/~/media/Files/Reports/2012/PIP_Older_
adults_and_internet_use.pdf.

7. Allstate/*National Journal* Heartland Monitor Poll XIII,
Conducted May 19-23, 2012, www.allstate
.com/Allstate/content/refresh-attachments/Heartland_
XIII_data.pdf.

8. T. W. Farnam, "Obama has aggressive Internet strategy to woo supporters," *The Washington Post*, April 6,
2012, www.washingtonpost.com/politics/obama-has-
aggressive-internet-strategy-to-woo-supporters/
2012/04/06/gIQAavB2zS_story.html.

9. Adam Mazmanian, "The Underdogs? Inside the
Romney Campaign's Digital Efforts," *The Atlantic*,
Aug. 22, 2012, www.theatlantic.com/politics/archive/
2012/08/the-underdogs-inside-the-romney-
campaigns-digital-efforts/261435.

10. For background, see Marcia Clemmitt, "Assessing
the New Health Care Law," *CQ Researcher*, Sept. 21,
2012, pp. 789-812.

11. Patrick Gaspard, https://twitter.com/patrickgas-
pard, and David Nakamura, "In a vicious campaign
year, apologies are in the air," *The Washington Post*,
Aug. 3, 2012, www.washingtonpost.com/politics/in-
a-vicious-campaign-year-apologies-are-in-the-
air/2012/08/03/cfe47e14-dd70-11e1-8e43-4a3c
4375504a_story.html.

12. Alyson Ward, "The politics of friendship: Have you
unfriended someone over their views?," *The Houston
Chronicle*, Sept. 24, 2012, p. 1, www.chron.com/
life/article/The-politics-of-friendship-Have-you-
unfriended-3881766.php.

13. "Politics on Social Networking Sites," Pew Research
Center, Sept. 4, 2012, p.19, http://pewinternet
.org/~/media/Files/Reports/2012/PIP_PoliticalLifeon
SocialNetworkingSites.pdf.

14. Tom Price, "Beyond Control: How Social Media
and Mobile Communication Are Changing Public
Affairs," Foundation for Public Affairs, 2011, http://
pac.org/system/files/FINAL%20Beyond%20
Control%20Report_0.pdf.

15. "The Digital Politico," ComScore Inc., April 2012,
www.comscore.com/Press_Events/Press_Releases/
2012/4/comScore_Releases_The_Digital_Politico_
Report.

16. "Social networking sites and politics," Pew Research
Center, March 12, 2012, p. 8, http://pewinternet
.org/~/media/Files/Reports/2012/PIP_SNS_and_
politics.pdf.

17. Allstate/*National Journal* Heartland Monitor Poll,
op. cit.

18. Mark McKinnon, "How a Tweet Can Beat a PAC,"
The Daily Beast, April 1, 2012, www.thedailybeast
.com/articles/2012/04/01/how-a-tweet-can-beat-a-
pac-social-media-gives-voters-muscle-in-politics.html.

19. For background, see Kenneth Jost, "Campaign Finance
Debates," *CQ Researcher*, May 28, 2010, pp. 457-480.

20. Brownstein, *op. cit.*

21. "2011 Public Affairs Pulse Survey," Public Affairs
Council, http://pac.org/pulse/report.pdf.

22. James Rainey, "Voters still tuned in to traditional
news media, poll finds," *Los Angeles Times*, Aug. 24,
2012, latimes.com/news/nationworld/nation/la-na-
media-poll-20120824,0,3396454.story.

23. Except where noted, information in this historical section was drawn from the following: Price, "Cyberpolitics," *op. cit.* Marcia Clemmitt, "Social Networking," *CQ Researcher*, Sept. 17, 2010, pp. 749-772; and John Allen Hendricks and Robert E. Denton Jr., *Communicator-in-Chief: How Barack Obama Used New Media Technology to Win the White House* (2010).

24. Josh Catone, "The Staggering Size of the Internet," *Mashable*, Jan. 25, 2011, http://mashable.com/2011/01/25/internet-size-infographic.

25. Price, "Cyberpolitics," *op. cit.*

26. *Ibid.*

27. *Ibid.*

28. Adam Nagourney, "The '08 Campaign: Sea Change for Politics as We Know It," *The New York Times*, Nov. 4, 2008, p. 1, www.nytimes.com/2008/11/04/us/politics/04memo.html.

29. "2008 Election: Presidential Candidate Barack Obama," Center for Responsive Politics, www.opensecrets.org/pres08/summary.php?cycle=2008&cid=N00009638. Chris Cillizza, "Is Obama overrated as a candidate?" *The Washington Post*, Oct. 7, 2013, www.washingtonpost.com/politics/decision2012/is-obama-overrated-as-a-candidate/2012/10/07/316c40f6-1087-11e2-ba83-a7a396e6b2a7_story.htm.

30. Philip Rucker, "Romney advisers, aiming to pop Obama's digital balloon, pump up online campaign," *The Washington Post*, July 13, 2012, www.washingtonpost.com/politics/romney-advisers-aiming-to-pop-obamas-digital-balloon-pump-up-online-campaign/2012/07/13/gJQAsbc4hW_story.html.

31. Sami Yenigun, "Presidential Campaigns Rock The Gamer Vote," "All Things Considered," NPR, Oct. 1, 2012, www.npr.org/2012/10/01/162103528/presidential-campaigns-rock-the-gamer-vote.

32. Nagourney, *op. cit.*

33. "The Digital Politico," ComScore Inc., April 30, 2012, www.comscore.com/DigitalPolitico.

34. Price, "Beyond Control," *op. cit.*

35. Jason Donner, "GOP Presidential Candidates to Debate in the 'Twitter-Sphere,' " foxnews.com, July 15, 2011, http://politics.blogs.foxnews.com/2011/07/15/gop-presidential-candidates-debate-twitter-sphere.

36. Micah Sifry, "How grass-roots social media are extending the GOP race," CNN, March 1, 2012, http://articles.cnn.com/2012-03-01/tech/tech_social-media-gop-sifry_1_social-media-conservative-voters-and-activists-social-networking?_s=PM:TECH.

37. *Ibid.*

38. Daniel Malloy, "Gingrich engages his 'tweeples' on social media," *The Atlanta Journal-Constitution*, March 10, 2012, www.ajc.com/news/news/local-govt-politics/gingrich-engages-his-tweeples-on-social-media/nQR5x.

39. Mazmanian, *op. cit.*

40. Romney-Ryan campaign, www.mittromney.com/we039re-almost-5-million-likes-x2013-help-us-get-there-quotlikequot-and-share.

41. Mazmanian, *op. cit.*

42. Data taken from the following sources: www.facebook.com/barackobama?ref=ts&fref=ts; www.facebook.com/mittromney; https://twitter.com/BarackObama; https://twitter.com/MittRomney; www.youtube.com/user/BarackObamadotcom?feature=g-all-a; and www.youtube.com/user/mittromney?feature=results_main.

43. Brittany Darwell, " 'People Talking About This' defined," *Inside Facebook*, Jan. 10, 2012, www.insidefacebook.com/2012/01/10/people-talking-about-this-defined.

44. "Inside Network," *PageData*, Sept. 30, 2012, http://pagedata.appdata.com/pages/leaderboard/fc/fan_count/type/78.

45. Alex Fitzpatrick, "Obama Has Millions of Fake Twitter Followers," *Mashable*, Aug. 24, 2012, http://mashable.com/2012/08/24/obama-has-13-million-fake-twitter-followers-report.

46. Dara Kerr, "Mitt Romney suspiciously gets 116K Twitter followers in one day," CNET, Aug. 6, 2012, http://news.cnet.com/8301-1023_3-57487861-93/mitt-romney-suspiciously-gets-116k-twitter-followers-in-one-day.

47. Fitzpatrick, *op. cit.*

48. Kerr, *op. cit.*

49. Mazmanian, *op. cit.*

50. Simon Owens, "No Strong Evidence Romney Is Beating Obama in Digital Media," *U.S. News & World Report*, Sept. 7, 2012, www.usnews.com/opinion/articles/2012/09/07/no-strong-evidence-romney-is-beating-obama-in-digital-media; Leigh Ann Caldwell, "Ann Romney created buzz on Twitter," CBS News, Aug. 29, 2012, www.cbsnews.com/8301-503544_162-57502597-503544/ann-romney-created-buzz-on-twitter.

51. Henry Blodget, "Romney's 47% Video Has Been Viewed 3 Times As Often As His Convention Speech," *Business Insider*, Sept. 28, 2012, www.business insider.com/romneys-47-viewed-more-than-convention-speech-2012-9; Brad Plumer, "Romney versus the 47 percent," *The Washington Post*, Sept. 17, 2012, www.washingtonpost.com/blogs/ezra-klein/wp/2012/09/17/romney-my-job-is-not-to-worry-about-those-people.

52. Jennifer Moire, "How Mitt Romney Upgraded to Facebook Timeline," *AllFacebook*, March 15, 2012, www.allfacebook.com/facebook-timeline-romney-2012-03.

53. Beth Fouhy, "Twitter plays outsize role in 2012 campaign," The Associated Press, May 7, 2012, http://news.yahoo.com/twitter-plays-outsize-role-2012-campaign-073847636.html;_ylt=Am7NGDL.3RobLkBs3JIjnwqs0NUE;_ylu=X3oDMTNhMXFvNXZqBG1pdAMEcGtnAzRmN2M3NzVlLWU0MWItMzA3Yy1hODBiLTI4NzQxMDAyN2M3NQRwb3MDNgRzZWMDbG5fQVBfZ2FsBHZlcgMwNzMyNGZlOS05ODU3LTExZTEtYmZiZi02NTMzZWYxYTZlZGQ-;_ylv=3.

54. Rucker, *op. cit.*

55. Farnam, *op. cit.*

56. Yenigun, *op. cit.*

57. Ann Romney, http://pinterest.com/annromney.

58. Michelle Obama, http://pinterest.com/michelleobama.

59. Adam Sharp, "Dispatch from the Denver debate," Twitter Blog, Oct. 4, 2012, http://blog.twitter.com/2012/10/dispatch-from-denver-debate.html.

60. *Ibid.*

61. For background see Peter Katel, "Voter Rights," *CQ Researcher*, May 18, 2012, pp. 449-476.

BIBLIOGRAPHY

Selected Sources

Books

Hendricks, John Allen, and Robert E. Denton Jr., eds., *Communicator in Chief: How Barack Obama Used New Media Technology to Win the White House*, **Lexington Books, 2010.**
This collection of scholarly essays looks at specific aspects of President Obama's 2008 campaign online, from email and YouTube to Twitter and video games.

Issenberg, Sasha, *The Victory Lab: The Secret Science of Winning Campaigns*, **Crown Publishers, 2012.**
A Washington journalist reveals the practical side of winning elections in the age of the Internet and powerful computers. One fascinating vignette: how, in the age of electronic communication, the Obama campaign decided to buy cardboard ads on buses on certain routes in 10 cities.

Panagopoulos, Costas, ed., *Politicking Online: The Transformation of Election Campaign Communications*, **Rutgers University Press, 2009.**
This collection of scholarly essays about politics and the Internet addresses campaigns in 2008 and earlier and elections in Europe as well as in the United States.

Trent, Judith S., Robert V. Friedenberg and Robert E. Denton Jr., *Political Campaign Communication: Principles and Practices*, **Rowman & Littlefield Publishers, 2011.**
Three communications scholars explore the full range of political communication, including various kinds of speeches, fundraising appeals, debates, advertising, communication among voters and use of the Internet.

Articles

Darwell, Brittany, "Does Romney have a better Facebook strategy than Obama?" *Inside Facebook*, **Aug. 28, 2012, www.insidefacebook.com/2012/08/28/does-romney-have-a-better-facebook-strategy-than-obama.**
Darwell, lead writer for an online magazine that covers all things Facebook, looks at Mitt Romney's and President Obama's Facebook operations and concludes that Romney is ahead.

McKinnon, Mark, "How a Tweet Can Beat a PAC," *The Daily Beast*, www.thedailybeast.com/articles/2012/04/01/how-a-tweet-can-beat-a-pac-social-media-gives-voters-muscle-in-politics.html.
A campaign communication adviser to both Democrats and Republicans argues that social media have the potential to "return power to all of the people."

Nagourney, Adam, "The '08 Campaign: Sea Change for Politics as We Know It," *The New York Times*, Nov. 4, 2008, p. 1, www.nytimes.com/2008/11/04/us/politics/04memo.html.
Writing on the eve of the 2008 general election, a veteran reporter reflects on how much the 2008 race changed campaigning.

Sifry, Micah, "How grass-roots social media are extending the GOP race," *CNN*, March 1, 2012, http://articles.cnn.com/2012-03-01/tech/tech_social-media-gop-sifry_1_social-media-conservative-voters-and-activists-social-networking?_s=PM:TECH.
An expert on politics and the Internet argues that social media played a key role in lengthening the race for the 2012 Republican presidential nomination.

Owens, Simon, "No Strong Evidence Romney Is Beating Obama in Digital Media," *U.S. News & World Report*, Sept. 7, 2012, www.usnews.com/opinion/articles/2012/09/07/no-strong-evidence-romney-is-beating-obama-in-digital-media.
The magazine's assistant managing editor examines the major presidential candidates' digital campaigns and concludes that despite Romney's best efforts, Obama has the edge.

Ward, Alyson, "The politics of friendship: Have you unfriended someone over their views?" *The Houston Chronicle*, Sept. 24, 2012, p. 1, www.chron.com/life/article/The-politics-of-friendship-Have-you-unfriended-3881766.php.
Texans describe how they're coping with the sometimes not-so-friendly political conversations encountered on Facebook and other social media.

Reports and Studies

"The Digital Politico: 5 Ways Digital Media is Shaping the 2012 Presidential Election," ComScore Inc., April 2012, www.comscore.com/Press_Events/Press_Releases/2012/4/comScore_Releases_The_Digital_Politico_Report.
ComScore, a firm that measures online activity, analyzes the impact of social media, digital advertising, Internet fundraising and actions online that earn coverage from traditional news organizations.

Price, Tom, "Beyond Control: How Social Media and Mobile Communication Are Changing Public Affairs," Foundation for Public Affairs, 2011, http://pac.org/system/files/FINAL%20Beyond%20Control%20Report_0.pdf.
The research and educational foundation examines how social media and mobile communications are causing businesses and activist groups to accept a more freewheeling world of public affairs. The author also is the author of this *CQ Researcher*.

Rainie, Lee, and Aaron Smith, "Social networking sites and politics," Pew Research Center, March 12, 2012, http://pewinternet.org/Reports/2012/Social-networking-and-politics.aspx; and "Politics on Social Networking Sites," *Pew Research Center*, Sept. 4, 2012, http://pewinternet.org/~/media//Files/Reports/2012/PIP_PoliticalLifeonSocialNetworkingSites.pdf.
Companion reports, based on a public opinion survey conducted early this year, explore how Americans use social media for political purposes.

For More Information

Association of Internet Researchers, 910 W. Van Buren St., #142, Chicago, IL 60607; www.aoir.org. Cross-disciplinary international academic association of scholars who study the Internet; conducts conferences and makes some research papers available for free on its website.

Berkman Center for Internet and Society at Harvard University, 23 Everett St., 2nd Floor, Cambridge, MA 02138; 617-495-7547; www.cyber.law.harvard.edu. Research center for studying the Internet and its impact on society; associates include faculty, students, fellows, entrepreneurs, lawyers and Internet practitioners.

Center for Democracy and Technology, 1634 I St., N.W., #1100, Washington, DC 20006; 202-637-9800; www.cdt .org. Advocacy group that promotes Internet freedom and individual privacy.

Center for Digital Democracy, 1621 Connecticut Ave., N.W., Suite 550, Washington, DC 20009; 202-986-2220; www.democraticmedia.org. Research, education and advocacy organization that promotes consumer protection and privacy.

Congressional Management Foundation, 513 Capitol Court, N.E., Suite 300, Washington, DC 20002; 202-546-0100; www.congressfoundation.org. Nonprofit organization that provides advice aimed at improving the way Congress works; publications include periodic reports on how Congress is — and should be — using the Internet.

Interactive Advertising Bureau, 116 East 27th St., 7th Floor, New York, NY 10016; 212-380-4700; www.iab.net. Trade association for companies that sell online advertising; website contains information about industry codes, public policy positions and research.

Personal Democracy Media, www.personaldemocracy.com. Promotes discussion about technology's impact on government, politics and society; publishes news and information on its website.

3

Farm Policy

Jennifer Weeks

A withered corn plant near Olmsted, Ill., on July 26, 2012, reflects the ravaging effects of a severe drought that has struck corn and soybean harvests throughout the Midwest. As of Aug. 1, 2012, the Agriculture Department had designated 1,452 counties as drought disaster areas. "A bad crop, ruined by a natural disaster or an unpredictable price collapse, can put a hard-working farm family out of business quickly," said Agriculture Secretary Tom Vilsack.

From *The CQ Researcher*, August 10, 2012.

When investigative journalist Tracie McMillan spent a year working in the U.S. food system — cutting garlic in California fields, cleaning produce at Walmart and garnishing plates at a chain restaurant — she learned a hard truth:

Healthy meals were barely affordable on wages of $8 per hour or less. Nutritious choices like fresh fruit and vegetables often were more expensive or less convenient than cheap processed options. And the working-class areas where McMillan lived had fewer grocery stores than did affluent suburbs.

"We're facing a dire public health problem related to poor diet," she writes in her 2012 book, *The American Way of Eating*. "Is it really in America's best interest to maintain a food system where eating well requires one to either be rich or to drive a total of thirty miles?"[1]

No single cause is to blame, McMillan concluded. Many factors make it hard for Americans to eat well, including "stagnating wages, skyrocketing income inequality and mushrooming health care costs; agricultural policies that pay farmers to exhaust our soils by growing food not to be eaten but to be burned [as biofuels]; an increasingly monopolized food infrastructure that gives the people selling our food little incentive to keep it affordable; and a population so strapped for time, cash and know-how that cooking dinner becomes a Herculean task rather than a simple and necessary chore."[2]

Congress is wrestling with many of those issues as it debates a new farm bill — a sprawling piece of legislation, enacted every five to seven years, that strongly influences what Americans eat, how the

Food Aid Topped 2008 Farm Bill Spending

The most recently enacted farm bill, which expires Sept. 30, was passed in 2008 at a total cost of $284 billion over five years. Most of that spending is for food aid, support for commodity producers, conservation and crop insurance. Smaller programs include rural development, forestry, horticulture and organic agriculture, livestock and research.

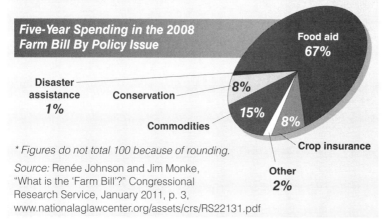

Five-Year Spending in the 2008 Farm Bill By Policy Issue

Food aid 67%

Disaster assistance 1%

Conservation 8%

Commodities 15%

8%

Crop insurance

Other 2%

* Figures do not total 100 because of rounding.

Source: Renée Johnson and Jim Monke, "What is the 'Farm Bill'?" Congressional Research Service, January 2011, p. 3, www.nationalaglawcenter.org/assets/crs/RS22131.pdf

food is grown and how much it costs. The 2012 bill will guide hundreds of billions of dollars in federal spending for programs including subsidies for farmers, food aid for needy families, land conservation, rural development and agricultural imports and exports.

Many current farm support programs are rooted in laws passed during the 1930s and '40s to implement President Franklin D. Roosevelt's New Deal. Through the 1980s, farm bills were shaped mainly by agricultural interests, including farm bureaus, trade associations for various crops and large agribusiness companies. More recently the debate has broadened. Today social welfare groups, nutrition advocates and many public officials see the farm bill as an opportunity to tackle food-related health issues that are widespread across the United States.

Food and farming issues "affect the health of residents in urban America because of hunger and food insecurity in low-income populations, lack of access to healthy food in low-income areas, [and] chronic diseases related to poor diet such as obesity, diabetes and cardiovascular diseases," the U.S. Conference of Mayors stated in a June 2012 resolution.[3] The group urged Congress to pass a farm bill that supports nutrition aid, sustainable farming practices and

programs to bring more fresh, healthy foods into urban areas.[4]

Environmentalists also are paying increased attention to farm policy. Along with academic experts and advocates for small- and mid-size family farms, they contend that large-scale agriculture focuses too heavily on a few major crops and relies too heavily on synthetic fertilizer, pesticides, herbicides and antibiotics for poultry and livestock.

Instead, environmentalists say, U.S. farm policy should provide more support for sustainable practices that protect the environment, such as farming organically and taking erosion-prone land out of production.

The last farm bill, enacted in 2008, authorized $24.1 billion over five years for conservation programs on farmland, which environmentalists view as an important and growing priority for the department.

"The Department of Agriculture needs more of a mandate to promote environmental protection," says Rebecca Klein, director of the Public Health and Agriculture Policy Project at Johns Hopkins University's Center for a Livable Future. "Farmers clearly have an interest in protecting water and soil, but they may not always be able to afford conservation measures that they would like to take. We need stronger policies to help make those actions feasible for them."

With billions of dollars at stake, farm bills inevitably generate heated debate about federal spending priorities. The Democratic-led Senate passed a farm bill in June that ends an especially controversial policy: direct subsidies paid for years to farmers and landowners, whether they grew crops or not. Instead, the bill puts greater emphasis on another safety-net measure for farmers: crop insurance subsidies. These programs help farmers qualify for financing by enabling them to pay back loans even if disasters destroy their harvests.

Farm advocacy groups say this shift will make federal agriculture policy more market-based. "We know there are a lot of concerns about direct payments to farmers and payments based on past production," says Dale Moore, deputy policy director with the American Farm Bureau Federation, a trade association for farms of all sizes. "We support an approach that lets producers make decisions based on their reading of markets and doesn't interfere with producers' planting decisions." However, the Farm Bureau says, farmers continue to need strong safety net programs — including crop insurance subsidies and marketing loans — to protect against catastrophes such as droughts and floods.[5]

Critics argue that like direct payments, crop insurance subsidies have outlived their purpose and support mainly large farms and insurance companies. "The federal government pays 60 percent of premiums, and payments are essentially uncapped," says Ariane Lotti, assistant policy director with the National Sustainable Agriculture Coalition. Moreover, she points out, crop insurance subsidies currently do not require farmers to follow conservation rules, although the Senate bill includes a provision that would create such a link. "We should be paying farmers for being good stewards of the land and selling products into their communities, not for their losses," Lotti contends.

Another flash point is the Supplemental Nutrition Assistance Program (SNAP), long known as food stamps, which is the main federal program designed to help low-income families afford adequate and nutritious foods. The Senate farm bill makes what supporters called modest reforms to SNAP, cutting $4.5 billion over 10 years. But House Republicans argue that many recipients abuse the program; the House farm bill, approved by the Agriculture Committee in July, cuts SNAP by $16 billion over 10 years. (*See graphic, p. 54.*)

"SNAP is the first line of defense against hunger," says Eric Olsen, senior vice president of Feeding America, the nation's largest domestic hunger-relief charity. "It's critically important for government to get its budget and spending under control, but past efforts have always exempted the safety net, and we think we can balance the budget without hurting poor people."

Cotton Farmers Benefit Most from Federal Insurance

More than 80 percent of cotton farms were covered by federal crop insurance in 2009. About 65 percent of farms specializing in peanuts and in such cash grains as corn, wheat and soybeans were covered. Hog and dairy farmers often grow crops to feed their livestock, and those crops are eligible for federal crop insurance.

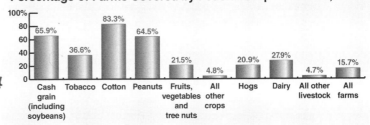

Percentage of Farms Covered by Federal Crop Insurance, 2009

Source: T. Kirk White and Robert A. Hoppe, "Changing Farm Structure and the Distribution of Farm Payments and Federal Crop Insurance," U.S. Department of Agriculture, February 2012, p. 16, www.ers.usda.gov/media/261681/eib91_1_.pdf

But the House recessed in early August without debating its version of the farm bill after Speaker John Boehner, R-Ohio, said the bill lacked enough support to pass. Most House Democrats oppose the bill's large cuts to SNAP funding, while many conservative advocates argue that the measure still spends too much money. The House passed a short-term drought relief package for ranchers, but Senate leaders say they want to debate a full farm bill rather than stopgap measures.[6]

Agriculture is a major sector of the U.S. economy, although the current drought could erode its position. Farm-sector earnings were strong through the 2008-2009 recession and generated a $42.5 billion trade surplus in 2011. The Obama administration's agriculture priorities include maintaining and boosting rural prosperity; conserving natural resources; strengthening local and regional food systems; and combating hunger and obesity, especially in children. Farm advocates say the administration has delivered reasonably well.

"They have not hindered growth in farm income, and many of their rural development and renewable-energy investments have directly contributed to farm income," says Roger Johnson, president of the National Farmers Union, which represents small- to medium-size and family-owned farms. "This administration has presided over a stretch of record farm-income years. Some say [it doesn't] deserve credit, but if prices were low there would be a lot of blame going around."

Presumptive Republican presidential nominee Mitt Romney released names of his agriculture advisory committee in March but did not take positions on specific agriculture issues. "I will work to ensure that our food supply will remain steady, safe and affordable for our citizens," Romney said.[7]

As Congress, advocacy groups and agriculture experts work to shape the 2012 farm bill, here are some issues they are considering:

Does U.S. farm policy need major reform?

The U.S. agricultural system is a vast network of about two million farms and ranches, from small family-owned holdings to huge operations that cover thousands of acres. It also includes agribusiness companies that produce farm equipment, seeds, pesticides, fertilizer and other production materials, as well as food processors and distributors. About 2 percent of all Americans live on farms.[8]

Supporters praise U.S. farmers for efficiently producing abundant quantities of safe and affordable food for both domestic consumption and export. "[T]here are just 210,000 Americans out there who are responsible for 80 percent of U.S. agricultural production," House Agriculture Committee chair Frank Lucas, R-Okla., said last year. "These Americans support our economy, help keep us secure and . . . answer . . . the question of how we are going to feed 9 billion people [worldwide] come the year 2050."[9]

But farm policy has many critics. Budget watchers say the federal government spends too much on farm support programs. Environmental groups want more support for land, water and soil conservation programs. And some public health and nutrition advocates argue that farm policy promotes unhealthy eating by generating vast quantities of cheap processed food, made primarily from heavily subsidized corn and soybeans. Many critics focus on Title I of the farm bill, which provides income support to farmers who raise major agricultural "commodities" such as wheat, corn, soybeans, cotton, rice, peanuts, sugar and dairy products. The 2008 farm bill authorized $41.6 billion for farm commodity support programs, about 15 percent of total spending in the bill.[10]

The critics argue that farm commodity programs have become welfare for large farms, which receive the biggest share of subsidies.[11] Both the Senate and House versions of the 2012 farm bill would save about $50 billion over 10 years by eliminating three commodity programs:

- Direct payments, which are based on past production and paid to farmers whether or not they actually plant crops;
- Countercyclical payments, which farmers receive when market prices fall below certain targets; and
- Average Crop Revenue Election payments, which farmers receive when actual revenue falls short of expected revenues.[12]

Instead, the bills increase support to help farmers buy crop insurance, which protects them against natural disasters.

"The most fundamental reform in [the Senate farm bill] is the shift away from direct payments and toward risk management for farmers," Senate Agriculture Committee chair Debbie Stabenow, D-Mich., said during floor debate on the bill. "[T]he current system, focused around direct and counter-cyclical payments, does not focus on actual risks and is no longer defensible or sustainable."[13]

Many public-interest groups want a bigger shift in priorities. "We subsidize too much of the wrong kinds of foods, especially commodity crops, and not enough local and healthy foods," says Justin Tatham, a lobbyist for the Union of Concerned Scientists (UCS), a national environmental advocacy group. The U.S. Department of Agriculture's (USDA's) MyPlate nutrition guidelines, published in 2011, recommend that fruits and vegetables make up 50 percent of every meal, but fruits and vegetables are grown on only about 2 percent of U.S. croplands.[14] (*See graphic, p. 53.*)

Instead, UCS advocates increased funding for farmers markets, production of specialty crops such as fruits and vegetables, organic agriculture and other programs to increase access to healthy foods. The Senate bill takes some steps in this direction, such as offering crop insurance on specialty crops for the first time. "But it doesn't really reform farm policy with respect to supports," Tatham says.

MyPlate Nutrition Guide Replaces Pyramid

MyPlate, the Agriculture Department's current nutrition guide, replaced the nearly two-decade-old food pyramid,* which critics said gave too much weight to high-fat foods (mainly dairy products and red meat) and carbohydrates such as white bread, rice and potatoes. The MyPlate guidelines, published in 2011, recommend that fruits and vegetables make up half of every meal. Critics note that those crops are grown on only about 2 percent of U.S. farmland and argue that farm support programs should be more closely aligned with nutrition goals.

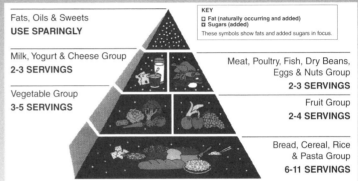

* A newer version of the food pyramid was introduced in 2005.

Source: "Food Groups," ChooseMyPlate.gov, U.S. Department of Agriculture, 2012, www.choosemyplate.gov/food-groups/

In a 2011 article in the journal *Science*, a dozen university researchers and several sustainable producers outlined a framework for an even broader transformation of U.S. agriculture. Truly sustainable farming, they argued, would provide abundant and affordable products, but also would:

- enhance natural resources and the environment;
- make farming financially viable; and
- promote the well-being of farmers, farm workers and rural communities.

"Most elements of the Farm Bill were not designed to promote sustainability," the authors contended. Farm policy, they argued, should be revised to provide more support for methods that balance all four sustainability goals, such as organic farming, grass-fed livestock production and growing of perennial grains instead of strains that are planted and harvested annually. They also called for reorienting federal agriculture research, arguing that most public and private agricultural science in the United States "is narrowly focused on productivity and efficiency."[15]

"We have the technology and the science right now to grow food in sustainable ways, but we lack the policies and markets to make it happen," lead author John Reganold, a soil scientist at Washington State University, said when the article was published.[16] But advocates of mainstream agriculture do not see the same need for radical change.

"Stretching food dollars to put meals on their tables is consumers' top concern," says the American Farm Bureau Federation's Moore. "We have a growing population around the world, so large-scale production technologies will be critical to help us feed that population."

Are crop insurance subsidies too large?

If a 2012 farm bill is enacted, it is likely to increase funding for crop insurance as an alternative to direct payments. In addition to paying farmers for unexpected losses, crop insurance helps farmers obtain credit to purchase seeds, fertilizer and equipment. When crops are insured, banks are more willing to lend money to farmers and let them use their expected harvests to secure the loans.

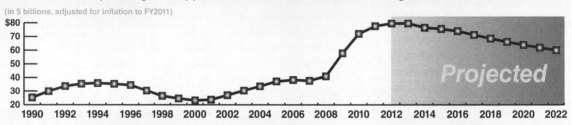

SNAP Spending Projected to Decline

After rising sharply over the past decade, especially during the recent recession, annual federal spending on the Supplemental Nutrition Assistance Program (SNAP) — formerly known as the food stamp program — is projected to decline by 25 percent as the economy improves over the next 10 years, from about $80 billion this year to $60 billion by 2022. The Senate's farm bill would cut $4.5 billion over 10 years, while a House version would cut $16 billion.

Federal Spending on Supplemental Nutrition Assistance Program, FY1990-FY2022

(in $ billions, adjusted for inflation to FY2011)

Projected

1990 1992 1994 1996 1998 2000 2002 2004 2006 2008 2010 2012 2014 2016 2018 2020 2022

Source: "The Supplemental Nutrition Assistance Program," Congressional Budget Office, April 2012, p. 4, www.cbo.gov/sites/default/files/cbofiles/attachments/04-19-SNAP.pdf

Supporters call crop insurance farmers' main shield against events such as the drought currently ravaging corn and soybean harvests. "High input costs mean agriculture will always remain a high risk," Agriculture Secretary Tom Vilsack said last year. "A bad crop, ruined by a natural disaster or an unpredictable price collapse, can put a hard-working farm family out of business quickly. These families rely on a strong safety net."

Sixteen companies have been designated by USDA to provide crop insurance for 2013 under a standard agreement with the Federal Crop Insurance Corp., a unit within USDA.[17] Taxpayers subsidize varying levels of farmers' crop insurance premiums, depending on how much coverage farmers buy. In 2011 subsidies covered about 62 percent of total premiums at a cost of about $7.4 billion (up from $1.5 billion in 2002), plus another $1.3 billion in administrative costs.[18] In contrast to direct payments — which typically were limited to $40,000 per recipient and were phased out for farms earning more than $750,000 — crop insurance subsidies have not had income or payment limits.[19]

Agriculture groups say crop insurance is a structured way of protecting farmers against disasters and market collapses. "Without crop insurance you'd have rampant, unfocused spending after disasters strike — aid programs would be ad hoc, not strategic," says Johnson of the National Farmers Union. "And farmers put some skin in the game — they buy the insurance and pay the premiums, although subsidies make it more affordable."

Moreover, recent farm bills have required farmers to buy crop insurance in order to qualify for disaster relief. "Farmers have been pressured for the past 15 years to use crop insurance instead of relying on government relief, so it's ironic that critics think crop insurance is running amok now," says the American Farm Bureau Federation's Moore.

Critics say the federal government spends too much mitigating risk for farmers and that because crop insurance reduces economic risk, it may promote harmful choices such as planting on marginal lands. A study by Iowa State University economist Bruce Babcock concludes that high federal crop insurance subsidies since 2000 (when subsidies were increased) have induced farmers to buy expensive coverage. Babcock argues that Congress could save $4.2 billion yearly by reverting to the old premium structure.

"[F]armers would still have access to the same types of insurance that they buy today, but eliminating the distorted incentives would encourage them to rely more heavily on alternative forms of risk management," Babcock writes. For example, they could vary the types of crops they plant or earn more income from nonfarm activities.[20]

The Senate-passed 2012 farm bill provides $5 billion for crop insurance over 10 years but includes some new limits. Sens. Richard Durbin, D-Ill., and Tom Coburn, R-Okla., offered an amendment cutting premium subsidies available to farmers with incomes over $750,000 by 15 percent, saving an estimated $1.1 billion. And Sen. Saxby Chambliss, R-Ga., offered an amendment requiring farmers to meet conservation compliance requirements in order to qualify for the subsidies. Both measures passed over objections from insurers and most commodity groups.[21]

According to UCS, too much spending for crop insurance goes to large commodity producers. "Organic and local farmers don't have any kind of federally supported risk management system," says UCS agricultural economist Jeffrey O'Hara. "They're managing risk on their own by growing a diverse array of crops, but they need insurance to help them get financing, and a better safety-net system."

USDA offers some crop-specific insurance policies for fruit and vegetable producers, but O'Hara believes more options are needed. "USDA needs to improve its 'whole-farm revenue' insurance program, which covers farmers who grow diverse products," he says. Moreover, many organic farmers are unable to buy insurance that values their crops at the premium prices that organic foods typically bring in the marketplace. "Those rates should be boosted, so farmers can insure their products at prices that reflect their market value," O'Hara says.

Although the National Farmers Union supports crop insurance as a safety net policy, Johnson acknowledges that costs are an issue. "I think Congress is torn between providing price protection through crop insurance or through some other mechanism," he says. "Over the long term Congress will have to grapple with the fact that crop insurance gets more expensive as prices go higher, because you're insuring the price of the crop as well as production of the crop. We believe that as prices go higher, the need for subsidies goes down. You need to be cautious about changing the system, but cost has to be addressed."

Should SNAP funding be cut?

If the House farm bill comes up for debate, one of the most controversial issues will be funding for the Supplemental Nutrition Assistance Program (SNAP).

SNAP is an entitlement program under which anyone who meets eligibility standards can receive benefits. SNAP program costs have grown sharply over the past decade, especially since the 2008-2009 recession. Critics say the program is too expensive, but supporters argue that SNAP is providing vital aid to millions of Americans.

The Senate-passed bill cuts SNAP by $4.5 billion between 2013 and 2022, while the House Agriculture Committee version would reduce SNAP funding by $16 billion. Legislators said the changes were necessary to protect the program's integrity and ensure that benefits went only to truly needy people.

Both bills tighten use of a policy known as "heat and eat," under which many states link the Low-Income Home Energy Assistance Program (LIHEAP) to SNAP benefits. LIHEAP helps poor people pay home energy bills.

Some states allow households that receive as little as $1 to $5 per month from LIHEAP to take a standard deduction for energy costs on their SNAP applications, which typically qualifies them for a higher level of SNAP benefits than they would receive otherwise. But under both pending farm bills, households must receive at least $10 per month from LIHEAP to be able to take the deduction. According to the Congressional Budget Office, this change will save about $4.5 billion in SNAP payments over 10 years and result in about 500,000 households in 15 states losing $90 per month in SNAP benefits.[22]

"[W]e did this in a very careful way to make sure we did not inadvertently hurt families who truly do have significant energy costs," Stabenow said during floor debate.

The House bill also tightens an option called "categorical eligibility," created in the 1996 welfare reform law, that allowed states to declare that families receiving Temporary Aid for Needy Families (TANF) support — the successor to federal welfare payments — were also eligible for SNAP. This approach allowed some low-income working families to qualify for SNAP even though their gross incomes were slightly above SNAP limits, in recognition that these families often spent substantial money on child care in order to work. Like "heat and eat," categorical eligibility was intended to simplify paperwork, align programs and reduce administrative costs for states.[23]

Stewart Kern waits to apply for food stamps at the Cooperative Feeding Program in Fort Lauderdale, Fla., on Feb. 10, 2011. Food stamps were first issued on an experimental basis from 1939 through 1942 as a substitute for cash relief payments to hungry families and a way to reduce agricultural surpluses. This year, federal spending on the food stamp program — now known as the Supplemental Nutrition Assistance Program (SNAP) — totals about $80 billion, nearly double the amount in 2008 as the economy sank into recession.

Restricting categorical eligibility in the House bill reduces SNAP costs by $11.5 billion and would eliminate SNAP benefits entirely for 1.8 million to 3 million people. In addition, about 280,000 children who currently receive free school lunches would become ineligible because they qualify for that benefit through their families' participation in SNAP.[24]

House Republicans say that in a tight fiscal climate no programs should be off-limits and emphasize that SNAP costs have risen sharply over the past decade. The number of Americans receiving SNAP benefits rose from 26 million (one in eleven) in 2007 to 45 million (one in seven) in 2011, a roughly 70 percent increase. Total spending on SNAP in 2011 was about $78 billion, the highest in the program's history.[25]

"Some say the cuts we propose to food stamps [SNAP] are not enough, while others say the cuts are too much. I believe most Americans would agree a 2 percent cut to food stamps is reasonable," committee chair Lucas said when the panel marked up its version of the farm bill last month.[26]

Food and nutrition advocates strongly oppose cuts to SNAP, especially at the House levels. They argue that SNAP costs have grown over the past decade mainly because of the punishing 2008-2009 recession. In their view, SNAP worked as designed, expanding as more Americans lost jobs and needed government support to feed themselves and their families. The Congressional Budget Office projects that SNAP costs will fall over the next several years as the U.S. economy gradually recovers.[27]

"We should fix the economy instead of blaming the program or people who need help while the economy is still recovering," says Olsen of Feeding America. The group operates more than 200 food banks across the United States, serving 37 million people annually, including 14 million children.

According to the Congressional Budget Office, the average household receiving SNAP benefits in 2010 had income below the federal poverty guidelines — about $18,500 for a family of three. The average recipient household earned about $8,800 per year, excluding SNAP benefits, which boosted gross monthly income by 39 percent for all households.[28] In other words, typical SNAP recipients are not well off.

"If your income is low, food competes against everything else in your life, so having a specific budget just for food can be really powerful," says journalist McMillan, who qualified for SNAP for a year while she was writing *The American Way of Eating*. "Healthy food is as important for subsistence as clean water, and we have public programs to make sure everyone gets clean water. We should start thinking about food in that way."

BACKGROUND

A Nation of Farmers

When the Department of Agriculture was established in 1862, President Abraham Lincoln called it "the people's department" because 90 percent of Americans lived on farms.[29] Over the next 150 years, as scientific and technical innovation made farming more and more productive, the fraction of Americans living on farms dwindled and the average size of U.S. farms steadily increased.

Farming helped settle the American continent. The Homestead Act of 1862 offered public lands for free (typically in 160-acre claims) west of the Mississippi to settlers who would live on the land and farm it for five years. The law was designed to populate Western territories with small independent farms. More than 270 million acres were "patented" (successfully claimed) under the law over the next 126 years.[30]

But farming was risky, especially in the West: More than half of all homestead efforts failed.[31] Some small farmers had trouble competing with land speculators who exploited loopholes in the law to create large estates. And the federal government encouraged farming in many areas where conditions were not suitable — for example, zones on the High Plains where it was too cold or arid to make a living on 160 acres.

By 1900 the number of Americans employed in agriculture had dropped to 41 percent. Many people moved to cities to escape the drudgery of farm labor and the isolation of rural life. In 1914 USDA created the Cooperative Extension Service, which sent agents into rural communities to help farmers adopt new techniques, based on federally funded agricultural research programs at colleges and universities. The extension service helped to nearly double U.S. wheat acreage during World War I and ease war-related labor shortages on farms at harvest times.[32]

Access to credit was a persistent problem for farmers, who needed money to plant and harvest their crops but had trouble getting long-term loans at low rates. In 1916 Congress passed the Federal Farm Loan Act, which created 12 Federal Land Banks and hundreds of National Farm Loan Associations to help farmers buy land and equipment. But these steps soon were superseded by an even larger problem. Aided by new inventions such as tractors and fertilizer, farmers were producing more goods than U.S. and world markets could absorb. These surpluses pushed down prices and made it hard for farmers to stay in business.

World export demand fell after World War I, causing a collapse in farm prices in 1920-21 that lasted throughout the decade. However, there was little political support for limiting production to balance supply and demand.

"Farmers had two choices: They could cut back, hoping supplies would tighten and prices would rise, or they could plant more as a way to make the same money on higher output," writes journalist Timothy Egan of the years leading to the Dust Bowl — a disaster that began in 1931, when millions of acres of over-plowed prairie soils dried up and blew away during a crippling eight-year drought. "Across the Southern plains, the response was overwhelming: The farmers tore up more grass. They had

Library of Congress/Arthur Rothstein

A farmer in Cimarron County, Okla., raises his fence to keep it from being buried by drifting sand during the Dust Bowl disaster, when millions of acres of over-plowed prairie soils dried up and blew away during a crippling eight-year drought in the 1930s. Along with the 1929 Wall Street crash and the ensuing Great Depression, the Dust Bowl helped to spur sweeping changes in U.S. farm policy.

debts to meet . . . for new tractors, plows, combines and land purchased or rented on credit. The only way for someone who made ten thousand dollars in 1925 to duplicate his earnings in 1929 was to plant twice the amount."[33]

Agriculture Transformed

Farmers' plights worsened with the Wall Street crash of 1929, the Great Depression that followed and the Dust Bowl.[34] These blows triggered sweeping changes in U.S. farm policy designed to help farmers earn fair prices for their products and protect them from recessions and natural disasters.

President Franklin D. Roosevelt (1933-1945) introduced a blizzard of legislation upon taking office, including the Agricultural Adjustment Act, passed in 1933 and first amended in 1938, which paid farmers to limit production. The goal was to raise prices of major commodities, including wheat, corn, cotton and tobacco, to the so-called "parity" level, or what farmers would have received in times when agricultural markets were strong. (The Agricultural Act of 1949 provided permanent authority for price supports and set parity levels.)

In the long run, according to historian Paul Conkin, subsidies would make farmland more valuable. That in turn would make it harder for small producers to enter

CHRONOLOGY

1860s-1914 *Agriculture evolves from small farms and local markets to a national industry.*

1862 U.S. Department of Agriculture (USDA) founded. . . . Homestead Act offers free 160-acre claims if applicants live on the land and farm it for five years.

1883 USDA begins conducting agricultural research.

1906 Pure Food and Drug Act gives government power to regulate food safety.

1914 Federal Extension Service is created to educate farmers about agricultural science.

1930-1979 *Responding to the Great Depression, new laws guarantee farm income and access to credit. Scientific and technical advances reduce need for farm labor.*

1930-33 Tractors begin to replace horse-based plowing. . . . Wall Street crash and Dust Bowl slash farm incomes by more than 50 percent. . . . Agricultural Adjustment Act pays farmers to limit production, authorizes USDA to buy and store food and crops, and creates price supports.

1941 USDA issues first recommended dietary allowances, with specific targets for calories, protein, iron, calcium and several major vitamins.

1945 Farm use of synthetic fertilizer and herbicides begins to rise dramatically.

1954 Agricultural Trade Development Assistance Act, later renamed Food for Peace, authorizes low-cost sales of surplus U.S. crops to foreign countries.

1956 Soil Bank Program pays farmers to take corn, cotton, wheat, tobacco, rice and peanuts out of production and conserve land. The program ends after three years due to farmer opposition.

1964 Congress passes Food Stamp Act of 1964; makes program permanent after several years.

1968 Hunger USA study finds widespread hunger and malnutrition among low-income Americans.

1979 Farmers jam National Mall with tractors to lobby for higher prices.

1980-Present *Vertical concentration increases. Concerns grow about continued viability of small farms.*

1985 Farm bill imposes strict rules for conservation grants and revives Conservation Reserve Program.

1990 Organic Foods Production Act creates framework for setting national standards.

1992 Food Pyramid Guide introduced.

1994 Farmers begin using satellite technology to analyze crop conditions and target their use of water and fertilizer.

1996 Freedom to Farm bill is designed to reduce subsidies but boosts federal farm support in 1998-99. . . . Welfare reform legislation requires states to deliver food stamps using electric benefit transfer cards instead of coupons by 2002.

2002 Farm Bill restores most support programs phased out under Freedom to Farm.

2005 Energy Policy Act mandates use of 4 billion gallons of biofuels in motor vehicles, rising to 7.5 billion gallons by 2012.

2007 Expandable Renewable Fuel Standard mandates use of 36 billion gallons of biofuels yearly by 2022.

2008 Federal Food Stamp Program is renamed Supplemental Nutrition Assistance Program (SNAP).

2011 Food Pyramid replaced with MyPlate diagram, recommending that fruits and vegetables make up half of Americans' daily food intake.

2012 Congress debates eliminating direct payments to farmers in 2012 Farm Bill. . . . Worst drought since the 1950s devastates crops. . . . Congress debates reducing SNAP program.

agriculture, speeding the exit of many small farmers. USDA's program mainly benefited large, affluent farmers, who were becoming more dominant in the 1930s and '40s.[35]

Roosevelt also reorganized the farm credit system; established the Rural Electrification Administration, which brought power to many remote areas; and subsidized farmers to carry out soil conservation. USDA created nationwide school lunch and milk programs to use up surplus food. Land-grant universities and USDA's agricultural extension service taught farm families home gardening, poultry production, marketing and other skills to help them survive the Depression.

Farm productivity rose sharply after World War II as mechanized equipment and synthetic chemical fertilizers became increasingly available. Antibiotics and artificial insemination enabled poultry and livestock farmers to greatly increase meat production. As meat, poultry and eggs became cheaper, most farmers bought them instead of raising their own animals. National electrification and the introduction of frozen foods reduced the need to grow vegetables and fruit at home. Farms became more specialized, often raising only one or two major crops.

From 1950 through 1970 the pace of change accelerated. Machinery, electrification, pesticides, fertilizers and plant and animal breeding — all supported by federally funded research — made agriculture less labor-intensive than ever. Corn, wheat and cotton yields per acre and milk production per cow all doubled or nearly doubled during this period. And the fraction of employed Americans working on farms fell from 16 percent of the labor force in 1945 to 4 percent in 1970.[36]

Questioning Growth

The transformation of agriculture filled American stores with thousands of food products, including time-savers such as cake mixes, canned soups and frozen "TV dinners" that contained a complete meal in a tray. But as a national environmental movement developed in the 1970s, some Americans began worrying about pesticides, food dyes and additives.[37] Others questioned how large-scale industrial production was affecting farmlands, and farmers.

"That one American farmer can now feed himself and fifty-six other people may be . . . a triumph of technology," Kentucky author and farmer Wendell Berry wrote in 1977. But, Berry argued, the impact on farms and farmers

was disastrous. "It has divided all land into two kinds — that which permits the use of large equipment and that which does not. And it has divided all farmers into two kinds — those who have sufficient 'business sense' and managerial ability to handle the large acreages necessary to finance large machines and those who do not."[38]

Farm production boomed in the 1970s, then ran into a deep economic recession in the first half of the 1980s. Payments to farmers — now based on the difference between target prices set by USDA and market prices — ballooned. In 1983 the Reagan administration instituted an emergency payment-in-kind program in which the government paid farmers who idled their land with USDA-held surplus crops.

Two years later Congress passed a farm bill that reduced price supports, imposed new rules for conserving vulnerable lands and revived the Conservation Reserve Program, an Eisenhower-era measure that paid farmers to set aside vulnerable lands as wildlife habitat.

In the late 1980s and '90s, as politicians and experts grew concerned about curbing federal spending, many started to question whether farm subsidy payments were producing much benefit when most of them went to large landholders. The United States and 116 other nations agreed in 1993 under the General Agreement on Tariffs and Trade (GATT) to reduce domestic farm subsidies and exports of subsidized commodities in order to promote free international trade. And in 1994 Republicans won control of both houses of Congress, pledging to cut federal spending.

These changes set the stage for so-called "Freedom to Farm" legislation in 1996, proposed by Rep. Pat Roberts, R-Kan., which lifted planting restrictions and decoupled farm subsidies from commodity prices in return for declining fixed payments over seven years. Free-market advocates called this the beginning of the end for farm subsidies, but when commodity prices fell shortly after the bill passed, Congress stepped in with billions of dollars in emergency farm assistance. Despite 50 years of radical change in U.S. agriculture, farm policy remained anchored to laws passed in 1938 and 1949.

Nutrition Debates

As policy makers struggled to guarantee farmers reasonable livings in a boom-and-bust industry, USDA was also shaping debates about nutrition in America. One of its

'Food Deserts' Provide Few Healthy Eating Options

Residents are forced to shop at small stores that don't offer fresh foods.

For most Americans, grocery shopping is a routine errand. But millions of consumers, especially people with low incomes, have trouble obtaining affordable and nutritious foods because they live in areas with few, if any, large grocery stores or supermarkets, and they may also lack transportation.

In these so-called food deserts, many health advocates warn that people are likely to eat fewer nutritious foods than recommended, which puts them at risk for such health problems as obesity and diabetes. However, other experts argue that food choices are shaped by many factors, not simply by distance to a supermarket.

In the 2008 farm bill, Congress directed the U.S. Department of Agriculture (USDA) to study the extent and impacts of low access to healthy foods. USDA found that 11.5 million Americans, or 4.1 percent of the U.S. population, have low incomes (at or below 200 percent of federal poverty thresholds) and live more than a mile from a supermarket or large grocery store (10 miles away in rural areas). As a result, people often shop at small markets or convenience stores that do not carry healthy foods such as fresh fruits, vegetables or seafood. And smaller stores typically charge more than supermarkets, so consumers get less food for their money. [1]

According to USDA's online Food Desert Locator, food deserts are widely distributed across the United States, from rural areas such as northern Maine to parts of Chicago, Los Angeles and other large cities. Urban food deserts often are in areas with high percentages of minority residents. [2]

"In North Chicago there are no grocery stores," said Rhonda Moore, who has Type 2 diabetes and struggles to eat a healthy diet. "Buses don't run on weekends. Cabs are expensive. I try to stock up on frozen things. I'd prefer to eat more salads and such, but you can't buy [fresh produce] in bulk. It only lasts so long." [3]

First lady Michelle Obama has made food deserts a focus of her "Let's Move" initiative to improve American health through better diets and exercise. "In so many neighborhoods, if people want to buy a head of lettuce or salad or some fruit for their kid's lunch, they have to take two or three buses, maybe pay for a taxicab, in order to do it," Obama said last October. [4] Large grocers pledged to open more than 1,000 new stores selling fresh produce in under-served areas, but action on that promise has lagged, with one notable exception: Walgreen's, a national pharmacy chain, is opening "food oasis" stores in urban areas that carry fresh produce along with more typical drugstore products. [5]

Still, some experts say the distance to a store is only one of many influences on Americans' food choices. Others include cultural preferences, work schedules and whether consumers have time to cook their own meals. Several recent studies have found only a weak relationship between foods sold near subjects' homes and what those people choose to consume. [6]

"Just because someone lives in a neighborhood doesn't mean they actually shop there. You need to do research on the ground to understand what's happening," says Rebecca

main tasks was administering the food stamp program, as the central federal food aid program was known for decades.

USDA first issued food stamps in an experimental program from 1939 through 1942 as a substitute for cash relief payments to hungry families and a way of reducing agricultural surpluses. The Kennedy administration revived the program in 1961 to address persistent concerns about hunger in America, and Congress made

it permanent in 1964, with the overall goal of ensuring that poor families could afford enough food for an adequate and nutritious diet. Participation grew rapidly, from 2.9 million people in 1969 to more than 20 million by the end of the 1970s. [39]

This expansion made the program a political target. President Ronald Reagan (1981-1989) frequently told stories of alleged "welfare queens" and other abusers of entitlement programs who used their benefits to buy goods

Klein, director of the Public Health and Agriculture Policy Project at John Hopkins University's Center for a Livable Future.

Journalist Tracie McMillan, who lived in several areas with relatively few supermarkets while researching her 2012 book *The American Way of Eating*, says the issue is more complex than the number of stores in a neighborhood. "The food desert concept is a shorthand for food distribution, which isn't just a matter of counting stores. It's the whole system for getting food into communities," she says. Most of the national transportation and storage systems that move food from farms to plates are controlled by a few large supermarket chains, which historically have not seen investing in low-income communities as a profitable business strategy. But McMillan does not think building more supermarkets in underserved areas will automatically solve the problem.

"Supermarkets do important things really well, but they tend to consolidate power. Their business model depends on offering a lot of processed foods, so you can shop there and buy a completely junk-food diet," McMillan contends. "It's important to bring more retail to communities that don't have enough access. But small grocers and farmers markets may do a better job connecting with people in their neighborhoods and understanding what kinds of foods those people appreciate and want to eat."

— *Jennifer Weeks*

First lady Michelle Obama and students from Bancroft Elementary School in Washington, D.C., harvest vegetables from the White House kitchen garden on the South Lawn of the White House on June 16, 2009. She has made "food deserts" a focus of her "Let's Move" campaign to improve Americans' health. "In so many neighborhoods, if people want to buy a head of lettuce or salad or some fruit for their kid's lunch, they have to take two or three buses, maybe pay for a taxicab, in order to do it," she said.

[1] "Access to Affordable and Nutritious Food: Measuring and Understanding Food Deserts and Their Consequences," Economic Research Service report summary, U.S. Department of Agriculture, June 2009, p. 2, www.ers.usda.gov/media/242654/ap036_reportsummary_1_.pdf.

[2] USDA Food Desert Locator, www.ers.usda.gov/data-products/food-desert-locator/go-to-the-locator.aspx.

[3] Malcolm Garcia, "For Diabetes Patients, Oases in the Food Desert," *Chicago Tribune*, Feb. 1, 2012, http://articles.chicagotribune.com/2012-02-01/health/ct-x-0201-diabetes-food-desert-20120201_1_food-desert-diabetes-patients-affordable-food.

[4] Steven Yaccino, "In Chicago, Michelle Obama Takes on 'Food Deserts,' " *The New York Times*, Oct. 25, 2011, http://thecaucus.blogs.nytimes.com/2011/10/25/in-chicago-michelle-obama-takes-on-food-deserts/.

[5] Leslie Patton, "Michelle Obama's Food Desert Plans Yield Few New Stores: Retail," Bloomberg.com, May 7, 2012, www.bloomberg.com/news/2012-05-07/michelle-obama-s-food-desert-plan-yields-few-new-stores-retail.html.

[6] Gina Kolata, "Studies Question the Pairing of Food Deserts and Obesity," *The New York Times*, April 17, 2012, www.nytimes.com/2012/04/18/health/research/pairing-of-food-deserts-and-obesity-challenged-in-studies.html.

like steaks and vodka.[40] These charges were often exaggerated, but some food stamp users did sell the coupons for cash.[41] In a 1996 overhaul of welfare policies, Congress ordered states to deliver food stamp benefits via electronic benefit cards instead of paper coupons to reduce fraud and abuse.

USDA also sought to help all Americans understand what types of foods made up a healthy diet, although its efforts were controversial. In 1992 the department published its first Food Pyramid, which recommended how many servings of each of six basic food groups should be eaten daily. Prominent nutrition experts argued that the diagram gave too much weight to high-fat foods such as whole milk and red meat, reflecting the influence that large agribusiness companies held over USDA.[42]

In 2005, with obesity reaching record levels across the United States, USDA revised the Food Pyramid, adding

USDA Seeks New Farmers

As older farmers retire, beginners need many kinds of support.

American agriculture is undergoing a generational shift, as older farmers leave the land and younger ones hoping to take their place confront a wide range of environmental, financial and regulatory challenges.

The average age of farm operators in America has been above 50 since at least 1974, and today more than half are over 55. [1]

"We're facing a major transition right now on our working lands in this country," said Kathleen Merrigan, deputy secretary of Agriculture. "It's not just about farming, it's about food safety, marketing, finance." [2]

Even on small farms, agriculture is a complex business that requires farmers to consider how financing, consumer demand, national and global commodity markets and many other factors will affect their profitability. And despite current record-high revenues, thanks to high world commodity prices, the basic economics of farming are daunting. "Profits are low, and agriculture is very capital-intensive," says National Farmers Union President Roger Johnson. "Both of those factors make it very hard to get started in farming."

The U.S. Department of Agriculture (USDA) defines beginning farmers and ranchers as those who have operated a farm for less than 10 years. About one-fifth of U.S. farms (roughly 450,000) fall into this category. [3]

Beginning farmers represent all age ranges and ethnic groups, but on average they are younger than established farmers. Like veteran farmers, the new farmers are concentrated in the Midwest and South, but also operate in the West and Northeast. On average, beginning farmers hold less land than established farmers (169 acres for a beginning farm, compared to 440 acres for an established one). Beginning farmers also are more likely than experienced farmers to have a college degree, and a larger fraction of their income comes from nonfarm activities. [4]

The 2008 farm bill contained several programs designed to help new farmers, including extra crop insurance subsidies, targeted loans and incentives for retiring farmers to transfer their operations to beginners. [5] Both versions of the 2012 farm bill would increase support for beginning farmers and ranchers, including providing about $50 million for research and outreach programs and $192 million for targeted crop insurance programs over 10 years.

The pending bills also boost support for specialty crops, such as fruits and vegetables, which will help new farmers, says Jeffrey O'Hara, an agricultural economist with the Union of Concerned Scientists. "Local foods are where farmers are coming in, growing the foods that people are demanding but can't get enough of. That's where the opportunities are for them. Supporting healthier foods supports the next generation of farmers."

Growth in local food networks backs that view. The number of farmers markets in the United States has more than quadrupled since 1994, from 1,744 to 7,864, and some markets have waiting lists of farmers seeking sales spaces. [6] (*See graphic, p. 63.*) Moreover, the USDA reported last year that it had been underestimating sales of local foods because it had focused on direct-to-consumer outlets, such as farmers markets and roadside stands, without counting sales to regional distributors, grocery stores and restaurants.

Counting those sales, farmers earned $4.8 billion in 2008 through local food marketing (including $877 million at direct-to-consumer outlets), according to USDA estimates. Local food sales could help promote economic development in many areas, especially near cities, the department said. [7]

Farmers and other agriculture experts were quick to respond early this year to a blog post by journalist Terence

a staircase to stress the importance of physical activity. This version was widely denounced as confusing and still overly focused on dairy and meat products. The agency scrapped the pyramid in 2011, replacing it with a new design called MyPlate, which advised that fruits and vegetables should constitute half of every meal.

CURRENT SITUATION

Drought and Delay

As much of the United States struggles through intense drought, the Obama administration and farm state legislators are pressing for Congress to pass the 2012

Loose, who listed agriculture, horticulture and animal science as three of the top five "useless degrees" for U.S. college students, along with fashion design and theater. He based his views on U.S. Department of Labor projections of job growth in those fields. [8]

Angry rebuttals went viral on the Internet. [9] Merrigan called the blog post "so out of touch with . . . what we know the situation to be," referring to the ongoing generational turnover in agriculture. [10] And a Facebook page titled "I Studied Agriculture and I Have a Job" collected thousands of "likes" within 24 hours of its creation. [11]

— Jennifer Weeks

---

[1] "Farm Household Well-Being: Labor Allocations and Age," U.S. Department of Agriculture, updated, May 27, 2012, www.ers.usda.gov/topics/farm-economy/farm-household-well-being/labor-allocations-age.aspx.

[2] "Merrigan Stresses Need for Young Leaders in Agricultural Pipeline," *Fresh Cut Magazine*, April 2, 2012, http://freshcut.com/index.php/news/release/16708/.

[3] Mary Clare Ahearn, "Potential Challenges for Beginning Farmers and Ranchers," *Choices*, 2nd Quarter 2011, www.choicesmagazine.org/choices-magazine/theme-articles/innovations-to-support-beginning-farmers-and-ranchers/potential-challenges-for-beginning-farmers-and-ranchers.

[4] "Farm Demographics," U.S. Department of Agriculture, www.start2farm.gov/usda/knowledge; "Farm Household Income and Characteristics: Characteristics of Principal Farm Operator Households by Experience of Operators, 2010," Economic Research Service, U.S. Department of Agriculture, www.ers.usda.gov/data-products/farm-household-income-and-characteristics.aspx.

[5] "2008 Farm Bill side-by-side: Provisions for Traditionally Underserved Groups," Economic Research Service, U.S. Department of Agriculture, http://webarchives.cdlib.org/sw1rf5mh0k/www.ers.usda.gov/FarmBill/2008/Titles/Underserved.htm.

[6] Tracie Cone, "Number of U.S. Farmers Markets Surges," The Associated Press, Aug. 3, 2012, www.timesrecordnews.com/news/2012/aug/03/apnewsbreak-number-us-farmers-markets-surges/.

[7] Sarah A. Low and Stephen Vogel, "Direct and Intermediated Marketing of Local Foods in the United States," Economic Research

Boom in Farmers Markets

There are nearly 7,900 farmers markets nationwide, four-and-a-half times more than in 1994 and 10 percent more than last year alone. Supporters of increased funding for farmers markets say they build distribution networks for small farmers and promote the production of fruits, vegetables and other healthy foods.

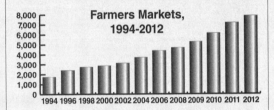

Farmers Markets, 1994-2012

Source: "Farmers Markets and Local Food Marketing," U.S. Department of Agriculture, August 2012, www.ams.usda.gov/AMSv1.0/ams.fetchTemplateData.do?template=TemplateS&leftNav=WholesaleandFarmersMarkets&page=WFMFarmersMarketGrowth&description=Farmers%20Market%20Growth&acct=frmrdirmkt

Report No. 128, U.S. Department of Agriculture, November 2011, pp. 2-3 and 13, www.ers.usda.gov/media/138324/err128_2_.pdf.

[8] Terence Loose, "College Majors That Are Useless," Yahoo.com, http://education.yahoo.net/articles/most_useless_degrees.htm.

[9] See, for example, Rebekah Bowen, "An Open Letter to Terence Loose on the Future of Agricultural Careers," http://rebekahbowen.wordpress.com/2012/01/19/an-open-letter-to-terence-loose-on-the-future-of-agriculture-careers/, and Holly Spangler, "Loose: Not Taking Questions," FarmProgress.com, Jan. 31, 2012, http://farmprogress.com/blogs-loose-taking-questions-2980.

[10] "Merrigan Stresses the Need for Young Leaders," *op. cit.*

[11] "Yahoo's 'Useless Degree' Article Draws Huge Response," Wisconsin Farm Bureau Federation, Jan. 26, 2012, http://wfbf.com/ag-newswire/yahoo%E2%80%99s-%E2%80%98useless-degrees%E2%80%99-article-draws-huge-response/.

farm bill. Because both the Senate-passed bill and the House Agriculture Committee's version would strengthen crop insurance programs and reauthorize USDA drought and disaster relief programs, advocates argue that enacting them would update important safety-net programs.

"While by no means perfect, this farm bill is needed for producers and those who rely on sound agriculture policy and nutrition programs during difficult economic times," a group of 78 House members (47 Republicans and 31 Democrats) wrote to House leaders on July 19.[43] Minority Leader Nancy Pelosi, D-Calif., echoed that view.

Getty Images/Scott Olson

Agriculture is a major sector of the U.S. economy, but farmers in the nation's midsection have been experiencing one of the worst droughts in more than 50 years. Here, Bill Kirklin sets up an irrigation system in his cornfield near Whiteland, Ind., on July 20, 2012. He and his brother, both sixth-generation farmers, raise about 1,500 acres of corn and soybeans on a farm founded by their family in 1835.

"Inaction means economic, nutritional and employment crisis throughout our rural communities," Pelosi said.[44]

But House Speaker Boehner has a record of voting against previous farm bills and has criticized the spending levels in the proposed 2012 bills. "We've got a Soviet-style dairy program in America today, and one of the proposals in the farm bill would actually make it worse," Boehner said in July.[45]

As of Aug. 1, 2012, USDA had designated 1,452 counties as drought disaster areas, with 66 percent of national hay acreage and 73 percent of cattle acreage affected and 48 percent of the corn crop rated as being in poor to very poor condition.[46] Losses of major crops such as corn, wheat, oats and soybeans will drive up the prices of many groceries, including breads, cereals, cooking oils and numerous processed foods that contain corn-based sweeteners. Corn and soybean meal also are major ingredients for animal feeds, so as corn and soybean prices rise, many livestock producers will further reduce their herds to cut costs. Smaller supplies will lead to higher meat, milk and egg prices.

"The bottom line is, food is a necessity," Purdue University agricultural economist Chris Hurt said last month. "[When] food extracts more of our disposable income, that's less dollars to be spent for other things."

Hurt predicted that food price inflation caused by the drought could increase overall inflation in the United States by several tenths of a percent, starting this fall.[47]

USDA has limited tools for providing quick relief to farmers hit hard by drought. The department is offering low-interest loans to farmers in drought disaster zones and letting ranchers cut hay and graze cattle on lands protected under the Conservation Reserve Program. Crop insurance will cover about 72 percent of yield and revenue losses for insured farmers, according to Agriculture Secretary Vilsack. "But it's the livestock producers that are in the biggest and most troubled situation because they simply don't have any disaster program, and there's no such thing as a crop insurance program for livestock producers," Vilsack said.[48]

Conserving Farm Lands

Farming can have many negative environmental impacts on soil, water supplies, air quality, wildlife and human health, especially when practiced on a large scale with heavy use of pesticides, herbicides, fertilizers and other chemicals. A 2004 study by Iowa State University economists estimated that the external costs of U.S. agriculture (costs that were not paid by farmers but instead were borne by society) ranged from $5.7 billion to $16.9 billion per year. "We pay for food in our utility bills and taxes and in our declining environmental and personal health," the authors observed.[49]

Environmental groups and sustainable-agriculture advocates have won increasing support for conservation programs in farm bills since 1985, when a conservation title was first added to the bill. Title II of the 2008 farm bill authorized $24.1 billion over five years for conservation programs, which fall into two main categories. Land retirement and easement programs pay farmers to take vulnerable lands out of crop production, while working lands programs help farmers protect natural resources on productive lands.

Now, however, these programs are under pressure. Both versions of the 2012 farm bill cut conservation programs in Title II by more than $6 billion over 10 years and consolidate 23 conservation programs into 13 programs. And market trends are undercutting the largest land retirement initiative: the Conservation Reserve Program (CRP), which pays farmers not to grow crops on sensitive lands, such as prairie wetlands and grasslands. Farmers

Does U.S. farm policy promote unhealthy eating?

YES

David Ludwig

Professor of Pediatrics, Harvard Medical School; Professor of Nutrition, Harvard School of Public Health

From "Reforming the 2012 Farm Bill," public forum, Oct. 20, 2011, Harvard School of Public Health

In the last century, there's been a progressive transformation to [our] traditional way of eating, such that we now have a massive number of products in our food supply. When you think of all of the prepared breakfast cereals alone, that could be hundreds on a store shelf, together with fast food, sugary drinks [and] a range of processed snacks.

And yet, they're all produced from literally four commodities: corn, wheat, soybeans [and] rice, or the animals that are fed [on] those commodities. That's the majority of calories in our diet now. This profound transformation of the diet has been driven by agricultural policies in general and, to some degree, specifically farm agricultural subsidies of commodities that have made these grains and soybeans that are inherently cheap to produce, even cheaper. . . .

The implications of this policy to public health are increasingly profound, for two reasons. One is that these ultra-processed products, based on commodities, are very dense in calories. Well, the calorie density, by itself, isn't inherently a problem. Nuts are calorie-dense, but they're also nutritious and satiating and have many benefits to health. It's the combination of concentrating calories and removing nutrients and other nutritional properties.

So . . . we might have, 50 years ago, had a child who ate a bowl of strawberries for an afternoon snack that provided 100 calories, [and] those strawberries would also have provided five or more grams of fiber, many vitamins and minerals, antioxidants and phytochemicals, in physiologically relevant doses. Today that child is probably eating strawberry-flavored Fruit Gushers, which have the same 100 calories in a tenth the size, [with] virtually no fiber, vitamins or minerals or anything of value.

The consequence, or what I saw today in the obesity clinic at Children's Hospital, are patients like the 8-year-old girl that I saw who weighed over 200 pounds, with triglycerides of 240, very high, and very low levels of HDL cholesterol, insulin resistance, fatty liver, and pre-diabetes. And this is not genetic; this is dietary. Ultimately, we are going to need to rethink agricultural policy to get us off this dependence primarily on these four products in order to improve the nutritional quality of the food supply, if we're going to do anything about the obesity epidemic and the epidemic of diseases related to obesity in the United States.

NO

Julian Alston

Professor of Agricultural and Resource Economics, University of California, Davis; Member, Giannini Foundation of Agricultural Economics, University of California

Written for *CQ Global Researcher,* August 2012

Many people blame federal farm subsidies for America's high obesity rates, but this view is rejected by my work with agricultural economists Brad Rickard and Abigail Okrent. Our careful quantitative analysis indicates that U.S. farm subsidy policies, for the most part, have not made food commodities significantly cheaper and have not had a significant effect on caloric consumption.

First, the effects of farm subsidies on food prices are muted because farm commodities used as ingredients represent a small share of the total cost of retail food products. On average, the farm commodity cost share is approximately 20 percent, but it varies widely: For grains, sugar and oilseeds, it is less than 10 percent; for soda, the share is approximately 2 percent.

Second, the effects on farm commodity prices are small and mixed. Subsidies have at times resulted in lower U.S. prices of some farm commodities, in particular grains, and consequently lower costs of producing breakfast cereal, bread or livestock products. But these effects have been contained by companion policies that restricted acreage. Moreover, U.S. import barriers that support farm prices for many commodities (such as sugar, dairy, orange juice and beef) also increase food prices domestically and discourage consumption. Consequently, eliminating all farm subsidies, including those provided indirectly by trade barriers, may, if anything, lead to an increase in annual per capita consumption of calories and an increase in body weight.

Third, the roles of policies affecting corn are misunderstood. Farm subsidies are responsible for the growth in the use of corn to produce high fructose corn syrup (HFCS) as a caloric sweetener, but not in the way it is often suggested. The culprit here is not corn subsidies; rather, sugar policy has restricted imports, driven up the U.S. price of sugar and encouraged consumers and food manufacturers to replace sugar with alternative caloric sweeteners, especially HFCS. Moreover, U.S. biofuels policy that also subsidizes corn producers has made corn much more expensive for food and feed. On net, corn and sugar policies have made caloric sweeteners more expensive, discouraging obesity.

U.S. farm policies might well be seen as unfair and inefficient. But whether we like these policies or not for other reasons, their effects on obesity are negligible. Farm subsidies are a red herring in the context of obesity, distracting attention from the real causes and potential solutions.

offer USDA bids to enroll specific parcels of land in the CRP program; the agency awards 10- to 15-year contracts, based on criteria designed to select the most environmentally sensitive lands. The average CRP land rental rate is currently $57.29 per acre, although rates vary widely from state to state.[50]

With crop prices rising, many farmers are not renewing CRP contracts. "We recognize that there are seven to 10 million acres in the CRP that could be productive," says the American Farm Bureau Federation's Moore. "The presumption is that farmers who hold expiring CRP contracts won't renew them, because expected returns [from planting on those acres] will be much greater."

Critics say that having crop insurance readily available is also a factor. "Crop insurance decreases risk for farmers, so it will probably motivate some farmers to plant on marginal land," says Johns Hopkins University's Klein. "Making conservation compliance a condition for receiving crop insurance subsidies will create a disincentive to plant those lands."

Some USDA conservation programs have historically been attached to the direct payments to farmers funded in Title I of the farm bill. But if Congress eliminates direct payments, those conservation incentives will no longer apply to the affected lands. These programs include Conservation Compliance, which requires farms operating on highly erodible land to use approved soil conservation techniques; Sodbuster, which bars farmers from plowing up highly erodible land without an approved soil conservation plan; and Swampbuster, which prohibits farms from converting wetlands to croplands.[51]

Instead, advocates say, crop insurance should come with conservation requirements. The American Farm Bureau Federation opposes this approach. "Almost every farmer out there is required to comply with some form of conservation program. But tying conservation to crop insurance raises the possibility that if you're not in compliance because of factors you can't control [for example, a natural disaster], you may not get crop insurance, which is a fundamental risk-management tool," says Moore.

But not all farmers support that position. In a June poll sponsored by the National Farmers Union, 61 percent of farmers surveyed said farmers should be required to meet some environmental standards to receive federal farm benefits such as crop insurance. And 71 percent agreed with the statement, "Conservation programs reduce costs and help farmers' bottom line," compared to 14 percent who believed that "conservation programs are a burden and hurt farmers' bottom line."[52]

The Disappearing Middle

Meanwhile, despite the continuing trend toward consolidation in American agriculture since the 1930s, many observers today say that with local food networks growing and consumers increasingly interested in the sources of their food, small farms are doing quite well overall. The sector of greatest concern is midsize farms — or as a national research initiative dubs them, "Agriculture of the Middle." Farms in this category are typically businesses where:

- Gross yearly sales total $50,000 to $500,000;
- Farming is the household's main income source, and one or more family members make most decisions and provide significant labor; and
- Farms sell to their markets through wholesale supply chains or other organizations such as co-ops, and often operate with high environmental standards.[53]

"We're seeing more really large farms that produce one or two crops on a lot of acres, and more small farms that produce diverse crops for local, regional or organic markets," says Lotti of the National Sustainable Agriculture Coalition. "Midsized family farms are declining — they can't make it with current farm policy and national and international market conditions." These farms often are too large to sell their products directly to consumers through outlets such as farmers markets, but too small to compete with large-scale producers.

Agriculture experts say strengthening local and regional food systems can create more outlets for products from medium-size farms. As one example, the state of Virginia's cooperative extension system recently pointed out that institutions such as colleges and universities, museums, hospitals and corporate cafeterias could not obtain enough locally grown Virginia products to meet customer demand. Better distribution systems could help meet that demand and create "Virginia-based value chains," thereby "linking people to their culture, land, agriculture and natural resources," according to two extension experts.[54]

Feed Versus Fuel

This summer's drought is reviving an intense debate over national production targets for ethanol, a biofuel made mainly from corn. Since 2005, the federal Renewable Fuels Standard (RFS) has required oil refiners to blend specific amounts of ethanol into motor gasoline yearly, a policy designed to reduce U.S. dependence on imported oil and bolster farm communities. Much conventional gasoline sold today across the United States contains 10 percent ethanol, a level that can be used in any car. Some cars and trucks are "flex-fuel" vehicles that can run on either gasoline or blends containing up to 85 percent ethanol.

The ethanol mandate becomes controversial when corn supplies are tight, because it creates competition between using corn to make animal feed or fuel. With the drought driving up corn prices, a coalition of meat and poultry producers petitioned the Environmental Protection Agency on July 30 to waive the RFS for a year. The groups estimated that meeting RFS targets (13.2 billion gallons of corn ethanol in 2012 and 13.98 billion gallons in 2013) could consume up to 40 percent of expected corn crops.[55]

"The combination of the drought and American ethanol policy will lead in many parts of the world to widespread inflation, more hunger, less food security, slower economic growth and political instability, especially in poor countries," University of California-Davis economist Colin Carter and Hoover Institution fellow Henry Miller wrote in support of a waiver.[56]

Ethanol advocates oppose waiving the RFS and say the law offers ways to handle any supply shortage. For example, refiners who earned credits in past years for blending more ethanol than the mandate required can use those credits toward current targets.

Waiving the RFS "will not make it rain in Indiana, bring pastures to life in the Plains, or meaningfully lower corn prices," Renewable Fuels Association President and CEO Bob Dinneen said in response to waiver requests.[57]

OUTLOOK

Big Shifts

U.S. agriculture is a vast system that is unlikely to change quickly — rather like turning an ocean liner — so many experts say the system may look much the same in a decade as it does today. "If momentum keeps building, we could get some big shifts within 20 years," says Klein of Johns Hopkins University.

But observers believe certain shifts are likely to continue — particularly the growth of small-scale local food networks and alternative production methods such as organic farming. They also expect increasing support for fruits and vegetables, after decades of focus on commodity crops.

"Ten years ago people thought organic agriculture was a niche market, but now it's much bigger. That's where we are now with local markets," says Robert Guenther, senior vice president of the United Fresh Produce Association. "Our goods go to market within two or three days of harvest, and we have to adjust to consumers' demands and needs. That will be a very important segment of our industry: more local and regional sourcing through outlets like roadside stands and farmers markets."

Growth will also continue at the large end, says Johnson of the National Farmers Union. "Big farms will keep getting larger, more concentrated and more specialized. But consumers will continue wanting to know more about where their food comes from, and that will provide more opportunities for people in areas where smaller operations can do direct marketing — for example, in the Northeastern states."

Much of the current energy in agriculture is at the small-scale end, observers say. Many predict that continued growth in the local and healthy food sector could have a disproportionate impact on health in America. "I expect the local food surge to continue, and it's very positive that people are talking about regional food systems. That's what we really need to achieve a diverse diet," says Klein.

One undervalued aspect of sustainable agriculture, advocates contend, is that it makes farmlands healthier and better able to withstand likely impacts from climate change, such as more frequent droughts. "Organic soils can withstand drought and absorb more water during flooding. On the crop side, if you diversify you have differently timed plantings and crops, so you're buffered against big losses," says Lotti of the National Sustainable Agriculture Coalition. "We should pay farmers for actions that would help mitigate future climate events, instead of just for production or losses the way we do today," she says.

Journalist McMillan says changes are needed beyond farmlands. "We should build more public capacity for quality food distribution and subsidize demand instead of production — for example, increasing programs that provide matching funds for money that low-income consumers spend at farmers markets," she says. "That would make it possible for smaller farmers to sell to smaller grocers in their areas. Small farmers and grocers can't develop cheap distribution systems like the big supermarkets, so a distribution system that brings quality food into communities will make it possible for them to sell directly to people who need it. That would transform the quality of food in a lot of communities, and it would diversify the food system."

NOTES

1. Tracie McMillan, *The American Way of Eating* (2012), p. 236

2. *Ibid.*, p. 237.

3. For background, see the following *CQ Researcher* reports: Nellie Bristol, "Preventing Disease," Jan. 6, 2012, pp. 1-24; Barbara Mantel, "Preventing Obesity," Oct. 1, 2010, pp. 797-820; Marcia Clemmitt, "Heart Health," Sept. 12, 2008, pp. 721-744; and Alan Greenblatt, "Obesity Epidemic," Jan. 31, 2003, pp. 73-104.

4. "Urging the Passage of a Farm Bill That Supports Healthy, Local, and Regional Food Systems," resolution adopted at 80th annual meeting, U.S. Conference of Mayors, June 13-16, 2012, http://usmayors.org/resolutions/80th_conference/chhs03.asp.

5. For background, see the following *CQ Researcher* reports: Peter Katel, "Water Crisis in the West," Dec. 9, 2011, pp. 1025-1048; and Chanan Tigay, "Extreme Weather," Sept. 9, 2011, pp. 733-756.

6. James Rowley and Derek Wallbank, "House Republicans Pass Drought Relief and Delay Farm Bill," Bloomberg News, Aug. 2, 2012, www.bloomberg.com/news/2012-08-02/house-republicans-seek-drought-relief-while-delaying-farm-bill.html.

7. "Mitt Romney Announces Agriculture Advisory Committee," March 13, 2012, www.mittromney.com/news/press/2012/03/mitt-romney-announces-agriculture-advisory-committee.

8. "Ag 101: Demographics," U.S. Environmental Protection Agency, www.epa.gov/oecaagct/ag101/demographics.html.

9. Opening statement, House Agriculture Committee hearing, Feb. 17, 2011, http://agriculture.house.gov/statements/lucas-statement-passing-stewart-doan.

10. Renée Johnson and Jim Monke, "What is the 'Farm Bill?'," *Congressional Research Service*, Jan. 3, 2011, p. 3, www.nationalaglawcenter.org/assets/crs/RS22131.pdf.

11. For background, see David Hosansky, "Farm Subsidies," *CQ Researcher*, May 17, 2001, pp. 433-456. Also see Reed Karaim, "Farm Subsidies," *CQ Global Researcher*, May 1, 2012, pp. 205-228.

12. For Congressional Budget Office (CBO) analyses of the 2012 bills, see www.cbo.gov/sites/default/files/cbofiles/attachments/hr6083.pdf (House bill), and www.cbo.gov/sites/default/files/cbofiles/attachments/s3240Passed.pdf (Senate bill).

13. Floor statement of Sen. Debbie Stabenow, June 6, 2012, p. 2, www.ag.senate.gov/newsroom/press/release/chairwoman-stabenow-floor-remarks-on-agriculture-reform-food-and-jobs-act-of-2012.

14. "Plant the Plate," Union of Concerned Scientists, May 1, 2012, www.ucsusa.org/food_and_agriculture/solutions/big_picture_solutions/plant-the-plate.html.

15. J. P. Reganold, *et al.*, "Transforming U.S. Agriculture," *Science*, vol. 332, May 6, 2011, pp. 670-671, www.sciencemag.org/content/332/6030/670.

16. "Expert Panel Calls for 'Transforming U.S. Agriculture:' Changes in Markets, Policies and Science Needed for More Sustainable Farming," *Science Daily*, May 5, 2011, www.sciencedaily.com/releases/2011/05/110505142600.htm.

17. For a list of the companies designated by USDA to provide crop insurance for 2013 and the master agreement, see www3.rma.usda.gov/tools/agents/companies/indexCI.cfm.

18. "Crop Insurance: Savings Would Result from Program Changes and Greater Use of Data Mining," U.S. Government Accountability Office (GAO), March 2012, pp. 1, 7, http://gao.gov/assets/590/589305.pdf; Bruce Babcock, "Impact of Scaling Back Crop

Insurance Premium Subsidies," Environmental Working Group, February 2012, p. 4, http://static.ewg.org/pdf/babcock_cropinsurancesubsidies.pdf.

19. GAO, *ibid.*, p. 3.

20. Babcock, *op. cit.*, p. 3.

21. Chris Clayton, "Senate Votes to Limit Crop Insurance Premium Subsidies," *DTN Progressive Farmer*, June 20, 2012, www.dtnprogressivefarmer.com/dtnag/view/ag/printablePage.do?ID=BLOG_PRINTABLE_PAGE&bypassCache=true&pageLayout=v4&blogHandle=policy&blogEntryId=8a82c0bc37ec102e01380c2a16280148&articleTitle=Senate+Votes+to+Limit+Crop+Insurance+Premium+Subsidies&editionName=DTNAgFreeSiteOnline.

22. Dorothy Rosenbaum and Stacy Dean, "House Agriculture Committee Farm Bill Would Throw 2 to 3 Million People Off of SNAP," Center on Budget and Policy Priorities, July 12, 2012, www.cbpp.org/files/7-6-12fa.pdf.

23. For background, see the following *CQ Researcher* reports: Peter Katel, "Child Poverty," Oct. 28, 2011, pp. 901-928; Peter Katel, "Straining the Safety Net," July 31, 2009, pp. 645-668; Thomas J. Billitteri, "Domestic Poverty," Sept. 7, 2007, updated April 27, 2011, pp. 721-744; Tom Price, "Child Welfare Reform," April 22, 2005, pp. 345-368; and Sarah Glazer, "Welfare Reform," Aug. 3, 2001, pp. 601-632.

24. *Ibid.*, pp. 2, 4, citing Congressional Budget Office estimates.

25. "The Supplemental Nutrition Assistance Program," Congressional Budget Office, April 2012, pp. 1, 4, http://cbo.gov/publication/43173.

26. Opening statement of Chairman Lucas, July 11, 2012, http://agriculture.house.gov/statements/opening-statement-chairman-lucas-business-meeting-consider-hr-6083-federal-agriculture.

27. "The Supplemental Nutrition Assistance Program," Congressional Budget Office, April 2012, p. 4, www.cbo.gov/sites/default/files/cbofiles/attachments/04-19-SNAP.pdf.

28. "The Supplemental Nutrition Assistance Program," CBO, *op. cit.*, p. 2.

29. "Troublesome Creek," "American Experience," PBS, www.pbs.org/wgbh/amex/trouble/timeline/index.html.

30. The Homestead Act was repealed in 1976 everywhere but Alaska, where homesteading continued until 1988.

31. "Legacy of the Homestead Act and Homesteading," U.S. Department of the Interior, Bureau of Land Management, www.blm.gov/wo/st/en/res/Education_in_BLM/homestead_act/legacy.html.

32. "Extension," National Institute of Food and Agriculture, U.S. Department of Agriculture, April 19, 2011, www.csrees.usda.gov/qlinks/extension.html#yesterday.

33. Timothy Egan, *The Worst Hard Time: The Untold Story of Those Who Survived the Great American Dust Bowl* (2006), p. 59.

34. For a timeline of the Dust Bowl, see "American Experience: Surviving the Dust Bowl," PBS, www.pbs.org/wgbh/americanexperience/features/timeline/dustbowl/.

35. Paul K. Conkin, *A Revolution Down on the Farm: The Transformation of American Agriculture Since 1928* (2008), pp. 124-125.

36. Carolyn Dimitri, *et al.*, "The 20th Century Transformation of U.S. Agriculture and Farm Policy," Economic Research Service, Economic Information Bulletin No. 3, U.S. Department of Agriculture, June 2005, http://ageconsearch.umn.edu/bitstream/59390/2/eib3.pdf.

37. Marian Burros, "Image of an Industry," *The Washington Post*, May 11, 1978, p. E1.

38. Wendell Berry, *The Unsettling of America: Culture and Agriculture* (1977), p. 33.

39. Margaret S. Andrews and Katherine L. Clancy, *The Political Economy of the Food Stamp Program in the United States* (1985), pp. 68-69, www.ifpri.cgiar.org/sites/default/files/pubs/pubs/books/ppa93/ppa93ch05.pdf.

40. Steven V. Roberts, "Food Stamps Program: How It Grew and How Reagan Wants to Cut It Back," *The New York Times*, April 4, 1981, www.nytimes.com/1981/04/04/us/food-stamps-program-it-grew-reagan-wants-cut-it-back-budget-targets.html; Donald M. Rothberg, "Senator Says Reagan Missing Point on Issues," The Associated Press, March 2, 1982, http://news.google.com/newspapers?nid=145

4&dat=19820302&id=AsssAAAAIBAJ&sjid=YBM EAAAAIBAJ&pg=3500,160234.

41. For background, see "Supplemental Nutrition Assistance Program: Payment Errors and Trafficking Have Declined, But Challenges Remain," GAO-10-956T, U.S. Government Accountability Office, July 28, 2010, www.gao .gov/products/GAO-10-956T.

42. Walter C. Willett and Meir J. Stampfer, "Rebuilding the Food Pyramid," *Scientific American*, January 2003, www.scientificamerican.com/article .cfm?id=rebuilding-the-food-pyram; Marion Nestle, "Why It's Good That the Food Pyramid Became a Plate," *Atlantic.com*, June 3, 2011, www.theatlantic .com/health/archive/2011/06/why-its-good-that-the-food-pyramid-became-a-plate/239889/.

43. "Noem and Welch lead bipartisan group of over 75 urging a vote on Farm Bill," office of Rep. Kristi Noem, U.S. House of Representatives, July 19, 2012, http://noem.house.gov/index.cfm/press-releases?ContentRecord_id=d0013f7a-1d75-4ef7-8c1e-76015e735156.

44. "Pelosi calls for swift action on farm bill before August recess," July 19, 2012, www.democrati cleader.gov/news/press?id=2694.

45. Russell Berman, "Speaker Says No Decision Has Been Made on Farm bill Vote," *The Hill.com*, July 12, 2012, http://thehill.com/blogs/on-the-money/1007-other/237557-boehner-no-decision-on-farm-bill-vote.

46. Press release, "Agriculture Secretary Vilsack Announces New Drought Assistance, Designates an Additional 218 Counties as Primary Natural Disaster Areas," U.S. Department of Agriculture, Aug. 1, 2012, www.usda .gov/wps/portal/usda/usdahome?contentid=2012/ 08/0260.xml&navid=NEWS_RELEASE&navtype=R T&parentnav=LATEST_RELEASES&edeployment_ action=retrievecontent.

47. "Severe Drought Hits the U.S.," "On Point," NPR, July 17, 2012, http://onpoint.wbur.org/2012/07/17/ severe-drought.

48. Press briefing by Press Secretary Jay Carney and Secretary of Agriculture Tom Vilsack, U.S. Department of Agriculture, July 18, 2012, www.usda

.gov/wps/portal/usda/usdahome?content id=2012/07/0244.xml.

49. Erin M. Tegtmeier and Michael D. Duffy, "External Costs of Agricultural Production in the United States," *International Journal of Agricultural Sustainability*, Vol. 2, No. 1, 2004, pp. 1-20, www.leopold.iastate.edu/sites/ default/files/pubs-and-papers/2004-01-external-costs-agricultural-production-united-states_0.pdf. Quote is from p. 14 of the study.

50. Kent Thiese, "CRP Sign-Up," MinnStar Bank, March 3, 2012, www.minnstarbank.com/blog/2012/ 03/crp-sign-up.

51. "Farm Bill: Protecting Environmental Compliance Programs: A Public Health Priority," Center for a Livable Future, The Johns Hopkins University, summer 2012, www.jhsph.edu/research/centers-and-insti tutes/johns-hopkins-center-for-a-livable-future/_pdf/ projects/ffp/farm_bill/Protect-Environmental-Compliance.pdf.

52. "U.S. Heartland Farmers Value Conservation Programs and Reject Cutting Farm Bill Conservation Funding," Greenberg Quinlan Rosner Research, June 25, 2012, http://nfu.org/news/201-energy-and-natural-resources/1129-poll-farmers-value-con servation-programs-and-reject-cutting-farm-bill-conservation-funding.

53. "Characterizing Ag of the Middle and Values-Based Food Supply Chains," Agriculture of the Middle, www .agofthemiddle.org/archives/2012/01/characterizing .html#more.

54. Eric Benfeldt and Kenner Love, "Can Virginia Communities and Counties Seize an Economic and Social Opportunity with Farm-based Local and Regional Economic Development?" Virginia Cooperative Extension, Oct. 7, 2009, http://pubs .ext.vt.edu/news/fbmu/2009/10/article_1.html.

55. "Petition Asks EPA for One-Year Waiver of Ethanol Production Mandate," National Cattlemen's Beef Association, July 30, 2012, www.beefusa.org/news releases1.aspx?NewsID=2591.

56. Colin A. Carter and Henry I. Miller, "Corn for Food, Not for Fuel," *The New York Times*, July 30, 2012, www.nytimes.com/2012/07/31/opinion/corn-for-food-not-for-fuel.html.

57. "RFS Waiver Calls 'Premature' and 'Void of Justification,'" Renewable Fuels Association, Aug. 2, 2012, www.ethanolrfa.org/news/entry/rfs-waiver-calls-premature-and-void-of-justification/.

BIBLIOGRAPHY

Selected Sources

Books

Allen, Will, with Charles Wilson, *The Good Food Revolution: Growing Healthy Food, People, and Communities*, Gotham, 2012.
The son of a sharecropper recounts his journey from professional sports and business to founding one of the nation's premier urban farms in Milwaukee and extols the benefits of strong community food systems.

Conkin, Paul, *A Revolution Down on the Farm: The Transformation of American Agriculture Since 1929*, University Press of Kentucky, 2008.
An emeritus professor of history at Vanderbilt University argues that the greatest industrial revolution in history has occurred in agriculture since 1929.

McMillan, Tracie, *The American Way of Eating: Undercover at Wal-Mart, Applebee's, Farm Fields and the Dinner Table*, Scribner, 2012.
An investigative report into American eating patterns and how they are shaped by employment patterns and incomes.

Salatin, Joel, *Folks, This Ain't Normal: A Farmer's Advice for Happier Hens, Healthier People, and a Better World*, Center Street, 2011.
Local, sustainable food production is the way of the future, argues a third-generation family farmer from Virginia who runs a "beyond organic, grass-fed" farm.

Articles

Bandow, Doug, "It's Time to Kick Farmers Off the Federal Dole," *Forbes*, July 18, 2011, www.cato.org/publications/commentary/its-time-kick-farmers-federal-dole.
A senior fellow at the libertarian Cato Institute calls for reducing direct payments, crop insurance subsidies and other forms of federal support to farmers.

Eligon, John, "Widespread Drought Is Likely to Worsen," *The New York Times*, July 19, 2012, www.nytimes.com/2012/07/20/science/earth/severe-drought-expected-to-worsen-across-the-nation.html?pagewanted=all.
As of mid-July, 55 percent of the continental United States was a federal drought disaster area. Grain prices are spiking because of crop losses, which also will drive up the cost of meat and dairy products.

Eng, Monica, "Politicians, Health Advocates Seek Transparency, Restrictions in Food Stamp Program," *Chicago Tribune*, June 20, 2012, www.chicagotribune.com/news/local/ct-nw-food-stamp-spending-20120620,0,3921977,full.story.
Under current rules participants in SNAP (Supplemental Nutrition Assistance Program) can use federal food credits to buy soda, chips and candy. Health advocates want to change the policy, but the Agriculture Department opposes limiting junk food purchases.

Freeland, Chrystia, "The Triumph of the Family Farm," *The Atlantic*, July/August 2012, www.theatlantic.com/magazine/archive/2012/07/the-triumph-of-the-family-farm/8998/.
Modern technology and global integration have driven most Americans off farms, but those who remain are thriving.

Reports and Studies

"Crop Insurance: Savings Would Result from Program Changes and Greater Use of Data Mining," U.S. Government Accountability Office, March 13, 2012, www.gao.gov/products/GAO-12-256.
Limits on total payments and more review of waste, fraud and abuse could save the federal government more than $1 billion annually in subsidies for crop insurance.

An, Ruopeng, and Roland Sturm, "School and Residential Neighborhood Food Environment and Diet Among California Youth," *American Journal of Preventive Medicine*, Vol. 42, Issue 2, February 2012, www.ajpmonline.org/article/S0749-3797(11)00849-X/abstract.
Rand Corp. researchers find no consistent relationship between the type of food that children and teens choose to eat and what is available nearby, calling into question the theory that living in "food deserts" increases obesity rates.

Carey, John, "The Case for Farm Bill Conservation Programs in the Great Lakes Region," National Wildlife Federation, February 2012, www.nwf.org/News-and-Magazines/Media-Center/Reports/Archive/2012/03-21-12-The-Case-For-Farm-Bill-Conservation-Programs-in-the-Great-Lakes-Region.aspx.
Programs that pay farmers to protect wetlands, manage fertilizer and waste effectively and take other conservation steps help protect the Great Lakes region's multibillion-dollar tourism, fishing and shipping industries and save millions of dollars in cleanup costs.

Carlson, Andrea, and Elizabeth Frazao, "Are Healthy Foods Really More Expensive? It Depends on How You Measure the Price," Economic Information Bulletin EIB-96, U.S. Department of Agriculture, May 2012, www.ers.usda.gov/publications/eib96/.
An analysis by the U.S. Department of Agriculture's Economic Research Service finds that healthy foods are cheaper than unhealthy foods when they are compared based on price by weight or price per average portion, rebutting the belief that healthy foods are expensive.

For More Information

American Farm Bureau Federation, 600 Maryland Ave., S.W., Suite 1000W, Washington, DC 20024; 202-406-3600; www.fb.org. Trade association for farm and ranch interests.

Feeding America, 35 E. Wacker Dr., Suite 2000, Chicago, IL 60601; 800-771-2303; www.feedingamerica.org. Nationwide network of food banks that advocates for policies to end hunger and food insecurity in the United States.

Harvard School of Public Health, 677 Huntington Ave., Boston, MA 02115; 617-432-8423; www.hsph.harvard.edu. Awards graduate degrees and conducts research on health issues, including nutrition and diet.

National Farmers Union, 20 F St., N.W., Suite 400, Washington, DC 20001; 202-554-1600; www.nfu.org. Advocates on behalf of small farms, ranchers and rural communities.

National Sustainable Agriculture Coalition, 110 Maryland Ave., N.E., Washington, DC 20002; 202-547-5754; www.sustainableagriculture.net. Alliance of grassroots organizations working to support small and midsize family farms, protect the environment and ensure access to healthy, nutritious foods.

Union of Concerned Scientists, 2 Brattle Square, Cambridge, MA 02138; 617-547-5552; www.ucsusa.org. National advocacy group combining scientific research and citizen action to achieve a healthy environment.

United Fresh Produce Association, 1901 Pennsylvania Ave., N.W., Suite 1100, Washington, DC 20006; 202-303-3400; www.unitedfresh.org. Trade association representing producers of fresh fruits and vegetables.

U.S. Department of Agriculture, 1400 Independence Ave., S.W., Washington, DC 20250; 202-720-2791; www.usda.gov. Lead federal agency on agriculture, food and nutrition policy; also manages national forests and grasslands and conducts research in partnership with public and land-grant universities.

4

U.S. Oil Dependence

Jennifer Weeks

President Obama, visiting a pipe storage facility in Cushing, Okla., on March 22, calls for expediting the southern leg of the Keystone XL pipeline, running from Oklahoma to the Gulf, but says the segment from Canada to Oklahoma needs more review. U.S. advocates say the pipeline would generate jobs and increase oil exports from a friendly ally. But environmentalists argue that producing oil from tar sands is harming Canadian forests and rivers and generating high carbon emissions.

From *The CQ Researcher*,
June 22, 2012.

A s gasoline hovered near $4 a gallon this past winter, Republican presidential hopeful Newt Gingrich made a bold assertion aimed at frustrated consumers: If elected, he said, he could reduce gas prices to $2.50 a gallon by boosting domestic oil production.

"Drilling here, drilling now so we can pay less and be independent of Middle East oil is just common sense," Gingrich declared.[1]

But President Barack Obama blasted the notion that any president can exert such quick control over what drivers pay at the pump. "It's the easiest thing in the world to make phony election-year promises about lower gas prices," he said. "What's harder is to make a serious, sustained commitment to tackle a problem that may not be solved in one year or one term or even one decade."[2]

The political squabbling — predictable as it may be in an election year — offers a backdrop to an important debate about the nation's energy future, its heavy dependence on petroleum to keep the economy moving and prospects for reducing our reliance on foreign oil.

Underlying that debate is a paradoxical set of facts. Oil currently accounts for 37 percent of U.S. energy use — more than any other fuel source — and 94 percent of transportation fuel.[3] Yet, although oil undergirds the economy, consumption has fallen to a 15-year low, due in part to the steep recession that began at the end of 2007 and rising sales of fuel-efficient cars. At the same time, domestic oil production, aided by technological advances, has cut oil imports from 60 percent of total U.S. consumption in 2005 to 44 percent at the beginning of 2012.[4]

Even as consumption declines and domestic production grows, however, the average price of gasoline was $3.61 per gallon in early

Western Hemisphere Provides Most U.S. Imports

Although the Middle East produces the largest share of world oil supplies (left), the United States is less dependent on those countries than it used to be. Today the largest share of U.S. imports comes from the Western Hemisphere (right), mainly Canada, Venezuela and Mexico.

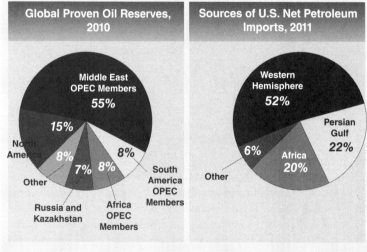

Global Proven Oil Reserves, 2010

Middle East OPEC Members 55%

15%

North America

8% 7% 8% 8%

Other

Russia and Kazakhstan

Africa OPEC Members

South America OPEC Members

Sources of U.S. Net Petroleum Imports, 2011

Western Hemisphere 52%

Persian Gulf 22%

6% Africa 20%

Other

* Figures do not total 100 because of rounding.

Source: "How Dependent Are We on Foreign Oil?" Energy Information Administration, May 2012, www.eia.gov/energy_in_brief/foreign_oil_dependence.cfm

June — a sign that Gingrich's focus on boosting production wouldn't have worked.

Many consumers see a disconnect in these conditions. Why, they ask, should gas prices remain high when oil consumption is down and domestic production is rising? But energy experts say the picture makes sense. Because oil is traded worldwide and prices can be influenced by geopolitical developments anywhere, they say, volatile energy costs are inescapable as long as America relies heavily on oil.

Every president since the 1970s has called for reducing U.S. dependence on oil, especially on imports. Until the 2008 recession drastically slowed world economic growth, imports accounted for a growing share of total U.S. oil consumption. (*See graph, p. 75.*)

Republicans and energy companies say the United States can produce more of its own oil if the federal government relaxes restrictions on exploration and development,

especially on public lands in the West and in federal coastal waters. "Many U.S. resources have been off-limits for decades," says Rayola Dougher, a senior adviser with the American Petroleum Institute, the oil industry's main trade group. "We won't be able to secede from the world oil market, but we'd be much more secure, and our balance of trade would be healthier, if U.S. companies could access these areas."

Presumed Republican presidential nominee Mitt Romney contends that the Obama administration has "put in place policies that are designed to reduce our production of fossil-based fuels and drive up the cost of energy" in order to push the nation toward alternative sources like wind and solar power. But although he now stresses production, as recently as 2010 Romney also supported the idea that higher oil prices could have a positive impact, motivating consumers to conserve energy and use less oil.[5]

President Obama says the right approach is an "all-of-the-above" policy that expands "responsible" oil and gas development but also reduces oil use and promotes renewable fuels and energy-efficient technologies.[6] In his first two years in office Obama focused on commercializing renewable energy sources and controlling carbon emissions from fossil fuel combustion — the largest driver of global climate change. But even before Republicans gained control of the House and expanded their ranks in the Senate in the 2010 midterm elections, Obama was looking for middle ground.

In April 2010 the president proposed opening the Atlantic Coast to offshore energy production from Maryland south, along with a swath of the eastern Gulf of Mexico and the north coast of Alaska. The administration canceled those plans after the *Deepwater Horizon* oil spill in the Gulf led it to tighten federal oversight of offshore drilling nationwide.[7] Now, however, the Interior Department is considering several leases along Alaska's north coast in the Beaufort and Chukchi seas. (*See sidebar, p. 82.*)

Obama is also under pressure to approve the Keystone XL pipeline, which would carry oil from so-called "tar sand" deposits in western Canada to refineries on the U.S. Gulf Coast. Canada is eager to move the oil, which is a heavy grade of crude, to processors with the specialized technology needed to refine it. And many U.S. advocates say the pipeline would generate jobs and increase oil exports from a friendly ally. But environmentalists strongly oppose the project. They argue that developing tar sand deposits is harming Canadian forests and rivers and generating unusually high levels of carbon emissions. (*See* "*At Issue*," *p. 89*.)

The State Department appeared likely to OK the pipeline (which needs federal approval because it crosses an international border) in 2011, but extended the process until after the 2012 election when critics raised problems with its environmental review.[8] Since last November the Republican-controlled House has voted four times to approve the pipeline on a fast track, while the Democratic-controlled Senate has narrowly supported the president.

In March Obama called for expediting the southern leg of the pipeline, which runs from Oklahoma to the Gulf, but argued that the segment from Canada to Oklahoma needed more review. "[A]nybody who suggests that somehow we're suppressing domestic oil production isn't paying attention," Obama said. Republicans countered that the president was taking credit for a project that did not even need federal approval since that segment of the pipeline lay entirely within the United States.[9]

Amid these controversies, the United States is starting to address its near-total reliance on oil for transportation. Last year Obama announced a new agreement with auto companies that will double the average fuel

Global Events Help Drive Oil Prices

Crude oil prices often are affected by events that have the potential to disrupt the flow of oil to the market. High global commodity prices pushed world oil prices up to $147 per barrel in June 2008, but then the financial crisis deflated them when economic growth stalled. Price shocks also followed the Arab Oil Embargo in 1973 and the start of the Iran-Iraq War in 1980.

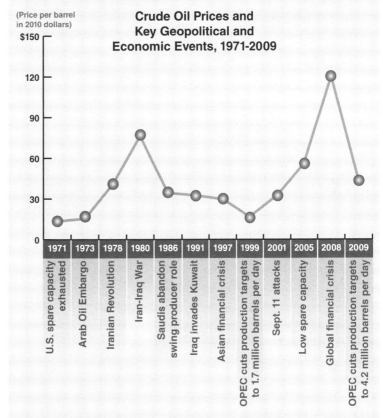

Crude Oil Prices and Key Geopolitical and Economic Events, 1971-2009

Source: "What Drives Crude Oil Prices?" Energy Information Administration, May 2012, www.eia.gov/finance/markets/spot_prices.cfm

efficiency of U.S. passenger vehicles by 2025, to more than 50 miles per gallon. And Toyota sold its one millionth Prius gas-electric hybrid car in the United States. Since the Prius was introduced in the United States in 2000, 13 other carmakers have brought hybrid models to market.[10]

Now manufacturers are introducing plug-in hybrids, which refuel at recharging stations, and battery-operated electric vehicles that operate entirely on battery power.

Bakken Boom Brings Mixed Blessings

Social stress tempers surge in jobs and wealth in North Dakota.

California had its Gold Rush in the 1840s and '50s, and now North Dakota and eastern Montana are at the center of their own rush — a pell-mell race for oil riches that has ignited a surge in jobs and tax revenues but also fueled worries about environmental damage and social upheaval.

Beneath the two-state region lies the Bakken Formation, a massive oil shale deposit that is the largest oil resource in the continental United States.

The Bakken contains approximately 3.6 billion barrels of oil, and perhaps as many as 4.3 billion barrels, according to the most recent U.S. Geological Survey (USGS) estimate, completed in 2008. [1] For comparison, the United States consumed roughly 6.8 billion barrels of petroleum products in 2011. [2] USGS is conducting another estimate because recent drilling in the formation suggests that it may hold even more oil. [3]

The Williston Basin, where the Bakken Formation is located, has been a well-known oil production region for decades. Until recently, however, most of the oil in the area was not economically recoverable because it was trapped tightly between rocky layers in shale beds. (In conventional oil formations, oil accumulates in a pool under a dome or vault of impermeable rock and can be pumped out more readily than it can be extracted from shale.)

Now, however, energy companies are using a combination of techniques to produce oil from tight shale. Engineers drill horizontally along seams in the oil-laced rock, then pump in massive quantities of water laced with chemicals to fracture the rock — a technique called hydraulic fracturing, or "fracking." Horizontal drilling and fracking have produced massive yields from U.S. natural gas fields in the past several years. But fracking is controversial because it also has the potential to pollute groundwater and creates huge quantities of wastewater. [4]

In 1995 the USGS estimated that the Bakken Formation contained about 150 million barrels of "technically recoverable oil" — oil that could be extracted with commercially available technology. The agency increased that estimate by a factor of 25 in its 2008 update, based on new insights into the area's geology derived from horizontal drilling.

"Horizontal drilling exposes more of the formation to the wellbore [the vertical shaft drilled from the surface], so you can get a much better picture of the resource," says Stephanie Gaswirth, USGS's task chief for the new assessment of the Williston Basin. "It's important to understand the source rock, which produces the oil, and also how . . . thick [the reservoir] is, whether there are spaces in it, the composition of the rock, how porous and permeable it is, and whether there are trapping mechanisms for oil."

USGS does not drill its own wells when it assesses formations, but the service uses data from energy companies, along with other geologic information such as seismic data. "In cases like the Bakken Formation, where there is a lot of production data, we use as much of it as we can to understand what energy producers are seeing," says Gaswirth. "We have several years to produce an assessment, but some people who work for private companies have been working this formation for their entire careers."

The Bakken boom has brought jobs and tax revenues to North Dakota. Oil companies are hiring hundreds of workers, who spend their earnings (including overtime pay) at local restaurants, bars, stores and motels. Many entry-level jobs in the oil region, such as waiting tables and stocking grocery shelves, pay $12 per hour or more. [5]

Auto industry leaders and the Obama administration have hailed new models, like the plug-in Chevy Volt, as evidence that American carmakers are shifting away from gas-guzzling models to more fuel-efficient cars. [11]

However, market prospects for electric cars are uncertain, and could weaken if gasoline prices ease over the next several years. Biofuels are also growing more slowly than many advocates projected, even with strong federal support: Under the Energy Policy Act of 2005 and subsequent laws, oil refiners are required to blend millions of gallons of biofuels into gasoline, and the industry also has received billions of dollars in subsidies. [12]

As the Obama administration, Congress and interest groups debate what kind of energy strategy the United States should pursue, here are some issues they are considering:

But energy booms also cause stresses, especially in rural areas. Sudden influxes of workers can lead to housing shortages, traffic jams and rising crime rates. Some rural counties in North Dakota are putting moratoriums on construction of new "man camps," where oil drillers and truckers live in temporary housing compounds. [6]

One community that has been especially hard-hit by the oil boom is the Fort Berthold Indian Reservation, home to the Mandan, Hidatsa and Arikara nations. Energy companies started leasing rights to develop underground oil and gas from residents of the reservation in 2007, and now many tribal members live on royalties. But critics say the federal Bureau of Indian Affairs — which is legally responsible for verifying that leases are in the best interests of the Indian mineral owners — has rubber-stamped leases that paid less than market value. And the tribe has spent most of its earnings from oil rights held in common on such expenses as repairing roads damaged by heavy trucks, building houses for oil workers and prosecuting energy companies that dump waste illegally. [7]

"These oil projects could dramatically change life on Fort Berthold," *The Bismarck* (N.D.) *Tribune* observed recently. "How that change goes down will be determined largely by how well federal, state and tribal agencies respond to the rapid growth. It will be a challenge all the way around." [8]

— *Jennifer Weeks*

An oil well is drilled near Tioga, N.D., amid the state's oil-rich Bakken Formation.

[1]"Assessment of Undiscovered Oil Resources in the Devonian-Mississippian Bakken Formation, Williston Basin Province, Montana and North Dakota, 2008," U.S. Geological Survey, http://pubs.usgs.gov/fs/2008/3021/pdf/FS08-3021_508.pdf.

[2]In 2011 the United States consumed 18.8 million barrels of petroleum per day, which equals approximately 6.862 billion barrels for the year. See, "How dependent are we on foreign oil?" U.S. Energy Information Administration, May 2, 2012, www.eia.gov/energy_in_brief/foreign_oil_dependence.cfm.

[3]"Bakken Formation Oil Assessment in North Dakota, Montana Will Be Updated by U.S. Geological Survey," U.S. Department of the Interior, May 19, 2011.

[4]For background see Daniel McGlynn, "Fracking Controversy," *CQ Researcher*, Dec. 16, 2011, pp. 1045-1072.

[5]Blake Ellis, "Double Your Money in the Middle of Nowhere, North Dakota," CNNMoney, Oct. 20, 2011, http://money.cnn.com/2011/09/28/pf/north_dakota_jobs/index.htm.

[6]A. G. Sulzberger, "Oil Rigs Bring Camps of Men to the Prairies," *The New York Times*, Nov. 25, 2011, www.nytimes.com/2011/11/26/us/north-dakota-oil-boom-creates-camps-of-men.html?pagewanted=all.; Jennifer Oldham, "North Dakota Oil Boom Brings Blight With Growth as Costs Soar," Bloomberg.com, Jan. 25, 2012, www.bloomberg.com/news/2012-01-25/north-dakota-oil-boom-brings-blight-with-growth-as-costs-soar.html.

[7]Sierra Crane-Murdoch, "The Other Bakken Boom: America's Biggest Oil Rush Brings Tribal Conflict," *High Country News*, April 16, 2012, www.hcn.org/issues/44.6/on-the-fort-berthold-reservation-the-bakken-boom-brings-conflict.

[8]"Reservation Oil Issues Look Familiar," *The Bismarck Tribune*, April 6, 2012, http://bismarcktribune.com/news/opinion/editorial/reservation-oil-issues-look-familiar/article_694aaeda-7fec-11e1-aee9-0019bb2963f4.html.

Will increasing U.S. oil production reduce gasoline prices?

Many politicians approach high gasoline prices as a simple supply-and-demand problem, although they frequently disagree on the solution.

Republicans typically argue that more exploration and drilling will lower prices by bringing more oil to the world market. For example, Gingrich this spring proposed a program to increase domestic production and eliminate the Environmental Protection Agency (EPA), which regulates some impacts of oil production. The former House speaker contended that his policies would ensure that "no future [U.S.] president will ever bow to a Saudi king." [13]

Congressional Republicans also support increasing domestic production and resist tighter environmental

Adding Up the Cost of Gas

Crude oil purchased by refiners comprises two-thirds of the average pump price of a gallon of regular gasoline. Refining costs (15 percent), federal and state taxes (8 percent) and distribution and marketing costs (8 percent) make up the rest.

Cost Components of a Gallon of Regular Gasoline
(Percentage of cost) (at average national retail price of $3.90/gallon, April 2012)

- Distribution and marketing: 8%
- Taxes: 11%
- Refining: 15%
- Crude oil: 66%

Source: "Gasoline and Diesel Fuel Update," Energy Information Administration, June 2012, www.eia.gov/petroleum/gasdiesel/

regulation of the oil industry. For example, they oppose requirements for new cleaner-burning gasoline blends, known as Tier 3 standards, and new restrictions on emissions from oil refineries.

"None of America's pain at the pump should be self-inflicted, which is why we must do more to increase domestic and North American oil supplies," Rep. Fred Upton, R-Mich., chairman of the House Energy and Commerce Committee, said in March. "Some in Washington claim that producing more domestic oil won't make any difference in prices, but the American people know better."[14]

Yet most mainstream economists say production decisions in the United States cannot affect world oil prices. "Oil is a global market in which America is a big consumer but a small supplier," wrote Richard H. Thaler, an economist at the University of Chicago. "We consume about 20 percent of the world's oil but hold only 2 percent of the oil reserves. That means we are, in economics jargon, 'price takers' " — that is, the United States must pay prevailing prices for its oil. "As producers, we are just too small to matter much," Thaler added. "And even if domestic oil companies further increased production, they would sell to the highest global bidder."[15]

In a statistical analysis of 36 years of monthly, inflation-adjusted gasoline prices and U.S. domestic oil

production rates, The Associated Press found no correlation between these two trends. In some years when production was high, prices were also high, and vice versa. Nor were average gasoline prices significantly different under Democratic or Republican presidents.[16]

That's because many factors that drive world oil prices are beyond American control, experts say. "Since 2005 we've had trouble increasing total world oil production, and in emerging economies like China and India consumption has risen drastically. That's a key fundamental, and it's not likely to change any time soon," says James Hamilton, an economist at the University of California-San Diego.

Moreover, Hamilton argues that although technology has helped open up new oil sources, such as Canadian tar sands and deepwater deposits, the gains should be kept in perspective. "These new sources are very expensive places to get oil, and their contribution is relatively modest compared to what we get from mature fields," he says.

Democrats typically put less faith in drilling, except for legislators from oil-producing states such as Louisiana and Alaska. But they also are concerned about the effect of rising gas prices on businesses and consumers, and often call for releasing oil from the Strategic Petroleum Reserve (SPR), a national emergency stockpile created after the OPEC oil shocks in the 1970s. Presidents released oil from the SPR in 1991 during the Persian Gulf War; in 2000 when rising world demand caused an oil price spike; and in 2005 after hurricanes Katrina and Rita damaged production facilities along the Gulf Coast.

President Obama released oil from the SPR in June 2011, when concern about political turmoil in Libya drove up world prices. In March 2012, three Northeastern Democratic House members — Reps. Peter Welch of Vermont, Ed Markey of Massachusetts and Rosa DeLauro of Connecticut — urged Obama to tap the reserve again, arguing that concerns about possible hostilities with Iran were triggering speculation on world oil markets and raising gas prices.

"As you know, releasing oil from the SPR has driven down prices in the past," the legislators wrote. "Releasing even a small fraction of that oil could again have a significant impact on speculation in the marketplace and on prices."[17]

Just the rumor that Obama had agreed with Britain in mid-March on a coordinated release of oil reserves caused oil prices to drop temporarily, although they partially recovered after the administration said the reports were wrong. Oil experts said that although a release could cause a "flash crash" in oil prices, it was not a long-term policy. "We do not think a reserve release is a sustainable solution to tame oil prices," said James Zhang, a commodity strategist with the Standard Bank Group in London.[18]

Should the U.S. use oil from tar sands?

The largest single source of U.S. imported crude oil is Canada's tar sands, also known as oil sands. Tar sands contain bitumen — a thick, heavy black form of oil — mixed with sand, clay and water. Canada is eager to develop more of its tar sands, and U.S. advocates call them an important new source that can reduce American dependence on other, less reliable suppliers. But critics argue that mining the tar sands and separating the oil consumes huge quantities of water and creates toxic wastes harmful to the environment. Rather than using more oil — especially a dirty form of oil — they say the United States should invest in cleaner sources such as energy efficiency and renewable fuels.

Canada's tar sands, located in Alberta Province north of Montana, extend over an area roughly the size of Florida. The deposits contain an estimated 170 billion barrels of oil — more than the total proven reserves of all other oil-producing countries except Saudi Arabia and Venezuela. But tar sand oil was too costly to develop until the mid-1990s, when the Alberta government slashed royalties and Canada's national government granted the oil industry an array of tax breaks. By 2005 the area was producing a million barrels of oil per day.[19]

Bitumen in tar sands is mingled with other materials, such as sand and clay, and cannot be pumped out like conventional oil. Instead it is mined in two ways. About one-fifth of Canada's tar sands lie near the surface and are

dug up with huge mechanical shovels and trucked to factories, where the bitumen is separated using a hot-water process. About two tons of tar sands are needed to produce one barrel of oil using this method.[20] To extract deeply buried tar sands, energy companies inject steam under high pressure into the ground, melting the bitumen so that it flows to an underground reservoir where it can be pumped out.

Heating water to make steam consumes huge quantities of natural gas. Both processes produce massive quantities of wastewater, which energy companies dispose of by injecting it deep underground, and tailings — liquid wastes containing chemicals and trace metals that are toxic to aquatic organisms and mammals. Tailings are stored in huge ponds at mining sites.

Although producing tar sand oil is energy intensive, advocates say, they see Canada's tar sands as a key new source. Canadian oil sands "have become a major engine of global oil supply growth — and the only growing supplier with a land-based connection to the U.S. market," said James Burkhard, managing director at the energy consulting firm IHS CERA.[21] Joe Oliver, Canada's minister of natural resources, called Canada "an emerging energy superpower."[22]

But tar sand development has heavy environmental costs. According to a 2011 summary by Environment Canada, the nation's environmental regulatory agency, they include:

• Excessive water withdrawals that could harm fish habitat in the 765-mile-long Athabasca River, which flows south from the Rocky Mountains through Canada's Jasper National Park;
• Contamination of the river with hydrocarbons and heavy metals that could endanger wildlife and communities downstream;
• Local air pollution from mining operations;
• Damage to forests and loss of habitat for caribou, whooping cranes and other vulnerable species; and
• Rising greenhouse gas emissions from tar sand production.[23]

Tar sand advocates assert that oil companies are improving their production processes so that they use less energy to extract and separate tar sand oil and generate less waste. "As the technology has evolved, it has become

Libyan rebels on July 20, 2011, attend the funeral of comrades killed in the battle for control of the oil-rich town of Brega. President Obama released oil from the Strategic Petroleum Reserve in June 2011, when concern about turmoil in Libya drove up world prices. In March 2012, three Democratic House members urged Obama to tap the reserve again, arguing that concerns about possible hostilities with Iran were triggering speculation on world oil markets and raising gas prices.

more efficient," said Karen Harbert, president of the Institute for 21st Century Energy at the U.S. Chamber of Commerce. "In fact, Albertan oil sands development has become so commonplace that it no longer even merits the designation of 'unconventional.'"[24]

U.S. environmentalists want to limit and eventually end imports of oil from tar sands. They strongly oppose the proposed Keystone XL pipeline.

"Over its entire lifecycle the synthetic crude oil from tar sands emits at least 20 percent more global warming pollution than conventional oil," the National Wildlife Federation, Sierra Club and four other national environmental groups commented on the initial Keystone XL proposal. "Furthermore, because tar sands oil is a heavier crude, the U.S. refineries that process it will produce higher levels of pollutants that damage human health and lead to more smog, haze and acid rain."[25] Building the pipeline, the groups argued, "would be detrimental to our country's national interests in building a clean-energy economy, curbing climate change and reducing national reliance on oil."[26]

Industry advocates say that if the United States does not approve Keystone XL, Canada will build new pipelines to the West Coast and ship tar sand oil to Asia instead. But Canadian analysts call that scenario unlikely

because the pipelines would have to go through British Columbia, where public support for environmental protection is much stronger than in Alberta.

"It will be extremely challenging to build an oil sand pipeline to the West Coast," says Nathan Lemphers, a senior analyst with the Pembina Institute, a Canadian think tank that promotes sustainable energy solutions. Two proposals to expand existing pipelines to the Pacific coast of Canada have generated widespread opposition, especially among aboriginal groups, which have strong legal leverage to intervene in the process.[27]

Since tar sand oil is already flowing to U.S. refineries in the Midwest, Lemphers says the United States should press Canada to clean up its production methods further. "We'd like to see a message to Canada and the oil sand industry that they have to improve their environmental performance if they want to expand," he says. "They're learning that on many fronts." For example, the European Union — which is working to reduce carbon emissions from energy use — is considering a rule that would classify oil from bitumen as more carbon-intensive than conventional crude oil. Canada's government strongly opposes the standard.[28]

"The U.S. has an opportunity to send a clear signal to Canada on managing its oil sands," says Lemphers.

Can the U.S. achieve independence from foreign oil?

For nearly 40 years, since the oil shocks of the 1970s, U.S. presidents and other elected officials have called repeatedly for steps to make the nation less dependent on imported oil. Advocates say cutting reliance on foreign oil would reduce the risk of supply interruptions from countries hostile to the United States or that are destabilized by conflicts, as occurred last year in Libya.

Today, with domestic oil production rising and consumption down, some experts say the United States can substantially reduce oil imports. The U.S. Energy Information Administration projects that imported oil will account for only 36 percent of the nation's liquid fuel supply (including biofuels) by 2035, down from 60 percent in 2005.[29] In a recent survey of energy executives by *Forbes* magazine, 27 percent of respondents said achieving energy independence was either very feasible or somewhat feasible.[30]

"We can probably reduce imports to around 5 million barrels per day, which would be dramatic," says Henry

CHRONOLOGY

1850s-1930s *U.S. oil industry expands from a fledgling venture into the nation's main energy source.*

1859 First U.S. oil well drilled in Titusville, Pa.

1870s-1880s Oil companies begin drilling and building refineries in Southern California.

1911 Supreme Court rules that Standard Oil Co. violates antitrust law and orders it broken into 34 companies.

1923 National Petroleum Reserve established near Prudhoe Bay, Alaska, as a potential emergency oil supply source.

1932 First federal gas tax enacted.

1950s-1960s *U.S. oil consumption swells during post-World War II boom.*

1950 Oil surpasses coal as main U.S. energy source.

1956 President Dwight D. Eisenhower signs Federal-Aid Highway Act, authorizing massive investments in a national Interstate Highway System.

1960 Iran, Iraq, Kuwait, Saudi Arabia and Venezuela form Organization of Petroleum Exporting Countries (OPEC) in an effort to influence global oil prices.

1970s-1980s *Arab oil shocks temporarily boost support for conservation and alternative fuels, but reforms fade when oil prices fall.*

1970 U.S. oil production peaks at 9.6 million barrels per day and begins a gradual decline, with imports accounting for a growing share of total consumption. . . . environmentalists hold first Earth Day (April 22) in response to events that include a major leak from an undersea oil well near Santa Barbara, Calif.

1973 Arab OPEC members embargo oil exports to the U.S., raising prices and triggering a national energy crisis.

1975 Congress creates Strategic Petroleum Reserve in underground salt caves along the Texas and Louisiana coasts as a buffer against future oil supply disruptions, and adopts fuel-economy (CAFE) standards requiring manufacturers to produce more fuel-efficient cars.

1977 President Jimmy Carter proposes energy conservation programs to reduce dependence on imported oil. . . . Oil from Alaska's North Slope reaches markets via the new Trans-Alaska Pipeline.

1978-1979 Revolution in Iran halts oil exports, triggering a second global oil shock and sharply raising U.S. energy prices.

1989 *Exxon Valdez* runs aground in Alaska's Prince William Sound, spilling 11 million gallons of oil and contaminating more than 1,000 miles of pristine shoreline.

1990s-Present *U.S. energy policy swings between conservation and production.*

1992 Congress passes Energy Policy Act, boosting funds for energy efficiency, renewable energy and alternative fuels.

1997 President Bill Clinton signs Kyoto Protocol, pledging to cut U.S. greenhouse gas emissions 7 percent below 1990 levels by 2012. Senate refuses to ratify the treaty, saying cutting carbon emissions will harm the economy.

2001 George W. Bush administration increases oil production on U.S. lands and offshore.

2008 Global oil consumption slackens as world economy enters a recession.

2010 Blowout at BP's *Deepwater Horizon* offshore well spills more than 200 million gallons of oil into Gulf of Mexico.

2011 Unrest in North Africa and Middle East drives world oil prices above $100 per barrel. . . . President Obama and major automakers agree to double fuel efficiency standards for passenger vehicles. . . . Obama blocks expedited permitting for the Keystone XL pipeline.

2012 TransCanada submits a new Keystone XL proposal that avoids the sensitive Nebraska Sandhills. . . . World oil prices drop below $84 per barrel in May-June.

Arctic Holds Energy Riches — and Environmental Peril

"Complacency is the biggest threat we have."

Rising world demand for oil is converging with another global trend — climate change — to spur competition for Arctic energy reserves. As warmer temperatures at the pole shrink Arctic sea ice, many nations see opportunity to drill for oil and gas that until recently were inaccessible. But environmentalists and many scientists worry that an Arctic oil rush could irreparably harm fragile polar ecosystems.

Scientists broadly agree that the Arctic is warming and that its sea ice — which partially melts during the summer and expands in winter — is shrinking. At its yearly low point from 1979 through 2000, Arctic sea ice covered 2.7 million square miles on average, according to NASA data. Since 2005, however, the ice has contracted to 2.3 million square miles or less each year. In September 2011 it shrank to 1.8 million square miles.[1] The United Kingdom's national weather service, the Met Office, projects that the Arctic could become ice free for part of the year sometime between 2040 and 2060, although scientific estimates vary.[2]

More than 400 onshore oil and gas fields already have been developed north of the Arctic Circle in Russia, Canada and Alaska. The fields contain about 240 billion barrels of oil and oil-equivalent natural gas, counting both what has already been extracted and the reserves that remain in the ground at these sites. But still more large oil and gas deposits in the Arctic may remain to be discovered. In 2008 the U.S. Geological Survey (USGS) published its first appraisal of undeveloped energy resources north of the Arctic Circle, which estimated that the region contained an additional 90 billion barrels of oil; 1.7 quadrillion cubic feet of natural gas; and 44 billion barrels of natural gas liquids — components

such as propane and butane that are extracted during processing. Most of these reserves are believed to lie offshore.[3]

As the U.S. prepares to allow Shell to drill test wells off Alaska this summer, other nations also are lining up Arctic ventures. (*See "Current Situation."*) Rosneft, Russia's state-owned oil company, has signed exploration agreements with Exxon Mobil, the Italian energy company Eni and Statoil, Norway's state energy company.[4] Greenland also has opened its onshore and offshore territory to drilling, although no company has recorded a major find yet.[5]

Many scientists say that much more information is needed before oil producers can operate safely in the Arctic Ocean. A 2011 USGS report identified a variety of important needs, including more research on important species, a better understanding of how cumulative impacts from multiple energy exploration projects will add up and a data-management system that allows researchers to share information about trends in many different areas.[6] In January 573 U.S. research scientists wrote to Interior Secretary Ken Salazar urging the Obama administration to act on the USGS's recommendations before approving offshore drilling in the Arctic.[7]

Energy companies say they take the challenges of operating in the Arctic seriously. At a conference last January in Norway, the International Association of Oil and Gas Producers announced a four-year, $20 million research program to address those issues. Because Russia is not participating, however, critics worry that Russian energy projects will fall short of international safety standards.[8]

Insurers also are tracking Arctic energy development. In April Lloyds of London, the world's largest insurer, and Chatham House, a British think tank, warned that cleaning

Lee, director of the Environment and Natural Resource Program at the Harvard Kennedy School of Government. In 2010 the United States consumed 19.2 million barrels of oil per day, of which 9.3 million barrels were imported.

In addition to lower oil demand since the recession and rising domestic production, U.S. cars are becoming

more fuel efficient. New standards negotiated by the Obama administration and major car manufacturers will boost average passenger car fuel efficiency to more than 50 miles per gallon by 2025 — double the 2010 level. "This is totally different from the perspective we had four years ago," says Lee.

up oil spills in the Arctic would involve unique and challenging risks and that a spill could irreversibly harm Arctic ecosystems. The groups called for major investments in research, infrastructure and monitoring to make development activities in the Arctic safe.

"In many areas — shipping, search and rescue — infrastructure is currently insufficient to meet the expected demands of economic development," Lloyd's and Chatham House warned. "Full-scale exercises based on worst-case scenarios of environmental disaster should be run by companies with government involvement and oversight" to test what operators know and make them more expert at operating in the Arctic.[9]

Marilyn Heiman, director of the Pew Environment Group's U.S. Arctic Program, points out another useful information source: Alaska, which took steps after the *Exxon Valdez* spill in 1989 to prepare for future disasters. Now industry trains fishermen to respond to oil spills, so that they have relevant qualifications, such as handling hazardous materials.[10]

The Oil Spill Pollution Act of 1990 also created citizen advisory councils after the *Exxon Valdez* disaster. "The councils are a great way to avoid complacency, which is the biggest threat we have," says Heiman. "They look over the shoulders of regulators, who can get complacent too, and provide real vigilance against future events."

— Jennifer Weeks

Drilling Being Considered on Alaska's North Coast

The Interior Department is considering granting several oil exploration leases this summer to Shell Oil Co. along Alaska's north coast in the Beaufort and Chukchi seas.

[1]"World of Change: Arctic Sea Ice," National Aeronautics and Space Administration, http://earthobservatory.nasa.gov/Features/WorldOf Change/sea_ice.php.

[2]Adam Vaughan, "Met Office: Arctic Sea-Ice Loss Linked to Colder, Drier UK Winters," *The Guardian*, March 14, 2012, www.guardian.co.uk/ environment/2012/mar/14/met-office-arctic-sea-ice-loss-winter.

[3]"Circum-Arctic Resource Appraisal: Estimates of Undiscovered Oil and Gas North of the Arctic Circle," U.S. Geological Survey, 2008, http://pubs.usgs.gov/fs/2008/3049/.

[4]Andrew E. Kramer, "Russian-Italian pact Opens Arctic Ocean to Drilling," *The New York Times*, April 25, 2012, www.nytimes.com/2012/ 04/26/business/global/russian-italian-pact-opens-arctic-ocean-to-drilling

.html; Melissa Akin and Vladimir Soldatkin, "Statoil to Drill with Rosneft in Russian Arctic," Reuters, May 5, 2012, www.reuters.com/ article/2012/05/05/rosneft-statoil-idUSL5E8G500X20120505.

[5]"Greenland: Offshore Drilling's Next Frontier," *24/7 Wall Street*, May 20, 2010, http://247wallst.com/2010/05/20/greenland-offshore-drillings-next-frontier/; Alex Hawkes, "Cairn Fails to Strike Oil Off Greenland," *The Guardian*, Nov. 30, 2011, www.guardian.co.uk/ business/2011/nov/30/cairn-fails-oil-greenland/print.

[6]Leslie Holland-Bartels and Brenda Pierce, eds., "An Evaluation of the Science Needs to Inform Decisions on Outer Continental Shelf Energy Development in the Chukchi and Beaufort Seas, Alaska," U.S. Geological Survey, 2011, http://pubs.usgs.gov/circ/1370/.

[7]Online at www.pewenvironment.org/uploadedFiles/PEG/ Publications/Other_Resource/ScientistsLetter-OCSDevelopment.pdf.

[8]Quirin Schiermeier, "The Great Arctic Oil Race Begins," *Nature*, Jan. 31, 2012, www.nature.com/news/the-great-arctic-oil-race-begins-1.9932.

[9]"Arctic Opening: Opportunity and Risk in the High North," Chatham House, 2011, p. 53, www.lloyds.com/-/media/Files/News%20and%20 Insight/360%20Risk%20Insight/Arctic_Risk_Report_20120412.pdf.

[10]For example, see Nicole Klauss, "Kodiak Fishermen Get Oil Spill Training," *Kodiak Daily Mirror*, April 7, 2012, www.newsminer.com/view/ full_story/18155840/article-Kodiak-fishermen-get-oil-spill-training-? instance=home_news_window_left_bullets.

The American Petroleum Institute estimates that constructing the Keystone XL pipeline and expanding access to U.S. oil and gas resources that are currently not open for development could make it unnecessary for the United States to import oil from any source other than Canada by 2024. Because Canada is a

neighbor, a democracy and a longtime U.S. ally and trading partner, U.S. energy producers say importing oil from Canada is the next-best alternative to drilling at home.

"For every dollar we spend on Canadian goods, they spend 90 cents in the U.S.," says API's Dougher. "Trade with Canada builds jobs here and expands our economy."

But some argue that even if the United States uses only oil produced in North America, it will still be vulnerable to economic shocks because oil prices are set in a global market. Achieving energy security, they contend, does not mean using less foreign oil. Rather, they say, it means using less oil, period.

"It's a misconception that we depend too much on the wrong suppliers," says Gal Luft, executive director of the Washington-based Institute for the Analysis of Global Security, which focuses on energy security. "We can do easily without Persian Gulf oil, which accounts for about 9 percent of our supply, and we don't import a drop from Iran, but we're still affected if something happens to Iran's oil supplies. There's less chance of embargoes by friendly countries like Canada, but importing from friends doesn't make us more economically secure."

Instead of focusing either on increased production or conservation, Luft and other "energy hawks" say the solution is to create competition for oil and make it less strategically important. To do that, they say, the United States should develop alternative fuels that can substitute for oil — including ethanol from corn and other plant sources and methanol from natural gas — and require auto makers to equip every car sold in the United States to run on any of those fuels, so that drivers can choose the cheapest option at the pump. Bills that would establish this policy, known as an open fuel standard, have been introduced in Congress several times in recent years and are currently pending in both the House and Senate.[31]

"Salt was a strategic commodity for thousands of years, the only way to preserve food until the 19th century," former Director of Central Intelligence R. James Woolsey said last October, comparing salt's role then to oil's today. But, he asserted, household electricity and refrigeration eventually offered a better and cheaper option. "Before that, people went to war over salt mines," Woolsey said. "We can do the same thing with oil. We can make oil boring."[32]

U.S. auto manufacturers oppose an open fuel standard, which they see as an extra regulatory burden, while advocates call it the best way to foster alternatives to oil.[33] Today about eight million cars in the U.S. are

"flex-fuel" models that can run on gasoline or ethanol. But since ethanol is sold mainly in the Midwest, where most of it is made, in practice many flex-fuel cars run solely on gasoline. On average, a flex-fuel vehicle in the United States consumes less than 20 gallons yearly of high-blend ethanol (fuel containing mainly ethanol, which is also blended at low concentrations into conventional gasoline).

The U.S. biofuel industry is gradually expanding, although it still produces mainly corn-based ethanol, which offers modest environmental benefits, at best, compared to gasoline.[34] Many plant and waste sources can be used to produce advanced cellulosic biofuels, which have lower carbon footprints than corn ethanol. But cellulosic biofuels cost more to manufacture than corn ethanol because the enzymes that can break down tough plant cell walls are expensive to produce. Corn, in contrast, contains mostly starch, which is easily broken down into sugars and fermented into ethanol. Progress on advanced biofuels has lagged behind early forecasts, even with federal subsidies and mandates, as companies work to bring down costs and find the most efficient production methods.[35]

In 2012 the Renewable Fuel Standard (RFS), established as part of the Energy Independence and Security Act of 2007, requires oil refiners to blend 15.2 billion gallons of renewable fuels into transportation fuels, replacing about 9.2 percent of the total supply. Of this amount, 8.6 million gallons must be cellulosic biofuels.[36] Refiners say the mandate sets unrealistic targets and argue that they should not have to buy "blending credits," as the law requires, to cover their quotas if they fall short.

In March the American Petroleum Institute sued EPA, arguing that the RFS was unachievable because cellulosic biofuels are not being manufactured on a commercial scale yet. EPA projects that manufacturers will be able to make the required amount of cellulosic biofuels in 2012, but acknowledges that it will be difficult.[37]

"We support the idea of using biofuels to diversify our fuel mix, but there's not enough cellulosic ethanol in the market now to meet the target, so refiners are paying a fine for failing to use a supply that doesn't exist," says API's Dougher.

A 2011 study by the National Research Council found that manufacturers were unlikely to meet the long-term RFS target of 36 billion gallons in 2022 without major technology breakthroughs or policy changes. The study also projected that making cellulosic biofuels cost-competitive with petroleum fuels would probably require some combination of high oil prices (well over $100 per barrel) and either a combination of government subsidies and mandates or a price on carbon emissions.[38]

Ethanol producers respond that the RFS has generated more than 90,000 direct jobs and 311,000 indirect jobs and reduced U.S. gasoline prices in 2011 by $1.09 per gallon.[39] The RFS "has been the most successful energy policy this nation has ever implemented," Renewable Fuels Association President Bob Dinneen said in April. "It should be vigorously defended and maintained and allowed to reach its full potential of 36 billion gallons of clean burning, renewable fuel."[40]

BACKGROUND

America's Dominant Fuel

Fossil fuels have powered the U.S. economy through much of the nation's history, enabling Americans to live increasingly comfortable and prosperous lives.

Wood was the main fuel source in the 17th and 18th centuries, but in the 1800s coal became the fuel of choice for powering factories, fueling trains and ships and heating homes. Scientists and entrepreneurs knew, however, that "rock oil" that seeped from the ground in some areas could be burned to generate light and heat. In 1859 the first U.S. well was drilled in Titusville, in northwestern Pennsylvania, making possible large-scale use of oil as fuel.

Because oil contains more energy per unit than coal and as a liquid is easier to transport, the industry grew rapidly, especially after the formation of Standard Oil Co. in 1870 by industrialist John D. Rockefeller. Over the next several decades Rockefeller built Standard Oil into a massive trust, buying dozens of smaller companies and most of the refining and pipeline capacity across the country. As Rockefeller used his monopoly power to control oil prices, Standard Oil became a reviled symbol of concentrated corporate wealth.

By the early 1900s U.S. oil producers were drilling in the Midwest, California, Oklahoma and Texas. The growing automobile industry created a massive new

Getty Images/Justin Sullivan

A gas station in Mill Valley, Calif., shows prices above $4 a gallon on June 12. Many consumers ask why gas prices are still high despite lower oil consumption and rising domestic production. But energy experts explain that because oil is traded worldwide and prices can be influenced by geopolitical developments anywhere, volatile energy costs are inescapable as long as the United States relies heavily on oil.

market for gasoline. America's first gas station opened in Ohio in 1912, just a year after the Supreme Court ordered Standard Oil broken apart to reduce its market power.[41] Oil was in such demand that despite the breakup, Standard's successor companies were soon worth more than the original trust.[42]

In 1929 the U.S. network of gas stations and garages had expanded to 300,000 outlets nationwide.[43] Cars quickly became so central to American life that even bankrupt farmers driven off their land by the Dust Bowl in the 1930s climbed into sedans or trucks to move West looking for work. Oil was the most important strategic resource for all sides during World War II: Germany and Japan, neither of which had large oil reserves, tried but failed to capture oil fields in eastern Europe and Asia, while the United States supplied much of the oil that powered Allied planes, tanks and ships to victory.

Wartime gasoline rationing was lifted in the United States within 24 hours of Japan's surrender in 1945, and in 1950 oil surpassed coal as the primary U.S. energy source. As demand swelled, driven by the postwar economic boom and expansion of the Interstate Highway System, America began to import oil from abroad, mainly from Saudi Arabia. Some U.S. officials, worried about the risks of depending on foreign suppliers, supported research into making synthetic fuels from large domestic coal supplies. But when it became clear that this option would cost several times more than importing cheap foreign oil, the program folded within several years.

In the late 1950s, as demand for domestic oil swelled, the United States cultivated relationships with oil-exporting countries, aided by American corporations such as Shell and Standard Oil of New Jersey. These linkages helped to expand the global oil industry. Oil prices fell throughout the 1950s and '60s as reserves were developed worldwide, fueling unprecedented international economic growth.

Environmental protection was not a concern for most Americans then, but as the impact of rapid industrial growth became clearer, some advocates began to call for action to reduce air and water pollution. The oil industry came under attack in 1969 when an undersea wellhead off Santa Barbara, Calif., suffered a blowout and, contaminated 35 miles of coastline with 200,000 gallons of oil. The spill helped to catalyze the first Earth Day rally in 1970 and led to state and federal bans on new offshore drilling.

Supply Crises

U.S. domestic oil production peaked in 1970 at 9.6 million barrels per day and began a slow decline. This did not mean that the nation was running out of oil; rather, it signaled that producers were drilling all of the reserves that could be developed profitably with the technology available at the time.[44] Imports filled the widening gap until Oct. 20, 1973, when Arab members of the Organization of Petroleum Exporting Countries (OPEC) shut off oil exports to the United States, responding to U.S. support for Israel in the Yom Kippur War. Oil prices shot up, and the Nixon administration was forced to ration gasoline. The embargo and resulting flow of wealth from Western industrialized countries to Middle East oil exporters triggered a deep economic recession lasting from November 1973 to March 1975.

To reduce America's dependence on imported oil, which accounted for 36 percent of national consumption when the embargo was imposed, the United States began building a pipeline to bring crude oil from Alaska's Prudhoe Bay to the lower 48 states. And in 1975 Congress imposed the first Corporate Average Fuel Economy (CAFE) standards, which required automakers to improve the fuel

efficiency of new cars to 27.5 miles per gallon on average (20.7 miles per gallon for light trucks) by 1987. Congress also established the Strategic Petroleum Reserve to safeguard against future supply disruptions.

President Jimmy Carter (1977-1981) labeled the energy crunch a national crisis and called for developing new sources such as wind, solar and nuclear power. Congress created a Cabinet-level Department of Energy and approved new energy-efficiency standards and tax incentives for investments in renewable energy sources. Carter also pressed for deregulation of oil and gas prices to encourage domestic exploration and production.

Before these measures could have much impact, however, a militant fundamentalist Islamic regime took power in Iran in the winter of 1978-79, shutting off Iranian oil exports and triggering a new wave of worldwide panic buying and price spikes. War broke out between Iran and Iraq in 1980, severely damaging both countries' oil industries. High energy prices helped create a condition dubbed "stagflation" (a stagnant economy with high inflation), contributing to Carter's re-election defeat by Ronald Reagan in 1980.

Reagan promised to revive the U.S. economy, but the second oil shock led to a worldwide recession in the early 1980s. One side effect, however, was reduced demand for oil, which undercut OPEC's power to affect world prices. Many industrialized countries turned to other fuels, such as coal, natural gas and nuclear power, and non-OPEC countries such as Britain and Mexico captured growing shares of global oil sales. In late 1985 OPEC abandoned production limits. World oil prices fell to $20 per barrel, rising only temporarily in 1990 when Iraq invaded Kuwait.

Environmental Impacts

As oil prices eased in the late 1980s, U.S. energy consumption once again began to climb. At the same time, however, policy makers began to focus on the environmental impacts of producing and using oil.

President George H. W. Bush (1989-93) supported oil drilling in the Arctic National Wildlife Refuge (ANWR), but public support waned after the *Exxon Valdez* oil tanker ran aground in Alaska's Prince William Sound in 1989, spilling 11 million gallons of oil and contaminating more than 1,000 miles of shoreline. Meanwhile, in the Clean Air Act Amendments of 1990, Congress mandated the use of specially formulated cleaner-burning fuels in cities with severe air pollution, forcing U.S. refineries to produce a wider range of products.

President Bill Clinton (1993-2001) took several steps to limit the environmental impacts of oil production. He opposed opening ANWR to oil exploration; designated nearly 10 million acres of federal lands as wilderness; and signed the Roadless Area Conservation Rule, which classified more than 58 million acres of national forest (at the time about one-third of the total) as roadless areas. These steps put large tracts of land off-limits for energy production, although millions of acres remained available.

Clinton supported increased funding for energy-efficiency programs and renewable fuels, but strong economic growth and low oil prices drove U.S. energy consumption to new highs in the 1990s. Americans shifted away from economy cars to larger, less-efficient models — especially sport utility vehicles (SUVs) and passenger vans, which benefited from a loophole in CAFE standards that classified those vehicles as "light trucks" and thus held them to weaker fuel-economy standards than passenger cars.

From Shock to Trance

In the late 1990s, oil prices started to rise again, driven by rapid economic growth in China and India. President George W. Bush (2001-2009), who had worked in the Texas oil industry early in his career, strongly advocated increasing supplies of oil and other fossil fuels, along with nuclear power. The Bush administration eliminated many regulatory barriers to oil production on public lands and lobbied vigorously for drilling in ANWR. Bush also called for speeding up the siting and construction of oil refineries and pipelines.

Bush cut spending on energy-efficiency programs and development of most renewable energy sources, over strong resistance from congressional Democrats and environmental advocates. Opponents of Bush's policies harshly criticized the administration for emphasizing production over conservation and downplaying environmental impacts of energy development.

High gasoline prices were a major debate topic during the 2008 presidential campaign. Former Alaska Gov. Sarah Palin, the Republican nominee for vice president, called for more domestic oil production, leading chants of "drill, baby, drill!" at campaign rallies. But then-Sen. Barack Obama, D-Ill., the Democratic nominee, argued that promoting

cleaner fuels and making cars more fuel-efficient was the right strategy.

"We go from shock to trance. You know, oil prices go up, gas prices at the pump go up, everybody goes into a flurry of activity. And then the prices go back down, and suddenly we act like it's not important, and we start, you know, filling up our SUVs again. And, as a consequence, we never make any progress," Obama said a week after his election.[45]

Within two years, however, Obama was battling Republicans in Congress who argued that his administration was hurting consumers through regulations that limited domestic energy production. In April 2010 Obama proposed expanding offshore oil drilling as part of a broad energy and climate change strategy. That policy was shelved weeks later when the *Deepwater Horizon* oil platform exploded in the Gulf of Mexico, triggering a spill that released nearly five million barrels of oil into some of the nation's richest fishing grounds.

Despite the spill, however, Obama continued to argue that his administration supported more production of all types of fuels, including expanded domestic drilling, while keeping environmentally sensitive areas such as ANWR off limits. "I believe this all-of-the-above approach is the only way we can continue to reduce our dependence on foreign oil and ultimately put an end to some of these gas spikes that we're going through right now," Obama said in March 2012.[46]

CURRENT SITUATION
Refinery Squeeze

Flagging U.S. oil demand has put the refining industry under pressure, threatening fuel supplies in some parts of the nation.

Over the past several decades oil companies have closed more than 100 refineries during periods when oil prices were low, and many smaller facilities became unprofitable. In 2011 the nation had 137 operable refineries, down from 254 in 1982.[47] U.S. refining capacity increased very slightly during that time, from 15.7 million barrels per day in 1985 to 17.7 million barrels per day in 2011, but today the U.S. has a smaller fleet of refineries that are clustered in fewer locations compared to the 1970s.[48]

As a result, regions located far from refineries, such as New England, are vulnerable to high gasoline prices and shortages. Several large refineries that service the Northeast have closed in the past year, raising fears of local gasoline shortages this summer.[49] In a surprise move, Delta Air Lines bought one of the refineries and announced that it would operate the plant itself, modifying it to boost its output of jet fuel.[50]

Planning in the refining industry also is complicated by federal policies, such as requiring refiners to produce specially blended "boutique fuels" to address air pollution issues in various areas. Refiners argue that environmental regulations are making it increasingly hard for them to survive in a low-margin industry where demand for oil products is already weak today. For example, the EPA is developing new Tier 3 standards for light-duty vehicle fuels that are designed to reduce a range of conventional air pollutant emissions from cars. A draft rule is scheduled for release in July.[51]

A study commissioned by the American Petroleum Institute estimates that complying with Tier 3 standards — which will require refiners to produce gasoline formulated to burn extremely cleanly — could increase the cost of gasoline by up to 25 cents per gallon, and in an extreme case could force several refineries to close if they were unable to afford the necessary upgrades. "U.S. refineries are under pressure for a combination of reasons, and increased regulatory costs are certainly a factor," API Group Director Robert Greco told Congress's Joint Economic Committee last month. Environmental regulations, Greco contended, "should focus on making regulation more efficient so it materially benefits the environment without impeding economic growth unnecessarily."[52]

But public health advocates argue that tighter air pollution standards for vehicles are worth the cost. "[I]n 2017, Tier 3 will reduce nitrogen oxide emissions by 260,000 tons, the equivalent to taking 33 million cars off our nation's roads," the American Lung Association and other health organizations wrote to EPA in January. "These benefits are a great bargain for the American people, costing less than 1 cent per gallon of gasoline and about one-half of a percent, or $150, of the cost of the average new car."[53]

New Offshore Drilling

Before the *Deepwater Horizon* oil spill in the Gulf of Mexico in 2010, Obama proposed to open large areas of U.S. coastline to offshore drilling, including many areas where drilling had never taken place. That proposal was derailed by the oil spill, which led to an overhaul of the federal office that regulates offshore energy production. Now, however, the administration is considering a much more limited expansion of offshore drilling.

In November 2011 the Interior Department released a proposed five-year plan for offshore oil drilling from 2012-2017, which expands open areas in the Gulf of Mexico and allows oil development off Alaska's north coast and in Cook Inlet on the south coast. Unlike the administration's previous plan, it does not allow drilling along the U.S. East Coast.

"This five-year program will make available for development more than three-quarters of [the] undiscovered oil and gas resources estimated on the [Outer Continental Shelf, OCS], including frontier areas such as the Arctic, where we must proceed cautiously, safely and based on the best science available," said Interior Secretary Ken Salazar.[54]

Conservationists say the United States should move extremely carefully in allowing drilling off the Alaska coast, where operating conditions are harsh and the environment is extremely vulnerable to spills. "In the Arctic you deal routinely with sub-zero temperatures, long periods of darkness, hurricane-force winds, and 20-foot seas. It's a very challenging place to work and operate equipment," says Marilyn Heiman, director of the Pew Environment Group's U.S. Arctic Program.

Because the Arctic shoreline is frozen for much of the year, there are no docks or infrastructure along the coast to support cleanup operations if a spill occurred offshore. "There are very few roads connecting villages along the coast, and the nearest port is 1,000 miles away. The U.S. Coast Guard has said that massing a spill response in the Arctic would be virtually impossible," says Heiman.

In February the Interior Department approved a spill response plan submitted by Shell Oil to support drilling leases in the Beaufort and Chukchi seas. Shell still needs permits for each individual well it plans to drill but could start operations in the Arctic later this year.[55] The company also has won legal injunctions against the environmental advocacy group Greenpeace, which often sends boats out to protest activities such as whaling and nuclear testing

Should the Keystone XL pipeline be built?

YES

Alex Pourbaix
President, Energy and Oil Pipelines,
TransCanada Corp.

From testimony before the House Committee on Energy and Commerce, Subcommittee on Energy and Power, Dec. 2, 2011.

When you boil down the debate on this project, I believe it comes down to a simple question for Americans: Do they want secure, stable oil from a friendly neighbor in Canada or do they want to continue importing high-priced conflict oil from unfriendly regions such as the Middle East or Venezuela?

Keystone XL will help secure that stable supply of oil by linking Canadian and U.S. crude supplies with the largest refining markets in the United States. Canada's oil reserves are vast — approximately 175 billion barrels are estimated to be recoverable at today's oil price. This compares to the United States' reserves, which are estimated to be around 19 billion barrels.

While transporting oil from Canada, Keystone XL will also ship domestic U.S. crude oil.

Keystone XL expects to move 100,000 [barrels per day] of American crude production from North Dakota and Montana to Cushing, Okla., or to the Gulf Coast, and further expects to move 150,000 barrels per day of U.S. crude from Cushing to the Gulf Coast. Growing domestic U.S. oil production has long been a goal in the United States. But that production cannot grow effectively if it cannot reach market. Keystone XL encourages domestic U.S. oil production by connecting areas with increased supply in Montana, North Dakota and Cushing, Okla., with the United States' largest refining center in the Gulf Coast. The fact that this pipeline access is needed is apparent in the significant price discount that U.S. inland producers have been receiving for their production compared to the price that Gulf Coast refiners pay for comparable grades of crude oil imported from other countries.

In addition to energy security, our project will also create valuable jobs for Americans. . . . Thousands of direct construction jobs were planned to begin next year, the overwhelming majority of which were union jobs. They would have started only a few months from now. Contracts and subcontracts were awarded to dozens of U.S. companies. Americans were hired and ready to go to work. Those Americans will now need to find other employment while we work through this delay. . . . Who speaks for these thousands of Americans and their families? Canadian crude oil will be produced regardless of whether Keystone XL is built. If it is not exported to the United States, it will be exported to other countries, from which there is no shortage in demand.

NO

Jane Fleming Kleeb
Founder, Bold Nebraska

From testimony before the House Committee on Energy and Commerce, Subcommittee on Energy and Power, Dec. 2, 2011.

This pipeline is risky. It is massive, and we literally have no long-term study on how tar sands affect land, water or our health. We have seen first-hand in Michigan, with the awful tar sands spill in the Kalamazoo River, how much more difficult and expensive it is to clean up tar sands and the chemicals mixed with this type of oil. Families have been displaced, and this oil is sticking to the bottom of the riverbed. This is not traditional oil that floats and can be skimmed with booms. We owe it to workers, our families, the environment and our water to do the right study to get us the answers we need.

I am asking for your help in getting a study on how tar sands affect our land, water and health. We need clarity on [whether] traditional pipelines, designed to carry conventional oil, can safely carry corrosive tar sands, especially since we have seen 14 spills in the past year on TransCanada's Keystone 1 when they told us we would see 11 leaks over the lifetime of the pipe. . . . It is hard to rationalize how a pipeline carrying oil across our nation to an unknown final destination can be in our national interest. We all know TransCanada and other tar sands companies need to get their oil to various ports in order to sell it to the highest bidder. In the end, we assume all of the risks and none of the rewards.

Yes, the process has taken a long time. It has been over three years since TransCanada started to contact landowners and threaten eminent domain even though they had no permit for their project, three years of threats from a powerful international company. Our state has been bombarded with misleading ads about the amount of jobs and money this pipeline would bring to our state. We will soon be releasing a report that shows how little in taxes TransCanada actually has paid to our counties compared to their promises. . . .

As a nation, we are facing our next moon challenge. Energy is our moon challenge. I want to look at my three little girls and tell them that I'm doing everything I can to ensure our energy is sustainable, that our energy is helping revitalize our communities, not destroy them, and that our energy is safe.

The TransCanada pipeline simply does not meet the challenge. It sets us on a path backward, not forward. We do not need to figure out ways to approve this pipeline. We need to figure out ways to ensure our land and water are protected . . . as we, together, figure out solutions for our country's energy and job needs.

at sea. Greenpeace boats were ordered to stay more than 3,200 feet away from oil rigs and 1,600 feet from support boats nationwide, and the court established a 25-yard safety zone around Shell's oil vessels in Dutch Harbor, Alaska, a staging area for operations in the region.[56]

Heiman argues that Interior has not improved oil spill response planning since the *Deepwater Horizon* spill and that the agency should require lessees to have more detailed spill response plans and gear in place before operations can start.

"We should have equipment and trained personnel in the region, plus containment systems and gear to drill relief wells," she says. "We also need standards for operating in Arctic conditions and responding to a worst-case discharge. There is no requirement now for future operations to have containment systems or relief rigs in the Arctic, or to have tested them in the Arctic."

Shell and Interior Department officials say they are committed to operating safely and protecting Alaska's fragile environment. When the Interior Department approved Shell's spill-response plan in February, Deputy Secretary David J. Hayes said the decision was "based on our new standards and our commitment to ensure the highest standard of safety and environmental preparedness in the world and our commitment to bringing science to all our activities in the Arctic."[57]

On the East Coast, officials and some residents in Virginia want Interior to open areas off the state's coast for drilling. "Energy production in the OCS has vigorous, bipartisan support among Virginians and their political leadership," Democratic U.S. Sens. James Webb and Mark Warner wrote to Salazar in January, citing approval from the state's congressional delegation, legislature, and Republican Gov. Bob McDonnell. Offshore drilling revenues, which are shared by the federal and state governments, could provide "a future source of funding for important State priorities such as transportation, land and water conservation and alternative energy development," the senators wrote.[58]

However, Virginia could face opposition from the Defense Department, which stated in 2010 that about three-quarters of the waters proposed for drilling off Virginia were crucial areas for Navy operations, including training, testing and gunnery exercises.[59] Virginia has large bases representing all four military services. Most notably, hundreds of ships and aircraft are based in the Norfolk/Newport News/Virginia Beach area at the mouth of the Chesapeake Bay, including aircraft carriers, destroyers and submarines.

Alt-Fuel Vehicles

In July 2011 the Obama administration and major auto manufacturers announced new fuel efficiency standards for U.S. cars and light trucks — the second increase during Obama's presidency. Previously, fuel economy standards had not changed since 1985. The new targets will double the average fuel efficiency of cars and light trucks to 54.5 miles per gallon by 2025, when fuel consumption will be an estimated 2.2 million barrels lower per day.[60]

Walter McManus, an economist at Oakland University's School of Business Administration in Michigan and a former market analyst at General Motors, calls the new standards a major breakthrough because they require manufacturers to make every class of vehicles they produce more efficient. Previously, auto makers could average the efficiency of different models across their fleets to meet an overall target, so car companies typically would offset sales of gas guzzlers by also offering smaller, more efficient models.

"Manufacturers will have to make everything lighter across their fleets, downsize engines, turbocharge them, and add features like stop-start systems [which turn engines off when vehicles stop, eliminating engine idling]. They'll have to address all of the ways that today's cars use energy, like tire inflation and wind resistance," says McManus.

The new fuel efficiency standards could boost so-called advanced-drive vehicles — gas/electric hybrids such as the popular Toyota Prius, plug-in hybrids and battery-powered electric vehicles. In November 2011, all of these categories combined accounted for just under 3 percent of monthly U.S. new car sales (27,897 vehicles), with more than two-thirds going to Toyota.[61] Electric vehicles entered mass production at the end of 2010, but started slowly: Combined sales for the Chevy Volt and Nissan Leaf plug-ins totaled about 26,000 cars for their entire first year.[62]

"Electric vehicles depend heavily on high gas prices, and they need to reduce battery costs almost threefold to be cost-competitive, which probably means developing and commercializing a brand-new technology," says Harvard's Lee. "They could make inroads in 2020 to 2030, but I wouldn't bet on it in the next few years."

McManus agrees that electric vehicles could help reduce U.S. oil dependence, but he says it will be in the long term. "If the goal is to use less fuel now, you can argue that the best way is to keep improving internal combustion engines by ratcheting up fuel economy targets, not by picking a technology," he says.

However, McManus does not expect a resurgence of SUVs and other gas-guzzling models in the wake of the recession. "Manufacturers are still making large pickup trucks and [large] SUVs, but they're making them mainly for commercial use. Households still buy pickups, but a lot of those owners are contractors, plumbers and electricians, and they are very concerned about fuel economy. SUVs are waning as a personal-use vehicle," he says.

OUTLOOK
No Choice

Over the past several decades Americans have snapped to attention during oil price spikes, then lapsed back into old ways once the crunches eased. But many experts say the recession that started in 2008, combined with rising world energy demand, may permanently alter U.S. attitudes toward oil use.

Energy companies are bullish about new production in the United States, even though domestic sources will not replace those like OPEC. "We're leaders in developing unconventional supplies at home and around the world, which has revolutionized supply," says the American Petroleum Institute's Dougher. She acknowledges that even if the United States becomes independent of oil produced outside North America, it would still pay world prices. Nonetheless, she contends, "What we can do by increasing production is get more control and reliable supplies and give the world more supply from stable sources."

Just because a source is large, however, may not make it reliable. "Energy security isn't just about supply — it's also about environmental impacts," says the Pembina Institute's Lemphers. "Operating costs to produce oil from Canadian tar sands are about four times higher than for Saudi crude oil. If global oil prices drop, this massive supply could become uneconomic to develop."

Although near-term market prospects for plug-in and battery-powered electric cars appear modest, Oakland University's McManus believes U.S. car makers have

learned that the era of gas guzzlers is over. "There's been a huge change in attitudes since the gasoline price rise from 2002-2006," he says. "Manufacturers started squeezing their big profit margins on SUVs, but they kept marketing them, which cost them a lot. Eventually they had to cut production dramatically. The only market for SUVs was here in North America, so we took the losses when they became hard to sell."

Now, in contrast, McManus believes that U.S. car companies support the mission of bringing smaller, more fuel-efficient cars to market — particularly Ford. "I think Ford definitely believes in this for the long term and is committed to sustainability because of the Ford family — they want to be in business 100 years from now," he says. "They want to be the fuel economy leader for every market segment that they compete in."

Energy hawks agree that fuel efficiency is important but strongly support an open fuel standard as a way to diversify the U.S. transportation sector away from gasoline. "An open fuel standard would create opportunity for sources like natural gas and methanol, which are much cheaper than oil. It's like switching from $100 per barrel oil to $18 per barrel oil, and it would break oil's monopoly," says Luft of the Institute for Analysis of Global Security. "Utilities switch between different fuels to make electricity, depending on prices, and we should aspire to something like that for transportation."

While experts may disagree on strategies, there is little argument that reducing U.S. oil dependence should be an important national priority. "Expanding world oil production will be very challenging, and demand will keep growing in China, India and other developing countries. We're not going to have a choice about using energy more efficiently," says University of California-San Diego economist James Hamilton. "We're seeing declines in U.S. consumption, and that's an ongoing process."

NOTES

1. Brian Montopoli, "Could Gingrich really lower gas to $2.50 per gallon?," CBS News, Political Hotsheet, March 13, 2012, www.cbsnews.com/8301-503544_162-57396671-503544/could-gingrich-really-lower-gas-to-$2.50-per-gallon/.

2. Kathleen Hennessey, "Obama scoffs at critics on gas prices, defends energy policy," *Los Angeles Times*, Feb. 23, 2012, http://articles.latimes.com/2012/feb/23/nation/la-na-obama-gas-prices-20120224.

3. "Primary Energy Consumption by Source and Sector, 2010," U.S. Energy Information Administration, http://205.254.135.7/totalenergy/data/annual/pecss_diagram.cfm.

4. Daniel Yergin, testimony before the Senate Energy and Natural Resources Committee, March 29, 2012, pp. 8-9, www.energy.senate.gov/public/index.cfm/files/serve?File_id=500012a0-c1a5-4c3f-87c4-16d3c06abcff.

5. Michael D. Shear, "Romney Faults Obama on Energy Costs, but Has cited Benefits of Rising Prices," *The New York Times*, April 2, 2012, www.nytimes.com/2012/04/03/us/politics/romney-faults-obama-for-rising-gas-prices.html?_r=1&pagewanted=print.

6. "Fact Sheet: Obama Administration's All-of-the-Above Approach to American Energy," Office of the Press Secretary, the White House, March 21, 2012, www.whitehouse.gov/the-press-office/2012/03/21/fact-sheet-obama-administration-s-all-above-approach-american-energy.

7. For background see Thomas J. Billitteri, "Offshore Drilling," *CQ Researcher*, June 25, 2010, pp. 553-580.

8. For details see Paul Parformak, *et al.*, "Keystone XL Pipeline Project: Key Issues," Congressional Research Service, R41668 (March 13, 2012), www.fas.org/sgp/crs/misc/R41668.pdf.

9. Padmananda Rama, "Obama Returns to Oklahoma Talking Oil," NPR, March 22, 2012, www.npr.org/blogs/itsallpolitics/2012/03/22/149161898/obama-returns-to-oklahoma-talking-oil.

10. "Toyota Sells One-Millionth Prius in the U.S.," Toyota USA Newsroom, April 6, 2011, http://pressroom.toyota.com/article_display.cfm?article_id=2959.

11. For background see Thomas J. Billitteri, "Auto Industry's Future," *CQ Researcher*, Feb. 6, 2009, pp. 105-128, update, Oct. 3, 2011.

12. For background see Jennifer Weeks, "Energy Policy," *CQ Researcher*, May 20, 2011, pp. 457-480.

13. Charles Riley, "Gingrich's $2.50 Gas Promise," CNN Money, Feb. 24, 2012, http://money.cnn.com/2012/02/24/news/economy/gingrich_gas_prices/index.htm.

14. Rep. Fred Upton, opening statement, March 7, 2012, p. 1, http://republicans.energycommerce.house.gov/Media/file/Hearings/Energy/20120307/HHRG-112-IF03-MState-U000031-20120307.pdf.

15. Richard H. Thaler, "Why Gas Prices Are Out of Any President's Control," *The New York Times*, March 31, 2012, www.nytimes.com/2012/04/01/business/gas-prices-are-out-of-any-presidents-control.html.

16. Jack Gillum and Seth Borenstein, "Fact Check: More U.S. Drilling Didn't Drop Gas Price," The Associated Press, March 21, 2012, http://0-news.yahoo.com.precise.petronas.com.my/fact-check-more-us-drilling-didnt-drop-gas-065231245.html.

17. Letter from Reps. Peter Welch, Ed Markey and Rosa DeLauro to President Barack Obama, March 16, 2012, p. 3, www.welch.house.gov/index.php?option=com_content&task=view&id=1930&Itemid=90.

18. Sam Fletcher, "Market Watch: Talk of SPR Release Drops Oil Prices," *Oil & Gas Journal*, March 16, 2012, www.ogj.com/articles/2012/03/market-watch-talk-of-spr-release-drops-oil-prices.html.

19. Andrew Nikiforuk, *Tar Sands: Dirty Oil and the Future of a Continent* (2008), pp. 25-27.

20. 2012 Oil Shale and Tar Sands Programmatic EIS Information Center, "About Tar Sands," U.S. Department of the Interior, http://ostseis.anl.gov/guide/tarsands/index.cfm.

21. Testimony before the House Energy and Commerce Committee, Subcommittee on Energy and Power, May 23, 2011, http://press.ihs.com/press-release/energy-power/congressional-testimony-significance-canadas-oil-sands.

22. "Minister Oliver Promotes Canadian Energy Interests in Kuwait," Marketwire, March 13, 2012, www.marketwatch.com/story/minister-oliver-promotes-canadian-energy-interests-in-kuwait-2012-03-13.

23. "Environment Canada and the Oil Sands," Environment Canada, May 2011, online at www.scribd.com/doc/76259666/Oilsands-Pollution.

24. Testimony before the House Committee on Science, Space and Technology, April 17, 2012, www.energy xxi.org/testimony-karen-harbert-house-committee-science.

25. "Public comments of the Sierra Club, *et al.*, on the TransCanada Keystone XL Pipeline Draft Environmental Impact Statement," July 2, 2010, p. 7, www.nebraskawildlife.org/Documents/NWF%20 Comments%20KeystoneXL%20DEIS%207.3.10.pdf.

26. *Ibid.*, p. 15.

27. Wendy Stueck, "Native Leaders Vow to Block Northern Gateway Pipeline," *The Globe and Mail*, Dec. 2, 2011, www.theglobeandmail.com/news/national/british-columbia/bc-politics/native-leaders-vow-to-block-northern-gateway-pipeline/article 2257573/; Doug Ward, "Feds Likely Could Push Pipelines Through B.C. After Long Legal Struggle," *Montreal Gazette*, May 1, 2012, /www.montreal gazette.com/news/Feds+likely+could+push+pipelines+ through+after+long+legal+struggle/6550161/story .html.

28. Max Paris, "EU Delays 'Anti-Oilsands' Fuel Quality Directive Decision," Canadian Broadcasting Corporation, April 29, 2012, www.cbc.ca/news/ politics/story/2012/04/20/pol-fuel-directive-europe-canada.html.

29. "Annual Energy Outlook 2012; Early Release Overview," U.S. Energy Information Administration, p. 1, http://205.254.135.7/forecasts/aeo/er/pdf/0383er %282012%29.pdf.

30. "2012 U.S. Energy Sector Outlook," *Forbes Insights*, p. 1, www.forbes.com/forbesinsights/energy_ sector_outlook_2012/index.html.

31. H.R. 1687, introduced by Rep. John Shimkus (R-Ill.), and S. 1603, introduced by Sen. Maria Cantwell (D-Wash.)

32. "OnPoint," E&E TV, Oct. 13, 2011, www.eenews .net/tv/transcript/1407.

33. "Automakers Say 'Enough!' on U.S. Flex-Fule Cars," *Biofuels Digest*, June 16, 2011, www.biofuelsdigest .com/bdigest/2011/06/16/automakers-say-enough-on-us-flex-fuel-cars/.

34. For background see Adriel Bettelheim, "Biofuels Boom," *CQ Researcher*, Sept. 29, 2006, pp. 793-816,

and Jennifer Weeks, "Energy Policy," *CQ Researcher*, May 20, 2011, pp. 457-480.

35. Todd Woody, "New Enzyme Could Make Cellulosic Ethanol Competitive With Fossil Fuels," *Forbes.com*, Feb. 22, 2012, www.forbes.com/sites/toddwoody/ 2012/02/22/new-enzyme-could-make-cellulosic-ethanol-competitive-with-fossil-fuels/; Jim Lane, "The Enzyme Wars," *Biofuels Digest*, Feb. 24, 2012, www.biofuelsdigest.com/bdigest/2012/02/24/ the-enzyme-wars/.

36. "EPA Finalizes 2012 Renewable Fuel Standards," Environmental Protection Agency Dec. 27, 2011, http://yosemite.epa.gov/opa/admpress.nsf/0/ A7CE72844710BE0A85257973006A20F3.

37. Kelsi Bracmort, "Meeting the Renewable Fuel Standard (RFS) Mandate for Cellulosic Biofuels: Questions and Answers," Congressional Research Service, Jan. 11, 2012, p. 7, www.fas.org/sgp/crs/ misc/R41106.pdf.

38. *Renewable Fuel Standard: Potential Economic and Environmental Effects of U.S. Biofuel Policy* (2011), National Research Council, pp. 3-4, www.nap.edu/ openbook.php?record_id=13105&page=3.

39. "Ethanol Keeps Gasoline Prices $1.09 Cheaper," Renewable Fuels Association, May 2012, http:// ethanolrfa.3cdn.net/794558c8d8f4826bb6_ alm6i6z9x.pdf, and "Don't Mess with the RFS," March 2012, http://ethanolrfa.3cdn.net/056f576c0 cb1b6388f_2om6b9rvl.pdf.

40. Testimony before the House Energy and Commerce Committee, Subcommittee on Environment and Economy, April 19, 2012, p. 2, http://ethanolrfa .org/page/-/objects/pdf/PublicPolicy/Official Statements/Dinneen%20E%26C%20Subcmte%20 Testimony%204-19-12.pdf?nocdn=1.

41. The case is *Standard Oil Co. of New Jersey v. United States*, 221 U.S. 1 (1911).

42. Daniel Yergin, *The Prize: The Epic Quest for Oil, Money & Power* (1991), pp. 112-113.

43. *Ibid.*, pp. 209-210.

44. "U.S. Field Production of Crude Oil," U.S. Energy Information Administration, May 30, 2012, www .eia.gov/dnav/pet/hist/LeafHandler.ashx?n=PET&s= MCRFPUS2&f=A.

45. Andrew Revkin, "Obama on the 'Shock to Trance' Energy Pattern," *The New York Times*, Nov. 17, 2008, http://dotearth.blogs.nytimes.com/2008/11/17/obama-on-shock-to-trance-energy-pattern/.

46. David Jackson, "Obama: Oil Drilling Has Increased on My Watch," *USA Today*, March 22, 2012, http://content.usatoday.com/communities/theoval/post/2012/03/obama-oil-drilling-up-on-my-watch/1#.T5mGb9USEuc.

47. "U.S. Number of Operating Refineries as of January 1," U.S. Energy Information Administration, http://205.254.135.7/dnav/pet/hist/LeafHandler.ashx?n=PET&s=8_NA_8OO_NUS_C&f=A.

48. "U.S. Operable Crude Oil Distillation Capacity," U.S. Energy Information Administration, http://205.254.135.7/dnav/pet/hist/LeafHandler.ashx?n=PET&s=MOCLEUS2&f=M.

49. Ron Scherer, "Why Gasoline Could Be in Short Supply this Summer on East Coast," *The Christian Science Monitor*, March 28, 2012, www.csmonitor.com/USA/2012/0328/Why-gasoline-could-be-in-short-supply-this-summer-on-East-Coast.

50. Jad Mouawad, "Delta Buys Refinery to Get Control of Fuel Costs," *The New York Times*, April 30, 2012, www.nytimes.com/2012/05/01/business/delta-air-lines-to-buy-refinery.html?pagewanted=print.

51. For details see "Control of Air Pollution from Motor Vehicles: Tier 3 Motor Vehicle Emission and Fuel Standards," Environmental Protection Agency, http://yosemite.epa.gov/opei/rulegate.nsf/byRIN/2060-AQ86#1.

52. Testimony before the Joint Economic Committee, April 26, 2012, p. 4, http://jec.senate.gov/public//index.cfm?a=Files.Serve&File_id=d2c7da82-7987-41e0-a43a-7a86dbea5636.

53. Letter online at www.lung.org/get-involved/advocate/advocacy-documents/letter-tier3-vechicle.pdf.

54. "Secretary Salazar Announces 2012-2017 Offshore Oil and Gas Development Program," U.S. Department of the Interior, Nov. 8, 2011, www.doi.gov/news/pressreleases/Secretary-Salazar-Announces-2012-2017-Offshore-Oil-and-Gas-Development-Program.cfm.

55. Kim Murphy, "Oil Drilling in Arctic Nears Reality: Shell Emergency Plan OKd," *Los Angeles Times*, Feb. 17, 2012, http://articles.latimes.com/2012/feb/17/nation/la-na-nn-arctic-oilspill-20120217; Sarah Blackman, "Drilling Arctic Oil: Do Shell's Response Plans Hold Water?" *Offshore Technology*, April 24, 2012, www.offshore-technology.com/features/featurethe-race-to-drill-arctic-oil-do-shells-response-plans-hold-water/.

56. Jim Paulin, "Shell Wins Injunction, Greenpeace Looks at Options," *Arctic Sounder*, April 6, 2012, www.thearcticsounder.com/article/1214shell_wins_injunction_greenpeace_looks_at.

57. John M. Broder, "Shell Clears Major Drilling Hurdle in Its Bid for New Arctic Drilling," *The New York Times*, Feb. 17, 2012, www.nytimes.com/2012/02/18/science/earth/us-tentatively-approves-shell-spill-plan-for-new-arctic-drilling.html.

58. Letter online at www.warner.senate.gov/public/index.cfm/pressreleases?ID=defcdc5f-27da-4766-8e3b-7e8d336bb223.

59. "Virginia Offshore Drilling Hits a Roadblock," *The Washington Times*, May 19, 2010, www.washingtontimes.com/news/2010/may/19/virginia-offshore-drilling-hits-a-roadblock/?page=all.

60. "Driving Efficiency: Cutting Costs for Families at the Pump and Slashing Dependence on Oil," The White House, 2011, www.whitehouse.gov/sites/default/files/fuel_economy_report.pdf.

61. John O'Dell, "Hybrid Sales Soar in November," *Edmunds.com*, Dec. 6, 2011, www.edmunds.com/industry-center/analysis/hybrid-sales-soar-in-november.html.

62. Steve LeVine, "Chevy Volt, Nissan Leaf: Will the Electric Car Ever Be a Success?" *Slate.com*, March 11, 2012, www.slate.com/articles/technology/future_tense/2012/03/chevy_volt_nissan_leaf_will_the_electric_car_ever_be_a_success_.html.

BIBLIOGRAPHY

Selected Sources
Books
Coll, Steve, *Private Empire: ExxonMobil and American Power*, Penguin, 2012.

A Pulitzer Prize winner tracks ExxonMobil's meteoric rise, focusing on the leader who remade the company's safety culture after the 1989 *Exxon Valdez* oil spill.

Mitchell, William J., Chris E. Borroni-Bird, and Lawrence D. Burns, *Reinventing the Automobile: Personal Urban Mobility for the 21st Century*, MIT Press, 2010.
A scholar at the Massachusetts Institute of Technology and two General Motors executives propose a new vision for urban transportation that relies on small cars, information technology and clean fuels to make cities cleaner and safer.

Nikiforuk, Andrew, *Tar Sands: Dirty Oil and the Future of a Continent*, Greystone, 2009.
An award-winning Canadian journalist argues that oil production from Alberta's tar sands is causing disastrous environmental, social and political harm and should be capped and limited.

Articles

"Ray Mabus, U.S. Navy Secretary, Defends Biofuels Investment," The Associated Press, March 13, 2012, www.huffingtonpost.com/2012/03/13/ray-mabus-navy-defends-biofuels_n_1341328.html.
The U.S. Navy is experimenting with expensive biofuels to power planes and ships, a strategy that Navy leaders say is a hedge against future oil price shocks.

Broder, John M., and Clifford Krauss, "New and Frozen Frontier Awaits Offshore Oil Drilling," *The New York Times*, May 23, 2012, www.nytimes.com/2012/05/24/science/earth/shell-arctic-ocean-drilling-stands-to-open-new-oil-frontier.html?ref=offshoredrillingandexploration.
The authors vividly describe the challenges of drilling off the Alaskan coast.

Bunkley, Nick, "Payoff for Efficient Cars Takes Years," *The New York Times*, April 4, 2012, www.nytimes.com/2012/04/05/business/energy-environment/for-hybrid-and-electric-cars-to-pay-off-owners-must-wait.html?scp=1&sq=Prius&st=cse.
Hybrids and electric vehicles save owners money on gas, but those savings are offset by high price tags.

Gillum, Jack, and Seth Borenstein, "Fact Check: More U.S. Drilling Didn't Drop Gas Price," The
Associated Press, March 21, 2012, www.cbsnews.com/8301-505145_162-57401456/more-us-drilling-didnt-drop-gas-price/.
A statistical analysis of 36 years of monthly, inflation-adjusted gasoline prices shows no relationship between U.S. domestic production levels and fuel costs.

Herron, James, "Citigroup Says Peak Oil is Dead," *Wall Street Journal*, Feb. 17, 2012, http://blogs.wsj.com/source/2012/02/17/citigroup-says-peak-oil-is-dead/.
Citigroup says new oil production from shale could one day make the United States and Canada self-sufficient in oil.

Jaffe, Amy Myers, "The Americas, Not the Middle East, Will Be the World Capital of Energy," *Foreign Policy*, September/October 2011, www.foreignpolicy.com/articles/2011/08/15/the_americas_not_the_middle_east_will_be_the_world_capital_of_energy.
Technical advances are making oil more accessible in the West at a time when political turmoil threatens Middle East production.

Moore, Jina, "After Oil: How We'll Live," *The Christian Science Monitor*, Oct. 10, 2011, www.csmonitor.com/Specials/Future-Focus-Energy.
A package of articles examines alternatives to fossil fuel, including electric cars and biofuels, and the Pentagon's push to reduce the armed forces' oil dependence.

Reports and Studies

"Keystone XL: Undermining Energy Security and Sending Tar Sands Overseas," Oil Change International and Natural Resources Defense Council, 2012, http://priceofoil.org/keystone-xl-undermining-energy-security/.
Two environmental organizations argue that building the Keystone XL pipeline will not improve U.S. energy security.

"Oil and Gas: Interior Has Strengthened Its Oversight of Subsea Well Containment, but Should Improve Its Documentation," U.S. Government Accountability Office, February 2012, www.gao.gov/assets/590/588961.pdf.
Since the 2010 *Deepwater Horizon* spill in the Gulf of Mexico, the Interior Department has tightened policies for

managing undersea well blowouts. But drilling off the coast of Alaska poses unique risks.

Lee, Henry, and Grant Lovellette, "Will Electric Cars Transform the U.S. Vehicle Market? An Analysis of the Key Determinants," Discussion Paper 2011-08, Belfer Center for Science and International Affairs, Harvard University, July 2011, www.belfercenter.ksg.harvard.edu/ files/LeeLovelletteElectricVehiclesDP2011web.pdf.
For electric cars to reduce U.S. oil use, gasoline prices would have to rise to $4.50-$5.50 per gallon and

battery technology improve, according to two Harvard scholars.

National Research Council, "Renewable Fuel Standard: Potential Economic and Environmental Effects of U.S. Biofuel Policy," National Academies Press, 2011.
Members of the National Academies of Science find that the United States is unlikely to meet its goals for producing advanced biofuels without major technical breakthroughs or policy changes.

For More Information

American Petroleum Institute, 1220 L St., N.W., Washington, DC 20005; 202-682-2000; www.api.org. National trade association for the oil and natural gas industry.

Harvard Kennedy School of Government, 79 John F. Kennedy St., Cambridge, MA 02138; 617-495-1100; www .hks.harvard.edu. Graduate school of government and public policy, with research programs on issues including environment and natural resources.

Institute for Analysis of Global Security, 7811 Montrose Rd., Suite 505, Potomac, MD 20854; 866-713-7527; www .iags.org. Nonprofit think tank focused on the connections between energy and national security.

Oak Ridge National Laboratory, P.O. Box 2008, Oak Ridge, TN 37831; 875-574-4160; www.ornl.gov. Multiprogram science and technology laboratory of the U.S. Department of Energy, focusing on clean energy and global security challenges.

Pembina Institute, 219 19th St., N.W., Calgary, Alberta T2N 2H9, Canada; 403-269-3344; www.pembina.org. Canadian think tank that conducts research, education and advocacy to promote sustainable energy solutions.

Pew Environment Group, 901 E St., N.W., Washington, DC 20004; 202-552-2000; www.pewenvironment.org. National environmental research and advocacy group, funded by the Pew Charitable Trusts.

U.S. Geological Survey, 12201 Sunrise Valley Dr., Reston, VA 20192; 703-648-5953; www.usgs.gov. Science agency within the U.S. Department of the Interior that collects, monitors and analyzes information about natural resource conditions, issues and problems.

University of Michigan Transportation Research Institute, 2901 Baxter Rd., Ann Arbor, MI 48109; 734-764-6504; www.umtri.umich.edu. Interdisciplinary research center that works to expand knowledge of transportation systems.

5

Genetically Modified Food

Jason McLure

California Right to Know

Boxes delivered to the Los Angeles County courthouse in May hold nearly one million signatures from California voters calling for a ballot initiative in November requiring labeling of genetically modified (GM) foods. Organic farmers and some consumer groups support the initiative, contending GM foods may pose health or environmental risks. The GM farming industry notes that scientific organizations ranging from the National Academy of Science to the World Health Organization say GM crops pose no more risk than conventional foods.

From *The CQ Researcher*,
August 31, 2012.

W hen California voters go to the polls Nov. 6, they'll be walking straight into a massive food fight.

On the ballot will be a highly contentious proposal to require special labels on foods produced with genetically modified ingredients — so-called GM foods. The federal government does not require that GM foods be labeled unless they change the nutritional content or add toxic or allergenic properties to food. Labeling advocates want any GM food to be labeled, as more than 40 countries do, including all of Europe, Japan and China.

California's labeling referendum has strong support from environmental and food-safety groups that say GM foods — made from crops that have had genetic material inserted or deleted in a laboratory to give them specific advantages, such as resistance to herbicides — may pose health or environmental risks.

Also among the staunchest labeling supporters are organic farmers, who compete with GM food producers. "People have a right to know what's in the food we eat and feed to our children," said Stacy Malkan, a spokeswoman for California Right to Know, a coalition that has spearheaded the ballot measure.[1]

But GM farming giants and other referendum foes argue that the health and environmental concerns are unfounded, and that the labeling effort is an attempt to demonize a technology with enormous potential benefits. They note that after extensive research, U.S. and international scientific organizations ranging from the National Academy of Science to the World Health Organization have concluded that GM crops don't inherently pose more risk than their conventional counterparts. What's more, they say genetically

Field Trials Focus on Corn and Other Big Crops

More than three-quarters of the crop field trials conducted by 24 developed countries (excluding China and India) from 2003-2008 were for big commodity crops, or crops bought and sold on futures exchanges. Only 15 percent of the trials were for GM fruits, vegetables, nuts and other specialty crops, which biotech companies have largely abandoned in favor of industrially grown commodities, such as corn and cotton.

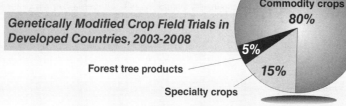

Genetically Modified Crop Field Trials in Developed Countries, 2003-2008

Commodity crops 80%

Forest tree products — 5%

Specialty crops 15%

Source: Jamie K. Miller and Kent J. Bradford, "The Regulatory Bottleneck for Biotech Specialty Crops," *Nature Biotechnology*, October 2010, p. 1014, www.nature.com/nbt/journal/v28/n10/full/nbt1010-1012.html

modified crops are more productive, pest-resistant and environmentally friendly than conventional crops — and they've been consumed by millions of people in the U.S. for nearly two decades without any documented health consequences.[2]

"Do you give the same scientific weight to evolution and creationism?" asks Adrian Dubock, director of the Golden Rice Project, which seeks to cut malnutrition and save millions of lives in the developing world through the use of GM rice varieties enriched with Vitamin A. "There's a point where the scientific controversy is over."

On the contrary, the opposition seems to be growing, says Douglas Gurian-Sherman, a senior scientist with the Union of Concerned Scientists, which favors labeling. "There is clearly more interest and momentum behind it than there was 10 years ago," he says.

Indeed, big agribusiness and biotechnology companies that engineer or produce GM crops are pouring resources into halting that momentum. By mid-August, Monsanto, Dupont Pioneer, Cargill and others had contributed nearly $25 million to defeat the statewide initiative — nearly 10 times the amount raised by supporters.[3]

California is the nation's biggest consumer market, and passage of the referendum could influence GM food policies nationwide. Labeling laws or ballot measures

have been proposed in 20 states in the past year, according to the Biotechnology Industry Organization (BIO), a trade group. And more than a million people signed a petition this year urging the Food and Drug Administration (FDA) to require labeling.

California's referendum campaign is part of a much bigger, two-decades-old debate about the safety, effectiveness and commercial viability of agricultural biotechnology. GM supporters argue that abundant peer-reviewed research shows GM crops are safe and that uninformed pressure groups and the organic-farming industry have thwarted GM progress. Opponents argue that the jury is still out on the safety and environmental effects of GM crops and that, at the very least, growers should better inform the public about the use of gene-transferring techniques in food.

The techniques, which have been perfected in laboratories over the past 40 years, include bombarding target cells with heavy metals coated with the gene to be transferred; using a naturally occurring bacterium to transfer genes into the host cell and using a pulse of electricity to introduce genes into the targeted cell.[4]

Two technologies currently dominate the GM farming industry:

- Some crops have been modified to be able to survive the weed-killer glyphosate, commonly sold under Monsanto's Roundup brand. So-called Roundup Ready crops decrease the need to till before planting, saving farmers time and money and reducing erosion and loss of soil moisture. Glyphosate is among the least toxic herbicides that can kill a broad spectrum of weeds, and thus is safer for farmworkers and less environmentally damaging than many chemical alternatives.[5]

- The introduction of genes from the soil bacterium *Bacillus thurengiensis* (Bt) produces a substance toxic to many pests but harmless to humans, wildlife and most beneficial insects, such as bees. While Bt has long been used by organic farmers, scientists have produced GM crops that manufacture their own Bt in the part of the plant susceptible to attack from pests — such as corn-plant roots prone to root-worm attack. Bt has allowed many farmers to reduce the use of harmful insecticides. In China alone, the use of Bt cotton has halved pesticide use since the crop was introduced in 1997, and the population of beneficial pest-eating insects such as ladybugs has increased, because they are resistant to Bt.[6]

The use of GM crops has become widespread among U.S. growers of commodities, or big crops sold on futures exchanges. Eighty-eight percent of corn and 94 percent of cotton, for example, came from GM strains in 2012.[7] Because corn and soy are ubiquitous in processed foods in the United States, from corn syrup-sweetened Coca-Cola to crackers made with soybean oil, it's likely that most Americans consume a product containing a genetically modified ingredient every day.

Nonetheless, GM agriculture has made uneven progress over the past two decades. At the dawn of the GM food revolution in the mid-1990s, scientists and industry officials predicted it would produce healthier food that would be slower to rot, taste better and reduce agriculture's impact on the environment. But some GM crops have failed to produce benefits, and some once-promising research has been abandoned. For instance, researchers have all but given up on developing GM fruits and other so-called specialty crops because the costs of gaining regulatory approval do not justify the potential economic rewards, plant scientists say.

They argue that valuable research has been hindered by consumer resistance to GM foods, due to either misunderstanding or confusion about the safety of the crops. Twenty-one percent of respondents to a 2010 Thomson Reuters and NPR poll thought GM food is safe, while 15 percent said it was unsafe. Nearly two-thirds weren't sure.[8] Some GM proponents contend that opponents resist GM crops because they oppose industrial farming, which is how most GM crops in the United States are grown.

Hundreds of Permits Issued for GM Crop Testing

Permits for U.S. field trials of genetically modified (GM) crops totaled 743 in 2008, more than six times the number in 1992. Most permits were for soybeans, corn and other commodity crops, which are far larger than specialty crops such as fruits and vegetables, and thus are more profitable. Successful field trials help the government decide whether to allow GM crops to be commercially produced.

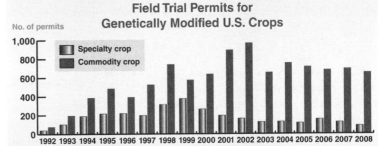

Field Trial Permits for Genetically Modified U.S. Crops

Source: Jamie K. Miller and Kent J. Bradford, "The Regulatory Bottleneck for Biotech Specialty Crops," *Nature Biotechnology,* October 2010, p. 1014, www.nature.com/nbt/journal/v28/n10/full/nbt1010-1012.html

Organic farmers, meanwhile, fear that their non-GM crops could be contaminated by the spread of genetically modified traits by wind and insect cross-pollination. Once those traits are in the agricultural gene pool, they say, there's no way to remove them.

"We believe that this technology doesn't make sense in the long run for the human species," says Bill Duesing, an organic farmer in Oxford, Conn., and Interstate Council president of the 5,000-member Northeast Organic Farming Association. "This is pollution with a life of its own; it spreads forever."

Environmental groups such as the Union of Concerned Scientists say the U.S. Department of Agriculture (USDA) does not adequately examine the environmental impacts of introducing new farming methods on millions of acres, such as possible resistance to Bt and Roundup by weeds and insects. In addition, some scientists complain that biotech companies deny access to their patent-protected GM technology if they suspect researchers may cast doubt on its effectiveness, a charge companies deny.[9]

Meanwhile, some consumers and organic farmers pose philosophical objections to GM plant-breeding methods. "It's the kind of breeding that would never happen in the wild," Duesing says. Resistance to genetic crop engineering ratcheted up a notch this summer after the House passed a version of a new farm bill that critics said would weaken the USDA's regulatory power over the industry while cutting funds for more stringent Environmental Protection Agency (EPA) regulations. The House bill would "create multiple backdoor approval mechanisms that would allow for the premature commercialization of untested biotech traits to enter our food system," charged Colin O'Neil, a policy analyst at the Center for Food Safety, a Washington-based advocacy group.[10]

But biotechnology researchers and industry advocates argue that environmental and food-safety groups are creating public confusion about GM foods long after scientific studies have established that the technology is safe. "We're seeing in the last couple years a vocal opposition to the technology, and food-labeling requirements are just one of the tactics being employed," says Cathleen Enright, vice president for food and agriculture at the Biotechnology Industry Organization.

Labeling initiatives, she says, are "essentially meant not to inform consumers about genetically engineered food but rather to eliminate the technology from agriculture in this country."

Ironically, for more than a decade some vaccines and life-saving medicines have been genetically engineered in the laboratory by creating new organisms that would never be created in nature — some even made by mixing plant and animal genes. Yet opposition to such products has been much more muted. Likewise, nongenetic engineered plant-breeding methods that would be impossible in nature, such as bombarding plants with radiation or carcinogenic chemicals to induce genetic change, have not attracted such widespread opposition.

Dubock says unfounded opposition to GM foods has caused needless delays in technologies that would potentially save hundreds of thousands of lives. Golden Rice was hailed on the cover of *Time* magazine a dozen years ago as having the potential to save a million children a year. That's because the rice strain was genetically modified to be rich in beta-carotene — a vitamin A precursor — that could help stave off blindness, infections and other maladies among impoverished children in countries like India and Bangladesh. Current estimates say widespread use of the crop could save up to 2.7 million children a year, according to Dubock, but it has not been

commercially planted due to suspicion about genetic engineering. That may change soon — the Philippines likely will permit cultivation in 2013.

"The activists have been very successful in promulgating their view," Dubock asserts. "We could have given it to farmers everywhere. We are not able to because of international regulations that prevent us from putting seeds in an envelope and mailing them to people who could use them."

As scientists, environmentalists, consumer advocates and organic farmers debate the effects of GM foods, here are some of the questions being asked:

Were the consumer benefits of GM crops oversold?

The future for genetically modified crops envisioned by biotech advocates in the 1990s looked substantially different from the GM landscape today.

Developing countries without reliable energy for refrigeration would have an additional supply of food "with no additional cost or environmental effect," Charles Gasser, a cellular biologist at the University of California-Davis and former Monsanto researcher, predicted optimistically in 1994. Biotechnology would provide such countries with slow-ripening fruits and vegetables with shelf lives up to five times longer than regular produce, he said.[11]

Not only have such technologies not been commercialized, but the scale of adoption of genetically modified crops has not matched earlier predictions, such as this one from Val Giddings, vice president for food and agriculture for the Biotechnology Industry Organization (BIO), who said in 1998: "Within five years — and certainly within 10 — some 90 to 95 percent of plant-derived food material in the United States will come from genetically engineered techniques." Furthermore, he predicted, "It'll take a little bit longer for these technologies to penetrate into the organic market, but it will. As the benefits become clearer, . . . opposition will be replaced by understanding, and adoption will follow."[12]

Instead, the organic foods industry — which rebuffed GM crops when they were first commercialized in the mid-1990s — has seen record growth, while GM crop research has slowed markedly. Biotech companies have largely abandoned pursuing genetically modified varieties of fruits, vegetables, nuts and other specialty crops in favor of industrially grown commodities, such as corn and cotton. Between 1994 and 1998, U.S. regulatory authorities approved 17 GM fruits and vegetables, which the USDA calls specialty crops. Over the next decade they approved only three, even though specialty crops account for 40 percent of U.S. agricultural revenues.[13]

Commercialized in 1996, Bt insecticidal crops and so-called Roundup Ready crops tolerant of herbicides became some of the most rapidly adopted agricultural technologies in history. But 16 years later, the two modifications are being used largely in only three row crops: corn, soybeans and cotton, which are grown on a large scale. The three commodities account for 94 percent of the world's acreage planted in GM crops.[14]

Critics of biotechnology say other GM varieties haven't been developed because researchers haven't been able to deliver the beneficial new products they promised. "This technology seems to me to be a fundamentally failed technology, because the science just didn't work," says Andrew Kimbrell, executive director of the Center for Food Safety, a Washington-based consumer group that has opposed GM crops and helped organize the labeling petition to the FDA.

In other words, he explains, while Roundup Ready and Bt insecticidal crops were extremely popular with large-scale commodity farmers, the crops haven't provided an identifiable benefit to consumers. "In 30 years, we've yet to come up with a single [genetic] trait that's advantageous to the consumer," Kimbrell adds. "It's not likely they're going to succeed in the near future."

Both opponents and supporters of the technology agree that the decision by biotech companies to first market herbicide-resistant and insecticidal commodity crops did not help to garner public acceptance and may have lowered perceptions of the potential consumer benefits of the technology.

"It's easy for consumers to reject GMOs [genetically modified organisms], because they don't taste better or

Genetic Engineering by the Numbers

400 million — Acres worldwide planted in genetically modified crops in 2011.

170 million — Acres of GM crops in U.S.

74.8 million — GM acres planted in 2011 by Brazil, the second-largest biotech nation after the U.S.

25 million — Dollars that companies that engineer or produce GM crops had contributed by mid-August to defeat the labeling initiative in California — nearly 10 times the amount raised by supporters.

2.7 million — Impoverished children in countries like India and Bangladesh whose lives could be saved by genetically engineered Golden Rice.

1 million-plus — People who signed a petition this year urging the Food and Drug Administration (FDA) to require labeling of GM foods.

20 — States in which labeling laws or ballot measures have been proposed in the past year.

12 — Percentage of the world's arable land planted in GM crops.

Sources: International Service for the Acquisition of Agri-Biotech Applications, Feb. 7, 2012; Biotechnology Industry Organization; United Nations; U.S. Department of Agriculture

smell any better, and they're not noticeably cheaper," says Robert Paarlberg, a political scientist at Wellesley College who researches the debate over biotech foods. "Most of the economic gains are not captured by the consumer but by the farmer and the biotech seed companies."

GM seed producer Monsanto tightly controls use of its product. Farmers who buy Monsanto GM seeds while they are covered by patents are barred from saving them from season to season as they may do with conventional crops.

Some organic farmers, who shun pesticides and GM crops, say the benefits of biotechnology touted by many scientists are illusory. "You keep being told the same promises or propaganda that you heard 20 years ago: It's going to reduce pesticides, it's going to be safer, it's going to produce more food," says Connecticut farmer Duesing.

But he says the way in which genetically engineered crops were developed in the United States — via monoculture industrial farming — has mainly benefited the

Most Acreage Used for GM Crops

More than 90 percent of the farmland for soybeans in the United States is dedicated to genetically modified (GM) herbicide-tolerant varieties. Most acreage for cotton and corn is also used for herbicide-tolerant or insect-resistant varieties, or both.

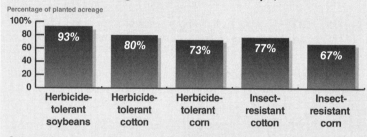

U.S. Acreage Dedicated to GM Crops, 2012

Percentage of planted acreage

Herbicide-tolerant soybeans	Herbicide-tolerant cotton	Herbicide-tolerant corn	Insect-resistant cotton	Insect-resistant corn
93%	80%	73%	77%	67%

Source: "Adoption of Genetically Engineered Crops in the U.S.," U.S. Department of Agriculture, July 2012, www.ers.usda.gov/data-products/adoption-of-genetically engineered-crops-in-the-us/recent-trends-in-ge-adoption.aspx

seed companies. "Nature works because of biodiversity," he says. Growing a single crop on thousands of acres "is the absolute opposite of biodiversity."

Others say the potential benefits of biotechnology to farmers in poor countries have been exaggerated. "Technology is not going to solve the problems of poor farmers," says Rachel Schurman, a sociologist at the University of Minnesota. Farming practices that dramatically boosted agricultural output during the "Green Revolution" in the 1960s and '70s — such as high-yield crop varieties, irrigation and heavy fertilizer and pesticide use — still have not trickled down to many of the poorest farmers in the developing world, she points out. "If they're going to devote all of these resources," she asks, "does it make economic sense to devote them to expensive technologies?"

While supporters of biotechnology may have overstated the possibilities of biotech foods, so too did opponents exaggerate the dangers, says Gregory Jaffe, biotechnology project director at the Center for Science in the Public Interest. "I don't think we've seen a lot of detrimental impacts on the environment yet," he says. "Similarly, we haven't seen some of the huge benefits that the industry had also suggested would happen."

Some biotech supporters blame the slow development of new GM varieties on opposition generated by food and environmental groups such as the Center for Food Safety and the Union of Concerned Scientists. The failure is "directly attributable" to "the people who are claiming this as a failure of biotech," says UC's Gasser. "The evidence was we could do it."

Others, like Harry Klee, a former Monsanto scientist who is now at the University of Florida, say progress in developing new crops — especially specialty crops like tomatoes — is impeded by high regulatory costs. Providing research data to make a single genetic alteration in a tomato variety, he says, can cost up to $15 million.

Dubock of the Golden Rice Project says the cost of regulatory approval has kept GM crops out of the hands of all but the best-funded multinational corporations.

"Do we want this technology to be only ruled by multinationals, or do we want it to be accessed by start-ups and developing countries?" he asks. "It's really a paradox that the attitudes promulgated by the activists against the technology reinforce the status of GM crops as row crops for the industrialized world."

Have existing GM crops caused environmental harm?

Most of the environmental concerns initially raised about biotech crops have not materialized. However, one worry — that the large-scale adoption of GM commodity crops would accelerate the natural development of resistance to the relatively safe Roundup herbicide and Bt insecticide — appears to have become reality.

Researchers have documented cases of resistance to Bt insecticide by the corn borer and corn rootworm, the two main pests killed by Bt corn — and a Roundup-resistant strain of a weed called waterhemp already has spread to 10 states.[15]

"In 2011, we saw glyphosate-resistant waterhemp explode across the Midwest," said Dan Westberg, a technical market manager at BASF, a maker of pesticides and biotech seeds. "It was a tipping point for farmers and another sign that we have to think beyond glyphosate alone for weed control."[16]

Experts say Roundup and Bt have become so widespread that resistant mutations have developed faster than they normally would in conventional crops because other types of controls are absent, an outcome that some GM opponents predicted.

A coalition of environmental groups published a report in 1990 predicting the rise of resistant weeds.[17] "We now know that inside the Trojan horse of biotechnology are just more herbicides and stronger weeds," Margaret Mellon, a biotechnology expert with the Union of Concerned Scientists, wrote in May.[18]

Farmers could have slowed the spread of resistance by planting "refuges," or small plots, of nonbiotech crops, which would allow some of the pests to survive and breed without generating resistance. Yet farmers growing Roundup Ready crops are not required by law to provide refuges, and those growing Bt crops are supposed to provide refuges equivalent to 20 percent of their acreage (or 50 percent for some types of Bt cotton). But a 2009 study found that up to 25 percent of corn farmers were not complying with refuge requirements.[19]

Opponents of biotechnology point out that resistance to existing GM products does not harm biotech multinationals like Monsanto, which already are developing crops resistant to other, more toxic pesticides. It's no coincidence, say the critics, that the new products will be coming on the market just as the patents for Roundup Ready crops expire, in 2014. When the patents expire, other companies can produce seed with the same technology, and farmers can legally plant seed harvested from Roundup Ready plants.

"It's a chemical arms race going backwards," says Kimbrell of the Center for Food Safety. "Now we have to close our eyes and hope we do find this magic, new herbicide. I don't think that's very good policy."

Many biotech supporters are equally worried about resistance to Bt and Roundup. But they say the problem is not biotechnology itself but American-style industrial farming, which allows a single crop to be planted year after year over vast swathes of land, which accelerates resistance to pesticides.

"If people had been smarter — the farmers, the companies and the U.S. Department of Agriculture — they could have easily developed rotations and minimal-use programs to avoid resistance," says Raoul Adamchak, the organic farm coordinator at UC-Davis and co-author of *Tomorrow's Table: Organic Farming, Genetics and the Future of Food.* "Those issues come up with herbicides all the time. If you develop an integrated control strategy, you can put resistance off for many years, or possibly even indefinitely."

Biotech opponents also discount the environmental benefits of replacing more toxic herbicides and pesticides with the relatively safe Roundup and Bt.

"There are now Roundup-resistant weeds on millions of acres that are creating problems for farmers," says Jaffe, of the Center for Science in the Public Interest. "What does that mean? That just means you're going back to other forms of weed killers that are toxic. But we did get 20 years of using the less-toxic weed killer."

U.S Leads in Biotech Agriculture

More than 170 million acres of biotech crops are under cultivation in the United States, more than twice Brazil's acreage, which ranks second. Experts credit faster technological advances, more lenient regulations and expanding economic benefits for the U.S. lead.

Biotech Acreage by Country, 2011

Country	Acres (in millions)	Biotech crops
United States	170.5	Corn, soybean, cotton, canola, sugarbeet, alfalfa, papaya, squash
Brazil	74.9	Soybean, corn, cotton
Argentina	58.6	Soybean, corn, cotton
India	26.2	Cotton
Canada	25.7	Canola, corn, soybean, sugarbeet
China	9.6	Cotton, papaya, poplar, tomato, sweet pepper
Paraguay	6.9	Soybean
Pakistan	6.4	Cotton
South Africa	5.7	Corn, soybean, cotton
Uruguay	3.2	Soybean, corn

Source: Clive James, "Global Status of Commercialized Biotech/GM Crops: 2011," International Service for the Acquisition of Agri-Biotech Applications, 2011, p. 2, www.isaaa.org/purchasepublications/itemdescription.asp?ItemType=BRIEFS&Control=IB043-2011

AFP/Getty Images/Noah Seelam

A Greenpeace activist campaigns against genetically modified eggplant (brinjal) at a farmers market in Hyderabad, India, on Jan. 19, 2010. The potential commercialization of a GM variety of the popular vegetable has drawn support and criticism. Cotton is currently the only GM crop permitted in India.

The increased productivity provided by biotech crops has also slowed deforestation, say GM proponents. "The reduced environmental impact and abundance in food supply that is offered with genetically engineered seed help to preserve biodiversity," says Enright, of the Biotechnology Industry Organization. "Instead of chopping down the Amazon or other pools of diversity, let's see what we can do on the land that we have."[20]

Roundup Ready crops also reduce the need for plowing to clear fields of weeds before planting, which saves topsoil. Bill Olthoff, who farms 1,800 acres of corn and soybeans in Kankakee, Ill., says that since switching to Roundup Ready soybeans he makes three fewer plowing runs over his field per crop, which conserves topsoil and tractor fuel, and he uses less herbicide. Additionally, he says, by using Bt corn he no longer has to use a more toxic insecticide, which can disrupt human and animal neurological systems.

"There's less use of fuel, less man-hours and less pesticide," says Olthoff.[21]

Should GM foods be labeled?

GM opponents say consumers have a right to know what they're eating and feeding their children. "Labeling is obvious — there is a fundamental physical change in the

plants that's patented," says Kimbrell of the Center for Food Safety. "There are novel proteins in the plants, never seen before in food."

The Just Label It campaign, which supports California's referendum and organized the labeling petition to the FDA, argues that U.S. consumers are being effectively used as guinea pigs in testing GM foods. "The debate about the benefits and risks of GE crops may go on for a long time," says the group's website, JustLabelIt.org. "Meanwhile, an entire generation will have grown up consuming them. We should all have a choice about whether we want to participate in this grand experiment with our bodies and our environment."

A large majority of consumers agree, according to a poll of 1,000 people commissioned earlier this year by Just Label It. It found that 92 percent support mandatory labeling, a figure that changed only slightly after respondents heard arguments for and against labeling.

Cynthia LaPier, a mental health counselor in Massachusetts, feels she has a right to know whether her food contains genetically modified components. "It just makes me nervous when you take genetic matter from something else that wouldn't have been done in nature and put it into food," she told *The New York Times* earlier this year, having spent part of her morning furtively applying stickers reading "Warning May Contain GMOs" to cereal boxes at her local supermarket. [22]

Just Label It argues that sufficient testing has not yet been done on the technology. The University of Minnesota's Schurman argues that even if there is no specific scientific evidence that GM crops are more harmful than conventional varieties, there is a legitimate case for labeling them.

"I don't think scientific concerns are the only reason we should be concerned about the impact of technology," she says. "We should be able to make decisions about the kind of society we live in, and we can't make those decisions if we don't have information. It's a question of democracy."

Gurian-Sherman, of the Union of Concerned Scientists, says GM crops have helped to push farming more toward industrial agriculture, and consumers who favor more sustainable methods should be able to decide which kinds of foods they want to buy.

"Both Bt and herbicide tolerance work in simplified crop systems," says Gurian-Sherman. "If your aim is to

be more and more efficient, you need to make agriculture [simpler], with many, many acres of one crop that is harvested with one type of machinery and simple pest control. All of those things are bad for the environment in a number of different ways."

Biotechnology supporters say labels will mislead consumers into believing there is something harmful to human health about GM foods. That's been the case in Europe, where labeling combined with public suspicion of genetically engineered foods has kept products containing GM crops off grocery store shelves.

Gasser, the UC Davis researcher, likens the debate to that over climate change, in which one side has overwhelming research data on its side but opponents are able to cast doubt on those findings with spurious arguments because the public has little understanding of the complex science involved.

"Climate science is the perfect example, because the anti-biotech people are on the wrong side of the argument both environmentally and scientifically," Gasser says.

He argues that since scientific research over the past two decades has vindicated genetic engineering in plant breeding, opponents are really left only with a philosophical argument about the so-called mutagenic techniques used to manipulate plant genes. Moreover, he says that GM opponents are hypocritical to single out genetic engineering in food crops as "unnatural." There are numerous conventional plant breeding methods that differ radically from how plants reproduce in the wild, including self-pollinating two different plant lines for seven or more generations and then crossing them; and triggering mutations through gamma rays, irradiation and carcinogenic chemicals.

Thousands of products have been developed using mutagenic techniques alone, according to the U.N.'s Food and Agriculture Organization, including more than 800 varieties of rice and familiar fruits such as the Rio Red grapefruit and a variety of the McIntosh apple.[23] Proponents say that, as with GM crops, there is no evidence that crops developed with mutagenic techniques are inherently more harmful to people or the environment than other crops.

"The fact that you're arguing about the one and not the other means your argument is not about safety it's about this religious view you have about biotech," says

Gasser. "It's only the people who don't understand it that are scared of it. Unfortunately that's most everyone."

Opponents of labeling also argue that it is unfair to conflate arguments against the environmental harm caused by industrial agriculture with a lab technique for creating better seeds — since farming is damaging to the environment no matter what kind of seeds are used. "If everyone's goal is to have a more sustainable agriculture, to reduce pesticide use and to reduce [fertilizer] run-off, then this labeling campaign doesn't make any improvements," says Adamchak, the UC-Davis organic farmer. "I'd much rather see people putting lots of energy into promoting sustainable agriculture."

BACKGROUND

'Green Revolution'

Humans began collecting seeds even before they settled in farming villages millennia ago in the Near East.

Ancient governments often played a major role in introducing new plants to civilizations. An inscription from Mesopotamia tells of the ruler Sargon journeying to Anatolia to collect figs, vines and roses to introduce to his country in the 24th century B.C. In 1495 B.C., Egypt's Queen Hatshepsut sent a team to what is now Ethiopia and Somalia to find the fragrant tree that produces frankincense.[24]

For centuries farmers have selected seeds and cross-bred plants to produce crops that had little in common with wild species. Yet it was not until 1856 that Gregor Johann Mendel, an Augustinian monk in Austria, began his famous study of garden peas that led to the identification of the factors that control heredity. Mendel's work ushered in the study of genetics.

Among other benefits, it laid the groundwork for the birth of modern agriculture in the early 20th century. In 1905 British researcher Roland Biffen showed that a type of wheat resistant to rust fungus could pass the trait on to future generations. Since then dozens of crops, from potatoes to parsnips, have been bred to resist disease and insects.[25]

Government investments in breeding and agricultural technologies helped lead to rapid productivity increases in the 20th century. For example, yields of English wheat took a thousand years to increase from 0.5 to 2 metric tons per hectare,* but jumped from 2 to 6 metric tons in just 40 years during the period.[26]

C H R O N O L O G Y

1950s-1960s *Scientists identify genes and begin investigating the role of DNA in plant development.*

1953 American biochemist James Watson and British biophysicist Francis Crick describe the structure of DNA, setting the stage for mapping the genetic code.

1967 Lenape potato, a new variety bred for making potato chips is withdrawn from experimental production after high levels of toxins are found.

1970s-1980s *Scientists begin experimenting with genetic transformation of plants and animals.*

1973 Scientists create first genetically engineered organism.

1983 Researchers transfer new DNA into plants, leading to the creation of genetically modified crops.

1989 Calgene Inc. receives U.S. patent for gene sequence in GM Flavr Savr tomato.

1990s *Biotech foods are marketed to the public despite environmental and health concerns.*

1992 FDA decides not to require labeling of most GM foods, sparking mistrust of the technology.

1993 FDA allows cows to be injected with bovine growth hormone (rBGH) made from genetically modified bacteria, setting off consumer protests.

1994 FDA approves Flavr Savr tomato, first GM food approved for sale to consumers.

1996 Monsanto introduces Roundup Ready soybeans, first of several popular herbicide-tolerant or insecticide-producing crops.

1998 European Union (EU) halts approvals of new GM crops in what is termed an "unofficial moratorium."

2000s *Genetically engineered foods face continued criticism despite growing scientific consensus that they do not pose greater safety risks than conventional crops.*

2000 Bowing to international demands, U.S. officials agree to label GM commodities for export. . . . Weeds resistant to Roundup discovered in Delaware. . . . Friends of the Earth, a major environmental group, reports that genes from StarLink corn, a GM crop approved only for animal consumption, have been discovered in taco shells. The discovery prompts recalls of corn products and lawsuits, but researchers are unable to document any human health effects. . . . Centers for Disease Control study concludes StarLink did not cause allergic reactions claimed by 28 people.

2002 National Center for Food and Agricultural Policy finds that GM crops in the United States produced four billion pounds of additional food and fiber on the same acreage, improved farm income by $1.5 billion and reduced pesticide use by 46 million pounds. . . . Monsanto announces it will delay introduction of GM wheat amid concerns from farmers that it will harm exports.

2003 Bollworms resistant to the Bt toxin, an insecticide produced by GM cotton, discovered in the South.

2004 Under U.S. pressure, EU drops de facto ban on GM crops but institutes mandatory labeling; many European stores won't stock GM foods because of consumer fears.

2008 Monsanto sells unit that produces rBGH, as major grocers including Walmart, Publix and Kroger decline to sell milk from cows treated with the product.

2010 After approving the sale of GM eggplant, India's environment minister declares a moratorium on the product because of public outcry.

2011 GM crops are grown on 395 million acres of farmland globally, though more than 90 percent is in just three crops: soybeans, corn and cotton.

2012 Anti-GMO groups file petitions containing more than 1 million signatures demanding that the FDA require GM foods be labeled. . . . Californian vote scheduled for Nov. 6 on ballot initiative requiring labeling for GM foods.

Beginning in the 1960s, higher yielding plant varieties, combined with increased use of fertilizer, pesticides and irrigation, led to a global boom in agricultural production — especially in the developing world — known as the "Green Revolution."

In the early 1970s scientists first learned how to replicate DNA in the lab and then to introduce foreign genetic material into living organisms, such as bacteria. Initially, concern that transferring genes among organisms could create dangerous microbes led scientists to establish a National Institutes of Health committee to oversee the approval of biotech research. It soon became evident, however, that genetic engineering tended to weaken bacteria rather than strengthen them. The NIH ended restrictions on genetic research in the 1980s, setting the stage for the commercialization of numerous genetically engineered drugs, such as synthetic insulin for diabetics.

In 1992 the commercialization of genetically modified foods was accelerated when limits were put on FDA oversight of GM foods. The new policy meant the agency would give GM crops no more scrutiny than it gave crops produced through conventional breeding.

The FDA's resulting program of "voluntary" consultation set off a controversy that endures today. Activist and economist Jeremy Rifkin, founder and president of the Foundation On Economic Trends, launched the Pure Food Movement, arguing that biotech crops were likely to be harmful to human health and destroy the natural environment.[27] The outcry led biotech companies to universally take part in the voluntary process for reviewing new crops, in addition to mandatory regulation by the Department of Agriculture and in some cases the EPA. Many groups argued that the tests required by federal regulators were insufficient and too reliant on studies supplied by the biotech industry.

Monsanto, a large, St. Louis-based chemical manufacturer, was among the first companies to capitalize on biotechnology for commercial farming. Its scientists inserted cow DNA into bacteria that then worked like millions of tiny factories to produce synthetic bovine growth hormone, known as rBGH or rBST. The hormone was then administered to cows to induce greater milk production. In 1993, the FDA approved the hormone for dairy production after the American Medical Association, National Institutes of Health and American

Academy of Pediatrics concluded milk from cows treated with the product was no different from other milk.[28]

Meanwhile, California-based Calgene Inc. developed a tomato that contained an extra bit of tomato DNA that had been altered in the lab. This new gene had been engineered to block production of an enzyme that makes tomatoes grow mushy and rot. Calgene's new Flavr Savr tomato was approved by federal regulators in 1994 and became the first genetically engineered food to be commercialized in the United States.[29]

But Flavr Savr turned out to be a failure. Activists wielding images of a tomato grafted onto a fish head, a reference to a different experimental tomato developed by another company that contained a fish gene for cold resistance, portrayed the Calgene product as Frankenfood. The company's bigger problem was that the Flavr Savr was more susceptible than other varieties to pests in the main tomato-growing states of Florida and California, and it could still bruise and become unappealing even without becoming mushy.[30] What's more, many consumers concluded it didn't taste good enough to justify the higher price. By 1997 Flavr Savr was off the market.

rBGH was more successful commercially, though it too faced strong resistance. By 1999, both Canada and the European Union had banned the hormone, citing public opposition to use of hormones on dairy cows and gaps in research.

In the United States, more than a fifth of dairy cows were being injected with the synthetic hormone biweekly by 2002, with milk production rising by about one gallon per day in lactating cows.[31] But advocacy groups opposed the hormone, pointing to studies showing it increased bovine udder infections and led to higher usage of veterinary antibiotics, which potentially could lead to human resistance to the drugs. Other research, including some sponsored by hormone producers, disputed the findings.[32]

Resistance to rBGH helped propel the organic dairy industry's rapid growth. The number of certified organic dairy cows rose to 249,766 in 2008 from zero in 1995, according to the USDA.[33] Companies such as Unilever's Ben & Jerry's Ice Cream and Oakhurst Dairy in Maine successfully marketed their products as rGBH-free.

Meanwhile, rGBH use declined from 22 percent of U.S. dairy cows in 2002 to 17 percent in 2007, and major retailers such as Walmart, Kroger and Publix agreed

Is Tampering With DNA Inherently Wrong?

Ethicists and religious scholars have differing opinions.

Many people recoil instinctively from the idea of taking genes from one plant or animal and inserting them into another — especially if the process inserts an animal gene into a plant's DNA, for instance. Some view the creation of such new part-plant, part-animal organisms as "playing God" or a violation of the natural order.

Several of these objections were first voiced by Jeremy Rifkin, a leading critic of genetic engineering, as early as 1977 when he published a book entitled *Who Should Play God? The Artificial Creation of Life and What it Means for the Human Race*. Rifkin expanded on concerns voiced in that book with later writings on the implications of cloning animals and the creation of plant and animal chimeras, or organisms with genes from both kingdoms.

"The globalization of commerce and trade makes possible the wholesale reseeding of the Earth's biosphere with a laboratory-conceived second Genesis, an artificially produced bioindustrial nature designed to replace nature's own evolutionary scheme," Rifkin wrote.[1] "A global life-science industry is already beginning to wield unprecedented power over the vast biological resources of the planet. Life-science fields ranging from agriculture to medicine are being consolidated under the umbrella of giant 'life' companies in the emerging biotech marketplace."

Ethics research into agricultural biotechnology focuses on two questions: whether the benefits of GM crops outweigh the drawbacks, and whether genetic engineering is inherently wrong. The tangible benefits and drawbacks of genetic engineering are often discussed in the media but the latter question is largely overlooked.

While Rifkin approaches the question from the secular perspective of genetic engineering violating the dignity of nature, theologians have also argued against genetic engineering from a religious perspective. Paul Ramsey, a prominent Christian ethicist who taught at Princeton University in the 1970s and '80s, was a leading advocate of the idea that genetic engineering was inherently unethical and that reducing people and other beings to a collection of genetic traits was a flawed concept. He also argued that since human beings are inherently fallible, they are poor custodians of the building blocks of life.

"We should not play God before we have learned to be men, and as we learn to be men we will not want to play God," Ramsey wrote.[2]

The technology also has implications for religious and dietary traditions established long before the advent of molecular biology. For instance, some vegetarians have questioned whether they can eat a vegetable containing one or more genes taken from an animal.

"The resulting vegetable is no longer a pure vegetable, but instead a chimera with properties taken from the original plant, plus some additional characteristics from an animal," according to Marcus Williamson, a London-based vegetarian who writes for the website www.gmfoodnews .com.[3]

Likewise, the world's 1 billion Hindus — many of whom are vegetarians and all of whom revere cows as sacred — might be concerned about eating a plant containing bovine genes, just as a Jew or Muslim might be concerned about eating a GM food containing pork genes.

---

to stop selling milk made from rBGH-treated cows in their private-label dairy products. With backlash against the hormone growing, Monsanto sold its rBGH division in 2008 to Eli Lilly & Co.[34]

The Roaring 1990s

More significant than the Flavr Savr or rBGH was Monsanto's introduction in 1995 and '96 of genetically engineered soybeans, corn and cotton that were either resistant to Roundup or contained Bt insecticide.

Many farmers rapidly switched to the new crops. In 1996 genetically engineered crops were grown in six countries on 4.2 million acres. By 2000 they were being grown on 109.2 million acres in 13 countries, though 68 percent of that acreage was in the United States, according to the Council for Biotechnology Information, an industry group.

While some food safety and environmental groups in the United States resisted the rapid growth of genetically modified foods, it set off a firestorm of protest in Europe. The reaction was due in part to bad luck: The first

Such alterations are potentially within the technology's reach: The use of jellyfish genes to create plant and animal organisms that "glow" under UV light has been used as a method of "marking" the transference of other genetic traits by researchers.[4]

According to a review of the issue, as of 2008 there was no consensus about biotechnology within the world's three main monotheistic faiths — Islam, Judaism and Christianity — on the ethical and moral issues surrounding GM foods.[5]

Other ethicists see arguments questioning the inherent immorality of genetic engineering as logically flawed. From a religious perspective, those who argue that genetic engineering is a violation of God's creation must explain why genetic engineering is not also an expression of God's will, since God gave humans "free will," including the ability to create technology, according to David Koepsell, a philosophy professor at Delft University of Technology in the Netherlands.[6]

Those who would argue that genetic engineering is a misuse of free will are plagued by a lack of sacred writings supporting that conclusion, says Koepsell. The Bible, for example, says nothing about recombinant DNA.

They must also explain why altering DNA through genetic engineering is bad, but other forms of altering DNA through other techniques are acceptable, given that it is arguably distinct only as a method. "The speed and predictability of the changes brought about by genetic engineering do surpass the speed and predictability of changes accomplished by selective breeding techniques, but that seems a poor argument for saying the former is contrary to God's will, while the latter is acceptable," Koepsell writes. "Is it God's will that modifying nature is acceptable, but only provided we proceed slowly and haphazardly?"

Likewise Koepsell contends that those who argue against genetic engineering from a secular perspective must explain why other forms of genetic change, such as evolution, are not affronts to the "natural" order of things. They also must show that there is an inherent dignity to the current genetic makeup of any given species and why that genetic makeup should only be changed by some forms of genetic alteration and not others.

Still, Koepsell and some other advocates of the technology allow that its effects on our world over the long term are difficult to predict and could yet prove harmful in unexpected ways. In that respect biotechnology is hardly unique: few in the 19th century would have foreseen that the invention of the internal combustion engine would contribute to rising global temperatures, melting polar ice caps and disappearing species 100 years later.

— Jason McLure

[1] Jeremy Rifkin, *The Biotech Century: Harnessing the Gene and Remaking the World* (1998), excerpted by *The New York Times*, www.nytimes.com/books/first/r/rifkin-biotech.html.

[2] Paul Ramsey, *Fabricated Man: The Ethics of Genetic Control* (1970), p. 151.

[3] Marcus Williamson, "Genetically Modified Food — Not Suitable for Vegetarians," Connectotel.com, undated, www.connectotel.com/gmfood/gm260401.txt.

[4] "Glowing Proteins — A Guiding Star for Biochemistry," The Royal Swedish Academy of Sciences, The Nobel Prize in Chemistry 2008, Oct. 8, 2008, www.nobelprize.org/nobel_prizes/chemistry/laureates/2008/press.html.

[5] Emmanuel Omobowale, Peter Singer and Abdallah Daar, "The Three Monotheistic Religions and GM Food Technology: An Overview of Perspectives," BMC International Health and Human Rights, 2009, www.biomedcentral.com/1472-698X/9/18.

[6] David Koepsell, "The Ethics of Genetic Engineering," Center for Inquiry, Aug. 28, 2007.

shipments of genetically modified soybeans from the United States to the U.K. coincided with a major outbreak of mad cow disease in Britain. The outbreak undermined the credibility of British food-safety officials, who had previously assured Britons that they could not get bovine disease from eating infected beef.[35]

The environmental organization Greenpeace and other groups opposed to GM crops found the European public receptive to arguments that the technology had not been adequately tested and was likely to be harmful in ways

not yet understood. "Mad cow disease was immediately used by the anti-biotech groups," says Jaffe, at the Center for Science in the Public Interest. "That was a big disadvantage, to the detriment of biotech. They were able to raise this specter of an unknown that could hurt you."

Emblematic of Europeans' skeptical attitudes was the response to a genetically modified tomato created by Zeneca, a British multinational company. Developed for lower water content to make it more suitable for tomato paste, it was sold in the U.K. from 1996 to 1999. The tomatoes cost 20 percent less than conventional ones used for tomato paste and labeled as genetically engineered. Initially they sold well, but demand collapsed following the airing of a documentary in which a Hungarian researcher said he had found that genetically modified potatoes led to biological changes in rats — research that has since been called into question.[36]

Surveys also indicated that the Europeans were skeptical of Monsanto, the company that led the charge to bring GM crops to Europe. To some, the company was an agent of American corporate imperialism. Many Europeans also perceived the technology as a threat to small farmers, who hold disproportionate political influence.

"In Europe they made a huge misstep by saying, 'Look, we're going to give this to you and you're going to accept it because America makes so much food and if you don't want it you're going to have to pay more for your food,' " says Klee, the former Monsanto researcher.

Resistance may also have reflected European values about the role of farms and nature, which Monsanto did little to address. In Europe, which lacks large forested areas, nature is more closely associated with agricultural land.[37]

"There was a bit of myopia in the industry," says the University of Minnesota's Schurman. "On Monsanto's part, they were so busy trying to get to the patent office that they didn't realize there were people organizing around environmental implications."

Rising resistance to GM crops in Europe led to adoption of the Cartagena Protocol in 2000, a U.N. treaty that updated a 1992 accord on biosafety to permit the use of the so-called precautionary principle in the regulation of biotech crops. That principle holds that when a technology has the potential to cause widespread harm to people or the environment, policymakers should delay approving it until it has been definitively proven safe.

In the wake of the accord, the United Nations Environmental Program began a $60 million training program for governments in the developing world on assessing the risks of biotechnology. Largely funded by European nations skeptical of the technology, the program promoted use of the precautionary principle. It also called for each nation to set up its own system of field trials of GM crops; rules on marketing, transport, packaging, labeling and disposal; and research on the crops' effects on traditional farming practices and implications for cultural and religious interests.[38]

StarLink Recall

A defining moment for GM crops came in 2000, when Taco Bell taco shells were found to contain traces of a genetically engineered corn variety not approved for human consumption, prompting recall of the shells and other consumer products.[39]

Developed by the French biotech company Aventis, the corn variety — known as StarLink — had been approved for animal consumption. But pollen from the corn had drifted into fields with other types of corn. Because one of the proteins in Starlink had not been in the human diet before, it was seen as a possible allergen.

"I view it as a very poignant cautionary tale that our regulatory system is not up to the task of preventing potential problems with genetically engineered food," Joseph Mendelson III, then the legal director of the Center for Food Safety, told *The New York Times*.[40]

Fallout from the controversy led to a temporary halt in U.S. corn exports, a recall of numerous corn products and lawsuits by dozens of consumers — some of whom reported having allergic reactions. However, medical studies have since been unable to document any harms from the protein.[41]

Similarly, in 2006 low levels of genetic material from a herbicide-resistant GM rice known as LibertyLink, which was not approved for human consumption, appeared in other U.S. rice. That led to a plunge in rice prices and temporary bans on imports of U.S. rice by Japan and the EU. The following year the Department of Agriculture concluded that LibertyLink posed no identifiable concerns for human health and the environment and approved it for human consumption, but farmers suffered extensive economic damage.[42] In 2011, Bayer CropScience, which had developed the rice, settled a class action suit with farmers for $750 million.[43]

Two other factors helped keep biotech agriculture in the spotlight. Monsanto, Dupont and Novartis — three of the biggest developers of biotech crops — all began buying up regional seed companies, greatly increasing their ability to spread the technology but also expanding their clout in the market. Their growing dominance raised concerns that a handful of large businesses would gain too much control over global agriculture.

Ethics and Genetically Modified Animals

Is there a difference between GM plants and animals?

In the Gulf of Mexico, a vast oxygen-depleted dead zone as large as New Jersey forms annually due to algae blooms caused by phosphorus and nitrogen run-off from farms in the Midwest. Similar blooms occur in the Great Lakes, killing fish and spoiling scenery. Genetic engineering could help with the problem, as Monsanto, DuPont and BASF are developing corn varieties that are more efficient at utilizing nitrogen fertilizers. A more provocative product is the Enviropig, a genetically modified Yorkshire pig developed in Canada that digests phosphorus more effectively and excretes less polluting nutrients.

The development of genetically modified animals presents just one of a myriad number of ethical problems that would have been hard to fathom even 50 years ago. From corporations patenting genetic sequences to inserting animal genes into plants, biotechnology has stretched into areas that are the province of dystopic novels.

Evaluating the ethics of creations such as the Enviropig involves weighing environmental benefits — such as a reduction in phosphorus in waterways — against concerns over manipulating the genes of a large mammal that is closely related to humans.

The Biotechnology Industry Organization argues that there is no ethical difference between genetically modified animals and genetically modified plants and that government regulators are wrong to delay approval of the first GM animal. "The market should determine whether there is a market for genetically modified animals," says Cathleen Enright, vice president for food and agriculture at the group.

Yet most societies do treat animals, especially large mammals such as pigs, as different moral beings than plants. No jurisdictions bar cruelty to soybeans. But as genetic engineering pushes further into human health care, it is possible that genetic modification of animals will seem less strange. Insulin produced by genetically engineered organisms has been used for diabetes patients since the early 1980s. Genetic engineering is expanding rapidly in health care, and people will likely benefit from therapeutic cloning of skin cells, heart tissue and even bones.[1]

University of Guelph

Genetically modified animals such as the Enviropig, a Yorkshire developed in Canada that excretes less polluting nutrients, raise perplexing scientific and ethical issues.

U.S. consumers are unlikely to be eating genetically modified animal products anytime soon. The Enviropig project was recently terminated due to a lack of commercial interest, and a salmon genetically engineered to grow nearly twice as fast as existing breeds is still awaiting approval nearly two years after the FDA reached a preliminary finding that it is safe for people and the environment. Yet some fear that continued resistance will cause the United States to fall behind other countries. Researchers in China are already studying transgenic sheep that produce more wool, cows resistant to foot-and-mouth disease and pigs that contain healthy omega-3 fatty acids in their meat.[2]

— Jason McLure

[1] "The Value of Therapeutic Cloning," Biotechnology Industry Organization, May 25, 2010, www.bio.org/articles/value-therapeutic-cloning-patients.

[2] Andrew Pollack, "An Entrepreneur Bankrolls a Genetically-Modified Salmon," *The New York Times*, May 21, 2012, www.nytimes.com/2012/05/22/business/kakha-bendukidze-holds-fate-of-gene-engineered-salmon.html?pagewanted=all.

Monsanto

Monsanto soybean seeds are genetically modified to resist disease and provide more yield per bushel. In the mid-1990s, the St. Louis agribusiness giant introduced GM soybeans, corn and cotton that were either resistant to Roundup or contained Bt insecticide. Environmental groups say the Department of Agriculture does not adequately examine the potential impacts of introducing GM farming methods on millions of acres, such as weed and insect resistance to Roundup and Bt.

Also controversial has been a decision by Monsanto to sue its own customers over the use of seeds gathered and saved from crops that originally were sown with the company's patented GM seeks. Saving and using seeds from subsequent crops violates contracts that farmers sign with the company.

To gather evidence against the farmers, Monsanto sent "seed police" to gather samples from fields that it suspected illegally contained plants with its patented genetic sequence. Since 1997, Monsanto says it has filed suit against 145 U.S. farmers — a relatively small number considering the 250,000 American farmers who buy the company's seed each year.[44] Monsanto sees itself as defending a technology it spent tens of millions of dollars to develop.

A spokesman for Monsanto declined to be interviewed for this article. However, on its website the company says it sues "to ensure a level playing field for the vast majority of honest farmers who abide by their agreements, and to discourage using technology illegally to gain an unfair advantage."

But critics see a corporate Goliath bullying farmers.

Gary Rinehart, a Missouri farmer suspected by Monsanto of violating a seed contract, said their message was: "Monsanto is big. You can't win. We will get you. You will pay."[45]

CURRENT SITUATION

In the Pipeline

With patents for common GM seeds, such as Roundup Ready crops, expiring, biotechnology companies are focusing on GM's next generation. Monsanto has recently gained regulatory approval for an early variety of drought-resistant corn, and both it and Syngenta are about five to seven years from commercializing additional drought-resistant strains, which could potentially aid farmers in the developing world and help mitigate the effects of increasingly frequent droughts linked to climate change.

Dupont's Pioneer Hi-Bred division and Monsanto also anticipate marketing GM soybean varieties rich in heart-healthy oils such as omega-3 fatty acids. Researchers also are in the advanced stage of developing new forms of Bt corn seed that provide non-Bt refuges for insects so as to slow the development of resistance. Virus-resistant strains of potatoes and beans are also less than a decade away, according to the industry's trade association.[46]

Other products could potentially be more environmentally damaging than today's GM crops, analysts say. These include corn and soybean varieties being developed by Dow AgroSciences that would be resistant to the herbicide 2,4-D. The new crops are being developed to provide farmers an alternative herbicide-resistant crop to battle Roundup-resistant weeds.

Yet 2,4-D is categorized as "moderately hazardous" by the World Health Organization, two steps more toxic than Roundup, which is considered "unlikely to present acute hazard" to people. Opponents of biotech note that the chemical was an ingredient in Agent Orange, a controversial defoliant used by the U.S. military during the

AT ISSUE

Should foods containing GM ingredients be labeled?

YES
Gary Hirshberg
Chairman and founding partner, Just Label It; Chairman and Co-Founder, Stonyfield Farm

Written for *CQ Global Researcher*, August 2012

Unlike more than 40 other countries — including all of Europe, Japan and China — the United States has no laws requiring labeling of genetically engineered (GE) foods. Yet most polls show that the vast majority (90 percent) of Americans believe GE foods should be labeled. For 20 years, however, we've been denied that right.

Reasons for wanting to know what's in our food vary, but the belief that it's our right unifies us. Without labeling, we can't make informed choices about our food. The Just Label It (JLI) campaign, a national coalition of more than 500 diverse organizations, was created to advocate for GE foods labeling.

Americans want labeling for many reasons, including health, safety, environmental and religious considerations, as well as the belief that the right to know is a core American value.

The Federal Food, Drug, and Cosmetic Act requires the Food and Drug Administration to prevent consumer deception by clarifying that a food label is misleading if it omits significant "material" information. In 1992 an FDA policy statement defined "material" as the ability to be sensed by taste, smell or other senses. The FDA determined that GE foods were "substantially equivalent" to conventional foods, so no labeling was required.

Twenty years later, this outdated policy remains in effect. This means a GE salmon designed to continuously produce hormones is not materially different from a non-GE salmon because it does not taste, smell or feel different, according to the FDA.

Mounting demand for the right to make informed decisions is responsible for the unprecedented success of Just Label It. In only 180 days, JLI generated more than 1.2 million comments on the FDA's labeling petition — the most comments on a food petition in the agency's history.

Despite the overwhelming support for GE foods labeling, our elected officials in the greatest democracy on earth have chosen to deny this right for the very people they represent. People on all sides of the political spectrum are voicing concern and distrust with how government and companies are making decisions.

We're living in a new era of transparency, and government can no longer justify keeping us in the dark. GE foods must be labeled so consumers can have the information they need to make informed decisions about the foods they eat and feed their families.

NO
Philip Nelson
President, Illinois Farm Bureau

Written for *CQ Global Researcher*, August 2012

Recently, there's been a lot of talk about the need to label foods that contain genetically modified organisms, or GMOs, as activist groups negatively label them. But why?

After all, the Food and Drug Administration (FDA) provides science-based labeling guidelines for all food and drugs produced and sold in the United States.

That's why the Illinois Farm Bureau supports FDA's guidelines. In particular, we support the fact that no special labeling is required unless a food is significantly different than its traditional counterpart or where a specific component is altered.

We also support FDA's use of nutritional information on labels, particularly where health effects of an ingredient are medically proven, including, for example, information on salt, trans fat and caffeine content and whether a food is calcium-enriched. Moreover, we support voluntary use of special labeling for specific characteristics of a food product or when certain ingredients are used to preserve the characteristics of a product throughout production and distribution, as they are in USDA-certified organic foods and even in some non-GMO foods.

The key is that we support voluntary labeling.

FDA guidelines do not require labeling for products of biotechnology — so-called GMOs. One reason is that biotechnology is not a product — it is a process that speeds up plant breeding. A second is that biotech products are not significantly different from conventional counterparts, nor are they allergens, which do require labeling. Biotech crops have been researched, grown and consumed for nearly 30 years. In that time, not a single allergy, sickness or reaction has occurred. What's more, thousands of scientists have attested to their safety.

The government determines how best to provide labels that protect consumers while also informing them. That is why details on labels are science-based and why most companies have additional information on their websites or information hotlines.

Finally, the organic industry does not include biotech production methods in its certification. Therefore, if people do not want to eat anything that includes GMO foods, they can choose organic products.

To start labeling for reasons other than science is a slippery slope that will result in less useful information, greater confusion and higher prices. Moreover, mandatory labeling of GM products will reduce organic market share and potentially decimate a market that farmers and the food industry alike worked to build.

Vietnam War that caused significant health problems — including cancer and birth defects — among Vietnamese villagers and U.S. soldiers exposed during the war. The USDA recently received 365,000 public comments opposing the approval of 2,4-D-resistant crops.[47]

Enright, of the Biotechnology Industry Organization, argues that such products will extend the life of Roundup by ridding fields of Roundup-resistant weeds with an herbicide sold under a variety of brand names such as Ortho's Weed B Gon Max. "Now what we're hearing is that farmers are going to be using Agent Orange. That's not true," says Enright. "Is 2,4-D new to consumers? No, they put it on their lawns every day."

Enright said she did not have enough information about 2,4-D to determine whether it would be worse for the environment if sprayed on the same scale as Roundup.

Others, however, are concerned about the prospect of a dramatic increase in 2,4-D spraying. "2,4-D is a much more toxic material," says Adamchak, the UC-Davis organic farm coordinator, who supports biotech research. "If the next generation is 2,4-D resistant, that's not making progress; that's going backwards."

Labeling Battle

The frontlines of the current debate are now in California, where the November ballot measure would require foods containing biotech crops to be labeled as "Partially Produced with Genetic Engineering," or "May Be Partially Produced with Genetic Engineering." Should it pass, the measure could have a broad impact nationwide if some food processors choose to stop using GM ingredients in order to avoid the stigma of a label in America's most populous state.

Supporters of the measure have momentum. It took them just 10 weeks to gather 971,126 signatures to put the question before voters.

The supporters argue labeling will put California in line with other developed nations. "More than 40 other countries — including all of Europe, Japan and even China — already label genetically engineered food," said Grant Lundberg, CEO of Lundberg Family Farms, a large, organic rice grower and processor. "Californians deserve to be able to make informed choices too."[48]

Consumers Union, publisher of *Consumer Reports* magazine, also supports labeling, arguing that there is uncertainty about the molecular characterization of some

GM crops and researchers' ability to detect potential allergens. The issue is one of consumers' ability to make choices about their products and protect themselves from potential harms, the group says.

"If foods are not labeled, it would be very difficult to even identify an unexpected health effect resulting from a [GM] food," Michael Hansen, a researcher with the group, wrote to the American Medical Association (AMA) this year.[49]

The California ballot measure includes several assertions that are misleading or at odds with peer-reviewed scientific research. "Government scientists have stated that the artificial insertion of DNA into plants, a technique unique to genetic engineering, can cause a variety of significant problems with plant foods," the ballot measure reads. "Such genetic engineering can increase the levels of known toxicants in foods and introduce new toxicants and health concerns."

It also states that the FDA "does not require safety studies of such food" and argues that some consumers — such as vegetarians, Muslims, Jews and Hindus —"can unknowingly violate their own dietary and religious restrictions" by eating genetically modified foods that might be created using animal genes.

Opponents of the measure point out that it doesn't explain that the FDA, World Health Organization, numerous national science academies and other prestigious research organizations have determined that GM crops aren't inherently less safe than other foods, which also aren't required to go through safety studies — nor does it mention that every product currently on the market has gone through FDA's voluntary regulatory process or that crops also are required to be approved by the USDA and in some cases the EPA. They also question concerns about violating religious dietary restrictions, given that no products on the market are made using genetic material from animals, nor have major Christian, Jewish or Muslim leaders raised significant opposition to the technology.[50]

In June the AMA opposed labeling and called for the FDA to strengthen pre-market safety testing for new GM products. "There is no scientific justification for special labeling of bioengineered foods, as a class, and voluntary labeling is without value unless it is accompanied by focused consumer education," the group said.[51]

The labeling referendum is likely to come down to a funding battle. Monsanto and other multinationals, for instance, spent $5.5 million campaigning against a similar measure in Oregon in 2002. Food processors and biotech giants have already dwarfed that figure, raising $25 million through Aug. 15, including seven-figure contributions from Monsanto, DuPont, PepsiCo., BASF Plant Science and Conagra Foods. This money is being largely spent on advertisements calling the labeling proposal a costly and needless burden on food companies.

Despite being outspent, labeling proponents include some heavy hitters. Organic food sales in the United States topped $31.5 billion in 2011,[52] nearly three times Monsanto's $11.8 billion in global biotech sales in 2011.[53] The board of directors of Just Label It, which is spearheading the California effort, includes representatives of Stonyfield Farms, an organic yogurt company that is majority-owned by Groupe Danon, the world's largest dairy company; Organic Valley, the largest U.S. organic dairy co-op with $715 million in sales; and the Organic Trade Association, a coalition of 6,500 organic businesses.

The growing political clout of the organic industry rankles conventional farmers like Olthoff, who say labeling unfairly demonizes GM crops. "I believe in testing; I want everything to be right, but I don't want people to badmouth biotech just to make money," he says.

Proponents have crafted the California measure more narrowly than Oregon's. The California initiative would allow several exemptions, including:

- restaurants;
- meat from animals fed GM crops;
- milk from cows injected with rBGH;
- food unintentionally contaminated with GM material;
- alcoholic beverages (such as wine made with genetically modified yeast); and
- cheeses and other foods made using genetically engineered enzymes.

"It's cleverly crafted to exempt those interests in California that could most readily influence consumers to reject the initiative," says Enright, of the biotech industry trade group.

The effectiveness of the FDA labeling petition, meanwhile, seems uncertain. Although organizers say more than a million people have sent comments and signed petitions to the agency, the FDA says it has only received

394 official comments. Even if thousands of people sign a form letter or a petition, the agency explains, their signatures are only counted as one person or "comment."

After the March deadline to respond to the petition passed, the agency said it needed more time to consider its response.

OUTLOOK
Conflict Ahead?

Some opponents of biotechnology foresee a difficult future for the seed-development technique.

Duesing, of the Northeast Organic Farming Association, predicts growing conflict between organic farmers and the biotech industry, particularly as GM alfalfa and sweet corn are grown in the Northeast, where small farms are often clustered closely together. Should GM varieties pollinate with nearby organic fields, organic farmers could lose their organic certification — and thus their price premium.

Duesing expects such situations to trigger an even stronger backlash against biotech companies, benefitting small farmers. "They've got their vision for the food system," he says. "They want control, and they don't want any other messy thing. Once we move away from Monsanto's technologies, people will be breeding for local conditions."

The Center for Food Safety's Kimbrell foresees greater environmental damage from GM crops and the expanded use of older and more toxic herbicides to fight Roundup-resistant weeds.

"I think the past is the future," he says. "You can't base good agriculture on bad science. That doesn't mean the corporations . . . won't keep pushing it."

Others predict that biotechnology will be able to achieve only modest gains in the near future as researchers struggle with the scientific challenges of producing higher-yielding and more drought-resistant crops. "We think breeding will considerably outpace genetic engineering for five to 10 years," says Gurian-Sherman, of the Union of Concerned Scientists. "For the foreseeable future I see genetic engineering being useful at the margins for society."

Some grain farmers disagree. "As far as we've come, I think we'll go further again, we'll double it," says Olthoff, the Illinois corn and soybean farmer. "I know Monsanto is working on drought-tolerant corn, which will be a boon for us and a boon for Africa."

Klee, the University of Florida molecular biologist, predicts research into fruit and vegetable crops likely will remain stymied for the foreseeable future by consumer resistance — even as crops that are components of processed foods are more widely adopted. "When someone picks up a GM fruit or vegetable and someone points out to them that this is a genetically modified food, there is a different attitude," says Klee.

The only exception is when specialty crops face crises, as when ringspot virus cut production by more than half in Hawaii's papaya industry, says Klee.

"In the late 1980s [the virus] took over everybody, and we were chopping down trees," says Ken Kamiya, a director of the Hawaii Papaya Industry Association. That led to the development of the Rainbow papaya, bred to be virus resistant. "Without GMOs we basically wouldn't have a papaya industry," he says.

The fact that public sentiment, spurred by advocacy groups and the rapidly growing organic sector, may be strong enough to pass a GM labeling law in California has the industry rethinking its public relations approach.

"They have a problem with industrial agriculture or with processed food," says Enright, of the industry trade group. "So to argue against either one of those they criticize biotech, because it's an easy target." The growth of social media has helped fuel anti-GM sentiment, she adds. "What we're all reconsidering right now is how do we talk about genetically engineered food. One of the results of all these calls for mandatory labeling has been to make us think about how we want our food products to be perceived."

Golden Rice may be the product that changes the dynamics of the debate, should it end up saving the lives, or sight, of hundreds of thousands of Vitamin A-deficient malnourished children each year. The Philippines now appears likely to approve the product for its first commercial planting in 2013, and China, Vietnam and Bangladesh may eventually approve it.

The Golden Rice Project's Dubock says researchers in the future will be able to create grain varieties that include nutrients such as folic acid. Deficiencies of the B-complex vitamins in pregnant women can lead to birth defects.

"It's important for a project like Golden Rice to be successful," says Dubock. "Twenty years from now, people will look back on it and say, 'What was all the fuss about?'"

NOTES

1. Elizabeth Weise, "Fight over genetically engineered crops on Calif. ballot," *USA Today*, June 12, 2012, www.usatoday.com/news/health/story/2012-06-12/genetically-engineered-food-california/55558352/1.

2. "20 questions on genetically modified foods," World Health Organization, 2012, www.who.int/foodsafety/publications/biotech/20questions/en/.

3. "Ag Giants Spend Big to Defeat Labeling Initiative," The Associated Press, Aug. 15, 2012, www.nytimes.com/aponline/2012/08/15/us/ap-us-california-food-labeling.html?hp.

4. Safety of Genetically Engineered Foods: Approaches to Assessing Unintended Health Effects, National Research Council and Institute of Medicine of the National Academies (2004), pp. 191-195.

5. Stephen Duke and Stephen Powle, "Glyphosate: A Once In a Century Herbicide," *Pest Management Science*, April 2008, http://ddr.nal.usda.gov/bitstream/10113/17918/1/IND44034731.pdf.

6. Damian Carrington, "GM Crops Good for the Environment, Study Finds," *The Guardian*, June 13, 2012, www.guardian.co.uk/environment/2012/jun/13/gm-crops-environment-study.

7. "Recent Trends in GE Adoption," Economic Research Service, U.S. Department of Agriculture, 2012, www.ers.usda.gov/data-products/adoption-of-genetically-engineered-crops-in-the-us/recent-trends-in-ge-adoption.aspx.

8. "National Survey of Healthcare Consumers: Genetically Engineered Food," Thomson Reuters PULSE, October 2010, www.factsforhealthcare.com/pressroom/NPR_report_GeneticEngineered Food.pdf.

9. Andrew Pollack, "Crop Scientists Say Biotech Research Companies are Thwarting Research," *The New York Times*, Feb. 19, 2009, www.nytimes.com/2009/02/20/business/20crop.html.

10. "Statement by Center for Food Safety at National Press Club Event Challenging House Farm Bill Biotech Riders," Center for Food Safety, July 17, 2012, www.centerforfoodsafety.org/2012/07/17/statement-by-center-for-food-safety-at-national-press-club-event-challenging-house-farm-bill-biotech-riders/. For background on the farm bill, see Jennifer Weeks, "Farm Policy," *CQ Researcher*, Aug. 10, 2012, pp. 693-716.

11. Quoted in Susan C. Phillips, "Genetically Engineered Foods," *CQ Researcher*, Aug. 5, 1994, pp. 673-696.

12. For background, see Kathy Koch, "Food Safety Battle: Organic Vs. Biotech," *CQ Researcher*, Sept. 4, 1998, pp. 761-784.

13. Jamie Miller and Kent Bradford, "The Regulatory Bottleneck for Biotech Specialty Crops," *Nature Biotechnology*, October, 2010.

14. Clive James, "Global Status of Commercialized Biotech/GM Crops: 2011," International Service for the Acquisition of Agri-Biotech Applications, 2011, p. 8 (web link in graphic on p. 724).

15. Dan Charles, "Insect Experts Issue 'Urgent' Warning on Using Biotech Seeds," NPR, March 9, 2012, www.npr.org/blogs/thesalt/2012/03/08/148227668/insect-experts-issue-urgent-warning-on-using-biotech-seeds.

16. "Survey: Waterhemp Top Weed to Watch in Midwest," Croplife.com, July 9, 2012, www.croplife.com/article/29047/survey-waterhemp-top-weed-to-watch-in-midwest.

17. Rebecca Goldburg, Jane Rissler, Hope Shand and Chuck Hassebrook, "Biotechnology's Bitter Harvest: Herbicide-Tolerant Crops and the Threat to Sustainable Agriculture," Biotechnology Working Group, March 1990, http://blog.ucsusa.org/wp-content/uploads/2012/05/Biotechnologys-Bitter-Harvest.pdf.

18. Margaret Mellon, "The Trojan Horse of Biotechnology," Union of Concerned Scientists, May 10, 2012, http://blog.ucsusa.org/the-trojan-horse-of-biotechnology/.

19. Gregory Jaffe, "Complacency on the Farm: Significant Noncompliance with EPA's Refuge Requirements Threatens the Future Effectiveness of Genetically Engineered Pest-Protected Corn," Center for Science in the Public Interest, November 2009, http://cspinet.org/new/pdf/complacencyonthefarm.pdf.

20. For background, see Doug Struck, "Disappearing Forests," *CQ Global Researcher*, Jan. 18, 2011, pp. 27-52.

21. For information on pesticides and toxicity see the Pesticide Action Network Database: www.pesticideinfo.org/.

22. Amy Harmon and Andrew Pollack, "Battle Brewing Over Labeling of Genetically Modified Food," *The New York Times*, May 25, 2012, www.nytimes.com/2012/05/25/science/dispute-over-labeling-of-genetically-modified-food.html?_r=2&ref=geneticallymodifiedfood.

23. For additional information on mutagenic crops see the International Atomic Energy Agency and the Food and Agriculture Organization's database on mutant-enhanced crops at http://mvgs.iaea.org/Search.aspx.

24. Calestous Juma, *The Gene Hunters* (1989), pp. 37-38.

25. See David Hosansky, "Biotech Foods" *CQ Researcher*, March 30, 2001, pp. 249-272.

26. B. R. Hazell, "Green Revolution: Curse or Blessing?" International Food Policy Research Institute, 2002, www.ifpri.org/pubs/ib/ib11.pdf.

27. Hosansky, *op. cit.*

28. Susan C. Phillips, "Genetically Engineered Foods, *CQ Researcher*, Aug. 5, 1994, pp. 673-696.

29. Phillips, *op. cit.*

30. Mark Youngblood Herring, *Genetic Engineering* (2005) pp. 71-73.

31. Andrew Pollack, "Maker Warns of Hormone in Dairy Cows," *The New York Times*, Jan. 27, 2004, www.nytimes.com/2004/01/27/business/maker-warns-of-scarcity-of-hormone-for-dairy-cows.html.

32. See also I. R. Dohoo, *et. al.*, "A Meta-Analysis Review of the Effects of Recombinant Bovine Somatotropin," *Canadian Journal of Veterinary Research*, October 2003, www.ncbi.nlm.nih.gov/pmc/articles/PMC280708/?tool=pmcentrez, and

Richard Raymond, *et al.*, "Recombinant Bovine Somatotropin (rbST): A Safety Assessment," ADSA-CSAS-ASAS Joint Annual Meeting, July 14, 2009, www.ads.uga.edu/documents/rbstexpertpaper-6.26.09-final.pdf.

33. "Organic Production Statistics," Economic Research Service, U.S. Department of Agriculture, www.ers.usda.gov/data-products/organic-production.aspx.

34. Andrew Martin and Andrew Pollack, "Monsanto Looks to Sell Dairy Hormone Business," *The New York Times*, Aug. 6, 2008, www.nytimes.com/2008/08/07/business/07bovine.html; Mike Barris, "Lilly to Pay $300 Million for Dairy-Hormone Business," *The Wall Street Journal*, Aug. 20, 2008, http://online.wsj.com/article/SB121923768836656505.html.

35. Sandra Blakeslee, "British Mad Cow Toll Rises, but the Cause is Unclear," *The New York Times*, March 19, 1999, www.nytimes.com/1999/03/19/world/british-mad-cow-disease-toll-rises-but-the-cause-is-unclear.html. For additional background, see Mary H. Cooper, "Mad Cow Disease," *CQ Researcher*, March 2, 2001, pp. 161-184.

36. G. Bruening and J. M. Lyons, "The Case of the FLAVR SAVR Tomato," *California Agriculture*, July-August, 2000, http://ucanr.org/repository/CAO/landingpage.cfm?article=ca.v054n04p6&fulltext=yes.

37. Michael Hertz, "Monsanto Europe, Case A: Monsanto Introduces GMOs to Europe with Unexpected Results: Draft," University of Virginia Darden School Foundation, May 17, 2001, www.docstoc.com/docs/50820240/Monsanto-Europe.

38. Robert Paarlberg, *Starved for Science: How Biotechnology is Being Kept Out of Africa* (2008), pp. 127-132.

39. Andrew Pollack, "Kraft Recalls Taco Shells With Bioengineered Corn," *The New York Times*, Sept. 23, 2000, www.nytimes.com/2000/09/23/business/kraft-recalls-taco-shells-with-bioengineered-corn.html?pagewanted=all&src=pm.

40. *Ibid.*

41. Andrew Pollack, "Study Raises Doubt About Allergy to Genetic Corn," *The New York Times*, Nov. 10, 2003, www.nytimes.com/2003/11/10/business/study-raises-doubt-about-allergy-to-genetic-corn.html.

42. "Conclusion on Rice Investigation," Animal and Plant Health Inspection Service, U.S. Department of Agriculture, October 2007.

43. Robert Patrick, "Genetic Rice Lawsuit in St. Louis Settled for $750 Million," *St. Louis Post-Dispatch*, July 2, 2011, www.stltoday.com/news/local/metro/genetic-rice-lawsuit-in-st-louis-settled-for-million/article_38270243-c82f-5682-ba3b-8f8e24b85a92.html.

44. "Saved Seed and Farmer Lawsuits," Monsanto.com, www.monsanto.com/newsviews/Pages/saved-seed-farmer-lawsuits.aspx.

45. Donald Barlett and James Steele, "Monsanto's Harvest of Fear," *Vanity Fair*, May 2008, www.vanityfair.com/politics/features/2008/05/monsanto200805.

46. "Plant Biotechnology Pipeline: PowerPoint Presentation," Biotechnology Industry Organization, May 2011.

47. "USDA Receives Over 365,000 Public Comments Opposing Approval of 2,4-D Resistant, Genetically Engineered Corn," Center for Food Safety, April 26, 2012, www.centerforfoodsafety.org/2012/04/26/usda-receives-over-365000-public-comments-opposing-approval-of-24-d-resistant-genetically-engineered-corn/.

48. "California Voters to Decide on GMO Labeling," California Right to Know press release, June 12, 2012, www.carighttoknow.org/california_voters_to_decide_on_gmo_labeling.

49. Michael Hansen, "Reasons for Labeling Genetically Engineered Foods," letter to American Medical Association Council on Science and Public Health, Consumers Union, March 19, 2012, http://truthinlabelingcoalition.org/AMA.GE.resolution.3.19.12[1]%20(1).pdf.

50. Emmanuel Omobowale; Singer, Peter and Daar, Abadallah, "The Three Main Monotheistic Religions and GM Food Technology: An Overview of Perspectives," BMC International Health & Human Rights, 2009, www.biomedcentral.com/1472-698X/9/18.

51. Rosie Mestel, "GMO Foods Don't Need Special Labels, American Medical Association Says," *Los Angeles Times*, June 21, 2012, http://articles.latimes .com/2012/jun/21/news/la-heb-gmo-foods-medi cal-association-20120620.

52. "Consumer-Driven U.S. Organic Market Surpasses $31 billion in 2011," Organic Trade Association, April 23, 2012, www.organicnewsroom.com/ 2012/04/us_consumerdriven_organic_mark.html.

53. Carey Gillam, "UPDATE 1 — DuPont Urges U.S. to Curb Monsanto Seed Monopoly," Reuters, Jan. 8, 2010, www.reuters.com/article/2010/01/08/ monsanto-antitrust-idUSN087196620100108.

BIBLIOGRAPHY

Selected Sources

Books

Brunk, Conrad, and Harold Coward, eds., *Acceptable Genes? Religious Traditions and Genetically Modified Foods*, State University of New York Press, 2009.
Brunk, a philosopher, and Coward, a historian, have gathered views on how practices such as the insertion of fish genes into tomatoes fit with religious dietary and ethical codes.

Engdahl, William F., *Seeds of Destruction: The Hidden Agenda of Genetic Manipulation*, Global Research, 2007.
Engdahl documents the effort by multinational companies and governments to exert greater control over the world's food supply through genetic engineering.

Federoff, Nina, and Nancy Marie Brown, *Mendel in the Kitchen: A Scientist's View of Genetically Modified Food*, Joseph Henry Press, 2006.
A molecular biologist and member of the National Academy of Sciences (Federoff) and a science writer (Brown) argue that biotechnology will help feed humanity for generations.

McHughen, Alan, *Pandora's Picnic Basket*, Oxford University Press, 2000.
A molecular geneticist at the University of California-Riverside clearly and objectively discusses the technologies underlying genetically modified food and the controversy over, among other things, labeling of GM foods.

Paarlberg, Robert, *Starved for Science: How Biotechnology is Being Kept Out of Africa*, Harvard University Press, 2008.
A Wellesley College political scientist argues that non-science-based fears about genetically modified crops in wealthy countries are slowing the adoption of beneficial crops in Africa.

Ronald, Pamela, and Raoul Adamchak, *Tomorrow's Table: Organic Farming, Genetics and the Future of Food*, Oxford University Press, 2010.
Combining memoir with argument, a California plant geneticist (Ronald) and an organic farmer (Adamchak) argue that the organic movement should adopt biotechnology in the interest of feeding the world's population sustainably.

Schurman, Rachel, and William Munro, *Fighting for the Future of Food: Activists Versus Agribusiness in the Struggle Over Biotechnology*, University of Minnesota Press, 2010.
A sociologist (Schurman) and a political scientist (Munro) explore differing views of the biotech industry.

Articles

Borrell, Brendan, "Food Fight: The Case for Genetically Modified Food," *Scientific American*, April 11, 2011, www.scientificamerican.com/article.cfm?id=food-fight.
The author argues in favor of increased use of genetically modified crops.

Levaux, Ari, "The Very Real Danger of Genetically Modified Foods," *The Atlantic*, Jan. 9, 2012, www .theatlantic.com/health/archive/2012/01/the-very-real-danger-of-genetically-modified-foods/251051/.
A food blogger argues that new research shows that genetically modified foods can be dangerous and merit greater regulation. The article generated extensive rebuttals from science writers at *Scientific American* and *Slate*.

Pollack, Andrew, "That Fresh Look, Genetically Buffed," *The New York Times*, July 12, 2012, www .nytimes.com/2012/07/13/business/growers-fret-over-a-new-apple-that-wont-turn-brown.html?page wanted=all.

A GM apple that doesn't bruise or turn brown has met resistance from others in the apple industry.

Willingham, Emily, "The Very Real Paranoia Over Genetically Modified Foods," *Slate,* **Jan. 17, 2012, www.slate.com/articles/health_and_science/medical_ examiner/2012/01/genetically_modified_foods_ari_ laux_s_alarmism_in_the_atlantic.html.**
A science writer attacks Levaux's widely read critique of GMO foods in *The Atlantic.* Her article led the magazine to admit "scientific inconsistencies" in his piece.

Reports and Studies

"A Decade of EU Funded GMO Research: 2001-2010," European Commission, Directorate-General for Research and Innovation, 2010, http://ec.europa .eu/research/biosociety/pdf/a_decade_of_eu-funded_ gmo_research.pdf.

A 262-page overview of 50 research projects on GM organisms concludes that food biotechnology carries no more environmental or health risks than other plant breeding methods.

"Genetically Engineered Food: An Overview," *Food & Water Watch,* **2012, www.foodandwaterwatch.org/ reports/genetically-engineered-food/.**
Genetically modified food should be labeled, and the U.S. government should stop approving new GM crops, an advocacy group argues.

"Impact of Genetically Modified Crops on Farm Sustainability in the United States," National Academy of Sciences, 2010, www.nap.edu/catalog.php?record_ id=12804.
The nation's most prestigious scientific body concludes that genetically engineered crops offer farmers substantial environmental and economic benefits.

For More Information

Biotechnology Industry Organization, 1201 Maryland Ave., S.W., Suite 900, Washington, DC 20024; 202-962-9200; www.bio.org. Trade group for agricultural and medical biotechnology companies.

Center for Science in the Public Interest, 1220 L St., N.W., Suite 300, Washington, DC 20005; 202-332-9110; www .cspinet.org. Food-safety group that advocates science-based government policies.

Greenpeace USA, 702 H St., N.W., Suite 300, Washington, DC 20001; 202-462-1177; www.greenpeace.org. Major global environmental group that opposes agricultural biotechnology.

International Food Policy Research Institute, 2033 K St., N.W., Washington, DC 20006-1002; 202-862-5600; www

.ifpri.org. Group supported by governments, foundations and international organizations that provides research and policy advice on regulation of biotech crops.

National Academy of Sciences, 500 Fifth St., N.W., Washington, DC 20001; 202-334-2000; www.nasonline .org. Society of scientists and engineers created by Congress to advise the government on scientific issues. NAS has published a number of reports assessing the risks of agricultural biotechnology.

Union of Concerned Scientists, Two Brattle Square, Cambridge, MA 02138-3780; 617-547-5552; www .ucsusa.org. Environmental group critical of agricultural biotechnology.

6

Internet Regulation

Marcia Clemmitt

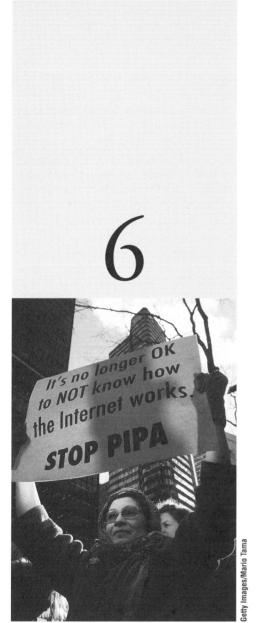

Protesters in New York City demonstrate on Jan. 18, 2012, against the proposed Protect Intellectual Property Act (PIPA) and the Stop Online Piracy Act (SOPA), which would block the unauthorized use of movies, TV shows, recorded music and other copyrighted material. The bills' opponents — including Wikipedia co-founder Jimmy Wales — argue they are too draconian and will lead to censorship.

From *The CQ Researcher*, April 13, 2012.

Wikipedia, the online encyclopedia written by its users, has become a dependable web presence — always there to answer questions on just about every conceivable subject, from aardvarks to Zoroaster. But on Jan. 18 Wikipedia disappeared, abruptly shutting down its U.S. site in a self-proclaimed "day of darkness."

The blackout came in protest of two Hollywood-backed proposals in Congress — the Stop Online Piracy Act (SOPA) and the Protect Intellectual Property Act (PIPA) — aimed at combating the unauthorized use or reproduction of movies, TV shows, recorded music and other copyrighted material.

Such pirating, which typically occurs on foreign-based rogue websites, has mushroomed into a global enterprise costing the entertainment industry and others billions of dollars a year in lost revenues and royalties.

But opponents of the proposed bills — including Wikipedia co-founder Jimmy Wales — argued they were so vague and draconian that they would force any website carrying user-generated content perceived to violate copyright laws to shut down at nearly a moment's notice.

What's more, opponents said, the bills would effectively block search engines from connecting to those sites and allow copyright owners to stop advertisers from doing business with them.

"I hope we send a broad global message that the Internet as a whole will not tolerate censorship in response to mere allegations of copyright infringement," said Wales.[1] Thousands of other websites also shut down in protest, while Google and Facebook, among

Top-Speed Internet Options Limited

Only about 15 percent of Americans will have a choice among top-speed broadband Internet service providers (ISPs) in 2012. Advocates of net neutrality, which would prevent ISPs from slowing delivery of some websites' content, say consumers won't be able to pressure ISPs to treat all content equally if they can't threaten to switch their business to other providers.

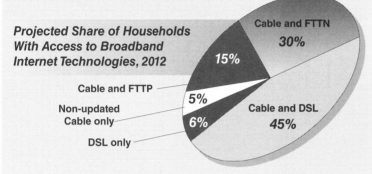

Projected Share of Households With Access to Broadband Internet Technologies, 2012

- Cable and FTTN **30%**
- **15%**
- Cable and FTTP **5%**
- Non-updated Cable only **6%**
- DSL only
- Cable and DSL **45%**

* Some telephone companies offer very high-speed broadband, but most service is slower. Fiber-to-the-premises (FTTP) is fastest — roughly as fast as current, upgraded cable. Fiber-to-the-node (FTTN) is somewhat slower, and digital subscriber line (DSL) is about a third as fast as top-speed cable and FTTP.

** Figures do not total 100 because of rounding.

Source: "Broadband Competition and Innovation Policy," Federal Communications Commission, 2010, www.broadband.gov/plan/4-broadband-competition-and-innovation-policy/

others, remained in operation but expressed support for Wikipedia's stand.

Debates on Internet regulation are heating up as cyber companies gain clout in Washington and the Internet penetrates every area of life. Besides the fight over copyright enforcement, a battle is raging over government attempts to bar Internet-service providers (ISPs) from delivering some websites' content to customers more slowly than others.

Government advocates argue that such "net neutrality" rules are needed to keep broadband ISPs — mostly cable TV and phone companies that provide high-speed Internet services but also are interested in supplying content to customers — from hurting small or upstart competitors in the content business. But the ISPs argue that such legislation impinges on their free-speech rights: After all, they argue, they own the transmission lines that carry the data. And besides, they say, slowing the flow of online traffic wouldn't be in their financial interest because it might make customers go elsewhere.

While the net neutrality debate can descend into the technical and arcane, Internet piracy is a subject that anyone who has knowingly watched a bootleg movie or illegally downloaded a Top 10 hit song can understand. Two days after Wikipedia's online protest, on Jan. 20, Congress postponed long-expected floor votes on House and Senate bills requiring online-payment companies, search engines and ISPs to cut their ties with websites alleged to be posting copyrighted material.

"The growing number of foreign websites that offer counterfeit or stolen goods continues to threaten American technology, products and jobs," said Rep. Lamar Smith, R-Texas, chief sponsor of the House bill. "Congress cannot stand by and do nothing while some of America's most profitable and productive industries are under attack."[2]

The 1998 Digital Millennium Copyright Act (DMCA) currently governs copyright infringement. Advocates of new legislation say it is outmoded because it doesn't cover the full range of Internet-piracy issues that have emerged over the past decade.

But others say the new bills go too far. "I'm not exactly a fan" of the DMCA, but it "has a process that at least gives people a hearing," says Jon Ippolito, an associate professor of new media at the University of Maine, in Orono. In contrast, proposed legislation risks "poisoning the very nature of the Internet" as a participatory medium by authorizing near-immediate shutdowns of websites with user-generated content, he says.

Meanwhile, after years of wrangling, the Federal Communications Commission (FCC), the federal agency that writes and enforces rules for telecommunications, last November required ISPs that deliver high-speed Internet service to observe "net neutrality" in managing their networks. While it's understood that ISPs may sometimes need to slow some data to avoid network congestion, they must publicly disclose the methods they use to manage traffic and may not block lawful websites or "unreasonably" discriminate among sites.

A congressional resolution to stop the regulation passed the House last year, but not the Senate, and lawmakers continue to fight over the issue.

The net neutrality rules are an unwarranted intrusion into an Internet market that functions well, wrote Gerald R. Faulhaber, professor emeritus of business and public policy at the University of Pennsylvania's Wharton School, and David J. Farber, professor of computer science and public policy at Carnegie Mellon University in Pittsburgh. The FCC's "successful policy of no regulation" for the past two decades has led to "the wildly successful Internet we have today" and should not be abandoned, they said.[3]

But net-neutrality advocates argue that broadband ISPs might have significant business motives for slowing some websites' traffic. The ISPs, too, would like to get into the Internet content game, which has brought big financial rewards to companies such as Facebook and Amazon. But the online services they could offer — video and phone service — also have competitors, such as the video company Netflix and the Internet phone company Skype.

Therefore, regulation advocates say, ISPs might consider it in their financial interest to slow content traffic to those competitors to gain an edge over them. For example, a phone company that offers broadband might be motivated to slow delivery of Internet-telephone services such as VoIP, and, in fact, several ISPs have been accused of such blocking in the past.[4]

"I don't pay Comcast for making Netflix inferior to [Comcast's] pay-per-view," says Robert Frieden, a professor of telecommunications and law at Pennsylvania State University, in University Park. "I don't want the intermediaries tilting things to favor their own content."

Edward W. Felten, a professor of computer science and public affairs at Princeton University and chief

One-Fourth of Downloads Are Illegal

Roughly one-fourth of global Internet traffic, and about 18 percent of U.S. traffic, illegally accesses copyrighted media through downloading methods that include file-sharing, video streaming and use of torrents, which are files that reveal the online location of copyrighted items.

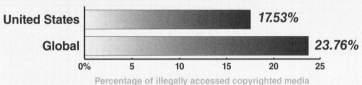

Internet Traffic Illegally Accessing Copyrighted Media

United States — 17.53%
Global — 23.76%

Percentage of illegally accessed copyrighted media

Percentages do not include pornography because its status can be difficult to assess.

Source: "Technical Report: An Estimate of Infringing Use of the Internet," Envisional, January 2011, pp. 2-3, documents.envisional.com/docs/Envisional-Internet_Usage-Jan2011.pdf

technologist at the Federal Trade Commission, says it remains an "open question whether government can police favoritism by Internet network operators." Nevertheless, he says that keeping the Internet neutral by some means would help small Internet providers get off the ground or thrive against their bigger rivals.

"The next generation of innovators, who need neutrality the most, are not at the bargaining table. They're hard at work in their labs or classrooms, dreaming of the next big thing, and hoping that the Internet is as open to them as it was to the founders of Google."[5]

As lawmakers, entrepreneurs and policy analysts consider the future of Internet regulation, here are some of the questions being debated:

Is Internet piracy harming the economy?

For advocates of tougher copyright regulation, the domino effect may be the most compelling argument for toughening anti-piracy laws: Piracy of copyrighted material not only robs creative artists of due compensation but harms the whole economy as lost revenues in one industry decrease sales in others, they argue.

However, many analysts argue that economic- and job-loss estimates cited by copyright-owners' groups such as the Recording Industry Association of America

New Technology Spurs Innovation — and Resistance

Critics say "dinosaurs" seek veto power over the future.

Jesse Jordan, a freshman at Rensselaer Polytechnic Institute in Troy, N.Y., got the idea for his new search engine in 2003. It would be a useful and harmless way for his fellow students to search each others' files in the "public file" section of the school's internal computer system.

But after some searches turned up copyrighted music files that students had stowed on the system, the Recording Industry Association of America (RIAA) — the music-industry trade group — sued Jordan for music piracy, demanding millions of dollars in damages. Ultimately, Jordan — who said his program wasn't intended for sharing music — paid $12,000 to settle the suit, without admitting wrongdoing.[1]

Jordan wasn't alone. In the early 2000s, RIAA filed or threatened dozens of lawsuits against college students around the country. The campaign was needed, said RIAA General Counsel Steven Marks, because "the enormous damage compounded with every illegal download is alarming — thousands of regular, working class musicians . . . out of work, stores shuttered, new bands never signed."[2]

But there was more to the lawsuit blitz than simply an effort to scare pirating students straight, says Kevin J. Greene, a professor at Thomas Jefferson School of Law, in San Diego. Among the schools where lawsuits were threatened were many that produce highly skilled technology majors, including Rensselaer, the Massachusetts Institute of Technology (MIT) and Carnegie Mellon University, in Pittsburgh. "That was not by chance," says Greene. RIAA officials "were trying to send a message to these high-tech kids" to back off from inventing new technology that would make it easier to copy and share music.

Attempts to slow the commercial impact of new communications technology have a long history.

In the 1930s, AT&T banned one of its engineers, Clarence Hickman of the telephone giant's famous research facility, Bell Labs, from continuing to work on an answering machine he'd invented that used magnetic tape to record messages. Worried that having conversations recorded would "lead the public to abandon the telephone," AT&T shut down Bell research on magnetic tape — the eventual source of audiocassettes, videocassettes and the first computer-storage systems. Eventually, "magnetic tape would come to America via imports of foreign technology, mainly German," wrote Tim Wu, a professor at Columbia Law School who specializes in technology issues.[3]

(RIAA) and the Motion Picture Association of America (MPAA) are inflated and based on minimal data.

"The accumulative impact of millions of songs downloaded illegally . . . is devastating" to a whole group of workers, including "songwriters, recording artists, audio engineers, computer technicians, talent scouts and marketing specialists, producers, publishers and countless others," said the RIAA.[6]

"More than 2.2 million hard-working, middle-class people in all 50 states depend on the entertainment industry for their jobs, and many millions more work in other industries that rely on intellectual property," Michael O'Leary, MPAA senior executive vice president, said in lauding the House Judiciary Committee's strong bipartisan support for SOPA.[7]

"Rogue websites that steal America's innovative and creative products . . . threaten more than 19 million American jobs," wrote Mark Elliot, executive vice president of the U.S. Chamber of Commerce.[8]

"The independent music community is impacted by . . . illegal downloading, even more so in many cases than major music labels or movie studios because [profit] margins are so thin for independent labels," according to the American Association for Independent Music (A2IM), a trade group that represents smaller, independent record labels. "Because we are not part of larger

Also in the 1930s, the young broadcast industry — at the time limited to AM radio — stymied the emergence of FM radio. David Sarnoff, president of RCA, a radio manufacturer and broadcast company, assigned noted inventor Edwin Armstrong of Columbia University to devise a way to eliminate the static that plagued AM broadcasts. Armstrong went one better, inventing an entirely new form of transmission that reduced broadcast noise and made high-fidelity music broadcasts possible. It did so by modulating radio waves' frequency, rather than their amplitude. It was called FM (frequency modulation) radio.

Because FM radio also operates at a much lower power, Armstrong's invention opened the way for more small broadcasters to get into the game. "You might think that the possibility of more radio stations with less interference would be generally recognized as an unalloyed good," wrote Wu. But, he added, "by this point the radio industry . . . had invested heavily in the status quo of fewer stations," which pleased advertisers by reaching many listeners with one ad buy.

To preserve their business model, industry leaders convinced federal regulators that FM transmission was not ready for prime time, and for six years the government banned its commercial use and limited its experimental use to one narrow band of frequencies. "There was no way for an FM station even to get started without breaking the law," Wu wrote.

In the 21st century, the RIAA successfully fought for new music-licensing rules to hamper expansion of so-called "Internet radio," wrote Harvard Law School Professor Lawrence Lessig. Internet technology allows a virtually unlimited number of "Internet radio stations" to "broadcast," potentially allowing a much wider range of musicians to find a worldwide audience.

But what technology does not limit, laws can, according to Lessig. The RIAA fought to expand copyright law to require Internet stations to pay licensing fees to both composers and the recording artists who perform their songs. Ordinary broadcast-radio stations pay composers only. (In an earlier amendment to the law, Congress had reasoned that radio play acts as advertising for singers and bands, so payment isn't needed.) [4]

The financial burden Internet stations face from the rule "is not slight," Lessig wrote. By one estimate, an Internet station delivering "ad-free popular music to ten thousand listeners, twenty-four hours a day," would owe $1 million a year in recording-artists' fees, while a traditional station doing the same thing would not, he argued.

It's not surprising that existing businesses fight technological change, Lessig wrote. But, he added, the resistance comes with a cost: "It gives dinosaurs a veto over the future."

— Marcia Clemmitt

[1] For background, see "Music Settlement," transcript, "American Morning," CNN.com, May 6, 2003, http://transcripts.cnn.com/TRANSCRIPTS/0305/06/ltm.03.html.

[2] "RIAA Sends More Law Pre-Lawsuit Letters to Colleges With New School Year," press release, RIAA, www.riaa.com/newsitem.php?id=36CA9067-8061-3114-41BB-491B8B32A357.

[3] Tim Wu, *Master Switch: The Rise and Fall of Information Empires* (2010), p. 106.

[4] Lawrence Lessig, *Free Culture: The Nature and Future of Creativity* (2005), p. 197.

corporations which might be able to offset losses during leaner years, making a living becomes that much more difficult."[9]

Recorded-music sales have declined significantly in most years since the advent of Internet downloading. In 2010, for example, worldwide music sales dropped by 8.4 percent — $1.45 billion. The decrease comes "as the industry continues to struggle with piracy and winning consumers over to legal download models," observes *The Guardian* newspaper in Britain.[10]

"The demand for new music seems as insatiable and diverse as ever, and record companies continue to meet it. But they are operating at only a fraction of their potential because of a difficult environment dominated by piracy," said Frances Moore, chief executive of the music-industry trade group International Federation of the Phonographic Industry (IFPI).[11]

"Piracy remains an enormous barrier to sustainable growth in digital music," according to IFPI. "Globally, one in four internet users (28%) regularly access unlicensed services," said the group.[12]

"I made a film called 'Naked Ambition: An R-rated Look at an X-rated Industry' " that Apple, Netflix and Warner Brothers distributed but that was widely pirated anyway, wrote photographer and independent filmmaker Michael Grecco. He received 107 Google alerts about online references to his movie that each named multiple websites where his film was available for free. The sites, which Grecco had not authorized to host his film, "made all the money; I have never seen a dime," he wrote.[13]

Piracy-related monetary and job losses are difficult to estimate, but the conservative, Lewisville, Texas-based think tank, Institute for Policy Innovation (IPI), founded by former House Majority Leader Dick Armey, R-Texas, has published perhaps the most oft-cited statistics. In 2005, industries that sell material whose copyrights they own, such as the film, TV and recording industries, lost at least $23.5 billion to piracy of music, video games and software, and retailers lost another $2.5 billion, the IPI calculated. The group also estimated that lost sales from pirating cost the United States the chance to add 373,375 jobs to the economy, about 120,000 in media- and software-creating industries and the rest in jobs that would have been supported by the 120,000 new media-industry workers.[14]

Skepticism about those estimates abounds, however. The Government Accountability Office (GAO), Congress' nonpartisan auditing arm, concluded in 2010 that while economic losses likely are "sizable," no existing estimates can be trusted. No public agencies collect their own data on piracy, industry groups often don't disclose the methods behind their estimates and numerous uncertainties cloud such questions as how much pirated material actually translates into lost sales, the GAO said. For example, a consumer who pays a low price for a counterfeit DVD wouldn't necessarily have paid the price of a non-counterfeit copy, it noted.[15]

Essentially, IPI argued that when a movie studio makes $10 selling a DVD, then passes on $7 to the company that manufactured it and $2 to the trucker who shipped it, the total value of the DVD is $10 plus $7 plus $2, or $19, wrote Timothy B. Lee, an adjunct scholar at the Cato Institute, a libertarian think tank in Washington. "Yet some simple math shows that this is nonsense," he wrote. After paying its subcontractors, "the studio is $1 richer, the trucker . . . $2, and the manufacturer . . . $7. . . . That adds up to $10."[16]

Sales of music CDs dropped steadily in the 2000s, but while the RIAA pins the blame on Internet piracy, the conclusion doesn't hold up because too many other factors likely play into the decrease, argued Lawrence Lessig, a Harvard Law School professor. For example, in the early 2000s, when RIAA reported a substantial drop in the number of CDs sold, fewer CDs than previously were being released and the per-CD price was rising, both solid reasons to expect fewer sales, Lessig wrote.[17]

Free downloading does sometimes replace a music sale, but it's misleading to count every free Internet download as an act of piracy that deprives a copyright owner of dollars, Lessig argued. For example, a large number of "pirated" downloads are of older music that has been taken off the market and is impossible to obtain legally, he wrote.

"This is still technically a violation of copyright, though because the copyright owner is not selling the content anymore, the economic harm is zero — the same harm that occurs when I sell my collection of 1960s 45-rpm records to a local collector."[18]

Figures about lost jobs from piracy don't add up, wrote Cato Institute Research Fellow Julian Sanchez. Research suggests that, for as many as 80 percent of free music downloads, the consumer would not actually have bought the music, even if a pirated copy had been unobtainable, he wrote. Those acts of piracy, then, cost the industry nothing, since they didn't replace potential sales, he said.

Meanwhile, in the 20 percent of cases in which piracy does replace a sale, the result is a loss to the music industry, "but not a [net] loss to the economy, since the money just ends up being spent elsewhere," Sanchez argued. That being the case, "there is no good reason to think eliminating piracy by U.S. users would yield any jobs on net."[19]

Should Congress crack down harder on digital piracy?

The entertainment industry argued forcefully over the past year that a much tougher system of copyright enforcement is imperative. However, critics of the stalled SOPA and PIPA bills contend that the legislation gives a few large businesses unwarranted power to shut down websites without due process.

SOPA and PIPA "would provide needed tools to combat foreign rogue websites," said MPAA's CEO, former Sen. Christopher Dodd, D-Conn.[20]

PIPA puts "muscle behind closing down foreign sites whose main purpose is to steal" and that cost "working professionals (not just corporations) hundreds of millions of dollars every year," wrote Grecco, the photographer and independent filmmaker.[21]

"Let's all agree that doing nothing is not an option any intellectual property creators can live with," said the independent-label group A2IM.[22]

Even some SOPA/PIPA critics want Congress to quickly craft tougher laws to combat piracy.

"While I'm relieved that the flawed SOPA and PIPA bills seem unlikely to pass in their current forms . . . rogue websites dedicated to the infringement of U.S. copyrights pose a public policy problem that merits . . . prompt (albeit prudent) legislative action," said Ryan Radia, associate director of policy studies at the Competitive Enterprise Institute, a free-market-oriented think tank.[23]

Others argue for more caution, however.

Trying to simply shut down sources of content is "bound to fail in today's increasingly interactive world," where new technologies and channels that facilitate information sharing come along continually, said Cato's Sanchez. "As the success of services like [the ad-supported video-streaming site] Hulu and [movie and TV-program distributor] Netflix suggests, consumers are only too happy to pay for content that's made available in a convenient form, and at a reasonable price," he said. "If the content industries want a genuinely effective way to reduce global piracy, they should spend less time and money lobbying for new regulations and focus on providing innovative services that make piracy unattractive."[24]

Many SOPA/PIPA critics view the bills as part of a long-running power grab by big media companies.

"I have first-hand knowledge of what the large media companies think of the Internet. They will never like it until they can control it 100 percent; of course ruining it in the process," wrote Joe Escalante, an entertainment lawyer and bassist for the punk band The Vandals. Escalante's band is being sued by the entertainment newspaper *Daily Variety* because websites unconnected to the band have posted images of album-cover art that the band withdrew from the market and scrubbed from

U.S. Internet Use Soars

More than three-fourths of Americans use the Internet, compared with fewer than half in 2000. About 240 million people are online, up from 124 million at the turn of the century.

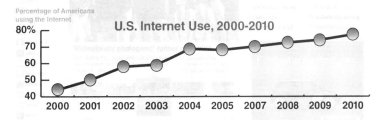

Percentage of Americans using the Internet

U.S. Internet Use, 2000-2010

Source: "United States of America: Internet Usage and Broadband Usage Report," Internet World Stats, February 2011, www.internetworldstats.com/am/us.htm

their own website after *Variety* complained that it constituted trademark infringement.[25]

"The *Daily Variety* will claim in front of a jury, presumably with a straight face, that mere 'links' to a site that posted artwork from a discontinued CD displaying an 'infringing parody' should result in the four members of the Vandals paying . . . upwards of a million dollars" in damages, Escalante said. "If the fear is that under SOPA, the media companies will take advantage of a legal anomaly that will permit them to shut down entire websites, with the burden of proving innocence placed on the defendant, based on trumped up claims and theories, I can tell you, it's not paranoia. It is a real-world certainty."[26]

Historically, media and entertainment companies have sought legal protection against every technology that has given the public freer access to copyrighted content, wrote Clay Shirky, a professor at New York University's interactive-telecommunications program, in New York City. "This is an industry that tried to kill Tivo [a device for recording TV shows]. . . . They tried to kill player pianos. They do this whenever a technology increases user freedom over media. Every time. Every single time."[27]

Should the government require Internet-service providers (ISPs) to treat all websites the same?

The FCC and some technology analysts want the government to enforce rules preventing ISPs, mainly phone and cable companies, from treating different

www.newline.com

The 2005 horror movie "Snakes on a Plane," starring Samuel L. Jackson, received a major marketing boost from bloggers and Internet movie-fan communities. After advance word of the movie leaked out, online fans distributed parodies, doctored photographs and mock videos, which the producers used to market the film and shape its plot.

websites differently by slowing data from some websites. The aim of the enforcement, they say, would be to prevent ISPs from slowing the flow of content from companies such as video distributors or Internet phone companies that compete with an ISPs' other lines of business or with its business partners. But others argue that such "net neutrality" rules would violate ISPs' rights to conduct business as they see fit over wires and cables they own.

Advocates of net-neutrality regulation have turned traditional arguments for free-speech protections on their head, said Adam Thierer, a senior research fellow in technology policy at George Mason University's Mercatus Center, which researches free markets. They argue that barring ISPs from treating different websites differently would guarantee free speech to website owners that supply content to users. But this is a "twisted theory" of the Constitution's free-speech guarantee, said Thierer. The Constitution is written to stop government from becoming the enemy of free speech and doesn't envision "private platforms" such as ISPs taking that role, he wrote.[28]

In fact, new rules would abridge ISPs' freedom of speech, Thierer said. ISPs are in the business of delivering content to consumers, and "the First Amendment . . . was not intended as a tool for government to control the editorial discretion of private . . . institutions."[29]

"Disappointing one's paying end-user customers is unlikely to be a great business model over time," so "it seems unlikely that broadband ISPs are going to intentionally make a practice of slowing or blocking access to select websites," wrote technology analyst Barbara Esbin, a former special counsel at the Federal Communications Commission. Thus net-neutrality rules are unnecessary, she said.[30]

The so-called "takings clause" in the Fifth Amendment to the Constitution bars the government from taking private property "for public use, without just compensation" to the owner, says Daniel Lyons, an assistant professor at Boston College Law School. Cable- and phone-company ISPs own the wires and cables that bring Internet data into individual homes and businesses — the so-called "last mile" of Internet-content delivery — and because of that, the takings clause may apply to Internet regulations, Lyons says. "Since the 1920s there's been a branch of law that says regulations that go too far are like a taking," and net-neutrality rules may fall into that category, meaning that the government would have to pay ISPs to abide by them, he argues.

(In 1982, the Supreme Court ruled that the public interest required a New York landlord to give a cable-TV company access to his roof to install a cable box, as state law required, but that he was entitled to "just compensation" for doing so. The court deemed "just compensation" in the case to be just one dollar; nevertheless, the court established the principle that regulatory requirements are similar to an actual taking, says Lyons.[31])

Many net-neutrality advocates argue that ISPs have solid business reasons for slowing some data relative to others, but that rules to control the behavior are necessary.

A cable-TV company that offers broadband might be strongly motivated to slow the online delivery of movies from a competing video vendor such as Netflix, for example, says Frieden, of Pennsylvania State.

Furthermore, it's already been done, Frieden says. ISPs have said, "We'll never do this. We have no incentive to throttle" traffic. But in 2007, when Comcast was accused of deliberately slowing data transmitted with peer-to-peer file-sharing technology — computer programs that allow individuals to send and receive digital-media files, including music and games — first the company "said it didn't do it, then it said it did. Players do have incentives to distort the market," says Frieden.

(Comcast has argued that many users of file-sharing technology were transferring very large files and that slowing them was necessary in order to keep Internet traffic overall flowing. Subsequently, the company has worked to develop methods of traffic management that would not depend on blocking content from specific websites.[32])

Furthermore, such distortion can be consequence-free for an ISP, Frieden says. "All the consumer knows is that Netflix isn't working well, and they'll blame Netflix," even if the real culprit were an ISP slowing traffic, he says.

ISPs enter contracts with consumers to deliver certain amounts of Internet content at certain rates of speed, and the government could establish some kind of consumer-protection system for those contracts, says Frieden. For example, Congress could explicitly give the FCC authority to do "light-handed" conflict resolution of specific consumer complaints about ISPs hindering traffic, he says.

Opponents of net-neutrality regulation argue that the consumer marketplace is the proper place to handle such problems, but that may not be feasible, says Jonathan Zittrain, a Harvard Law School professor of Internet law.

"If access to Facebook is important to you, and an ISP provides poor (or no) connectivity to Facebook, you can fire your ISP. That is how markets work." But there's a catch, he continues. "There have to be meaningful alternatives" to your nonperforming ISP, and "you have to *know* that you are getting less than you want so you are motivated to switch. Both assumptions may turn out to be wrong." There is less ISP competition than many had hoped for, and rather than blaming one's ISP for slow connections, "you might just think the site itself doesn't have its act together."[33]

BACKGROUND

Communications Wars

Struggles over control of communications and media businesses have been among the most intense in economic history. Owners of older, dominant technologies have repeatedly fought innovations that threatened their businesses.[34]

In the mid-19th century, for example, Americans communicated long distances using a single technology — the telegraph — controlled by a single company, Western

Union. When, around 1880, the fledgling telephone caused telegraphy to lose its role as virtually the only swift, viable distance-communications technology, Western Union faced potential collapse. Thus, "no sooner had the firm realized the potential of the Bell company's technology to overthrow the telegraph monopoly" than it made an all-out attempt "to kill or devour Bell," wrote Tim Wu, a professor of Internet, media and communications law at Columbia Law School in New York.[35]

Western Union's effort failed, but the pattern would repeat itself many times, frequently slowing development of innovations, sometimes for decades.[36] (*See sidebar, p. 134.*)

At times, the government has stepped in to keep communications companies from snuffing out new competitors.

Beginning in the 1890s, some entrepreneurs strung their own wires through communities — attaching them to supports such as farms' barbed-wire fences — to provide local phone service. The companies prospered, especially in rural areas and small remote towns not served by the Bell system, and in the early 1900s began banding together into larger systems.

AT&T President Theodore Vail feared for his business and believed the small companies would provide inferior service. He began offering independent companies membership in the Bell system, on the condition that they adopt its technical standards and pay to use its long-distance lines. Many companies, which knew they were hamstrung without long-distance service, took the deal, even though AT&T did not promise to connect any calls to non-Bell customers.

The federal government, however, viewed the deals as antitrust violations, intended to snuff out AT&T's competition. To avoid sanctions, Vail agreed to allow independents access to AT&T's lines without joining the company and, more important, to operate AT&T henceforth as a "common carrier" — a company deemed so important to the public good that it must be required to do business in a nondiscriminatory way.[37]

Copyright Disputes

Over the years, numerous legal fights have arisen over protecting the rights of copyright owners, such as composers and filmmakers, when emerging technology has provided new ways for others to copy, alter or publish their intellectual property.

In 1909, Congress amended copyright law for music to ensure that composers were paid for "mechanical reproductions" of their works, such as phonograph records and player-piano rolls. Previous law had granted composers the exclusive right to control whether, when and how their music was performed in public. Under the new law, however, once a composer authorized any recording of a composition, subsequent musicians had the right — the "license" — to record and distribute new recordings of the piece, as long as they paid the composer a fee set by law.

Such licensing arrangements still prevail, and over time lawmakers have expanded their use in an attempt to balance the interests of original intellectual-property owners and those of others who want to use the works. Without such balance, "the monopoly power of rights holders . . . would stifle follow-on creativity," such as the creativity of musicians arranging old music into a new style, wrote Harvard's Lessig.[38]

In recent years, intellectual-property owners have argued for controlling or even banning the use of some technology.

Soon after VCRs — machines that could record TV shows and play tapes of movies for home viewing — hit the market in the 1970s, for example, the movie and television industries sought a ban. "The VCR is to the American film producer and the America public as the Boston strangler is to the woman home alone," Motion Picture Association of America (MPAA) President Jack Valenti told Congress in 1982.[39]

Movie studios sued VCR inventor Sony Corp., alleging that the machines were made for the sole purpose of copyright infringement. In 1984, the Supreme Court narrowly decided the case in Sony's favor, ruling that the recorders were most likely to be used to record TV programs to watch when convenient, a benign purpose that wouldn't harm original creators.[40]

Media Converging

The birth of digital media intensified past struggles.

When the digital revolution began, communications and media executives, like most people, viewed computers as calculating tools and scientific instruments. They missed the fact that, as computers gained more memory, everyday users not only would be able to access all kinds of media — including sound, graphics and video — through a single computer but also could manipulate those media as they wished.

The secret is "digitization" — the fact that a photograph, audio recording or any other piece of information can be converted into a two-digit "binary code" that computers can store, process and manipulate.

Coded digital information, no matter how complex, is expressed as a sequence containing only zeroes and ones. Digital technology means that "I don't use . . . different kinds of digits for representing music than I use for representing video or . . . documents," said Princeton's Felten. So "where I previously had . . . separate sets of technology" for producing and viewing video and audio, for example, a home computer now becomes "a universal machine" that can access any media and "cause a great earthquake in the media business."[41]

Peer-to-peer file-sharing (P2P) was one of the quake's first tremors.

Via cassette tapes and photocopiers, people have long shared their favorite copyrighted media with friends, but in 1999, the first P2P website for music sharing, Napster, came on the scene. Within months millions were using the site. Some downloaded others' copies of hard-to-obtain music, such as older songs that record companies had taken off the market, and amateur recordings, such as bootleg concert recordings.

But many also downloaded new music without paying for it. Heavy-metal band Metallica sued Napster after leaked copies of their unreleased music appeared on the site. The trade association Recording Industry Association of America (RIAA) also sued Napster for copyright infringement, and in 2000 a federal court ordered the website to close.[42]

The universal power of digital computing has led to a boom in the so-called "remix" culture — the creation of new art by copying and manipulating the old. Amateur and professional artists can manipulate photographs and paintings to create their own collages and animated videos, and young movie buffs intercut scenes from digitized commercial films with their own video to create unauthorized sequels to classic movies such as "Star Wars." (*See sidebar, p. 132.*)

To blunt computers' power to share and remix media, one bill introduced in Congress — but not enacted — would have required that computers come with software that can determine whether online content is copyrighted and keep copyrighted material from being shared.[43]

C H R O N O L O G Y

1990s *Introduced in 1969 as a network linking a few research centers, the Internet attracts millions of users.*

1996 Phone companies unsuccessfully seek congressional ban on Internet telephone service. . . . Congress passes the Telecommunications Act, classifying cable-TV broadband Internet providers as lightly regulated "information services" but saying little else about the Internet.

1998 Congress passes Digital Millennium Copyright Act, toughening penalties for online piracy.

1999 Millions of users begin sharing music, much of it copyrighted, on Napster, first peer-to-peer file-sharing website.

2000s *Copyright owners worry as online file-sharing booms. Advocates push for requiring broadband Internet service providers (ISPs) to practice "net neutrality" by not blocking lawful content.*

2000 Judge orders Napster to shut down in wake of lawsuits by musicians and the Recording Industry Association of America (RIAA).

2003 RIAA sues or threatens lawsuits against thousands of students for alleged music piracy; Rensselaer Polytechnic Institute freshman Jesse Jordan is among those sued.

2005 Supreme Court rules that cable broadband providers don't have to open their lines to competitors. . . . FCC announces that phone companies providing broadband Internet service can operate under the same rules as cable broadband ISPs. . . . FCC will monitor all broadband ISPs to ensure that consumers can access the websites and applications they choose.

2006 Congress considers net-neutrality legislation.

2008 FCC orders cable broadband provider Comcast to stop blocking peer-to-peer file-sharing programs; Comcast complies but sues, arguing the FCC had no authority to issue the order. . . . RIAA announces it will end mass lawsuits against college students.

2009 Congress is split on net neutrality. Sen. John McCain, R-Ariz., introduces legislation to prohibit the FCC from regulating the Internet; Rep. Edward Markey, D-Mass., introduces a bill to make net neutrality national policy.

2010s *As Internet speeds rise and video streaming increases, movie and TV studios worry about illegal downloads.*

2010 Federal appeals court overturns FCC ruling in 2008 Comcast case. . . . FCC announces an "Open Internet Order," requiring ISPs to disclose their methods for managing Internet traffic and to not discriminate among websites; because of their capacity limitations, wireless broadband providers get more leeway to slow traffic.

2011 FCC Open Internet Order takes effect. . . . House passes resolution calling for the order to be rescinded; a similar measure fails in the Senate. . . . Phone company ISP Verizon sues the FCC over the order, arguing that the agency has no authority to issue it. . . . Countries including the United States, Australia, Canada, Japan and South Korea sign the Anti-Counterfeiting Trade Agreement (ACTA), requiring stronger cross-border antipiracy enforcement.

2012 Motion Picture Association of America urges Congress to toughen anti-piracy legislation. . . . Congress puts two anti-piracy bills, the Stop Online Piracy Act (SOPA) and the Protect Intellectual Property Act (PIPA), on a fast track, but House and Senate leaders pull the measures from consideration two days after Wikipedia and other websites close for a day to protest them. . . . After protests, several European countries delay signing the Anti-Counterfeiting Trade Agreement (ACTA). . . . Department of Justice shuts down Hong Kong-based Megaupload file-sharing site for violating the Digital Millennium Copyright Act. . . . Comcast announces that traffic from its Xbox streaming video service won't count against users' monthly data caps, but other video-streaming will; net-neutrality advocates say Comcast's policy endangers the Internet's standing as a neutral medium fostering economic competition.

'Remix' Culture Worries Copyright Owners

Software allows anyone to manipulate works of art.

After young fans of British author J. K. Rowling began posting renditions of her wildly popular *Harry Potter* story on their own Potter-related websites, Warner Brothers — producer of the book's film version — fought back.

Even though Rowling and her publisher, Scholastic, said they supported the young fans' creative impulses, Warner Brothers tried to block some of the websites, many of them run by children or teenagers, arguing that it wanted to prevent audience confusion about which sites were official.[1]

Heather Lawver, a young American fan, circulated a petition to stop Warner's crackdown and debated a company executive on television. "There are dark forces afoot, darker even than [Potter's evil nemesis] He-Who-Must-Not-Be-Named, . . . daring to take away something so basic, so human, that it's close to murder," she wrote. "They are taking away our freedom of speech."[2]

Warner Brothers backed off.

The episode underscored the increasingly uneasy relationship between copyright owners and others with a financial stake in creative works and a so-called "remix" culture that creates new art by copying, building upon and altering older art.

"Remix culture is in fact not an invention of the digital age," noted Edward W. Felten, a professor of computer science and public affairs at Princeton University.[3] Shakespeare, after all, famously borrowed virtually every plot twist of his play "Julius Caesar" from the Roman historian Plutarch.

New, however, is the breadth of older works that artists can incorporate, now that all art can be digitized and software allows virtually anyone to access, remix and manipulate it, altering visual art pixel by pixel, for example.

Furthermore, while the ability to publish was once the province of professionals, today everyone can publish their creations online.

As a result, traditional distinctions between artist and audience are breaking down.

"Once upon a time . . . the edge of the stage was there. The performers are on one side. The audience is on the other side, and never the twain shall meet," said Eric Kleptone, a Brighton, England-based producer of mashups — recordings that blend tracks from other songs into new music. As media-manipulating software such as Pro Tools, for music, and Photoshop, for graphics, allows people to put their own stamp on art they love, the creator-audience dichotomy is changing, he said. Increasingly, the media-buying public expect "that they should be able to personalize [purchased media] or manipulate it in some way. Or at least have the freedom to do so."[4]

By allowing amateurs to share their creations and get feedback, the Internet spurs more amateur remixes — and makes it easier for copyright owners to find — and object to — such uses of their creative output, according to Henry Jenkins, a professor of communications at the University of Southern California. In the past, "nobody minded, really, if you copied a few songs and shared the dub tape with a friend," he wrote. "But, as those transactions came out from behind closed doors, they represented a visible, public threat to the absolute control the culture industries asserted over their intellectual property."[5]

For the most part, copyright owners' response has been to ask Congress to "massively" increase "regulation

Such attempts are doomed, however, according to Lessig. Any technological fix "will likely be eclipsed" in short order by new technologies that make it even easier for consumers to access and adapt media, he wrote.[44]

Net Neutrality

The Internet was born in the 1960s when engineers at the Rand Corp., a think tank that focused on military issues, sought to devise a communications network that could survive a nuclear war.

Traditional networks — like the phone system and U.S. Postal Service — route messages through central switching points and can break down completely if vital nodes are knocked out. Rand's Paul Baran proposed a network with no central switch points but merely many smaller, widely dispersed nodes, each of which could route of creativity in America," wrote Lawrence Lessig, a professor at Harvard Law School. As a result, "To build upon or critique the culture around us one must ask . . . for permission first. Permission is, of course, often granted — but it is not often granted to the critical or the independent."[6]

Crackdowns on amateur expression risk snuffing out a vital source of cultural progress, argued Lessig. In the past, "The ordinary ways in which ordinary individuals shared and transformed their culture — telling stories, reenacting scenes from plays or TV, participating in fan clubs, sharing music, making tapes — were left alone by the law." It was "a tradition that, for at least the first 180 years of our Republic, guaranteed creators the right to build freely upon their past."[7]

As the realization dawns that the Internet is nearly impossible to control, some copyright holders may be casting a friendlier eye on remixers, some analysts say.

Warner Brothers' subsidiary New Line Cinema, for example, actually collaborated with bloggers and Internet movie-fan communities in the making and marketing of the 2005 horror movie "Snakes on a Plane," wrote Aram Sinnreich, an assistant professor at Rutgers University's School of Communication and Information.

"After advance word of the film was leaked . . . the one-two punch of its absurd title and a star turn by Samuel L. Jackson (perhaps the most remixed and mashed-up actor in cyberspace) attracted legions" of fans to share online "video mash-ups and remixes, doctored photographs," parodies and more, which the studio used to shape both its marketing campaign and the plot of the film itself, Sinnreich said.[8]

— *Marcia Clemmitt*

Getty Images/Jeff J. Mitchell

Young fans of Harry Potter author J. K. Rowling posted their own Harry Potter spin-offs, raising copyright concerns.

[3] Edward Felten, quoted in Carlos Ovalle, transcript, "Rip, Mix, Burn, Sue: Technology, Politics and the Fight to Control Digital Media," a lecture, Oct. 12, 2004, (transcript by Carlos Ovalle), www.cs.princeton .edu/~felten/rip.

[4] Quoted in Aram Sinnreich, *Mashed Up: Music, Technology, and the Rise of Configurable Culture* (2010), p. 109.

[5] Jenkins, *op. cit.*, p. 137.

[6] Lawrence Lessig, *Free Culture: The Nature and Future of Creativity* (2005), p. 71.

[7] *Ibid.*, p. 8.

[8] Sinnreich, *op. cit.*, p. 79.

[1] Henry Jenkins, *Convergence Culture: Where Old and New Media Collide* (2006), p. 137.

[2] Quoted in *ibid.*, p. 87.

data to another node until a message finally reached its destination. Each message would be chopped into tiny "packets" of digital code, and each separately addressed packet would travel on its own to the destination, where a computer would reassemble all the packets into a coherent message.

Each digital packet "would be tossed like a hot potato from node to node to node, more or less in the direction

of its destination, until it ended up in the proper place," explained technology and science fiction writer Bruce Sterling. "If big pieces of the network had been blown away, that simply wouldn't matter; the packets would still stay airborne, lateralled wildly across the field by whatever nodes happened to survive."[45]

Soon the fledgling network was up and running, with packets traveling over telephone wires. The seven

Entertainment Industry Seeks New Business Plan

"There is a slow and grudging march toward progress."

You might say the pirate hunters engaged in a little piracy of their own. At the Sundance Film Festival, in Park City, Utah, this past January, VEVO — a video website owned by music-industry giants Sony Music Entertainment and Universal Music Group — streamed a pirated ESPN football game for guests, according to technology writer Jason Kincaid. Like many who pirate, VEVO likely streamed the game illegally because doing so was convenient and because a legal stream at a reasonable price wasn't available, Kincaid said.[1]

Sony and Universal have been at the forefront of protecting profits and fighting music and movie piracy, but as VEVO's display of the game underscores, they could be fighting a losing battle. Eventually, the Internet could make a wide variety of media — movies, TV programs, music CDs and other offerings — more easily and cheaply accessible to everyone, on demand, even if it means streaming content illegally.

Yet, while conventional wisdom says that such a trend would be financially devastating for media companies, the sales effects of piracy — and of laws that crack down on it — aren't as clear-cut as they might seem, some experts argue.

For example, in one study, researchers found that while pirated movies released before a film's debut significantly reduce opening-weekend box-office revenues, the piracy had no impact on the box-office take after that. That might have been because only fervent fans who attend openings want to see movies pre-release.[2]

In France, where an ultra-tough three-strikes-and-you're-banned-from-the-Internet law was adopted in 2009, aimed at individual users, piracy rose after enactment, as illegal downloaders switched to websites not explicitly targeted by the law. Furthermore, some of the most active music pirates in the study were also among the most frequent music buyers, so banning them from the Internet could wind up depressing sales, the researchers said.[3]

Of course, big media companies that rely on above-the-board sales of movies and music would rather see piracy disappear. But Internet sales of creative works may not be as gloomy as some may think, thanks in large part to an expanding online marketplace.

"It's true that CD sales are down precipitously," but the size of the music sector overall "actually grew last year," says Aram Sinnreich, an assistant professor at Rutgers University's School of Communication and Information. While some

research-university computers that constituted the entire network in 1969 expanded to thousands by the early 1970s and millions by the early 1990s. Users paid to use phone lines to transmit their data, but, otherwise, phone companies showed no interest in the medium.

As a result, the Internet initially developed without the strife that attended the early spread of such technologies as the telephone.

"There were no . . . Internet service providers . . . no commercial anything. So nobody . . . saw the original Internet initiative as a threat to their business," said Robert Kahn, an early Internet developer.[46]

In 1972, AT&T actually turned down an offer from the federal government to run the Internet.[47]

As late as 1996, when Congress undertook its first major overhaul of telecommunications law since 1934, lawmakers, too, ignored the Internet, mentioning it only a handful of times. Instead, the Telecommunications Act of 1996 focused on provisions lawmakers hoped would create more competition within each of the different forms of data transport, such as cable-TV or local landline phone service. The law also set up different regulatory structures for the various modes of information transfer, with cable companies operating under a completely different set of rules than telephone companies.[48]

growth came from a rebounding economy, he said, the rest was likely due to the growing universe of online venues for accessing music conveniently and economically.

At Apple's iTunes site, listeners can buy the exact songs they like for a wallet-friendly $1.29 per tune. At the London-based ad- and subscription-supported website Spotify, users can stream and share songs the company has licensed from record labels, without buying, if they choose, says Sinnreich.

In addition, "music publishers are having a field day," as downloads provide an unprecedented opportunity to sell the reams of older music to which they own rights, Sinnreich says. "Back catalogs used to be a hassle. You wouldn't distribute [CDs by 1970s singer-songwriter] Dan Fogelberg to Walmart" because too few would buy them, he says. But the CDs can be sold as downloads because no manufacturer or store shelf space is needed. And with computer tools that break recorded music into individual tracks and put it back together in new ways, "you can have [digital music producer] Danger Mouse do a remix of Dan Fogelberg" that may sell to a new generation.

What's needed, say many Internet experts, are new business and copyright models that reasonably compensate artists while helping consumers take advantage of online streaming, sharing and buying.

Such models might involve "licensing" — with websites buying the right to distribute songs, films or TV shows by selling ads or subscriptions and forwarding payment to industry groups such as the Recording Industry Association of America (RIAA) to distribute among the artists in proportion to how much their creative works were used.

Historically, that's been the solution to disputes between copyright holders and new technology, says David Touve, an assistant professor of business administration at Washington and Lee University, in Lexington, Va. "Radio is a massive infringer of copyright — except that they have a license," he quips. The challenge is "figuring out at what license value both copyright owners and others will be willing to participate," then devising an appropriate licensing scheme, he says.

Online technologies could help more artists get paid for their work, says Sinnreich. According to the RIAA, under "today's copyright-intensive system, only one in 10 albums make back their money" and, "if they don't, artists don't get paid. Can we develop a model that compensates a greater number of musicians?"

Websites such as TuneCore, which helps musicians place music on retail download sites such as Amazon, and CD Baby — a sales site for independent artists — show that payment can be distributed more widely and fairly among individual copyright holders, Sinnreich says. "There is a slow and grudging march toward progress on the economic front."

— *Marcia Clemmitt*

[1] Jason Kincaid, "Music Labels' Joint Venture, VEVO, Shows Pirated NFL Game at Sundance," *TechCrunch*, Feb. 9, 2012, http://techcrunch.com/2012/02/09/music-labels-joint-venture-vevo-shows-pirated-espn-game-at-sundance.

[2] "Selected Research Findings," "Digital Media," Heinz College iLab website, www.heinz.cmu.edu/ilab/research/digital-media/index.aspx.

[3] For background, see David Murphy, "French Anti-Piracy Law Actually Increasing Piracy," *PC Magazine*, March 28, 2010, www.pcmag.com/article2/0,2817,2361925,00.asp.

Lawmakers failed to grapple with the rapidly materializing prospect that the Internet would soon become a competitor to cable-TV and phone companies, transmitting video and audio data. They also did not foresee that Internet data would soon be carried by numerous modes, including TV cables, phone wires, high-speed wires, fiber-optic cables and wireless transmitters, some of which their new law had put under separate, very different, systems of regulation.

The main Internet-related provision in the 1996 law, which continues to have significant consequences, stems from these different levels of regulation. Specifically, the law states that cable-TV companies' broadband — or "high-speed" — Internet service will operate as a loosely regulated "information service" rather than a tightly regulated "telecommunications carrier," such as a phone company.

"Telecommunications carriers" — like the "common carriers" of old — must offer access to their lines to anyone who seeks it, including competing businesses. For this reason, slow, dial-up Internet service — which travels over regular phone lines — has been offered by many independent ISPs to whom phone companies are required to open their lines.

By contrast, in dubbing cable broadband Internet an "information service," Congress lumped it with "luxuries, non-essentials that don't need the same level of protection," says Pennsylvania State's Frieden. That decision — plus

German Web entrepreneur Kim Dotcom, founder of Megaupload. com, a file-sharing website, leaves an Auckland, New Zealand, court on Feb. 22, 2012, after being released on bail. He was arrested at the request of the U.S. Justice Department, which is seeking to extradite him on online piracy charges.

fast-moving technological change — set up the so-called "net neutrality" debate that has raged ever since.

For one thing, soon after passage of the 1996 law, phone companies joined cable TV companies as providers of high-speed Internet, laying down their own technologically advanced networks — DSL, or digital subscriber lines, and, later, wireless networks and fiber-optic cable.

Furthermore, in the late 1990s and accelerating in the 2000s, the Internet's importance to public life and business soared as it became a one-stop shop for media and communications, as well as business functions such as shopping and banking. For many observers, this raised the question of whether the public's growing political and economic dependence on online access required all ISPs to operate as a kind of common carrier.

Further complicating matters, so-called packet-sniffing technology was developed that gave ISPs the ability to find out what kind of data a website was transmitting and, to some degree at least, slow or speed up that data.

In the early 2000s, calls began for the government to require all ISPs — including the lightly regulated cable companies — to abide by a principle of "net neutrality," treating data from all websites the same. In 2005, however, the Supreme Court and the FCC moved the other way. In a key ruling based on Congress' classification of cable broadband as an "information service," the Supreme Court ruled 6-3 that a cable company had no obligation to open its lines to a competing, independent ISP.[49]

The ruling opened the door for telephone companies to argue that if cable broadband was not obliged to follow common-carrier-type rules, their broadband services shouldn't be required to do so either.

In 2005, the FCC agreed. Beginning in August 2006, phone companies would no longer be required to offer competing ISPs, such as AOL, free access to their DSL connections. Dial-up Internet would still travel free over regular phone lines, however.[50]

The FCC was not entirely comfortable with leaving ISPs with so much discretion to block competitors, however. It announced that it would monitor ISPs to protect consumers' right to access and run any lawful websites, applications or services and link to the Internet any devices that would not harm the ISP network.

In 2008, the U.S. Court of Appeals for the District of Columbia ruled that cable giant Comcast had violated those policies when it selectively blocked some users' peer-to-peer file-sharing, which Comcast said it did to prevent Internet bottlenecks. In 2010, however, the same court decreed that, under the 1966 law, the FCC had no authority to impose common-carrier-type rules on cable broadband.[51]

Lawmakers are sharply divided. In 2009, Sen. John McCain, R-Ariz., introduced a bill that, with a few exceptions, would have banned the FCC from issuing any rules governing the Internet. That same year Rep. Edward Markey, D-Mass., introduced legislation to establish net neutrality as national policy.

Technical complexity hampers the progress, says Princeton's Felten. "There's a general consensus" that requiring ISPs to be evenhanded has value, "but how do you draw the line between reasonable network management and discrimination? That's hard to talk about" in legislative language, he says.

In December 2010, the FCC adopted an "Open Internet Order," proposing to maintain net neutrality through three rules. Network operators must:

- publicly disclose methods for managing network traffic;
- not block legal applications or websites, except as required for network management;
- not practice "unreasonable discrimination" among websites.

Only the "no blocking" and public-disclosure rules will apply to wireless broadband. Unlike wired transmission, wireless leaks a large amount of its signal into the air, experiences significant signal interference and can't easily add more capacity, as wired networks can. Therefore, as Internet traffic increases, wireless networks might become hopelessly congested without aggressive traffic management, the agency noted.[52]

The order took effect on Nov. 20, 2011.

CURRENT SITUATION

Going Dark

After seeming to be on the fast track toward enacting strict new online copyright enforcement, Congress has backed away amid protests by individuals and some major Internet players, including Google and Wikipedia. Meanwhile, some lawmakers are vowing to stop the FCC's net-neutrality order.

In January, Congress postponed long-expected floor votes for SOPA (H.R. 3261), introduced last year in the House by Smith, the Texas Republican — and PIPA — the Protect Intellectual Property Act (S. 968), introduced last year by Sen. Patrick Leahy, D-Vt.[53]

The bills were intended to help copyright owners fight media piracy that websites such as the Swedish site The Pirate Bay facilitate. The Pirate Bay and other sites host so-called bit-torrent files and other software that allow users to share massive audio and video files, many of which are copyrighted. Entertainment industries want enhanced enforcement to stop it.

Posting copyrighted files online without paying is already illegal under the 1998 Digital Millennium Copyright Act (DMCA).[54] The entertainment industry argues, however, that, because the law is tougher on individual copyright infringers than on websites where the material is posted, it goes after small-time pirates while passing up the chance to shut off piracy at its source by forcing entire piracy-facilitating websites offline.

SOPA would give the government a quick path to order advertising networks and online-payment companies such as PayPal to cut off service to websites where copyright infringement is alleged to occur. It would bar search engines from linking to those sites and require ISPs to block access to them. Copyright owners themselves could order advertising and payment companies to stop doing business with websites that post copyrighted material and sue if companies don't comply.

PIPA takes a similar approach but differs in some particulars. For example, it would not require search engines to remove infringing sites from their indexes and would set up a different legal process for seeking court orders.

PIPA is "a strong and balanced approach to protecting intellectual property through a . . . system that leverages the most relevant players in the Internet ecosystem," Leahy said in early January.[55]

Only a few days later, though, thousands of website owners staged a dramatic protest against what many called copyright owners' overreach. On Jan. 18, sites including Wikipedia, the social-media site Reddit, and Boing Boing shut down for the day, redirecting visitors to explanations of their objections to the bills. Other sites, including Google, expressed support for the protests, and millions signed online petitions against the legislation.[56]

"It's not hard to imagine . . . that a service provider, acting with abundance of caution and out of its own self-interest, will simply cut off services to entire sites that have been accused of infringement, even if the court order only applies to a portion of the site," wrote Christine Montgomery, president of the Online News Association, a digital journalists' organization.[57]

The ferocity of the fight is driven by the movie industry, says Kevin J. Greene, a professor of intellectual-property and entertainment law at Thomas Jefferson School of Law, in San Diego. The MPAA spent around $1 million a month fighting for the legislation during the last four to six months before Congress dropped the bills, he says. "Their fears are legitimate," though, especially when it comes to how piracy affects global sales, he says. "In the online world, it's said that if you have a video game to sell in China, you'll sell one copy" because the rest will be pirated.

Nevertheless, the MPAA "said that the problem they were going after was foreign websites, but the language in the bill was so broad" that it casts doubt on that claim, says Greene. "It looks more like they just wanted more weapons in their arsenal" against copyright infringement in general, even though "that arsenal has been getting bigger and bigger for years." (The MPAA did not respond to *CQ Researcher*'s request for comment.)

On Jan. 20, congressional leaders withdrew the bills from consideration.[58]

Should lawmakers support the FCC's net-neutrality rules?

YES — Gigi B. Sohn
President, Public Knowledge

From testimony before the House Judiciary Subcommittee on Intellectual Property, Competition and the Internet, Feb. 15, 2011

An open Internet is vitally important to political discourse, societal interactions, commercial transactions, innovation, entrepreneurship and job creation in the United States. However, past actions by incumbent broadband Internet access providers have threatened the preservation of an open internet resulting in the need for clear, enforceable baseline network-neutrality rules.

Network-neutrality rules are necessary to protect consumers against the monopoly and duopoly behavior of broadband Internet access providers in our country. Contrary to assertions by industry incumbents that consumers enjoy competition when it comes to broadband access choice and can simply switch, the Federal Communications Commission's (FCC's) National Broadband Plan reported that 13 percent of Americans have only one broadband access provider, and 78 percent of Americans have only two broadband Internet access providers.

Cable and telephone incumbents have asserted that network-neutrality rules are unnecessary and that the market has never demonstrated the need for rules. However, there is a documented history of harmful actions taken by broadband Internet access providers. The commission observed that it had acted on two high-profile incidents of blocking but recounted evidence of numerous other incidents. . . .

AT&T blocked certain applications, such as SlingBox video streaming, Skype and Google voice, from its mobile network while permitting its own streaming and voice products to use the same network. Cox and RCN both admitted to slowing or degrading Internet traffic at times. Both providers deny wrongdoing and claim that these practices are designed to handle congestion, but in neither case did providers disclose their traffic-management practices to subscribers. It is ironic that providers which publicly proclaim they have no intention of ever actually blocking or degrading content routinely include statements in their terms of service that would allow them to engage in precisely these practices — and without prior notice to consumers.

I want to mention Public Knowledge's concern with recent discussions in Congress to invoke the Congressional Review Act (CRA) to repeal the FCC network-neutrality rules. Enactment of a CRA repeal of the FCC's network-neutrality rules would virtually eliminate the agency's authority to protect an open Internet.

I urge members of the committee to recognize that the economic benefits of the Internet are entirely based on ensuring that it remains an open and free marketplace and that the federal government has an integral role to play in that regard.

NO — Larry Downs
Senior Adjunct Fellow, TechFreedom

From testimony before the House Judiciary Subcommittee on Intellectual Property, Competition and the Internet, Feb. 15, 2011

Proponents of net-neutrality regulation argue that the Internet's defining feature — and the key to its unarguable success — is the content-neutral routing and transport of individual packets throughout the network by Internet service providers, Internet backbones and other individual networks that make up the Internet.

As evidenced in all of my writings on the digital revolution, I share the enthusiasm for the open internet. I just don't believe there is any evidence of a need for regulatory intervention to "save" this robust ecosystem, or that the Federal Communications Commission (FCC) had the authority to do so.

As with any lawmaking involving disruptive technologies, moreover, the risk of unintended consequences is high.

There was no need for new regulation. Despite thousands of pages of comments from parties on all sides of the issue, in the end the [FCC] majority could only identify four incidents in the last 10 years of what it believed to be non-neutral behavior. All four were quickly resolved outside the agency's adjudication processes. Yet these four incidents provide the sole evidence of a need to regulate. With no hint of market failure, the majority instead has issued what it calls a "prophylactic rule" it hopes will deter any actual problems in the future.

But maybe these four incidents are not what's really driving the push for FCC regulation of Internet access. Maybe the real problem is, as many regulatory advocates argue vaguely, the lack of "competition" for broadband. According to the National Broadband Plan, 5 percent of the U.S. population still doesn't have access to any wireless broadband provider. In many parts of the country only two providers are available, and in others the offered speeds of alternatives vary greatly, leaving users without high-speed alternatives.

If lack of competition is the problem, though, why not solve the problem? Multiple technologies have been used to deliver broadband access to consumers, including DSL, coaxial cable, cellular, wireless and broadband over power lines (BPL). But rather than promote multiple technologies, the FCC has done just the opposite. For example, the agency has sided with some state governments who argued successfully that they can prevent municipalities from offering telecommunications service. And the commission has dragged its feet on approving trials for BPL.

Why does anyone believe the FCC can "prophylactically" solve a problem dealing with an emerging, rapidly evolving new technology that has thrived in the last decade in part because it was unregulated?

The protests themselves were a kind of watershed in Internet history — "the first time the Internet rose to defend itself," says Ippolito, of the University of Maine.

Others doubt that grassroots activism played much of a role, however. In the end, the dispute was "monopoly against monopoly, a clash of very big players," with Google and Facebook pitted openly against entertainment-industry giants such as Sony for the first time, says Robert W. Gehl, an assistant professor of communication at the University of Utah, in Salt Lake.

Progress toward an anti-piracy treaty once thought to be on the fast track to adoption also slowed this year.

In October 2011, countries including Australia, Canada, Japan, Morocco, New Zealand, Singapore, South Korea and the United States signed the Anti-Counterfeiting Trade Agreement (ACTA), which would set tough international standards for pursuing copyright enforcement and other anticounterfeiting actions.[59] This year, however, protests in countries such as the U.K., Germany, Poland and the Netherlands have led several European countries to postpone signing the measure.[60]

The White House Office of the U.S. Trade Representative promises that the compact will "support American jobs in innovative and creative industries."[61]

But opponents argue that while the treaty targets "commercial-scale piracy," its language is so vague that it might criminalize small-scale noncommercial file-sharing that involves no financial gain and is handled in civil courts today.[62]

Net Neutrality in Court

The FCC's plan to monitor ISPs for possible discrimination against particular websites remains under fire. In 2011, a joint congressional resolution disapproving the rule — and ordering the agency to refrain from regulating the Internet altogether until Congress issues directions for how to do so — passed the House but failed in the Senate.[63]

Lawsuits questioning the order are proceeding.

On Sept. 30, 2011, New York City-based Verizon Communications filed suit, arguing that the order is unnecessary and that the FCC had no legal authority to promulgate it. "We are deeply concerned by the FCC's assertion of broad authority to impose potentially sweeping and unneeded regulations on broadband networks and services and on the Internet itself," said Senior Vice President Michael E. Glover.[64]

CQ Press/Screenshot

Boing Boing and thousands of other websites, including Wikipedia and Reddit, shut down on Jan. 18, 2012, to protest proposed legislation to block pirating of online copyrighted material. The sites oppose the Stop Online Piracy Act and the Protect Intellectual Property Act, which they claim would amount to censorship. Posting copyrighted files online without paying is already illegal, but supporters of the legislation, principally the entertainment industry, argue tougher laws are needed to stop piracy at its source.

Yet, the Massachusetts-based media-reform advocacy group Free Press also has filed suit, arguing that the rule doesn't go far enough. "The final rules . . . fail to protect wireless users from discrimination," an "arbitrary distinction" between regulations for wireless and wired Internet that is "unjustified," said Policy Director Matt Wood.[65]

Some analysts say Congress must act to clarify the situation for consumers, the FCC and the courts.

ISP subscribers "don't expect anybody to mess with" their data delivery, says Frieden, of Pennsylvania State. For that reason, "Congress needs to clarify the law," stipulating exactly what power the FCC has to settle disputes between consumers and ISPs, he says. "You can revile government and hate the courts but you need some kind of referee here."

OUTLOOK
Continuing Battles

It's anybody's guess how the ongoing battles over control of digital intellectual property and management of the Internet's traffic flows will turn out.

This year's heated debate over SOPA and PIPA, however, did reveal something new, says Greene, of Thomas

Jefferson Law School. For the first time in a fight over copyrights, "the motion picture industry was up against somebody as well financed as they are" — Internet giants such as Google and Facebook — and that fact is what slowed the bills down, he says.

If SOPA or PIPA were enacted, it would break a "deal cut in 1998" when Congress, the entertainment industry and Internet businesses negotiated the Digital Millennium Copyright Act, Greene says. At that time, everyone agreed that "there's a lot of piracy online but also that we don't want ISPs to actually have to police it," he says.

Recently, however, MPAA came back with new proposals, asking Congress to require ISPs to do just that. In the past, they've gotten what they wanted through back-room channels, Greene says. This time, though, the Internet industry "has more power and money than the entertainment industry."

Many analysts worry that the concerns of the public and of small business won't be heard in the debates.

"Nobody, except for some poorly funded organizations" such as the San Francisco-based Electronic Frontier Foundation — which advocates on civil-liberties issues related to computers —"are standing up for the consumer and citizen," says Aram Sinnreich, an assistant professor at Rutgers University's School of Communication and Information. And those groups have trouble enlisting support "since it's difficult to make these arguments in terms that make sense to non-policy wonks," he says.

Ironically, while the goal of net-neutrality advocates is ensuring that new, small organizations with good ideas get a chance to grow online, such organizations are left out of legislative discussions, says Felten, of Princeton. "When it comes to small companies in the startup culture, and small business as an engine of growth, there's less understanding than there could be" of what's needed. "People in government look to large, established companies" for guidance on shaping the laws, he says.

Most alarming to some is the likelihood that powerful industries' desire to control online behavior — such as by detecting downloads of copyrighted media —"will overlap with a political interest in overseeing citizens' online behavior," says Sinnreich.

"As committed as we are to freedom, our government and every other government in the world has a prevailing interest in surveillance and control, which is truly scary if it aligns with corporate interest in the same thing."

NOTES

1. Quoted in Emma Barnett, "Wikipedia Founder Jimmy Wales Defends SOPA Protest Blackout," *The Telegraph* [UK], Jan. 17, 2012, www.telegraph.co.uk/technology/wikipedia/9020053/Wikipedia-founder-Jimmy-Wales-defends-SOPA-protest-blackout.html.

2. Lamar Smith, "Why We Need a Law Against Online Piracy," CNN.com, Jan. 20, 2012, www.cnn.com/2012/01/20/opinion/smith-sopa-support/index.html.

3. Gerald R. Faulhaber and David J. Farber, "The Open Internet: A Customer-Centric Framework," *International Journal of Communication*, 2010, pp. 302-342, http://ijoc.org/ojs/index.php/ijoc/article/view/670/388.

4. For background, see "10 ISPs and Countries Known to Have Blocked VoIP," *VoIP Providers List*, Feb. 2, 2009, www.voipproviderslist.com/articles/others/10-isps-and-countries-known-to-have-blocked-voip.html.

5. Edward Felten, "'Neutrality' Is Hard to Define," Room for Debate blog, *The New York Times*, Aug. 10, 2010, www.nytimes.com/roomfordebate/2010/8/9/who-gets-priority-on-the-web/net-neutrality-is-hard-to-define.

6. "Who Music Theft Hurts," Recording Industry Association of America, www.riaa.com/physicalpiracy.php?content_selector=piracy_details_online.

7. "MPAA Statement on Strong Showing of Support for Stop Online Privacy Act," Motion Picture Association of American, Inc., press release, Dec. 16, 2011, www.mpaa.org/resources/5a0a212e-c86b-4e9a-abf1-2734a15862cd.pdf. See also, "Intellectual Property and the U.S. Economy: Industries in Focus," U.S. Commerce Department, March 2012, www.esa.doc.gov/sites/default/files/reports/documents/ipandtheuseconomyindustriesinfocus.pdf.

8. Mark Elliot, letter to the editor, *The New York Times*, Nov. 18, 2011, www.nytimes.com/2011/11/19/opinion/rogue-web-sites.html.

9. "Protect IP and SOPA Legislation — Obama Administration Announcement," A2IM website, Jan. 16, 2012, http://a2im.org/tag/sopa.

10. Mark Sweney, "Global Recorded Music Sales Fall Almost $1.5 bn Amid Increased Piracy," *The Guardian* [UK], March 28, 2011, www.guardian.co.uk/business/2011/mar/28/global-recorded-music-sales-fall.

11. Quoted in *ibid.*

12. "IFPI Publishes Digital Music Report 2012," press release, International Federation of the Phonographic Industry, Jan. 23, 2012, www.ifpi.org/content/section_resources/dmr2012.html.

13. Michael Grecco, "Michael Grecco Is Pro Protect IP and SOPA," MichaelGrecco.com, Jan. 20, 2012, http://michaelgrecco.com/michael-grecco-blog/michael-grecco-is-pro-protect-ip-and-sopa.

14. Stephen E. Siwek, "The True Cost of Copyright Industry Piracy to the U.S. Economy," Institute for Policy Innovation, October 2007, www.ipi.org/IPI%5CIPIPublications.nsf/PublicationLookupFullTextPDF/02DA0B4B44F2AE9286257369005ACB57/$File/CopyrightPiracy.pdf?OpenElement.

15. "Observations on Efforts to Quantify the Economic Effects of Counterfeit and Pirated Goods," Government Accountability Office, April 2010, www.gao.gov/new.items/d10423.pdf.

16. Tim Lee, "Texas-sized Sophistry," The Technology Liberation Front website, Oct. 1, 2006, http://techliberation.com/2006/10/01/texas-size-sophistry.

17. Lawrence Lessig, *Free Culture: The Nature and Future of Creativity* (2005), p. 71.

18. *Ibid.*, p. 67.

19. Julian Sanchez, "How Copyright Industries Con Congress," Cato at Liberty blog, Jan. 3, 2012, www.cato-at-liberty.org/how-copyright-industries-con-congress.

20. Christopher Dodd, "These Two Bills Are the Best Approach," Room for Debate blog, *The New York Times*, Jan. 18, 2012, www.nytimes.com/roomfordebate/2012/01/18/whats-the-best-way-to-protect-against-online-piracy/these-two-bills-are-the-best-approach.

21. Grecco, *op. cit.*

22. "Protect IP and SOPA Legislation — Obama Administration Announcement," *op. cit.*

23. Ryan Radia, "Are Rogue Websites Really So Bad After All?" The Technology Liberation Front, Jan. 23, 2012, http://techliberation.com/2012/01/23/are-rogue-websites-really-so-bad-after-all.

24. Julian Sanchez, "Focus on Innovation Instead," Room for Debate blog, *The New York Times*, Jan. 18, 2012, www.nytimes.com/roomfordebate/2012/01/18/whats-the-best-way-to-protect-against-online-piracy/the-content-industry-should-focus-on-innovation-instead.

25. For background, see Vickie Chang, "Painful Parody," *OC Weekly*, Sept. 9, 2010, www.ocweekly.com/2010-09-09/music/vandals-vs-daily-variety/.

26. Joe Escalante, "Does Daily Variety Validate SOPA Fears?" *Huffington Post*, Jan. 23, 2012, www.huffingtonpost.com/joe-escalante/sopa-copyright_b_1222058.html.

27. Clay Shirky, "Pick up the Pitchforks: David Pogue Underestimates Hollywood," Shirky.com, Jan. 20, 2012, www.shirky.com/weblog/2012/01/pick-up-the-pitchforks-david-pogue-underestimates-hollywood.

28. Adam Thierer, "Net Neutrality Regulation & the First Amendment," The Technology Liberation Front, Dec. 9, 2009, http://techliberation.com/2009/12/09/net-neutrality-regulation-the-first-amendment.

29. *Ibid.*

30. Barbara Esbin, "Net Neutrality: A Further Take on the Debate," The Progress & Freedom Foundation, December 2009, http://papers.ssrn.com/sol3/papers.cfm?abstract_id=1529090.

31. For background, see *Loretto v. Teleprompter Manhattan CATV Corp.*, 458 U.S. 419, 434-35 (1982), http://caselaw.lp.findlaw.com/cgi-bin/getcase.pl?navby=case&court=US&vol=458&invol=419&pageno=436.

32. For background, see K. C. Jones, "Comcast Removes Blocks on File Sharing," *Information Week*, Jan. 7, 2009, www.informationweek.com/news/internet/policy/212701122; Ryan Paul, "FCC to Investigate Comcast BitTorrent Blocking," *Ars Technica*, http://arstechnica.com/tech-policy/news/2008/01/fcc-to-investigate-comcast-bittorrent-blocking.ars.

33. Jonathan Zittrain, "Net Neutrality as Diplomacy," Jan. 23, 2011, http://papers.ssrn.com/sol3/papers.cfm?abstract_id=1729424.

34. For background, see Tim Wu, *Master Switch: The Rise and Fall of Information Empires* (2010); Marcia

Clemmitt, "Controlling the Internet," *CQ Researcher*, May 12, 2006, pp. 409-432; Kenneth Jost, "Copyright and the Internet," *CQ Researcher*, Sept. 29, 2000, pp. 769-792.

35. Wu, *op. cit.*, p. 27.

36. *Ibid.*, p. 10.

37. *Ibid.*, p. 58.

38. Lawrence Lessig, *Free Culture: How Big Media Uses Technology and the Law to Lock Down Culture and Control Creativity* (2004), p. 57.

39. Quoted in Carlos Ovalle, transcript, "Rip, Mix, Burn, Sue: Technology, Politics and the Fight to Control Digital Media," a lecture by Edward Felten, Oct. 12, 2004, www.cs.princeton.edu/~felten/rip.

40. *Sony Corp. v. Universal City Studios*, 464 U.S. 417 (1984), http://supreme.justia.com/cases/federal/us/464/417.

41. Ovalle, *op. cit.*

42. For background, see Steve Knopper, "Napster Wounds the Giant," *Rocky Mountain News*, Jan. 2, 2009, www.rockymountainnews.com/news/2009/jan/02/napster-wounds-the-giant.

43. Lessig, *Free Culture: How Big Media Uses Technology*, *op. cit.*, kindle location 5476, Chap. 12, footnote 11.

44. *Ibid.*, p. 193.

45. Bruce Sterling, "Internet," *The Magazine of Fantasy and Science Fiction*, February 1993, archived at Electronic Frontier Foundation website, w2.eff.org/Net_culture/internet_sterling.history.txt.

46. Quoted in "Putting It All Together With Robert Kahn," Computer and Computer History website, http://66.14.166.45/history/network/Robert%20Kahn%20Interview%20-%20Putting%20it%20all%20Together%20with%20Robert%20Kahn.pdf.

47. For background, see Scott Bradner, "Blocking the Power of the Internet," *Network World*, Jan. 16, 2006, www.networkworld.com/columnists/2006/011606bradner.html.

48. For background, see Charles B. Goldfarb, "Telecommunications Act: Competition, Innovation, Reform," Congressional Research Service, Aug. 12, 2005, http://digital.library.unt.edu/ark:/67531/metacrs7798/m1/1/high_res_d/RL33034_2005Aug12.pdf.

49. For background, see *National Cable & Telecommunications Assn. v. Brand X Internet Services*, 545 U.S. 967 (2005), www.law.cornell.edu/supct/html/04-277.ZS.html.

50. For background, see Angele A. Gilroy, "Access to Broadband Networks: The Net Neutrality Debate," Congressional Research Service, Oct. 25, 2011, www.fas.org/sgp/crs/misc/R40616.pdf.

51. For background, see *Comcast Corp. v. FCC*, 600 F.3d 642, www.cadc.uscourts.gov/internet/opinions.nsf/EA10373FA9C20DEA85257807005BD63F/$file/08-1291-1238302.pdf.

52. For background, see Matthew Lasar, "It's Here: FCC Adopts Net Neutrality (Lite)," *Ars Technica*, 2011, http://arstechnica.com/tech-policy/news/2010/12/its-here-fcc-adopts-net-neutrality-lite.ars, and Elliott Drucker, "Tech Insights — Sizing Up Wireline Vs. Wireless Performance," *Wireless Week*, Jan. 16, 2011, www.wirelessweek.com/Articles/2011/02/Drucker-Sizing-Up-Wireline-Vs-Wireless-Performance.aspx.

53. For background, see bill text, H.R. 3261, Thomas, Library of Congress, http://thomas.loc.gov/cgi-bin/query/z?c112:H.R.3261:, and bill text versions, S. 968, Thomas, Library of Congress, http://thomas.loc.gov/cgi-bin/query/z?c112:S.968.

54. For background, see "The Digital Millennium Copyright Act of 1998," U.S. Copyright Office, December 1998, www.copyright.gov/legislation/dmca.pdf.

55. Quoted in Mike Masnick, "Senator Leahy Hopes to Rush Through PIPA By Promising to Study DNS Blocking . . . Later?" *TechDirt*, Jan. 12, 2012, www.techdirt.com/articles/20120112/14322317392/senator-leahy-hopes-to-rush-through-pipa-promising-to-study-dns-blocking-later.shtml.

56. For background, see Sean Poulter and Rob Waugh, "Wikipedia Protest Hits Home: U.S. Senators Withdraw Support for Anti-piracy Bills as 4.5 Million Sign Petition," *Daily Mail Online* [UK], Jan. 19, 2012, www.dailymail.co.uk/news/article-2087673/Wikipedia-blackout-SOPA-protest-US-senators-withdraw-support-anti-piracy-bills.html.

57. Christine Montgomery, "Letter from the President: Why ONA Opposes Sopa," Online News Association

website, Jan. 5, 2012, http://journalists.org/2012/01/05/ona-on-sopa.

58. For background, see SOPA/PIPA Timeline, *Pro Publica*, http://projects.propublica.org/sopa/timeline.

59. For background, see "Anti-Counterfeiting Trade Agreement," www.mofa.go.jp/policy/economy/i_property/pdfs/acta1105_en.pdf.

60. For background, see "Timeout for Finland in Ratifying ACTA," *Valtioneuvosto*, Finnish Government, March 9, 2012, http://valtioneuvosto.fi/ajankohtaista/tiedotteet/tiedote/fi.jsp?oid=352766&c=0&toid=1802&moid=1803; Dave Lee, "ACTA Protests: Thousands Take to Streets Across Europe," BBC News, Feb. 11, 2012, www.bbc.co.uk/news/technology-16999497; Raphael Satter and Venssa Gera, "Anonymous Protests ACTA, Attacks FTC and Other U.S. Agencies' Sites," Associated Press/*Huffington Post*, Feb. 17, 2012, www.huffingtonpost.com/2012/02/17/anonymous-acta-ftc_n_1285668.html; Anti-Counterfeiting Trade Agreement, Foreign Affairs and International Trade Canada, www.international.gc.ca/trade-agreements-accords-commerciaux/fo/intellect_property.aspx?view=d; Glyn Moody, "Brazil Drafts and 'Anti-ACTA': A Civil-Rights-Based Framework for the Internet," *Tech Dirt*, www.techdirt.com/articles/20111004/04402516196/brazil-drafts-anti-acta-civil-rights-based-framework-internet.shtml.

61. "Anti-Counterfeiting Trade Agreement," Office of the U.S. Trade Representative, www.ustr.gov/acta.

62. Dan Mitchell, "Meet SOPA's Evil Twin, ACTA," CNN Money, Jan. 26, 2012, http://tech.fortune.cnn.com/2012/01/26/meet-sopas-evil-twin-acta.

63. For background, see S.J.Res. 6, Open Congress, www.opencongress.org/bill/112-sj6/show.

64. Quoted in Marguerite Reardon, "Verizon Sues Again to Block Net Neutrality Rules," CNET, Sept. 30, 2011, http://news.cnet.com/8301-30686_3-20114142-266/verizon-sues-again-to-block-net-neutrality-rules.

65. Quoted in Grant Gross, "Free Press Files Lawsuit on FCC's Net Neutrality Rules," *Computer World*, Sept. 28, 2011, www.computerworld.com/s/article/9220367/Free_Press_files_lawsuit_on_FCC_s_net_neutrality_rules.

BIBLIOGRAPHY
Selected Sources
Books

Downes, Larry, *The Laws of Disruption: Harnessing the New Forces that Govern Life and Business in the Digital Age*, Basic Books, 2009.
A business and legal consultant describes how digitization and the Internet are disrupting the traditional economy. He argues against hasty government regulation of new technologies and for allowing a new legal system suitable to the digital era to emerge on its own.

Lessig, Lawrence, *Free Culture: The Nature and Future of Creativity*, Penguin, 2004.
A Harvard University law professor argues that copyright law favors copyright owners, empowering media companies to strangle creative digital opportunities.

Wu, Tim, *The Master Switch: The Rise and Fall of Information Empires*, Vintage, 2011.
A Columbia University law professor describes the history of American communications industries as one in which inventors create powerful industries that then fight to suppress competing innovations.

Articles

Ferreira, Heather, "What Do Directors Think When People Make a Torrent for Their Movie?" *Huffington Post*, Feb. 22, 2012, www.huffingtonpost.com/quora/what-do-directors-think-w_b_1292760.html.
An independent filmmaker argues that anti-piracy legislation serves the interests of big film studios and the highest-paid tier of Hollywood talent but not those of independent creators.

Hachman, Mark, "Comcast's Xfinity-on-Xbox Plans Draw Net Neutrality Fire," *PCMag.com*, March 26, 2012, www.pcmag.com/article2/0,2817,2402149,00.asp.
Net-neutrality advocates say Comcast's policy of not counting video streaming from its Xbox subsidiary toward customers' monthly data-usage caps violates the principle of an open Internet.

Jardine, Nick, "Meet the Man Who Founded the Pirate Party That Is Spreading Through European Parliaments,"

Business Insider, Dec. 5, 2011, http://articles.business insider.com/2011-12-05/europe/30477454_1_new-movement-young-voters-protest.
A Swedish-based political movement that aims to legalize online file-sharing is gaining support, especially among young people.

Wortham, Jenna, and Amy Chozick, "The Piracy Problem: How Broad?" *The New York Times*, Feb. 8, 2012, www.nytimes.com/2012/02/09/technology/in-piracy-debate-deciding-if-the-sky-is-falling.html?pagewanted=all.
Copyright-owning industries such as the movie and music businesses cite huge financial losses from piracy, but many consumers say they resort to pirating only when they can't conveniently access what they want at a reasonable price.

Reports and Studies

Benkler, Yochai, "Seven Lessons from SOPA/PIPA/Megaupload and Four Proposals on Where We Go From Here," techpresident, Jan. 25, 2012, http://techpresident.com/news/21680/seven-lessons-sopapipamegauplaod-and-four-proposals-where-we-go-here.
A Harvard law professor argues that anti-piracy bills in Congress this year were an over-reach by copyright-owning industries and that protests that slowed the bills' progress show how consumers are learning to use the Internet to accomplish political goals.

Esbin, Barbara S., "Net Neutrality: A Further Take on the Debate," Progress on Point, The Progress and Freedom Foundation, December 2009, http://papers.ssrn.com/sol3/papers.cfm?abstract_id=1529090.
A media lawyer and former Federal Communications Communication official argues that the fast-evolving nature of the Internet and its openness to new businesses and new ideas would be hampered if the government chose to regulate it.

Felten, Edward W., "Rip, Mix, Burn, Sue: Technology, Politics, and the Fight to Control Digital Media," video lecture, Princeton University, Oct. 12, 2004, www.cs.princeton.edu/~felten/rip; transcript, www.ischool.utexas.edu/~i312co/copyright/felten.html.
A Princeton University professor of computer science and public affairs discusses how digitization changes the game for media and communications businesses.

Gilroy, Angele A., "Access to Broadband Networks: The Net Neutrality Debate," *Congressional Research Service*, April 15, 2011, http://opencrs.com/document/R40616.
An analyst for Congress' nonpartisan research office describes the history and legislative, regulatory, judicial and commercial issues involved in the debate over net neutrality.

Thierer, Adam, "Net Neutrality Regulation & the First Amendment," The Technology Liberation Front, Dec. 9, 2009, http://techliberation.com/2009/12/09/net-neutrality-regulation-the-first-amendment.
A libertarian telecommunications analyst argues that net-neutrality advocates turn the Constitution's First Amendment on its head when they argue that in order to preserve freedom of speech Internet service providers (ISPs) must treat all content the same. In fact, he writes, net-neutrality rules would assault ISPs' free-speech rights by substituting government rules for ISPs' own editorial judgment.

For More Information

Chilling Effects Clearinghouse, www.chillingeffects.org. University-supported website that provides information on and analysis of digital-media issues.

Electronic Frontier Foundation, 454 Shotwell St., San Francisco, CA 94110-1914; 415-436-9333; www.eff.org. Advocates for media-related civil liberties, such as open access to the Internet.

Federal Communications Commission, 445 12th St., S.W., Washington, DC 20554; 888-225-5322; www.fcc.gov. Federal agency that sets rules for communications industries.

Motion Picture Association of America, 1600 Eye St., N.W., Washington, DC, 20006; 202-293-1966; www.mpaa .org. Trade association that represents the major American motion-picture and television studios.

Progress and Freedom Foundation, www.pff.org. Archives of a free-market-oriented think tank that analyzed digital media policy until October 2010.

Public Knowledge, 1818 N St., N.W., Suite 410, Washington, DC 20036; 202-861-0020; www.publicknowledge.org. Advocates for net neutrality and copyright policies that balance the interests of intellectual-property owners and media consumers.

Recording Industry Association of America, 1025 F St., N.W., 10th Floor, Washington, DC 20004; 202-775-0101; www.riaa.com. Trade association that represents major music-recording companies.

Technology Information Front, http://techliberation.com. Website of commentary by libertarian analysts that opposes government regulation of the Internet.

7

Youth Unemployment

Reed Karaim

Rioting that lasted for five days in London and other British cities last summer was blamed in part on the lack of jobs — particularly among the young. Many believe if the issue of youth joblessness isn't addressed, countries around the globe will see further upheavals, but analysts differ on how closely youth unemployment can be connected to social unrest.

From *CQ Researcher*,
March 6, 2012.

The line of hopeful South Africans stretched for more than a mile. Many of the thousands standing outside the University of Johannesburg in January had come long distances and been waiting since the middle of the night.

But when the campus gate finally opened, the crowd surged forward so violently that a woman was trampled to death; several others were seriously injured.

In a country with a youth unemployment rate of 70 percent, the chance to get one of a few hundred openings at a South African public university is intensely competitive. For the prospective students — many accompanied by their parents — who rushed the gate, a college education is a crucial requirement for getting a decent job.[1]

The incident capped a year in which the frustrations of young people were on display from Tahrir Square in Cairo to the streets of Athens, Madrid and London. With youth unemployment stuck at staggering levels in many countries, finding work for an ever-growing number of jobless youths has become a pressing international issue, with economic prosperity, regime survival and social stability at stake.

While the average unemployment rate for people ages 15 to 24 stood at 12.6 percent worldwide in 2011, it was much higher in some individual countries, according to the International Labour Organization (ILO). The latest statistics for Spain and Greece, for instance, show youth joblessness rates of about 50 percent, and parts of the Middle East and North Africa had rates of more than 30 percent.[2] In both Europe, with a rate of 20.9 percent, and the United States, with an 18.4 percent rate, youth unemployment was about double the overall levels of joblessness.[3] (*See graph, p. 153.*)

Youth Unemployment Highest in Arab World

Joblessness was higher among youths in the Middle East and North Africa over the past three years than in any other region and twice the global average of 12.7 percent, according to the most recent data available. Developed economies and the European Union also have above-average rates, with some individual countries — such as Spain and Greece — suffering from rates of around 50 percent.

Average Youth Unemployment Rates, by Region, 2008–2010

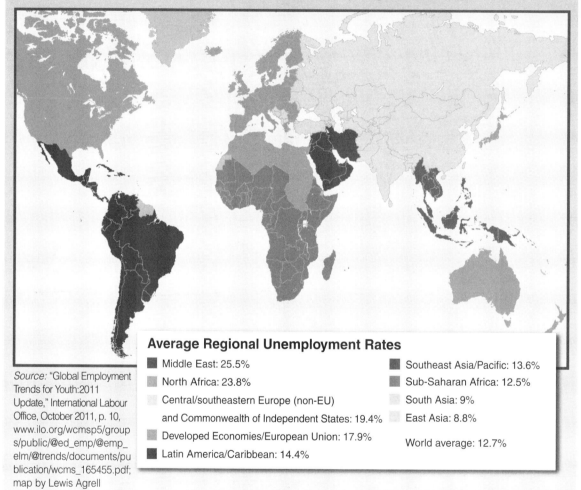

Average Regional Unemployment Rates

- Middle East: 25.5%
- North Africa: 23.8%
- Central/southeastern Europe (non-EU) and Commonwealth of Independent States: 19.4%
- Developed Economies/European Union: 17.9%
- Latin America/Caribbean: 14.4%
- Southeast Asia/Pacific: 13.6%
- Sub-Saharan Africa: 12.5%
- South Asia: 9%
- East Asia: 8.8%
- World average: 12.7%

Source: "Global Employment Trends for Youth:2011 Update," International Labour Office, October 2011, p. 10, www.ilo.org/wcmsp5/groups/public/@ed_emp/@emp_elm/@trends/documents/publication/wcms_165455.pdf; map by Lewis Agrell

The difficulties facing young people looking for work are so severe that analysts describe the prospect of "a lost generation," whose delayed entry into the job market will leave them far behind, even after the world economy recovers.[4]

But experts disagree on how closely youth unemployment can be tied to social unrest. (*See "At Issue," p. 162.*) Most analysts see at least some link.

"There is a demonstrated link between youth unemployment and social exclusion that can translate into political and social instability," says Susana Puerto Gonzalez, officer-in-charge of the Geneva-based Youth Employment Network, a joint effort by the World Bank, ILO and United Nations to promote jobs for young people. "The inability to find employment creates a sense of uselessness and idleness that can trigger crime, mental health problems, violence and conflicts."

Educated young people were in the vanguard of the revolutions that marked the Arab Spring last year, which many observers say reflects disillusionment that Arab governments have failed to stimulate enough jobs for their growing youth populations.[5] "You grow up having faith in this idea that I'm going to study hard and get my college education and I'll be fine. But now they find out that isn't enough," says Sara Elder, an ILO economist in Geneva who studies youth employment. "The fallout of that is mistrust in the socioeconomic system, which is exactly what we're seeing."

Economists, demographers and political scientists debate the degree to which various factors cause high youth unemployment, but all agree the global economic downturn has played a leading role.

"At the peak of the crisis period in 2009, the global youth unemployment rate saw its largest annual increase on record," notes the ILO. Between 2008 and 2009, the rate rose from 11.8 to 12.7 percent — the largest annual increase over the 20 years of available global estimates.[6]

Young people usually are "the first out and the last in" during recessions, says Elder. Their lack of seniority makes them the easiest to let go, and their inexperience means companies are often reluctant to hire them when they begin refilling jobs.

Experts also point to more deeply rooted problems, particularly in the Middle East, parts of Europe and Southeast Asia. In Europe, for instance, generous job benefits and government policies that protect workers can make it more expensive to hire new employees. Wealthier societies also cushion the blow of unemployment, reducing the urgency

Youth Unemployment Remains High

Global youth unemployment declined during the economic boom in 2002-2007 and then began climbing again during the Great Recession. The projected 2011 rate is 12.6 percent — a full percentage point over the 2007 level, when unemployment fell almost to 1992 levels.

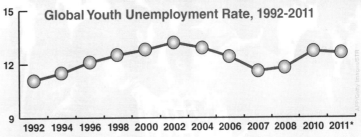

Global Youth Unemployment Rate, 1992-2011

* *Projected*

Source: "Global Employment Trends for Youth: 2011 Update," International Labour Organization, October 2011, p. 2, www.ilo.org/wcmsp5/groups/public/@ed_emp/@emp_elm/@trends/documents/publication/wcms_165455.pdf

of finding a job. "In developed countries, your parents are going to take care of you, the state is going to take care of you," notes Elder. "To some degree, you have the luxury of being unemployed."

Some analysts blame the problem on a disconnect between college curriculums and job markets in certain regions, notably the Middle East. Schools there "have been turning out people who are well-credentialed, but they don't have job skills," says Nader Kabbani, director of the Syrian Development Research Centre in Damascus.

In many developing countries, youth unemployment is driven in part by a surge in the number of younger citizens — what demographers call the "youth bulge" — which is particularly acute across the Middle East and North Africa. From Morocco to Iran, about 30 percent of the population is between the ages of 15 and 29, while only 20 percent of Western Europe's population is in that age group.[7]

Many countries in sub-Saharan Africa and South Asia also are seeing youth bulges, caused when death rates fall faster than birth rates. (*See Background, p. 158.*) These increases in youth population pose a particular challenge.

"Two or three years ago, when people were really beginning to focus on the youth bulge, we talked about a billion new jobs being necessary to absorb the bulge," says William Reese, president of the International Youth Foundation, a worldwide youth development organization based in Baltimore, Md. "Well, about 90 percent of those billion jobs needed to be found in the developing world."

And while official unemployment numbers in many developing countries aren't as high as in Europe and the Middle East, analysts say that's often because people are scraping by in the "shadow" economy (which exists off the books), so they're only marginally employed and don't show up as seeking work. In developing countries, "people can't afford to be unemployed," says John Weeks, a distinguished professor of geography at San Diego State University and the co-editor of the book *The Youth Bulge: Challenge or Opportunity.* "If you're unemployed, you're dead."

Even when choices aren't that stark, millions of young people face difficult decisions as they confront their national job markets. For some, looking for work abroad has become the best option. Statistics on job-related migration are hard to come by, but economists and demographers agree it's gone up dramatically since the advent of the financial crisis. (*See sidebar, p. 156.*)

For those who stay at home, frustration continues to mount, especially for the college educated, who once believed their degrees were a ticket to a better life. Abdul Rahim Momneh is one of a group of young Moroccans who stage almost daily protests in Rabat, the capital, with the hope of forcing their government to give them jobs.

"I have a degree, a master's degree in English," he said, "and I'm here . . . idle without a job, without dignity, without anything."[8]

As economists, demographers and political leaders try to deal with youth unemployment, here are some of the questions they are weighing:

Are we facing a "lost generation" of workers?

Analysts say the high unemployment rates for young people do not capture the full extent of the problem, because large numbers of young people have stopped looking for work.

In a report on youth employment, the ILO suggested the situation could lead to a "'lost generation' made up of young people who detach themselves from the labour market altogether." And even those who eventually find work can suffer lasting consequences, the study said.

> **"I have a degree, a master's degree in English," he said, "and I'm here . . . idle without a job, without dignity, without anything."**
>
> — *Abdul Rahim Momneh, one of a group of youths who demonstrate almost daily in Rabat, Morocco, demanding jobs.*

"Numerous studies show how entering labour markets during recession can leave permanent scars on the generation of youth affected."[9]

The report touched off a wave of international commentary about the possibility that the lives of today's jobless youths could be permanently blighted. A delayed entry into the job market or a sustained period of unemployment early in someone's working life can have long-term consequences, which economists call "scarring."

Scarring occurs because wages rise for most people as they gain experience and seniority. Being unable to find work at the beginning puts people behind in their career track. "They will have lost precious time. Their skills will have depreciated. They're likely to have to accept jobs below their qualifications," says Glenda Quintini, an economist with the Organisation for Economic Co-operation and Development (OECD), a Paris-based coalition of 34 developed nations that works to promote democracy and free markets.

According to a British study, people who were unemployed for a year before age 22 were still earning 12 to 15 percent less — 20 years later — than they would have been earning if they'd not been unemployed. Shorter bouts of unemployment resulted in a smaller wage scar, but repeated periods of joblessness early in life had a cumulative effect that persisted for decades.[10]

"There are definitely going to be long-term consequences," Quintini says of the current rates of youth unemployment in many OECD nations.

Other analysts, however, believe young workers can catch up more quickly and say worries about a "lost generation" are exaggerated. "Young people who enter the labor market as a downturn is coming take about 10 years to catch up in wages," says Wendy Cunningham, a World Bank economist who formerly managed the

Helping Jobless Youth Develop "Soft" Skills

Punctuality and being a team player are highly valued.

Finding and holding down a job involves more than mastering a technical skill that is in high demand, say job-training experts. Equally important, they say, is having "soft" skills — the habits and social behaviors that make an employee a valuable part of the team.

Around the globe, in small programs and large, private groups are working to solve the youth unemployment problem, and helping young people develop soft skills is a big part of that campaign.

Two widely heralded approaches that have been the most effective are Entra21 — developed by the Baltimore-based International Youth Foundation (IYF), a worldwide youth development organization — and the smaller, Washington-based Education for Employment program.

With support from the Inter-American Development Bank (IDB) and the World Bank, both based in Washington, D.C., Entra21 has provided 20,000 young people with employment training and job placement services through 35 pilot projects in Latin America. The program targets "out-of-school, out-of-work teenagers," most of whom have attended school for only six or seven years, says William Reese, IYF president and CEO.

The youths receive 400-500 hours of training, including technical skills for jobs that are in high demand in the local community. Teens also receive training in life and professional skills, such as punctuality, working in teams and taking the initiative in problem-solving. The final stage is an internship with a company.

Initially, the World Bank and IDB thought teaching technical skills was the most important component of the program, Reese says. But employer surveys indicated that "all those softer things that are harder to put your finger on . . . were absolutely essential," he says.

The World Bank had hoped that at least 40 percent of the graduates would still be employed six months after graduating from the program. Instead, 55 percent were still employed and another 25 percent had gone back to school to get more training. "The bank was thrilled," Reese says.

Education for Employment, which has had similar results, operates on a smaller scale in the Middle East and targets "young people from very poor incomes and backgrounds," says Jamie McAuliffe, president and CEO. An

applicant must have been out of work for six months and considered unlikely to find a job without the program.

Founded by Ron Bruder — a U.S. entrepreneur who became concerned about the lack of jobs for young Arabs after the 9/11 attacks — Education for Employment designs training courses for mostly mid-sized to larger private employers in the Middle East.

The program first started in Jordan in 2002 and now operates in six countries in the region. "We've graduated 2,500 young people and placed roughly 80 percent in jobs," says McAuliffe.

He attributes the program's success to the close working relationships the group has developed with potential employers, who commit to hiring acceptable trainees. As with Entra21, developing soft skills often turns out to be the "most critical and transformational" part of the program, McAuliffe says. "Time and time again our partners come back to us to say, 'We've just seen a real difference in the way your graduates are able to present themselves and operate in a business environment.' "

Education for Employment hopes to scale up its program in the next couple of years. McAuliffe says working with local partners has been critical for both financing and establishing credibility. And success depends on finding participants willing to be flexible about their future employment, he adds.

Economists debate the effectiveness of job-training programs, and critics say they show little long-term effectiveness. But Reese says he has found that the components of a successful youth jobs program include:

- Training in both professional and personal, or soft, skills,
- Providing the latest technical training based on local employer needs,
- Helping participants gain real-world experience through internships, and
- Providing job placement services.

"We know what works," says Reese. "What's missing is the political and financial commitment to take these things to scale."

— *Reed Karaim*

Getty Images/Gallo Images/Sowetan

Thousands of students and parents push to get through the main gates at the University of Johannesburg in South Africa on Jan. 9, 2012, in a desperate attempt to register for the new academic year. A woman was trampled to death and several others were seriously injured during the stampede. In a country where 70 percent of the youths are unemployed and a college education is required to get a decent job, competition is stiff for one of the public university's few hundred openings.

children and youth division. "They do catch up, but not immediately."

Kabbani, at the Syrian Development Research Centre, has studied the impact of unemployment on young Syrians. He believes the long-term situation is not so bleak, particularly for young people in Europe and the Middle East, which have a substantial portion of the world's unemployed college graduates. "It's definitely a loss, but I wouldn't go so far to put it in generational terms," he says. "They're smart people; they're fairly well educated. Many of them will eventually catch up."

But as the global economic downturn drags on in Europe and elsewhere, some fear that when employers finally do return to hiring they will look toward the newest crop of graduates, bypassing those with lengthy periods of unemployment or a series of "make-do" jobs on their resumes. "There is some concern they will be skipped over," notes ILO economist Elder. That's what happened in Japan, which experienced rising youth unemployment in the 1990s and early 2000s.[11] In effect, many employers chose to start fresh with unscarred young workers.

And even if they return to the job force, workers may be "lost" as fully productive members of society in others ways. Studies show that prolonged joblessness can have long-term

mental health and even physical implications. A study in the 1980s found that many of the formerly unemployed suffered lingering feelings of failure and doubts about their abilities, which persisted after they returned to work.[12]

"The long-term scars of unemployment can be cruel, particularly as regards mental health, confidence and assertiveness," says Gonzalez, at the Youth Employment Network.

Unemployment also can affect life expectancy. A study of workers who lost their jobs in the 1970s and '80s found that they had a lower life expectancy, and the impact was greater for young unemployed workers.[13]

Other researchers say the mental-health impact of unemployment has been overstated and that even those who are unemployed for a lengthy period usually recover over time.[14] "In fact, most people cope well with this event and report few long-term effects on their overall well-being," said lead author Isaac Galatzer-Levy, a psychiatric researcher now at the New York University Langone Medical Center.[15]

However, Galatzer-Levy and his colleagues confined their study to the unemployed who were at least 21 years old. Younger people, they found, responded more poorly to not being able to find work.

In any case, lasting effects limiting the ability of younger workers to realize their full potential in life have ramifications that go beyond their individual struggles, say several analysts.

"You can imagine that there's a generation of young people in some countries that is scarred in this way, and that's very expensive for all of us," says Mattias Lundberg, senior economist in the Human Development Network at the World Bank. "If we have to sacrifice the economic gains from productive employment of young people, that's an enormous loss to the entire country."

Does education reduce youth unemployment?

A college education has long been considered the ticket to a better job. That belief is so fundamental it has fueled an explosion in the number of young people enrolling in higher education around the world.[16] "The literature is just plain overwhelming on the benefits of going to college," said Philip Altbach, director of the Center for International Higher Education at Boston College.[17]

But some analysts say youth unemployment trends in several countries indicate that higher learning no longer guarantees that a college graduate will be in more demand when he enters the job market. "There have always been expectations that a good education leads to a good career. This is no longer the case," says Gonzalez of the Youth Employment Network in Geneva. "The link between youth employment and education is more and more weak, as other factors come into play."

She cites unemployment trends in several Middle Eastern and North African countries that have invested heavily in education. The average number of years of schooling in the region "have grown nearly five times over the last five decades," she says. Yet the area's youth unemployment rates were among the highest in the world, even before the worldwide recession that began in 2008. In 2010, a quarter of the region's youths had no jobs, compared to the worldwide rate, which was half that.[18] Those countries now have "millions of young, educated unemployed," Gonzalez notes.

Higher education in these countries has not kept up with the changing nature of the job market, says Ragui Assaad, a professor of public affairs at the University of Minnesota, currently studying Egyptian labor market reforms in Cairo. Most of their economies have been government controlled and most of the best jobs — which provide better benefits and lifetime employment — were in government bureaucracies.

Today, however, only about 15 percent of college graduates in Egypt will be able to get a public-sector job, Assaad says, which remains the goal of most graduates. "This is the legacy of 40 years of policy in which the public sector was the dominant force in the economy," he says. "There was an implicit promise that anyone who got a college degree, or even a high school degree, would get a job in this sector."

Universities and students have reflected that bias by focusing on degrees, such as Arabic studies or English literature, that confer societal prestige but have little connection to the private job market, says Kabbani, of the Syrian Development Research Centre. Schools also have

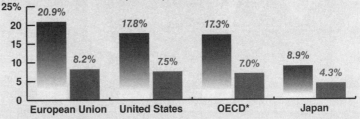

Youth Joblessness is Double Adult Rate

The jobless rates for youths in Europe, Japan and the United States are more than twice the adult rates. Similar disparities exist in the developed countries that make up the Organisation for Economic Co-operation and Development (OECD).

Youth (15-24) and Adult (25-54) Joblessness in Selected Countries and Regions
(First quarter, 2011)

* Includes Japan, United States, 21 EU countries and 11 other developed countries.

Source: "OECD Employment Outlook 2011," Organization for Economic Cooperation and Development, 2011, www.oecd.org/document/46/0,3746, en_2649_33729_40401454_1_1_1_1,00.html

poor job-placement services, and graduates have little idea what private employers require in terms of performance and behavior.

As a result, ironically, the more education you have in Egypt and other countries in the region, the more likely you are to be unemployed. Frustration over that realization played a significant role in the region's political upheavals last spring, observers say. "There is a sense of a broken social contract," says Assaad.

But the World Bank's Lundberg says inadequate education remains a barrier to productive employment in much of the developing world, particularly sub-Saharan Africa and South Asia, where secondary and higher education lags behind the rest of the world and illiteracy rates remain high.[19]

And even in other parts of the globe, labor experts say the right education still makes a big difference.

"It's not about the quantity of education, it's about the quality of education," says the World Bank's Cunningham. "We have the most educated youth ever, when you're talking about average education, but . . . we're increasingly hearing [from] employers that young people don't have the skills they want." Technical

British musicians Ms. Dynamite and Charlie Simpson demonstrate in London, on Oct. 11, 2011, to help raise awareness of Britain's 1 million unemployed youths. The coalition government recently announced creation of a "Youth Contract" program to spend £1 billion subsidizing private youth employment, but some economists say government programs do little to increase jobs for young people.

and vocational skills remain in high demand, she says, but vo-tech education programs often are stigmatized as a lesser career path.

The OECD's Quintini notes that the high number of unemployed youth means many European employers are placing a premium on educational attainment. "Having a secondary qualification [equivalent to a U.S. high school diploma] is now essential," she says. "The basic requirement is to reach that level of education. In fact, some countries are starting to impose compulsory education up to 18." And in the United States, research continues to indicate that college graduates are more likely to be employed.[20]

Still, it's not just the Middle East and North Africa where a diploma, even a college diploma, no longer means what it once did. China has strong economic growth with relatively low unemployment, but the number of Chinese students attending universities or other institutions of higher learning has mushroomed.

"Within the last 10 years, the share of China's population with higher education degrees has more than doubled," says Anke Schrader, a researcher at The Conference Board's China Center for Economics and Business in Beijing. Yet, even though the number of jobs in industries

requiring highly skilled labor — such as finance, scientific research and information technology — is growing rapidly, "China's overall employment base is still built largely on low-cost, low-skilled type work," she says.

At the end of 2010, the 9.3 percent official unemployment rate for college graduates was more than double the official average jobless rate in urban areas. Chinese official unemployment rates are calculated somewhat differently than in the West. With the annual output of graduates, "the urban labor market has not kept up with creating equal numbers of high-skilled, high-paid jobs for workforce entrants without work experience," she notes.

In several European nations, lack of economic growth and an entrenched, older work force has forced many college graduates to settle for temporary work or make-do jobs outside of their chosen professions. The situation is particularly difficult in Greece, Italy, Spain and Ireland.[21]

Iris Murumagi, 28, is grappling with the kinds of challenges often faced by even highly educated young people in those countries. She has a graduate degree in biology and previous work experience in microbiology in her native Estonia. After moving to Ireland to be near her boyfriend, she began applying for jobs last March.

"I applied for loads and loads of jobs," she says. "I applied for a job a day but got less than an interview a month."

After 10 months, Murumagi found work. "It's a fundraising job, asking people to sign up for charities," she says. "It's a tough job. It's not my profession or anything. But it's a job."

Should governments do more to address youth unemployment?

In Spain, more than half of the workers between ages 16 and 24 are unemployed — the highest youth unemployment rate in the developed world.[22] Nearly half of Greece's young people are unemployed, as are youths in Italy, Ireland and parts of Eastern Europe.[23]

With such high unemployment rates, it's not surprising that some of the most strident calls for increased government action on youth unemployment have come from inside the European Union. The European Youth Forum, an organization of national youth councils and nongovernmental youth groups from across the continent, has called for a "standardized youth guarantee that will offer young people a job, training or retraining within four months of unemployment."[24]

CHRONOLOGY

Early 20th Century *As world population explodes, economic growth manages to keep pace in the West. Swelling younger populations add to social unrest.*

1900 World population stands at 1.6 billion.

1930s U.S. and European birth rates fall during the Great Depression, when unemployment rates top 20 percent in developed nations.

1946-1964 Western world experiences baby boom after World War II ends.

Mid-to-Late 20th Century *China has a baby boom as it recovers from failed "Great Leap Forward" economic program.*

1964-1968 Led by baby boomers, youth protests break out in the West over civil rights and the Vietnam War.

1989 Chinese baby boomers' grown children demand greater freedom during demonstrations in Beijing's Tiananmen Square; army crushes the protests.

2000-2009 *Younger populations soar in the developing world. Youth unemployment drops during a booming economy but rises again as Great Recession strikes.*

2000 World population reaches 6.1 billion. Higher-education enrollment reaches 100 million worldwide, 200 times the number of a century earlier, providing the world with the largest educated pool of young job seekers in history.

2002-2007 Despite youth bulges around the world, youth joblessness falls during strong economic growth, reaching its lowest rate in 2007.

2008 Worst global economic downturn since the Great Depression takes hold. Youth unemployment begins to climb.

2009 Overall youth unemployment jumps from 11.8 to 12.7 percent, the biggest one-year increase on record, with some countries experiencing significantly higher rates.

2009 Ireland's youth joblessness triples in two years; 30,000 young Irish workers leave the country each year seeking work abroad.

October 2009 U.S. teen joblessness hits 27.6 percent, a post-WWII high.

2010-Present *Youth joblessness remains high. Social unrest, led by young people, spreads across Arab World.*

2010 World population reaches 6.9 billion, with most of the growth in developing countries, where half the population is under 25.

August 2010 International Labour Organization (ILO) warns of "lost generation" of youths due to lack of jobs.

Dec. 19, 2010 Mohammed Bouazizi, a 26-year-old Tunisian fruit seller, frustrated at police harassment, sets himself on fire. His act triggers Arab Spring protests and revolutions.

2011 Massive rallies protesting the lack of opportunity and injustice spread to Egypt, Algeria, Libya, Yemen and other countries, including Syria. Jobless Egyptian college graduates play leading role in ousting President Hosni Mubarak, toppled after 20 years in power. . . . In May, protests by jobless youths sweep across Spain as youth unemployment climbs past 45 percent. . . . Riots break out among young people in London and other English cities in August. Analysts debate how much high youth joblessness is to blame. By November, youth unemployment in Britain tops a record high 1 million, as joblessness reaches 21.9 percent among young people.

2012 ILO warns the world must create 600 million new jobs in the next 10 years to cope with existing unemployment and young people joining the workforce. . . . Youth unemployment in Spain reaches 51 percent, the highest in Europe. European leaders pledge on Jan. 30 to use untapped funds to address youth unemployment.

Desperate Youths Emigrate to Seek Work

But they don't always get a warm welcome.

Liam Allen, a 23-year-old Irishman who went to college to become a videographer, graduated into an Irish job market devastated by the global financial crash. "There's just no room in the industry for new people to come in," he says.

Determined to find a job in his profession, he chose the route embraced by a growing number of young people in many nations with high youth unemployment: He went abroad to search for work.

Youth joblessness in Ireland jumped from 9 percent in 2007 to 27.5 percent in 2010, but the International Labor Organization (ILO) believes it would be 19.3 percent higher if many Irish young people hadn't decided to remain in school or simply stopped looking for work. [1]

Migrating in search of a better life has a long tradition, of course, and had been on the rise even before the economic downturn. In the past, immigration primarily had been from developing to developed countries. Between 2000 and 2005-2006, the influx of migrants from Latin America and Africa into 34 developed nations jumped more than 30 percent, according to the Organisation for Economic Co-operation and Development in Paris. [2]

But the Great Recession and its aftermath changed the picture. Although overall numbers are hard to come by, analysts agree that job-seeking young Europeans increasingly are looking outside their national borders.

The National Youth Council of Ireland, for example, noted that between 2004 and 2009, the number of emigrants under 25 nearly doubled — from 15,600 to 30,000. [3] Spain, which has long been a magnet for immigrants from Spanish-speaking developing countries, recorded a net emigration of 50,000 people in 2011. Argentina, with its strong economy, is a popular destination, especially for Spanish-speaking emigrants. [4]

Greece, Italy and Portugal also are seeing a significant exodus. "Italy is one of the worst. There's absolutely no possibility of advancement for so many educated young people there, so they're just leaving," says Sara Elder, an economist with the International Labour Organization in Geneva, Switzerland. "They're all leaving, and they leave with a great sense of sadness."

At the same time, increased immigration has roused political passions in the countries where the job-seekers are moving. In Great Britain, MigrationWatch UK stirred up controversy when it blamed much of the country's youth unemployment problem on immigration from Eastern Bloc nations. The group pointed out that during the same period that British youth unemployment was rising by nearly 450,000, the number of Eastern European migrants working in the U.K. growing by 600,000. [5]

But Britain's Institute for Public Policy Research pointed out that immigration had been increasing for some time before youth unemployment soared and accused MigrationWatch of cherry-picking the years in order to blame foreigners for England's problems. [6]

In the United States, illegal migration remains a potent political issue, blamed by many for growing U.S. unemployment. But during the recession, government data indicate that illegal immigration was declining significantly when youth and overall unemployment in the United States was soaring. [7]

The group also has called for more scholarships to help young people go back to school and sufficient support through European government safety nets to keep young people from falling into poverty. Finally, the organization believes "young people should have the right to personalized career counseling and guidance . . . to help find a tailored solution to unemployment."[25]

But proposed programs for dealing with rising youth unemployment in Europe have faced a backlash from those who believe government should get out of the way of free enterprise. In Great Britain, the coalition government's announcement last winter of a "Youth Contract," designed to spend £1 billion subsidizing private youth employment drew a dismissive retort from Eamonn Butler, director of the Adam Smith Institute, a conservative think tank in London.

"Another . . . government 'initiative' is not the way to get young people into work," Butler said. Instead, he said the government should "reduce the cost and the risk that employers face when taking on young people. We need

While the public often views immigrants as a threat and laments the exodus of its own young people, Wendy Cunningham, a World Bank analyst, notes the actual effects are less clear. Migrants often send significant amounts of money back home while filling labor needs in their new home countries.

"There's a big question about whether migration is good for the sending country and good for the receiving country," she says. "It's not at all settled."

As for Irishman Allen, he found a videographer job in New York City. But he was hardly alone. "I met a lot of people, Irish people, who left college over there and came to New York to find a job," he says. "It was crazy." Allen returned to Ireland after his visa expired but hopes to return to Manhattan, where his former employer has promised him a job as soon as he can get a new work visa. He is upbeat about his prospects, joking that leaving the country to look for work has become "almost a coming-of-age thing" in Ireland.

Yet, he also sums up the frustration of many young people when he compares his circumstances to those of past college graduates. "You look at those people who are five to 10 years senior, and you think, you guys just had it all," Allen says. "You came out at the right time."

— *Reed Karaim*

With high rates of unemployment in their home countries, many young people are going abroad to find work, such as Stephen Masterson, 23, from Northern Ireland, who found a construction job in Nantucket, Mass.

[3]"Youth Unemployment in Ireland: The Forgotten Generation," National Youth Council of Ireland, January 2011, www.youth.ie/sites/youth.ie/files/Youth_Unemployment_in_Ireland_web.pdf.

[4]Wolf Richter, "Europe's Youth Unemployment Crisis is Leading to an Exodus," *Business Insider*, Feb. 1, 2012, http://articles.businessinsider.com/2012-02-01/europe/31011916_1_immigrants-oil-and-diamonds-angola.

[5]Macer Hall, "East European Surge Blamed for 1M Young Britons Being On Dole," *The Daily Express*, Jan. 9, 2012, www.express.co.uk/posts/view/294457/East-European-surge-blamed-for-1m-young-Britons-being-on-dole.

[6]Matt Cavanaugh, "The right tries to blame youth unemployment on immigration — again," *The New Statesman*, Jan. 9, 2012, www.newstatesman.com/blogs/the-staggers/2012/01/immigration-unemployment.

[7]Julia Preston, "Number of Illegal Immigrants in U.S. Fell, Study Says," *The New York Times*, Sept. 1, 2010, www.nytimes.com/2010/09/02/us/02immig.html.

[1]"Global Employment Trends for Youth: 2011 update," International Labour Organization, 2011, p. 4, www.ilo.org/empelm/pubs/WCMS_165455/lang--en/index.htm.

[2]Sarah Widmaier and Jean-Christophe Dumont, "Are Recent Immigrants Different? A New Profile of Immigrants in the OECD based on DIOC 2005/06," Organisation for Economic Co-operation and Development, Nov. 29, 2011, www.oecd-ilibrary.org/social-issues-migration-health/are-recent-immigrants-different-a-new-profile-of-immigrants-in-the-oecd-based-on-dioc-2005-06_5kg3ml17nps4-en.

to get rid of the minimum wage, which is pricing young people out of starter jobs, and radically cut back workplace regulation."[26]

But at an appearance in January at the World Economic Forum, ILO Director-General Juan Somavia said the size of the youth unemployment problem demands a wide-ranging response from both governments and the private sector. He suggested incentives to promote youth employment, including hiring subsidies, training grants and career guidance.[27]

Somavia rejected the notion that government regulations have made it too difficult for employers to hire or fire employees. "The problem is not the flexibility of the labor markets," he said. "The problem is how do we agree that job creation is the central objective of economic policy. The question is how do we change the mix of policies [to help young people] because if we continue this way, the issue of a lost generation is going to be real."[28]

James Sherk, a senior policy analyst in labor economics at the conservative Heritage Foundation think tank in Washington, says government job programs aren't the answer. "Most youth employment programs have been shown not to work," he told a joint U.S. congressional economic committee.[29]

Previous U.S. jobs programs such as Job Corps, Job Start and the Job Training and Partnership Act were ineffective, he said. And the record is even clearer across the Atlantic, he continued. "European nations have created far more extensive youth job programs than America has because they have much higher youth unemployment," he said. "Evaluations of these programs come to similar conclusions. Public training, wage subsidies and direct government job creation have generally not worked."

Sherk echoed Butler's call for a lower minimum wage and said reducing government barriers to entrepreneurship and wealth creation will spur employers to hire. "A stronger overall labor market is the best way to help young and low-skilled workers," he said.

The ILO sharply rejected that view in its 2011 update on youth unemployment. "It is not enough to give the economy a little boost and then step back and let the recovery take its own course to eventually absorb the bulk of young jobseekers. Such an approach might have worked if the current recession was not proving to be as deep and structurally rooted as it is," the report concluded.

"Short term fixes are not enough," it continued. "Sustained support of young people, through expansion of the social protection system, long-term investment in education and training, hiring subsidies to promote employment of young people, employment intensive investment, sectoral policy, etc., is needed now more than ever."[30]

European Union leaders recently announced plans to use part of 82 billion euros in untapped EU funds to address youth unemployment, although they did not specify what actions they might take except pledging to help establish apprentice programs.[31]

Still, the ILO's Elder has been encouraged by government proposals around the world to address the problem. "I do think they're trying," she says, citing President Obama's proposal, The American Jobs Act, which would provide tax credits for hiring the long-term unemployed and subsidize successful approaches to hiring low-income youth and adults. "Obama's doing a lot of what we would advise," she adds. "Targeting the long-term unemployed is a good idea."

The Youth Employment Network's Gonzalez, however, cautions that research into the impact of youth employment programs, including the U.S. Jobs Corps, indicates their benefits deteriorate over time — participants enjoy a boost from initial employment but show scant improvement in long-term earnings or employment.

"There is little evidence on what works to support young workers," she says, adding there is a need for careful evaluations "that can give us an idea of what and why certain interventions help youth to find or stay in a job."

BACKGROUND

Youth Bulges

Many countries had to deal with youth bulges in the 20th century, providing both lessons and warnings for countries struggling with the frustrations of unemployed youth today.

A youth bulge is not the same as having a young population. In fact, throughout most of human history, the average age of the population was younger than today, because disease and hardship killed many people before they could grow old. In *The Youth Bulge: Challenge or Opportunity*, the authors point out that, until the early 20th century, life expectancy was rarely more than 40 years and was closer to 20 in most societies. Infant mortality was so high women had to have many children just to keep the population from dying out.[32]

That began to change, first in Western nations, with advances in modern hygiene, sanitation and medicine. Increased prosperity and the establishment of relatively stable political systems also played a role. But the authors, San Diego State University's Weeks and adjunct professor of geography Debbie Fugate, note that children benefit the most when conditions improve and death rates decline. When infant and child death rates fall, families eventually begin having fewer children — but it takes a while for families to change their behavior.

The result is a youth bulge — a generation significantly larger than those before and after it, which moves through society as it ages like a pig in a python. The "baby boom" that followed World War II in America and other Western nations was one example. Japan experienced a similar boom at about the same time; Korea had one in the mid-1950s and a Chinese baby boom peaked in the late 1960s and early '70s.[33]

Youth bulges present challenges to a society throughout their existence. When the mass of young people begins moving into adult society and looking for work, a nation can find itself struggling to absorb the influx.

"A bulge in itself isn't a problem, a bulge coupled with a low job-growth rates is a problem," says the World Bank's Cunningham.

Indeed, Weeks, Fugate and others point out that in a vibrant economy a youth bulge can bring an infusion of energy and talent that leads to even greater prosperity, as occurred in the 1960s, when the baby boomers came of age in the West. "The economic progress made in these already-rich countries would not have been nearly so dramatic had [they] not responded positively to the challenges created by the baby boomers and turned those challenges into opportunities," Weeks and Fugate observe.[34] Japan, South Korea and China also managed to put youth bulges to work, benefiting their societies overall.

But many of those countries had advantages that countries now dealing with youth bulges lack: They were already comparatively wealthy and had free-market economies. Most were also democracies, generally more able to respond to the changing demands of their populations.

The economies in many less developed parts of the world have not been able to keep pace with their growing populations, a situation exacerbated because demographic shifts are occurring more quickly as medical knowledge and other advances rapidly move from country to country, Weeks notes. "The population of the average country in sub-Saharan Africa, for example, is currently growing at a rate of 2.5 percent per year," he and Fugate write. "These countries can expect that 41 percent of their population will be under age 15, with 68 percent under the age of 30."[35]

At that rate, a country's population doubles in 40 years, or about a generation and a half. Demographers and other analysts note that when a youth bulge presents the greatest potential for social disruption as it reaches the age range of 15 to 29 — old enough to take part in adult society but not necessarily to have settled into a job or family life. If such a generation feels alienated or unfairly treated, it may believe it has nothing to lose.

"It certainly is dry tinder, ready to burn. All it takes is a spark. Quite literally, that's what we saw in Tunisia," says Weeks, referring to the self-immolation of Tunisian

> ## "They will have lost precious time. Their skills will have depreciated. They're likely to have to accept jobs below their qualifications."
>
> — *Glenda Quintini, Economist, Organisation for Economic Co-operation and Development, Paris, France*

peddler Mohamed Bouazizi. The 26-year-old vegetable vendor set himself on fire after a policewoman confiscated his cart and officials refused to listen to his appeal, part of a pattern of harassment that had frustrated his efforts to support his family.

Bouazizi's death is widely seen as having triggered the Arab Spring.[36] The young people that spilled into the streets in Tunisia were at the forefront of a regional revolution, but they also harkened back to a long history in which young people have manned the barricades against what they perceived as injustice.

Joblessness and Unrest

Educated, frustrated youths were at the forefront of revolutions throughout modern history, according to Jack Goldstone, a sociologist at George Mason University School of Public Policy in Arlington, Va., who specializes in social movements. "It was true in the Puritan revolution in 1640s" in England, Goldstone says. "It was true in the French Revolution in the 1780s and all across Europe in the revolutions of 1848." But a large youth population does not necessarily mean social unrest or revolution, he points out.

However, youths are less patient with perceived injustice and inequality in a society and more prone to react, even in a wealthy democracy. A wave of civil rights and anti-war protests swept through the United States as the first American baby boomers reached adulthood in the 1960s.

But, he notes, educated young people can't sustain a revolution on their own. The 1989 Tiananmen Square protests were led by college-age Chinese born during a similar baby boom in China; but without the support of the larger public, their protest was crushed by the army. During the Arab Spring, however, educated young people were joined by working class people of all ages with similar

> **"There have always been expectations that a good education leads to a good career. This is no longer the case. The link between youth employment and education is more and more weak."**
>
> — *Susana Puerto Gonzalez, Officer in charge, Youth Employment Network, Geneva, Switzerland*

frustrations. "Then you have a situation in which the youth are kind of like a hammer pounding on a table that's already cracking," he says.

In the past, Goldstone notes, educated youths often were in the vanguard because they were attending university, which brought together a concentration of young people being educated to think about big issues. But in today's wave of unrest, social media such as Facebook and Twitter have replaced the college coffee shop. In the Middle East, "young people who had more education and more access and comfort with social media were concentrated in the cities," he says, "and they were the easiest to bring out."

While the technology has changed, many of the motives remain the same, however. In the revolutions that swept across Europe in the 1840s, young people were frustrated because they felt their progress was being blocked by privileged groups who monopolized wealth and power, Goldstone points out. While in the past, "it might have been nobility and church leaders" who monopolized power, in Arab countries today, "the privileged groups were cronies of the leaders."

Some analysts do not find a direct connection between high youth unemployment and social unrest or violence, while other studies find that a lack of opportunity played a role in the discontent, such as in last summer's riots in London.[37] The riots, which included widespread looting and arson over the course of five days, began after police shot Mark Duggan, a 29-year-old man in Tottenham, North London, during an arrest. But the protests soon spread to include other parts of London and other cities. Much of the violence was concentrated in poorer neighborhoods with higher rates of unemployment.

The OECD's Quintini sees further evidence in other violent protests. "There seems to be a relationship and a correlation," she says. "If you think of France and the

social unrest we had a few years ago, you would have seen that it came from areas of high unemployment."

The ILO's Elder, however, notes that youth unemployment has been high in Arab nations for 30 years, and young people had remained largely passive about the situation. "You have to ask yourself what has changed," she says. "I would say the unemployment of young people is a definite factor, but there is something bigger that brought them out into the street, and that has to do with social networking and this movement of social democracy. They've realized they're not alone, and they've finally gotten over their fear."

Youth unemployment is higher in several European nations, including Spain and Ireland, than in the Middle East, yet protests in those countries have been relatively peaceful. The same is true in sub-Saharan Africa, which is experiencing youth bulges that are as transformative as those in the Arab world.

CURRENT SITUATION

Developed Nations

The Great Recession still casts a giant shadow over millions of unemployed youths, but today's youth unemployment also is tied to longer-term cultural and political problems. Until the global economy recovers, analysts say, youth unemployment also is likely to remain a significant problem, especially in countries with the worst youth joblessness.

But even when the economy recovers, other issues will remain, experts say, with different countries facing different types of labor market challenges. Europe, for instance, includes countries at both extremes of the youth unemployment picture. Spain and Greece have two of the highest youth joblessness rates, but the rates in Germany, Austria and the Netherlands — which have extensive apprenticeship programs — are under 10 percent.[38]

Apprenticeships give youths work experience before they enter the job market. In Germany, a quarter of employers provide apprenticeships and nearly two-thirds of students take advantage of them. Students in vocational schools work as paid, part-time employees for two to four years while in school. The government and the employer share the cost. At the end, most apprentices expect their positions to turn into full-time jobs.[39]

"It's creating high quality jobs and a very positive image for their vocational education system," says Quintini of the German apprenticeship system. "Even the best of their students will go into it, and at the end, they actually have a job waiting for them."

Spain, in contrast, adopted a system of "temporary" contracts for younger workers, essentially creating a separate category of employees who can be let go and replaced more easily than permanent employees. Because Europe's labor protection laws and generous job benefits make it difficult and expensive to hire and fire full-time employees, temporary contracts were supposed to make it easier for companies to give younger workers a chance, which could then lead to full-time employment.

Instead, says the World Bank's Cunningham, "What seems to be happening . . . is young people just live from temporary contract to temporary contract." Temporary workers get little chance to advance their careers, and the high EU administrative costs for hiring or firing an employee work against younger people when a full-time opening becomes available. "Employers feel safer hiring somebody with references, a background where they can observe their previous experience," Quintini says.

Studies also have found that some European youth unemployment is caused by "churning," or trying out different jobs before settling on a career, Cunningham notes. The relatively generous benefits of European welfare states cushion the blow of unemployment, allowing young people to be choosier. "A more generous social safety net allows you to search in better conditions, so it's not such a bad thing in one sense," says Quintini, "but it can create an incentive to remain unemployed for a longer time."

Often, in countries with the highest youth unemployment, the older, permanent employees have set up barriers to protect their jobs. For instance, a 1992 Greek law established higher payroll taxes for new employees (and their employers) than those paid by workers who already have a job. More than two-thirds of Greek employees are at least 43 years old, according to one tally.[40] An Italian plan to relax rules for laying people off, which the government hopes will make it easier to hire young people, has drawn heated union opposition.

"This would damage the rights of all workers in order to help the young," said Vincenzo Scudiere, an official with CGIL, Italy's largest union.[41]

Youths in Asia's developed economies have fared better than those in most European nations during the downturn. Japan and South Korea had youth unemployment rates of about 10 percent in the latest ILO report.[42] South Korea's economy has remained strong, while Japanese corporations traditionally avoid layoffs by offering early retirement and reducing hours or salaries.[43]

Although the U.S. labor market is generally considered more flexible than Europe's, the United States still had an 18.4 percent youth unemployment rate in 2010, nearly double the rate for the nation's overall labor force.[44] But youth unemployment in the United States is concentrated in a younger age group than in Europe.

"In the U.S. you see record levels of teenage unemployment, particularly concentrated among some minorities," says Quintini. In fact in October 2009, U.S. teenage unemployment reached 27.6 percent, the highest since World War II, according to the OECD.[45]

U.S. teenage unemployment began to decline in 2010, although it continued to climb for some minorities. The unemployment rate of African-American teenagers, for instance, reached 43 percent in the first 11 months of 2010. "Historically, youth in this group have had the worst prospects on the labour market," the OECD notes, "and the recent rise in unemployment increases the risk that they will withdraw from the labour market and remain trapped in inactivity for a number of years."[46]

Emerging Nations

China, Brazil and India — the three largest emerging world economic powers — all rebounded quickly from the global downturn. Yet, the sheer size of their populations (China and India are the two most populous nations in the world, while Brazil ranks fifth) presents a continuing employment challenge. Despite their growing economies, for example, large segments of their populations still earn mostly a subsistence living.

In India, for instance, more than half of the population works on farms, and 30 percent of the population was surviving on less than $1.25 a day.[47] Many work in the informal economy, so their employment does not figure into unemployment statistics. Youth and overall unemployment is estimated at around 10 percent, but the larger problem remains underemployment and the lack of education of poorer workers.[48]

Does high youth joblessness lead to political instability?

YES
Henrik Urdal
Senior Researcher, Peace Research Institute, Oslo, Norway, and Research Fellow, Harvard Kennedy School

Written for *CQ Global Researcher*, March 2012

When Tunisian vegetable vendor Mohamed Bouazizi self-immolated in December 2010, he set fire to a movement that transformed the Arab world. Frustrated young people — like the underemployed 26-year old Bouazizi — fueled the Arab Spring with their rage against undemocratic governments whose failed policies have created some of the world's highest youth joblessness rates.

Demography links youth unemployment to political instability. Statistical studies indicate that exceptionally large youth populations — or "youth bulges" — are associated with an elevated risk of armed conflict and other forms of instability.

Studies also have shown that large youth bulges experience higher rates of joblessness, on average, than smaller ones. And when the labor market cannot absorb a sudden surplus of young job seekers, a large pool of unemployed youths will generate high levels of frustration that could morph into protest movements or rebel organizations.

What can governments do to avoid instability in the face of youth bulges? Notably, a plentiful youth population can be a demographic bonus, given the right conditions. For instance, large youth bulges accounted for a third of the miraculous economic growth of the "Asian Tiger" economies of South Korea, Taiwan and Singapore. The bonus opportunity arises as fertility declines, if that decline is accompanied by stable political conditions and the availability of educated workers.

Governments often respond to youth bulges by expanding education, which works, to some degree. An empirical analysis of 120 countries over 40 years showed that boosting secondary education significantly lowered a country's risk that a youth bulge would ignite conflict. But expanding education also can lead to "elite overproduction" if such expansion is not matched by job opportunities. The result can be a large group of politically and economically alienated but highly mobilizable youth. Arguably, that may have contributed to last year's Arab Spring, since the most educated Arab youths experienced the highest unemployment rates.

Youth bulges will continue to challenge frail governments. In troubled countries such as Afghanistan, Yemen and the Palestinian areas, the number of youth ages 15 to 24 will grow by more than 40 per cent over the next 10 years. Providing greater economic opportunities to youth will not only build the economy of these countries but also significantly reduce the risk of political instability.

NO
Mattias Lundberg
Senior economist for Human Development Network, Children and Youth, World Bank

Based on an address to the Alliance for International Youth Development in October, 2011

Reports of joblessness and disaffection among youths are growing across the globe, from China to Egypt to London. Does this mean unemployed young people are prone to violence to achieve their goals and redress grievances?

After the World Bank completed the World Development Report in 2007, I went on a sort of book tour, and among the few things that came up in conversation everywhere — almost a refrain or chorus — were jobs and violence. Implicitly, and sometimes explicitly, the link was made between the two. This concern was uppermost in the minds of public officials: If we don't find something for the young people to do, they'll get angry and throw us out of office. Well, in many cases they were right.

That said, I want to refute the widely-held belief that unemployment among young people necessarily leads to violence. The argument makes intuitive sense — that young people are tempted to engage in violence — both as a mechanism for the expression of frustration and because unemployment lowers the opportunity cost of criminal and violent activity. There's even a new book on the "precariat" class — the growing pool of increasingly frustrated and ostensibly dangerous young people and migrants.

But this intuition is not borne out by the evidence. As Christopher Cramer's background paper for the 2011 World Development Report on violence said: "There is no remotely convincing evidence . . . to support the claim that unemployment is a mechanistic causal factor in violent conflicts in developing countries. The evidence on youth unemployment is even weaker."

So why does youth unemployment matter? It matters because it determines welfare, equity, productivity, growth, personal and collective identity and social cohesion. Unemployment at any point in life makes people unhappy. Unemployment while young lowers morale and self-esteem and increases the rate of depression; it makes people ill, increasing the likelihood of poor physical health, including heart disease, in later life. Unemployment in early life reduces lifetime earnings and increases the risk of future unemployment. This is costly for the young person and a waste to society.

These should be sufficient grounds for decisive policies to foster labor demand and structural shifts in employment, provide opportunities for expression and improve the lives of millions of young men — and especially young women — stuck at the bottom of the labor market pile.

Likewise, Brazil's economy has a huge informal sector, which is "the main labor market segment to receive the unemployed," even though "they do not want to be there," according to Cunningham.[49] Brazil's 2009 youth unemployment rate of 17.8 percent is roughly three times as high as the country's overall jobless rate.[50] And while the country has expanded private higher education dramatically in recent years, many young people still cannot find formal employment.

In Latin America, the overall youth unemployment rate was 18.5 percent in 2009, but the impact of the global recession is reflected in the fact that nearly 20 percent of young people in the region are neither studying nor looking for work, according to the ILO. "Fewer young people were looking for jobs . . . when [youths] perceive there are no jobs, they just don't look for one," said Jurgen Weller, an economist at the Economic Commission for Latin America and the Caribbean in Santiago, Chile.[51]

China has a complicated youth employment situation. The growing number of un- or under-employed college graduates present a challenge, but the continued growth in manufacturing has led to strong demand for unskilled labor, much of which is supplied by the ongoing migration of young people from rural areas to urban centers, where manufacturers seek young, affordable employees.

"To a certain degree this trend improves bargaining power for young, low-skilled workers" the China Board's Schrader observes. Overall unemployment rates remain remarkably low compared to other nations.

Developing Nations

Although countries as disparate as Egypt and Ethiopia often are grouped together as part of the developing world, their economies and educational systems are different enough that one cannot generalize about the youth unemployment problems.

In sub-Saharan Africa and the poorest parts of Latin America and Asia, the World Bank's Lundberg notes, youth unemployment is closely linked to the challenge of boosting overall economic development. Many of these countries have high illiteracy rates and largely agricultural economies. Their ongoing youth bulges are a huge challenge.

"Sub-Saharan Africa and South Asia . . . are the areas where the United Nations Population Division projects that virtually all population growth between now and the half century is going to occur," says San Diego State University's Weeks.

China's Huzhong University of Science and Technology graduates a small academic army — more than 7,780 students — on June 23, 2010, joining the more than 6 million students who graduated from college in China in 2010. The share of China's population with university degrees has more than doubled in a decade, but the country's employment base is still built largely on low-cost, low-skilled jobs. Thus, China's 9.3 percent unemployment rate for college graduates in 2010 was more than double the nation's average in the cities.

Vusi Gumede, an associate professor in development studies at the University of Johannesburg in South Africa, offers one of the harshest assessments of conditions for young people in the region. "The troubles confronting young people are, arguably, Africa's most vexing policy challenge," he wrote. "A striking common thread is that the young person in Africa is poor, unemployed, out-of-school, and living in a rural area — and possibly angry."[52]

Yet Lundberg notes that, despite high levels of youth unemployment, most of these countries so far have avoided the kind of mass unrest that occurred last year in the Middle East and North Africa. After last year's revolutions, young workers in that region face a vastly different political scene than they did just a year ago.

Yet, several cultural conditions that led to chronic high youth unemployment still remain, contributing to uncertainty about the future. Although educated youths were in the forefront of the mass protest movements that overturned governments from Egypt to Tunisia, surveys indicate that a majority of college graduates still hope to get a public sector job.

Cultural pride and family support make college graduates less likely to take a job that they feel is beneath their status. In the Middle East and North Africa there is "this kind of tolerance — the family structure is set up so you can just stay at home for years, not working, until you get a job," says Cunningham.

If Arab graduates want better job prospects, experts say, they must start looking for jobs in the private sector and adjust to lives without the guaranteed lifetime employment their parents enjoyed working for the government. They also will have to embrace a more entrepreneurial spirit and be willing to take on new career challenges, employment experts say.

But these changes won't be easy. "The question is, 'Can you, at a real basic level, renegotiate the social contract [and] change social norms?' " says Kabbani. "It's not just about another youth program."

Kabbani's research included a survey of young people in Syria, which found that despite the nation's political upheavals, roughly four out of five still felt they had a right to employment in the public sector. The persistence of old attitudes is also on display in Morocco's capital of Rabat where the regular protests by unemployed graduates are aimed at getting government jobs, not more opportunity in the private sector. And every so often, government responds by hiring some of the graduates.

Still, a euphoric feeling of new possibilities has gripped the young in several Middle Eastern countries after their successful protests last spring. Salmin Eljawhari, a 22-year-old from Benghazi, Libya, says many of her friends had looked for work for years, but "they didn't give up." She recently entered a dental training program herself, but she views the emergence of a new civil society in Libya as the most "beautiful" thing she has seen.

"The role of the youth in the Arab spring revolutions and especially in Libya was the most important, because they had the real desire for change," she says. "I am sure things will be better. Sure, it will take time. Maybe longer then we expect, but in the end we will take our rights and fight corruption everywhere to have a better future for us and for the next generation."

OUTLOOK

Global Resource

Whether it's in families or nations, the young are generally regarded as the best hope for the future. The recent youth unrest that has roiled many countries,

> "So we have a billion young people, mostly underemployed," he says. "That's a wealth of human capital and talent that we'll find a way to take advantage of sooner or later."
>
> — Mattias Lundberg, Senior Economist, Human Development Network, World Bank

particularly in the Middle East, has cast the young in a different light — frustrated and deeply skeptical of social and political structures they believe have limited their opportunities.

But many of the experts continue to see the current population of young people just beginning their working lives as a global resource. The World Bank's Lundberg notes that there are more than 1 billion people today between the ages of 15 and 25, the largest youth population in human history, with the great majority of them in developing countries. "So we have a billion young people, mostly underemployed," he says. "Wouldn't you think, if we take a step back, that's a fantastic opportunity? That's a wealth of human capital and talent that we'll find a way to take advantage of sooner or later."

While attention has been focused on the Arab nations and Europe, Lundberg notes that several African countries have been making progress in establishing civil societies and laying the groundwork for stronger, more diversified economies. He hopes these seeds will bear fruit 10 or 15 years down the road.

"Ethiopia is a good case in point," Lundberg says. "They've been investing in education and health. I really hope they will become better integrated into the world economy, and young people will be able to take advantage of the opportunities that come with that. I hope there are factory jobs in Ethiopia. That would be a fantastic outcome."

Looking at the future from Cairo, Professor Assaad believes things will get better. "I'm pretty optimistic, if you're looking that far down the road, because the youth bulge will translate into a high working population, with people in their productive years. They will have made the transition into the labor market, so demographically we're going to be in a better position than we are now."

Weeks, of San Diego State University, also sees some reason for optimism about the Middle East, pointing out that the birth rates already are declining in the region. But he is less optimistic about the future of sub-Saharan Africa and parts of Asia, where the vast bulk of population growth is projected to occur between now and 2050.

"You've got countries that are growing rapidly without an apparent job base that can support all these young people," he says. "The resources, at the moment, just aren't there."

In the developed world, an economic recovery is expected eventually to bring down unemployment. Once strong growth resumes, "there will be a sense of a much brighter future," Weeks predicts.

ILO economist Elder, however, points out that the toll for many jobless individuals will likely be felt for some time, citing studies showing it can take a decade to recoup lost earnings. "Even 10 years is quite significant," she says.

And even with a growing global economy, Cunningham believes many countries, particularly in Europe, will need to adopt new labor rules and approaches to help integrate young people into their job markets. Education and attitudes about work also must change to fully address the problem.

"There isn't a quick fix for the youth unemployment problem," she says. "We need to accept that there isn't, and this isn't going to change overnight. There just isn't a magic bullet."

NOTES

1. Lydia Polgreen, "Fatal Stampede in South Africa Points Up University Crisis," *The New York Times*, Jan. 10 2012, www.nytimes.com/2012/01/11/world/africa/stampede-highlights-crisis-at-south-african-universities.html.

2. "Global Employment Trends for Youth: 2011 Update," International Labor Office, 2011, p. 1, www.ilo.org/empelm/pubs/WCMS_165455/lang--en/index.htm. Also see "Eurozone unemployment hits Euro-era high," The Associated Press, Jan. 31, 2012, www.cbc.ca/news/world/story/2012/01/31/eu-record-unemployment.html.

3. "Unemployment Statistics," Eurostat website, Dec. 15, 2011, http://epp.eurostat.ec.europa.eu/statistics_explained/index.php/Unemployment_statistics. See also, *ibid.*, table 6.

4. Naomi Powell, "Europe's Lost Generation: No Jobs or Hope for the Young," *The Globe and Mail*, Sept. 10, 2011, www.theglobeandmail.com/report-on-business/international-news/european/europes-lost-generation-no-jobs-or-hope-for-the-young/article2228489/singlepage/. Also see "The jobless young: Left behind," *The Economist*, Sept. 10, 2011, www.economist.com/node/21528614.

5. For background, see Roland Flamini, "Turmoil in the Arab World," *CQ Global Researcher*, May 3, 2011, pp. 209-236.

6. "Global Employment Trends for Youth: 2011 Update," *op. cit.*, p. 1.

7. Edward Sayre and Samantha Constant, "The Whole World Is Watching, Why the Middle East's own "youth bulge" is key to the region's economic and political stability," *The National Journal*, Feb. 21, 2011, www.nationaljournal.com/magazine/why-the-middle-east-s-youth-bulge-is-key-to-the-regions-stability-20110221.

8. Deborah Amos, "In Morocco, Unemployment Can Be A Full-Time Job," Morning Edition, NPR, Jan. 27, 2012, www.npr.org/2012/01/27/145860575/in-morocco-unemployment-can-be-a-full-time-job.

9. Sarah Elder, *et al.*, "Global Employment Trends for Youth: Special issue on the impact of the global economic crisis on youth," International Labour Organization, August 2010, p. 1, www.ilo.org/wcmsp5/groups/public/@ed_emp/@emp_elm/@trends/documents/publication/wcms_143349.pdf.

10. Paul Gregg and Emma Tominey, "The Wage Scar from Unemployment," Centre for Market and Public Organisation, University of Bristol, 2004, www.bris.ac.uk/cmpo/publications/papers/2004/wp97.pdf.

11. "The Jobless Young: Left Behind," *op. cit.*

12. Stephen Fineman, "The middle class: Unemployed and underemployed," in Unemployment: Personal and social consequences, S. Fineman (ed.), Tavistock, 1987, p. 74.

13. Daniel Sullivan and Till Von Wachter, "Job Displacement and Mortality: An Analysis Using Administrative Data," *The Quarterly Journal of Economics*, August 2009, www.columbia

.edu/~vw2112/papers/sullivan_vonwachter_resubmission.pdf.

14. Isaac R. Galatzer-Levy, *et al.*, "From Marianthal to Latent Growth Mixture Modeling: A Return to the Exploration of Individual Differences in Response to Unemployment," *Journal of Neuroscience, Psychology and Economics*, 2010, Vol. 3, No. 2, http://apa.ba0.biz/pubs/journals/releases/npe-3-2-116.pdf.

15. Jeanette Mulvey, "Unemployment Has Little Long-term Effect on Mental Health," *Business News Daily*, Dec. 14, 2010, www.businessnewsdaily.com/490-unemployment-has-little-long-term-effect-on-mental-health.html.

16. For background, see Reed Karaim, "Expanding Higher Education," *CQ Global Researcher*, Nov. 15, 2011, pp. 525-572.

17. *Ibid.*, p. 559.

18. "Global Unemployment Trends for Youth: 2011 Update," *op. cit.*, p. 3.

19. "Human Development Report 2011," United Nations, Table 9, p. 158, http://hdr.undp.org/en/reports/global/hdr2011/download/en/.

20. "Education pays . . .," U.S. Bureau of Labor Statistics, www.bls.gov/emp/ep_chart_001.htm.

21. Fiona Ortiz and Feliciano Tisera, "Southern Europe's Lost Generation Stuck in Junk Jobs," Reuters, Oct. 17, 2011, www.reuters.com/article/2011/10/17/us-europe-junkjobs-idUSTRE79G4RJ20111017.

22. Fiona Govan, "Spain's lost generation: youth unemployment surges above 50 percent," *The Telegraph*, Jan. 27, 2012, www.telegraph.co.uk/news/worldnews/europe/spain/9044897/Spains-lost-generation-youth-unemployment-surges-above-50-per-cent.html.

23. "Eurozone unemployment hits Euro-era high," *op. cit.*

24. "Youth Employment in Europe: A Call for Change," The European Youth Forum, December 2011, p. 19, http://issuu.com/yomag/docs/a_call_for_change.

25. *Ibid.*

26. Eamonn Butler, "On Nick Clegg's 'youth contract,'" blog, Adam Smith Institute, Nov. 25, 2011, www.adamsmith.org/blog/welfare/on-nick-cleggs-youth-contract.

27. "Somavia puts the accent on youth employment in Davos," ILO News, Jan. 27, 2012, www.ilo.org/global/about-the-ilo/press-and-media-centre/news/WCMS_172255/lang--en/index.htm.

28. "Davos 2012 — Averting a Lost Generation" panel discussion, World Economic Forum, Jan. 27, 2012, www.livestream.com/worldeconomicforum03.

29. James Sherk, testimony before the Joint Economic Committee, U.S. Congress, June 1, 2010, www.heritage.org/multimedia/video/2010/05/sherk-cspan-5-26-10.

30. "Global Employment Trends for Youth: 2011 Update," *op. cit.*, p. 7.

31. "EU: Pledges Action on Youth Unemployment, Credit Flows," *The Wall Street Journal*, Jan. 30, 2012, http://online.wsj.com/article/BT-CO-20120130-711890.html.

32. John Weeks and Debbie Fugate, *The Youth Bulge: Challenge or Opportunity*, International Debate Education Association, March 2012, p. 3.

33. "China's population by age and sex in 1990," ChinaProfile, www.china-profile.com/data/fig_p_19a_m.htm.

34. Weeks and Fugate, *op. cit.*, p. 8.

35. *Ibid.*, p. 5.

36. Rania Abouzeid, "Bouazizi: The Man Who Set Himself and Tunisia on Fire," *Time*, Jan. 21, 2011, www.time.com/time/magazine/article/0,9171,2044723,00.html.

37. Matthew Taylor, Simon Rogers and Paul Lewis, "England rioters: young, poor and unemployed," *The Guardian*, Aug. 18, 2011, www.guardian.co.uk/uk/2011/aug/18/england-rioters-young-poor-unemployed.

38. "Table 1: Youth unemployment figures, 2008-2011Q3," Eurostat website, http://epp.eurostat.ec.europa.eu/statistics_explained/index.php/Unemployment_statistics.

39. "The jobless young: Left behind," *op. cit.*

40. "Youth unemployment in Mediterranean Europe: It's grim down South," *The Economist*, Sept. 11, 2011, www.economist.com/node/21528616.

41. Deborah Ball, "Italy Seeks to Tackle Youth Jobless Problem," *The Wall Street Journal*, Aug. 22, 2011,

http://online.wsj.com/article/SB100014240531119 0427900457652231182474934.html.

42. "Global Employment Trends for Youth: 2011 Update," *op. cit.*, p. 4.

43. Kazushi Minami, "Tackling Youth Unemployment in Japan," Youth Think! Blog, World Bank, Nov. 16, 2010, http://youthink.worldbank.org/issues/employment/tackling-youth-unemployment-japan.

44. "ILO Youth Unemployment: 2011 Update," *op. cit.*, p. 13.

45. "OECD (2010) — Off to a Good Start? Jobs for Youth, United States," www.oecd.org/dataoecd/22/54/46729274.pdf.

46. *Ibid.*

47. "India Country Overview — September 2011," The World Bank, www.worldbank.org.in/WBSITE/EXTERNAL/COUNTRIES/SOUTHASIAEXT/INDIAEXTN/0,,contentMDK:20195738~pagePK:141137~piPK:141127~theSitePK:295584,00.html.

48. India profile, *The World Factbook*, Central Intelligence Agency, Jan. 12, 2012, https://www.cia.gov/library/publications/the-world-factbook/geos/in.html.

49. Wendy Cunningham, "Unpacking Youth Unemployment in Latin America," The World Bank, August 2009, http://inec.usip.org/resource/unpacking-youth-unemployment-latin-america.

50. "Youth unemployment rate, aged 15-24, both sexes," Millennium goal indicators, United Nations Statistics Division, http://unstats.un.org/unsd/mdg/SeriesDetail.aspx?srid=630&crid=76.

51. Sara Miller Llana, "Unemployment among Latin America youths fuels 'lost generation,' " *The Christian Science Monitor*, March 12, 2010, www.csmonitor.com/World/Americas/2010/0312/Unemployment-among-Latin-America-youths-fuels-lost-generation.

52. Vusi Gumede, "Policies letting the youth down in Africa," Vusi Gumede Thinkers Network, Aug. 5, 2010, www.vusigumedethinkers.com/pages/acpapers_log/8.html.

BIBLIOGRAPHY

Selected Sources

Books

Papademetrious, Demetrios, Madeleine Sumption and Aaron Terrazas, eds., *Migration and the Great Recession: The Transatlantic Experience*, Migration Policy Institute, June 15, 2011.
Case studies trace the disproportionate impact of the financial crisis on young people and the effect their emigration has on the receiving countries.

Standing, Guy, *The Precariat: The New Dangerous Class*, Bloomsbury USA, July 24, 2011.
A professor of social and policy sciences at the University of Bath in England believes the global economy has created a growing "precariat" class — people living precariously, often with a series of short-term jobs that offer little security or standing.

Weeks, John, and Debbie Fugate, eds., *The Youth Bulge: Challenge or Opportunity?* International Debate Education Association, March 1, 2012.
Two San Diego State University professors examine the ramifications of demographic "youth bulges" — disproportionately young populations.

Articles

"The Jobless Young: Left Behind," *The Economist*, Sept. 10, 2011, www.economist.com/node/21528614.
The article examines the long-term consequences of high youth unemployment, for both the jobless and society as a whole.

Allen, Katie, " 'Bad luck' generation will be blighted by youth unemployment for several years," *The Guardian*, Oct. 19, 2011, www.guardian.co.uk/business/2011/oct/19/generation-scarred-by-youth-unemployment.
The International Labour Organization says nearly 50 percent of young people are jobless in many countries.

Coy, Peter, "The Youth Unemployment Bomb," *Businessweek*, Feb. 2, 2011, www.businessweek.com/magazine/content/11_07/b4215058743638.htm.
The growing problem of youth unemployment around the world could cause social unrest.

Klein, Matthew, "Educated, Unemployed and Frustrated," *The New York Times*, March 20, 2011, www.nytimes.com/2011/03/21/opinion/21klein.html.
The uprisings in the Middle East and North Africa are a warning for the developed world, says a 24-year-old research associate at the Council on Foreign Relations.

Llana, Sara Miller, "Unemployment among Latin American youths fuels 'lost generation,'" *The Christian Science Monitor*, March 12, 2010, www.csmonitor.com/World/Americas/2010/0312/Unemployment-among-Latin-America-youths-fuels-lost-generation.
While official youth unemployment rates in Latin America are high, they do not include the high number of young people who have given up looking for work.

Taylor, Mathew, Simon Rogers and Paul Lewis, "England Rioters: Young, Poor and Unemployed," *The Guardian*, Aug. 18, 2011, www.guardian.co.uk/uk/2011/aug/18/england-rioters-young-poor-unemployed.
The writers examine the link between economic hardship and last summer's riots in London.

Wessel, David, and Chip Cummins, "Arab World Built Colleges, but Not Jobs," *The Wall Street Journal*, Feb. 5, 2011, http://online.wsj.com/article/SB10001424052748704709304576124320031160648.html.
The lack of opportunity for college graduates in many Arab countries played a role in the region's "Arab Spring" revolutions last year.

Studies and Reports

"Global Employment Trends for Youth: 2011 Update," International Labour Organization, October 2011, www.ilo.org/wcmsp5/groups/public/@ed_emp/@emp_elm/@trends/documents/publication/wcms_165455.pdf.
The report updates the ILO's exhaustive 2010 study on global youth employment trends, which examined how people aged 15 to 24 years fared during the economic recession.

"OECD Employment Outlook 2011," Organisation for Economic Co-operation and Development, Sept. 15, 2011, www.oecd.org/document/46/0,3746,en_2649_33729_40401454_1_1_1_1,00.html.
The latest annual assessment of labor market developments and prospects in the organization's 34 member countries focuses on youth unemployment.

Cramer, Christopher, "Unemployment and Participation in Violence," World Development Report 2011 background paper, Nov. 16, 2010, http://wdr2011.worldbank.org/sites/default/files/pdfs/WDR%20Background%20Paper%20-%20Cramer.pdf.
A professor of politics, economics and development at the University of London concludes that there is no firm evidence linking youth unemployment to violence and social instability.

For More Information

AFL-CIO, 815 16th St., N.W., Washington, DC, 20006; 202-637-5000; www.afl-cio.org. A federation of 56 national and international unions; maintains extensive information on youth work and unemployment.

European Union, 00 800 6789 1011; http://europa.eu/. A political and economic partnership between 27 European nations; website includes the latest statistics on unemployment and the responses of individual countries and EU itself.

European Youth Forum, Rue Joseph II Straat 120, B-1000 Brussels, Belgium; + 32 2 230 64 90; www.youthforum.org. An umbrella organization established by national youth councils and international nongovernmental youth organizations to tackle youth employment in Europe.

International Labour Organization, 4 Route des Morillons, CH-1211, Geneva 22, Switzerland; +41 (0) 22 799 6111; www.ilo.org. An U.N. agency that deals with labor issues and conducts research on employment and other labor issues.

International Trade Union Confederation, Boulevard du Roi Albert II, 5, Bte 11210 Brussels, Belgium; 32 (0) 2 224 0211; www.ituc-csi.org. International trade organization representing about 175 million workers in 151 countries; website includes an international "young workers" blog.

International Youth Foundation, 32 South St., Baltimore, MD 21202; 410-951-1500; www.iyfnet.org. A nonprofit organization that aims to help young people become productive, engaged members of society; has several job-training efforts in different parts of the globe.

Organisation for Economic Co-operation and Development, 2, rue André Pascal 75775, Paris Cedex 16, France; 33 1 45.24.82.00; www.oecd.org. Promotes economic and social well-being among its membership, consisting of 34 developed countries.

The World Bank, 1818 H St., N.W., Washington, DC 20433; 202-473-1000; www.worldbank.org. International financial organization that lends money to developing countries for anti-poverty programs; studies and supports jobs programs around the globe.

Voices From Abroad:

BAN KI-MOON

Secretary-General, United Nations

Start with the young

"Today we have the largest generation of young people the world has ever known. They are demanding their rights and a greater voice in economic and political life. We need to pull the U.N. system together like never before to support a new social contract of job-rich economic growth. Let us start with young people."

Gulf News (United Arab Emirates), February 2012

DAVID CAMERON

Prime Minister, United Kingdom

A continuing problem

"Of course today's unemployment figures are a matter of great regret, and it's a great regret particularly in terms of higher youth unemployment. Youth unemployment has been a problem in this country for well over a decade, in good years and in bad. . . . What we have to do is sort out all of the things that help young people get back into work."

Leicester Mercury (England), February 2011

ELIAS MASILELA

CEO, Public Investment Corp., South Africa

Impatience leads to problems

"We must look at the way we invest and take account of youth unemployment. If the youth become impatient, then it is very difficult to stop them."

Business Day (South Africa), September 2011

ALHAJI ALIKO DANGOTE

Chairman, National Job Creation Committee, Nigeria

A new Arab Spring?

"Our [Nigerian] youth are underemployed, unemployed or unemployable at the peak of their productivity. As we

have seen in the Maghreb countries of Tunisia, Egypt, Libya and now spreading to the Emirates of the Middle East, youth unemployment is a very effective catalyst for social unrest that has brought down entire governments."

This Day (Nigeria), April 2011

MARYAM HOBALLAH

Economist, Lebanon

The 'brain drain' solution

"The constraints on the economy, job market and business environment for the youth exacerbate Lebanon's 'Brain Drain.' The youth live in a society where they feel their basic needs are not met. The most logical solution is to leave Lebanon for a better life and become one more number in the ever-growing 'Brain Drain.' "

Daily Star (Lebanon), August 2011

CLARIS MADHUKU

Director, Platform for Youth Development, Zimbabwe

Political perceptions

"It would appear the bigger politicians are not interested in addressing this problem for fear they will not have ready youths to use, misuse, abuse and dump. The situation portrays youths as unorganised, violent and an undisciplined lot."

Financial Gazette (Zimbabwe), May 2011

PAUL BROWN

Director of Communications, The Prince's Trust (youth charity), England

A 'dripping tap'
"Youth unemployment is like a dripping tap, costing tens of millions of pounds a week through benefits and lost productivity. And, just like a dripping tap, if we don't do something to fix it, it's likely to get much worse."

The Independent (England), October 2011

SHARON NAKANDHA

Attorney, Uganda

Education's role
"We should also recognise that our education system is partly responsible for the problem of youth unemployment and therefore needs to be reviewed. The system is still archaic and unresponsive to Uganda's growing needs."

The Monitor (Uganda), June 2011

THABO KUPA

Board Member, National Youth Development Agency, South Africa

The youth must lead
"If we know we are 'sitting on a ticking' time bomb then surely we must tackle the problem of youth unemployment with the same vigour and dedication used to bring about the demise of apartheid. As the most affected group, young people are expected to take the lead in fighting against unemployment."

Sowetan (South Africa), October 2011

8

Financial Misconduct

Kenneth Jost

Angelo Mozilo, founder of Countrywide Financial Corp., testifies before a congressional committee in 2008. The next year the Securities and Exchange Commission charged Mozilo with securities fraud and insider trading for selling off his Countrywide stock despite his worries about the quality of subprime loans Countrywide had helped create and popularize. In 2010, Mozilo agreed to pay a $67.5 million fine and never again serve as a director or officer of a publicly traded company.

From *The CQ Researcher*, January 20, 2012.

The Securities and Exchange Commission (SEC) exuded confidence last fall when it announced a $285 million settlement with the financial conglomerate Citigroup for misleading investors about a $1 billion package of toxic mortgages sold in early 2007.

In its 25-page complaint filed Oct. 19, the federal agency depicted Citigroup as hatching a devious scheme to offload around $500 million of subprime mortgages to institutional investors without disclosing that Citi would be betting that the package would go bust.

Which it did. The investors — hedge funds and others — lost "several hundred millions of dollars" when the package defaulted in November 2007, according to the SEC. But Citigroup pocketed $160 million in profits by selling the mortgages with the expectation they would plunge in value — along with the original $34 million management fee for structuring and marketing the package.

The SEC had successfully brought similar securities-fraud complaints within the past 15 months against two other Wall Street giants: Goldman Sachs and JP Morgan Chase. The allegations underscored one dark side of the housing-market bust that led to the financial crisis of 2008. Big financial firms trading in securitized mortgages tried to profit or shield themselves from losses by concealing their own fears that many of the mortgages were likely to default.

Some news accounts, however, noted one potential stumbling block for the SEC's enforcement action against Citigroup. The case

SEC Targets Insider Trading

The Securities and Exchange Commission has brought more than 500 insider-trading cases against individuals and entities over the past 10 years, including 57 in fiscal 2011. Defendants include hedge fund managers, corporate insiders, attorneys and government employees who allegedly traded securities on nonpublic information.

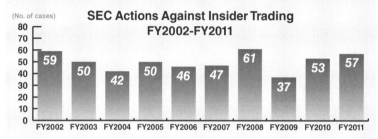

(No. of cases)

SEC Actions Against Insider Trading FY2002-FY2011

FY2002: 59, FY2003: 50, FY2004: 42, FY2005: 50, FY2006: 46, FY2007: 47, FY2008: 61, FY2009: 37, FY2010: 53, FY2011: 57

Source: "Year-by-Year SEC Enforcement Actions," Securities and Exchange Commission, www.sec.gov/news/newsroom/images/enfstats.pdf

had been assigned to a federal judge in New York, Jed Rakoff, who — *The New York Times* pointed out — had previously "taken a hard line on SEC settlements." In February 2010, Rakoff had approved a $150 million settlement the agency negotiated with Bank of America for inadequate disclosure about the details of its acquisition of the former investment firm Merrill Lynch, but only after criticizing the deal as "half-baked justice at best."

The caveat proved to be prophetic. On Nov. 28, Rakoff stunned the SEC and Citigroup alike by refusing to sign off on the accord. In a 15-page decision, Rakoff blasted the agency for allowing Citigroup to resolve the complaint without admitting allegations that, the judge added, had been inadequately laid out. The settlement was "pocket change" for Citigroup, Rakoff said, while the agency was seeking only "a quick headline" instead of fulfilling its "statutory mission to see that the truth emerges."[1]

Rakoff's rebuff to one of the key federal agencies charged with protecting the public from financial misconduct came just six days before a nationally televised news program blasted the U.S. Justice Department for failing to prosecute high-level executives responsible for the financial crisis. The CBS program "60 Minutes" showcased would-be whistleblowers from Citigroup and Countrywide Financial, the nation's largest mortgage lender until its collapse in 2008. Former Countrywide

executive Eileen Foster and former Citigroup vice president Richard Bowen told correspondent Steve Kroft that the Justice Department had shown no interest in hearing their accusations.[2]

The unrelated episodes exemplify a sentiment widely shared by the public that the financial crisis stemmed at least in part from violations of the law and that the government has failed to bring the wrongdoers to justice. "We know there are insiders within the companies who say there is strong evidence that the companies committed criminal wrongdoing that should have warranted prolonged investigations and that should have resulted in actions by now," says Russell Mokhiber, editor of *Corporate Crime Reporter*, a Washington, D.C.-based newsweekly founded in 1987. "And we have no actions."

The SEC and Justice Department both reject the criticism. The SEC has brought charges against 87 companies and individuals stemming from the financial crisis, including 39 CEOs, chief financial officers or other senior officers. The agency, which can bring civil but not criminal charges, said financial penalties and "other monetary recovery" in the actions total nearly $2 billion.[3] (*See graph, p. 175.*)

In the "60 Minutes" program, Assistant Attorney General Lanny Breuer, who heads the department's Criminal Division, insisted the government was pursuing investigations without any outside interference, but noted the difficulties of making a criminal case.

"I find the excessive risk-taking to be offensive," Breuer said. "I find the greed that was manifested by certain people to be very upsetting. But because I may have an emotional reaction and I may personally share the same frustration that American people all over the country are feeling, that in and of itself doesn't mean we bring a criminal case."[4]

Legal experts acknowledge some of the difficulties of bringing criminal prosecutions in cases based on complex and arcane financial transactions. Indeed, the government suffered a black eye in its most high-level prosecution when a federal jury acquitted two hedge fund managers at the defunct investment firm Bear Stearns of obstructing justice in November 2009.

Still, many experts agree with the public perception that the government could and should do more. "They aren't bringing as many cases against public firms for [misleading] financial statements as they could," says Jennifer Arlen, a securities law expert at New York University Law School. "And they haven't been as aggressive in going against senior individuals as they could."

William Black, an associate professor of economics and law at the University of Missouri-Kansas City and a former federal regulator, strongly seconds Rakoff's criticism of the SEC practice of allowing defendants to settle complaints without admitting wrongdoing. "When something doesn't work and doesn't work profoundly, you really should reconsider," says Black, who worked with the former Office of Thrift Supervision in cleaning up the savings and loan crisis of the 1980s. "And the SEC hasn't worked for a very long time."

Some experts, however, dispute the widespread assumption that criminal conduct was at the heart of the financial crisis. "People think that because there's a scandal that people ought to go to jail," says Thomas Gorman, a Washington lawyer who publishes a blog on SEC litigation. "That's not necessarily true."

The SEC has helped win prison sentences for some Wall Street figures by referring insider-trading cases to the Justice Department for prosecution. Most notably, Raj Rajaratnam, the head of the Galleon Group hedge fund, was sentenced to 11 years in prison in October for orchestrating a large insider-trading scheme at Galleon over a six-year period. Rajat Gupta, a prominent Wall Streeter formerly at Goldman Sachs, was indicted later that month for tipping off Rajaratnam to valuable inside information about corporate deals. (*See sidebar, p. 184.*)

In the latest insider-trading case, the U.S. attorney's office in Manhattan announced charges on Jan. 18 against a prominent hedge fund manager and six others

Financial Crisis Sparks SEC Charges

The Securities and Exchange Commission has charged 87 entities and individuals — including 45 CEOs or other senior corporate officers — with financial misconduct in connection with the financial crisis that began in 2008. Penalties and other monetary relief total nearly $2 billion.

SEC Enforcement Actions Related to Financial Crisis*	
Number of entities and individuals charged	87
Number of CEOs, CFOs and other senior corporate officers charged	45
Total penalties, disgorgement and other monetary relief	$1.97 billion

* As of Dec. 16, 2011

Source: "SEC Enforcement Actions Addressing Misconduct That Led to or Arose From the Financial Crisis," Securities and Exchange Commission, December 2011, www.sec.gov/spotlight/enf-actions-fc.shtml

in a scheme that allegedly netted nearly $62 million in illicit profits in 2008 and 2009 — rivaling the $70 million-plus in illicit gains that Rajaratnam was alleged to have realized. Anthony Chiason, co-founder of Level Global Investors LP, was charged along with others in a plot that allegedly used inside information from a paid tipster at Dell, the big computer maker, to trade in Dell stock. The tipster and two others pleaded guilty and were cooperating with authorities, the U.S. attorney's office said.[5]

Apart from the insider-trading cases, however, the only prominent Wall Street figure to be prosecuted successfully since the financial crisis hit is Bernard Madoff, who is now serving a 150-year prison sentence for turning his wealth-management business into a Ponzi scheme that cost investors $18 billion or more. Madoff's prosecution brought no kudos to the SEC, however. A report by the SEC's inspector general showed the agency failed to detect Madoff's crimes despite a succession of ever-more-detailed tips going as far back as 1992. (*See sidebar, p. 178.*)

Madoff's offenses were tangential, however, to the financial crisis. To date, no prominent executive who played a central role in the events leading up to the crisis has been prosecuted. The SEC did file civil complaints in December, however, against the former chief executives and four other top managers of the two government-sponsored mortgage lenders: Fannie Mae and Freddie Mac. The complaint, announced on Dec. 17, charges the executives with misleading investors about the extent of subprime mortgages in their portfolios.

The SEC is appealing Rakoff's rejection of its proposed Citigroup settlement, but at the same time somewhat revising its policy of allowing defendants to avoid admitting wrongdoing in resolving civil complaints. Under a new policy announced Jan. 6, the SEC will not allow a defendant to stand mute on the substance of a civil complaint if it already has admitted wrongdoing in a related criminal case.[6]

Meanwhile, the nation's biggest banks are squared off with attorneys general from all 50 states over legal remedies for allegedly having used improper procedures to evict delinquent borrowers from their homes as the financial crisis deepened. The banks had been close to an agreement last summer, calling for a $20 billion settlement, but some states balked at their demand to be shielded from any further liability.

Another federal agency also is entering the field of policing financial misconduct with President Obama's appointment of a director for the newly established Consumer Financial Protection Board (CFPB). Obama named former Ohio Attorney General Richard Cordray to head the new agency on Jan. 4, using his power to make a recess appointment after Senate Republicans had stalled action on the nomination. GOP senators disputed the move, saying the Senate was technically in session. The legal wrangling masks a bigger issue, however, about whether the agency's powers to regulate non-bank financial institutions — such as payday lenders — will actually benefit consumers. (*See "At Issue," p. 189.*)

As the various legal proceedings continue, here are some of the questions being debated:

Was illegal conduct a major cause of the financial crisis?

Ralph Cioffi and Matthew Tannin were pulling down seven-figure salaries for managing hedge funds for the Wall Street firm Bear Stearns until the funds, heavily invested in mortgage securities, went belly up in July 2007. Federal prosecutors charged the two with securities fraud in June 2008, alleging that they knowingly misled investors about the funds' exposure to potentially toxic assets.

Cioffi and Tannin defended themselves in a three-week trial in fall 2009 by contending that they and their

funds were victims of an unforeseeable market meltdown. Federal court jurors apparently agreed, finding the pair not guilty after barely six hours' deliberation. Columbia University securities law expert John Coffee called the result "a total rebuff to the prosecution."[7]

The too-clever-by-half financial deals that came crashing down in the summer and fall of 2008 naturally led many of the victims — investors left holding the bag, homeowners stuck with underwater mortgages — to assume that laws had been violated. But experts and financial-crisis watchers from President Obama down caution that illegal conduct was not necessarily to blame.

Answering a question at a press conference on Oct. 6 about the lack of major prosecutions, Obama replied: "One of the biggest problems about the collapse of Lehmans" —a reference to the investment bank Lehman Brothers, which declared bankruptcy in September 2008 — "and the subsequent financial crisis and the whole subprime lending fiasco is that a lot of that stuff wasn't necessarily illegal, it was just immoral or inappropriate or reckless."[8]

Assessing the verdict in the Bear Stearns case, financial journalists Bethany McLean and Joe Nocera voiced a similar view. "Much of what took place during the crisis was immoral, unjust, craven, delusional behavior—but it wasn't criminal," McLean and Nocera write in their book, *All the Devils Are Here.*[9]

Other experts, however, are less inclined to give a legal pass to the companies and individuals whose actions helped topple respected Wall Street firms, forced the government to bail out the nation's biggest banks, caused millions of homeowners to lose their homes and left hundreds of thousands of others owing more than their homes were worth.

"Accounting-control frauds drove this financial crisis, as they did the two prior financial crises: the Enron era fraud [of the early 2000s] and the S&L debacle," says Black, the former regulator from the S&L crisis. "What caused the crisis was overwhelmingly garden-variety fraud, which can and should be prosecuted."

Fraud was widely seen as a major factor in the 1980s S&L crisis, but the extent to which fraud caused the collapse of so many thrift institutions defies simple calculation. Early on, the government suggested that fraud was a factor in 70 to 80 percent of the thrift failures. But a study by the Resolution Trust Corporation, the government-owned company organized to manage the assets of the failed thrifts, estimated more conservatively that fraud played a significant role in the failure of about a third of the institutions. Officials estimated that fraud was to blame for about 10 percent to 15 percent of net losses from the crisis.[10]

Any firm conclusion about how much fraud or other illegal conduct was to blame for the latest financial crisis is years away. For now, Arlen, the New York University professor, acknowledges uncertainty. "It does seem to me clear that there were disclosure problems," Arlen says, "but I'm not yet in a position to know whether the problems relate to judgment calls that are inherently part of the accounting profession or to actual fudging."

Lawyers who defend white-collar-crime cases voice doubts about the extent of fraud in the recent events. "In most of these cases, I don't see fraud," says David Douglass, a Washington lawyer and chair of the government enforcement and compliance committee of the defense bar organization DRI. "In most of these cases, I see why people would be unhappy with the results, but it's not fraud."

"You're talking about companies taking huge risks, companies being hugely leveraged," says Gorman, the lawyer with the securities litigation blog. "You might categorize that as reckless mismanagement or breach of fiduciary duty, but it's not criminal."

Even years from now, any assessment of the issue may be elusive, in part because of the difficulties of proving fraud or financial wrongdoing in court. "It is enormously problematic for prosecutors to prove beyond a reasonable doubt that the executives of a company acted with fraudulent intent," says Michael Perino, a professor at St. John's University School of Law in Jamaica, N.Y., and a former Wall Street litigator. "That is what you need to show a criminal prosecution under the federal security law."

But Black points out that federal regulatory agencies have referred far fewer cases for possible prosecution in the current scandal than the 10,000-plus criminal referrals that were made during the S&L crisis. As of November 2011, Black counted no referrals from the Office of Thrift Supervision, three from the Office of the Comptroller of the Currency and three from the Federal Reserve.[11]

"Yes, these are difficult cases," Black says. But, he adds, "Without criminal referrals there are no police on elite white-collar criminals."

Have federal agencies been tough enough in prosecuting financial wrongdoing?

Angelo Mozilo helped found Countrywide Financial in 1969 and built it over the next three decades into the largest lender of single-family home loans in the country. By 2006, however, Mozilo was worrying about a possible decline in home prices and the quality of some of the subprime loans his company had helped create and popularize.

Publicly, however, Mozilo voiced confidence in his company right up to its collapse in late 2007 and acquisition in January 2008 by Bank of America at the fire-sale price of $4 billion. As the storm clouds grew, the SEC in June 2009 charged Mozilo in a civil suit with securities fraud and insider trading for selling off his stock in Countrywide.

In October 2010, the SEC negotiated a settlement with Mozilo that included a $67.5 million fine and a permanent ban on his serving as a director or officer in a publicly traded company. Robert Khuzami, director of the SEC's Division of Enforcement, said the "record penalty" was a "fitting outcome" in the case. But observers noted that the agreement allowed Mozilo to avoid any admission of wrongdoing. And the government's criminal investigation was quietly shelved a few months later.[12]

The decision to bring no criminal charges against Mozilo exemplifies what *The New York Times* called in a 4,000-word overview last spring the "dearth of prosecutions" in connection with the financial crisis.[13] The story by two of the *Times*' veteran financial reporters, Gretchen Morgenson and Louise Story, noted that under President George W. Bush, Attorney General Michael Mukasey declined to create a nationwide task force on financial crimes — as was done during the S&L crisis. A task force created by Obama's attorney general, Eric Holder, was given a broad mandate but no additional resources.

Black, who was prominently quoted in the story, continues to speak out about the lack of prosecutions. "There has been no prosecution of an elite Wall Street figure who played a major role" in the crisis, Black says today. "That's an astonishing fact."

Statistics compiled by the private Transactional Records Access Clearinghouse at Syracuse University

Madoff Eluded SEC for 16 Years

Despite tips, agency failed to halt $18 billion Ponzi scheme.

The Securities and Exchange Commission (SEC) got its first tip about something fishy in Bernard Madoff's investment operations in 1992. The next, very detailed tip came in 2000, followed by four more reports before Madoff sons' accusations against their father in December 2008 finally got the agency to stop what appears to have been the largest Ponzi scheme in U.S. history.*

The missed opportunities to stop a scheme that bilked investors out of $18 billion in cash — and higher amounts in claimed but nonexistent profits — are catalogued in a damning report issued in late August 2009 by the SEC's inspector general. SEC investigators repeatedly failed to grasp the significance of tipsters' information, according to the 450-page report, and never took some rudimentary steps that could have verified the suspicions. [1]

Two years later, the agency confirmed on Nov. 11 that it had disciplined eight employees for mishandling the investigation, but fired no one. A ninth employee resigned before disciplinary action could be taken, according to *The Washington Post*'s account. Victims of Madoff's fraud denounced the disciplinary steps as inadequate. [2]

Madoff, now 73, is serving a 150-year sentence in a federal prison in North Carolina even as a court-appointed trustee seeks to recover and return to victims some of the misappropriated funds. As of December, an estimated $11 billion had been recovered. [3]

The inspector general's report clears the SEC of any conflicts of interest or inappropriate interference in the investigations but ends with an understated critique of the agency's thoroughly botched response to tips it received.

---

* A Ponzi scheme, named after the early 20th-century swindler Charles Ponzi, is a fraudulent investment operation in which investors are paid gains from money deposited by new investors. The schemes typically collapse when new investors cannot be recruited or a large number of investors try to cash out all at once.

"The SEC never properly examined or investigated Madoff's trading and never took the necessary, but basic, steps to determine if Madoff was operating a Ponzi scheme," the report states. "Had these efforts been made with appropriate follow-up at any time beginning in June 1992 until December 2008, the SEC could have uncovered the Ponzi scheme well before Madoff confessed."

The report prompted sharp criticism of the agency from members of Congress from both parties. Sen. Charles E. Schumer, D-N.Y., said the report showed "a level of incompetence unseen since [the Federal Emergency Management Agency's] handling of Hurricane Katrina." Sen. Charles Grassley, R-Iowa, said the agency's "utter failure" to follow up on the tips was "further evidence of a culture of deference toward the Wall Street elite." [4]

"The SEC was properly chastised," says Thomas Gorman, a Washington lawyer who publishes a blog on SEC litigation. "They had multiple opportunities to find that case. They simply failed to analyze the information."

Jennifer Arlen, a securities law professor at New York University, is more sympathetic to the agency's investigators' difficulties in dealing with what she calls "huge numbers of tips" of varying quality and credibility. "They're making tradeoffs between, 'Here are these things that I know something wrong's going on,' and 'Here's something big but it could be something or it could be nothing.'"

The first of the tips against Madoff came in June 1992 from customers of an investment firm suspicious that the firm was claiming "100%" safe investments with "extremely high and consistent" rates of return. The firm's investments, it turned out, were managed exclusively by Madoff. "Inexperienced" investigators suspected a Ponzi scheme, the inspector general's report states, but failed to conduct a thorough investigation.

Eight years later, the SEC received the first of three detailed complaints about Madoff from Harvey Markopolos, a securities executive-turned-independent financial fraud investigator

show an uninterrupted, decade-long decline in the number of federal prosecutions for financial institution fraud. In a report in late 2011, the clearinghouse showed more than 3,000 such prosecutions per year in the 1990s but only 1,349 for fiscal 2011. [14] (*See graph, p. 180*)

In the "60 Minutes" segment, former Countrywide vice president for fraud investigations Eileen Foster said there was "systemic" fraud at the company — specifically, loan officers approving mortgages based on forged or manipulated statements of borrowers' incomes and assets.

in Boston. Markopolos' reports grew from an eight-page complaint in May 2000 to a longer version in October 2005 with the headline, "The World's Largest Hedge Fund Is a Fraud."

In each report, Markopolos said he had attempted but failed to replicate Madoff's claimed returns based on Madoff's reports of his investment strategy. Markopolos has forcefully criticized the agency in interviews and in his first-person account, *No One Would Listen*, published in 2010. [5]

By the third of his reports, Markopolos was being taken seriously by SEC investigators, according to the inspector general's report. They focused, however, more on the question of whether Madoff needed to register as an investment adviser than on whether he was operating a Ponzi scheme as Markopolos believed.

In addition, the report states, SEC investigators failed to take the basic step of attempting to verify through third parties whether Madoff actually was making the trades that he said he was making. "A simple inquiry . . . could have immediately revealed the fact that Madoff was not trading in the volume he was claiming," the report states.

Other complaints came to the SEC from "a respected hedge fund manager," an anonymous informant and a "concerned citizen," who first contacted the agency in December 2006 and again in March 2008. The last communication included the damning detail — later confirmed — that Madoff kept two sets of records, "the most interesting of which is on his computer which is always on his person."

Even when SEC investigators began probing his operations, Madoff, the one-time chairman of the NASDAQ stock exchange, fended them off in an interview, according to the report, by lording his credentials and knowledge over the less experienced agency personnel. Supervisors closed the investigation in January 2008 and declined to reopen it after receiving the report about double sets of books two months later.

Madoff's scheme finally unraveled when he confessed in December 2008 to his sons, Andrew and Mark, who reported him to federal authorities. Madoff was arrested on Dec. 10; he pleaded guilty on March 12, 2009, to 14 federal felonies, including securities fraud. In court, Madoff said he began his Ponzi scheme in 1991. Judge Denny Chin sentenced him three months later.

AFP/Getty Images/Timothy A. Clary

Bernard Madoff, once a prince of Wall Street, pleaded guilty to running a Ponzi scheme that bilked investors out of $18 billion. He is serving a 150-year prison sentence.

Madoff has apologized for his conduct, but his son Andrew has said he will never forgive his father. Mark Madoff committed suicide by hanging himself in his Manhattan apartment. He was found dead on Dec. 11, 2010, two years to the day after his father's arrest.

— *Kenneth Jost*

[1]"Investigation of Failure of SEC to Uncover Bernard Madoff's Ponzi Scheme — Public Version," U.S. Securities and Exchange Commission's Office of Investigations, Aug. 31, 2009, www.sec.gov/news/studies/2009/oig-509.pdf. The executive summary is found at pp. 20-41. For coverage, see David Stout, "Report Details How Madoff's Web Ensnared S.E.C.," *The New York Times*, Sept. 3, 2009, p. B1; Zachary A. Goldfarb, "The Madoff Files: A Chronicle of SEC Failure," *The Washington Post*, Sept. 3, 2009, p. A1.

[2]See David S. Hilzenrath, "SEC disciplines 8 employees for Madoff failures," *The Washington Post*, Nov. 12, 2011, p. A1; "SEC's disciplinary steps in Madoff case enrage fraud victims," *The Washington Post*, Nov. 17, 2011, p. A17.

[3]See Diana B. Henriques, "A Lasting Shadow," *The New York Times*, Dec. 12, 2011, Business, p. 1.

[4]See Sean Lengell, "Schumer: Boost SEC's budget to fight fraud," *The Washington Times*, Sept. 4, 2009, p. 9; Marcy Gordon, "SEC bungled Madoff probes, agency watchdog says," The Associated Press, Sept. 3, 2009.

[5]Harry Markopolos with Frank Case, Neil Chelo, Gaytri Kachroo, and Michael Ocrant, *No One Would Listen: A True Financial Thriller* (2010).

However, she told correspondent Kroft, she was never interviewed by the Justice Department.

In the second part of the segment, Richard Bowen, a former senior vice president in Citigroup's consumer-lending division, said he warned Citi's top executives in

November 2007 that a high percentage of mortgages in its portfolio were "defective" and that the company was understating its financial risks. Kroft went on to suggest that Citi's CEO Vikrim Pandit and Chief Financial Officer Gary Crittenden may have violated a central

Financial Fraud Prosecutions on the Decline

Federal prosecutions for financial institution fraud have declined sharply over the past 20 years. They totaled 1,251 in the first 11 months of fiscal 2011 and were projected to reach 1,365 for the full year if trends continued. That would be 29 percent fewer than in 2006 and 58 percent fewer than a decade ago.

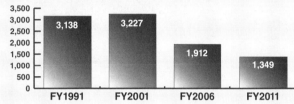

Criminal Fraud Prosecutions of Financial Institutions FY1991-FY2011

Source: Transactional Records Access Clearinghouse, Syracuse University, November 2011, trac.syr.edu/tracreports/crim/267/

provision of the post-Enron Sarbanes-Oxley Act by certifying inaccurate financial statements to the SEC. Kroft quoted the company as defending the statements.

Commenting generally, New York University's Arlen sharply criticizes the failure to bring legal actions against individual executives. "You can't safeguard the market unless securities fraud doesn't pay, and it has to not pay for the individuals who do it," Arlen says. "You need people to be personally afraid of the consequences of lying."

SEC officials insist the agency is not shying away from going after individual executives. In announcing the civil suit against the former Fannie Mae and Freddie Mac executives, enforcement chief Khuzami promised that "all individuals" would be held accountable for financial misrepresentations "regardless of their rank or position."[15]

The SEC also is touting its recent crackdown on insider-trading cases. In testimony to congressional committees in December, Khuzami described insider trading as "one of the Division of Enforcement's highest priorities" and listed several initiatives aimed at spotting suspicious trading patterns and abusive market practices.[16]

Private lawyers Douglass and Gorman both give the SEC credit for its insider-trading initiatives. "It's aggressive and innovative," says Douglass. "It captured the attention of the business community." Overall, however, Douglass, an assistant U.S. attorney before going into

private practice, calls the government's prosecution policies in the financial crisis "feckless."

"Insider trading should be prosecuted, but I don't think you can link insider-trading cases to these other kinds of fraud," Douglass says. "It undermines people's faith in the legal system when prosecutors say they're going to hold people accountable and they fail to do so."

Should mortgage lenders be punished for their role in improper foreclosures?

Among the more than 5 million home foreclosures since the financial crisis, banks and other mortgage lenders are now known to have completed a substantial number with procedures more akin to a factory assembly line than to a court of law. Banks, lenders and mortgage-servicing companies acknowledge the practice — dubbed "robo-signing" when first disclosed in October 2010 — where loan officers routinely signed foreclosure papers en masse without having read them.

Consumer advocates and some state attorneys general say the procedures amounted to "foreclosure fraud." Major banks admitted but somewhat minimized the problems even as they halted foreclosures for a while in order to clean up procedures. Investigations by news organizations and others, however, indicate that robo-signing and other documentation discrepancies continue.[17]

Banks hoping to put the issue behind them have been negotiating with representatives of state attorney general offices since spring 2011, looking to a multibillion-dollar settlement that would also limit their liability in further investigations. An accord looked close last fall, but the likelihood of agreement dimmed as some state attorneys general split off from the talks to take a tougher line.

In the most significant development, Massachusetts Attorney General Martha Coakley sued the nation's five largest mortgage lenders in state court on Dec. 1. The 57-page complaint charges the banks — Bank of America, Citigroup, GMAC Mortgage and its parent company Ally Financial, JP Morgan Chase and Wells

Fargo — with having seized properties unlawfully. It asks for a court order that they change their practices and correct defects in previous foreclosures. [18]

In announcing the suit, Coakley said she pulled out of the settlement talks because the banks had failed to take responsibility for what she called "the devastation" on individual homeowners and communities. Critics of the lenders' practices similarly say the proposed settlement — which is being pushed by the Obama administration — would allow the banks to escape accountability for throwing people out of their homes without proper procedures.

"We should have prosecutions," says Yves Smith, who writes critically about financial industry news on the popular blog *Naked Capitalism.* "You don't settle unless you know what the crime was," she continues. "The attorneys general don't know what they're settling for, so they don't have any bargaining leverage."

Smith sharply criticizes the banks' effort to limit further legal exposure. "The banks have continued to ask for more and more and more," she says. Black, the law professor and former S&L regulator, agrees. "I would not have believed it possible in the United States that we would actually immunize them," Black says.

Banks involved in the negotiations have generally declined to comment about the talks. Spokesmen for three of the banks — Bank of America, JP Morgan Chase and Wells Fargo — all expressed disappointment with the filing of the Massachusetts suit. "We continue to believe that the collaborative resolution rather than continued litigation will most quickly heal the housing market and help drive economic recovery," BofA spokesman Lawrence Grayson said.

GMAC was more combative. "GMAC Mortgage believes it has strong legal and factual defenses," the company said in a statement, "and "will vigorously defend its position in court."[19]

The value of the proposed settlement as reported could reach $25 billion if all 50 states participate, most of it apparently in the form of principal write-downs, interest-rate reductions and other benefits to homeowners. Some cash penalties could be imposed on the banks. The settlement would be reduced if some states — most notably, California — balk at the accord.[20]

California is one of five states — all with Democratic attorneys general — that have pulled out of the talks to pursue separate legal actions. Besides Massachusetts, the others are Delaware, Nevada and New York.

Obama administration officials, including Treasury Secretary Timothy Geithner and Housing and Urban Development Secretary Shaun Donovan, have been pushing the settlement in the interest of stabilizing the banks and the housing market. Without commenting on the specifics of the proposed settlement, Christopher Mayer, a real estate finance expert at Columbia Business School, agrees on the importance of resolving the issues.

"Settling this is incredibly important because there's an enormous backlog of delinquent mortgages," Mayer says. "The process of doing nothing is a loser for everybody. We need to reduce uncertainty."

Mayer says most of the foreclosures are justified in economic terms. "The vast, vast majority of people who are involved are people who are not paying their mortgages," he says.

But Smith insists that the banks' actions are more than "innocent" mistakes. "These are not mistakes," she says. "They happened on too large a scale to be mistakes."

BACKGROUND

Policing the Markets

Federal regulation of the banking, housing and securities industries dates from the Great Depression, the economic calamity touched off by the stock market crash of 1929 that cost millions of Americans their homes, farms, jobs or life savings. The legislative and regulatory regimes set up to insure bank deposits, protect investors and support home mortgages appeared to serve the country's financial system well for half a century. By the 1970s, however, the Supreme Court began to balk at some of the SEC's expansive applications of anti-fraud rules. Since then, marketplace changes have combined with deregulatory initiatives and out-and-out dishonesty to jolt the financial system, first in the 1980s and twice already in the 21st century.[21]

The stock market crash of October 1929 — a 25 percent drop in two days — came unexpectedly after a decade of boom times. The subsequent congressional investigation documented abuses that, if known, might have foretold the collapse — in particular, risky investments in securities by banks. Over a four-year period,

CHRONOLOGY

Before 1960 *Federal regulation of banks, securities established.*

1933, 1934 Financial disclosure required to offer stock, other securities (Securities Act). . . . Commercial, investment banking separated; federal deposit insurance instituted (Glass-Steagall Act). . . . Securities and Exchange Commission (SEC) established.

1938 Federal National Mortgage Association ("Fannie Mae") created by Congress; becomes private company in 1968; Federal Home Loan Mortgage Corporation ("Freddie Mac") established as competitor in 1970.

1960s-1970s *SEC becomes more aggressive, meets Supreme Court resistance.*

1961 SEC prescribes "disclose or abstain rule" to bar insider trading.

1976 Supreme Court rules that securities fraud requires intent to deceive, not mere negligence.

1980s-1990s *Savings and loan crisis: government bailout, tightened rules.*

1980, 1982 Congress passes, two presidents sign legislation to deregulate thrift industry to aid competition with commercial banks.

Mid-1980s Hundreds of S&Ls fail; speculative loans, looting by executives blamed.

1989 Congress reregulates thrift industry, approves bailout of failed S&Ls (Financial Institutions Reform, Recovery and Enforcement Act). . . . Bailout cost later put at $88 billion; more than 1,800 S&L officials prosecuted, more than 1,000 sent to prison.

1996, 1998 Congress limits private securities-fraud suits in federal, state courts.

1999 Congress repeals Glass-Steagall; allows banks, securities firms to merge (Gramm-Leach-Bliley).

Early 2000s *Enron, accounting scandals followed by reforms.*

2001 Enron forced into bankruptcy after accounting frauds; top executives later prosecuted, convicted.

2002 Congress requires top executives to personally certify financial statements, creates agency to oversee accounting profession (Sarbanes Oxley).

2008-Present *Financial crisis freezes markets, brings financial overhaul, calls for tougher government action.*

2008 Government forces Bear Stearns fire-sale to JP Morgan Chase (March 16). . . . Government takes over Fannie Mae, Freddie Mac (Sept. 7). . . . Lehman Brothers declares bankruptcy (Sept. 15). . . . Treasury Secretary Henry Paulson strong-arms major banks to agree to bailout; Congress OKs plan (Emergency Economic Stabilization Act) (September/October). . . . Bernard Madoff charged with Ponzi scheme (Dec. 10).

2009 Madoff pleads guilty (March 12); later sentenced to 150 years in prison. . . . SEC Office of Inspector General says investigators could have stopped Madoff after first tip in 1992 (Aug. 31). . . . Bear Stearns hedge fund managers acquitted (Nov. 9).

2010 Goldman Sachs agrees to $550 million penalty in marketing subprime mortgages (July 15). . . . Dodd-Frank Act gives government more power to seize failing banks; creates Consumer Financial Protection Bureau (July 21). . . . Countrywide founder Angelo Mozilo settles with SEC for $67.5 million (Oct. 15).

2011 Meltdown could have been avoided, Financial Crisis Inquiry Commission says; Republican members file dissent (Jan. 27). . . . Hedge fund manager Raj Rajaratnam convicted in insider-trading case (May 11); later draws 11-year sentence; two dozen others convicted. . . . JP Morgan Chase agrees to $154 million penalty for rigged subprime mortgage package (June 21). . . . Citigroup agrees to $285 million settlement in toxic mortgage deal (Oct. 19), but judge balks at deal (Nov. 28).

2012 President Obama uses recess appointment to name Richard Cordray to head Consumer Financial Protection Bureau; Republican senators object (Jan. 4).

43 percent of the 24,970 U.S. banks failed or were merged out of existence.[22]

The investigation by the so-called Pecora Commission — named after its lead investigator, Ferdinand Pecora — helped build support for new laws regulating banking and securities. The Glass-Steagall Act, passed in 1933, separated commercial from investment banking and also established the Federal Deposit Insurance Corporation (FDIC) to insure individual depositors' accounts. In the same year, Congress passed the Securities Act, which required disclosure of financial information by companies issuing stock or other securities. A year later, the Securities Exchange Act created the SEC, regulated securities trading and gave the SEC power to write anti-fraud rules.

Congress also sought to bolster home mortgages. The Federal Home Owners' Loan Corporation was created in 1933 to repurchase foreclosed homes and reinstate former mortgages; the Federal Housing Administration was established in 1934 to insure those mortgages. Meanwhile, deposit insurance was extended in 1934 to savings and loan associations, the main source of mortgage funds. Then in 1938, the Federal National Mortgage Association — dubbed "Fannie Mae" — was founded as a government-sponsored enterprise to invest in mortgages. Fannie Mae was transformed into a private corporation in 1968; that change prompted Congress two years later to create a competitor: the Federal Home Loan Mortgage Corporation, dubbed "Freddie Mac."

Despite congressional and law enforcement investigations, the Depression-era financial turmoil spawned only a "small handful" of criminal prosecutions, according to St. Johns professor Perino. "The point of the Pecora Commission was to show that the laws and regulations were inadequate," he explains. The highest profile prosecutions failed. Bank executive Charles Mitchell of National City Bank was found not guilty of tax evasion; utility tycoon Samuel Insull of Commonwealth Edison was acquitted of mail fraud and antitrust charges. The only big name to go to prison was Richard Whitney, president of the New York Stock Exchange from 1930 to 1935, who embezzled money from the exchange's gratuity fund to cover heavy investment losses. He pleaded guilty to state charges in 1938 and served three years in prison.

The banking and securities regulations remained controversial through the 1930s. In a memoir, Pecora warned in 1939 against allowing Wall Street to go back to the time "before Uncle Sam stationed a policeman at its corner."[23]

Over the next several decades, however, the regulatory regimes appeared to gain general acceptance. With FDIC insurance, runs on banks by worried depositors became a relic of history. Investors grew accustomed to the financial disclosures required from companies issuing securities. By the 1950s and '60s, the SEC was being criticized not for over- but for under-regulating. President John F. Kennedy responded to a report by former SEC Chairman James Landis that called for strengthening regulatory agencies by increasing the SEC staff and appointing an activist-minded corporate law expert, William Cary, as chairman.

Cary laid the basis for the SEC's insider-trading enforcement with an administrative ruling in November 1961 sanctioning a broker who sold a company's stock based on advance word of a dividend cut that he learned from a partner who was on the company's board of directors. The ruling in *In re Cady, Roberts & Co.* established a so-called "disclose or abstain" rule: insiders had to disclose material information about a company's finances or abstain from trading on the basis of the information. In 1968 the rule gained judicial endorsement from the New York-based Second U.S. Circuit Court of Appeals in a case, *SEC v. Texas Gulf Sulphur Co.*, where company insiders had bought up stock and stock options in advance of an announcement of a major discovery of copper and zinc deposits. The appeals court interpreted the anti-fraud Rule 10b-5 to require that all investors have "relatively equal access to material information."[24]

The Supreme Court, which left the Texas Gulf Sulphur ruling in place by rejecting the company's appeal, had been generally supportive of SEC authority since the 1930s but began to shift in the 1970s. In a succession of rulings, the court cut back on SEC litigating positions. In 1976, for example, the court ruled 6-2 that the SEC's anti-fraud rule required proof of an intent to deceive, not mere negligence. A 1980 ruling rejected the SEC's attempt to expand the definition of insider to include people with no fiduciary relationship to the company.[25] Despite the adverse court rulings, however, the SEC increased its insider-trading enforcement, thanks in part to the creation of a computerized tracking system to monitor stock trading, corporate filings and news items.[26]

Losing Control

Twice over the next quarter century, the United States experienced seeming epidemics of financial misconduct,

'Test Drive' for Wiretaps in Insider-Trading Case

Galleon hedge fund founder made more than $70 billion in illegal gains.

Federal prosecutors in New York City have used wiretaps and a wired informant to help win more than two dozen convictions in a sprawling insider-trading investigation, including a record-setting prison term against the billionaire hedge-fund founder at the center of the case.

Dozens of recorded telephone calls provided the critical evidence that netted Raj Rajaratnam an 11-year prison sentence after his May 11 conviction in federal court in New York on nine counts of insider trading and five counts of conspiracy.

Rajaratnam, founder of the now defunct Galleon Group, made more than $70 million in illegal profits over a six-year period, according to prosecutors, by trading on inside information gathered from multiple contacts in Wall Street and corporate circles. [1]

One of Rajaratnam's major sources is alleged to have been Rajat Gupta, a friend and former head of the giant consulting firm McKinsey & Co. Gupta was charged in a six-count indictment unsealed on Oct. 26 with passing valuable inside information to Rajaratnam from his position as a director with Goldman Sachs, a big investment firm constantly involved in potential corporate mergers and acquisitions.

Among the lesser figures in the investigation was Brien Santarlas, formerly a patent attorney with a New York law firm, whose secretly recorded conversations with other conspirators helped win convictions in June of a key stock trader linked to Rajaratnam and two other defendants. Santarlas, who pleaded guilty to securities fraud charges in November 2009, was given a reduced, six-month sentence on Nov. 30, 2011, based on his cooperation with the prosecution. [2]

The government's first extensive use of wiretaps in an insider trading case — a tactic usually associated with organized crime and public corruption investigations — is one of the issues being raised on appeal by lawyers for Rajaratnam. Patricia Millett, a Washington lawyer and veteran appellate litigator, previewed her argument in an unsuccessful attempt in late November to win bail for Rajaratnam pending appeal.

Millett told a panel of the Second U.S. Circuit Court of Appeals on Nov. 30 that the government had not filed a proper request for the taps. Assistant U.S. Attorney Jonathan Streeter said the requests had been proper and noted that the trial judge had considered the issue before admitting the tapes at the start of Rajaratnam's seven-week trial. The appeals court denied bail for Rajaratnam the next day without comment. [3]

The prosecution made the most of the tapes during the trial. "You heard the defendant commit his crimes time and time again in his own words," Assistant U.S. Attorney Reed Brodsky said in closing arguments. Former government

followed each time by strengthened federal regulation and criminal prosecutions of prominent corporate executives. The savings and loan crisis of the 1980s required a $100 billion federal bailout to stabilize the thrift industry. By one count, more than 100 executives were prosecuted for various offenses. The accounting scandals of the early 2000s forced thousands of companies to revise their financial statements and led to prison terms for several top corporate managers. Meanwhile, Congress and the Supreme Court significantly tightened the rules governing civil suits for securities fraud while Congress also approved legislation to loosen regulation of abstruse financial instruments known as derivatives.

The S&L crisis stemmed from the competitive pressure on the thrifts created by the rise in interest rates in the late 1970s and a regulatory cap on interest they could pay on deposits. To aid the thrifts, Congress in 1980 and 1982 passed deregulatory legislation that, among other provisions, uncapped interest rates for most deposits, permitted adjustable-rate mortgages and allowed more speculative investments. Initially, the thrifts seemed to fare well, but many investments went bad as the real estate boom subsided. The thrifts also fell prey to high-flying entrepreneurs, some of whom simply looted the funds for personal benefit. By the end of the decade, more than 1,000 had failed, sticking the government with a $100 billion bailout bill. By 1995, the Justice Department had conducted 1,852 prosecutions of S&L officials, with 1,072 sentenced to prison.[27]

lawyers had praise after the verdict for the tactic. Prosecutors "took wiretaps for a test drive, and I'd say it was a resounding success," Stephen Miller, a former federal prosecutor in private practice in Philadelphia, told The Associated Press.[4]

Santarlas, who got into the insider-trading racket in October 2007 as a young associate at the New York office of the Boston-based firm Ropes & Gray, agreed to cooperate with the government in his first meeting with FBI agents in November 2009. He admitted being paid for tips about pending corporate deals gathered from confidential information at his firm. In the later trial, Santarlas testified that he was instructed to use a pre-paid cell phone to relay information and then to cut the phone into pieces and throw the pieces into the river.

Santarlas testified, along with fellow lawyer-turned-tipster Arthur Cutillo, in the trial of stock trader Zvi Goffer, who had worked for Rajaratnam before starting his own firm. Goffer and two others who worked for him — his brother Emanuel and lawyer Michael Kimelman — were convicted on June 13 on multiple counts of securities fraud and conspiracy. Zvi Goffer later received a 10-year prison sentence, Emmanuel Goffer a three-year term, and Kimelman a 30-month sentence.

Cutillo, who like Santarlas pleaded guilty to a single count of conspiracy, was sentenced on June 30 to 30 months in prison. Both lawyers apologized at sentencing for their offenses. "I know what I did was terribly wrong," Cutillo said in the June 30 hearing. Five months later, Santarlas said he was "ashamed," "embarrassed" and "humiliated" about what he had done. "It's something I'll never forgive myself for," he said.

— Kenneth Jost

Getty Images/Spencer Platt

Former Goldman Sachs director Rajat Gupta is facing charges of passing inside information to hedge fund founder Raj Rajaratnam, who was convicted on fraud and conspiracy charges in connection with his making $70 million in illegal profits.

---

[1] Press releases on individual developments in the case can be found by date on the website of the U.S. attorney for the Southern District of New York: www.justice.gov/usao/nys/pressreleases/. Details on Rajaratnam's trial and conviction taken from Tom Hays and Larry Neumeister, "Hedge fund founder convicted in inside-trade case," The Associated Press, May 11, 2011.

[2] See Larry Neumeister and Tom Hays, "NY jury convicts 3 in NYC hedge fund trial," *ibid.*, June, 13, 2011; Tom Hays, "Tipster sentenced in NYC insider trading case," *ibid.*, Nov. 30, 2011.

[3] Larry Neumeister, "Fund boss loses bid to stay free during appeal," *ibid.*, Dec. 1, 2011.

[4] Quoted in Larry Neumeister and Tom Hays, "Wiretaps key in conviction of ex-hedge fund giant," *ibid.*, May 11, 2011.

Congress and President George H. W. Bush responded to the S&L crisis by enacting the Financial Institutions Reform, Recovery and Enforcement Act of 1989. In addition to authorizing the $100 billion bailout by the newly established Resolution Trust Corporation, the law revamped deposit insurance, raised capital requirements for thrifts and placed them under the authority of the newly established Office of Thrift Supervision within the Treasury Department.

In contrast to the heightened regulation of the thrift industry, Congress and the Supreme Court were erecting barriers in the 1990s to private lawsuits aimed at enforcing federal securities laws. Congress responded to business-community complaints about supposedly baseless securities class action suits by enacting, over President Bill Clinton's

veto, the Private Securities Litigation Reform Act of 1996. The act raised the initial burden of proof for private securities-fraud suits to proceed and tightened various rules governing federal class action suits. When plaintiffs' lawyers tried to circumvent the law by bringing suits in state courts, Congress responded with a second law, the Securities Litigation Uniform Standards Act, effectively preempting state court jurisdiction over securities cases.

Earlier, the Supreme Court in 1994 had issued a closely divided ruling that barred extending civil liability for aiding and abetting securities fraud to outsiders, such as accountants, attorneys or other professionals.[28] In 1997, however, the court boosted both private and criminal enforcement against insider trading by endorsing the SEC's

With Richard Cordray at his side, President Obama addresses staffers at the new Consumer Financial Protection Bureau on Jan. 6, 2012. Obama used a recess appointment to install the former Ohio attorney general as the agency's head after Republicans blocked action on the nomination. Cordray is laying out an aggressive initiative for the agency despite potential legal challenges to his appointment.

so-called misappropriation theory, which barred anyone — not just corporate insiders — from trading on confidential company information. The ruling in *United States v. O'Hagan* upheld the 57-count conviction of a Minneapolis lawyer who made $4.3 million in profits while trading in Pillsbury stock in advance of a planned tender offer by a corporate client of his firm.[29]

As the decade ended, Congress approved two additional deregulatory initiatives that helped set the stage for the later financial crisis. The Gramm-Leach-Bliley Act of 1999 effectively repealed the Glass-Steagall Act by allowing banks and financial holding companies to own both commercial banking and securities firms as well as insurance companies. A year later, the Commodity Futures Modernization Act blocked the Commodity Futures Trading Commission from asserting regulatory authority over the complex financial instruments known as over-the-counter derivatives. Clinton signed both measures after they had won bipartisan support in Congress.

The financial scandals of the early 2000s were embodied most dramatically in the story of Enron, a Houston-based energy trading company that used creative accounting tricks to conceal shaky finances until being forced late in 2001 to issue financial restatements and then seek bankruptcy protection. Top Enron executives were prosecuted,

along with the company's outside accounting firm Arthur Andersen. Similar accounting scandals forced a succession of other companies to issue restatements, and a few other top executives faced criminal charges. The image of a corporate crime wave was heightened by a spike in unrelated cases of garden-variety insider trading and misappropriation of corporate funds.[30]

Even as criminal prosecutions were getting under way, Congress and President George W. Bush responded by overhauling corporate accounting practices. The bipartisan Sarbanes-Oxley Act — named after its principal Senate and House sponsors — included provisions to strengthen auditors' independence from corporate boards and to require top executives to take individual responsibility for the accuracy of financial statements. It also established a new, quasi-independent agency, the Public Company Accounting Oversight Board, to oversee accounting firms' compliance with the act. In signing the bill, Bush called it "the most far-reaching reforms of American business practices since the time of Franklin D. Roosevelt."

Digging Out

The financial crisis of 2008 formed under the surface for several years before emerging into public view in March when the government forced the sale of cash-strapped Bear Stearns to JP Morgan Chase for a paltry $2 a share. By year's end, Lehman Brothers had collapsed, Fannie Mae and Freddie Mac had been nationalized and the nation's nine biggest banks had been ordered to take billions in bailouts in exchange for a commitment to unfreeze the frozen credit markets. Government regulators and federal prosecutors then went to work, looking for culpability. The government won some significant victories but endured constant second-guessing from critics about the pace of investigations and the penalties imposed.[31]

Meanwhile, Congress was working on legislation aimed at preventing another financial meltdown. As signed into law by President Obama on July 21, 2010, the Wall Street Reform and Consumer Protection Act — more commonly, the Dodd-Frank Act after its principal Senate and House sponsors — gives the government more power to seize and wind down big financial firms. It also requires companies that sell mortgage-backed securities generally to retain at least 5 percent of the risk of the products. The bill also mandates regulation of over-the-counter derivatives and requires hedge funds to register with the SEC. And it established the Consumer Financial Protection Bureau as an independent agency within the Federal Reserve to enforce consumer-protection laws against not only banks and mortgage lenders but also credit card issuers, payday lenders and other financial-service companies.[32]

The charges against the ex-Bear Stearns hedge fund managers Cioffi and Tannin in June 2008 marked the first financial crisis-related prosecution to hit Wall Street directly. The pair were arrested June 19 on a fraud and conspiracy indictment based largely on e-mails showing undisclosed doubts about their funds' strength. Mark Mehrson, head of the FBI's New York office, told reporters the case was about "premeditated lies to investors and lenders." Lawyers for Cioffi and Tannin foreshadowed their successful defense by insisting their clients were victims of an unexpected crisis in financial markets. After the acquittals, a former Enron fraud prosecutor told *The New York Times* that the verdict showed the weakness of relying on " 'smoking gun' e-mails" to make a white-collar crime case.[33]

Once in office, the Obama administration made a public show of going after financial misconduct with the creation of an interagency task force on financial fraud in November 2009. Holder, accompanied by SEC Chairwoman Mary Schapiro and Cabinet colleagues Geithner from Treasury and Donovan from HUD, promised that the task force would be "relentless" in investigating and prosecuting corporate and financial wrongdoing. But Black, the Missouri law professor, notes that in addition to the task force getting no additional resources, its mission was extended beyond Wall Street. In April 2011, for example, a task force working group was formed to study the causes of rising oil and gas prices.[34]

The SEC, meanwhile, was achieving some success with civil actions carrying nine-figure settlements in cases against Goldman Sachs and JP Morgan Chase. Both companies were charged with securities fraud by misleading investors in subprime mortgage packages. The $550 million settlement that Goldman agreed to in July 2010 was described as one of the biggest penalties in SEC history. The agency charged Goldman with marketing a package of mortgages picked by the prominent hedge fund manager, John Paulson, who later bet against the bonds. News reports after the settlement disclosed that the five-member agency had split along party lines in initiating the complaint and approving the settlement, with three Democrats in favor and two Republicans against. Almost a year later, the agency won a $154 million settlement against Morgan in a similar case. In both cases, the firms neither admitted nor denied wrongdoing.[35]

Despite complaints in the press and from observers about the lack of prosecutions, the government was winning some significant convictions. It won a big case in April 2011 when a federal jury in Alexandria, Va., convicted Lee Farkas, the former majority owner of the big mortgage company Taylor, Bean & Whitaker, in a $3 billion fraud that toppled the Florida-based firm as well as the Alabama-based Colonial Bank. Farkas was sentenced on June 30 to 30 years in prison.[36]

In May 2011, the government notched a higher-profile victory with the conviction of prominent hedge fund manager Rajaratnam on 14 counts of securities fraud and conspiracy. Rajaratnam received an 11-year prison sentence in October — said to be the longest ever for insider trading — even as Gupta, one of his sources, a former chief executive of the giant consulting firm McKinsey & Co., was awaiting trial himself for insider trading.[37]

The SEC was still basking in the publicity glow from the Rajaratnam and Gupta cases when Judge Rakoff caught the agency by surprise by rejecting the proposed settlement with Citigroup. Two weeks later, on Dec. 15, the SEC announced that it would ask the Second U.S. Circuit Court of Appeals to overturn Rakoff's decision. "We believe the district court committed legal error by announcing a new and unprecedented standard that inadvertently harms investors by depriving them of substantial, certain and immediate benefits," enforcement chief Khuzami said in a statement accompanying the court filing.[38]

The next day, the agency shifted from defense to offense with its civil complaint charging the former Fannie and Freddie executives with fraud. The executives misled investors by understating their exposure to subprime mortgages, Khuzami said. In a briefing, Khuzami said the case was the 38th action brought by the commission in connection with the financial crisis.[39]

CURRENT SITUATION

Blaming Fannie, Freddie?

The SEC's fraud complaint against the former Fannie Mae and Freddie Mac executives is renewing the debate over the government-sponsored mortgage companies' responsibility for the subprime mortgage crisis, even as lawyers for the defendants call the charges baseless.

The parallel complaints, filed in federal district court in New York City, charge the former chief executives and two other ranking executives at each of the companies with making "materially false and misleading public disclosures" by understating the companies' exposure to subprime mortgage loans.

Named in the 59-page complaint against Fannie Mae executives are former CEO Daniel Mudd; Enrico Dallavecchia, former chief risk officer; and Thomas Lund, former executive vice president of Fannie's single-family mortgage business. The 49-page complaint against Freddie Mac executives names former CEO Richard Syron; Patricia Cook, former executive vice president and chief business officer; and Donald Bisenius, executive vice president for its single-family business.

The suits both seek disgorgement of profits, unspecified civil penalties and "other necessary and appropriate relief," which could include bans on their serving as officers or directors of publicly traded companies. The Fannie Mae case was assigned to Judge Robert Carter, the Freddie Mac case to Judge Richard Sullivan.[40]

None of the defendants has filed any response to the complaints, but Mudd and lawyers for Syron denied the allegations after the SEC announcement. "The SEC is wrong, and I look forward to a court where fairness and reason — not politics — is the standard for justice," Mudd said. Representing Syron, attorneys Thomas Green and Mark Hopson contended Freddie's filings had "no shortage of meaningful disclosures." They called the SEC's case "fatally flawed" and "without merit."[41]

The cases apparently will turn on how broadly to define the risks of unconventional loans offered by the two mortgage companies during the two-year period covered in the complaints up to their takeover by the government in August 2008. A chart accompanying the SEC's news release depicts Fannie as reporting $8 billion and Freddie $6 billion in subprime exposure as of second-quarter 2008, when their actual exposure to risky loans was $110 billion and $250 billion, respectively.

In the Fannie Mae complaint, the agency elaborates that its disclosures did not include so-called Alt-A reduced-documentation mortgages and loan products targeted to borrowers with weaker credit histories — also known as Expanded Approval or EA loans. Such loans, the complaint

states, "were exactly the type of loans that investors would reasonably believe Fannie Mae included when calculating its exposure to subprime loans." Similarly, the Freddie Mac complaint says the company failed to include loans referred to internally as "subprime," "otherwise subprime" or "subprime-like."

The role played by the two mortgage giants — sometimes referred to as "government-sponsored enterprises" or GSEs — had been a partisan issue on Capitol Hill and elsewhere since the financial crisis emerged. Republicans and conservative experts argued that Fannie and Freddie led mortgage lenders into the subprime swamp in order to satisfy 1990s-era statutory and regulatory mandates to provide access to affordable housing. Democrats generally defended the affordable-housing mandates and depicted the mortgage companies' problems as due to profit-driven recklessness. Days after the SEC filing, Peter Wallison, a longtime critic of the GSEs and a senior fellow at the conservative American Enterprise Institute (AEI), wrote in an op-ed in *The Wall Street Journal* that the legal actions vindicated his critique. "For the first time in a government report, the complaint has made it clear that the two government-sponsored enterprises (GSEs) played a major role in creating the demand for low-quality mortgages before the 2008 financial crisis," Wallison wrote.[42]

In a sharp reply to Wallison's argument even before the op-ed appeared, *New York Times* columnist Joe Nocera argued that Wallison was wrong in blaming the two GSEs for what he called "imagined" mistakes. "Fannie and Freddie got into subprime mortgages, with great trepidation, only in 2005 and 2006, and only because they were losing so much market share to Wall Street," Nocera wrote. He went on to call the SEC's case "extraordinarily weak," insisting that the agency was exaggerating the amount of risky loans and ignoring the companies' relatively low default rates.[43]

As part of the legal action, the SEC agreed not to prosecute the two companies, and both agreed to cooperate with the agency in pursuing the case. The filing appeared to be drawing generally positive reaction. Appearing on the PBS "NewsHour," Lynn Turner, a former SEC chief accountant, called the complaints "a very positive development" that showed the government "is willing to go after and hold accountable the people at the very top."[44]

Less approvingly, Black, the former regulator from the S&L crisis, acknowledges that the agency has a lower burden of proof in a civil case than the government would

Will the Financial Protection Bureau benefit consumers?

YES
Robert L. Borosage
Co-director, Campaign for America's Future

Written for *CQ Global Researcher*, January 2012

The best tribute to the potential of the Consumer Financial Protection Bureau (CFPB) is the millions the banking lobby expended in an unrelenting campaign to block its creation and cripple it once it was established. The reason for the resistance is simple. The CFPB has one mission: to protect consumers against abuse by large banks and other previously unregulated nonbank financial institutions.

The CFPB consolidates consumer protections previously scattered across the federal government into one agency devoted to their enforcement. Every other financial regulatory agency gives priority to protecting the "safety and soundness" of the banks they supervise. The result, witnessed to catastrophic effect in the housing bubble, has been an utter failure to protect consumers, allowing what the FBI called an unchecked "epidemic of fraud" in subprime mortgages that cost consumers trillions and drove the economy into recession.

One of CFPB's priorities will be to police nonbanking institutions, particularly the payday lenders that levy obscene charges — effective interest rates of 400 percent or more and onerous penalties and fees — on the most vulnerable workers who live paycheck to paycheck. If it simply exposes the big banks engaged in these practices, while requiring and enforcing clear notice of costs, the CFPB can make a dramatic difference.

Already the CFPB is stepping up scrutiny of lenders peddling loans to students at profit-making colleges, many of which project 50 percent default rates. The CFPB also has set up special sections to monitor abuses of seniors and active-duty military personnel who are often targeted by predatory lenders.

The CFPB already has begun to develop clear "know before you owe" notifications of terms for mortgages, credit cards and student loans. Currently consumers sign forms that are purposefully too long, detailed and arcane to be read or understood. By forcing simplification, the CFPB will allow consumers to police the tricks and traps now used on unwary borrowers.

Despite the claims of the bank lobby and Republicans, the concern about the CFPB isn't that it is unaccountable, but that it will be constrained by budgetary limits and unique oversight requirements. Its rule-making can be overturned by a Financial Oversight Council, made up of traditional banking regulators, all more concerned about protecting the solvency of banks than fairness to consumers.

But an active CFPB will garner immense public support as it cracks down on financial predators. No wonder the banking lobby continues to try to weaken it.

NO
Diane Katz
Research Fellow in Regulatory Policy, Heritage Foundation

Written for *CQ Global Researcher*, January 2012

Some unknown number of individuals may benefit from the Consumer Financial Protection Bureau (CFPB). But the new agency's unparalleled powers — magnified by an absence of accountability — bodes ill for most consumers.

President Obama's recess appointment of Richard Cordray to direct the bureau demonstrates the indiscretion to which the CFPB is prone. To the extent its regulations unduly restrict the availability of financing, economic growth will be constricted. And when unnecessarily stringent regulation raises the cost of credit, consumers are forced to find alternatives that entail greater cost and risk than conventional sources.

Researchers have long documented these dynamics, which are also inherent in other provisions of the Dodd-Frank regulatory statute. For example, the so-called Durbin amendment, which imposed price controls on the fees that banks charge retailers to process debit card transactions, has led to higher fees for checking accounts and other bank services. Higher fees, in turn, force low-income Americans from banks and to less conventional lenders of the very sort regulatory advocates warn against.

Imbued with ill-defined powers and unparalleled independence, the bureau is the epitome of regulatory excess. Well-intended or otherwise, its proponents are wholly invested in saving us from ourselves, and thus disposed to overreach. That increases the likelihood that consumers will be lulled into a false sense of security and makes the absence of bureau oversight all the more problematic.

The CFPB is ensconced within the Federal Reserve, its funding set by statute. Therefore, its budget is not subject to the same congressional control as most other federal agencies. And the bureau's status within the Fed also effectively precludes presidential oversight.

Its accountability is also minimized by the vague language of its statutory mandate. It is empowered to punish "unfair, deceptive and abusive" business practices. While *unfair* and *deceptive* have been defined in other regulatory contexts, the term *abusive* is largely undefined, granting the CFPB officials inordinate discretion.

The financial crisis did not result from any lack of regulation over consumer financial products. Therefore, creation of the CFPB will not help to prevent a future crisis. But it will limit consumer choices. Congress should abolish the CFPB's funding mechanism and subject it instead to congressional control, strike the undefined term *abusive* from the list of practices under CFPB purview, and require the bureau to apply definitions of *unfair* and *deceptive* practices in a manner consistent with consumer choice.

have in a criminal case. But he still complains about the lack of criminal prosecutions. "The Department of Justice still has failed to prosecute any of the elite accounting-control frauds that drove this crisis," he says.

New Agency Under Way

The head of the new Consumer Financial Protection Bureau is promising to make full use of the agency's regulatory and enforcement powers even as Republicans and industry groups challenge his recess appointment to the post.

"It's a valid appointment," Richard Cordray said in remarks to the Brookings Institution on Jan. 5, the day after President Obama named him to the position. "I'm now director of the bureau."[45]

Cordray, a former Ohio attorney general, is signaling an initial priority to extend federal regulation to what he calls in a press release the "thousands" of so-called non-banks. The non-depository financial businesses include mortgage lenders, mortgage servicers, payday lenders, consumer reporting agencies, debt collectors and money-services companies such as currency exchanges and traveler's check and money order issuers.

"This is an important step forward for protecting consumers," Cordray said in a Jan. 5 release. "Holding both banks and nonbanks accountable to consumer financial laws will help create a fairer, more transparent market for consumers. It will create a better environment for the honest businesses that serve them. And it will help the overall economic stability of our country."[46]

The debate over Obama's invocation of his recess-appointment power adds to the controversies surrounding the new agency, created as part of the Dodd-Frank Act passed by the Democratic-controlled Congress and signed by the president in 2010. Senate Republicans had blocked action on Cordray's nomination and Obama's previous selection of Harvard law professor Elizabeth Warren in an effort to change the structure and powers of the agency as provided in the law. Warren, now running as a Democrat for the U.S. Senate seat from Massachusetts, was a prime architect of the new agency.

Obama named Cordray the day after the Senate formally convened on Jan. 3 (as required by law) and then resumed a long holiday break. But the Senate had been conducting pro forma sessions every two to three days during the interval. Minority Leader Mitch McConnell of Kentucky and other GOP senators say the Senate's pro

forma sessions during the period barred the president from invoking his power under the Constitution to fill positions while the chamber is in recess.

A week after the appointment, the Justice Department released a memorandum from the Office of Legal Counsel supporting Obama's action. "[T]he convening of periodic pro forma sessions in which no business is to be conducted does not have the legal effect of interrupting an intrasession recess," assistant attorney general Virginia Seitz wrote in the 23-page opinion. Administration officials said Seitz had summarized her conclusion to Obama before his appointment.

Seitz acknowledged "substantial arguments" on the opposite side and possible "litigation risks" to the action. Sen. Charles Grassley of Iowa, ranking Republican on the Judiciary Committee, called the memorandum "unconvincing."[47]

The law establishes the CFPB as an independent agency within the Federal Reserve to be headed by a single director. Senate Republicans want to provide instead for a multimember board, comparable to other regulatory agencies. They also criticize the agency's independent budget authority. Democrats counter that Republicans should have tried to amend the law instead of blocking action on the nomination. If valid, Obama's recess appointment would allow Cordray to stay in the post through the remainder of the year.

In assuming the office, Cordray is making special efforts to solicit input from consumers and whistleblowers. In a two-minute video posted on the CPFB web site (www.consumerfinance.gov), Cordray personally invites consumer complaints. "Tell us your story today," he says in closing. In his remarks at Brookings, Cordray said the agency "will make clear that there are real consequences to breaking the law."

A week later, Cordray briefed reporters on plans to scrutinize the student loan business, particularly non-traditional lenders to students at for-profit and trade schools. Cordray said the bureau has seen evidence of loans made by lenders even though they knew borrowers would be unlikely to be able to pay off the loans.[48]

OUTLOOK

No Way to Know?

Ben Bernanke wrapped up his first meeting as chairman of the Federal Reserve Board of Governors in March 2006 with cautious optimism about what he described as the "cooling" in the housing market. Transcripts of the March 27-28 meeting — released in accord with the Fed's practice five years afterward — show Bernanke expected the economy's "strong fundamentals" to offset any reduced spending from homeowners as house prices sagged. "I think it would take a very strong decline in the housing market to substantially derail the strong momentum for growth that we are currently seeing in the economy," Bernanke concluded.[49]

Instead of the "soft landing" that Bernanke predicted, the United States' decades-long housing bubble burst dramatically and plunged the nation into recession by the end of 2007. Four years later, the economy has yet to recover. Many victims of the recession — those who lost their jobs, homes or both — naturally blame mortgage lenders and other financial institutions for driving the market catastrophically to unsustainable levels.

The financial industry has responded in general by insisting that it did not know — and could not have known — that the bubble would burst as it did. In the industry's view, all of the people at banks and investment firms who sliced and diced mortgages into marketable investment packages hardly could have known that they were selling what turned out to be "toxic assets."

The law enforcement agencies going through the wreckage — chiefly, the SEC and Justice Department at the federal level — have found plenty of cases of unmistakable financial misconduct, such as Bernard Madoff's giant Ponzi scheme or the flurry of insider-trading cases. In one of the most recent cases, the government is trying to determine what happened to $1.2 billion in customer money when the New York-based brokerage firm MF Global headed into bankruptcy in October 2011.[50]

The SEC also has found evidence of deception at some of the nation's banks in marketing securitized mortgages — deception that could amount to fraud under federal securities law. Two banks, Goldman Sachs and JP Morgan Chase, agreed to nine-figure payments to resolve such charges, and Citigroup was prepared to do the same until Judge Rakoff balked at the settlement. But the SEC may face an uphill fight in making a similar case against the former Fannie Mae and Freddie Mac executives if they contend that they cannot be held responsible for failing to spot the housing market crash that Bernanke and his Federal Reserve colleagues did not see coming.

Based on his experience in the S&L crisis, Black thinks the evidence of prosecutable "garden-variety fraud" is there for the looking. He sees a lack of political will to pursue cases. "It's the Wall Street folks who were the frauds, and nowadays they are the leading contributors to both parties," he says.

At the Justice Department, Breuer denies any political interference. "This Department of Justice is acting absolutely independently," he told correspondent Kroft in the "60 Minutes" interview. "Every decision that's being made by our prosecutors around the country is being made 100 percent based on the facts of that particular case and the law that we can apply."[51]

Gorman, the Washington lawyer and SEC litigation blogger, thinks the critics are exaggerating the extent of criminal activity involved. "It's one thing to run your business in a reckless way," Gorman says. "It's another thing to actually violate the law."

Washington defense lawyer Douglass thinks the government itself is to blame for feeding the public perception of serious wrongdoing. "If they think there's fraud, they should go out and build those cases," he says. "It's not that hard. It's just a heavy lift."

The government has been "pretty ineffective," says David Skeel, a professor of corporate law at the University of Pennsylvania in Philadelphia. "The pattern of enforcement and nonenforcement has been depressing, to put it mildly."

When Skeel was interviewed for *The New York Times* overview in March 2011, he said the lack of prosecutions led to "the whole perception that Wall Street was taken care of, and Main Street was not." Today, he says he is "hopeful but pessimistic" that the government will improve on its record.

"My fear is that two years from now the 2007-2008 crisis will seem to have been a long time ago," Skeel says. "The sense of urgency that regulators ought to have about stepping in will have dissipated."

NOTES

1. The decision is *U.S. Securities and Exchange Commission v. Citigroup Global Markets, Inc.*, 11 Civ. 7387 (JSR), U.S. Dist. Ct., S.D.N.Y., Nov. 28, 2011, www.scribd.com/doc/74040599/Rakoff-Citigroup.

For coverage, see Edward Wyatt, "Judge Rejects an S.E.C. Deal With Citigroup," *The New York Times*, Nov. 29, 2011, p. A1; David S. Hilzenrath, "Judge rebukes SEC on Citigroup deal," *The Washington Post*, Nov. 29, 2011, p. A1. For the SEC press release, and links to the complaint, see "Citigroup to Pay $285 Million to Settle SEC Charges for Misleading Investors About CDO [Collateralized Debt Obligation] Tied to Housing Market," Oct. 19, 2011, www.sec.gov/news/press/2011/2011-214.htm. For coverage, see Edward Wyatt, "Citigroup to Pay Millions to End Fraud Complaint," *The New York Times*, Oct. 20, 2011, p. B1. For coverage of the Bank of America case, see Louise Story, "Bank's Deal With S.E.C. Is Approved," *The New York Times*, Feb. 23, 2010, p. B1.

2. "Prosecuting Wall Street," "60 Minutes," Dec. 4, 2011, www.cbsnews.com/8301-18560_162-57336042/prosecuting-wall-street/?tag=contentMain;cbsCarousel (video, script, and 'Web extras').

3. "SEC Charges Stemming From Financial Crisis," Oct. 19, 2011, www.sec.gov/news/press/2011/2011-214-chart-stats.pdf. For background on the financial crisis, see these *CQ Researcher* reports: Marcia Clemmitt, "Financial Industry Overhaul," July 30, 2010, pp. 629-652; Thomas J. Billitteri, "Financial Bailout," Oct. 24, 2008, pp. 865-888, updated July 30, 2010; Kenneth Jost, "Financial Crisis," May 9, 2008, pp. 409-432.

4. "Prosecuting Wall Street," *op. cit.* The interview with Breuer ends the segment.

5. "Manhattan U.S. Attorney and FBI Assistant Director-in-Charge Announce Charges Against Seven Investment Professionals for Insider Trading Scheme That Allegedly Netted more than $61.8 Million in Illegal Profits," U.S. Attorney, Southern District of New York, Jan. 18, 2012, www.justice.gov/usao/nys/pressreleases/January12/newmantodetalchargespr.pdf; Jenny Strasburg, Michael Rothfeld and Susan Pulliam, "Federal Officials Charge Seven in Insider Probe," *The Wall Street Journal*, Jan. 18, 2012, http://online.wsj.com/article/SB10001424052970204468004577168450897919374.html?mod=WSJ_hp_LEFTTopStories.

6. See Edward Wyatt, "S.E.C. Changes Policy on Firms' Admissions of Guilt," *The New York Times*, Jan. 7, 2012, p. B1.

7. Quoted in E. Scott Reckard, "Pair are cleared of fraud charges," *Los Angeles Times*, Nov. 11, 2009, p. B1; see also Zachery Kouwe and Dan Slater, "2 Bear Stearns Funds Leaders Are Acquitted," *The New York Times*, Nov. 11, 2009, p. A1. For an account of the rise and fall of the funds, see Bethany McLean and Joe Nocera, *All the Devils Are Here: The Hidden History of the Financial Crisis* (2010), pp. 285-295.

8. "News Conference by the President," Oct. 6, 2011, www.whitehouse.gov/the-press-office/2011/10/06/news-conference-president.

9. McLean and Nocera, *op. cit.*, p. 362. McLean is a contributing editor at *Vanity Fair*, Nocera a columnist with *The New York Times*.

10. See Kitty Calavita, Henry N. Pontell, and Robert H. Tillman, *Big Money Crime: Fraud and Politics in the Savings and Loan Crisis* (1997), p. 29.

11. Quoted in Bruce Maiman, "Occupy protest should focus on the bank," *Sacramento* (Calif.) *Bee*, Nov. 8, 2011.

12. For coverage, see Gretchen Morgenson, "Leading Magnate Settles Charges for $67 Million," *The New York Times*, Oct. 16, 2010, p. A1; Walter Hamilton and E. Scott Reckard, "Countrywide execs settle fraud charges," *Los Angeles Times*, Oct. 16, 2010, p. A1. Under an indemnification agreement, Bank of America will pay $20 million of Mozilo's fine. Background drawn from McLean and Nocera, *op. cit.*, *passim*, esp. pp. 219-221, 230-31.

13. Gretchen Morgenson and Louise Story, "A Financial Crisis With Little Guilt," *The New York Times*, April 14, 2011, p. A1.

14. "Criminal Prosecutions for Financial Institution Fraud Continue to Fall," Transactional Records Access Clearinghouse, Nov. 15, 2011, http://trac.syr.edu/tracreports/crim/267/. The report showed 1,251 prosecutions for the first 11 months of fiscal 2011; a separate update for the final month (September 2011) showed 98 more, for a total of 1,349. The pictured chart projected 1,365 cases.

15. "SEC Charges Former Fannie Mae and Freddie Mac Executives With Securities Fraud," Dec. 16, 2011, www.sec.gov/news/press/2011/2011-267.htm. For coverage, see David S. Hilzenrath and Zachary

Goldfarb, "SEC charges ex-Fannie, Freddie chiefs," *The Washington Post*, Dec. 17, 2011, p. A1; Azam Ahmed and Ben Protess, "Ex-Fannie, Freddie Chiefs Accused of Deception," *The New York Times*, Dec. 17, 2011, p. A1.

16. "Statement on the Application of Insider Trading Law to Trading by Members of Congress and Their Staffs," testimony to Senate Committee on Homeland Security and Government Affairs, Dec. 1, 2011, www.sec.gov/news/testimony/2011/ts120111rsk.htm. Khuzami delivered similar testimony to the House Committee on Financial Services on Dec. 6.

17. Background drawn in part from " 'Robo-Signing' Paperwork Breakdown Leaves Many Houses in Foreclosure Limbo," PBS "NewsHour," Oct. 6, 2010, www.pbs.org/newshour/bb/business/july-dec10/foreclosures_10-06.html; Scot J. Paltrow, "Banks Continue 'Robo-Signing' Foreclosure Practices In Spite Of Promises to the Contrary: Investigation," Reuters Thomson, July 18, 2011, updated Sept. 17, 2011, published in *Huffington Post*, www.huffingtonpost.com/2011/07/18/robo-signing-foreclosure-banks_n_902140.html?page=1/.

18. The lawsuit is *Commonwealth v. Bank of America et al.*, Suffolk County Superior Court, B.L.S. 1-4363, www.mass.gov/ago/docs/press/ag-complaint-national-banks.pdf. The suit is also against Mortgage Electronic Registration System Inc., a widely used mortgage recording firm, and its parent company. For coverage, see Jenifer B. McKim, "State sues big US lenders," *Boston Globe*, Dec. 2, 2011, p. 1; Gretchen Morgenson, "Massachusetts Sues 5 Major Banks Over Foreclosure Practices," *The New York Times*, Dec. 2, 2011, p. B1.

19. Reactions from McKim, *op. cit.*, and Morgenson, *op. cit.* (Dec. 2, 2011).

20. See Ruth Simon, Nick Timiraos and Dan Fitzpatrick, "Banks in Push for Pact," *The Wall Street Journal*, Dec. 13, 2011, p. C1.

21. Some background drawn from "Fair to All People: The SEC and the Regulation of Insider Trading," Nov. 1, 2006, www.sechistorical.org/museum/galleries/it/.

22. Cited in Robert J. Samuelson, "Fed bashing slander," *The Washington Post*, Dec. 12, 2011, p. A21. For background, see Hoyt Gimlin, "Wall Street: 40 Years After the Crash," *Editorial Research Reports*, Oct. 8, 1969, and Richard Boeckel, "Stock Exchanges and Security Speculation," *Editorial Research Reports*, Feb. 1, 1930; both available in *CQ Researcher Plus Archive*.

23. Ferdinand Pecora, *Wall Street Under Oath: The Story of Our Modern Money Changers* (1939), p. xi. For Perino's account of the commission's investigation, see *The Hellhound of Wall Street: How Ferdinand Pecora's Investigation of the Great Crash Forever Changed American Finance* (2010).

24. The citation is 401 F.2d 833 (2nd Cir. 1968). The Supreme Court declined to hear the company's appeal.

25. The cases are *Ernst & Ernst v. Hochfelder*, 425 U.S. 185 (1976); *Chiarella v. United States* — 445 U.S. 222 (1980).

26. See story by Judith Miller, no headline available, *The New York Times*, March 7, 1980, sec. 4, p. 1 (SEC begins crackdown on 'insiders').

27. U.S. Department of Justice, "Attacking Financial Institution Fraud: A Report to the Congress of the United States," June 30, 1995, June 30, 1995, cited by incomplete name in Gillian Tett, "Insight: A Matter of Retribution," *Financial Times*, Sept. 30, 2009.

28. The decision is *Central Bank of Denver v. First Interstate Bank of Denver*, 511 U.S. 164 (1994). For coverage, see Kenneth Jost, *Supreme Court Yearbook*, 1993-1994.

29. The citation is 521 U.S. 642 (1997). For coverage, see Jost, *Supreme Court Yearbook, 1996-1997*.

30. For background, see "Corporate Crime," *op. cit.* For a later listing of some companies implicated, see Perry E. Wallace, "Accounting, Audit and Audit Committees After Enron, *et al.*: Governing Outside the Box Without Stepping Off the Edge in the Modern Economy," *Washburn Law Review*, Vol. 94 (January 2004), pp. 102-103 & accompanying notes.

31. For a dramatized overview of the events of 2008, see Frontline, "Inside the Meltdown," PBS, originally aired Feb. 17, 2009, www.pbs.org/wgbh/pages/frontline/meltdown/.

32. See Brady Dennis, "Obama ushers in new financial era," *The Washington Post*, July 22, 2010, p. A13; "Historic Financial Overhaul Creates Bureau, Expands Oversight of Banks," *2010 CQ Almanac*, pp. 3-3 to 3-9.

33. Mehrson, defense lawyers Edward Little (Cioffi) and Susan Brune (Tannin) quoted in Tom Hays, "2 Former Bear Stearns Hedge Fund Managers Charged," The Associated Press, June 20, 2008; ex-Enron prosecutor John Hueston quoted in Kouwe and Slater, *op. cit.*

34. Government releases: SEC, www.sec.gov/news/press/2009/2009-249.htm; Justice Department: www.justice.gov/opa/pr/2011/April/11-ag-500.html.

35. See Sewell Chan and Louise Story, "S.E.C. Settling Its Complaints With Goldman," *The New York Times*, July 16, 2010, p. A1; David S. Hilzenrath, "J.P. Morgan to pay $153.6 million to settle fraud suit," *The Washington Post*, June 22, 2011, p. A14.

36. For the trial, see Matthew Barakat, "Jury convicts exec in $3B mortgage fraud case," The Associated Press, April 19, 2011.

37. For the trial, see Tom Hays and Larry Neumeister, "Hedge-fund founder convicted in inside-trade case," The Associated Press, May 11, 2011.

38. See Edward Wyatt, "Citing 'Legal Error,' S.E.C. Says It Will Appeal Rejection of Citigroup Settlement," *The New York Times*, Dec. 16, 2011, p. B3.

39. Quoted in Ahmed and Protess, *op. cit.*

40. The cases are *SEC v. Mudd et al.*, Case No. 11 CIV 9202 (S.D.N.Y., Dec. 18, 2011),

41. www.sec.gov/litigation/complaints/2011/comp-pr2011-267-fanniemae.pdf; *SEC v. Syron et al.*, Case No. CIV 9201 (S.D.N.Y., Dec. 18, 2011), www.sec.gov/litigation/complaints/2011/comp-pr2011-267-freddiemac.pdf.

42. Mudd quoted in Andrew Strickler and Josh Bernstein, "FBI Launches Probe of Fannie, Freddie," *The Daily*, Dec. 17, 2011, www.thedaily.com/page/2011/12/17/121711-news-fannie-fredie-1-2/; Syron's lawyers quoted in Ahmed and Protess, *op. cit.*

43. Peter J. Wallison, "The Financial Crisis on Trial," *The Wall Street Journal*, Dec. 21, 2011, p. A19.

Wallison served under President Ronald Reagan as general counsel for the Treasury Department and White House counsel and played a significant role in the administration's unenacted proposals to deregulate the financial services industry. As a member of the Financial Crisis Inquiry Commission, he joined with other Republican appointees in dissenting from the majority report.

44. Joe Nocera, "An Inconvenient Truth," *The New York Times*, Dec. 20, 2011, p. A33. See also Joe Nocera, "The Big Lie," *ibid.*, Dec. 24, 2011, p. A21.

45. "Former Fannie, Freddie Officials Face 'Significant' Fraud, Lying Charges," PBS "NewsHour," Dec. 16, 2011 (interview by Judy Woodruff), www.pbs.org/newshour/bb/business/july-dec11/fanniefreddie_12-16.html.

46. See Edward Wyatt, "New Consumer Chief Promises Strong Agenda," *The New York Times*, Jan. 6, 2012, p. B3; Suzh Khimm, "Cordray Proceeds Despite Appointment Challenges," *The Washington Post*, Jan. 6, 2012, p. A16. See also Edward Wyatt, "Appointment Clears the Way for Agency to Act," *The New York Times*, Jan. 5, 2012, p. A16.

47. "Consumer Financial Protection Bureau launches nonbank supervision program," Jan. 5, 2012, www.consumerfinance.gov/pressrelease/consumer-financial-protection-bureau-launches-nonbank-supervision-program/. See also Peggy Twohig and Steve Antonakes, "The CFPB launches its nonbank supervision program," Jan. 5, 2012 (blog), www.consumerfinance.gov/the-cfpb-launches-its-nonbank-supervision-program/.

48. The memorandum is entitled "Lawfulness of Recess Appointments During a Recess of the Senate Notwithstanding Periodic Pro Forma Sessions," Jan. 6, 2012, www.justice.gov/olc/2012/pro-forma-sessions-opinion.pdf. Grassley is quoted in Charlie Savage, "Justice Dept. Defends Obama Recess Appointments," *The New York Times*, Jan. 13, 2012, p. A19. See Lyle Denniston, "First challenge on new Obama appointees," SCOTUSBlog, Jan. 13, 2012, www.scotusblog.com/2012/01/first-challenge-on-new-appointees/.

49. See Edward Wyatt, "Some Lenders to Students to Face Greater Scrutiny," *The New York Times*, Jan. 13,

2012, p. B3. For background, see Marcia Clemmitt, "Student Debt," *CQ Researcher*, Oct. 21, 2011, pp. 877-900; and Barbara Mantel, "Career Colleges," *CQ Researcher*, Jan. 7, 2011, pp. 1-24.

50. "Meeting of the Federal Open Market Committee, March 27-28, 2006, www.federalreserve.gov/monetarypolicy/files/FOMC20060328meeting.pdf. Bernanke's concluding comments begin at p. 95. For coverage, see Zachary A. Goldfarb, "As financial crisis brewed, Fed appeared unconcerned," *The Washington Post*, Jan. 13, 2012, p. A1; Binyamin Appelbaum, "Inside the Fed in '06: Coming Crisis, and Banter," *The New York Times*, Jan. 13, 2012, p. A1.

51. See Ben Protess and Azam Ahmed, "U.S. Inquiry of MF Global Gains Speed," *The New York Times*, Jan. 10, 2012, p. B1.

52. "Prosecuting Wall Street," *op. cit.*

BIBLIOGRAPHY

Selected Sources

Books

McLean, Bethany, and Joe Nocera, *All the Devils Are Here: The Hidden History of the Financial Crisis*, Portfolio/Penguin, 2010.
Veteran business journalists trace the origins and course of the financial crisis of 2008 from the invention of securitized mortgages through the proliferation of subprime mortgages and their dispersal to financial institutions and investors with limited disclosure of the financial risks. McLean is a contributor editor to *Vanity Fair*, Nocera a columnist for *The New York Times*. No notes or bibliography.

Morgenson, Gretchen, and Joshua Rosner, *Reckless Endangerment: How Outsized Ambition, Greed, and Corruption Led to Economic Armageddon*, Times Books, 2011.
The book focuses critically on the role played by Fannie Mae, the giant, government-sponsored mortgage company, in marketing subprime mortgages, especially loans written by its primary partner, Countrywide Financial. Morgenson is a Pulitzer Prize-winning reporter and columnist for *The New York Times*; Rosner is a consultant and early critic of the role of Fannie Mae and the other

government-sponsored mortgage company, Freddie Mac. No notes or bibliography.

Articles

"Prosecuting Wall Street," 60 Minutes (Steve Kroft, correspondent; James Jacoby, producer), CBS News, Dec. 4, 2011, www.cbsnews.com/8301-18560_162-57336042/prosecuting-wall-street/?tag=contentMain;cbsCarousel.
Two whistleblowers — former executives with Countrywide Financial and Citigroup — tell Kroft that they know of financial misconduct at their former companies but have not been questioned by government investigators.

Morgenson, Gretchen, and Louise Story, "A Financial Crisis With Little Guilt," *The New York Times*, April 14, 2011, p. A1.
The 4,000-word story details, in text and informative graphics, the lack of criminal prosecutions against companies or individuals involved in the financial crisis.

Reports and Studies

"The Financial Crisis Inquiry Report: Final Report of the National Commission on the Causes of the Financial and Economic Crisis in the United States," January 2011, www.gpoaccess.gov/fcic/fcic.pdf.
The congressionally appointed panel concluded that the financial crisis could have been avoided if the financial industry and public officials had heeded warnings and properly understood and managed evolving risks in the financial system. Republican members of the commission did not support the conclusions.

On the Web

"Chasing the Devil Around the Stump: Securities Regulation, the SEC, and the Courts," SEC Historical Society, Dec. 1, 2011, www.sechistorical.org/museum/galleries/ctd/.
The "gallery" in the SEC Historical Society's virtual museum and archive provides a compact, up-to-date overview of the Securities and Exchange Commission's regulatory activities and philosophy in the context of court decisions that alternately approve or disapprove of the agency's efforts at expansive enforcement. For a longer historical account, see the earlier gallery, "Fair to

All People: The SEC and the Regulation of Insider Trading," Nov. 1, 2006, www.sechistorical.org/museum/galleries/it/.

Books on the Financial Crisis

The financial crisis of 2008 and the developments that led up to it have been chronicled and analyzed in a veritable flood of books. Here is a list of some that have drawn the most attention, with brief notations of the topics covered; all have been republished in paperback.

Cohan, William E., *House of Cards: A Tale of Hubris and Wretched Excess on Wall Street*, Doubleday, 2009. [Bear Stearns]

—-, *Money and Power: How Goldman Sachs Came to Rule the World*, Anchor, 2011.

Lewis, Michael, *The Big Short: Inside the Doomsday Machine*, W.W. Norton, 2010. [bond and real estate derivative markets]

Lowenstein, Roger, *The End of Wall Street*, Reed Elsevier, 2010. [2008 financial collapse]

Sorkin, Andrew Ross, *Too Big to Fail: The Inside Story of How Wall Street and Washington Fought to Save the Financial System — and Themselves*, Viking, 2009. [2008 financial collapse]

Tett, Gillian, *Fool's Gold: How the Bold Dream of a Small Tribe at J.P. Morgan Was Corrupted by Wall Street Greed and Unleashed a Catastrophe*, Free Press, 2009.

Wessel, David, *In Fed We Trust: Ben Bernanke's War on the Great Panic*, Crown Business, 2009. [Federal Reserve]

Zuckerman, Gregory, *The Greatest Trade Ever: The Behind-the-Scenes Story of How John Paulson Defied Wall Street and Made Financial History*, Broadway Books, 2009. [hedge fund manager Paulson].

For More Information

American Bankers Association, 1120 Connecticut Ave., N.W., Washington, DC 20036; 1-800-226-5377; www.aba.com. Nation's largest banking trade association.

Campaign for America's Future, 1825 K St., N.W., Suite 400, Washington, DC 20006; 202-955-5665; www.ourfuture.org. Progressive political organization that opposes the influence of financial institutions in politics.

Consumer Financial Protection Bureau, 1500 Pennsylvania Ave., N.W., Washington, DC 20220; 202-435-7000; www.consumerfinance.gov. Independent agency within Federal Reserve that enforces consumer-protection laws against banks, mortgage lenders, credit card issuers, payday lenders and others.

Department of Justice, 950 Pennsylvania Ave., N.W., Washington, DC 20530; 202-514-2000; www.justice.gov. Federal executive department responsible for enforcing laws against financial misconduct.

Heritage Foundation, 214 Massachusetts Ave., N.E., Washington, DC 20002; 202-546-4400; www.heritage.org. Conservative think tank working to repeal financial reforms it says interfere with free enterprise.

Mortgage Bankers Association, 1919 Pennsylvania Ave., N.W., Washington, DC 20006; 202-557-2700; www.mbaa.org. National association promoting residential and commercial real estate markets and increased homeownership.

Securities and Exchange Commission, 100 F St., N.E., Washington, DC 20549; 202-942-8088; www.sec.gov. Federal agency that oversees publicly traded companies and enforces securities laws.

U.S. Chamber of Commerce, 1615 H St., N.W., Washington, DC 20062; 202-659-6000; www.uschamber.com. Lobbying group for businesses and trade associations.

9

Future of Public Universities

By Robert Kiener

University of Virginia President Teresa A. Sullivan was fired last year, reportedly for not applying more business principles to the university's operations. Sullivan said she refused to make "deep, top-down cuts" that would threaten the university's mission. After faculty and students protested, Sullivan was reinstated, but the debacle is seen as reflecting the massive challenges facing the nation's public colleges and universities.

From *The CQ Researcher*, January 18, 2013.

B y most accounts, students, faculty and administrators enthusiastically greeted Teresa A. Sullivan's appointment as president of the University of Virginia (UVA) in 2010. They viewed the noted scholar, educator and college administrator as especially well prepared to deal with several challenges facing the prestigious public university: steep government funding cuts, the growing role of technology in higher education and pressure to align UVA's curriculum more closely with students' career interests and needs.

Sullivan promptly made big changes at UVA. As *The Washington Post* noted, she "set about reshaping it, shifting power to academic departments, exploring online education and re-energizing the admissions office, yielding the freshman class with the highest scores in history." A little more than a year into Sullivan's term, Rector Helen Dragas, head of UVA's Board of Visitors — the school's governing body — lauded her as a "very talented" administrator.[1]

But the praise didn't last. On June 14, less than two years after her appointment, the board — led by Dragas — sacked Sullivan in a move so controversial that some called it a higher education "coup d'etat."[2] The reasons for the board's dissatisfaction were murky, but reportedly some board members faulted Sullivan for not applying more business and corporate principles to the university's finances and operations.[3] Sullivan blamed the move on her refusal to follow the board's mandate to make "deep, top-down cuts" that she felt would threaten the university's mission.

"A university that does not teach the full range of arts and sciences will no longer be a university," Sullivan declared.[4]

States Slash Funding for Research Universities

State funding for public research universities declined in 43 states from 2002 to 2010. On average the funding dropped 20 percent per student and then declined to a 25-year low in 2011. Helping to drive the decline have been the recent economic recession and the rising cost of state needs and mandated requirements unrelated to higher education.

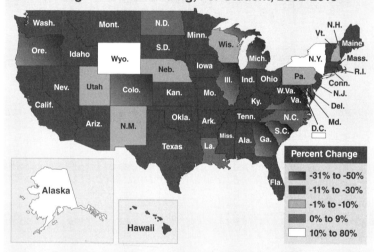

Change in State Funding, Per Student, 2002-2010

Percent Change
- -31% to -50%
- -11% to -30%
- -1% to -10%
- 0% to 9%
- 10% to 80%

Source: "Diminishing Funding and Rising Expectations: Trends and Challenges for Public Research Universities," National Science Board, July 2012, p. 21, www.nsf .gov/nsb/publications/2012/nsb1245.pdf

Faculty and students expressed such outrage at Sullivan's sudden dismissal that the board reversed itself and reinstated her 12 days later. In December UVA's accrediting body * sanctioned the university for allegedly violating governance requirements related to her ouster.[5]

The UVA debacle has resonated throughout the world of higher education because it underscores the massive challenges facing the nation's public colleges and universities. "The interest in the Virginia case proves how much

anxiety there is about the future of higher education," says Jeff Selingo, editor at large at *The Chronicle of Higher Education* and author of the forthcoming book, *College (Un)bound: The Future of Higher Education and What It Means for Students.* "Across the country, university administrators are under intense pressure to transform how colleges do business."

Numerous forces are driving that pressure:

- Widespread cuts in government funding;
- Soaring operating costs that have led to higher tuition;
- Growing demand for "vocationally relevant" training;
- Increasing competition from for-profit, community and other educational models;
- Questions about the role of fast-evolving technology in higher education.

In particular, technological innovations such as so-called MOOCs — massive open online courses — allow thousands of students to take high-quality courses online simultaneously for free and are forcing universities to rework their traditional pedagogical models.

A 2012 poll of senior college and university administrators found that a staggering 96 percent believe higher education is in crisis.[6] And more than a third of university presidents believe the higher-education industry they lead is "heading in the wrong direction."[7]

"The American [university] model is beginning to creak and groan, and it may not be the model the rest of the world wants to emulate," warned James J. Duderstadt, president emeritus of the University of Michigan at Ann Arbor.[8]

Public universities need a "new strategy for the funding and the structure and the dynamics of higher education," said Gordon Gee, president of Ohio State University.

---

* The Commission on Colleges of the Southern Association of Colleges and Schools is the recognized regional accrediting body in the 11 U.S. Southern states (Alabama, Florida, Georgia, Kentucky, Louisiana, Mississippi, North Carolina, South Carolina, Tennessee, Texas and Virginia) and in Latin America for institutions that award associate, baccalaureate, master's or doctoral degrees.

"There's a real urgency about what we need to do in higher education."[9]

Public colleges and universities educate about 80 percent of the nation's higher-education students and perform more than 60 percent of the nation's academic research and development.[10] And although private universities are experiencing many of the same problems as their public counterparts, they often have the advantage of large endowments and the freedom to operate and raise their tuitions free of political restrictions.

The financial challenges facing universities are complex. State and local spending on public university students dropped to a 25-year-low in 2011, and states provided, on average, only $6,290 per student enrolled at a public institution compared with $8,025 in 1986 after adjusting for inflation.[11] Since 2008 total state funding for higher education has dropped 15 percent, adjusted for inflation, to an estimated $72.5 billion in 2012.[12]

Many of the cuts have been drastic:

• UVA's state funding has dropped 22 percent since 2008.[13]

• New Hampshire's university system lost almost half its state funding in 2011-2012, and the University of New Hampshire now receives only 7 percent of its funding from the state, compared with 32 percent two decades ago.[14]

• Louisiana has slashed its funding for Louisiana State University by $92 million, or 43 percent, since 2009.[15]

• Florida recently announced it was cutting $300 million from its state university budgets. Since fiscal 2008, funding for the flagship University of Florida alone plunged by about $189 million, or nearly 29 percent.[16]

Auxiliary Enterprises Boost Revenues

Public research universities traditionally have received most of their funding from state and local appropriations. But government budget cuts have forced schools to rely more on other revenue sources, including tuition and non-academic auxiliary enterprises such as university hospitals, athletic programs and bookstores. Auxiliary enterprises can be expensive to run, however. Nearly one-fourth of expenditures in the 2008-2009 academic year went to such enterprises.

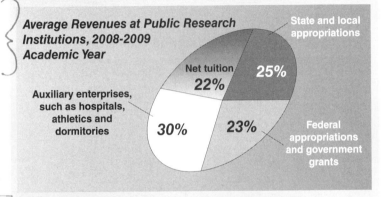

Average Revenues at Public Research Institutions, 2008-2009 Academic Year

State and local appropriations 25%
Net tuition 22%
Auxiliary enterprises, such as hospitals, athletics and dormitories 30%
Federal appropriations and government grants 23%

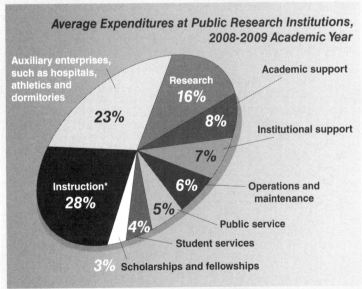

Average Expenditures at Public Research Institutions, 2008-2009 Academic Year

Auxiliary enterprises, such as hospitals, athletics and dormitories 23%
Research 16%
Academic support 8%
Institutional support 7%
Operations and maintenance 6%
Public service 5%
Student services 4%
Scholarships and fellowships 3%
Instruction* 28%

* Includes office supplies, administration of academic departments and the portion of faculty salaries going to research and public service.

Source: "Diminishing Funding and Rising Expectations: Trends and Challenges for Public Research Universities," National Science Board, July 2012, p. 9, 15, www.nsf.gov/nsb/publications/2012/nsb1245.pdf

MOOCs Offer Free Courses to All

The rising cost of a traditional college education has helped spur the rise of so-called MOOCs — massive open online courses. Offered for free, they are available to anyone with Internet access but currently do not provide credit toward a degree. Some organizations offering MOOCs, such as Coursera and edX, have partnered with universities to create courses taught by their professors. Others, such as Udacity and Khan Academy, create their own instructional videos. Many experts say the popularity of MOOCs will force public universities to change if they want to remain relevant.

Select Organizations Offering Online Courses

Name	Founded	Enrollment	Model	Details
Coursera (www .coursera .org)	2012	2.3 million	For profit	Allows students to watch free lectures at partner universities. Offers more than 200 courses across a wide range of disciplines. Plans to charge for select services, such as certification for completed courses, in the future.
edX (www .edx.org)	2012	570,000	Non-profit	Collaborative enterprise between Harvard and MIT offering free online courses at six universities. Currently offers 23 courses. Researches how students learn and how technology can transform learning.
Udacity (www .udacity .com)	2012	800,000	For profit	Offers free courses primarily in computer science. For a fee, provides corporate recruiters with names of students who are the best fit for specific jobs.
Open Learning Initiative (oli.cmu .edu)	2002	55,000	Non-profit	Grant-funded project at Carnegie Mellon University offering free access to course materials for select courses. Students use the materials to teach themselves at their own pace and do not work with an instructor. Currently offers 17 courses across several disciplines.
Khan Academy (www.khan academy. org)	2008	4.6 million unique website visitors (Dec. 2012)	Non-profit	Offers 3,800 free pre-recorded video lectures primarily for K-12 math and science students. Also offers a free software platform for math exercises.

Sources: individual organizations

Faced with such massive cuts, universities have raised tuition, often at a dizzying pace. Over the past decade, in-state tuition and fees at four-year public colleges have climbed at an inflation-adjusted 5.6 percent annually, according to the College Board. [17] Even at the depths of the recent recession, public universities continued to hike their tuition and fees, raising them 8.3 percent in 2011 alone, says Stuart Butler, director of the Center for Policy Innovation at the Heritage Foundation, a conservative think tank in Washington, and a critic of what he views as public universities' lack of innovation. "It's no wonder students and parents are facing sticker shock and taking on massive debt," he says.

Student debt has topped $1 trillion, and Americans now owe more on student loans than on credit cards. [18] And students are not alone in taking on debt. Since 2001 debt shouldered by cash-strapped colleges has risen 88 percent, to $307 billion. [19]

Political pressure also is buffeting public higher education. Some politicians — particularly conservatives — argue that because only about 30 percent of Americans get college degrees, public universities are becoming "elite" institutions that don't merit as much state support as in the past. [20] During the Republican presidential primaries, candidate Rick Santorum — holder of an MBA and law degree — labeled President Obama "a snob" for wanting all Americans to go to college, saying Obama "wants to remake you in his image." [21]

Others question public universities' curricula, complaining that courses often fail to prepare graduates for the workplace. Many politicians are pressing universities to focus more on readying students for careers in "employable" fields by offering a more vocational curriculum.[22]

"Parents, desperate to ensure their kids' futures, remortgage their houses to pay for college, only to have their young graduates return home and begin their working lives in run-of-the-mill service jobs," Mark C. Taylor, chairman of the Department of Religion at Columbia University, said in his 2010 book *Crisis on Campus*. "At the graduate level, universities are producing a product for which there is no market," such as candidates for teaching jobs that don't exist, he wrote.[23]

As they face mounting financial and political pressures, public universities also are being challenged to explore, adopt — and in some cases compete with — technological innovations such as online learning that are rapidly growing in scale and scope. "The public university's traditional business model is coming under attack from new kinds of institutions that offer more efficient methods of learning," says Butler.

New ventures are attracting millions of students. They include Khan Academy, a nonprofit online educational organization; the for-profit open-enrollment University of Phoenix; Coursera, a for-profit supplier of online higher education courses, and various MOOCs. Emerging business models will further chip away at the student market, experts say.

"To compete with newly emerging educational competition and to become more efficient and better at what we do, public universities have to be open to innovation," says Daniel Mark Fogel, president of the University of Vermont from 2002-2011.

Although many academics charge that their online competitors often lack educational quality and limit teacher-student contact, education experts say traditional faculty discount the technological revolution in education at their peril. "I wouldn't be surprised if in 10 to 15 years half of the institutions of higher education will have either merged or gone out of business" because of rising competition and costs, said Michael Horn, education executive director of the Innosight Institute, a consulting firm that focuses on improving education and health care.[24]

Experts predict that the public university landscape will be vastly different in coming years. Some believe

Gordon Gee, president of Ohio State University, earns nearly $2 million; he was one of three public university presidents to earn more than $1 million in 2011. Many analysts cite escalating administrative salaries as a key reason college tuitions are skyrocketing. The median total compensation of public university presidents was $421,395 in the 2010-2011 academic year — up about 3 percent from the previous year.

that technology will completely transform it. "Higher education will be universally accessible, mediated by technology, probably offered through a variety of commercial platforms and very, very inexpensive," wrote Richard A. DeMillo, director of the Center for 21st Century Universities at the Georgia Institute of Technology and author of *Abelard to Apple: The Fate of American Colleges and Universities.*

"If there's anything that will be significantly different 25 years from today," said Cameron Evans, chief technology officer at MicroSoft Education, "it's that people won't go to school for knowledge."[25]

Others claim that technology should be only a tool to aid learning and that eliminating the university residential model would be a mistake. "I love technology, but it isn't a replacement for the kind of learning that goes on where you're interacting. It's an enhancement," said Lillian Taiz, a history professor at California State University, Los Angeles, and president of the California Faculty Association, which launched the Campaign for the Future of Higher Education, a national faculty campaign to support quality higher education.[26]

Tenure Disappearing at U.S. Colleges

The proportion of full-time tenured or tenure-track college faculty has fallen sharply since 1975 while the share of part-timers has surged. In 1975 more than half of faculty held full-time tenured positions or were on track to receive tenure. By 2007, that proportion had shrunk to less than a third.

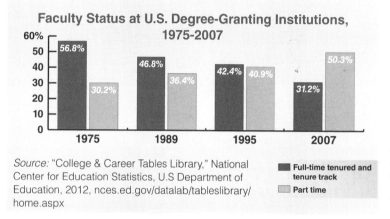

Faculty Status at U.S. Degree-Granting Institutions, 1975-2007

Source: "College & Career Tables Library," National Center for Education Statistics, U.S Department of Education, 2012, nces.ed.gov/datalab/tableslibrary/home.aspx

■ Full-time tenured and tenure track
▨ Part time

As politicians, administrators and others continue to debate the future of public higher education, here are some of the questions they are asking:

Are public universities to blame for their present problems?

Whether its predicament is described as a "challenge," a "crisis" or a "learning opportunity," public higher education clearly is in the midst of profound change — and introspection. At countless venues across the nation, faculty and administrators are attending conferences, workshops and seminars on the future of higher education. Speaker after speaker offers a perspective, but few answer the fundamental question: "Who got us into this mess?"

"That's simple," says Andrew Hacker, a Queens College political science professor and co-author of the 2010 book *Higher Education: How Colleges Are Wasting Our Money and Failing Our Kids — and What We Can Do About It.* "The universities are absolutely responsible. For years they have been spending like drunken sailors.

"Consider salaries at public — not private — institutions," Hacker continues. "The average salary for a full professor at the University of Maryland is $142,600, and $166,000 at the New Jersey Institute of Technology.[27] And remember, that's the average. . . . No wonder they're

in financial trouble." At Queens College, where Hacker teaches, the average salary for full time professor is a more modest $84,000.

But the American Association of University Professors said salaries of full-time faculty fell an average of 1.2 percent in 2011-2012 after adjusting for inflation. Over the past decade, it said, salaries of public-college professors rose less than 1 percent at doctoral and baccalaureate institutions and fell more than 5 percent at master's-level universities, after adjusting for inflation.[28]

At the University of Michigan, Ann Arbor, where full professors make an average of $148,000, the administration defends the pay level. "The quality and reputation of the university depends on the strength of the faculty and staff. Maintaining competitive salaries is an important component of our ability to retain the best faculty and staff," said Provost Phil Hanlon.[29]

Administrators' pay also is on the rise. In 2010-2011, median total compensation for public-institution presidents was $421,395, up about 3 percent from the previous academic year. Topping the list at nearly $2 million was Ohio State's Gee, one of three public university presidents to earn more than $1 million in 2011.[30]

According to James C. Garland, author of the 2009 book *Saving Alma Mater: A Rescue Plan for America's Public Universities*, about 70-80 percent of university budgets typically are spent on salaries, wages and benefits, but that figure is for all employees.[31] Data appear to be scarce on what percentage of university budgets is spent on faculty and administrator salaries.

Public universities also are accused of poor financial planning and overspending on expansion. "Higher education is now being forced to make up for the mistakes it made in the industry's 'lost decade,' from 1999 to 2009," says *The Chronicle of Higher Education*'s Selingo. "Public universities expanded so much during these boom years that they doubled their debt and kept hiking up tuition. Instead of preparing for the inevitable economic downturn, they thought 'the model will continue forever so let's take on more debt.' Much of the industry lost its way."

A study by the Washington-based American Institutes for Research, a nonprofit behavioral and social science research organization, found that university spending rose every year from 1999 through 2008 and by 2008 was at "historic highs across most functions of four-year public colleges and universities."[32]

"The future investment strategy for higher education has to include regular, transparent attention to cost restructuring: reducing spending overall, while generating new sources of capital to pay for the instructional expansions and innovations that have to take place," the study found. "If current trends persist, in 2025 the United States will have lower levels of educational attainment than much of the rest of the developed world."

Michigan's state universities are a good example of how public universities increased their spending. From 2005-2010, spending on administrative positions jumped $260 million, or 30 percent on average. The number of administrative jobs increased by 19 percent, and faculty compensation rose 22 percent, even though state funding stayed roughly steady.[33]

However, university administrators defend rising expenditures such as faculty pay increases. As University of Michigan President Mary Sue Coleman explained recently, "I am not going to punish people for doing a good job. . . . We want the best and work hard to keep them."[34]

Peter McPherson, president of the Association of Public and Land Grant Universities (APLU), says, "Spending has risen, but the real problem is that state funding has dropped. We have to convince states to fund research universities at realistic and competitive levels."

Yet critics accuse many public university administrators of adhering to "Bowen's Law," devised by the late economist and college president Howard Bowen: "Colleges raise all the money they can, and spend all the money they can raise."

"Many institutions have suffered from their own 'edifice complex,' building ever larger and more grandiose facilities," says the Heritage Foundation's Butler. "When the economy crashed, they were in trouble."

A recent study of nearly 1,700 public and nonprofit colleges by the Boston-based management consulting firm Bain & Co. found that a third have been on an "unsustainable financial path" in recent years and another 28 percent are "at risk of slipping into an unsustainable condition." Bain criticized institutions for adhering to a "Law of More," arguing that they "have operated on the assumption that the more they build, spend, diversify and expand, the more they will persist and prosper. But instead, the opposite has happened: Institutions have become overleveraged."[35]

Universities say they are being forced to expand and improve facilities and offer a broader curriculum partly because of competition for new students. As tuition goes up to compensate for state spending cuts and rising expenses, universities say they are caught in a bind: On the one hand, they need to expand and improve their facilities to attract and cater to students who have become more demanding; on the other, these new facilities and other expenditures have forced them to raise tuition.

In 2003 David Rood, a spokesman for the National Association of College Auxiliary Services, observed: "There is a lot of one-upmanship going on. Whatever the students want is pretty much what they're getting."[36]

Critics charge that not only have universities overspent but that in many cases faculty are mired in bureaucracy and resist change. "Change is difficult for many faculty members," says Selingo. "Because a university operates differently from any other organization, it's harder to implement change and innovation."

Some critics say tenure compounds the problems universities face — not only resulting in higher salaries and expensive benefits for full-time professors but also breeding resistance to change that makes it difficult for administrators to remain nimble in the face of a shifting higher-education landscape. (*See sidebar, p. 212.*)

Still, many educators say states have contributed to dysfunction in higher education by trying to overregulate it.

"Ironically, even as state support has declined, the effort to regulate universities and hold them accountable has increased," said former University of Michigan president Duderstadt.[37] "It's bad enough to starve your institutions . . . to death but to strangle them through bureaucracy at the same time is adding insult to injury."[38]

Fogel, the former University of Vermont president, recalled that a "rapid turnover of trustees, and even the board's chair, often complicated getting things done during my tenure."

Can public universities survive?

For years the conventional wisdom has said that no matter how expensive tuition is, a college education is almost certainly a ticket to prosperity and a good job. With easy credit making rising tuition less of an immediate burden for students, colleges have been able to keep upping their prices, and students have eagerly responded.

Lately, however, more and more jobless graduates have begun asking, as *The Economist* magazine noted, "whether a degree in religious and women's studies is worth the $100,000 debt incurred to pay for it."[39]

Experts say many debt-laden graduates are finding that their costly educational investments are not paying off in the jobs they had hoped for. Already, analysts say, universities are suffering as demand for expensive degrees declines. "Enrollment numbers are softening [and] students are becoming more reluctant to borrow money to pay for [an] education," said Glenn Reynolds, author of *The Higher Education Bubble*.[40]

While enrollments at flagship public universities are stable, that is not always the case at smaller schools. "State by state, enrollments appear to be down, mostly at community colleges and at some four-year schools as well," noted Richard Vedder, an economics professor at Ohio University and author of the 2004 book *Going Broke by Degree: Why College Costs Too Much*. "In Ohio, preliminary numbers from the Board of Regents of the University System of Ohio show a 5.9 percent decline, and the dropoff at one community college [Hocking in Nelsonville] was so precipitous (more than 20 percent) that it had to dismiss staff. In other Midwest states, such as Michigan and Wisconsin, enrollments at some institutions have fallen as well. In Arizona, one large Tucson-area community college (Pima) shows a decline of 11 percent."[41]

Based on demographics alone, the numbers may keep dropping. After peaking in 2009, the number of high school graduates is declining. Enrollment fell at more than 40 percent of colleges and universities last year, according to the credit-rating firm Moody's, and at least 375 institutions had vacancies for the 2012-2013 academic year, the largest number in a decade, according to the National Association for College Admission Counseling.[42] In another recent Moody's study, 15 percent of the 127 public universities surveyed projected a decline in net tuition revenue, due to a drop in enrollment.[43]

The Chronicle of Higher Education's Selingo says the bursting bubble, coupled with state funding cutbacks, competition from new education models and other forces, will inevitably kill off some "weaker," less prestigious public colleges and universities. "I think you will see some 'bottom tier' colleges and universities going out of business," he says. "The larger universities, in part because they are more subsidized, will survive."

Few doubt that any large, prestigious public flagships will fail. "There's so much demand that they aren't in danger of disappearing," says Neal McCluskey, associate director of the Center for Educational Freedom at the Cato Institute, a libertarian think tank in Washington. "You might see them dropping some majors, such as languages or the classics, but they will survive."

Significant demand for public higher education comes from out-of-state and foreign students, who pay much higher fees than in-state students. Some 764,000 foreign students are enrolled in U.S. public and private undergraduate and graduate schools.[44] They include about 158,000 Chinese undergraduate students, compared with just 9,955 four years ago.[45] Total undergraduate enrollment in the United States is about 14.5 million.

Some experts foresee more consolidation among public universities, especially among lower-ranked institutions. "For some schools, mergers will allow administrators to cut costs and make them more efficient," says the Heritage Foundation's Butler. Georgia recently announced the consolidation of eight public institutions into four and said more may be affected.[46]

Mergers not only can cut costs but also can encourage administrators and faculty to innovate and modernize, advocates say. New Jersey offers an example.[47] Christopher Molloy, the provost overseeing a merger between Rutgers University and the University of Medicine and Dentistry of New Jersey, said the union was "a chance for both of our universities to get together to do things better. It's a chance to really create a university, in some ways, from the ground up."[48]

Critics say universities' survival is threatened not only by financial problems but also by bureaucracies that thwart innovation and whose "inertia" makes them vulnerable to emerging competition from new, nontraditional online models. "At some state schools, where the faculty runs everything and a patronage system is in place, change is almost impossible," says Butler. "These

CHRONOLOGY

1700s-1901 *Public universities spread across the new nation.*

1785 University of Georgia becomes nation's first chartered public university.

1795 University of North Carolina becomes first state university to hold classes.

1862 Morrill Land Grant Act calls for public land to be donated for colleges that emphasize agricultural, mechanical arts and military training.

1870 Fewer than 15,000 students are enrolled in higher education.

1890 Second Morrill Act increases funding for public universities and establishes "separate but equal" colleges for blacks.

1895 Nearly 25,000 students are attending land-grant colleges and universities.

1900 Nearly 240,000 U.S. residents attend higher education institutions.

1901 The first two-year junior (community) college is founded in Joliet, Ill.

1940s-1970s *Post-World War II baby boom and GI benefits trigger surge in college enrollment.*

1940 Public institutions are educating almost half of college students.

1944 GI Bill makes higher education possible for millions of veterans.

1952 Korean War GI Bill is passed, eventually helping 2.4 million veterans attend college or receive vocational training.

1958 National Defense Education Act increases funding for public universities and helps boost enrollment.

1965 Higher Education Act provides financial aid to students; enrollment climbs to 5.6 million.

1978 Higher Education Act is amended to include Pell Grants, designed to help low-income college students.

1980s-1990s *Tuition begins to rise in response to funding cuts.*

1980 With the election of President Ronald Reagan and a tax revolt, states begin to reduce their funding of public colleges and universities.

1991 Sixty-three percent of high school graduates go directly to college, compared with 46 percent in 1973.

1992 Number of for-profit colleges jumps after federal regulation makes them eligible for federal student aid.

2000-Present *Tuition continues to rise; universities expand as competition from for-profit and online learning heats up.*

2000 Tuition and fees at four-year public colleges and universities average $8,653.

2005 Per-student funding of public colleges and universities hits quarter-century low.

2008 First massive online open course (MOOC) is offered to 2,300 students.

2010 Median total compensation for public-college presidents is $421,395. . . . For-profit universities triple enrollments to 1.8 million students from 2000 to 2010. . . . Federal government accuses some for-profit institutions of fraud.

2011 Average student debt has grown to $23,000. . . . Per-student state and local spending drops to 25-year low of $6,290. . . . Texas pledges to create a "$10,000 degree." . . . Pell Grant maximum is raised to $5,500.

2012 Teresa A. Sullivan is fired from presidency of University of Virginia for refusing to cut academic programs, then rehired. . . . Fewer than 60 percent of students graduate within six years. . . . Online learning makes inroads into higher education via startup ventures such as Coursera and edX. . . . A study of nearly 1,700 public and nonprofit colleges finds that one-third have been on an "unsustainable financial path" in recent years, and an additional 28 percent are "at risk of slipping into an unsustainable condition."

Big Spending on Sports Scrutinized

Does it waste precious dollars or attract students and donations?

It's no secret that big-time college sports — particularly some high-profile football and basketball programs — rake in millions of dollars. For example, in 2011 the University of Alabama athletic programs, thanks largely to revenues from the school's legendary "Crimson Tide" football team, had a $31.7 million surplus; the University of Michigan's program netted $26.6 million and Ohio State's $18.6 million.[1]

But those are the exception. In fact, only 22 of 227 public universities in the National Collegiate Athletic Association's (NCAA) highly competitive Division I made a profit in 2011.[2]

"The truth is, most college athletic programs are money-losers," says Andrew Hacker, a Queens College political science professor and co-author of *Higher Education? How Colleges Are Wasting Our Money and Failing Our Kids — and What We Can Do About It.*

Battered by rising costs and falling financial support, public universities with money-losing athletic programs increasingly are finding it harder to justify them. "It's about time that public universities stopped funding these programs that have gobbled up resources that should have gone to the schools' academic mission," says Hacker.

"We've gotten ourselves in a terrible situation with intercollegiate athletics, with the cost of running a program really out of proportion to the basic purpose of our universities," said William E. "Brit" Kirwan, chancellor of the University System of Maryland and a co-chairman of the Knight Commission on Intercollegiate Athletics, a group formed in 1989 that seeks to reform college sports by making sure they operate within schools' educational missions.[3]

Much of the money generated by football and basketball programs stays within the athletic departments and supports lower-profile sports, such as track, swimming and tennis. Even when athletic programs produce a surplus, the amount often is a pittance: The University of Tennessee's athletic revenues topped $102 million in 2011, but after figuring in costs, the surplus amounted to only $15,000.[4] There are rare exceptions, however: Ohio States' athletic department has contributed $4 million to support the university's main library.[5]

Most college athletic departments lose money, critics say, because of big spending — often driven by the desire to field winning teams that will help them reap lucrative broadcast fees and big donations from excited backers. Sports-related spending is rising almost twice as much as academic spending, according to the Knight Commission. Schools are building bigger and bigger stadiums and other athletic facilities at the very time college debts are soaring.

Others cite soaring college athletic salaries: Nick Saban, the University of Alabama's football coach and the highest-paid NCAA coach, earns $5.5 million, followed by the University of Texas at Austin's Mack Brown at $5.4 million. In 2006, only 42 major college football coaches made $1 million or more; today 42 make at least $2 million.[6]

In fact, coaches' pay has risen faster than that of corporate executives. While CEO compensation — including salaries, stock options, bonuses and other pay — rose 23 percent between 2007 and 2011, coaches' pay increased 44 percent.[7] Proponents of college athletic programs often point out that some of those coaches' salaries are paid in part by "booster" donations or from money the schools earn for selling the rights to broadcast their games.[8]

Proponents of athletic programs argue, however, that they attract alumni donations. "Athletic events are the biggest draw to bring alumni back to campus, and alumni philanthropy is becoming a major and desperately needed source of funds for universities," said Eric Barron, president of Florida State University.[9] According to an NCAA study, alumni and booster donations made up 27 percent of a typical athletic department's revenues.[10]

Cutting athletics would reduce donations, say some experts. "Presidents are obligated to raise money, and it's the football and basketball events that bring the big donors and trustees in," said R. Scott Kretchmar, a Pennsylvania State University professor of exercise and sport sciences who served as the university's faculty athletic representative to the NCAA for 10 years. "There's virtually nothing else at the university that has the caché and excitement that big-time sports does. Presidents are saying, 'I can't go down that road of scaling back big-time sports.' Unilateral disarmament is nothing that will fly."[11]

As the debate over soaring athletic spending continues, the University of Maryland recently announced its athletic program had run up a deficit of $4.7 million that was projected to reach $17.6 million by 2017 if nothing was done. Instead of trimming its costly NCAA football program, whose coaching salaries alone had risen from $18.7 million to $24.3 million between 2005 and 2010, it cut seven of its 27 varsity teams such as swimming and diving, cross country and tennis.[12] It also announced its football team would jump to the Big Ten conference, hoping for a possible $100 million windfall by 2020 from higher Big Ten television-rights revenues.[13]

Some see the school's move as a risky decision and one that is far removed from a university's original mission. "Let's stop the farce of having university presidents try to manage large, commercial sports programs," said Steven Salzberg, a *Forbes* columnist and professor of medicine and biostatistics in the Institute of Genetic Medicine at Johns Hopkins University's School of Medicine. "Let them get back to focusing on research and education, topics on which they actually have some expertise."[14]

— *Robert Kiener*

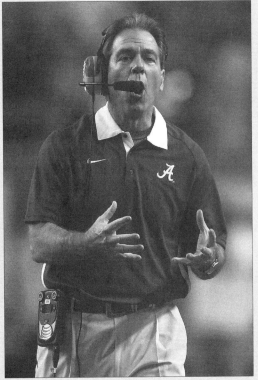

Getty Images/Mike Ehrmann

University of Alabama head football coach Nick Saban earns $5.5 million a year — more than any other college football coach. Critics complain that while state governments are slashing college budgets, coaches' salaries are rising faster than those of corporate executives.

[1]Tom Karol, "Big money in college athletics," *The Daily Caller*, July 12, 2012, http://dailycaller.com/2012/12/07/big-money-in-college-athletics/#ixzz2EzhWXKl7.

[2]Liz Clarke, "Maryland athletics' financial woes reveal a broken college sports revenue model," *The Washington Post*, June 28, 2012, www.washingtonpost.com/sports/colleges/maryland-athletics-financial-woes-reveal-a-broken-college-sports-revenue-model/2012/06/28/gJQAmEvx9V_story.html. For background, see Kenneth Jost, "College Football," *CQ Researcher*, Nov. 18, 2011, pp. 977-1000; and Chanan Tigay, "Women and Sports," *CQ Researcher*, March 25, 2011, pp. 265-288.

[3]*Ibid.*

[4]Karol, *op. cit.*

[5]Rich Exner, "Ohio state's athletic department is one of the few nationally to pay its own bills," *The Plain Dealer*, Oct. 13, 2011, www.cleveland.com/datacentral/index.ssf/2011/10/ohio_states_athletic_departmen.html.

[6]Erik Brady, Steve Berkowitz and Jodi Upton, "College football coaches continue to see salary explosion," *USA Today*, Nov. 20, 2012, www.usatoday.com/story/sports/ncaaf/2012/11/19/college-football-coaches-contracts-analysis-pay-increase/1715435/.

[7]*Ibid.*

[8]Mark Yost, "Who pays the college coach?" *The Wall Street Journal*, Dec. 6, 2008, http://online.wsj.com/article/SB122853304793584959.html.

[9]Alexander Heffner, "Athletics over academics: an improper equation for state universities," *Washington Monthly*, Feb. 9, 2011, www.washingtonmonthly.com/college_guide/blog/athletics_over_academics_an_im.php?page=all.

[10]"NCAA Div I Intercolegiate Athletics Program Report," National Collegiate Athletic Association, 2010, www.ncaapublications.com/productdownloads/REV_EXP_2010.pdf.

[11]Clarke, *op. cit.*

[12]*Ibid.*

[13]Pete Thamel, "Marlyand in line for huge financial bump in wake of Big Ten move," *SI.com*, Nov. 19, 2012, http://sportsillustrated.cnn.com/2012/writers/pete_thamel/11/19/maryland-big-ten-money/index.html.

[14]Steven Salzberg, "Football is corrupting America's universities: It needs to go," *Forbes.com*, Nov. 26, 2011, www.forbes.com/sites/stevensalzberg/2011/11/26/football-is-corrupting-americas-universities-it-needs-to-go/.

bureaucracies prevent universities like this from changing and adapting to the new market forces."

But many universities are in fact innovating, says McPherson at the Association of Public and Land-Grant Universities, citing institutions such as Arizona State University and the University of South Carolina, which have adopted online teaching and other technological developments.

Arizona State President Michael Crow, admitting that the rigid organization of a typical university had become "ossified," eliminated some academic departments and broke down divisions between others to create a multidisciplinary environment.[49] As Crow noted, "Education and innovation are the only way forward . . . The world is changing really fast. And we've got to be out on the edge."[50]

According to the authors of the Bain study, change is much more difficult in academia than in the corporate world. "In the corporate ecosystem, power resides largely with the executive team and cascades down," the Bain study said. "In academia, power usually emanates from the faculty and works its way toward the central administration. The concept of shared governance, combined with academic autonomy and tenure, leads to an organization where broad change cannot be mandated. Instead, change on a large scale can only be achieved by working with the faculty to build a compelling case and a clear path forward — one that supports the mission of the institution, but copes effectively with ? scal constraints."[51]

While some see online learning as a new educational tool for public institutions, others see it as a threat. Butler argues that public colleges and universities are especially vulnerable to changes in higher education. He points out that it is precisely the public institutions' market — students who are more price sensitive than those at elite private universities — that is "ideally suited to the online education and flexible approaches to instruction offered by low-cost upstarts."[52]

If these institutions refuse to adopt new technologies such as online learning that can result in lower costs, they could lose their market, wrote Harvard Business School professor Clayton Christensen and Mormon educator Henry B. Eyring, co-authors of *The Innovative University.* "Faced with an either-or choice, many young college students will follow the lead of adult learners: They'll take the affordable online option over the socially preferable but financially inaccessible traditional college experience."[53]

Should the mission of public universities be changed?

Last July 2 marked the 150th anniversary of the landmark Morrill Land-Grant Act, the 1862 legislation that laid the foundation for the nation's public colleges and universities. The law was intended to make higher education accessible to the general public. "With public universities under threat, the anniversary is an excellent time to ask if they are still fulfilling the act's missions," says Fogel, the former University of Vermont president.

Given the huge range of the nation's 1,700 two- and four-year public universities and colleges, critics say there is no common agreement on exactly what that mission is today. "First, higher education needs to figure out what we want public universities to do," says Selingo of *The Chronicle of Higher Education.* "In some cases we want them to do great research and solve 'the next big problem.' In others we want them to simply educate the state's residents."

Selingo and others say many public universities have strayed from the Morrill Act's intention "to promote the liberal and practical education of the industrial classes in the several pursuits and professions in life."[54] "Too many public universities are trying to be the next Harvard — chasing prestige instead of teaching," Selingo says. He quotes the late University of Georgia professor of education J. Douglas Toma, who said, "Prestige is to higher education as profit is to corporations."

As Christensen and Eyring argued, "Even schools of relatively small size and modest means have outstretched themselves, often in an attempt to be more like Harvard and other great research institutions."[55]

Many critics say public universities should return to basics by putting more resources into the so-called STEM fields — science, technology, engineering and mathematics — and reduce their focus on liberal arts and general studies. "Some claim that the mission of a university is to educate good citizens," says the Cato Institute's McCluskey. "That's a fine idea, but students also have to earn a living after they graduate. There should be a shift away from the present liberal arts core requirement for everyone and a more vocational focus that gives students the skills they need to get a job."

But Queens College's Hacker, although an outspoken critic of many of higher education's current priorities, disagrees with the push for more vocational training. "Presently over half of all undergraduates are already in vocational — that's different from educational — training programs, from nursing to engineering to majors such as resort management and fashion merchandising," he says. He also notes that bachelor's degrees are awarded at various schools in baking and pastry arts, welding technology and medical-office assisting.

"These students may be learning something, but are they being educated?" Hacker asks. A strong proponent of the liberal arts, Hacker has written, "College should be a cultural journey, an intellectual expedition, a voyage confronting new ideas and information, expanding and deepening our understanding of ourselves and the world."[56]

As politicians reduce funding for public institutions, many are attacking such nonvocational departments as humanities, arts and social sciences. Last year Republican Florida Gov. Rick Scott said, "We're spending a lot of money on education, and when you look at the results, it's not great. . . . Do you want to use your tax money to educate more people who can't get jobs in anthropology? I don't."[57]

Selingo says there can be drawbacks to cutting programs such as classics or foreign languages in favor of more vocational courses. "The labor market changes so fast that it's not easy to predict what will be needed in five to 10 years," he says.

In what they see as a race for prestige to emulate the flagship private research universities, some critics claim that many public institutions have lost sight of their original mission of educating undergraduates. Instead, they charge, schools have put increasing emphasis on — and investment in — their more prestigious graduate departments. "It's almost as if teaching undergraduates is disdained," argues Hacker. "More and more professors simply refuse to teach introductory or other undergraduate courses."

Filling this void are part-time, lower-paid adjunct teachers or graduate assistants. In fact, the bulk of undergraduate teaching is now performed by these part-timers, a trend often described as "the dirty little secret" of higher education.[58]

According to the American Federation of Teachers (AFT), three-quarters of college and university faculty

are part-timers on limited-term contracts. Some are paid as little as $800 per course. And many lack retirement benefits and health insurance. Although adjuncts at some institutions have joined national labor unions, such as the AFT, most have not.[59]

The pressure for full-time professors to produce original research, as a prerequisite for obtaining tenure, is one reason for the greater reliance on adjunct faculty in undergraduate courses, experts say. Because tenure-track faculty must "publish or perish," says Hacker, they often view teaching as a necessary evil.

"As publication became a symbol of achievement, ambitious colleges and universities adjusted teaching loads downward to enable faculty members to spend more time on their research and writing," said Columbia's Taylor.[60]

Given the pressures they face, many universities must "effectively change their DNA," Christensen and Eyring wrote. "Most will need to become more focused on undergraduate students, cutting back on graduate programs that serve relatively few students while consuming much faculty time and generating little of the prestige hoped for when they were created."[61]

BACKGROUND
Early Beginnings

Public institutions of higher education did not flourish in the United States until the Morrill Act of 1862 was enacted and a successor act in 1890 provided widespread funding to establish colleges. But government aid for education is nearly as old as the nation.

In 1785, just two years after the Revolutionary War, the Congress of Confederation passed the Northwest Ordinance, which reserved a portion of land allocated to each Western township "for the maintenance of public schools."[62] Two years later, the Northwest Ordinance of 1787, which established the Northwest Territory, reinforced the importance of the government's support of education, mandating that "religion, morality and knowledge, being necessary to good government and the happiness of mankind, schools and the means of education shall forever be encouraged."[63]

The University of Georgia, which held its first classes in 1801, had become the nation's first chartered public university in 1785. To this day the university describes itself as "the birthplace of the American system of public higher education."[64] But establishing which institution was the "first" public university is complicated. For example, the first state university to hold classes was the University of North Carolina, in 1795, but it wasn't chartered until 1789.

Likewise, some of today's public universities were established as private institutions before the University of Georgia was founded. The now-public College of William and Mary was founded, for instance, as a private school in 1693, making it the nation's second-oldest university after Harvard (established in 1636). The University of Tennessee was chartered in 1794 as the private Blount College (with tuition of $8 a term), but it didn't become a state institution until 1807, when it was renamed East Tennessee College.[65] Most of these early institutions — like Harvard, Yale and the earlier colonial colleges — were devoted to the teaching of religion and the classics.

Throughout the 1800s a growing movement advocated for affordable higher education. Jonathan Baldwin Turner, a Yale graduate, wrote about the need for public universities that would serve the "industrial working classes" during the middle of the century. He urged farmers to press Congress "to create and endow . . . a general system of popular Industrial education, more glorious in its design and more beneficent in its results than the world has ever seen before."[66] Although this effort did not result in federal funding, it did pave the way for Justin Smith Morrill's historic push for public higher education.

Morrill, a Vermont-born member of Congress, was a passionate champion of public higher education. Citing a need for educating American farmers, he introduced a bill in 1857 to provide each state with public lands that could be sold to fund the creation of "land grant" universities, specializing in agriculture, mechanics and military tactics.

"He framed the bill as a matter of 'public justice' and believed that agricultural colleges would allow the United States to compete with foreign nations," says a recent historical review of the Morrill Act. "Morrill saw that vast amounts of American soil were being exhausted. He believed that agricultural colleges could teach new techniques and foster innovation and experimentation. Noting that numerous European countries had similar schools, Morrill called for the United States to develop a similar system. He believed the country should do 'something for every owner of land . . . and something to increase the loveliness of the American landscape.' "[67]

President James Buchanan vetoed the bill, but after Morrill reintroduced it, President Abraham Lincoln signed it. The Morrill Land Grant Act of 1862 allotted 30,000 acres of federal land to each state for every representative it had in Congress. The land could then be used for the creation — and financing — of public universities. In 1890 Congress passed another Morrill-sponsored bill, which increased funding to public universities and established "separate but equal" colleges for blacks in Southern states.

Thanks to visionaries suclike Turner and Morrill, the nation's higher-education landscape blossomed. Morrill's 1862 bill helped create 48 colleges that, as he noted, were "sending forth a large number of vigorous young men to scientific, agricultural, mechanical, educational and other industrial careers."[68]

In 1870, fewer than 15,000 Americans were enrolled in institutions of higher learning of any type. By 1895 nearly 25,000 students were attending land-grant colleges and universities alone.[69]

After being largely the reserve of the elite, university educations were now accessible to many. "We . . . implemented a less elite system, in which students were less likely to be tracked at an early stage into vocational tasks," wrote University of Massachusetts-Amherst economics professor Nancy Folbre, author of *Saving State U*.[70]

The rise of public institutions dominated higher education in the early 20th century. The colleges grew larger as more students were enrolled and states increased funding. By 1940 public institutions were educating almost half of higher-education students, compared with 22 percent in 1897.[71]

And curricula reflected a new interest in practical research. "These were truly state-based institutions," said Folbre. "In the Midwest and West, land-grant institutions tended to promote the research that would serve their local economies best: the University of Wisconsin promoted dairy science . . . [and] the University of Colorado pursued mining technology. Taxpayers in a state were likely to capture the benefits of their investments. More than three-quarters of all students attended college in the same state in which they were born."[72]

GI Bill

Just as the Northwest ordinances and the Morrill acts established and democratized higher education, the 1944 GI Bill opened the doors of both private and public higher education to millions of returning veterans. It also ushered in what many refer to as the golden age of higher education, a period of unparalleled expansion that lasted until the mid-1970s.

The GI Bill, officially the Servicemen's Readjustment Act, provided grants to veterans to cover the full cost of three years of college. Millions took advantage of these benefits. By 1947, 49 percent of college students were veterans. When the bill's benefits ended in 1956, nearly half of the 16 million eligible veterans had used them for higher education or job training.[73] Between 1940 and 1950 the number of U.S. college and university degrees doubled. The percentage of Americans with at least a bachelor's degree rose from 4.6 percent in 1945 to 25 percent by the end of the century.[74]

Thanks to a surging economy and the growth of Cold War-era research at universities, public enrollment continued to increase during the 1950s, '60s and — aided by the post-World War II baby boom — into the 1970s. For example, the 1958 National Defense Education Act, passed in part as a reaction to the Soviet Union's launching of the unmanned *Sputnik* satellite the year before, boosted funding to public universities and helped increase enrollments, especially in mathematics, science and modern foreign languages.

The great public research universities flowered. "The act put the federal government, for the first time, in the business of subsidizing higher education directly, rather than through contracts for specific research," Louis Menand wrote in *The Marketplace of Ideas*. "Before 1958 public support for higher education had been administered at the state level (which is one reason why there are state universities in the United States but no national university)."[75]

The baby boom also increased demand; the number of 18-24-year-olds jumped from 15 million in 1955 to 25 million by 1970.[76]

College enrollment continued to grow quickly; between 1960 and 1975, the number of students enrolled in public institutions grew 20 percent.[77] To keep up with demand, more universities — mostly public — were opened. Between 1960 and 1975 the number of public higher-education institutions roughly doubled.[78] Many existing public universities were transformed into massive and complex institutions. State funds and federal research money helped feed the growth.

The composition of public universities began to change as more women, minorities and lower-income applicants enrolled. Minorities, aided by passage of the Civil Rights Act of 1964, made greater inroads into previously

Bangladeshi-American educator Salman Khan created Khan Academy in 2006 to provide "a high quality education to anyone, anywhere." The nonprofit website supplies more than 3,600 free online video tutorials on subjects ranging from mathematics and history to medicine and computer science. The popular site is one of a growing number of online educational models offering quality instruction, including Coursera, edX, Udacity and StraighterLine.

segregated colleges and public institutions. The growing availability of financial aid, including the Higher Education Act of 1965 and the Education Amendments of 1972, made college even more accessible.

As universities "democratized" and opened their doors to a larger variety of students, the public's perception of a higher-education degree began to shift from what was seen largely as a "private good" to a "public good." There was a "movement away from the notion of education for an 'elite' group of American youth to education for the masses, providing the near-universal access that has earned American higher education this reputation," according to a Stanford University report.[79] The general view was that investing in universities by funding them was in the public interest because a better educated populace would improve the nation's economy.

Enrollment began to drop with the end of the Vietnam War draft in 1973; many male students had enrolled in

Tenure Under Intense Scrutiny

Is it a luxury public higher education can no longer afford?

Tenure, which rewards professors with guaranteed lifetime employment, is under fire. To faculty members, it is a traditional, hard-earned feature of academic employment that provides job security and protects academic freedom.

But in today's cash-strapped world of higher education, many administrators see it as an indefensible throwback. In a recent survey, 69 percent of college leaders said they prefer that most faculty work under long-term or annual contracts instead of receiving tenure.[1]

On most campuses, professors can earn tenure — if they are in a tenure-track position — after a six-year trial period and if their departmental peers deem them worthy. Faculty members turned down for tenure must leave an institution a year later. It is, literally, a make-or-break situation for professors. Once tenure is granted, however, a faculty member is essentially "fireproof" — immune from dismissal for anything but ethical or criminal transgressions.

Critics say tenure can foster complacency and make it difficult to dismiss incompetent faculty. "Tenured faculty members often use their power to stifle innovation and change," reducing intellectual diversity, said Richard Vedder, director of The Center for College Affordability and Productivity, a higher-education think tank in Washington. "Many ideologically driven tenured professors use their job security to aggressively thwart efforts to increase alternative viewpoints being taught."[2]

The tenure process also can pressure tenure applicants to be overly cautious, says Andrew Hacker, a professor of political science at Queens College in New York City and co-author of *Higher Education: How Colleges Are Wasting Our Money and Failing Our Kids — and What We Can Do About It.* "Tenure is the enemy of spontaneity and intellectual freedom."

In his book, co-written with *New York Times* journalist Claudia Dreifus, Hacker asserted that "few junior faculty are willing to try unconventional research or break with the orthodoxies of their discipline, espouse dissenting ideas, indeed do anything that might otherwise displease their seniors."[3]

Opponents also claim tenure is expensive and limits opportunities for younger faculty members. "With tenured professors earning such large salaries and staying on longer and longer, they are eating up the payroll that could be used to hire younger academics," says Hacker. "Instead of retiring, they stay put, protected by tenure. What they will not admit is that they are preventing young, untenured, people from joining the faculty." Hacker, who retired after being tenured for 40 years, teaches full-time now on a yearly contract.

"As with other people, tenure came automatically when I was promoted to associate professor, and I didn't think to question it anymore than I did my health benefits," Hacker says. "In retrospect, knowing what I know now, I would have not gotten it."

However, proponents of tenure say doing away with it would stifle academic freedom. Tenure ensures "that faculty members can speak forthrightly in their classes without fear of retribution," according to Cary Nelson, a professor of English at the University of Illinois at Urbana-Champaign and past president of the American Association of University Professors. Tenure helped "make American classrooms places where students can be challenged and inspired."[4]

Some proponents argue that tenure allows professors to be outspoken critics of their administrators or politicians. "Indeed, what's disappearing along with tenure, say its

college as a way of avoiding the draft. Moreover, as the baby boom drew to a close, the college-age population leveled off.

As the shift continued, the golden age of college enrollment was ending. As the University of Massachussetts' Folbre wrote, "The widespread political support that many of us had taken for granted began to be gradually, unevenly,

but relentlessly, withdrawn. . . . A backlash against public higher education was underway."[80]

When a conservative mood swept across the country with the 1980 election of President Ronald Reagan, more voters began to demand tax reform at the state and national levels, and states began to reduce their funding of public colleges and universities. Also, explained Robert M.

advocates, is the ability of professors to play a strong role in running their universities and to object if they think officials are making bad decisions," said *The Chronicle of Higher Education.*[5]

"One of the jobs of tenured faculty is to raise a lot of questions and make people uncomfortable," Martin J. Finkelstein, a professor of higher education at New Jersey's Seton Hall University," told *The Chronicle.* "Non-tenured faculty are very cautious. They want to be retained."[6]

Tenured faculty also see tenure as part of their compensation package and might be tempted to switch colleges if they lost it, some proponents say. "Removing tenure would result in a chaotic upheaval of faculty at some universities," says Robert Zemsky, a professor of education at the University of Pennsylvania and co-author of *Remaking the American University.* "You'd see thousands leaving their positions for jobs at universities that offer tenure."

But tenure critics disagree. Hacker contends that while some elite professors might leave their jobs, the majority would not because "they are not getting offers from other colleges. The question you have to ask is, 'Who wants them?' "

Universities have cut back hiring, and tenured professors are staying in their jobs longer. According to the Bureau of Labor Statistics, the number of professors age 65 and over doubled between 2000 and 2011.[7]

As the debate continues, the number of tenured professors continues to fall. In 1969, 68 percent of the nation's faculty were either tenured or on a tenure track. Today that has dropped to 33.5 percent.[8]

Universities say they cannot afford to keep hiring tenure-track professors and so increasingly are offering only non-tenure track or part-time positions. In 1960, three-fourths of faculty were full time or tenure-track professors; today adjunct instructors (or graduate assistants) account for two-thirds of the faculty.[9]

The average pay for an adjunct teacher is $2,987 for a three-credit course, according to a recent survey, and some make under $1,000. In the same survey, 79 percent of respondents reported they didn't receive health insurance benefits from their colleges.[10]

"I think the financial pressures are so severe that — other than the selective, wealthy liberal-arts colleges and the public and private flagship research universities — tenure is just going to be a vanishing species," said Ronald G. Ehrenberg, a professor of industrial and labor relations at Cornell University.[11]

— *Robert Kiener*

[1]Jack Stripling, "Most presidents prefer no tenure for majority of faculty," *The Chronicle of Higher Education,* May 15, 2011, http://chronicle.com/article/Most-Presidents-Favor-No/127526/.

[2]Richard Vedder, "Reducing Intellectual Diversity," *The New York Times,* Nov. 23, 2010, www.nytimes.com/roomfordebate/2010/07/19/what-if-college-tenure-dies/tenure-reduces-intellectual-diversity?gwh=4AB1D5DF16B0977B6DBFC72F465BA8ED.

[3]Andrew Hacker and Claudia Dreifus, *Higher Education: How Colleges Are Wasting Our Money and Failing Our Kids — and What We Can Do About It* (2010), p. 146.

[4]Cary Nelson, "At stake: freedom and learning," *The New York Times,* July 20, 2010, www.nytimes.com/roomfordebate/2010/7/19/what-if-college-tenure-dies/tenure-protects-freedom-and-students-learning.

[5]Robin Wilson, "Tenure, RIP: What the vanishing status means for the future of education," *The Chronicle of Higher Education,* July 4, 2012, http://chronicle.com/article/Tenure-RIP/66114/.

[6]*Ibid.*

[7]Audrey Williams June, "Aging professors create a faculty bottleneck," *The Chronicle of Higher Education,* March 18, 2012, https://chronicle.com/article/Professors-Are-Graying-and/131226/.

[8]Robin Wilson, "2 tracks for faculty," *The Chronicle of Higher Education,* Oct. 12, 2012, http://chronicle.com/article/What-If-There-Were-2-Tracks/135050/.

[9]Samantha Stainburn, "The Case of the Vanishing Full-Time Professor," *The New York Times,* Dec. 30, 2009, www.nytimes.com/2010/01/03/education/edlife/03strategy-t.html?ref=edlife&_r=0.

[10]Audrey Williams June and Jonah Newman, "Adjunct project reveals wide range in pay," *The Chronicle of Higher Education,* Jan. 4, 2013, http://chronicle.com/article/Adjunct-Project-Shows-Wide/136439/.

[11]Wilson, "Tenure, RIP," *op. cit.*

Berdahl, chancellor of the University of California, Berkeley, "the notion developed that the chief beneficiaries of universities were the students educated, not the public at large, so that it should be the students themselves who bore a larger portion of the cost of education."[81]

As state appropriations for public higher education dropped, universities scrambled to make up the shortfall.

Tuition rose and kept climbing until it outpaced the rate of inflation. Eventually, higher education became inaccessible for many lower- and even middle-income students.

Expanding Bubble

As tuition increased in the 1990s and the first decade of the 21st century, so did talk about a "higher-education

Peter Struck, an associate professor of classical studies at the University of Pennsylvania, records a lecture on Greek mythology on Nov. 15, 2012. The video will be offered free to 54,000 students around the world taking a massive open online course (MOOC) provided by the university. Struck says he is reaching more students through the MOOC than all the tuition-paying students he taught in 15 years of traditional classes.

bubble." Students, many of whom were fortified with private and government loans, kept paying more and more for tuition. But as the economy worsened jobs grew scarcer, and suddenly those costlier degrees seemed like less of a good investment. Talk of a higher-education bubble, similar to the dot-com and real estate bubbles of the recent past, became commonplace.

Compounding the problem, students piled on more debt to pay their tuition. By 2011 the average student debt was $23,300, and the amount of federal loans grew by more than 60 percent between 2007 and 2012.[82]

Meanwhile states kept cutting funding. In 2005, per-student funding at public colleges and universities was its lowest in a quarter century, after adjusting for inflation.[83] Financial aid — including federal Pell grants, which were created in 1972 to help low-income families afford higher education — was covering less of the tab for four years of college. In the program's first year the maximum Pell Grant was $452; by 1990 it had reached $2,300 and $5,550 in 2012.[84] From covering nearly all of a year's tuition at a typical two-year public university, a Pell Grant now covers only about 36 percent.[85]

In President Obama's 2008 stimulus bill, designed to boost the flagging U.S. economy, Pell Grants were increased to a maximum of $5,350. To save awardees having to pay interest rates imposed by the banks, the Obama administration elected to award the federal grants directly in 2010. (*See "At Issue," p. 215.*) When they took over the House in 2011, Republicans sought to cut them by $5.7 billion, or a maximum cut of $845 per grantee, but the attempt failed. The grants were cut during the summer of 2011 during a budget standoff and then raised again in the Budget Control Act of 2011.

As *The New York Times* noted, "the Obama administration has given out more grants and loans than ever to more and more college students with the goal of making the United States first among developed nations in college completion."[86]

During the boom years between 1999 and 2009, both tuition and higher-ed spending rose. Institutions added new facilities, expanded programs and increased salaries.

Meanwhile, as public universities were flourishing in the latter half of the 20th century, a new model — for-profit colleges — had entered the marketplace. Led by the success of the University of Phoenix, which was started as a largely online venture in 1976, schools such as DeVry, Capella and Kaplan universities aggressively3 marketed themselves to potential students. Between 2000 and 2010, enrollment in for-profit institutions nearly quadrupled from 673,000 to 2.6 million. The University of Phoenix, the largest of the for-profits, grew to 455,600 students by 2010, making it the nation's second-largest higher-education system, after the State University of New York.[87]

However, the rise of the for-profits stalled when a 2012 congressional report found "exorbitant tuition, aggressive student recruiting and abysmal student outcomes," all subsidized by taxpayers. The report characterized the $32 billion the schools received in tuition aid during 2009-2010 as a poor investment for taxpayer money.[88]

Although some of the for-profit colleges have announced they would self-regulate, there has been no industry-wide effort to reform or institute new standards. Enrollment began falling, however, and last October Phoenix announced it would close nearly half its campuses and satellite operations; Kaplan closed nine.[89]

CURRENT SITUATION
Rise of the MOOCs

Online learning has come a long way since 1989, when the University of Phoenix started its online degree program.

Did expansion of the Pell Grant program lead to tuition hikes?

YES
Neal P. McCluskey
Associate Director, Center for
Educational Freedom, Cato Institute.

Written for *CQ Global Researcher*, January 2013

Give most people free money to buy something and they'll demand more frills and willingly pay higher prices. With that in mind, President Obama's expansion of the Pell Grant program has almost certainly enabled colleges to inflate tuition.

Numerous variables are at play in college pricing beyond Pell, including federal loans, scholarships, state subsidies, etc. And, because not-for-profit colleges call last year's spending this year's "costs," it is hard to nail down the precise inflationary effect of Pell, especially over the short term. Long term, however, it is pretty clear that Pell and other aid have fueled tuition escalation.

Over the last quarter-century, inflation-adjusted aid ballooned from $4,452 per student to $14,745. Much of that took the form of loans, but grants moved from $2,264 to $6,994. Concurrently, average tuition, fees and room-and-board charges increased from $8,453 to $17,860 at public colleges and from $21,048 to $39,518 at private institutions. In absolute terms, aid has increased by $10,293 per student — very close to the $9,407 rise in public-college prices.

This strongly suggests that aid, including Pell, enables tuition inflation. Other research indicates that private colleges not only raise prices in response to the availability of aid but also dollar-for-dollar in response to increases in Pell Grants. So, too, do public colleges for out-of-state students.

Which brings us to academia's favorite inflation scapegoat: cuts in state and local support, which supposedly are forcing the price hikes. In the short term, there is probably some truth to this. The long-term evidence, however, is quite different.

First, the explanation doesn't apply to private schools, which like publics have raised their charges at rates that greatly exceed normal inflation. More directly, state and local funding overall, adjusted for inflation, has risen about 29 percent over the last 25 years, although on a per-pupil basis it has fallen. However, for every dollar that per-pupil subsidies have dropped, schools have raised two dollars through tuition.

But isn't Pell aimed at truly low-income students, and therefore likely to have no effect on sticker prices, even if overall aid is inflationary? Pell has become less targeted but probably has little direct effect on maximum prices. However, schools likely replace their own aid money with Pell, and redirect theirs to less needy students. That redirection, in turn, enables them to increase sticker prices.

So has Pell expansion provided inflationary fuel? It's hard to prove but is almost certainly the case.

NO
Peter McPherson
President, Association of Public and
Land-grant Universities

Written for *CQ Global Researcher*, January 2013

Both tuition and federal financial aid have risen over the past decade, but it is a mistake to conclude that parallel timing proves causality. Many have examined this possible relationship and have concluded that increasing student financial aid does not cause higher tuition. One study concluded that an increase in the maximum Pell Grant results in less unmet need so it puts *downward* pressure on tuition growth.

The dynamics of financial aid and tuition differ among the various higher education sectors. For public universities, the critical figure is per-student education expenditures. If increases in financial aid caused higher tuition, then presumably higher tuition would contribute to increased education expenditures. However, per-student education expenditures at public universities have been almost flat, at 1 percent above inflation, for 20 years, according to U.S. Department of Education data. Increased financial aid has not produced higher per-student education expenditures, so increased federal student aid is not why tuition has risen at public universities.

The driving force behind increases in public university tuition has been the reduction in per-student appropriations by state governments. Education expenditures at public universities are typically paid for with revenues from student tuition, financial aid and state appropriations. Over the past decade, state appropriations per student have declined by 32 percent. Public universities have raised tuition primarily to fill the funding gap left by this significant change in revenues.

At the same time, the number of public university students has increased by 23 percent since 2000. Many of these students come to college with fewer financial resources and are unable to contribute as much toward their tuition as previous students. This has strained public universities' finances as they strive to maintain stable education expenditures per student. Federal financial aid has expanded access and made college affordable for more students. In short, financial aid shifted how students paid their tuition but did not generally increase the total revenue (tuition plus state appropriations) per student received by the university.

In summary, the increased availability of financial aid for students has not caused higher tuition at public universities. Rather, increased financial aid has provided an opportunity to millions of low-income students who otherwise would not have enrolled in college.

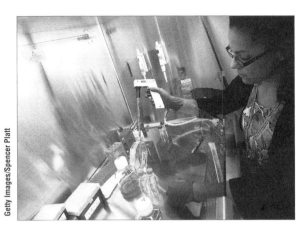

Geneticist Kristen Martins-Taylor conducts stem cell research at the University of Connecticut's Stem Cell Institute in Farmington. Critics say public colleges and universities — which conduct more than 60 percent of the nation's academic research — focus too much on research and not enough on their original purpose: to provide an educated workforce by giving a "liberal and practical education" to the "industrial classes."

Nearly seven million students now participate in some form of online learning at U.S. colleges and universities.[90]

While many educators were initially dismissive of the idea, the popularity — and adaptability — of online learning has compelled them to consider its potential to help public colleges and universities cut costs and expand enrollment.

Nonprofit and for-profit innovators — such as Coursera, edX, Udacity, StraighterLine, Khan Academy and others — are teaming with major universities to offer quality online courses to the public. "The elite, pace-setting universities have embraced the Internet," said *New York Times* columnist David Brooks. "Not long ago, online courses were interesting experiments. Now online activity is at the core of how these schools envision their futures."[91]

MOOCs — massive open online courses — are the latest online learning trend, offering millions of online students around the world a wide variety of courses, ranging from artificial intelligence to poetry, taught by some of the world's top faculty.[92]

Unlike regular online courses, in which students pay a fee to take a course online for credit toward a degree, MOOCs are free for anyone who signs up but do not, currently, count toward completion of a traditional degree.

MOOCs are evolving, and it is not yet clear how big a role they and other forms of online learning will play in public colleges and universities, especially since MOOCs have a low completion rate — only about 10 percent.[93]

"Because higher education is not a monolith, different schools face different problems," says *The Chronicle of Higher Education*'s Selingo. "MOOCs will not be for everybody." Harvard and other top-flight institutions may not be attracted to the money-saving aspects of MOOCs, but smaller schools, pressured to cut costs and become more efficient, may find them irresistible. "These lower-tier colleges could drop their poorest-quality courses and save money by replacing them with prestige courses from other institutions via MOOCs," says Selingo.

Other questions abound. First and foremost, say skeptics, will MOOC courses erode the existing financial model of universities, eventually forcing schools to start charging for them? Will they "dilute the brand" of prestigious degrees? And can high dropout rates and cheating be minimized?

"The real question is, if you start to get very good online MOOCs, why do you need a university?" said Joseph A. Burns, dean of faculty at Cornell. "And what does an Ivy League university bring to the table? What do you give to students that they can't get sitting at home and eating potato chips?"[94]

While MOOCs have yet to prove how applicable they can be to degree programs at universities, other online-learning developments are already changing the university model. Semester Online, a consortium of the University of North Carolina at Chapel Hill, Duke University and eight other prominent institutions, this fall will begin offering 30 online for-credit courses to both their own students and students who will pay more than $4,000 per course. Using a virtual classroom that allows students to raise their hands to ask questions and form their own study sessions, the courses are designed to mirror the classroom experience.[95]

The University of South Carolina designed its distance-learning program — Palmetto College — to attract a niche market: adults who had dropped out of any of its branches. The online college offers a bachelor's-degree program in such vocational fields as nursing, education and business and is open to those who have completed at least 60 credits at other higher-education institutions. The program is similar to those at Pennsylvania State, North Carolina State and elsewhere.[96]

$10,000 Degree

In his 2011 State of the State address, Texas Republican Gov. Rick Perry challenged the state's higher-education institutions to create bachelor's degree programs that would cost students no more than $10,000 and be designed to better help them land jobs after graduation. Perry noted that tuition at Texas public colleges and universities has increased an average of 5 percent per year since 1994 and now averaged $27,000.[97]

Perry called for more than tuition limits. His plan links funding to degree completion, encourages online learning, advocates paying faculty on the basis of performance and could limit perks such as tenure.

Educators resisted. Peter Hugill, president of the Texas Conference of the American Association of University Professors, reflected the opinion of many academics when he said, "I don't think it's a very practical idea. Do you really want a stripped-down, bare-bones degree?"[98]

Hunter Rawlings, president of the Association of American Universities, recently labeled Perry's plan "an assault" whose effect is "essentially to treat research universities as vocational schools, diploma mills and grant-getters."[99]

But Perry has prevailed. So far 10 Texas public colleges and universities have begun or announced $10,000 degree programs. They include a five-year, general-degree "pipeline" program that combines high school, community college and four-year university credits. Also included is a program that relies on competency-based assessments to allow students to complete an organizational leadership degree in as little as 18 months.[100]

Other Republican governors are looking with interest at Perry's ideas. Florida's Scott recently announced, "I am issuing a challenge to our state colleges to find innovative ways to offer a bachelor's degree at a cost of just $10,000 in fields that will provide graduates with the best opportunity for employment."[101]

Wisconsin Republican Gov. Scott Walker also recently announced plans to tie higher-education funding to how well schools prepare students for "open and needed" jobs in the state. "We're going to tie our funding in our technical colleges and our University of Wisconsin System into performance and say if you want money, we need you to perform, and particularly in higher education, we need you to perform not just in how many people you have in the classroom," said Walker. "In higher education, that means not only degrees, but are young people getting degrees in jobs that are open and needed today, not just the jobs that the universities want to give us, or degrees that people want to give us?"[102]

OUTLOOK
Old Order Passes

Whether one describes the issues buffeting public higher education as a "crisis," a "perfect storm" or "disruptive innovation," one thing is clear: The changes they are bringing will ensure tomorrow's model will be far removed from today's. "What we will see is the passing of the old order," says Hacker of Queens College. "We're in for some massive changes."

Here are some of the changes that experts in public higher education envision over the next decades:

Online Learning — As the composition, delivery and eventual accreditation of online courses improve, more and more institutions will accept online learning as a viable alternative to the "brick and mortar" classroom model. Students will be able to learn at their own pace from elite teachers and will take a mix of online and classroom studies.

Structure — Higher education will be "unbundled." Different suppliers may provide separate features, and institutions will assemble these components according to the specific needs of students. For example, a student may spend a year on campus, a year working in a field of study, then attend another institution — freeing the student from being limited to one college's facilities and course offerings. Today's college counselors will be replaced by "organizers."

Students — Thanks to technological advances and other efficiencies, lower-income students will be better able to afford higher education. Older students and distant learners will be able to complete degree courses with the help of advances in online learning. The expense of living away from home for four years will push more and more students online or to regional, satellite institutions. Students will be less brand loyal to institutions and quicker to question the value of degrees.

Curriculum — Interdisciplinary curricula will be widespread as colleges knock down traditional "walls" separating disciplines. The trend toward a more "vocational" curriculum, such as STEM courses, and the "attack" on the liberal arts will accelerate. More training programs will be available for students seeking technical degrees so they can bypass theory and more quickly apply their knowledge. Universities, especially those in the lower tier, will discontinue many of their costlier graduate programs.

Faculty — As tenured faculty members retire, universities will offer fewer tenure-track positions. Multiyear contracts will, in many cases, replace tenure. Universities will re-emphasize the importance of teaching (especially of undergraduates), and rewards and promotions will be based on both teaching and research. Sabbaticals will be curtailed.

Administration — With states slashing funds, expenses rising and competition heating up, more and more public universities will be run by CEO-like presidents skilled in marketing products, raising money and balancing budgets.

Degrees — Increasingly, degrees awarded for knowledge in a subject — not merely for having completed a course of studies — will be accepted. For example, students with experience in a subject who pass a competency test could count that experience toward a degree, saving money and expanding overall degree completion. The three-year degree, already in place at some colleges, will become more widespread.

As rapid technological and economic factors challenge academia's traditionally slow pace of change, Ohio State's Gee said if universities don't change how they operate, changes will be imposed upon them by outside forces.

"We are elephants," he said. "We have to become ballerinas or else we're going to become dinosaurs."[103]

NOTES

1. Paula C. Squires, "What happened," *Virginia Business*, June 12, 2012, www.virginiabusiness.com/index.php/news/article/what-happened/319835/. See also Marc Fisher and Daniel de Vise, "Question in U-Va. tumult: What should premier public universities be?" *The Washington Post*, June 23, 2012, www.washingtonpost.com/local/question-in-u-va-tumult-what-should-premier-public-universities-be/2012/06/23/gJQA1o6qxV_story.html.

2. Jeff E. Schapiro, "Sullivan's ouster a coup d'etat at U. Va," *Richmond Times Dispatch*, June 13, 2012, www.timesdispatch.com/archive/schapiro-sullivan-s-ouster-a-coup-d-etat-at-u/article_376502f6-09b6-59b3-8f0d-c8888076905b.html.

3. Richard Perez-Peña, "Ousted head of university is reinstated in Virginia," *The New York Times*, June 26, 2012, www.nytimes.com/2012/06/27/education/university-of-virginia-reinstates-ousted-president.html?pagewanted=all&_r=0.

4. Susan Milligan, "The deeper problem with ousting of UVA president Teresa Sullivan," *U.S. News & World Report*, June 19, 2012, www.usnews.com/opinion/blogs/susan-milligan/2012/06/19/the-deeper-problem-with-ousting-of-uva-president-teresa-sullivan.

5. Jenna Johnson, "U-Va. Receives warning from accreditors after failed ouster of president in June," *The Washington Post*, Dec. 11, 2012, www.washingtonpost.com/local/education/u-va-receives-warning-from-accreditors-after-failed-ouster-of-president-in-june/2012/12/11/3a5553d0-43b1-11e2-8e70-e1993528222d_story.html.

6. Josh Sanburn, "Higher-education poll," *Time*, Oct. 18, 2012, http://nation.time.com/2012/10/18/higher-education-poll/.

7. Karin Fischer, "Crisis of confidence threatens colleges," *The Chronicle of Higher Education*, May 15, 2011, http://chronicle.com/article/A-Crisis-of-Confidence/127530/. The poll surveyed more than 1,000 university presidents.

8. Karin Fischer and Ian Wilhelm, "Experts Ponder the Future of the American University," *The Chronicle of Higher Education*, June 21, 2010, http://chronicle.com/article/Experts-Ponder-the-Future-o/66011/.

9. "Public universities grapple with money, technology and mission," PBS, June 27, 2012, www.pbs.org/newshour/bb/education/jan-june12/uva_06-27.html.

10. Eighty percent figure is from Daniel Luzer, "The state funding problem," *Washington Monthly*, May 16, 2012, www.washingtonmonthly.com/college_guide/blog/the_state_funding_problem.php. Research and development figure is from Daniel Mark Fogel and Elizabeth Malson-Huddle, *Precipice or Crossroads* (2012), p. xxix.

11. Jilian Mincer, "U.S. recession's other victims: public universities," Reuters, July 19, 2012, www.reuters.com/article/2012/07/19/us-funding-state-idUSBRE86I04V20120719.

12. Jack Nicas and Cameron McWhirter, "Universities feel the heat amid cuts," *The Wall Street Journal*, June 14, 2012, http://online.wsj.com/article/SB10001424052702303734204577466470850370002.html.

13. *Ibid.*

14. Mincer, *op. cit.*

15. "LSU Budget Information," Louisiana State University, www.lsu.edu/budget/.

16. Nathan Crabbe, "Scott agrees to $300 million cut in university funding," *The Gainesville Sun*, April 17, 2012, www.gainesville.com/article/20120417/ARTICLES/120419629.

17. Stuart Butler, "The coming higher-ed revolution," *National Affairs*, Winter, 2012, www.nationalaffairs.com/publications/detail/the-coming-higher-ed-revolution.

18. "Student Loans," *The New York Times*, Sept. 12, 2012, http://topics.nytimes.com/top/reference/timestopics/subjects/s/student_loans/index.html?inline=nyt-classifier. For background, see Marcia Clemmitt, "Student Debt," *CQ Researcher*, Oct. 21, 2011, pp. 877-900.

19. Jeff Selingo, "Fixing College," *The New York Times*, June 25, 2012, www.nytimes.com/2012/06/26/opinion/fixing-college-through-lower-costs-and-better-technology.html.

20. U.S. Census Bureau, 2012, www.census.gov/prod/2012pubs/p20-566.pdf.

21. William Selway and Timothy R. Homan, "Santorum 'snob' attack on college collides with wage gains," *Business Week*, Feb. 29, 2012, www.bloomberg.com/news/2012-02-29/santorum-snob-attack-on-obama-s-college-pitch-collides-with-wage-gains.html.

22. For background, see Thomas J. Billitteri, "The Value of a College Education," *CQ Researcher*, Nov. 20, 2009, pp. 981-1004.

23. Mark C. Taylor, *Crisis on Campus* (2010), p. 5.

24. Butler, *op. cit.*

25. Tanya Roscoria, "What will higher education look like in 25 years?" *Government Technology*, Nov. 12, 2012, www.govtech.com/What-Will-Higher-Education-Look-Like-in-25-Years.html?page=1.

26. *Ibid.*

27. Kaustuv Basu, "Slow Recovery," *Inside Higher Ed*, April 9, 2012, www.insidehighered.com/news/2012/04/09/aaup-releases-faculty-salary-data.

28. Audrey Williams June, "Professors seek to reframe salary debate," *The Chronicle of Higher Education*, April 8, 2012, http://chronicle.com/article/faculty-salaries-barely-budge-2012/131432/.

29. Kellie Woodhouse, "Pay comparison: Full University of Michigan professors average $149K per full academic year," *AnnArbor.com*, May 10, 2012, www.annarbor.com/news/full-university-of-michigan-professors-make-149k-per-year-on-average/.

30. Jack Stripling and Andrea Fuller, "Presidential pay is still a potent political target," *The Chronicle of Higher Education*, May 17, 2012, http://chronicle.com/article/Presidents-Pay-Remains-Target/131914/.

31. James C. Garland, *Saving Alma Mater: A Rescue Plan for America's Public Universities* (2009), p. 11, excerpted at www.press.uchicago.edu/Misc/Chicago/283869.html.

32. "Trends in college spending: 1998-2008," Delta Cost Project, 2010, www.deltacostproject.org/resources/pdf/Trends-in-College-Spending-98-08.pdf.

33. David Jessee, "Amid tougher times, spending on payroll soars at Michigan universities," *Detroit Free Press*, March 27, 2011, www.freep.com/article/20110327/NEWS06/103270503/Amid-tougher-times-spending-payroll-soars-Michigan-universities.

34. "University of Michigan Response," *CAPCON: Michigan Capitol Confidential*, Jan. 6, 2012, www.michigancapitolconfidential.com/16260.

35. Jeff Deneen and Tom Dretler, "The financially sustainable university," Bain & Co., 2012, www.bain.com/Images/BAIN_BRIEF_The_financially_sustainable_university.pdf.

36. Greg Winter, "Jacuzzi U? A battle of perks to lure students," *The New York Times*, Oct. 5, 2003, www .nytimes.com/2003/10/05/us/jacuzzi-u-a-battle-of-perks-to-lure-students.html?pagewanted= all&src=pm.

37. James J. Duderstadt, "Creating the future; the promise of public research universities for America," in Fogel and Malson-Huddle, *op. cit.*, p. 223.

38. Nathan Crabbe, "UF trustees ponder how to survive budget cuts while students protest tuition hikes," *The Gainesville Sun*, March 29, 2012, www .gainesville.com/article/20120329/ARTICLES/ 120329466?p=2&tc=pg.

39. "The college-cost calamity," *The Economist*, Aug. 4, 2012, www.economist.com/node/21559936.

40. Glenn Reynolds, "Sunday reflection: What comes after the high education bubble?" *Washington Examiner*, May 5, 2012, http://washingtonexaminer .com/sunday-reflection-what-comes-after-the-higher-education-bubble/article/572421# .UO42IeTAfTo.

41. Richard Vedder, "Five reasons college enrollments might be dropping," Bloomberg, Oct, 22, 2012, www.bloomberg.com/news/2012-10-22/ five-reasons-college-enrollments-might-be-dropping.html.

42. Jon Marcus, "Colleges freeze, reduce tuition as public balks at further price hikes," NBC News, Aug. 1, 2012, http://usnews.nbcnews.com/_news/ 2012/08/01/13070188-colleges-freeze-reduce-tuition-as-public-balks-at-further-price-hikes?lite.

43. Michael Corkery, "Colleges lose pricing power," *The Wall Street Journal*, Jan. 9, 2013, http:// online.wsj.com/article/SB1000142412788732444 23045782319221596026766.html.

44. Katy Hopkins, "International students continue to flock to U.S. colleges, grad schools," *U.S. News & World Report*, Nov. 12, 2012, www.usnews .com/education/best-colleges/articles/2012/11/12/ international-students-continue-to-flock-to-us-colleges-grad-schools.

45. Adrienne Mong, "Chinese applications to U.S. schools skyrocket," NBC News, Jan. 11, 2012, http://behindthewall.nbcnews.com/_news/2012/ 01/11/9679479-chinese-applications-to-us-schools-skyrocket?lite.

46. Jeanne Bonner, "More university mergers possible," GBP News, Nov. 14, 2012, www.gpb.org/ news/2012/11/14/more-university-mergers-possible.

47. Kelly Heyboyer, "Rutgers boards approve historic UMDNJ merger," *The Star Ledger*, Nov. 19, 2012, www.nj.com/news/index.ssf/2012/11/rutgers_ boards_approve_umdnj_m.html.

48. Kelly Heyboyer, "Rutgers board to vote on UMDNJ merger, sealing all-but-done deal," *The Star Ledger*, Nov. 18, 2012, www.nj.com/news/index.ssf/ 2012/11/rutgers_boards_to_vote_on_umdn.html.

49. Jack Stripling, "As the crow flies," *Inside Higher Ed*, July 16, 2010, www.insidehighered.com/ news/2010/07/16/crow.

50. Gary Nelson, "ASU's Crowe: Arizona should tout strengths," *The Arizona Republic*, Sept. 2, 2012, www.azcentral.com/community/tempe/ articles/20120829asu-crow-arizona-strengths.html.

51. Deneen and Dretler., *op. cit.*, p. 9.

52. Butler, *op. cit.*

53. Clayton Christensen and Henry Eyring, "How to save the traditional university, from the inside out," *The Chronicle of Higher Education*, July 24, 2011, http://chronicle.com/article/How-to-Save-the-Traditional/128373/.

54. "Transcript of Morrill Act 1862," www.our documents.gov/print_friendly.php?flash=true&page =transcript&doc=33&title=Transcript+of+Morrill+ Act+(1862).

55. Christensen and Eyring, *op. cit.*

56. Andrew Hacker and Claudia Dreifus, *Higher Education? How Colleges Are Wasting Our Money and Failing Our Kids — and What We Can Do About It* (2010), p. 3.

57. Aaron Deslatte, "Scott: Anthropology and journalism don't pay and neither do capes," *Orlando Sentinel*, Oct. 11, 2011, http://blogs.orlandosentinel.com/ news_politics/2011/10/scott-anthropology-and-journalism-dont-pay-and-neither-do-capes.html.

58. Rob Capriccioso, "Help wanted: low-cost adjuncts," *Inside Higher Ed*, Oct. 31, 2005, www.inside highered.com/news/2005/10/31/adjunct.

59. Jonathan Rees, "Guest commentary: Adjunct professors are hiding in plain sight," *The Denver Post*, April 29, 2012, www.denverpost.com/headlines/ci_20490316/guest-commentary-adjunct-professors-are-hiding-plain-sight.

60. Taylor, *op. cit.*, p. 182.

61. Christensen and Eyring, *op. cit.*

62. "Land Ordinance of 1785," http://thehistoryprofessor.us/bin/histprof/misc/1785landord.html.

63. "Northwest Ordinance July 13, 1787," The Avalon Project, Yale Law School, http://avalon.law.yale.edu/18th_century/nworder.asp.

64. "Point of Pride; Facts," University of Georgia, www.uga.edu/profile/pride/.

65. "History of the University of Tennessee," www.tennessee.edu/aboutut/history/index.html.

66. Quoted in Fogel and Malson-Huddle, *op. cit.*, p. 7.

67. Stephen O'Hara, "Lincoln and Morrill: passing the 1862 Morrill Act," Virginia Tech, www.vt.edu/landgrant/essays/lincoln-morrill.html.

68. Quoted in Fogel and Malson-Huddle, *op. cit.*, p. 12.

69. David Masci, "Liberal Arts Education," *CQ Researcher*, April 10, 1998, pp. 313-336.

70. Nancy Folbre, *Saving State U* (2010), p. 31.

71. *Ibid.*, p. 35.

72. *Ibid.*

73. "GI Bill," City University of New York, www.cuny.edu/archive/cc/higher-education/gi-bill.html.

74. "Servicemen's Readjustment Act 1944," *Our Documents*, www.ourdocuments.gov/doc.php?flash=true&doc=76.

75. Louis Menand, *The Marketplace of Ideas* (2010), pp. 66-67.

76. *Ibid.*, p. 69.

77. Patricia J. Gumport, *et al.*, "Trends in United States higher education from massification to post massification," National Center for Postsecondary Improvement, Stanford University, 1997, p. 3, www.stanford.edu/group/ncpi/documents/pdfs/1-04_massification.pdf.

78. *Ibid.*, p. 9.

79. *Ibid.*, p. 12.

80. Folbre, *op. cit.*, p. 45.

81. Robert M. Berdahl, "The Privatization of Public Universities," speech at Erfurt University, Erfurt, Germany, May 23, 2000, http://cio.chance.berkeley.edu/chancellor/sp/privatization.htm.

82. Andrew Martin and Andrew W. Lehren, "A generation hobbled by the soaring cost of college," *The New York Times*, May 13, 2012, www.nytimes.com/2012/05/13/business/student-loans-weighing-down-a-generation-with-heavy-debt.html?pagewanted=all.

83. Folbre, *op. cit.*, p. 45.

84. "Pell Grant Historical figures," FinAid, www.finaid.org/educators/pellgrant.phtml.

85. Tyler Kingkade, "Pell grants cover smallest portion of college costs in history as GOP calls for cuts," *The Huffington Post*, Aug. 27, 2012, www.huffingtonpost.com/2012/08/27/pell-grants-college-costs_n_1835081.html.

86. Martin and Lehren, *op. cit.*

87. Robin Wilson, "For profits change higher education's landscape," *The Chronicle of Higher Education*, Feb. 7, 2010, http://chronicle.com/article/For-Profit-Colleges-Change/64012/.

88. For background, see Barbara Mantel, "Career Colleges," *CQ Researcher*, Jan. 7, 2011, pp. 1-24. Also see John Hechinger and Oliver Staley, "For-profit colleges shortchange taxpayers, Senate study says," Bloomberg, July 30, 2012, www.bloomberg.com/news/2012-07-30/for-profit-colleges-shortchange-taxpayers-senate-report-finds.html.

89. "Enrollment falling at for-profit campuses," *eCampusNews*, Oct. 23, 2012, www.ecampusnews.com/top-news/enrollment-falling-at-for-profit-colleges/.

90. "Changing Course: Ten Years of Tracking Online Education in the United States," The Sloan Consortium, 2013, http://sloanconsortium.org/publications/survey/survey04.asp.

91. David Brooks, "The campus tsunami," *The New York Times*, May 3, 2012, www.nytimes.com/2012/05/04/opinion/brooks-the-campus-tsunami.html?_r=0.

92. See Tamar Lewin, "Students Rush to Web Classes, but Profits May Be Much Later," *The New York*

Times, Jan. 6, 2013, www.nytimes.com/2013/01/07/education/massive-open-online-courses-prove-popular-if-not-lucrative-yet.html?pagewanted=2&_r=0&hp&pagewanted=print.

93. *Ibid.*

94. Nick Anderson, "Elite education for the masses," *The Washington Post*, Nov. 3, 2012, www.washington post.com/local/education/elite-education-for-the-masses/2012/11/03/c2ac8144-121b-11e2-ba83-a7a396e6b2a7_story_1.html.

95. Hannah Seligson, "University consortium to offer small online course for credit," *The New York Times*, Nov. 16, 2012, www.nytimes.com/2012/11/16/education/duke-northwestern-to-offer-semester-online-classes.html.

96. Alina Mogiulyanskaya, "U. of South Carolina crafts an online degree that students can afford," *The Chronicle of Higher Education*, Sept. 23, 2012, http://chronicle.com/article/U-of-South-Carolina-Crafts-an/134566/?cid=at&utm_source=at&utm_medium=en.

97. Thomas Lindsay, "Texas tries to make college cheap," *Real Clear Policy*, Oct. 16, 2012, www.realclearpolicy.com/articles/2012/10/16/making_public_colleges_affordable_once_again_321.html.

98. Ralph K. M. Haurwitz, "Perry's call for $10,000 bachelor's degrees stumps educators," *Austin American Statesman*, Feb. 11, 2011, www.statesman.com/news/news/state-regional-govt-politics/perrys-call-for-10000-bachelors-degrees-stumps-edu/nRXWb/.

99. Nick Anderson, "Head of major university group weighs in on U-Va.," *The Washington Post*, Oct. 25, 2012, www.washingtonpost.com/blogs/college-inc/post/head-of-major-university-group-weighs-in-on-u-va/2012/10/25/be27a594-1ea6-11e2-9cd5-b55c38388962_blog.html.

100. Lara Seligman, "Does Texas have an answer to sky-high tuition?" *National Journal*, Nov. 23, 2012, http://nationaljournal.com/domesticpolicy/does-texas-have-an-answer-to-sky-high-tuition—20121123?page=1,s.

101. Reeve Hamilton, "Perry's $10,000 degree challenge spreads to Florida," *Texas Tribune*, Nov. 28, 2012, www.texastribune.org/texas-education/higher-education/perrys-10000-degree-challenge-spreads-florida/.

102. Dee J. Hall and Samara Kalk Derby, "Gov. Scott Walker unveils agenda for Wisconsin during speech in California," *Wisconsin State Journal*, Nov. 19, 2012, http://host.madison.com/wsj/news/local/govt-and-politics/gov-scott-walker-unveils-agenda-for-wisconsin-during-speech-in/article_a35a1378-31ed-11e2-bb6c-0019bb2963f4.html.

103. "Public universities grapple with money, technology and mission," PBS, June 27, 2012, www.pbs.org/newshour/bb/education/jan-june12/uva_06-27.html.

BIBLIOGRAPHY

Selected Sources

Books

Clawson, Dan, and Max Page, *The Future of Higher Education*, **Routledge, 2011.**
Two public university professors analyze the contemporary public higher education landscape by asking who pays for it, who can afford it and who governs it and offer a plan for radically revising it.

Fogel, Daniel Mark, and Elizabeth Malson-Huddle, eds., *Precipice or Crossroads? Where America's Great Public Universities Stand and Where They Are Going Midway Through Their Second Century*, **SUNY Press, 2012.**
Experts in higher education discuss whether the quality of the nation's public institutions, and of American life and democracy, can be sustained.

Folbre, Nancy, *Saving State U: Why We Must Fix Higher Education*, **The New Press, 2010.**
An economics professor at the University of Massachusetts, Amherst, examines the debates surrounding the future of state-funded public higher education.

Hacker, Andrew, and Claudia Dreifus, *Higher Education: How Colleges Are Wasting Our Money and Failing Our Kids — and What We Can Do About It*, **Times Books, 2010.**

Visiting campuses across the country, Queens College professor (Hacker) and *New York Times* journalist Dreifus investigate how American higher education has "lost its way."

Menand, Louis, *The Marketplace of Ideas: Reform and Resistance in the American University*, W.W. Norton, 2010.
A *New Yorker* staff writer and Harvard English professor details how the American college curriculum has evolved and explores how it, and other elements of higher education, should be modernized.

Taylor, Mark C., *Crisis on Campus: A Bold Plan for Reforming Our Colleges and Universities*, Alfred A. Knopf, 2010.
A noted writer and philosophy professor argues that higher education needs to do away with tenure, restructure academic departments, encourage interdisciplinary cooperation and emphasize teaching if it hopes to remain relevant.

Articles

Butler, Stuart M., "The Coming Higher-Ed Revolution," *National Affairs*, winter 2012, www.nationalaffairs.com/publications/detail/the-coming-higher-ed-revolution.
The higher education industry is on the verge of a transformative re-alignment. Its fate will be decided by how universities respond to financial, technological, academic and societal factors.

Fischer, Karin, "Crisis of Confidence Threatens Colleges," *The Chronicle of Higher Education*, May 15, 2011, http://chronicle.com/article/A-Crisis-of-Confidence/127530/.
A survey of more than 1,000 college and university presidents reveals a deep divide between the various sectors of American higher education.

Grafton, Anthony, "Can the Colleges Be Saved?" *The New York Review of Books*, May 24, 2012, www.nybooks.com/articles/archives/2012/may/24/can-colleges-be-saved/?pagination=false.
The rich history of American higher education has been improved and damaged colleges, but survival of the nation's higher education depends on how it builds on that past.

Pappano, Laura, "The Year of the MOOC," *The New York Times*, Nov. 2, 2012, www.nytimes.com/2012/11/04/education/edlife/massive-open-online-courses-are-multiplying-at-a-rapid-pace.html?pagewanted=all&_r=0.
Although massive open online courses (MOOCs) have been around for several years, they have recently been attracting more attention as schools examine how MOOCs can be designed for maximum benefit to both students and institutions.

Selingo, Jeff, "The Fiscal Cliff for Higher Education," *The Chronicle of Higher Education*, Aug. 12, 2012, http://chronicle.com/blogs/next/2012/08/12/the-fiscal-cliff-for-higher-education/.
A recent conference offered numerous suggestions on how to address the financial crisis in American higher education.

Reports and Studies

Deneen, Jeff, and Tom Dretler, "The Financially Sustainable University," Bain & Co., 2012, www.bain.com/publications/articles/financially-sustainable-university.aspx.
College presidents and administrators must reshape and reinvent their industry if they are to cope successfully with the financial crises facing colleges and universities.

King, Gary, and Maya Sen, "The Troubled Future of Colleges and Universities," Harvard University, Sept. 13, 2012, http://gking.harvard.edu/files/distruptu_0.pdf.
Political, economic and educational forces threaten to undermine the business model, governmental support and operating mission of traditional colleges.

McKeown, Karen, "Can Online Learning Reproduce the Full College Experience?" Heritage Foundation, March 13, 2012, www.heritage.org/research/reports/2012/03/can-online-learning-reproduce-the-full-college-experience.
Despite the claims of some critics, some aspects of online learning may provide a better experience for some students than traditional brick-and-mortar colleges offer.

For More Information

Association of American Colleges and Universities, 1818 R St., N.W., Washington, DC 20009; 202-387-3760; www.aacu.org. Has more than 1,200 public and private member institutions; focuses on ensuring the quality of undergraduate liberal arts education.

Association of Public and Land-Grant Universities, 1307 New York Ave., N.W., Suite 400, Washington, DC 20005-4722; 202-478-6040; www.aplu.org. A research and advocacy organization of public research universities, land-grant institutions and state university systems.

Center for College Affordability and Productivity, 1150 17th St., N.W., Suite 910, Washington, DC 20036; 202-375-7831; http://centerforcollegeaffordability.org. Independent, nonprofit think tank that analyzes college finances and spending.

College Board, 45 Columbus Ave., New York, NY 10023; 212-713-8000; www.collegeboard.com. Nonprofit organization that manages college admissions testing and collects data on college costs and student debt.

Education Trust, 1250 H St., N.W., Suite 700, Washington, DC 20005; 202-293-1217; www.edtrust.org. A nonprofit promoting high academic achievement at all levels — especially among low-income and minority students.

Office of Postsecondary Education, Department of Education, 1990 K St., N.W., Washington, DC 20006; 202-401-2000; www2.ed.gov/about/offices/list/ope. Formulates policy and administers programs designed to increase access to quality postsecondary education.

Project on Student Debt, Institute for College Access and Success, 405 14th St., 11th Floor, Oakland, CA 94612; 510-318-7900; http://projectonstudentdebt.org. Independent research and education group.

10

Gun Control

Barbara Mantel

Colorado supporters of gun ownership, including Theresa White of Estes Park, demonstrate at the state Capitol in Denver on Jan. 9, 2013. The nation's state lawmakers are divided on new gun legislation. Many favor tougher background checks, but others oppose limits on assault weapons and high-capacity magazines. The public strongly favors expanding background checks to private gun sales, but reinstating a federal ban on assault weapons seems unlikely.

From *The CQ Researcher*, March 8, 2013.

The debate over gun control has been inescapable since last December, when Adam Lanza used a so-called assault rifle* to kill 20 first-graders and six adults at Sandy Hook Elementary School in Newtown, Conn., before taking his own life in one of the most horrific mass shootings in the nation's history.

The fallout from the massacre has been widespread and relentless: marches and protests, fiery advertisements, celebrity endorsements, contentious congressional and state hearings, proposed federal and state legislation and a tough, new gun-control law in New York state.

But whether the shooting will spur Congress to pass stricter nationwide controls remains a toss-up — some support exists, even among conservatives, for expanding background checks to include private firearm sales, but a federal ban on assault weapons seems to be a nonstarter. Meanwhile, more than 1,000 firearm-related bills have been introduced in state legislatures, but only New York has passed one to date.

In late January, more than 2,000 people descended on Connecticut's statehouse in Hartford for a packed public hearing that ran more than 17 hours. In a visual symbol of the revived and often rancorous discussion of gun violence, gun-rights advocates sported round yellow stickers reading "Another Responsible Gun

---

*Federal and state laws banning semiautomatic weapons with detachable magazines and military-style features use the term "assault weapon" to describe such firearms. But gun-rights advocates say only fully automatic firearms, such as machine guns, are true assault weapons.

Concealed-Carry Laws Sweep Nation

Forty-nine states now allow gun owners to carry concealed firearms, compared with 31 in 1981. Thirty-five states — up from two in 1981 — have adopted "shall issue" laws, which require concealed-carry permits to be granted to gun owners who meet minimum qualifications. Meanwhile, the number of states with "may issue" laws, which allow officials to deny concealed-carry permits at their discretion, has declined by more than half.

Concealed-Weapon Laws by State, 1981 and 2013*

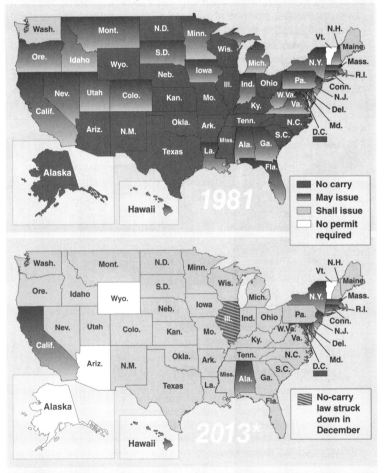

* As of March 6, 2013

Sources: "Guns in Public Places: The Increasing Threat of Hidden Guns in America," Law Center to Prevent Gun Violence, August 2011, smartgunlaws.org/guns-in-public-places-the-increasing-threat-of-hidden-guns-in-america/; "State Concealed Weapons Permitting," Law Center to Prevent Gun Violence, January 2012, smartgunlaws.org/category/state-concealed-weapons-permitting/

Owner," while gun-control supporters wore green ribbons in remembrance of Newtown.[1]

Advocacy groups on both sides testified, along with gun industry representatives, gun-violence victims and private citizens. Parents of children killed at Sandy Hook, though joined in mourning, were not always united in their testimony.

"I believe in a few simple gun laws. I think we have more than enough on the books," said Mark Mattioli, whose son James, 6, was killed.

"That wasn't just a killing. That was a massacre," said Neil Heslin, who lost his 6-year-old son, Jesse Lewis. Heslin told lawmakers that private citizens have no need for assault weapons like the one Lanza used to kill his son.[2]

But an impassioned Henson Ong, a Waterbury, Conn., resident, said that if Korean shop owners had not armed themselves with semiautomatic weapons with large-capacity magazines during the 1992 riots in Los Angeles, many of their stores would have been burned to the ground. "Their's stood because they stood their ground," said Ong, who told lawmakers he was an immigrant and an American by choice.[3]

Fresh memories of the Newtown shootings formed the backdrop for the public hearing. Lanza, a withdrawn 20-year-old, shot his way into the school wearing combat gear and armed with two semiautomatic pistols, a Bushmaster AR-15 semiautomatic rifle and numerous large-capacity ammunition magazines, each holding 30 rounds. (*See glossary, p. 229, and diagram, p. 227.*) Lanza used the rifle to shoot his victims, all of them multiple times, in under 10 minutes. The guns were legally owned by his mother, Nancy, whom Lanza had shot dead earlier in the day.

"We're going to have to come together and take meaningful action to prevent more tragedies like this, regardless of the politics," President Obama said that afternoon.[4]

After a week-long silence, Wayne LaPierre, executive vice president of the National Rifle Association of America (NRA), the country's leading gun-rights organization, headquartered in Fairfax, Va., blamed "vicious, violent video games" and lax law enforcement for violent crime.[5]

"The only thing that stops a bad guy with a gun is a good guy with a gun," said LaPierre. He called for placing armed security officers — whether police or trained volunteers — at every public school in the nation.[6] But according to the Justice Department, nearly half of the nation's public schools already had assigned police officers even before the Newtown massacre. Few reliable studies have been done on their effectiveness.[7]

Unlike other recent mass shootings, which spurred outrage but no federal legislation, Newtown is different, say gun-control advocates. "People are really feeling like they have had enough of this violence and these deaths," says Laura Cutilletta, a senior staff attorney with the San Francisco-based advocacy group Law Center to Prevent Gun Violence.

Several members of Congress with "A" ratings from the NRA have re-evaluated their positions on gun control. Sen. Joe Manchin, D-W.Va., told a radio host that "everything is on the table."[8] Sen. Mark Warner, D-Va., said, "there's got to be a way that we can do a bit more."[9]

Meanwhile, the NRA continues to oppose all gun-control proposals. The debate has gotten only more heated since mid-January, when Obama unveiled sweeping recommendations from a gun-violence working group

Anatomy of an AR-15 Rifle

Gun-control advocates say firearms such as the Rock River Arms AR-15 rifle in this photo illustration have features that make them "assault weapons." Such features can include a threaded barrel for mounting a silencer or flash suppressor, which reduces the visible flash that emanates from the muzzle when the gun is fired; a pistol grip that gives the shooter added control, and a detachable magazine. This rifle is similar in style to the Bushmaster AR-15 used by Adam Lanza in his deadly attack on schoolchildren at Sandy Hook Elementary School in Newtown, Conn., on Dec. 14, 2012. However, assault-style weapons account for only a small fraction of gun crimes, experts say.

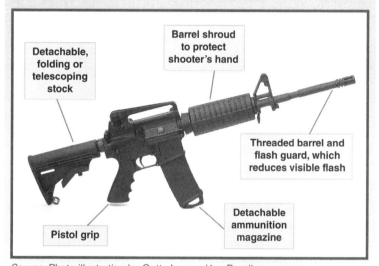

Source: Photo illustration by Getty Images/Joe Raedle

headed by Vice President Joseph Biden. Obama called on Congress to mandate universal background checks, ban the sale of assault weapons and large-capacity magazines and stiffen penalties for gun trafficking. Obama also announced 23 more modest executive actions, including launching a national safe and responsible gun ownership campaign and improving mental-health care.[10]

Gun-control advocates uniformly praised Obama's proposals. "It's really unprecedented in its scope and complexity," said Matt Bennett, co-founder of Third Way, a centrist think tank in Washington.[11] But many Republicans were highly critical of the proposals, including Senate Minority Leader Mitch McConnell, R-Ky., who sent a recorded message to gun owners across his state: "Their efforts to restrict your rights, invading your personal privacy and overstepping their bounds with executive orders, is just plain wrong."[12] The NRA sponsored attack advertisements against the administration's proposals, including one warning of a middle class left defenseless against "madmen, drug cartels and home-invading killers."

Meanwhile, the Senate Judiciary Committee is preparing gun-control legislation, and lawmakers in several states have introduced bills to toughen gun laws. At the same time, legislators in two dozen Western and Midwestern states have introduced bills to block enforcement of any forthcoming federal gun control within their borders.

Mass shootings such as Newtown garner national headlines but account for a small fraction of gun violence, much of which is concentrated among inner-city minorities. "In 2012, for the first time, there will probably be more firearm-related homicides and suicides than motor vehicle traffic fatalities," said Garen Wintemute, director of the Violence Prevention Research Program at the University of California Davis Medical Center.[13]

Nevertheless, the homicide rate in America, while dramatically higher than in many other Western democracies, is falling.[14] "We are at a 45-year historic low in terms of our murder rate," says political scientist Patrick Egan of New York University. Since reaching a peak of 10.2 reported murders per 100,000 people in 1980, the rate steadily declined during the next 20 years, plateaued through 2007, then dropped to 4.7 in 2011.[15]

About two-thirds of murders are committed with firearms — mostly handguns — and the gun-related homicide rate has dropped as well. Researchers say possible reasons include violence-prevention programs, a decline in the crack-cocaine market, the nation's aging population and the use of community policing, among others. Suicides by gun account for more than half of firearm-related deaths, and that rate also has fallen.[16]

In addition, individual gun ownership is at or near all-time lows, says Egan. "Back in the 1970s, about one in two households kept a gun, and these days it's more like one in three," he says, citing data from the University of Chicago's General Social Survey (GSS). Egan attributes the trend to increasing urbanization; an increase in households headed by single women, who are less likely

to own guns than men; and a resulting decline in the number of children who inherit the habit of gun ownership from parents.

While fewer individuals own guns today, more guns are in circulation, a trend that accelerated after Newtown, as gun buyers flocked to retailers and gun shows in expectation of future restrictions. "Our best guess is that fewer people are owning more guns," says Egan.

Americans own about 300 million guns today, up from just under 200 million 20 years ago, according to the Bureau of Alcohol, Tobacco, Firearms and Explosives (ATF).[17]

Data on gun violence, ownership and sales have been used to marshal arguments on all sides of the debate. However, such data are often "unreliable" and "inadequate," and the lack of dependable information severely hampers research, according to a National Academy of Sciences report.[18]

For instance, how many U.S. households own guns? While the GSS says about one-third, other surveys put it higher. How many guns are in circulation? Because no national gun registry exists, the ATF's 300 million number is only an estimate.

How about the number of stolen guns? "We really don't know," says economist David Hemenway, director of the Boston-based Harvard Injury Control Research Center. If the aggregate figure is unknown, researchers certainly can't know "the who, what, when, where and how," he says. Since 2004, Congress has restricted the ATF from releasing information from its Firearms Tracing System database. The restriction is known as the "Tiahrt Amendment," after its principal sponsor, former Rep. Todd Tiahrt, R-Kan.

Even FBI crime data can be incomplete because local, county, state, tribal and federal law enforcement agencies provide it voluntarily.

The lack of extensive gun-violence research dates to the early 1990s. After two studies funded by the Centers for Disease Control and Prevention (CDC) showed that a gun in the home is associated with increased risks of homicide and suicide in the home, the NRA pressed a Republican-controlled Congress in 1996 to strip the CDC of the $2.6 million funding for such research. It then succeeded in casting the CDC's gun research as motivated by support for gun restrictions, getting the following sentence into 1997 legislation: "None of the funds made available for injury prevention and control at the Centers for Disease Control and Prevention may be used to advocate or promote gun control."[19]

The CDC stopped funding research on gun violence, and other sources have not picked up the slack. As one of his executive actions, Obama has directed the CDC to resume research into causes and prevention of gun violence, saying it is not "advocacy," and has asked Congress for $10 million in funding.

Against this backdrop, here are some of the questions researchers, gun-rights and gun-control advocates, elected officials and law enforcement are asking:

Would a ban on assault weapons reduce gun violence?

The semiautomatic rifle that Lanza used is one of the most popular rifles in America. But the gun — a civilian version of the military's fully automatic M-16 rifle — also has been the weapon of choice in several other recent rampages. Jacob Tyler Roberts, 22, used one to kill two people and wound another before taking his own life in an Oregon shopping mall in December.[20] James Holmes, 24, is accused of using one, along with a 12-gauge shotgun, to open fire in a Colorado movie theater last July, killing 12 and wounding 58.[21]

So-called long guns — shotguns and rifles — are not the only firearms used in mass shootings, defined by the FBI as incidents in which four or more victims are killed. Forty-year-old Wade Michael Page, for example, used a semiautomatic handgun equipped with a 19-round magazine last August to kill six people and wound three at a Sikh temple in Wisconsin.[22]

In January, Sen. Dianne Feinstein, D-Calif., introduced a ban on assault weapons and large-capacity magazines that hold more than 10 rounds of ammunition.

"If 20 dead children in Newtown wasn't a wakeup call that these weapons of war don't belong on our streets, I don't know what is," she said. A press release from her office claimed that a previous ban, the Federal Assault Weapons Ban of 1994 in effect until 2004, "was effective

Types of Firearms

Semiautomatic: Each pull of the trigger results in a complete firing cycle, from discharge through reloading. Most guns sold in the United States, including handguns, are semiautomatic.

Automatic: Loads, discharges and reloads as long as the trigger remains depressed. Machine guns, for example, are automatic.

Assault weapon: Gun-rights advocates say only automatic firearms are assault weapons. Others say the definition also includes semiautomatic firearms with detachable magazines and at least one military-style feature, such as a bayonet mount or threaded barrel for attaching a silencer.

AFP/Getty Images/Joe Klamar

at reducing crime and getting these military-style weapons off our streets."[23]

The NRA's LaPierre has called Feinstein's proposal "a phony piece of legislation" that is "built on lies" and said the previous ban had no impact on lowering crime.[24]

Both Feinstein and LaPierre were selectively quoting from a Department of Justice analysis of the 1994 law, which banned the manufacture, transfer and possession of 18 specific models by name and all other semiautomatic firearms that fell under its general definition of assault weapons: those that could accept a detachable magazine and had at least two specified military-style features, such as a bayonet mount, folding rifle stock and a threaded barrel for attaching silencers.[25] (*See diagram, p. 227.*)

While the ban was in effect, "the percentage of crime guns that were assault weapons went down by a third or more," says Christopher Koper, the report's principal investigator and a professor of criminology at George Mason University in Fairfax, Va. However, prior to the ban assault weapons had been used in only a small fraction of gun crimes — about 2 percent — his study showed.

The law also prohibited large-capacity magazines holding more than 10 rounds of ammunition. Many non-banned semiautomatics accept such magazines, and such guns represented up to 26 percent of crime guns prior to the ban.

A newspaper's analysis of Virginia data found a reduction in the number of large-capacity magazines seized by police during the ban.[26] But more generally, "we found that it was inconclusive whether the use of large-capacity magazines declined in any real way," says Koper. "That,

Public Backs Most Gun-Control Proposals

A majority of Americans support requiring background checks for gun-show and private gun sales, establishing a federal database to track gun sales, barring people who are mentally ill from purchasing guns and putting police in more schools. However, most oppose arming more teachers.

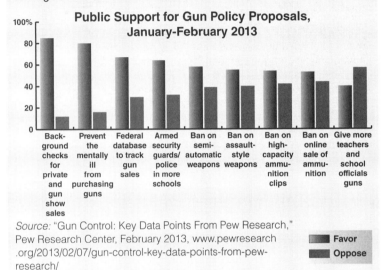

Public Support for Gun Policy Proposals, January-February 2013

Source: "Gun Control: Key Data Points From Pew Research," Pew Research Center, February 2013, www.pewresearch .org/2013/02/07/gun-control-key-data-points-from-pew-research/

of course, has to be linked to the grandfathering provision in the law."

Indeed, the law had a huge loophole. Any banned magazine or assault weapon manufactured before the law took effect remained legal to own or sell. There were nearly 1.5 million assault weapons privately owned in the United States at the time, along with nearly 25 million guns equipped with large-capacity magazines.[27]

Did the ban reduce gun crime? "We didn't really expect to see a reduction in the rate of gun crime overall," Koper says. "People could substitute other guns for the ones that were banned. But by forcing that substitution, we thought it could reduce the number of gunshots and the number of victims."

But, there was no evidence that it did, Koper says. "However, if the law had been in place longer and we had had a drop in the use of large-capacity magazines, would you then see more of an impact on gun deaths and gun injuries?" he asks.

Feinstein's proposed legislation tries to correct what gun-control advocates believe were the expired law's weaknesses. It would ban 157 specific weapons by name. And it would reduce the number of military-style features that define a semiautomatic weapon as an assault weapon from two to one, making it more difficult for gun manufacturers to make cosmetic changes to elude the ban, as they did under the expired law. As before, large-capacity magazines holding more than 10 rounds of ammunition would be prohibited.

While the law would exempt assault weapons lawfully possessed at the date of enactment, it would require purchasers of such weapons to undergo a background check, and it would prohibit the sale or transfer of grandfathered large-capacity magazines. In addition, the law would not automatically expire.[28]

"We are very supportive of the bill," says Cutilletta of the Law Center to Prevent Gun Violence. "The hope is that even the grandfathered weapons and magazines will at least be regulated and their potential damage will be curtailed."

But gun-rights groups say Feinstein's bill wouldn't reduce gun violence. "There would be instant weapon substitution," says Alan Gottlieb, executive vice president of the Second Amendment Foundation, a legal-action group in Bellevue, Wash., that promotes gun rights. "A shotgun can do as much damage as a so-called assault weapon."

Gottlieb says the ban on large-capacity magazines wouldn't reduce gun violence either because someone intent on inflicting mass damage could use many smaller magazines. "It takes a whopping three seconds to change a magazine," says Gottlieb.

Koper offers this assessment. "In the long run, the bill, if passed, would probably not affect the overall rate of gun crime. But it could result in a small reduction in shootings because you are forcing offenders to substitute less-lethal weapons and magazines. By small, I don't mean trivial."

The Johns Hopkins Center for Gun Policy and Research also warned of the need to be realistic about the likely impact of any ban, pointing to a study in Jersey City, N.J., that found 10 or more rounds were fired in fewer than 5 percent of gun incidents. Still, the center said, "We have decided to regulate the design of numerous consumer products, such as cribs and small, high-powered magnets, in order to prevent far fewer deaths than could be prevented with a ban of [large-capacity magazines]."[29]

But gun-rights advocates say Feinstein's law would contradict a 2008 ruling by the U.S. Supreme Court in *District of Columbia v. Heller*, in which the court struck down the District's handgun ban.[30] "The *Heller* case said that guns that are in common use by law-abiding people are protected by the Second Amendment," says Virginia attorney Stephen Halbrook, who has successfully argued gun-rights cases before the court. "And the kinds of guns that are being banned are very much in common use."

"That's a reasonable interpretation of the *Heller* case," says Adam Winkler, a constitutional law professor at UCLA School of Law, "yet I think the counterargument is that the Supreme Court might interpret the common-use requirement to only apply when needed for self-defense." The firearms banned under Feinstein's bill are not self-defense weapons, says Winkler.

Would mandatory background checks of all gun buyers keep guns away from criminals and other dangerous people?

Federal law prohibits possession of firearms by — among others — felons, fugitives, certain categories of domestic-violence offenders, drug addicts and those found mentally incompetent or a danger to themselves or others because of mental illness or who have been involuntarily committed to a mental institution. The 1994 Brady Handgun Violence Prevention Act requires gun buyers to submit to background checks — usually taking just a few minutes — but only if purchasing through a federally licensed gun dealer. Private sales — at gun shows, online or person-to-person — are exempt, yet they may account for 30 to 40 percent of firearms sales, according to 1994 survey data, the most recent available.[31]

The proposal to expand background checks to include private firearms sales — a less controversial idea than banning assault weapons or large-capacity magazines — is gathering bipartisan momentum, at least in the Senate. Judiciary Committee Chairman Patrick Leahy, D-Vt., is a strong supporter, and a

diverse group of four senators — including Democratic Sen. Charles Schumer of New York, a liberal, Republican Sen. Tom Coburn of Oklahoma, an NRA member and strong conservative, and moderate GOP Sen. Mark Kirk of Illinois — has been meeting privately to work out a compromise. "We'll get something, I hope. I'm praying for it," said Sen. Manchin of West Virginia, one of the participants.[32] Sen. Coburn's resistance to requiring private sellers to keep a record of transactions is apparently holding up the compromise.

"Until you close this loophole, you're giving people with a propensity for violence an opportunity to buy guns without any background check," says Ladd Everitt, director of communications for the Washington-based advocacy group Coalition to Stop Gun Violence. "It makes no sense."

A survey of state prison inmates convicted of crimes committed with a handgun found that nearly 80 percent said they got their guns from private sources — either friends or families or from street or black-market suppliers. Another 10 percent said they stole their gun; one in 10 said they purchased a gun from a licensed dealer.[33]

The NRA is opposed to expanding background checks. "Let's be honest, background checks will never be 'universal' because criminals will never submit to them," said LaPierre.[34]

Everitt calls that response the anarchy argument: "They say that criminals don't obey laws, so why should we have laws?" But that misses the point, he says. "There still would be ways for criminals to get around background checks, but the people who sold them the gun would be held accountable. Now they are not."

The NRA argument also assumes that criminals are smart, determined and informed, says Philip Cook, a professor of economics and sociology at Duke University in Durham, N.C. "A large percentage of criminals are youthful, not very well educated and very impatient, and even if you put small obstacles in their path that might discourage them from getting guns, it would help."

Gun-control advocates say the Brady Act, even with the private-sales exemption, has been effective. "By blocking 2 million attempts to purchase [since 1994], we have placed a barrier," says Becca Knox, director of research at the Washington-based Brady Campaign to Prevent Gun Violence. "The estimate is that half of those denials are to felons."

But a study of the law's first five years, conducted by Cook and Jens Ludwig, director of the University of Chicago Crime Lab, a research institute, found "no evidence of a reduction in the homicide rate that could be attributed to Brady." The researchers compared homicide rates in 32 states directly affected by the Brady Act with the 18 states that already had their own similar laws on the books.

Homicide rates were dropping nationwide before the act was passed, due in part, experts say, to the end of the crack cocaine epidemic, changes in policing and increased imprisonment rates. The trends were remarkably similar in both groups of states, and the researchers found the trends in homicide rates remained remarkably similar after the Brady Act was passed.[35]

So how do the researchers reconcile the Brady Act's lack of a detectable impact on homicide rates with the millions of people denied handguns through background checks since the act became law? "We did some back-of-the-envelope calculations using what we know about the people who attempt to buy a gun from a dealer even though they are disqualified — how likely they are to go commit homicide," says Cook. Using data from California and extrapolating nationwide, he estimates that the 60,000 annual denials in the five years he studied would have prevented roughly 40 homicides — or about eight per year.

Cook blames "the private-sale loophole" primarily for the Brady Act's lack of detectable impact on homicide rates. "And we can close that," he says. In addition, a majority of adults who end up committing a crime with a gun did not fall into any of the categories that would have disqualified them from buying the gun, says Cook. "In Cook County [Ill.] data, only 40 percent of defendants in murder cases were disqualified by having a felony conviction."

That's why many criminologists want Congress to expand the list of people ineligible to possess a gun to include those convicted of violent misdemeanors, such as misdemeanor assault and battery, which are generally punishable with jail time of up to one year. "The Brady Campaign is in favor of that expansion," says Knox.

The gap in records that states voluntarily submit to the FBI's National Instant Criminal Background Check System, particularly mental health records, also prevents the Brady Act from having a more measurable impact on homicide rates. As a result of that gap, buyers who should be disqualified slip through the system, people on all sides of the gun debate agree. (*See sidebar, p. 236.*)

California, Rhode Island and New York have completely closed the background-check loophole, requiring such checks for every gun purchase. (New York just did so in January). Yet Cook says researchers don't know how effective those laws been in stemming gun violence. "There is no money for these evaluations," says Cook.

In any case, it's not easy to conduct such evaluations because guns flow from states with lax laws to states with strict laws. At gun shows in Reno, Nev., "a third of the cars in the parking lot are from California," said gun violence expert Wintemute.[36]

Do state laws allowing citizens to carry concealed weapons make communities safer?

More than 76,000 Ohio residents received licenses to carry concealed weapons last year, the highest number since the state began licensing in 2004, according to Ohio Attorney General Mike DeWine. Six out of seven were new licenses and the rest renewals. "As a strong supporter of the Second Amendment, I am pleased to see more Ohioans than ever before are exercising their rights under Ohio's concealed carry law," DeWine said.[37]

Over the past 30 years, states have drastically loosened their "right-to-carry" laws, which allow citizens who can legally own firearms to carry concealed weapons in public, often except in parks, schools, government offices, bars and places of worship. (*See maps, p. 226.*) For example:

- Nineteen states prohibited concealed carry in 1981; today none do. (Washington, D.C. does ban it.) In December, the Seventh U.S. Circuit Court of Appeals in Chicago told Illinois its ban was unconstitutional and gave it until early June to draft a concealed-carry law.
- In 1981, 28 states had "may-issue" permit laws, which allow officials to grant or deny a concealed-carry permit; today 10 states have such laws.
- In 1981, two states had "shall-issue" permit legislation, which require officials to issue a concealed-carry permit to anyone meeting minimum qualifications; today, 35 states have such laws.
- In 1981, only Vermont did not require a gun owner to have a permit to carry a concealed firearm; today Alaska, Arizona, Vermont and Wyoming require no permit.[38]

Gun-rights advocates say right-to-carry laws, especially "shall-issue" laws, reduce crime. "The presence of a gun in the hands of good person makes us all safer. It's true. History proves it," said the NRA's LaPierre.[39] He and others argue that not only can gun-carrying individuals ward off attackers, but criminals are deterred because they don't know who does or does not carry a concealed weapon. In most states, the percentage of adults with active concealed-carry permits is in the single digits. For example, in Ohio the figure is 3.2 percent.[40]

Gun-control advocates could not disagree more. "Carrying guns in public puts American families and communities at risk of more gun deaths and injuries, as opposed to providing greater protection," says Knox of the Brady Campaign, which opposes shall-issue permit laws.

It's a fierce debate that was turbocharged in 1997, when economist John Lott concluded, based on his analysis of nationwide county data, that right-to-carry laws deter violent crime. The NRA and state legislatures have used Lott's research to justify right-to-carry legislation.

Lott's work triggered a tremendous number of followup studies. "There have been more than two dozen, each claiming to be somewhat superior to the others," says Harvard's Hemenway. Some researchers lined up with Lott while many others found serious problems with the data and analysis. The National Academy of Sciences' 2004 report found "no credible evidence that the passage of right-to-carry laws decreases or increases violent crime."[41]

One persistent Lott critic, John Donohue of Stanford Law School, revisited the issue in 2010 and concluded, again, that right-to-carry laws do not deter crime. In fact, he said, "aggravated assault rises when [such] laws are adopted."[42]

"Screening is very weak, and you have people getting these permits who have some type of criminal record, who have mental health history, a history of drug abuse or a history of domestic violence," says Everitt of the Coalition to Stop Gun Violence. In addition, "The presence of a gun can turn something that should have been a fistfight into something far more lethal."

Donohue and fellow researcher Ian Ayres of Yale Law School have said that arming citizens could encourage an "arms race" in which criminals "respond to shall-issue laws by packing more heat and shooting quicker." And with as many as one million or more guns stolen each year, "putting more guns in the hands of the law-abiding population necessarily means that more guns will end up in the hands of criminals," they wrote.[43]

The majority of shall-issue states recognize permits from other states, but most states with may-issue permit laws do not.[44] The U.S. House of Representatives passed a bill in 2011 that would create reciprocity in every state that gives citizens the right to carry concealed weapons.

"It's something that we absolutely oppose," says Knox. "This would be a race to the bottom. The state with the loosest regulations would be driving who could carry."

BACKGROUND

Early Gun Culture

Gun-control and gun-rights regulations share a long history in the United States. Adult white men in the American colonies had the right to own firearms for hunting and self-defense and, in fact, were required to use them in the service of local militias, often in battles with Native Americans. But the colonies also placed restrictions on gun ownership.

In 1637 about 100 Massachusetts Bay colonists were ordered to surrender their "guns, pistols, swords, powder, shot & match" on suspicion of being heretics, wrote journalist Craig Whitney.[45] Maryland barred Roman Catholics from possessing firearms, and Pennsylvania disarmed Loyalists during the Revolutionary War. These were not "criminals or traitors who took up arms on behalf of the British" but "ordinary citizens exercising their fundamental right to freedom of conscience," wrote UCLA's Winkler.[46]

Colonies also forbade slaves, free blacks and people of mixed race — who in some states far outnumbered whites — from owning firearms, fearing they might revolt. Combine their numbers with the up to 40 percent of the population who were Loyalists, and the colonies "were perfectly willing to confiscate weapons from anyone deemed untrustworthy — a category so broadly defined that it included a majority of the people," wrote Winkler.[47]

After the Revolution, the Founding Fathers addressed gun rights in the Second Amendment, part of the Bill of

CHRONOLOGY

1920s-1930s *States and Congress pass gun-control legislation.*

1926 American Bar Association commission, with National Rifle Association (NRA) support, adopts model state legislation regulating the concealed carry and sale of handguns; Pennsylvania is among the first to adopt it.

1934 National Firearms Act of 1934 — first federal gun-control law — levies $200 tax on the manufacture or sale of machine guns and "sawed-off" shotguns; owners must register them with the U.S. Treasury Department.

1938 National Firearms Act of 1938 requires interstate gun dealers to be licensed and to record sales; prohibits gun sales to convicted felons. . . . Carrying concealed handguns is either prohibited or permitted only with a license in every state but two.

1960s-1990s *Democratic administrations sign major gun-control legislation into law. Republican President Ronald Reagan promotes gun rights.*

1968 After the assassinations of President John F. Kennedy, Democratic presidential candidate Sen. Robert F. Kennedy and the Rev. Martin Luther King Jr, President Lyndon B. Johnson signs the Gun Control Act of 1968; it prohibits convicted felons, drug users and the seriously mentally ill from buying guns, raises the age to purchase guns from a federally licensed dealer to 21 and expands dealer licensing requirements.

1986 Reagan signs Firearm Owners' Protection Act limiting the Bureau of Alcohol, Tobacco and Firearms from inspecting licensed gun dealers more than once a year and forbidding the government from creating a national registry of gun owners.

1990 Gun-Free School Zones Act makes it a federal crime to knowingly bring a gun within 1,000 feet of a school or fire a gun within that zone. In 1995 the U.S. Supreme Court rules that punishment of gun possession or use near schools is a state matter.

1993 President Bill Clinton signs Brady Handgun Violence Act requiring licensed gun dealers to conduct background checks of buyers; unlicensed private sellers are exempt.

1994 Violent Crime Control and Law Enforcement Act of 1994 (often called the "assault weapons ban") prohibits the manufacture and sale of semiautomatic assault weapons for 10 years; it also bans ammunition magazines holding more than 10 rounds.

2000s *Gun-control advocates face defeats in Congress and Supreme Court, but massacre of 20 children in Newtown, Conn., in December reignites gun-control debate.*

2003 Congress passes Tiahrt Amendment prohibiting law enforcement from releasing data showing where criminals bought their firearms.

2004 "Assault weapons" ban expires.

2005 President George W. Bush signs Protection of Lawful Commerce in Arms Act granting gun manufacturers immunity from civil lawsuits involving crimes committed with guns.

2008 Supreme Court holds that Americans have an individual right under the Second Amendment to posses firearms for self-defense within the home.

2012 Federal appeals court rules that Illinois' ban on concealed carry of firearms is unconstitutional and gives the state until early June to draft a concealed carry law (Dec. 11). . . . Adam Lanza kills 20 children and six adults at Sandy Hook Elementary in Newtown, Conn., sparking national outrage and renewing gun-control debate (Dec. 14).

2013 President Obama proposes sweeping gun-control legislation. . . . Congress begins gun-control hearings. . . . Sen. Dianne Feinstein, D-Calif., introduces legislation to ban assault weapons and large-capacity ammunition magazines. . . . New York legislature passes one of the nation's strictest gun-control laws. Thirty-four of 62 New York counties pass resolutions demanding that lawmakers repeal the act; a state court has agreed to review whether the new law was rushed through the legislature in violation of the state constitution.

Rights attached to the U.S. Constitution in 1791. The amendment reads: "A well regulated Militia being necessary to the security of a free State, the right of the people to keep and bear Arms shall not be infringed." Various states drafted constitutions with similar provisions. Their intended meaning became the subject of debate in the early 19th century as states enacted "the first comprehensive laws prohibiting handguns and other concealed weapons," according to historian Saul Cornell.[48]

In 1813, Kentucky and Louisiana became the first states to ban the carrying of concealed weapons. Indiana did so in 1820, followed over the next two decades by Georgia, Tennessee, Virginia and Alabama.[49] The Southern states were responding to the extraordinary violence in the region, where an honor culture meant "that insults could not be safely ignored," wrote historian Clayton Cramer. "If someone insulted you publicly, or cast doubts about your honor, you challenged them to a duel" or pulled out a gun or Bowie knife to "settle the matter right on the spot."[50]

These early gun-control laws spawned legal challenges asserting constitutional rights to bear arms for individual self-defense. Most courts disagreed and upheld the laws, interpreting the right to bear arms as a community duty and not an individual right. However, "a few courts embraced the new ideology of gun rights," wrote Cornell.[51]

While some states were tightening gun regulations, "others, such as Mississippi and Connecticut, were writing into their constitutions more robust statements affirming the right of individuals to have weapons for self-defense," he wrote. At the same time, "Other states rejected the new language and reaffirmed the traditional civic model of the right to bear arms." For example, Maine's constitution, adopted in 1820, declared that "every citizen has a right to keep and bear arms for the common defense."[52]

Federal Gun Control

The NRA was not initially a gun-rights organization. "Dismayed by the lack of marksmanship shown by their troops [during the Civil War], Union veterans Col. William C. Church and Gen. George Wingate formed the National Rifle Association in 1871," reads the NRA website. Its primary goal would be to "promote and encourage rifle shooting on a scientific basis," according to Church.[53]

The NRA held target-shooting competitions and sponsored gun clubs and shooting ranges. Membership swelled between World War I (1914-1918) and World War II (1939-1945), when the U.S. military gave more than 200,000 surplus rifles to NRA members for free or at government cost.

The NRA also helped write model state gun-control legislation containing some provisions similar to those vehemently opposed by the association today. The Uniform Firearms Act, produced by an American Bar Association commission in 1926, applied mostly to handguns. It recommended that states require individuals to apply for a license to carry a concealed gun in public and that states issue such licenses with discretion. Handgun sellers had to be licensed, keep sales records and forward them to law enforcement officials and refrain from selling guns to those convicted of violent crimes.[54]

The NRA promoted this model legislation nationwide, and numerous states adopted it in whole or in part. In fact, a 1938 scholarly article concluded: "Today the carrying of concealed pistols is either prohibited absolutely or permitted only with a license in every state but two."[55]

Congress came later to gun control. The federal government's first major attempt occurred in the 1930s as Prohibition-era gangsters with compact machine guns outgunned city police, and notorious criminals such as John Dillinger, Bonnie Parker and Clyde Barrow, George "Machine Gun" Kelly, Charles "Pretty Boy" Floyd and Kate "Ma" Barker used guns and cars for crime sprees across state lines.

The National Firearms Act of 1934, signed into law by President Franklin D. Roosevelt, imposed a $200 tax on the manufacture, sale or transfer of machine guns and "sawed-off" shotguns and rifles with barrels less than 18 inches long. Anyone possessing such guns had to register them with the U.S. Treasury Department. While no one expected criminals to comply, their failure to do so meant that if caught with such a gun, a criminal could be jailed for tax evasion or non-registration, and "the government wouldn't have to prove that the person had killed anyone," wrote Winkler.[56]

The Roosevelt administration initially wanted to include handguns in the law, a provision the NRA opposed because it said it would make it difficult for ordinary citizens to defend themselves against criminals. After a massive

Background-Check System Has Serious Gaps

Crucial mental-health and drug-abuse records are not included in the database.

The nation's system for checking the background of gun buyers is supposed to help keep firearms out of the hands of felons, fugitives, drug abusers, people legally determined to be dangerous or incompetent to manage their affairs due to mental illness or those who have been committed to a mental institution, among others. Licensed firearms dealers call or email the National Instant Criminal Background Check System (NICS) and usually receive an immediate answer about whether to deny or allow a sale.

But the NICS database has serious gaps. Crucial mental-health and drug-abuse records are missing because states are not required to share them with NICS. They do so voluntarily. "Unfortunately, as long as these gaps remain, they are going to be fatal," says John Feinblatt, chairman of New York-based Mayors Against Illegal Guns, a coalition of 800 mayors that issued a recent report on gaps in the background system.

The report points to two mass killers who eluded the background check system:

- Seung Hui Cho passed several background checks to purchase the guns he used to kill 32 people and himself at Virginia Tech University in 2007, despite a judge's earlier determination that he was mentally ill. Virginia had never entered his mental-health records in the NCIS system.
- Jared Loughner had a history of drug abuse, according to media accounts, that was never reported to NCIS before he passed background checks to purchase guns he used to kill six people and critically wound 13 others — including Rep. Gabrielle Giffords, D-Ariz., in Tucson in 2011. [1]

Before the Virginia Tech shootings, only Alabama, Colorado, Connecticut and Georgia required agencies to share relevant mental-health records with NCIS. After the shootings, 19 additional states — including Virginia — adopted such laws. [2]

The federal government also increased funding to help states with record keeping and reporting after the Virginia Tech shootings.

Since then, the gap has narrowed. From 2004 to 2011, states increased the number of mental-health records available to NICS for background checks by 500 percent. However, according to the Government Accountability Office (GAO), a federal watchdog agency, "this progress largely reflects the efforts of 12 states." Most states, the GAO said, "have made little or no progress in providing these records." [3]

"Many states are still performing poorly," says Feinblatt. For instance, 23 have reported fewer than 100 mental-health records to the federal background-check database since its creation in 1999, and 44 states have submitted fewer than 10 records about drug abuse. As a result, Mayors Against Illegal Guns has concluded that millions of records identifying drug abusers and people with serious mental illness are absent from the system. [4]

But even if the background check system worked perfectly, it would have only a marginal impact on gun violence, says Jeffrey Swanson, a professor of psychiatry at Duke University and a leading expert in the causes and control of violence. "It would probably reduce overall gun violence against others by 4 or 5 percent," says Swanson, because the mentally ill account for a very small fraction of violent crime.

NRA-organized letter writing campaign, Congress dropped the handgun provision.

The NRA supported the law because it was an "indirect" approach to controlling gun violence. "I think that under the Constitution the United States has no jurisdiction to legislate in a police sense with respect to firearms," NRA president Karl T. Frederick testified at a 1934 congressional hearing before the law was passed. "I think that is exclusively a matter for state regulation, and I think that the only possible way in which the United States can legislate is through

its taxing power, which is an indirect method of approach, through its control over interstate commerce, which was perfectly proper, and through control over importations."[57]

Four years later, Congress expanded the federal government's reach, requiring gun sellers to obtain a license from the Internal Revenue Service and prohibiting the sale of guns and ammunition to felons — provisions the NRA supported.

"After this flurry of activity, Congress and the NRA went back to their respective corners and more or less left

While the mentally ill are responsible for close to 20 percent of mass shootings, said Michael Stone, a New York forensic psychiatrist, "most mass murders are done by working-class men who've been jilted, fired or otherwise humiliated — and who then undergo a crisis of rage and get out one of the 300 million guns in our country and do their thing." [5]

In an article earlier this year, Swanson and his colleagues detailed other flaws in assumptions underlying the background-check system. [6] For example, the small fraction of the mentally ill who are dangerous often don't seek treatment before doing something harmful, so they would not show up in a background-check database. And even when they do seek help, doctors often can't identify them as dangerous, according to studies. "Psychiatrists are just not very good at predicting who is going to be violent or not," says Swanson. "It's not much better than chance."

Despite that record, New York's newest gun-control law requires a doctor, psychologist, registered nurse or licensed clinical social worker who determines that a patient is a danger to himself or others to report that patient to the government. The government may then decide to prevent the person from possessing a firearm or revoke an existing license. [7] Under current professional guidelines, only involuntary hospitalizations and direct threats made by patients are required to be reported to state authorities, who then share the information with the federal background-check database, according to *The New York Times*. [8]

Many mental-health professionals oppose this new provision, fearing that people will avoid treatment or not reveal their true thoughts in therapy. "If people with suicidal or homicidal impulses avoid treatment for fear of being reported in this way, they may be more likely to act on those impulses," said Paul Appelbaum, director of law, ethics and psychiatry at New York's Columbia University Medical Center. [9]

Some experts say it's debatable whether mental-health professionals will take the reporting requirement seriously, because the law does not hold them liable if the decision to report or not to report a patient to authorities is made — in the statute's wording — "reasonably and in good faith." [10]

— *Barbara Mantel*

[1]"Fatal Gaps," Mayors Against Illegal Guns, November 2011, p. 2, www.mayorsagainstillegalguns.org/downloads/pdf/maig_mimeo_revb .pdf.

[2]*Ibid.*, p. 14.

[3]"Sharing Promising Practices and Assessing Incentives Could Better Position Justice to Assist States in Providing Records for Background Checks," Government Accountability Office, July 2012, p. 9, www.gao .gov/assets/600/592452.pdf.

[4]"Fatal Gaps," *op. cit.*, p. 3.

[5]Benedict Carey and Anemona Hartocollis, "Warning Signs of Violent Acts Often Unclear," *The New York Times*, Jan. 15, 2013, www.nytimes .com/2013/01/16/health/breaking-link-of-violence-and-mental-illness .html?_r=0.

[6]Jeffrey W. Swanson, *et al.*, "Preventing Gun Violence Involving People with Serious Mental Illness," *Reducing Gun Violence in America: Informing Policy with Evidence and Analysis* (2013), p. 36.

[7]"Program Bill #1," New York Legislative Bill Drafting Commission, pp. 19-20, www.governor.ny.gov/assets/documents/GPB_1_GUNS_ BILL_LBD_12007_03_3.pdf.

[8]Carey and Hartocollis, *op. cit.*

[9]"Experts: Tougher N.Y. gun control law may discourage therapy," The Associated Press, Jan. 16, 2013, www.usatoday.com/story/news/ nation/2013/01/15/ny-gun-law-therapy/1836323.

[10]"Program Bill #1," *op. cit.*, p. 20.

each other alone," wrote journalist Osha Gray Davidson. The NRA's "lobbying wing remained incidental to the organization's primary mission of serving hunters and target shooters."[58]

Gun Debate

That changed dramatically three decades later. "The 1960s were the turning point for the cultural war over guns as we know it," wrote Whitney. Rising crime, racial tensions and a loss of public confidence in the police "led millions of Americans to buy weapons for personal protection," he wrote.

Despite more guns and more homicides, Congress was "reluctant to pass gun laws that would be taken as a threat to the lawful use of weapons by ordinary Americans," said Whitney.[59]

Congress took no action on guns after the assassination of President John F. Kennedy in Dallas in 1963. But public opinion shifted a few years later, as race riots engulfed the nation's cities and members of the revolutionary Black

Getty Images/Mark Wilson

Wayne LaPierre, the executive vice president of the National Rifle Association (NRA), has criticized proposed gun-control legislation, although a January Pew Research Center poll shows 85 percent of gun owners support making private gun sales subject to background checks. Only 43 percent of gun owners, however, said they support a ban on assault-style weapons.

Panther Party openly — and legally — displayed their guns in public to attract media attention. And after the assassinations of civil rights leader Dr. Martin Luther King Jr. and Democratic senator and presidential candidate Robert F. Kennedy two months apart in 1968, President Lyndon B. Johnson pleaded with Congress to pass gun-control legislation "in the name of sanity, in the name of safety and in the name of an aroused nation."[60] In October, he signed into law the Gun Control Act of 1968.

The statute requires all persons manufacturing, importing or selling firearms as a business to be federally licensed; prohibits the interstate sale of firearms through the mail; bans all interstate sales of handguns; lists categories of people to whom firearms may not be sold, including convicted felons and the seriously mentally ill; and requires dealers to maintain records of gun sales.

Franklin Orth, NRA executive vice president — the seat of power at the organization — testified before Congress in favor of the law. "We do not think any sane American, who calls himself an American, can object to placing into this bill the instrument which killed the president of the United States," he said.

But a growing number of NRA members were furious at Orth. "Their objections didn't so much stem from opposition to any specific sections of the legislation; it was the concept of gun control itself that they disliked, even hated," wrote Davidson.[61]

The 1968 dispute was "the opening volley in what was to become an all-out war, one that would split the gun group wide open over the next decade," wrote Davidson. The division pitted mostly older members who believed the NRA should focus on teaching gun safety and organizing shooting competitions and hunting clinics against younger members who wanted the NRA to focus on blocking any and all gun-control measures as violations of the Second Amendment. At the organization's 1976 annual meeting in Cincinnati, the young "hard-liners" took control, using parliamentary procedure to shift power from officials to the membership, which then voted out the old guard and voted in the new.

"The Cincinnati Revolt (as the episode became known) changed forever the face of the NRA," according to Davidson. It "became more than a rifle club. It became the Gun Lobby."[62]

In 1986, the NRA scored a victory when President Ronald Reagan signed into law the Firearm Owners' Protection Act. It prohibits civilian transfer or possession of machine guns but legalizes shipments of ammunition through the mail; allows gun owners to transport firearms through states where they are banned; prohibits the federal government from maintaining a registry of guns and their owners; and mandates that the Bureau of Alcohol, Tobacco and Firearms (ATF) inspect licensed gun dealers for compliance with the 1968 law no more than once a year. The NRA had complained that ATF agents had been harassing dealers.

The pendulum swung the other way under President Bill Clinton. In December 1993 he signed the Brady Handgun Violence Prevention Act instituting background checks for gun purchases through licensed dealers. The law was named after Reagan Press Secretary James Brady, who was seriously wounded in an assassination attempt on Reagan in 1981. And in 1994 Clinton signed a measure banning what it defined as assault weapons and large-capacity ammunition magazines. The NRA vehemently opposed both laws. After the Brady Act was passed, the NRA told its members that rogue government agents will start to "go house to house, kicking in the law-abiding gun owners' doors."[63]

Congress has passed no major gun-control legislation since then. In 2008, the Supreme Court surprised gun-control advocates in its *District of Columbia v. Heller* ruling, which nullified Washington, D.C.'s ban on handgun ownership by declaring that individuals have a Second Amendment right to possess firearms "for traditionally lawful purposes, such as self-defense within the home." But the court made it clear that its opinion did not "cast doubt" on a wide variety of gun-control laws that regulated who could possess firearms, where they could be carried and how they could be sold. The court also recognized limitations on "dangerous and unusual" weapons but did not define them.[64]

"The court went out of its way to make clear that the right to bear arms can co-exist with gun control," says Winkler.

CURRENT SITUATION

New York Is First

New York has become the first — and so far only — state to pass gun-control legislation since the Newtown shootings. "I'm proud to be a New Yorker because New York is doing something — because we are fighting back," Democratic Gov. Andrew M. Cuomo said in mid-January as he signed the New York Secure Ammunition and Firearms Enforcement Act, or SAFE Act, into law.[65]

The act makes the state's already-strict gun regulations some of the nation's toughest. It broadens the definition of banned assault weapons; requires owners of existing assault weapons, grandfathered under the law, to register them with the New York State Police; reduces the limit on magazine capacity from 10 rounds of ammunition to seven; requires background checks of not only gun purchasers but also ammunition buyers; expands background checks to private sales, except between immediate family members; and establishes tougher penalties for the use of illegal guns.

The legislation won praise from gun-control advocates, including New York City Mayor Michael R. Bloomberg,

who said it "protects the Second Amendment rights of people, and at the same time it makes all New Yorkers safer."[66]

But 34 of 62 New York counties have passed resolutions demanding that lawmakers repeal the act.[67] And a state court has agreed to review whether the new law was rushed through the legislature in violation of the state constitution. "To have Cuomo dictate to the honest gun owners of New York because of the few criminals is criminal in itself," says Harold "Budd" Schroeder, chairman of the Shooters Committee on Political Education (SCOPE), a volunteer gun-rights organization with 12 chapters across the state.

In addition, "the law is unworkable," says Schroeder. While Feinstein dropped from her proposed federal assault-weapons ban a requirement that owners of grandfathered weapons register their guns, New York state's law kept a registration provision. "If you don't require registration, someone could say that they had the gun when the ban went into effect, and there is no way to prove that they didn't. It's an enforcement tool," says Cutilletta of the Law Center to Prevent Violence.

Schroeder, like the NRA, calls registration the first step toward firearms confiscation. However, seven states and Washington, D.C., require registration of some or all firearms and "no guns have been confiscated," says Cutilletta. "It's either paranoia or it's a political argument to try to scare people."

Nevertheless, a civil disobedience movement is brewing. "The sense I get from all the gun owners I have been talking to is that the [New York] law says register your long guns — and that is not going to happen," says Schroeder. According to the *New York Post*, gun-club leaders, gun dealers and Second Amendment advocacy groups are organizing a registration boycott. While the boycott's size won't be known until the registration deadline of April 15, 2014, the state expects "widespread violations," an unnamed Cuomo-administration source told the newspaper. "Many of these assault-rifle owners aren't going to register; we realize that," the source said. Failing to register is a class-A misdemeanor, punishable by up to a year in prison.[68]

More State Action

Currently, few states have strict gun-control measures on the books. Six states and Washington, D.C., require

State Gun Laws Vary Widely

Since the massacre at Sandy Hook Elementary School, state legislatures have been debating various proposals for changing gun laws, but so far only New York's has acted. It joins California, Rhode Island and the District of Columbia in adopting some of the nation's toughest gun measures, including requiring "universal" background checks on all gun purchases, some of which are now exempt under the federal Brady Act.

Key State Gun Laws*

Universal Background Checks
(Checks required for sales by both licensed dealers and private sellers)

- California, New York, Rhode Island and Washington, D.C., require universal background checks on sales of all classes of firearms.
- Maryland requires universal background checks on purchases of handguns and assault weapons.
- Connecticut and Pennsylvania require universal background checks on all handgun sales.

Licenses and Permits

- Anyone buying or owning a gun in Hawaii, Illinois, Massachusetts or New Jersey must get a license or permit.
- California, Connecticut, Iowa, Michigan, New York, North Carolina and Rhode Island require a license or permit for handguns only.

Safety Training and Exams

- Massachusetts requires gun buyers to take a firearms safety course before buying a gun.
- California, Connecticut, Hawaii, Michigan and Rhode Island also require gun-safety training, but only for handgun purchasers or owners.

Assault Weapons

- Although the definitions of "assault weapon" vary, the following states ban sales of assault weapons: California, Connecticut, Massachusetts, New Jersey, New York and the District of Columbia.
- Hawaii and Maryland ban assault pistols.
- Maryland, Minnesota and Virginia regulate the sale and use of assault weapons.

Large-Capacity Ammunition Magazines

- New York has banned magazines holding more than seven rounds.
- California, Hawaii, Massachusetts and the District of Columbia ban magazines holding more than 10 rounds. New Jersey bans magazines holding more than 15 rounds.
- Maryland bans magazines holding more than 20 rounds.

* includes the District of Columbia

Source: "Search Gun Laws By Policy," Law Center to Prevent Gun Violence, 2013, smartgunlaws.org/search-gun-law-by-gun-policy/

universal background checks — for private firearm sales and sales through licensed dealers — but in some states the requirements don't apply to all types of guns. Four states require licenses for anyone buying or owning any firearm, while seven states require only handgun buyers and owners to be licensed. Seven states and Washington, D.C., ban variously defined assault weapons, while six of those states also ban large-capacity ammunition magazines.[69]

But by the first week of March, 1,159 firearms-related bills had been introduced in state legislatures, 308 more than during the same period in 2012, according to Cutilletta. Slightly more than half of this year's proposals would expand gun controls. Some would for the first time ban assault weapons or limit magazine size, such as proposals in Vermont, South Carolina and Virginia; others would tighten existing bans, as New York did. Several would require background checks on private firearms sales, such as a measure introduced in New Mexico.

"Regulating ammunition sales is also popular," says Cutilletta, "like banning Internet sales or mail-order sales of ammunition or requiring a background check before buying ammunition — that's been introduced in California." Gun safety also is being addressed; laws that would regulate the way guns are stored have been introduced in Montana, Nebraska, California, Missouri and South Carolina.

Perhaps no state is being watched more closely by both sides of the gun debate than Colorado, a historically pro-gun state and home to two of the nation's most notorious mass shootings: the 1999 Columbine High School massacre and last year's killing spree at an Aurora movie theater.[70] In late February, the state's Democratic-controlled House approved a package of bills that would require background checks for all gun transactions, paid for by the purchaser; ban ammunition magazines with more than 15 rounds; and allow colleges to ban concealed weapons on campus. No Republicans voted for the bills, and several Democrats crossed party lines to vote against them.

"This is part of our heritage," Democratic Rep. Ed Vigil said during the debate, explaining why he opposed the measures. "This is part of what it took to settle this land. I cannot turn my back on that." The bills have moved to the state Senate, where Democratic control is much slimmer.[71]

Meanwhile, pressure is building on Connecticut's elected officials to strengthen the state's gun-control laws in the wake of the Newtown shootings. A bipartisan legislative task force has missed a self-imposed deadline to recommend consensus gun-control measures, and a separate task force appointed by Democratic Gov. Dannel P. Malloy is not expected to produce its recommendation until later this month.

"The public is demanding they act," said Scott McLean, an analyst with the Quinnipiac University Polling Institute in Hamden, Conn. In mid-February, 5,500 people rallied for gun control at the statehouse. Soon after, Malloy announced his own proposals — expanded background checks, lower magazine limits and a broader definition of assault weapons — and vowed to push his plan through the legislature. "I think it's time to lay it out on the table and get it done," Malloy said.[72]

Nullification

Just under half of the firearm-related measures introduced in states this year would loosen gun controls. Some would allow guns to be carried in public schools, and others attempt to nullify new, and in some cases existing, federal gun-control laws. For instance, Alaska Republican state Rep. Michael Kelly has proposed the Alaska Firearm Freedom Act, which would make it illegal for federal agents to enforce new gun-control legislation on Alaskan soil. Similar legislation has been introduced in 23 other states. In two — Montana and Wyoming — such bills have passed the House, and a nullification measure has passed the Senate in Kentucky.[73]

These bills are being promoted by a national states'-rights group called the Tenth Amendment Center, which argues that states do not have to enforce laws they believe are unconstitutional.* But the U.S. Supreme Court has repeatedly rejected state nullification laws. "The states can't simply choose to defy and override a valid federal law," said Allen Rostron, a professor of constitutional law at the University of Missouri-Kansas City. The U.S. Constitution deems federal statutes "the supreme law of the land," he said.[74]

Liability Insurance

In at least six states legislators have proposed bills requiring gun owners to purchase liability insurance. Backers hope insurers would reward safe behavior — such as having a trigger lock — with lower premiums, according to *The New York Times*. "I believe that if we get the private sector and insurance companies involved in gun safety, we can help prevent a number of gun tragedies every year," said David P. Linsky, a Democratic state representative in Massachusetts. "Insurance companies are very good at evaluating risk factors and setting their premiums appropriately."

However, the insurance industry is wary of such proposals, according to the paper, especially if they require coverage for damages resulting not just from negligence but also from "willful acts," such as shooting an intruder, which are generally not covered.[75]

"Insurance will cover you if your home burns down in an electrical fire, but it will not cover you if you burn down your own house, and you cannot insure yourself for arson," said Robert P. Hartwig, president of the New York-based Insurance Information Institute.[76]

OUTLOOK
Political Reality

Broad public support exists for certain gun-control measures, and a sharp partisan divide separates the public on others, according to a Pew Research Center poll. Eighty-three percent of Americans support background checks for private and gun-show sales, a position for which there is bipartisan agreement. But only slightly more than half of Americans support proposals to ban

Should all gun sales be registered in a national database?

YES
Garen Wintemute
Baker-Teret Chair in Violence Prevention, University of California, Davis

Written for *CQ Global Researcher*, March 2013

An estimated 478,422 firearm-related violent crimes occurred in 2011, including 11,101 homicides. To help prevent such violence, federal statute prohibits felons and certain others from acquiring or possessing firearms. People who acquire firearms from licensed gun dealers and pawnbrokers must provide identification and undergo a background check to verify they can legally own them. The retailer keeps a permanent record of the transaction.

Our current system is plagued by two major shortcomings. First, perhaps 40 percent of all firearm acquisitions, and at least 80 percent of those made with criminal intent, are made from private parties. No identification need be shown, no background check conducted, no record kept.

Second, licensed retailers keep their records to themselves. If a firearm is used in a crime and an effort is made to trace its chain of ownership, the trace ordinarily ends with the first retail purchaser. Yet 85 percent of the time, the criminal who used the firearm is someone else. Without an archive of transactions, the firearm cannot be traced beyond its first purchaser.

Background checks and purchase denials are very effective, reducing by approximately 25 percent the risk of the buyer committing new firearm-related or violent crimes. Six states already require all firearm transfers to be routed through licensed retailers, so background checks are completed and records are kept.

In California, handgun transaction records are archived by the state's Department of Justice; records for rifles and shotguns will be added in January 2014. Comprehensive background-check policies interfere with the criminal acquisition of firearms and disrupt firearm trafficking. In California, traces of a firearm used in a crime end with the most recent purchaser, not the first. Cold cases become hot cases.

The United States should set a single, simple, equitable standard for firearm transfers. It should require all transfers (with certain exceptions for those within a family) to include a background check and a permanent record. The policy should not be limited to acquisitions at gun shows, which account for only a small proportion of private-party firearm transfers. To make it easier for law enforcement to trace firearms used in crimes, retailers should report to the FBI the make, model, caliber and serial number of the firearms they sell; they shouldn't have to report the purchasers, except for the first. Law enforcement can then trace a firearm used in a crime to its most recent transaction and obtain more information from the retailer.

NO
Stephen P. Halbrook
Attorney; Author, The Founders' Second Amendment

Written for *CQ Global Researcher*, March 2013

"your papers are not in order!" It's five years in prison for not registering to exercise a constitutional right. Unthinkable for any other right, but not the "right" to keep and bear arms — just ignore the "shall not be infringed" part of the Second Amendment.

Attorney General Eric Holder proposed that punishment for not registering a firearm in the District of Columbia when he was U.S. attorney there. Sen. Dianne Feinstein demands the registration of millions of "assault weapons," which means anything she wants it to mean. Right now, in the Southern Border States, anyone buying more than one semiautomatic rifle per week is reported to the Bureau of Alcohol, Tobacco, Firearms and Explosives.

New York City required registration of hunting rifles and other "long guns" in the 1960s. It later declared them "assault weapons" and sent the police to confiscate them. New York state just passed a law saying countless ordinary rifles have "assault" traits needing registration. California even records purchases of duck-hunting guns and single-shot rifles.

Criminals don't register guns. That's why, even where registration is required, the police don't check registration records before responding to crime scenes. Canada just abolished its billion-dollar gun-registration system because it never solved a single crime.

Germany just implemented a central database of all lawful firearms, a European Union diktat. The German interior minister promised very high security for handling the data, while a skeptic said "everything that is registered can be taken away by the government." Sound familiar? A year before the Nazis seized power, Germany decreed gun registration, and the Interior Minister warned at the time: "Precautions must be taken that these lists not . . . fall into the hands of radical elements." Hitler then used them first to disarm democratic "enemies of the state" and then, in 1938, the Jews during the violent pogrom known as Kristallnacht.

In France, Prime Minister Pierre Laval decreed gun registration. After France fell to Germany in 1940, Laval guided the French police to collaborate with the Nazis, who executed anyone failing to surrender firearms in 24 hours.

Americans were well aware of these events. Just before Pearl Harbor, Congress forbade registration of guns used for sport or self-defense. It did the same in the Firearms Owners' Protection Act of 1986 and Brady Act of 1993.

The purpose of registration is confiscation. Until then, the records are fodder for exploitation by hackers and burglars.

assault weapons and high-capacity ammunition magazines, and those opinions break along party lines.[77]

Similar thinking is reflected in the Democratic-controlled U.S. Senate, where the gun-control debate is currently centered. "I'm very optimistic about legislation on universal background checks, [because] you see even conservative politicians coming forward and supporting it," says Everitt of the Coalition to Stop Gun Violence. In fact, Republican Sen. John McCain of Arizona told NBC's "Meet the Press" on Feb. 17, "I think most of us will be able to support" bipartisan gun-control legislation whose centerpiece is an expansion of background checks.[78]

Support also is growing in the Senate for increased penalties for illegal gun trafficking and "straw purchases," in which an individual buys a gun through a licensed dealer and then passes the gun to someone who typically would not pass a background check. The Senate Judiciary Committee was scheduled to consider bills addressing those issues — plus school-safety measures, universal background checks and an assault-weapons ban — on March 7.

But the chances of Congress banning assault weapons are close to zero, says Gottlieb of the Second Amendment Foundation. "This is not going to go anywhere," he says. Many political analysts agree chances are slim and doubt that the controversial ban would become part of any gun-control legislation emerging from the Senate Judiciary Committee.

As an alternative, Feinstein could offer her legislation banning assault weapons and limiting large-capacity magazines on the floor of the Senate as an amendment. However, "If it's just offered as a floor amendment it's likely to fail, because it's a stand-alone provision and Republicans will filibuster and it will be almost impossible for Democrats to get 60 votes," said Darrell West, director of governance studies at the Washington-based Brookings Institution.[79] (A filibuster is a procedure to delay or block a vote by one or more senators speaking on any topic for as long as they wish. It takes 60 Senators to agree to end a filibuster.)

While Everitt favors a ban on assault weapons, his highest priority is a requirement for universal background checks. "Universal background checks are a staple of any civilized country's gun laws, and one that we've never had on the books and should have been done decades ago in this country," he says.

Meanwhile, the Republican-controlled House is waiting to see what the Senate does before it takes up the issue of gun violence. "They feel if we're able to do something, there might be a chance," said Senate Judiciary Committee Chairman Leahy." "If we're unable, frankly, they're not going to try anything at all. I think that's a political reality."[80]

NOTES

1. Ray Rivera and Peter Applebome, "Sandy Hook Parents' Testimony to Legislature Reflects Divide on Guns," *The New York Times*, Jan. 28, 2013, www.nytimes.com/2013/01/29/nyregion/connecticut-legislature-hearing-on-gun-violence.html.

2. Mattioli and Heslin quotes are from *ibid.*

3. "Gun Violence Prevention Testimony — Henson," YouTube, Feb. 27, 2013, www.youtube.com/watch?v=sJt-yrXKYG4&feature=endscreen.

4. "President Obama Makes a Statement on the Shooting in Newtown, Connecticut," The White House, Dec. 14, 2012, www.whitehouse.gov/photos-and-video/video/2012/12/14/president-obama-makes-statement-shooting-newtown-connecticut.

5. For background, see Sarah Glazer, "Video Games," *CQ Researcher*, Nov. 10, 2006, pp. 937-960; updated, Sept. 23, 2011. For background on gun debates, see the following *CQ Researchers*: Kenneth Jost, "Gun Violence," May 25, 2007, pp. 457-480; Bob Adams, "Gun Control Debate," Nov. 12, 2004, pp. 949-972.

6. National Rifle Association press conference, Dec. 21, 2012, www.washingtonpost.com/blogs/post-politics/wp/2012/12/21/nras-wayne-lapierre-put-armed-police-officers-in-every-school/.

7. Barbara Raymond, "Assigning Police Officers to School," U.S. Department of Justice, April 2010, pp. 1, 7, www.cops.usdoj.gov/Publications/e041028272-assign-officers-to-schools.pdf.

8. "The Andrea Tantaros Show," Jan. 14, 2013, www.trn1.com/tantaros-audio.

9. "Gun Rights Supporter Sen. Mark Warner Says Tighter Firearms Laws Needed," "Newshour," PBS,

Dec. 18, 2012, www.pbs.org/newshour/bb/politics/july-dec12/warner_12-18.html.

10. "Now is the Time: Gun Violence Reduction Executive Actions," The White House, Jan. 26, 2013, www.whitehouse.gov/sites/default/files/docs/wh_now_is_the_time_actions.pdf.

11. Ruby Cramer, "Gun Control Advocates: Obama's Proposals 'Unprecedented,' " *Buzzfeed*, Jan. 16, 2013, www.buzzfeed.com/rubycramer/gun-control-advocates-obamas-proposals-unpreced.

12. Joseph Gerth, "Mitch McConnell vows to block President Obama's gun control initiatives," *The Courier-Journal*, Jan. 20, 2013, www.courier-journal.com/article/20130119/NEWS010605/301190088/Mitch-McConnell-vows-block-President-Obama-s-gun-control-initiatives?nclick_check=1.

13. Garen J. Wintemute, "Tragedy's Legacy," *The New England Journal of Medicine*, Jan. 31, 2013, p. 397, www.nejm.org/doi/full/10.1056/NEJMp1215491.

14. Letter, The University of Chicago Crime Lab, Jan. 10, 2013, p. 1, http://crimelab.uchicago.edu/sites/crimelab.uchicago.edu/files/uploads/Biden%20Commission%20letter_20130110_final.pdf.

15. "Crime in the United States 2011," Table 1, FBI, www.fbi.gov/about-us/cjis/ucr/crime-in-the-u.s/2011/crime-in-the-u.s.-2011/tables/table-1; "Uniform Crime Reporting Statistics Data Building Tool," FBI, www.ucrdatatool.gov/Search/Crime/State/TrendsInOneVar.cfm.

16. "WISQARS Injury Mortality Reports, 1981-1991," Centers for Disease Control and Prevention, http://webappa.cdc.gov/sasweb/ncipc/mortrate9.html; "WISQARS Injury Mortality Reports, National and Regional, 1999-2010," Centers for Disease Control and Prevention, http://webappa.cdc.gov/sasweb/ncipc/mortrate10_us.html.

17. William Krouse, "Gun Control Legislation: Executive Summary," Congressional Research Service, Nov. 14, 2012, p. 8, www.fas.org/sgp/crs/misc/RL32842.pdf.

18. "Firearms and Violence: A Critical Review," National Research Council of the National Academies, December 2004, p. 3, www.nap.edu/openbook.php?record_id=10881&page=2.

19. Zachary Roth, "Blackout: How the NRA suppressed gun violence research," MSNBC, Jan. 14, 2013, http://tv.msnbc.com/2013/01/14/blackout-how-the-nra-suppressed-gun-violence-research.

20. Jordan Yerman, "Jacob Tyler Roberts IDed as Oregon mall shooter: Photos," examiner.com, Dec. 12, 2012, www.examiner.com/article/jacob-tyler-roberts-ided-as-oregon-mall-shooter-photos.

21. "Mass Shooting Incidents in America (1984-2012)," Citizens Crime Commission of New York City, www.nycrimecommission.org/initiative1-shootings.php.

22. *Ibid.*

23. "Feinstein Introduces Bill on Assault Weapons, High-Capacity Magazines," The Office of Senator Dianne Feinstein, U.S. Senate, Jan. 24, 2013, www.feinstein.senate.gov/public/index.cfm/press-releases?ID=5dffbf07-d8e5-42aa-9f22-0743368dd754.

24. Eric Lichtblau, "N.R.A. Leaders Stand Firm Against Gun Restrictions," *The New York Times*, Dec. 23, 2012, http://thecaucus.blogs.nytimes.com/2012/12/23/n-r-a-leaders-defiant-in-television-appearances; "Wayne LaPierre Testimony Before the U.S. Senate Committee," National Rifle Association, Jan. 31, 2013, http://home.nra.org/classic.aspx/blog/350.

25. Christopher S. Koper, "An Updated Assessment of the Federal Assault Weapons Ban: Impacts on Gun Markets and Gun Violence, 1994-2003," U.S. Department of Justice, June 2004, p. 1, www.sas.upenn.edu/jerrylee/research/aw_final2004.pdf.

26. David S. Fallis and James V. Grimaldi, "In Virginia, high-yield clip seizures rise," *The Washington Post*, Jan. 23, 2011, www.washingtonpost.com/wp-dyn/content/article/2011/01/22/AR2011012204046.html.

27. Koper, *op. cit.*

28. "Assault Weapons Ban of 2013," The Office of Senator Dianne Feinstein, U.S. Senate, Jan. 24, 2013, www.feinstein.senate.gov/public/index.cfm/assault-weapons-ban-summary.

29. Daniel W. Webster, *et al.*, "The Case for Gun Policy Reforms in America," Johns Hopkins Center for Gun Policy and Research, October 2012, p. 10, www.jhsph.edu/research/centers-and-institutes/

johns-hopkins-center-for-gun-policy-and-research/
publications/WhitePaper102512_CGPR.pdf.

30. For background see Kenneth Jost, "Gun Rights Debates," *CQ Researcher*, Oct. 31, 2008, pp. 889-912; updated July 22, 2010.

31. Philip J. Cook and Jens Ludwig, "Guns in America: Results of a Comprehensive National Survey on Firearms Ownership and Use," Police Foundation, 1996, p. 27, www.policefoundation.org/content/guns-america.

32. "Keystone of Obama gun control plan gains steam as Dem, GOP senators seek background check pact," The Associated Press (*The Washington Post*), Feb. 8, 2013.

33. Daniel W. Webster, *et al.*, "Preventing the Diversion of Guns to Criminals through Effective Firearm Sales Laws," *Reducing Gun Violence in America: Informing Policy with Evidence and Analysis* (2013), p. 110.

34. "Wayne LaPierre Testimony Before the U.S. Senate Committee," *op. cit.*

35. Philip J. Cook and Jens Ludwig, "The Limited Impact of the Brady Act: Evaluation and Implications," *Reducing Gun Violence in America: Informing Policy with Evidence and Analysis* (2013), pp. 22-25.

36. Wintemute, *op. cit.*, p. 398.

37. "Attorney General's Concealed Carry Report Shows Record Number of Licenses Issued in 2012," press release, Office of Ohio Attorney General, Feb. 27, 2013, www.ohioattorneygeneral.gov/Media/News-Releases/February-2013/Attorney-General's-Concealed-Carry-Report-Shows-Re.

38. "Guns in Public Places: The Increasing Threat of Hidden Guns in America," Law Center to Prevent Gun Violence," July 1, 2011, http://smartgunlaws.org/guns-in-public-places-the-increasing-threat-of-hidden-guns-in-america.

39. "NRA EVP and CEO Wayne LaPierre — Speech to CPAC 2011," YouTube, Feb. 10, 2011, www.youtube.com/watch?v=Bg_uy9_2a1U.

40. "Gun Control: States' Laws and Requirements for Concealed Carry Permits Vary across the Nation," U.S. Government Accountability Office, July 2012, pp. 75-76, www.gao.gov/assets/600/592552.pdf.

41. "Firearms and Violence: A Critical Review," *op. cit.*

42. Abhay Aneja, John J. Donohue III and Alexandria Zhang, "The Impact of Right-To-Carry Laws and the NRC Report: Lessons for the Empirical Evaluation of Law and Policy," Social Sciences Research Network, June 29, 2010, http://papers.ssrn.com/sol3/papers.cfm?abstract_id=1632599.

43. Ian Ayres and John J. Donohue III, "Shooting Down the 'More Guns, Less Crime' Hypothesis," *Stanford Law Review*, April 2003, pp. 1204-1205, http://islandia.law.yale.edu/ayers/Ayres_Donohue_article.pdf.

44. "Gun Control: States' Laws and Requirements for Concealed Carry Permits Vary across the Nation," *op. cit.*, p. 19.

45. Craig R. Whitney, *Living with Guns: A Liberal's Case for the Second Amendment* (2012), pp. 45-47.

46. Adam Winkler, *Gun Fight: The Battle Over the Right to Bear Arms in America* (2011), p. 116.

47. *Ibid.*

48. Saul Cornell, *A Well Regulated Militia: The Founding Fathers and the Origins of Gun Control in America* (2006), p. 4.

49. Clayton E. Cramer, *Concealed Weapon Laws of the Early Republic: Dueling, Southern Violence, and Moral Reform* (1999), pp. 2-3.

50. *Ibid.*, pp. 6-7.

51. Cornell, *op. cit.*, p. 4.

52. *Ibid.*, pp. 142-143.

53. "A Brief History of the NRA," www.nrahq.org/history.asp.

54. Winkler, *op. cit.*, pp. 208-209.

55. Sam B. Warner, "The Uniform Pistol Act," *Journal of Criminal Law and Criminology*, November-December 1938, p. 530.

56. Winkler, *op. cit.*, pp. 203-204.

57. "Hearings Before the Committee on Ways and Means," House of Representatives, Seventy-third Congress, on H.R. 9066, April and May 1934, p. 53, www.keepandbeararms.com/nra/nfa.htm#KarlT.

58. Osha Gray Davidson, *Under Fire: the NRA & the Battle for Gun Control* (1993), p. 29.

59. Whitney, *op. cit.*, p. 3.

60. *Ibid.*, pp. 5-6.

61. Davidson, *op. cit.*, p. 30.

62. *Ibid.*, pp. 30-31, 36.

63. Winkler, *op. cit.*, pp. 71-72.

64. "Personal Guns and the Second Amendment," *The New York Times*, Dec. 17, 2012, www.nytimes.com/2012/12/18/opinion/the-gun-challenge-second-amendment.html.

65. Thomas Kaplan, "Sweeping Limits on Guns Become Law in New York," *The New York Times*, Jan. 15, 2013, www.nytimes.com/2013/01/16/nyregion/tougher-gun-law-in-new-york.html.

66. *Ibid.*

67. "Documenting County and Town resolutions on the NY SAFE act," NY SAFE Resolutions, www.nysaferesolutions.com.

68. Fredric U. Dicker, "Hit us with your best shot, Andy!" *New York Post*, Jan. 21, 2013, www.nypost.com/p/news/local/hit_us_with_your_best_shot_andy_5rxZg0gYBJJhkLBtiTPMfJ.

69. "Private Sales Policy Summary," Law Center to Prevent Gun Violence, http://smartgunlaws.org/private-sales-policy-summary; "Licensing of Gun Owners and Purchasers Policy Summary," Law Center to Prevent Gun Violence, http://smartgunlaws.org/licensing-of-gun-owners-purchasers-policy-summary; "Summary of State Assault Weapon Laws," Law Center to Prevent Gun Violence, http://smartgunlaws.org/assault-weapons-policy-summary; "Large Capacity Ammunition Magazines Policy Summary," Law Center to Prevent Gun Violence, http://smartgunlaws.org/large-capacity-ammunition-magazines-policy-summary.

70. For background, see Kathy Koch, "Zero Tolerance," *CQ Researcher*, March 10, 2000, pp. 185-208. Also see Kathy Koch, "School Violence," *CQ Researcher*, Oct. 9, 1998, pp. 881-904.

71. Amanda Paulson, "Gun-control bills pass Colorado House: Was Aurora a tipping point?" *The Christian Science Monitor*, Feb. 20, 2013, www.csmonitor.com/USA/2013/0220/Gun-control-bills-pass-Colorado-House-Was-Aurora-a-tipping-point-video.

72. Laura Nahmias, "Malloy Charts New Course on Gun Laws," *The Wall Street Journal*, Feb. 21, 2013, http://online.wsj.com/article/SB10001424127887324048904578316573460812236.html.

73. "2nd Amendment Preservation Act: 2013 Legislation," Tenth Amendment Center, http://tracking.tenthamendmentcenter.com/2ndamendment.

74. John Hancock and Brad Cooper, "Legislators in Missouri, Kansas and elsewhere look to nullify federal laws," *The Kansas City Star*, Jan. 23, 2013, http://midwestdemocracy.com/articles/states-looking-to-nullify-the-feds.

75. Michael Cooper and Mary Williams Walsh, "Buying a Gun? States Consider Insurance Rule," *The New York Times*, Feb. 21, 2013, www.nytimes.com/2013/02/22/us/in-gun-debate-a-bigger-role-seen-for-insurers.html.

76. *Ibid.*

77. "Gun Control: Key Data Points from Pew Research," Pew Research Center, Feb. 7, 2013, www.pewresearch.org/2013/02/07/gun-control-key-data-points-from-pew-research.

78. Peter Grier, "Which gun control measures are gaining momentum in Congress?" *The Christian Science Monitor*, Feb. 19, 2013, www.csmonitor.com/USA/DC-Decoder/Decoder-Wire/2013/0219/Which-gun-control-measures-are-gaining-momentum-in-Congress-video.

79. Alexander Bolton, "Senate Dems face gun-control dilemma," *The Hill*, Feb. 6, 2013, http://thehill.com/homenews/senate/281343-senate-democrats-face-gun-dilemma.

80. Grier, *op. cit.*

BIBLIOGRAPHY

Selected Sources

Books

Cornell, Saul, *A Well Regulated Militia: The Founding Fathers and the Origins of Gun Control in America*, Oxford University Press, 2006.
A constitutional historian examines the origins of the Second Amendment and the ensuing constitutional debate.

Webster, Daniel W., and Jon S. Vernick, eds., *Reducing Gun Violence in America: Informing Policy with Evidence and Analysis*, The Johns Hopkins University Press, *2013*.
Leading experts summarize relevant research and recommend policies to reduce gun violence, including expanding background checks to private firearms sales and prohibiting more categories of criminals from possessing firearms.

Whitney, Craig R., *Living with Guns: A Liberal's Case for the Second Amendment*, PublicAffairs, *2012*.
A journalist explores the history behind today's polarized debate about guns and concludes that both more guns and more gun control would help reduce violence.

Winkler, Adam, *Gun Fight: The Battle Over the Right to Bear Arms in America*, W.W. Norton & Co., Inc., *2011*.
An expert in constitutional law examines America's four-century political battle over gun control and the right to bear arms.

Articles

Dicker, Fredric U., "Hit us with your best shot, Andy!" *New York Post*, Jan. 21, 2013, www.nypost.com/p/news/local/hit_us_with_your_best_shot_andy_5rxZg0gYBJJhkLBtiTPMfJ.
Gun-rights advocates and gun dealers are organizing a boycott of New York's new gun-control law.

Gerth, Joseph, "Mitch McConnell vows to block President Obama's gun control initiatives," *The Courier-Journal*, Jan. 20, 2013, www.courier-journal.com/article/20130119/NEWS010605/301190088/Mitch-McConnell-vows-block-President-Obama-s-gun-control-initiatives?nclick_check=1.
In a taped call to Kentucky gun owners, the Senate minority leader promises to block the president's gun-control proposals.

Grier, Peter, "Which gun control measures are gaining momentum in Congress?" *The Christian Science Monitor*, Feb. 19, 2013, www.csmonitor.com/USA/DC-Decoder/Decoder-Wire/2013/0219/Which-gun-control-measures-are-gaining-momentum-in-Congress-video.

Support in the Senate is growing for expanded background checks, but backing for the more controversial ban on assault weapons is slim.

Redden, Molly, "Meet John Lott, the Man Who Wants to Arm America's Teachers," *The New Republic*, Dec. 19, 2012, p. 1, www.newrepublic.com/blog/plank/111263/meet-john-lott-the-man-who-wants-to-arm-teach-ers-carry-guns.
Economist John Lott argues that carrying concealed weapons makes communities safer.

Roth, Zachary, "Blackout: How the NRA suppressed gun violence research," MSNBC, Jan. 14, 2013, http://tv.msnbc.com/2013/01/14/blackout-how-the-nra-suppressed-gun-violence-research.
In the 1990s, the National Rifle Association helped insert language into federal legislation restricting government-sponsored research on gun violence.

Reports & Studies

"Firearms and Violence: A Critical Review," National Research Council of the National Academies, December 2004, www.nap.edu/openbook.php?record_id=10881&page=2.
A prominent research council finds that reliable data and research on gun violence and gun control are lacking.

"Gun Control: States' Laws and Requirements for Concealed Carry Permits Vary Across the Nation," U.S. Government Accountability Office, July 2012, pp. 75-76, www.gao.gov/assets/600/592552.pdf.
An independent congressional agency evaluates states' concealed-carry laws.

"Guns in Public Places: The Increasing Threat of Hidden Guns in America," Law Center to Prevent Gun Violence, July 1, 2011, http://smartgunlaws.org/guns-in-public-places-the-increasing-threat-of-hidden-guns-in-america.
A gun-control advocacy group analyzes states' concealed-carry laws and concludes they lead to increased violence.

Koper, Christopher S., "An Updated Assessment of the Federal Assault Weapons Ban: Impacts on Gun Markets and Gun Violence, 1994-2003," U.S. Department of Justice, June 2004, www.sas.upenn.edu/jerrylee/research/aw_final2004.pdf.

A criminology professor finds that the federal ban on assault weapons had a negligible impact on crime.

Webster, Daniel W., *et al.*, "The Case for Gun Policy Reforms in America," Johns Hopkins Center for Gun Policy and Research, October 2012, p. 10, www.jhsph **.edu/research/centers-and-institutes/johns-hopkins-center-for-gun-policy-and-research/publications/ WhitePaper102512_CGPR.pdf.** A group of academic researchers argues for gun-control legislation.

For More Information

Brady Campaign to Prevent Gun Violence, 1225 Eye St., N.W., Suite 1100, Washington, DC 20005; 202-289-7319; www.bradycampaign.org. Education and advocacy group that works to pass federal and state laws to reduce gun violence.

Gun Owners of America, 800 Forbes Pl., Suite 102, Springfield, VA 22151; 703-321-8585; http://gunowners.org. Lobbying organization that works to preserve Second Amendment rights of gun owners.

Harvard Injury Control Research Center, 677 Huntington Ave., Boston, MA 02115; 617-432-8080; www.hsph .harvard.edu/hicrc. Academic research center that studies the causes of injury, as well as intervention strategies and policies.

Johns Hopkins Center for Gun Policy and Research, Bloomberg School of Public Health, 615 N. Wolfe St., Baltimore, MD 21205; 410-955-6878; www.jhsph.edu/ research/centers-and-institutes/johns-hopkins-center-for-gun-policy-and-research. Academic research center that works to reduce gun-related injuries and deaths.

Law Center to Prevent Gun Violence, 268 Bush St., #555, San Francisco, CA 94104; 415-433-2062; http://smartgun laws.org. National law center that promotes gun-control legislation and policies.

Mayors Against Illegal Guns, Mayor of New York City, City Hall, 260 Broadway, New York, NY 10007; 212-788-2958; www.mayorsagainstillegalguns.org. Coalition of 800 mayors supporting policies and laws to keep guns away from criminals.

National Rifle Association of America, 11250 Waples Mill Rd., Fairfax, VA 22030; 800-672-3888; http://nra.org. Membership organization that promotes gun ownership rights and trains firearm users.

National Shooting Sports Foundation, 11 Mile Hill Rd., Newtown, CT 06470; 203-426-1320; www.nssf.org. Trade association whose members include firearms manufacturers, distributors, retailers, shooting ranges, clubs and publishers.

Second Amendment Foundation, 12500 N.E. 10th Pl., Bellevue, WA 98005; 425-454-7012; www.saf.org. Advocacy group that promotes gun ownership rights through education and legal action.

Tenth Amendment Center; www.tenthamendmentcenter. com. Think tank advocating states' rights and the decentralization of federal government power.

Violence Policy Center, 1730 Rhode Island Ave., N.W., Suite 1014, Washington, DC 20036; 202-822-8200; www .vpc.org. Advocacy and research organization working to reduce gun violence.

11

Immigration Conflict

Kenneth Jost

Arizona residents rally in Phoenix on July 31, 2010, in support of the state's hard-hitting immigration law, which gives police new responsibilities to look for immigration law violators. Five states last year followed Arizona's lead. The U.S. Supreme Court will hear arguments on the disputed Arizona measure on April 25.

From *The CQ Researcher*, March 9, 2012.

Micky Hammon minced no words when he urged his fellow Alabama legislators to enact what would become the toughest of a batch of new state laws cracking down on illegal immigrants. "This bill is designed to make it difficult for them to live here so they will deport themselves," Hammon, leader of the Alabama House of Representatives' Republican majority, said during the April 5, 2011, debate on the bill.[1]

Immigrant-rights groups say the law, which took effect Sept. 28 after partly surviving a court challenge, is as tough as Hammon hoped — and more. "It's been pretty devastating," says Mary Bauer, legal director of the Southern Poverty Law Center in Montgomery, Alabama's capital. "Tens of thousands of people have left, and the people who remain are completely terrorized by this law."

Among other provisions, Alabama's law requires state and local law enforcement officers to determine the immigration status of anyone arrested, detained or stopped if there is a "reasonable suspicion" that the person is an alien "unlawfully present" in the United States. Failure to carry alien-registration papers is made a state crime, punishable by up to 30 days in jail for a first offense.

Alabama, with an estimated 120,000 unlawful aliens living within its borders as of 2010, was one of five states that last year followed Arizona's lead a year earlier in giving police new responsibilities to look for immigration law violators.* Republican-controlled legislatures in each of the states said they were forced to act because the federal government was not doing enough to control illegal immigration at the border or in U.S. workplaces. Opponents

West Has Highest Share of Unlawful Aliens

Undocumented immigrants comprise at least 6 percent of the population of Arizona, California, Nevada and Texas and at least 3.8 percent of the population of New Mexico, Oregon and Utah. Unlawful immigrants also make up sizable percentages of several other states' populations, including New Jersey and Florida. The nationwide average is 3.7 percent.

Unauthorized Immigrants as a Share of State Population, 2010

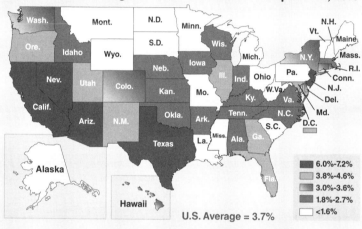

6.0%-7.2%
3.8%-4.6%
3.0%-3.6%
1.8%-2.7%
<1.6%

U.S. Average = 3.7%

Source: Jeffrey Passel and D'Vera Cohn, "Unauthorized Immigrant Population: National and State Trends, 2010," Pew Research Center, February 2011, p. 29, www.pewhispanic.org/files/reports/133.pdf

warned the laws risked profiling Latinos, including U.S. citizens and aliens with legal status.

All six of the laws are being challenged in federal court, with the "stop and check" provisions blocked except in Alabama's case. In the most important case, the Arizona measure is scheduled to be argued before the U.S. Supreme Court on April 25 after a federal appeals court struck some of the law enforcement provisions as interfering with federal immigration policy.[2] (*See chart, p. 254.*)

Alabama's law includes a unique provision that prohibits unlawful aliens from entering into any "business transaction" with state or local governments. Some public utilities in the state interpreted the provision to require proof of immigration status for water or electricity service. Until a federal judge's injunction on Nov. 23, some counties were applying the law to prevent unlawful immigrants from renewing permits for mobile homes.[3]

Once the law went into effect, school attendance by Latino youngsters dropped measurably in response to a provision — later blocked — requiring school officials to ascertain families' immigration status. The fear of deportation also led many immigrants in Alabama to seek help in preparing power-of-attorney documents to make sure their children would be taken care of in case the parents were deported, according to Isabel Rubio, executive director of the Hispanic Interest Coalition of Alabama. "You have to understand the sheer terror that people fear," Rubio says.

The law is having a palpable effect on the state's economy as well, according to agriculture and business groups. With fewer migrant workers, "some farmers have planted not as much or not planted at all," says Jeff Helms, spokesman for the Alabama Farmers Federation. Jay Reed, president of Associated Builders and Contractors of Alabama, says it has been harder to find construction workers as well.

Reed, co-chair of the multi-industry coalition Alabama Employers for Immigration Reform, wants to soften provisions that threaten employers with severe penalties, including the loss of operating licenses, for hiring undocumented workers. He and other business leaders also worry about the perception of the law outside the state's borders. "Some of our board members have expressed concern about our state's image and the effect on economic-development legislation," Reed says.

Reed says the state's Republican governor, Robert Bentley, and leaders in the GOP-controlled legislature are open to some changes in the law. But the two chief sponsors, Hammon and state Sen. Scott Beason, are both batting down any suggestions that the law will be repealed or its law enforcement measures softened.

"We are not going to weaken the law," Hammon told reporters on Feb. 14 as hundreds of opponents of the measure demonstrated outside the State House in

Montgomery. "We are not going to repeal any section of the law."[4]

On the surface, Alabama seems an improbable state to take a leading role in the newest outbreak of nativist concern about immigration and immigrants. Alabama's unauthorized immigrant population has increased nearly fivefold since 2000, but the state still ranks relatively low in the proportion of unauthorized immigrants in the population and in the state's workforce.

Alabama's estimated 120,000 unauthorized immigrants comprise about 2.5 percent of the state's total population. Nationwide, the estimated 11.8 million unauthorized immigrants represent about 3.7 percent of the population. Alabama's estimated 95,000 unauthorized immigrants with jobs represent about 4.2 percent of the workforce. Nationwide, 8 million undocumented workers account for about 5.2 percent of the national workforce.[5]

Americans Want Less Immigration

More than 40 percent of Americans say they favor a lower level of immigration, reflecting a view that has prevailed over most of the past half-century. About one in six want immigration to increase, while about one-third favor the current level.

Should immigration be kept at its present level, increased or decreased?

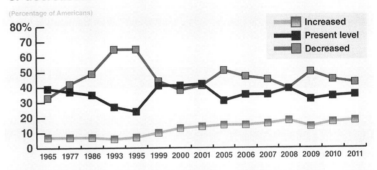

Sources: Jeffrey M. Jones, "Americans' Views on Immigration Holding Steady," Gallup, June 2011, www.gallup.com/poll/148154/americans-views-immigration-holding-steady.aspx; Roger Daniels, Guarding the Golden Door, Hill and Wang Press, December 2004, p. 233

Nationwide, the spike in anti-immigrant sentiment is also somewhat out of synch with current conditions. Experts and advocates on both sides of the immigration issues agree that the total unauthorized immigrant population has fallen somewhat from its peak in 2007, mainly because the struggling U.S. economy offers fewer jobs to lure incoming migrant workers.

"The inflow of illegals has slowed somewhat," says Mark Krikorian, executive director of the Center for Immigration Studies (CIS) in Washington. The center describes its stance as "low-immigration, pro-immigrant."[6]

Jobs were a major focus of the debate that led to Alabama's passage of the new law. "This is a jobs bill," Beason said as the measure, known as HB 56, reached final passage in June. "We have a problem with an illegal workforce that displaces Alabama workers. We need to put those people back to work."[7]

Today, Beason, running against an incumbent congressman for the U.S. House seat in the Birmingham area, credits the law with helping Alabama lower its unemployment rate from 9.8 percent in September to

8.1 percent in December. "I promised that the anti-illegal immigration law would open up thousands of jobs for Alabamians, and it has done that," Beason said in a Jan. 26 statement.

A University of Alabama economist, however, doubts the law's claimed effect on unemployment. Samuel Addy, director of the university's Center for Business and Economic Research in Tuscaloosa, notes that unemployment actually has increased, rather than declined, in the four sectors in the state viewed as most dependent on immigrant labor: agriculture, construction, accommodation and food and drinking places.[8]

In a nine-page study released in January, Addy contends instead that the immigration law is likely to hurt the state's economy overall. After assuming that 40,000 to 80,000 workers leave the state, Addy calculated that the law could reduce the state's gross domestic product by $2.3 billion to $10.8 billion. State income and sales taxes could take a $56.7 million to $265.4 million hit, Addy projected, while local sales tax revenue could decline by $20.0 million to $93.1 million. Hammon dismissed the report as "baloney."[9]

Five months after it took effect, however, the law's impact may be ebbing. Police appear not to have enforced the law vigorously, perhaps stung by the nation-wide embarrassment when a visiting Mercedes-Benz executive from Germany carrying only a German identi-fication card was held after a traffic stop until he could retrieve his passport. With police enforcement lagging, some of the immigrants who left appear to be coming back. "Some people have returned," Rubio says.[10]

Meanwhile, attorneys for the Obama administration and the state were preparing for arguments on March 1 before the federal appeals court in Atlanta in the govern-ment's suit challenging the state law on grounds of fed-eral pre-emption, the doctrine used to nullify state laws that conflict with U.S. laws and policies. The Hispanic Interest Coalition had challenged the law on broader grounds in an earlier suit, represented by the American Civil Liberties Union and other national groups.

In a massive, 115-page ruling, U.S. District Court Judge Sharon Blackburn upheld major parts of the law on Sept. 28 and then allowed the upheld parts to go into effect even as the government and civil rights groups appealed. Blackburn blocked half a dozen provisions on pre-emption grounds but found no congressional intent to prevent states from checking the immigration status of suspected unlawful aliens.[11]

With the legal challenges continuing, the political debates over immigration are intensifying. Republican presidential candidates generally agree on criticizing the Obama administration for failing to control illegal immi-gration even though the administration has increased the number of immigrants deported to their home countries. The Republican hopefuls disagree among themselves on the steps to deal with the problem.

For his part, Obama concedes that Congress will not approve a broad immigration overhaul in this election year. But he used his State of the Union speech to call for pas-sage of a bill — the so-called DREAM Act — to allow legal status for some immigrants who have served in the U.S. military or completed college. (*See "At Issue," p. 265.*)

As the immigration debates continue, here are some of the major questions being considered:

Is illegal immigration an urgent national problem?

As the anti-illegal immigration bill HB 56 was being signed into law, Alabama's Republican Party chairman

depicted the measure as needed to protect the state's tax-payers and the state's treasury. "Illegal immigrants have become a drain on our state resources and a strain on our taxpaying, law-abiding citizens," Bill Armistead declared as Republican governor Bentley signed it into law on June 9, 2011.[12]

Today, Republican officials continue to defend the law in economic terms. "Unemployment was sky high, especially in areas where there's high concentration of these undocumented workers," says Shana Kluck, the party's spokeswoman. Kluck also points to the cost on public treasuries. "The public-assistance budgets were bursting at the seams," she says. "That's why HB 56 was necessary."

Nationally, groups favoring tighter immigration con-trols make similar arguments about immigrants' eco-nomic impact, especially on jobs and wages for citizen workers. "We need to slow down immigration," says Dan Stein, president of the Federation for American Immigration Reform (FAIR), pointing to the current high levels of unemployment and underemployment.

"Immigration helps to decimate the bargaining lever-age of the American worker," Stein continues. "If you use a form of labor recruitment that bids down the cost of labor, that leads you to a society where a small number are very, very rich, there's nobody in the middle, and eve-ryone is left scrambling for crumbs at the bottom."

"The longer this economic doldrum continues, the more likely you are to see some real pushback on immi-gration levels as such, not just illegal immigration," says Krikorian with the low-immigration group Center for Immigration Studies. The group's research director, Steven Camarota, said if illegal immigrants are forced to go back to their home countries, there is "an ample sup-ply of idle workers" to take the jobs freed up.[13]

Pro-immigration groups say their opponents exagger-ate the costs and all but ignore the benefits of immigrant labor. "They never take into account the contributions that undocumented immigrants make," says Mary Giovagnoli, director of the American Immigration Council's Immigration Policy Center.

"We've had an economy that depends on immigra-tion," says Ali Noorani, executive director of the National Immigration Forum. "It would be an eco-nomic and social disaster for 11 million people to pick up and leave."

Immigration Law Basics

Even experts find it confusing.

Immigrating legally to the United States is difficult at best for those who fit into categories defined in mind-numbing detail by federal law and impossible for those who do not. Here is a primer on a body of law that is complex and confusing even to immigration experts, and all the more so for would-be Americans.

The Immigration and Nationality Act — sets an overall limit of 675,000 permanent immigrants each year. The limit does not apply to spouses, unmarried minor children or parents of U.S. citizens, but the sponsoring U.S. citizen must have an income above the U.S. poverty level and promise to support family members brought to the United States.

Who gets visas — Out of the 675,000 quota, 480,000 visas are made available under family-preference rules, and up to 140,000 are allocated for employment-related preferences. Unused employment-related visas may be reallocated to the family-preference system.

The family-sponsored visas are allocated according to a preference system with numerical limits for each category. Unmarried adult children of U.S. citizens are in the first category, followed, in this order, by spouses and minor children of lawful permanent residents; unmarried adult children of lawful permanent residents; married adult children of U.S. citizens; and brothers and sisters of U.S. citizens. No other relatives qualify for a family preference. Again, the sponsor must meet financial and support requirements.

Visa categories — The employment-based preference system also sets up ranked, capped categories for would-be immigrants. The highest preference is given to "persons of extraordinary ability" in the arts, science, education, business or athletics; professors and researchers; and some multinational executives. Other categories follow in this order: persons with professional degrees or "exceptional" abilities in arts, science or business; workers with skills that are in short supply and some "unskilled" workers for jobs not temporary or seasonal; certain "special immigrants," including religious workers; and, finally, persons who will invest at least $500,000 in a job-creating enterprise that employs at least 10 full-time workers.

In addition to the numerical limits, the law sets a cap of 7 percent of the quota for immigrants from any single country. The limit in effect prevents any immigrant group from dominating immigration patterns.

Refugees — Separately, Congress and the president each year set an annual limit for the number of refugees who can be admitted based on an inability to return to their home country because of a fear of persecution. Currently, the overall ceiling is 76,000. The law also allows an unlimited number of persons already in the United States, or at a port of entry, to apply for asylum if they were persecuted or fear persecution in their home country. A total of 21,113 persons were granted asylum in fiscal 2010. Refugees and asylees are eligible to become lawful permanent residents after one year.

Debate over the rules — An immigrant who gets through this maze and gains the coveted "green card" for lawful permanent residents is eligible to apply for U.S. citizenship after five years (three years for the spouse of a U.S. citizen). An applicant must be age 18 or over and meet other requirements, including passing English and U.S. history and civics exams. About 675,000 new citizens were naturalized in 2010, down from the peak of slightly more than 1 million in the pre-recession year of 2008.

Applying for citizenship — Immigration advocates say the quotas are too low, the rules too restrictive and the waiting periods for qualified applicants too long. Low-immigration groups say the record level of legal and illegal immigration over the past decade shows the need to lower the quotas and limit the family-reunification rules.

— Kenneth Jost

Madeleine Sumption, a senior labor market analyst with the pro-immigration Migration Policy Institute in Washington, acknowledges that immigration may have what she calls a "relatively small" impact on employment and wages for citizen workers. But the costs are more than offset, she says, by the benefits to employers, consumers and the overall economy.

The benefits can be seen particularly in sectors that employ large numbers of immigrants, according to Sumption. "The United States has a large agriculture

Major State Immigration Laws in Court

Five states have followed Arizona's lead in giving state and local police a role in enforcing federal immigration law. With some variations, the laws authorize or require police after an arrest, detention or stop to determine the person's immigration status if he or she is reasonably suspected of being unlawfully in the United States. In legal challenges, federal courts have blocked major parts of five of the laws; the Supreme Court is set to hear arguments on April 25 in Arizona's effort to reinstate the blocked portions of its law.

State	Bill, date signed	Legal challenge
Arizona	S.B. 1070: April 23, 2010	*United States v. Arizona* Major parts enjoined; pending at Supreme Court
Utah	H.B. 497: March 15, 2011	*Utah Coalition of La Raza v. Herbert* Major parts blocked; suit on hold pending Supreme Court ruling in Arizona case
Indiana	SB 590: May 10, 2011	*Buquer v. City of Indianapolis* Major parts blocked; suit on hold pending Supreme Court ruling in Arizona case
Georgia	HB 87: May 13, 2011	*Georgia Latino Alliance v. Deal* Major parts blocked; on hold at 11th Circuit
Alabama	HB 56: June 9, 2011	*United States v. Alabama* Major parts upheld; on hold at 11th Circuit
South Carolina	S20: June 27, 2011	*United States v. South Carolina* Major parts blocked; suit on hold pending Supreme Court ruling in Arizona case

Sources: National Conference of State Legislatures, http://www.ncsl.org/issues-research/immig/omnibus-immigration-legislation.aspx; American Civil Liberties Union; news coverage.

industry," she says. "Without immigration labor, it would almost certainly not be possible to produce the same volume of food in the country." The health care industry also employs a high number of immigrants, especially in low-end jobs, such as home-health aides and hospital orderlies. "These are jobs for which there is a growing demand and an expectation of an even more rapidly growing demand in the future," Sumption says.

In Alabama, Rubio with the Hispanic coalition and the leaders of the agriculture and construction groups all discount Camarota's contention that citizen workers are available to take the jobs currently being filled by immigrants. "We did not have a tomato crop [last] summer because the immigrants who pick that crop weren't there," Rubio says. "This is hard work, and many people don't want to do it."

Reed, president of the state's builders and contractors' organization, says construction companies similarly cannot find enough workers among the citizen labor force. "Traditionally, in our recruitment efforts we have unfortunately not found those that are unemployed are ready and willing to perform these kinds of jobs that require hard labor in extreme weather conditions," Helms says.

The claimed costs and benefits from immigration for public treasuries represent similarly contentious issues. Low- or anti-immigration groups emphasize the costs in government services, especially education and medical care. Pro-immigration groups point to the taxes that even unlawful aliens pay and the limits on some government benefits under federal and state laws. In an independent evaluation of the issue, the nonpartisan Congressional Budget Office in 2007 found a net cost to state and local governments but called the impact "most likely modest."[14]

The cost-benefit debates are more volatile in stressed economic times, according to David Gerber, a professor of history at the University of Buffalo and author of a primer on immigration. "People get angry when they feel that immigrants are competing for jobs of people in the United States or when they feel that immigrants are getting access to social benefits that the majority is paying for," Gerber says. "In harder times, it makes people angrier than in times of prosperity."[15]

Even so, David Coates, a professor at Wake Forest University in Winston-Salem, N.C., and co-editor of a book on immigration issues, notes that fewer undocumented workers are entering the United States now than in the peak year of 2007, and the Obama administration has been deporting unlawful aliens in significantly greater numbers than previous administrations. Asked whether illegal immigration should be less of an issue for state legislators and national politicians, Coates replies simply: "Yes, in terms of the numbers."

Should state and local police enforce immigration laws?

Alabama's HB 56 was stuffed with more provisions for state and local governments to crack down on illegal immigrants than the Arizona law that inspired it or any of the copy-cat laws passed in four other states. Along with the stop-and-check section, the law includes provisions making it a state crime for an unauthorized alien to apply for work and barring unauthorized aliens from court enforcement of any contracts. Another provision made it illegal to conceal, harbor or rent to an illegal immigrant or even to stop in a roadway to hire workers.

Opponents harshly criticized the enforcement provisions as they were signed into law. "It turns Alabama into a police state where anyone could be required to show their citizenship papers," said Cecillia Wang, director of the ACLU's Immigrant Rights Project. Noorani, with the National Immigration Forum, called the law "a radical departure from the concepts of fairness and equal treatment under the law," adding, "It makes it a crime, quite literally, to give immigrants a ride without checking their legal status."[16]

Today, even with the harboring provision and several others blocked from taking effect, opponents say the law is having the terrorizing effect that they had predicted on immigrants both legal and illegal as well as U.S. citizens of Hispanic background. "We've heard numerous accounts of people who have been stopped under very suspicious circumstances, while driving or even while walking on the street," says Justin Cox, an ACLU staff attorney in Atlanta working on the case challenging the law.

The law "has had the effect that it was intended to have," Cox says, "which was to make immigration status a pervasive issue in [immigrants'] everyday lives."

Supporters of the law are defending it, but without responding to specific criticisms. "We've seen an awful lot of illegal immigrants self-deport," House Majority Leader Hammon said as opponents rallied in Montgomery on Feb. 14. "We're also seeing Americans and legal immigrants taking these jobs."[17]

When questioned by a Montgomery television station about critical documentaries prepared for the progressive group Center for American Progress, Hammon declined to look at the films but attacked the filmmaker. "We don't need an activist director from California to come in here and tell us whether this law is good or not," Hammon said. "The people in Alabama can see it for themselves."[18]

Nationally, immigration hawks view the new state laws as unexceptional. "They're helping the feds to enforce immigration laws," says Center for Immigration Studies executive director Krikorian. "The question is [whether] local police use immigration laws as one of the tools in their tool kit to help defend public safety."

"Every town is a border town, every state is a border state," Krikorian continues. "Immigration law has to be part of your approach, part of your strategy in dealing with some kind of a significant problem."

FAIR president Stein strongly objects to the Obama administration's legal challenges to the state laws. "It should be a massive, industrial-strength issue that the Obama administration" has attacked the laws on grounds of federal pre-emption. But Giovagnoli with the pro-immigration American Immigration Council says the state laws should be struck down. "Congress has established that immigration enforcement is a federal matter," she says. "The more states get into the mix, the more you create a real patchwork of laws that don't make sense together."

As Krikorian notes, federal law already provides for cooperative agreements between the federal government and state or local law enforcement agencies to enforce immigration laws. U.S. Immigration and Customs Enforcement (ICE), the successor agency to the Immigration and Naturalization Service, touts the so-called 287(g) program on its website as one of the agency's "top partnership initiatives." The program, authorized by an immigration law overhaul in 1996, permits the federal agency to delegate enforcement power to state or local law enforcement after officers have received training on federal immigration law.[19]

Pro-immigration groups say the training requirement distinguishes 287(g) programs from the broader roles being given state and local police by the new state laws. "State and local law enforcement officers are not trained to do this kind of work," says Cox. "Inevitably, they're

Unlawful Immigration High Despite Dip

Despite a dip beginning in 2007, an estimated 11.2 million unauthorized immigrants live in the United States, one-third more than a decade ago (top graph). An estimated 8 million are in the civilian labor force, a 45 percent increase since 2000 (bottom graph).

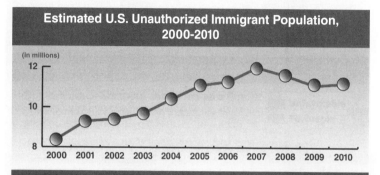

Estimated U.S. Unauthorized Immigrant Population, 2000-2010

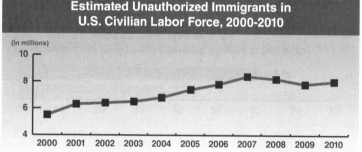

Estimated Unauthorized Immigrants in U.S. Civilian Labor Force, 2000-2010

Source: Jeffrey Passel and D'Vera Cohn, "Unauthorized Immigrant Population: National and State Trends, 2010," Pew Research Center, February 2011, pp. 1, 17, www.pewhispanic.org/files/reports/133.pdf

going to rely on pernicious stereotypes about what an undocumented immigrant looks like." The result, Cox continues, "is a breakdown of trust between the immigrant community and law enforcement, which ultimately affects all of us. It undermines public safety."

Alabama Republicans, however, insist that the state law fulfills a 2010 campaign pledge that helped the GOP gain control of both houses of the state legislature and that it remains popular despite the criticisms and legal challenges. "We've definitely been criticized," party spokeswoman Kluck acknowledges, but she blames the criticisms on "misinformation." As for possible changes in the law, Hammon and other legislative leaders are guarding details until a bill with proposed revisions can be completed by late March.

Should Congress make it easier for illegal immigrants to become citizens?

With many Republican primary and caucus voters viewing illegal immigration as a major issue, presidential candidate and former Massachusetts Gov. Mitt Romney says he has a simple solution: Get undocumented immigrants to "self-deport" to their home countries and then get in the legal waiting line for U.S. citizenship. But one of his rivals for the Republican nomination, former House speaker Newt Gingrich, pushing stronger enforcement at the border, mocks Romney's belief that 11 million unlawful aliens will go back home voluntarily. Speaking to a Spanish-language television network in late January on the eve of the Florida presidential primary, Gingrich called Romney's plan "an Obama-level fantasy."[20]

Pro-immigration groups agree that Romney's stance is unrealistic. "It's a fantasy to think that people are going to self-deport," says the National Immigration Forum's Noorani. Unlike border-control advocates, however, Noorani and other pro-immigration advocates and experts say the solution is "a path to legal citizenship" for the undocumented.

"We need a functioning legal immigration system, a system that has the necessary legal channels for a person to immigrate here whether for a job or his family," Noorani says. "That doesn't exist here." Without "a solution," Noorani says, "the only ones who are winning are the crooked employer who is more than happy to exploit the undocumented, poor third-country worker."

Immigration hawks quickly denounce any broad legalization proposal as an "amnesty" that they say is neither workable nor deserved. "All amnesties attract future immigration," says the CIS's Krikorian. "All amnesties reward lawbreakers." As evidence, immigration critics point to the broad amnesty granted under the 1986 immigration act to some 3 million immigrants — and its evident failure within a matter of years to stem the flow of illegal immigrants from across the country's Southern borders.

As an alternative to broader proposals, pro-immigration groups are pushing narrower legislation that in its current form would grant conditional legal status to immigrants who came to the United States before age 16 and have lived in the United States for at least five years. The so-called DREAM Act — an acronym for the Development, Relief and Education for Alien Minors Act — had majority support in both chambers of the Democratic-controlled Congress in 2010 but failed to get a Senate floor vote in the face of Republican opposition.

The DREAM Act starts with the assumption that immigrants who came to the United States as children have grown up as Americans and are innocent of any intentional immigration violations. They would be eligible for a conditional permanent residency and could then earn a five-year period of temporary residency by completing two years in the U.S. military or two years in a four-year college or university.

"The intent of the DREAM Act is to provide legal status for individuals who are enlisting in our armed services or pursuing higher education," says Noorani. "Whether they came here at age 5 or 15, I think we only stand to benefit."

"It's a good way to show that if you provide legal status to folks like this, the world is not going to fall apart," says Giovagnoli with the American Immigration Council. "In fact, the country would be better off if these people were in the system."

Similar proposals have been introduced in Congress since 2001. Immigration hawks acknowledge the proposals' appeal and argue over details. "The concept that people who have been here from childhood, that it might be prudent to legalize people in that position, is a plausible one," says Krikorian. But, he adds, "As it exists, it is not a good piece of legislation."

As one change, Krikorian says the eligibility age should be lowered, perhaps to age 10 or below. "The reason they pick 16 is it legalizes more," he says. Paradoxically, Krikorian also says the bill is too narrow by allowing temporary residency only by joining the military or going to college. "What if you're not college material?" he asks.

AP Photo/*Montgomery Advertiser*/Mickey Welsh

Republican Alabama Gov. Robert Bentley addresses lawmakers at the state capitol on June 9, 2011, before signing the state's new immigration law. Republican cosponsors of the law, Sen. Scott Beason (left), and state Rep. Micky Hammon (right), both oppose softening or repealing the law. But state business interests want to ease provisions that threaten employers with severe penalties for hiring undocumented workers. They also worry about the perception of the law outside the state.

Krikorian also dismisses the idea of absolving those who arrived as youngsters of any responsibility for immigration violations. "The parents . . . did know what they were doing," he says. The bill needs to be changed, he says, "to ensure that no parent would ever be able to benefit" under family-reunification rules.

Gingrich and some GOP lawmakers favor a narrower version of the DREAM Act that would extend legal status for serving in the military but not for going to college. Supporters oppose the narrower version. "If you read the bill carefully, it would actually allow a fewer number of immigrants to enlist in the military than the original," Noorani says. Krikorian also dismisses the alternative. He calls it "phony," adding that it would help "only a few thousand people a year."

The White House pushed hard for the bill in the Democratic-controlled Congress's lame-duck session in December 2010 but fell short in the Senate. Obama continues to speak out for the bill, most prominently in his State of the Union address. "[I]f election-year politics keeps Congress from acting on a comprehensive plan, let's at least agree to stop expelling responsible young people who want to staff our labs, start new businesses, defend this country," Obama said near the end of the Jan. 24

speech. "Send me a law that gives them the chance to earn their citizenship. I will sign it right away."[21]

BACKGROUND

Constant Ambivalence

The United States is a nation of immigrants that has been ambivalent toward immigration through most of its history. Immigrants are alternately celebrated as the source of diversity and criticized as agents of disunity. Immigrants were recruited to till the soil, build the cities and labor in the factories, but often criticized for taking jobs from and lowering wages for the citizen workforce. The federal government reflected popular sentiment in restricting immigration in the late 19th and early 20th century, only to draw later criticism for exclusionary policies. Today, the government is drawing criticism for liberalized policies adopted in the 1960s and for ineffective border enforcement from the 1980s on.[22]

African slaves were the first source of immigrant labor in America, but Congress banned importation of slaves in 1808. Otherwise, the United States maintained an open-door policy on immigration until the late 19th century. Europe's mid-century agricultural crisis drove waves of German and Irish peasants to the United States in the 1840s and '50s. Many were met by ethnic and anti-Catholic hostility, embodied in the first nativist political movement: the American or so-called Know-Nothing Party. The party carried one state in the 1856 presidential election and then faded from history.

Significant Chinese immigration began with the California Gold Rush of 1849 and increased with the post-Civil War push to complete the transcontinental railroad. Stark warnings of the "Yellow Peril" led to a series of restrictions at the federal level — most notably, the Chinese Exclusion Act of 1882, which suspended immigration of Chinese laborers and barred citizenship for those already in the United States. Significantly for present-day debates, efforts to deport those in the country or to seal the borders against new Chinese immigrants were no more than partly successful.[23]

Congress laid the basis for present-day immigration law and policy in a series of increasingly restrictive enactments from the 1890s through the early 1920s that coincided with the great waves of immigration from

Europe, including regions previously unrepresented in the American polity. The Immigration Act of 1891 established the Bureau of Immigration, then under the Treasury Department, and provided for border inspections and deportation of unlawful aliens. Additional laws prescribed admission procedures, created categories of inadmissible immigrants and tightened the exclusion of immigrants from Asia.

The restrictive policies drew support from nativists worried about assimilation, pro-labor groups concerned about the impact on jobs and wages and progressive leaders fearful of the impact on the urban environment. The restrictions culminated in the passage of the first and second Quota Acts in 1921 and 1924, which established the first quantitative limitation on immigration (350,000, lowered to 150,000) and a national-origins system that favored immigrants from Northern and Western Europe. In reporting the bill in 1924, a House committee stated: "If the principle of liberty . . . is to endure, the basic strain of our population must be preserved."[24]

The Quota Acts' exception for Western Hemisphere immigrants combined with the unrest associated with the Mexican Revolution (1910-1929) to produce what Stanford historian Albert Camarillo calls "a tsunami" in immigration across the United States' Southern border. Camarillo says 1.5 million Mexicans — one-tenth of the country's population — relocated to the United States by the end of the 1930s.[25] The influx fueled ethnic prejudice embodied in the derogatory term "wetback" to refer to the Mexican immigrants, most of whom actually entered by crossing arid regions rather than fording the Rio Grande River.

During the Great Depression of the 1930s, the federal and state governments — concerned about the impact on jobs for Anglo workers — sent tens of thousands of Mexicans back to their home country, sometimes with force and little regard for due process. During World War II, however, the government worked with Mexico to establish the so-called bracero program to use temporary immigrant labor for agricultural work. The "temporary" program continued into the 1960s.

Congress liberalized immigration law with a 1952 statute that included restrictionist elements as well and then, dramatically, with a 1965 law that scrapped the Eurocentric national-origins system and opened the gate to increased immigration from Latin America and Asia.

CHRONOLOGY

Before 1960 *Congress establishes immigration quotas.*

1920s Quota Act (1921), Johnson-Reed Act (1924) establish national-origins quota system, favoring Northern European immigrants over those from Southern Europe, elsewhere.

1952 McCarran-Walter Act retains national-origins system but adds small quotas for some Asian countries.

1960s *Congress opens door to immigration from outside Europe.*

1965 Immigration and Nationality Act of 1965 abolishes national-origins quota system dating from 1920s; allows dramatic increase in immigration from Central and South America, Asia.

1980s-1990s *Illegal immigration increases, becomes major public issue.*

1986 Immigration Reform and Control Act allows amnesty for many unlawful aliens, prohibits employers from employing undocumented workers; enforcement proves elusive.

1996 Illegal Immigration Reform and Immigrant Responsibility Act seeks to strengthen border security, streamline deportation proceedings; creates optional E-Verify system for employers to electronically check immigration status of workers and job applicants.

2000-Present *Illegal immigration increases; immigration reform falters in Congress; state laws to crack down on illegal immigration challenged in court.*

2001 Al Qaeda 9/11 attacks on U.S. soil underscore national security threat from failure to track potential terrorists entering United States (Sept. 11); USA Patriot Act gives immigration authorities more power to exclude suspected terrorists (Oct. 26).

2005-2006 Immigration reform measures fail in GOP-controlled Congress despite support from Republican President George W. Bush; Congress approves Secure

Fence Act, to require double-layer fence on U.S.-Mexico border.

2007 Immigration reform measure dies in Senate; three motions to cut off debate fail (June 7). . . . Arizona legislature passes employer-sanctions law; companies threatened with loss of operating license for knowingly hiring undocumented aliens, required to use federal E-Verify system; signed into law by Democratic Gov. Janet Napolitano (July 2). . . . Unauthorized immigrant population in United States peaks near 12 million.

2008 Democrat Barack Obama elected president after campaign with little attention to immigration issues (Nov. 4); Obama carries Hispanic vote by 2-1 margin.

2009 Obama endorses immigration reform, but without specifics; issue takes back seat to economic recovery, health care.

2010 Arizona enacts law (S.B. 1070) to crack down on illegal immigrants; measure requires police to check immigration status if suspect or detainee is reasonably believed to be unlawful alien; makes it a crime to fail to carry alien registration papers; signed by Republican Gov. Jan Brewer (April 23); federal judge blocks parts of law (July 28). . . . DREAM Act to allow legal status for unlawful aliens who entered U.S. as minors approved by House of Representatives (Dec. 8) but fails in Senate: 55-41 vote is short of supermajority needed for passage (Dec. 18).

2011 Utah, Indiana, Georgia follow Arizona's lead in giving state, local police immigration-enforcement powers (March, May). . . . Federal appeals court upholds injunction against parts of Arizona's S.B. 1070 (April 11). . . . Supreme Court upholds Arizona's employer-sanctions law 5-3 (May 21). . . . Alabama enacts nation's toughest state law on illegal immigrants, HB 56 (June 9). . . . Federal judge blocks some parts of HB 56, allows others to take effect (Sept. 28).

2012 Immigration is flashpoint for Republican presidential candidates. . . . Obama urges passage of DREAM Act (Jan. 24). . . . Alabama, Georgia laws argued before U.S. appeals court (March 1). . . . Supreme Court to hear arguments on Arizona's S.B. 1070 (April 25); ruling due by end of June.

Journalist Reveals His Immigration Secret

"There's nothing worse than being in limbo."

When journalist-turned-immigration rights activist Jose Antonio Vargas traveled to Alabama with a documentary filmmaker, he found a Birmingham restaurant patron who strongly supported the state law cracking down on undocumented aliens. "Get your papers or get out," the patron said.

"What if I told you I didn't [have papers]?" Vargas is heard asking off camera. "Then you need you get your ass home then," the patron rejoined.[1]

Vargas says he is home — in America, where he has lived since his Filipina mother sent him, at age 12, to live in California with his grandparents in 1993. "I'm an American without papers," says Vargas, who came out as an undocumented immigrant in dramatic fashion in a 4,300-word memoir in *The New York Times Magazine* in June 2011.[2]

In the story, Vargas recounts how he learned at age 16 that he was carrying a fake green card when he applied for a driver's license. The DMV clerk let him go. Back home, Vargas confronted his grandfather, who acknowledged the forgery and told Vargas not to tell anyone else.

For the next 14 years, Vargas kept his non-status secret from all but a handful of enablers as he completed high school and college and advanced rapidly from entry-level newspaper jobs to national-impact journalism at *The Washington Post*, *Huffington Post* and glossy magazines. His one attempt at legal status ended in crushing disappointment in 2002 when an immigration lawyer told him he would have to return to the Philippines and wait for 10 years to apply to come back.

Vargas was inspired to write about his life by the example of four undocumented students who walked from Miami to Washington, D.C., in 2010 to lobby for the DREAM Act, the status-legalizing proposal for immigrants who came to the United States as minors. Vargas's story,

Journalist Jose Antonio Vargas disclosed in *The New York Times* in June 2011 that he was an undocumented immigrant.

Getty Images/Justin Sullivan

published by *The Times* after *The Washington Post* decided not to, quickly went viral in old and new media alike.

In the eight months since, Vargas has founded and become the public face for a Web-based campaign, Define American (www.defineamerican.org). "Define American brings new voices into the immigration conversation, shining a light on a growing 21st century Underground Railroad: American citizens who are forced to fill in where our broken immigration system fails," the mission statement reads. "Together, we are going to fix a broken system."

The DREAM Act fell just short of passage in Congress in December 2010 and has gotten little traction since. Broader proposals to give legal status to some of the 11 million unlawful aliens are far off the political radar screen. Vargas is critical of Alabama's law cracking down on illegal immigration but acknowledges the states' frustration with federal policies. "At the end of the day, the federal government hasn't done anything on this issue," he says.

In the meantime, Vargas waits. "There's nothing worse than being in limbo," he says. In the story, he cited some of the hardships for the undocumented. As one example, he cannot risk traveling to the Philippines, so he has yet to meet his 14-year-old brother. But Vargas says he has no plan to "self-deport." "I love this country," he says.

— Kenneth Jost

---

[1] "The Two Faces of Alabama," http://isthisalabama.org/. The films by director Chris Weitz were prepared under the auspices of the Center for American Progress. Some comments from Vargas are from a Feb. 15, 2012, screening of the videos at the center.

[2] Jose Antonio Vargas, "Outlaw," *The New York Times Magazine*, June 26, 2011, p. 22. Disclosure: the author is a professional acquaintance and Facebook friend of Vargas.

The 1952 law preserved the national-origins system but replaced the Chinese Exclusion Act with very small quotas for countries in the so-called Asia-Pacific Triangle. The act also eliminated discrimination between sexes. Over the next decade, immigration from European countries declined, seemingly weakening the rationale for the national-origins system. Against the backdrop of the civil rights revolution, the national-origins system seemed to many also to be antithetical to American values. The result was the Immigration Act of 1965, which replaced the national-origins system with a system of preferences favoring family reunification or to lesser extents admissions of professionals or skilled or unskilled workers needed in the U.S. workforce.

Quickly, the demographics of immigration shifted — and dramatically. Immigration increased overall under the new law, and the new immigrants came mostly from Latin America and Asia. By 1978, the peak year of the decade, 44 percent of legal immigration came from the Americas, 42 percent from Asia and only 12 percent from Europe.[26]

Cracking Down?

Immigration to the United States increased overall in the last decades of the 20th century, and illegal immigration in particular exploded to levels that fueled a public and political backlash. Congress and the executive branch tried to stem the flow of undocumented aliens first in 1986 by combining employer sanctions with an amnesty for those in the country for several years and then a decade later by increasing enforcement and deportations.

Then, in the wake of the Sept. 11, 2001, terrorist attacks on the United States, Congress and President George W. Bush joined in further efforts to tighten admission procedures and crack down on foreigners in the country without authorization.

Estimates of the number of immigrants in the United States illegally are inherently imprecise, but the general upward trend from the 1980s until a plateau in the 2000s is undisputed. As Congress took up immigration bills in the mid-1980s, the Census Bureau estimated the number of those undocumented at 3 million to 5 million; many politicians used higher figures. The former Immigration and Naturalization Service put the number at 3.5 million in 1990 and 7.0 million a decade later. Whatever the precise number, public opinion polls registered increasing concern about the overall level of immigration. By the

mid-1990s, Gallup polls found roughly two-thirds of respondents in favor of decreasing the level of immigration, one-fourth in favor of maintaining the then-present level and fewer than 10 percent for an increase.[27]

The congressional proposals leading to the Immigration Reform and Control Act in 1986 sought to stem illegal immigration while recognizing the reality of millions of undocumented immigrants and the continuing need for immigrant labor, especially in U.S. agriculture. The law allowed legal status for immigrants in the country continuously since 1982 but aimed to deter unauthorized immigration in the future by forcing employers to verify the status of prospective hires and penalizing them for hiring anyone without legal status. Agricultural interests, however, won approval of a new guest worker program. Some 3 million people gained legal status under the two provisions, but illegal immigration continued to increase even as civil rights groups warned that the employer sanctions would result in discrimination against Latino citizens.

The backlash against illegal immigration produced a new strategy for reducing the inflows: state and federal laws cutting off benefits for aliens in the country without authorization. California, home to an estimated 1.3 million undocumented aliens at the time, blazed the path in 1994 with passage of a ballot measure, Proposition 187, that barred any government benefits to illegal aliens, including health care and public schooling. The education provision was flatly unconstitutional under a 1982 ruling by the U.S. Supreme Court that guaranteed K-12 education for school-age alien children.[28]

The measure mobilized Latino voters in the state. They contributed to the election of a Democratic governor in 1998, Gray Davis, who dropped the state's defense of the measure in court in his first year in office. In the meantime, however, Congress in 1996 had approved provisions — reluctantly signed into law by President Bill Clinton — to deny unauthorized aliens most federal benefits, including food stamps, family assistance and Social Security. The law allows states to deny state-provided benefits as well; today, at least a dozen states have enacted such further restrictions.

The centerpieces of the 1996 immigration law, however, were measures to beef up enforcement and toughen deportation policy. The Illegal Immigration Reform and Immigrant Responsibility Act authorized more money for

AFP/Getty Images/Mark Ralston

A Maricopa County deputy arrests a woman following a sweep for illegal immigrants in Phoenix on July 29, 2010. The police operation came after protesters against Arizona's tough immigration law clashed with police hours after the law went into effect. Although the most controversial parts of the law have been blocked, five other states — Utah, Indiana, Georgia, Alabama and South Carolina — last year enacted similar laws.

the Border Patrol and INS, approved more funding for a 14-mile border fence already under construction and increased penalties for document fraud and alien smuggling. It sought to streamline deportation proceedings, limit appeals and bar re-entry of any deportee for at least five years. And it established an Internet-based employer verification system (E-Verify) aimed at making it easier and more reliable for employers to check legal status of prospective hires. The law proved to be tougher on paper, however, than in practice. The border fence remains incomplete, deportation proceedings backlogged and E-Verify optional and — according to critics — unreliable. And illegal immigration continued to increase.

The 9/11 attacks added homeland security to the concerns raised by the nation's porous immigration system. In post-mortems by immigration hawks, the Al Qaeda hijackers were seen as having gained entry into the United States with minimal scrutiny of their visa applications and in many cases having overstayed because of inadequate follow-up.[29] The so-called USA Patriot Act, enacted in October 2001 just 45 days after the attacks, gave the INS — later renamed the U.S. Citizenship and Immigration Service and transferred to the new Department of Homeland Security — greater authority to exclude or detain foreigners suspected of ties to terrorist organizations. The act also

mandated information-sharing by the FBI to identify aliens with criminal records. Along with other counterterrorism measures, the act is viewed by supporters today as having helped prevent any successful attacks on U.S. soil since 2001. Illegal immigration, however, continued to increase — peaking at roughly 12 million in 2007.

Getting Tough

Congress and the White House moved from post-9/11 security issues to broader questions of immigration policy during Bush's second term, but bipartisan efforts to allow legal status for unlawful aliens fell victim to Republican opposition in the Senate. As a presidential candidate, Democrat Obama carried the Hispanic vote by a 2-1 margin over Republican John McCain after a campaign with limited attention to immigration issues. In the White House, Obama stepped up enforcement in some respects even as he urged Congress to back broad reform measures. The reform proposals failed with Democrats in control of both the House and the Senate and hardly got started after Republicans regained control of the House in the 2010 elections.

Bush lent support to bipartisan reform efforts in the Republican-controlled Congress in 2005 and 2006 and again in the Democratic-controlled Congress in his final two years in office. Congress in 2006 could agree only on authorizing a 700-mile border fence after reaching an impasse over a House-passed enforcement measure and a Senate-approved path-to-citizenship bill. Bush redoubled efforts in 2007 by backing a massive, bipartisan bill that would have allowed "earned citizenship" for aliens who had lived in the United States for at least eight years and met other requirements. As in the previous Congress, many Republicans rejected the proposal as an unacceptable amnesty. The bill died on June 7 after the Senate rejected three cloture motions to cut off debate.[30]

Immigration played only a minor role in the 2008 presidential campaign between Obama and McCain, Senate colleagues who had both supported reform proposals. Both campaigns responded to growing public anger over illegal immigration by emphasizing enforcement when discussing the issue, but the subject went unmentioned in the candidates' three televised debates. McCain, once popular with Hispanics in his home state of Arizona, appeared to have paid at the polls for the GOP's hard line on immigration. Exit polls indicated that Obama won 67 percent of a record-size Hispanic vote; McCain got 31 percent — a significant drop from Bush's 39 percent share of the vote in 2004.[31]

With Obama in office, Congress remained gridlocked even as the president tried to smooth the way for reform measures by stepping up enforcement. The congressional gridlock had already invited state lawmakers to step into the vacuum. State legislatures passed more than 200 immigration-related laws in 2007 and 2008, according to a compilation by the National Conference on State Legislatures; the number soared to more than 300 annually for the next three years.[32]

The numbers included some resolutions praising the country's multi-ethnic heritage, but most of the new state laws sought to tighten enforcement against undocumented aliens or to limit benefits to them. Among the earliest of the new laws was an Arizona measure — enacted in June 2007, two weeks after the Senate impasse in Washington — that provided for lifting the business licenses of companies that knowingly hired illegal aliens and mandated use of the federal E-Verify program to ascertain status of prospective hires. Business and labor groups, supported by the Obama administration, challenged the law on federal preemption grounds. The Supreme Court's 5-3 decision in May 2011 to uphold the law prompted several states to enact similar mandatory E-Verify provisions.[33]

The interplay on immigration policy between Washington and state capitals is continuing. In Obama's first three years in office, the total number of removals increased to what ICE calls on its website "record levels." Even so, Arizona lawmakers and officials criticized federal enforcement as inadequate in the legislative debate leading to SB 1070's enactment in April 2010. Legal challenges followed quickly — first from a Latino organization; then from a broad coalition of civil rights and civil liberties groups; and then, on July 6, from the Justice Department. The most controversial parts of the law have been blocked, first by U.S. District Court Judge Susan Bolton's injunction later that month and then by the Ninth Circuit's decision affirming her decision in April 2011. The legal challenges did not stop five other states — Utah, Indiana, Georgia, Alabama and South Carolina — from enacting similar laws in spring and early summer 2011. Civil rights groups and the Justice Department followed with similar suits challenging the new state enactments.

As the 2012 presidential campaign got under way, immigration emerged as an issue between Republican candidates vying for the party's nomination. The issue posed difficulties for the GOP hopefuls as they sought to appeal to rank-and-file GOP voters upset about illegal immigration without forfeiting Latino votes in the primary season and in the general election. Presumed front-runner Mitt Romney took a hard stance against illegal immigration in early contests but softened his message in advance of winning the pivotal Jan. 31 primary in Florida with its substantial Hispanic vote.

Despite differences in details and in rhetoric, the three leading GOP candidates — Romney, Newt Gingrich and Rick Santorum — all said they opposed the DREAM Act in its present form even as Obama called for Congress to pass the bill in his State of the Union speech.

CURRENT SITUATION

Obama's Approach

The Obama administration is claiming success in increasing border enforcement and removing unlawful aliens while injecting more prosecutorial discretion into deportation cases. But the mix of firm and flexible policies is resulting in criticism from both sides of the issue.

U.S. Immigration and Customs Enforcement (ICE) counted a record 396,906 "removals" during fiscal 2011, including court-ordered deportations as well as administrative or voluntary removals or returns. The number includes a record 216,698 aliens with criminal convictions.[34]

Meanwhile, Homeland Security Secretary Janet Napolitano says illegal border-crossing attempts have decreased by more than half in the last three years. In a Jan. 30 speech to the National Press Club in Washington, Napolitano linked the decline to an increase in the number of Border Patrol agents to 21,000, which she said was more than double the number in 2004.

"The Obama administration has undertaken the most serious and sustained actions to secure our borders in our nation's history," Napolitano told journalists. "And it is clear from every measure we currently have that this approach is working."[35]

Immigration hawk Krikorian with the Center for Immigration Studies gives the administration some, but only some, credit for the removal statistics. "They're not making up the numbers," Krikorian says. But he notes that immigration removals increased during the Bush administration and that the rate of increase has slowed under Obama.

In addition, Krikorian notes that new figures compiled by a government information tracking service indicate the pace of new immigration cases and of court-processed deportations slowed in the first quarter of fiscal 2012 (October, November and December 2011). A report in early February by Syracuse University's Transactional Records Access Clearinghouse (TRAC) shows 34,362 court-ordered removals or "voluntary departures" in the period, compared to 35,771 in the previous three months — about a 4 percent drop.

A separate TRAC report later in the month showed what the service called a "sharp decline" in new ICE filings. ICE initiated 39,331 new deportation proceedings in the nation's 50 immigration courts during the first quarter of fiscal 2012, according to the report, a 33 percent decline from the 58,639 new filings in the previous quarter.[36]

"The people in this administration would like to pull the plug on enforcement altogether," Krikorian complains. "They refuse to ask for more money for detention beds and then plead poverty that they can't do more."

From the opposite perspective, some Latino officials and organizations have been critical of the pace of deportations. When Obama delivered a speech in favor of immigration reform in El Paso, Texas, in May 2011, the president of the National Council of La Raza tempered praise for the president's position with criticism of the deportation policy.

"As record levels of detention and deportation continue to soar, families are torn apart, innocent youth are being deported and children are left behind without the protection of their parents," Janet Murguía said in a May 10 press release. "Such policies do not reflect American values and do little to solve the problem. We can do better."[37]

Latinos disapprove of the Obama administration's handling of deportations by roughly a 2-1 margin, according to a poll by the Pew Hispanic Center in December 2011. Overall, the poll found 59 percent of those surveyed opposed the administration's policy while 27 percent approved. Disapproval was higher among foreign-born Latinos (70 percent) than those born in the United States (46 percent).[38]

Napolitano and ICE Director John Morton are both claiming credit for focusing the agency's enforcement on the most serious cases, including criminal aliens, repeat violators and recent border crossers. Morton announced the new "prosecutorial discretion" policy in an agency-wide directive in June 2011.[39]

TRAC, however, questions the claimed emphasis on criminal aliens. The 39,331 new deportation filings in the first quarter of fiscal 2012 included only 1,300 against aliens with convictions for "aggravated felonies," as defined in immigration law. "Even this small share was down from previous quarters," the Feb. 21 report states. Aliens with aggravated felony convictions accounted for 3.3 percent of deportations in the period, compared to 3.8 percent in the previous quarter.[40]

The administration is also being questioned on its claim — in Obama's El Paso speech and elsewhere — to have virtually completed the border fence that Congress ordered constructed in the Secure Fence Act of 2006.[41] The act called for the 652-mile barrier to be constructed of two layers of reinforced fencing but was amended the next year — with Bush still in office — to give the administration more discretion in what type of barriers to use.

As of May 2011, the barrier included only 36 miles of double-layer fencing, according to PolitiFact, the fact-checking service of the *Tampa Bay Times*. The rest is single-layer fencing or vehicle barriers that critic Krikorian says are so low that a pedestrian can step over them. PolitiFact calls Obama's claim "mostly false."[42]

Meanwhile, the administration is preparing to extend nationwide its controversial "Secure Communities" program, which tries to spot immigration law violators by matching fingerprints of local arrestees with the database of the Department of Homeland Security (DHS). A match allows U.S. Immigration and Customs Enforcement (ICE) to issue a so-called detainer against violators, sending their cases into the immigration enforcement system. The administration touts the program as "a simple and common sense" enforcement tool. Critics note, however, that it has resulted in wrongful detention of U.S. citizens in a considerable but unknown number of cases. One reason for the mistakes: The DHS database includes all immigration transactions, not just violations, and thus could show a match for an immigrant with legal status.[43]

Should Congress pass the DREAM Act?

YES Walter A. Ewing
*Senior Researcher, Immigration
Policy Center American Immigration Council*

Written for *CQ Global Researcher*, March 2012

The Development, Relief and Education for Alien Minors Act is rooted in common sense. To begin with, it would benefit a group of unauthorized young people who, in most cases, did not come to this country of their own accord. Rather, they were brought here by their parents. The DREAM Act would also enable its beneficiaries to achieve higher levels of education and obtain better, higher-paying jobs, which would increase their contributions to the U.S. economy and American society. In short, the DREAM Act represents basic fairness and enlightened self-interest.

More than 2 million young people would benefit from the DREAM Act, and their numbers grow by roughly 65,000 per year. They came to the United States before age 18, many as young children. They tend to be culturally American and fluent in English. Their primary ties are to this country, not the countries of their birth. And the majority had no say in the decision to come to this country without authorization — that decision was made by the adult members of their families. Punishing these young people for the actions of their parents runs counter to American social values and legal norms. Yet, without the DREAM Act, these young people will be forced to live on the margins of U.S. society or will be deported to countries they may not even know.

Assuming they aren't deported, the young people who would benefit from the DREAM Act face enormous barriers to higher education and professional jobs because of their unauthorized status. They are ineligible for most forms of college financial aid and cannot work legally in this country. The DREAM Act would remove these barriers, which would benefit the U.S. economy.

The College Board estimates that over the course of a working lifetime, a college graduate earns 60 percent more than a high school graduate. This higher income translates into extra tax revenue flowing to federal, state and local governments.

The DREAM Act is in the best interest of the United States both socially and economically. It would resolve the legal status of millions of unauthorized young people in a way that is consistent with core American values. And it would empower these young people to become better-educated, higher-earning workers and taxpayers. Every day that goes by without passage of the DREAM Act is another day of wasted talent and potential.

NO Mark Krikorian
*Executive Director, Center for
Immigration Studies*

Written for *CQ Global Researcher*, March 2012

The appeal of the DREAM Act is obvious. People brought here illegally at a very young age and who have grown up in the United States are the most sympathetic group of illegal immigrants. Much of the public is open to the idea of amnesty for them.

But the actual DREAM Act before Congress is a deeply flawed measure in at least four ways:

• Rather than limiting amnesty to those brought here as infants and toddlers, it applies to illegal immigrants who arrived before their 16th birthday. But if the argument is that their very identity was formed here, age 7 would be a more sensible cutoff. That is recognized as a turning point in a child's psychological development (called the "age of reason" by the Catholic Church, hence the traditional age for First Communion). Such a lower-age cutoff, combined with a requirement of at least 10 years' residence here, would make a hypothetical DREAM Act 2.0 much more defensible.

• All amnesties are vulnerable to fraud, even more than other immigration benefits. About one-fourth of the beneficiaries of the amnesty granted by Congress in 1986 were liars, including one of the leaders of the 1993 World Trade Center bombing. But the DREAM Act specifically prohibits the prosecution of anyone who lies on an amnesty application. So you can make any false claim you like about your arrival or schooling in America without fear of punishment. A DREAM Act 2.0 would make clear that any lies, no matter how trivial, will result in arrest and imprisonment.

• All amnesties send a signal to prospective illegal immigrants that, if you get in and keep your head down, you might benefit from the next amnesty. But the bill contains no enforcement provisions to limit the need for another DREAM Act a decade from now. That's why a serious proposal would include measures such as electronic verification of the legal status of all new hires, plus explicit authorization for state and local enforcement of immigration law.

• Finally, all amnesties reward illegal immigrants — in this case including the adults who brought their children here illegally. A credible DREAM Act 2.0 would bar the adult relatives of the beneficiaries from ever receiving any immigration status or even a right to visit the United States. If those who came as children are not responsible, then those who are responsible must pay the price for their lawbreaking.

Supreme Court Action

All eyes are on the Supreme Court as the justices prepare for arguments on April 25 in Arizona's effort to reinstate major parts of its trend-setting law cracking down on illegal immigrants.

The Arizona case is the furthest advanced of suits challenging the six recently enacted state laws that give state and local police responsibility for enforcing federal immigration laws. After winning an injunction blocking major parts of the Arizona law, the Obama administration filed similar suits against Alabama's HB 56 as well as the Georgia and South Carolina measures.

The ACLU's Immigrants Rights Project, along with Hispanic and other civil rights groups, has filed separate challenges on broader grounds against all six laws. Federal district courts have blocked parts of all the laws, though some contentious parts of Alabama's law were allowed to take effect.

District court judges in the Indiana, South Carolina and Utah cases put the litigation on hold pending the Supreme Court's decision in the Arizona case. Alabama and Georgia asked the Eleventh U.S. Circuit Court of Appeals to postpone the scheduled March 1 arguments in their cases, but the court declined.

Judge Charles R. Wilson opened the Atlanta-based court's March 1 session, however, by announcing that the three-judge panel had decided to withhold its opinion until after the Supreme Court decides the Arizona case. "Hopefully, that information will help you in framing your arguments today," Wilson told the assembled lawyers.[44]

Wilson and fellow Democratic-appointed Circuit Judge Beverly B. Martin dominated the questioning during the three hours of arguments in the cases. Both judges pressed lawyers defending Alabama and Georgia on the effects of their laws on the education of children, the ability of illegal aliens to carry on with their lives while immigration courts decided their cases and what would happen if every state adopted their approach to dealing with immigration violations. The third member of the panel, Richard Voorhees, a Republican-appointed federal district court judge, asked only three questions on technical issues.

Opening the government's argument in the Alabama case, Deputy Assistant U.S. Attorney General Beth Brinkmann said the state's law attempts to usurp exclusive federal authority over immigration. "The regulation of immigration is a matter vested exclusively in the national government," Brinkman said. "Alabama's state-specific regulation scheme violates that authority. It attacks every aspect of an alien's life and makes it impossible for the alien to live."

Alabama Solicitor General John C. Neiman Jr. drew sharp challenges from Wilson and Martin even before he began his argument. Wilson focused on the law's Section 10, which makes it a criminal misdemeanor for an alien unlawfully present in the United States to fail to carry alien registration papers.

"You could be convicted and sent to jail in Alabama even though the Department of Homeland Security says, 'You're an illegal alien, but we've decided you're going to remain here in the United States?' " Wilson asked.

Neiman conceded the point. "If the deportation hearing occurred after the violation of Section 10, then yes," Neiman said. "Someone could be held to be in violation of Section 10 and then later be held not removable."

Wilson also pressed Neiman on the potential effects on the federal government's ability to control immigration policy if states enacted laws with different levels of severity. "These laws could certainly have the effect of making certain states places where illegal aliens would be likely to go," the state's attorney acknowledged.

Representing the ACLU in the separate challenge, Immigrants Rights Project director Wang sharply attacked the motive behind the Alabama law. The law, she said, was written to carry out the legislature's stated objective "to attack every aspect of an illegal immigrant's life so that they will deport themselves." *

In Washington, lawyers for Arizona filed their brief with the Supreme Court defending its law, SB 1070, in early February. Among 20 *amicus* briefs filed in support of Arizona's case is one drafted by the Michigan attorney general's office on behalf of 16 states similarly defending the states' right to help enforce federal immigration law. A similar brief was filed by nine states in the Eleventh Circuit in support of the Alabama law.

The government's brief in the Arizona case is due March 19. Following the April 25 arguments, the Supreme Court is expected to decide the case before the current term ends in late June.

Meanwhile, legal challenges to other parts of the state's law are continuing in federal court in Arizona.

In a Feb. 29 ruling, Bolton blocked on First Amendment grounds a provision prohibiting people from blocking traffic when they offer day labor services on the street.[45]

OUTLOOK

A Broken System

The immigration system is broken. On that much, the pro- and low-immigration groups agree. But they disagree sharply on how to fix it. And the divide defeats any attempts to fix it even if it can be fixed.

Pro-immigration groups like to talk about the "three-legged stool" of immigration reform: legal channels for family- and job-based immigration; a path to citizenship for unlawful aliens already in the United States; and better border security. Low-immigration groups agree on the need for better border controls but want to make it harder, not easier, for would-be immigrants and generally oppose legal status for the near-record number of unlawful aliens.

Public opinion is ambivalent and conflicted on immigration issues even as immigration, legal and illegal, has reached record levels. The nearly 14 million new immigrants, legal and illegal, who came to the United States from 2000 to 2010 made that decade the highest ever in U.S. history, according to the low-immigration Center for Immigration Studies. The foreign-born population reached 40 million, the center says, also a record.[46]

Some public opinion polls find support for legal status for illegal immigrants, especially if the survey questions specify conditions to meet: 66 percent supported it, for example, in a Fox News poll in early December 2011. Three weeks earlier, however, a CNN poll found majority support (55 percent) for concentrating on "stopping the flow of illegal immigrants and deporting those already here" instead of developing a plan for legal residency (42 percent).[47]

Other polls appear consistently to find support for the laws in Arizona and other states to crack down on illegal immigrants — most recently by a 2-1 margin in a poll by Quinnipiac University in Connecticut.[48] "Popular sentiment is always against immigration," says Muzaffar Chishti, director of the Migration Policy Institute's office at New York University School of Law and himself a naturalized U.S. citizen who emigrated from his native India in 1974.

Pro-immigration groups say the public is ahead of the politicians in Washington and state capitals who are pushing for stricter laws. State legislators "have chosen to scapegoat immigration instead of solving tough economic challenges," says Noorani with the National Immigration Forum. "There are politicians who would rather treat this as a political hot potato," he adds, instead of offering "practical solutions."

From the opposite side, the Federation for American Immigration Reform's Stein says he is "pessimistic, disappointed and puzzled" by what he calls "the short-sighted views" of political leaders. Earlier, Stein says, "politicians all over the country were touting the virtues of engagement in immigration policy." But now he complains that even Republicans are talking about "amnesty and the DREAM Act," instead of criticizing what he calls the Obama administration's "elimination of any immigration enforcement."

Enforcement, however, is one component of the system that, if not broken, is at least completely overwhelmed. In explaining the new prosecutorial discretion policy, ICE director Morton frankly acknowledged the agency "has limited resources to remove those illegally in the United States."[49] The nation's immigrant courts have a current backlog of 300,225 cases, according to a TRAC compilation, double the number in 2001.[50]

Employers' groups say the system's rules for hiring immigrants are problematic at best. In Alabama, Reed with the contractors' group says employers do their best to comply with the status-verification requirements but find the procedures and paperwork difficult. The farm federation's Helms says the same for the rules for temporary guest workers. "We're working at the national level to have a more effective way to hire legal migrant workers to do those jobs that it's hard to find local workers to do," he says.

The rulings by the Supreme Court on the Arizona law will clarify the lines between federal and state enforcement responsibilities, but the Center for Immigration Studies' Krikorian says the decision is likely to increase the politicization of the issue. A ruling to uphold the law will encourage other states to follow Arizona's lead, he says, but would also "energize the anti-enforcement groups." A ruling to find the state laws pre-empted, on the other hand, will mobilize pro-enforcement groups, he says.

The political and legal debates will be conducted against the backdrop of the nation's rapidly growing Hispanic population, attributable more to birth rates than to immigration.[51] "Whoever the next president is, whoever the next Congress is, will have to address this issue," says Giovagnoli with the American Immigration Council. "The demographics are not going to allow people to ignore this issue.

"I do believe we're going to reform the immigration system," Giovagnoli adds "It's going to be a lot of work. Even under the best of circumstances, it's a lot of work."

NOTES

1. Quoted in Kim Chandler, "Alabama House passes Arizona-style immigration bill," *The Birmingham News*, April 6, 2011, p. 1A.

2. The case is *Arizona v. United States*, 11-182. Background and legal filings compiled on SCOTUSblog, www.scotusblog.com/case-files/cases/arizona-v-united-states/?wpmp_switcher=desktop.-

3. See Human Rights Watch, "No Way to Live: Alabama's Immigration Law," December 2011, www.hrw.org/news/2011/12/13/usalabama-no-way-live-under-immigrant-law.

4. Quoted in David White, "Hundreds rally at State House seeking immigration law repeal," *The Birmingham News*, Feb. 15, 2012, p. 1A.

5. See "Unauthorized Immigrant Population: State and National Trends, 2010," Pew Hispanic Center, Feb. 1, 2011, pp. 23, 24, www.pewhispanic.org/files/reports/133.pdf. The U.S. Department of Homeland Security estimates differ slightly; for 2010, it estimates nationwide unauthorized immigrant population at 10.8 million.

6. For previous *CQ Researcher* coverage, see: Alan Greenblatt, "Immigration Debate," pp. 97-120, updated Dec. 10, 2011; Reed Karaim, "America's Border Fence," Sept. 19, 2008, pp. 745-768; Peter Katel, "Illegal Immigration," May 6, 2005, pp. 393-420; David Masci, "Debate Over Immigration," July 14, 2000, pp. 569-592; Kenneth Jost, "Cracking Down on Immigration," Feb. 3, 1995.

7. Quoted in David White, "Illegal immigration bill passes," *The Birmingham News*, June 3, 2011, p. 1A.

8. See Dana Beyerle, "Study says immigration law has economic costs," *Tuscaloosa News*, Jan. 31, 2012, www.tuscaloosanews.com/article/20120131/news/120139966. For Beason's statement, see http://scottbeason.com/2012/01/26/beason-statement-on-the-impact-of-hb-56-on-alabama-unemployment-rate/.

9. Samuel Addy, "A Cost-Benefit Analysis of the New Alabama Immigration Law," Center for Business and Economic Research, Culverhouse College of Commerce and Business Administration, University of Alabama, January 2012, http://cber.cba.ua.edu/New%20AL%20Immigration%20Law%20-%20Costs%20and%20Benefits.pdf; Hammon quoted in Brian Lyman, "Studies, surveys examine immigration law's impact," *The Montgomery Advertiser*, Feb. 1, 2012.

10. See Alan Gomez, "Immigrants return to Alabama," *USA Today*, Feb. 22, 2012, p. 3A; Jay Reeves, "Immigrants trickling back to Ala despite crackdown," The Associated Press, Feb. 19, 2012.

11. The decision in *United States v. Alabama*, 2:11-CV-2746-SLB, U.S.D.C.-N.D.Ala. (Sept. 28, 2011), is available via *The New York Times*: http://graphics8.nytimes.com/packages/pdf/national/112746memopnentered.pdf. For coverage, see Brian Lyman, "Judge allows key part of immigration law to go into effect," *The Montgomery Advertiser*, Sept. 29, 2011; Brian Lawson, "Judge halts part of immigration law," *The Birmingham News*, Sept. 29, 2011, p. 1A. The Alabama Office of the Attorney General has a chronology of the legal proceedings: www.ago.state.al.us/Page-Immigration-Litigation-Federal.

12. Quoted in Eric Velasco, "Immigration law draws praise, scorn," *The Birmingham News*, June 10, 2011, p. 1A.

13. Steven A. Camarota, "A Need for More Immigrant Workers?," Center for Immigration Studies, June 2011, http://cis.org/no-need-for-more-immigrant-workers-q1-2011.

14. "The Impact of Unauthorized Immigrants on the Budgets of State and Local Governments," Congressional Budget Office, Dec. 6, 2007, p. 3, /www.cbo.gov/sites/default/files/cbofiles/ftpdocs/87xx/doc8711/12-6-immigration.pdf.

15. David Gerber, *American Immigration: A Very Short Introduction* (2011).

16. Quoted in Velasco, *op. cit.*

17. Quoted in White, *op. cit.* Hammon's office did not respond to several *CQ Researcher* requests for an interview.

18. "Alabama's Illegal Immigration Law Gets Hollywood's Attention," WAKA/CBS8, Montgomery, Feb. 21, 2012, www.waka.com/home/top-stories/Alabamas-Illegal-Immigration-Law-Gets-Attention-From-Hollywood-139937153.html. The four separate videos by Chris Weitz, collectively titled "Is This Alabama?" are on an eponymous website: http://isthisalabama.org/.

19. See "Delegation of Immigration Authority 287(g) Immigration and Nationality Act," www.ice.gov/287g/ (visited February 2012).

20. See Sandhya Somashekhar and Amy Gardner, "Immigration is flash point in Fla. Primary," *The Washington Post*, Jan. 26, 2012, p. A6.

21. Text available on the White House website: www.whitehouse.gov/the-press-office/2012/01/24/remarks-president-state-union-address.

22. General background drawn from Gerber, *op. cit.*; Otis L. Graham Jr., *Unguarded Gates: A History of America's Immigration Crisis* (2004). Some country-by-country background drawn from Mary C. Waters and Reed Ueda (eds.), *The New Americans: A Guide to Immigration Since 1965* (2007).

23. Roger Daniels, *Guarding the Golden Door: American Immigration Policy and Immigrants Since 1882* (2004), pp. 19-22.

24. Quoted in Graham, *op. cit.*, p. 51.

25. Albert M. Camarillo, "Mexico," in Waters and Ueda, *op. cit.*, p. 506.

26. Figures from *INS Statistical Yearbook*, 1978, cited in Daniels, *op. cit.*, p 138.

27. Polls cited in Daniels, *op. cit.*, p. 233.

28. See *Plyler v. Doe*, 452 U.S. 202 (1982).

29. See Graham, *op. cit.*, Chap. 17, and sources cited therein.

30. "Immigration Rewrite Dies in Senate," *CQ Almanac 2007*, pp. 15-9 — 15-11, http://library.cqpress.com/cqalmanac/cqal07-1006-44907-2047763.

31. See Julia Preston, "Immigration Cools as Campaign Issue," *The New York Times*, Oct. 29, 2008, p. A20, www.nytimes.com/2008/10/29/us/politics/29immig.html; Mark Hugo Lopez, "How Hispanics Voted in the 2008 Election," Pew Hispanic Research Center, Nov. 5, 2008, updated Nov. 7, 2008, http://pewresearch.org/pubs/1024/exit-poll-analysis-hispanics.

32. "Immigration Policy Report: 2011 Immigration-Related Laws and Resolutions in the States (Jan. 1-Dec. 7, 2011)," National Conference of State Legislatures, www.ncsl.org/issues-research/immigration/state-immigration-legislation-report-dec-2011.aspx.

33. The decision is *Chamber of Commerce v. Whiting*, 563 U.S. — (2011). For coverage, see Kenneth Jost, *Supreme Court Yearbook 2010-2011*, http://library.cqpress.com/scyb/document.php?id=scyb10-1270-72832-2397001&type=hitlist&num=0.

34. See "ICE Removals, Fiscal Years 2007-2011," in Mark Hugo Lopez, *et al.*, "As Deportations Rise to Record Levels, Most Latinos Oppose Obama's Policy," Pew Hispanic Center, Dec. 28, 2011, p. 33, http://pewresearch.org/pubs/2158/latinos-hispanics-immigration-policy-deportations-george-bush-barack-obama-administration-democrats-republicans. The report notes that ICE's statistics differ somewhat from those released by DHS, its parent department.

35. "Secretary of Homeland Security Janet Napolitano's 2nd Annual Address on the State of America's Homeland Security: Homeland Security and Economic Security," Jan. 30, 2012, www.dhs.gov/ynews/speeches/napolitano-state-of-america-homeland-security.shtm.

36. "Share of Immigration Cases Ending in Deportation Orders Hits Record Low," *TRAC Reports*, Feb. 7, 2012, http://trac.syr.edu/immigration/reports/272/; "Sharp Decline in ICE Deportation Filings," Feb. 21, 2012, http://trac.syr.edu/immigration/reports/274/. For coverage, see Paloma Esquivel, "Number of deportation cases down by a third," *Los Angeles Times*, Feb. 24, 2012, p. AA2, http://articles.latimes.com/2012/feb/24/local/la-me-deportation-drop-20120224.

37. Text of La Raza statement, www.nclr.org/index.php/about_us/news/news_releases/janet_murgua_president_and_ceo_of_nclr_responds_to_president_obamas_speech_in_el_paso_texas/. For coverage of the

president's speech, see Milan Simonich, "In El Paso, President Obama renews national immigration debate, argues humane policy would aid national economy," *El Paso Times*, May 11, 2011.

38. Lopez, *op. cit.*, p. 16.

39. U.S. Immigration and Customs Enforcement: Memorandum, June 17, 2011, www.ice.gov/doclib/secure-communities/pdf/prosecutorial-discretion-memo.pdf. For coverage, see Susan Carroll, "ICE memo urges more discretion in immigration changes," *Houston Chronicle*, June 21, 2011, p. A3.

40. "Sharp Decline," *op. cit.*

41. For background, see Reed Karaim, "America's Border Fence," *CQ Researcher*, Sept. 19, 2008, pp. 745-768.

42. "Obama says the border fence is 'now basically complete,'" PolitiFact, www.politifact.com/truth-o-meter/statements/2011/may/16/barack-obama/obama-says-border-fence-now-basically-complete/. The original rating of "partly true" was changed to "mostly false" on July 27, 2011.

43. See "Secure Communities," on the ICE website: www.ice.gov/secure_communities/; Julia Preston, "Immigration Crackdown Snares Americans," *The New York Times*, Dec. 14, 2011, p. A20, www.nytimes.com/2011/12/14/us/measures-to-capture-illegal-aliens-nab-citizens.html?pagewanted=all.

44. Coverage of the hearing by contributing writer Don Plummer. For additional coverage, see Brian Lawson, "11th Circuit won't rule on Alabama/Georgia laws until after Supreme Court rules on Arizona," *The Huntsville Times*, March 2, 2012; Jeremy Redmon, "Court to rule later on Georgia, Alabama anti-illegal immigrant laws," *The Atlanta Journal-Constitution*, March 2, 2012.

45. See Jacques Billeaud, "Judge blocks day labor rules in AZ immigration law," The Associated Press, March 1, 2012.

46. Steven A. Camarota, "A Record-Setting Decade of Immigration, 2000-2010," Center for Immigration Studies, October 2011, www.cis.org/articles/2011/record-setting-decade.pdf.

47. Fox News poll, Dec. 5-7, 2011, and CNN/ORC International poll, Nov. 18-20, 2011, cited at www.PollingReport.com/immigration.htm.

48. Quinnipiac University poll, Feb. 14-20, 2011, cited *ibid.*

49. ICE memo, *op. cit.*

50. "Immigration Court Backlog Tool," Transactional Records Access Clearinghouse, http://trac.syr.edu/phptools/immigration/court_backlog/ (visited March 2012).

51. "The Mexican-American Boom: Births Overtake Immigration," Pew Hispanic Center, July 24, 2011, www.pewhispanic.org/files/reports/144.pdf. The report depicts the phenomenon as "especially evident" among Mexican-Americans; it notes that Mexican-Americans are on average younger than other racial or ethnic groups and that Mexican-American women have more children than their counterparts in other groups. For background, see David Masci, "Latinos' Future," *CQ Researcher*, Oct. 17, 2003, pp. 869-892.

BIBLIOGRAPHY

Selected Sources

Books

Coates, David, and Peter M. Siavelis (eds.), *Getting Immigration Right: What Every American Needs to Know*, Potomac, 2009.
Essays by 15 contributors representing a range of backgrounds and views examine, among other issues, the economic impact of immigration and proposed reforms to address illegal immigration. Includes notes, two-page list of further readings. Coates holds a professorship in Anglo-American studies at Wake Forest University; Siavelis is an associate professor of political science there.

Daniels, Roger, *Guarding the Golden Door: American Immigration Policy and Immigrants Since 1882*, Hill and Wang, 2004.
A professor of history emeritus at the University of Cincinnati gives a generally well-balanced account of developments and trends in U.S. immigration policies from the Chinese Exclusion Act of 1882 through the immediate post-9/11 period. Includes detailed notes, 16-page bibliography.

Gerber, David, *American Immigration: A Very Short Introduction*, Oxford University Press, 2011.
A professor of history at the University of Buffalo gives a compact, generally positive overview of the history of immigration from colonial America to the present. Includes two-page list of further readings.

Graham, Otis L. Jr., *Unguarded Gates: A History of America's Immigration Crisis*, Rowman & Littlefield, 2004.
A professor emeritus at the University of California-Santa Barbara provides a critical account of the United States' transition from an open-border policy with relatively small-scale immigration to a system of managed immigration that he views today as overwhelmed by both legal and illegal immigration. Includes notes.

Reimers, David M., *Other Immigrants: The Global Origins of the American People*, New York University Press, 2005.
A New York University professor of history emeritus brings together new information and research about the non-European immigration to the United States, emphasizing the emergence of "a new multicultural society" since 1940. Individual chapters cover Central and South America, East and South Asia, the Middle East, "new black" immigrants and refugees and asylees. Includes extensive notes, six-page list of suggested readings.

Waters, Mary C., and Reed Ueda (eds.), *The New Americans: A Guide to Immigration Since 1965*, Harvard University Press, 2007.
The book includes essays by more than 50 contributors, some covering broad immigration-related topics and others providing individual portraits of immigrant populations by country or region of origin. Includes detailed notes for each essay, comprehensive listing of immigration and naturalization legislation from 1790 through 2002. Waters is a professor of sociology at Harvard University, Ueda a professor of history at Tufts University.

Articles

"Reap What You Sow," *This American Life*, Jan. 27, 2012, www.thisamericanlife.org/radio-archives/episode/456/reap-what-you-sow.
The segment by reporter Jack Hitt on the popular public radio program found that Alabama's law to encourage undocumented immigrants to self-deport was having unintended consequences.

Kemper, Bob, "Immigration Reform: Is It Feasible?," *Washington Lawyer*, October 2011, p. 22, www.dcbar.org/for_lawyers/resources/publications/washington_lawyer/october_2011/immigration_reform.cfm.
The article gives a good overview of recent and current immigration debates, concluding with the prediction that any "permanent resolution" will likely prove to be "elusive."

Reports and Studies

"No Way to Live: Alabama's Immigrant Law," Human Rights Watch, December 2011, www.hrw.org/reports/2011/12/14/no-way-live-0.
The highly critical report finds that Alabama's law cracking down on illegal immigrants has "severely affected" the state's unlawful aliens and their children, many of them U.S. citizens, as well as "the broader community linked to this population."

Baxter, Tom, "Alabama's Immigration Disaster: The Harshest Law in the Land Harms the State's Economy and Society," Center for American Progress, February 2012, www.americanprogress.org/issues/2012/02/pdf/alabama_immigration_disaster.pdf.
The critical account by journalist Baxter under the auspices of the progressive Center for American Progress finds that Alabama's anti-illegal immigration law has had "particularly harsh" social and economic costs and effects.

Passel, Jeffrey S., and D'Vera Cohn, "Unauthorized Immigrant Population: National and State Trends, 2010," *Pew Hispanic Center*, Feb. 1, 2011, www.pewhispanic.org/files/reports/133.pdf.
The 32-page report by the Washington-based center provides national and state-by-state estimates of the unauthorized immigrant population and the number of unauthorized immigrants in the workforce.

For More Information

American Civil Liberties Union, Immigrant Rights Project, 125 Broad St., 18th floor, New York, NY 10004; 212-549-2500; www.aclu.org/immigrants-rights. Seeks to expand and enforce civil liberties and civil rights of immigrants.

American Immigration Council, 1331 G St., N.W., 2nd floor, Washington, DC 20005; 202-507-7500; www.american immigrationcouncil.org. Supports sensible and humane immigration policies.

America's Voice, 1050 17th St., N.W., Suite 490, Washington, DC 20036; 202-463-8602; http://americasvoiceonline.org/. Supports "real, comprehensive immigration reform," including reform of immigration enforcement practices.

Center for Immigration Studies, 1522 K St., N.W., Suite 820, Washington, DC 20005-1202; 202-466-8185; www.cis.org. An independent, nonpartisan research organization that supports what it calls low-immigration, pro-immigrant policies.

Define American, www.defineamerican.com/. Founded by journalist and undocumented immigrant Jose Antonio Vargas, the web-based organization seeks to fix what it calls a "broken" immigration system.

Federation for American Immigration Reform, 25 Massachusetts Ave., N.W., Suite 330, Washington, DC 20001; 202-328-7004; www.fairus.org. Seeks "significantly lower" immigration levels.

Migration Policy Institute, 1400 16th St., N.W., Suite 300, Washington, DC 20036; 202-266-1940; www.migration policy.org. A nonpartisan, nonprofit think tank dedicated to analysis of the movement of people worldwide.

National Council of La Raza, 1126 16th St., N.W., Suite 600, Washington, DC 20036-4845; 202-785-1670; www.nclr.org. The country's largest national Hispanic advocacy and civil rights organization.

National Immigration Forum, 50 F St., N.W., Suite 300, Washington, DC 20001; 202-347-0040; www.immigration forum.org. Advocates for the values of immigration and immigrants to the nation.

Pew Hispanic Center, 1615 L St., N.W., Suite 700, Washington, DC 20036; 202-419-4300; www.pewhispanic.org/. Seeks to improve understanding of the U.S. Hispanic population and to chronicle Latinos' growing impact on the nation.

12

Gay Marriage Showdowns

Kenneth Jost

Kate Sheppard and Kory O'Rourke celebrate with their children after obtaining a marriage license at San Francisco City Hall on June 17, 2008. A California Supreme Court ruling in May made California the second state, after Massachusetts, to legalize same-sex marriage. Opponents quickly gained approval to put a state constitutional amendment on the Nov. 4 ballot that would allow marriage in California only "between a man and a woman."

Getty Images/Justin Sullivan

From *The CQ Researcher*,
September 26, 2008 (updated May 29, 2012).

Jennifer Pizer and Doreena Wong met on their first day at New York University Law School in 1984. They graduated in 1987 and moved to California together three years later.

Jenny and Doreena were still together on May 15, 2008, when the California Supreme Court issued its stunning, 4-3 decision establishing a constitutional right to marriage for same-sex couples in the state. As one of the Lambda Legal Defense and Education Fund lawyers in the case, Pizer spoke at a press conference in San Francisco after the decision was released and then flew home to Los Angeles for a rally in the heart of gay West Hollywood.

"You're not going to do anything funny, are you?" Doreena asked Jenny in the car as they drove to the rally. Pizer feigned ignorance even as she was thinking that the event was the perfect time to pop "the question."

So, as she finished her remarks, Pizer looked down toward her partner's face in the crowd and said, "Now, I'd like to ask a question I've waited 24 years to ask: Doreena Wong, will you marry me?"

"Yes, of course," Wong replied. Standing at the microphone, Pizer relayed the answer to the cheering crowd: "She said yes!"

Television cameras recorded the moment, but Pizer admits months later that she has yet to see the full video clip. For even as gay rights advocates are celebrating the victory — and Jenny and Doreena are planning their Oct. 5 wedding in Marin County — opponents of gay marriage are working hard to reverse the state court's decision.

Less than three weeks after the decision, opponents won legal approval to put a state constitutional amendment on the Nov. 4 ballot

Most States Ban Gay Marriage

Voters in 26 states have approved constitutional amendments banning marriage for same-sex couples.* Most of the measures may also ban other forms of recognition, such as domestic partnership or civil unions; some may ban legal recognition for unmarried opposite-sex couples as well. Arizona, California and Florida will be voting on Nov. 4 on constitutional amendments to define marriage as the union of one man and one woman.

Seventeen other states have enacted statutory bans on same-sex marriage since 1995. Iowa's ban was ruled unconstitutional by a state trial court; the state's appeal is pending. In addition, pre-existing laws in Maryland, New York, Wyoming and the District of Columbia have been interpreted to limit marriage to opposite-sex couples.

California and Massachusetts are the only states recognizing same-sex marriage. Some states with gay-marriage bans recognize civil unions or domestic partnerships. Two states — New Mexico and Rhode Island — appear not to have addressed the issue.

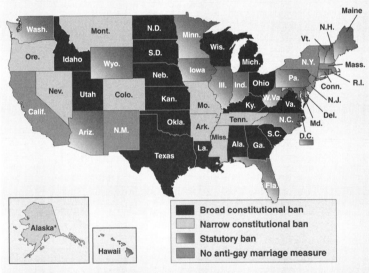

Legend:
- Broad constitutional ban
- Narrow constitutional ban
- Statutory ban
- No anti-gay marriage measure

*CQ Researcher *follows the National Gay and Lesbian Task Force in not counting Hawaii as a constitutional ban state, unlike* Stateline.org *and the Williams Institute. Hawaii adopted a constitutional amendment in 1998 authorizing the legislature to define marriage in opposite-sex terms, and the legislature did so. However, the point of the constitutional bans is to preclude change, and Hawaii's amendment does not.*

Sources: National Gay and Lesbian Task Force; Williams Institute, UCLA School of Law; Stateline.org

for gay and lesbian couples in California and bar recognition of same-sex marriages from other states as well.

"Marriage has always been understood as the union of one man and one woman by California citizens and by other people in the country," says Mathew Staver, founder and chairman of Liberty Counsel, a Christian public-interest law firm, and one of the lawyers who argued against gay marriage before the California Supreme Court. "That provides the best environment for society."

"We absolutely agree that marriage is a special word for a special institution," Pizer responds. "We disagree that the social institution should be available only in a discriminatory manner and that it serves any social purpose to exclude gay and lesbian couples."

The debate over the ballot measure has not deterred but in fact has encouraged gay and lesbian couples in California to get to the altar — or to city hall. By one estimate, some 5,000 same-sex couples got married in California within the first week after the court ruling became effective on June 17. The first-week spike receded, but the weddings are continuing — spurred by the widespread assumption that marriages performed before Nov. 4 will remain valid even if Proposition 8 is approved.

Hollywood celebrities have been among those tying the knot, including TV talk show host Ellen de Generes and ex-"Star Trek" actor George Takei. De Generes wed Portia de Rossi, her girlfriend of the past four years, in an intimate, picture-book ceremony at their Beverly Hills home on Aug. 16. Takei and his longtime partner Brad Altman exchanged self-written vows in a more lavish ceremony at the Japanese American National Museum in downtown Los Angeles on Sept. 14. "May equality long

that would allow marriage in California only "between a man and a woman." If accepted by a simple majority of the state's voters, Proposition 8 would prohibit marriage live and prosper," Takei said as he left the ceremony amid a horde of photographers and well-wishers.[1]

Most of the newlyweds, however, are non-celebrities, many of them in long-term relationships that had already been registered under a 2003 California law as domestic partnerships with nearly complete marriage-like rights and responsibilities. "There's almost no change" over domestic partnership status, explains David Steinberg, news desk copy chief at the *San Francisco Chronicle*, who married his longtime partner Gregory Foley in July. Steinberg says he and Foley, a nurse at Kaiser Permanente, decided to get married anyway "because they might take it away."

The state high court decision made California the second state, after Massachusetts, to allow marriage for same-sex couples. The Supreme Judicial Court of Massachusetts issued a 4-3 decision in November 2003, holding that the state had "no constitutionally adequate reason" for denying same-sex couples the legal benefits of marriage. The court gave the legislature 180 days to respond but later issued an advisory opinion saying that civil union status would not be an adequate substitute for marriage. When the legislature failed to act by the deadline, the high court decision took effect, and same-sex marriages began in Massachusetts on May 17, 2004.[2]

The California Supreme Court ruled similarly but more directly that the state's constitution guarantees a "fundamental right to marry" to "all Californians, whether gay or heterosexual, and to same-sex couples as well as opposite-sex couples." The majority opinion — written by the Republican-appointed chief justice, Ronald George — specifically rejected civil union or domestic partnership status.[3]

Ten States, D.C. Recognize Same-Sex Unions

Ten states and the District of Columbia grant some legal recognition to same-sex couples, ranging from limited spousal rights in Hawaii to fully recognized marriages in California and Massachusetts. Hawaii was the first to recognize same-sex couples' rights in 1997. An estimated 85,000 same-sex couples have gained legal recognition under the various laws.

State	Date	Provisions
California	2008	Marriage approved by California Supreme Court; Proposition 8 on Nov. 4 ballot would overturn ruling
Connecticut	2005	Civil unions approved by legislature; marriage suit pending before Connecticut Supreme Court
District of Columbia	2002	Limited domestic partnership law enacted by D.C. Council in 1992; delayed by Congress until 2002
Hawaii	1997	"Reciprocal beneficiaries" (limited spousal rights)
Maine	2004	Limited domestic partnership law approved by legislature
Massachusetts	2004	Marriage legalized as required by November 2003 ruling by Supreme Judicial Court; constitutional amendment to overturn ruling failed to qualify for ballot
New Hampshire	2007	Civil unions approved by legislature
New Jersey	2006	Civil unions approved by legislature to comply with October 2006 ruling by New Jersey Supreme Court
Oregon	2007	Domestic partnership law approved by legislature
Vermont	2000	Civil unions approved by legislature following ruling by Vermont Supreme Court in December 1999
Washington	2007	Limited domestic partnership law approved by legislature; marriage suit rejected by state Supreme Court, July 2006

Sources: National Gay and Lesbian Task Force; Williams Institute, UCLA Law School

The ruling invalidated a statutory initiative to define marriage as between one man and one woman approved by slightly over 61 percent of the state's voters as Proposition 22 in March 2000. Gay marriage opponents had already begun circulating an initiative to write the

An anti-gay protester demonstrates against same-sex marriage during the 38th annual LA Pride Parade on June 8, 2008, in West Hollywood, Calif. Constitutional amendments that would deny marriage rights to same-sex couples are on the ballot in Arizona and Florida, as well as California.

Besides Massachusetts and California, eight other states and the District of Columbia permit some legal recognition for same-sex couples, including four that permit civil unions with virtually the same rights and responsibilities as marriage. (*See chart, p. 275.*) On the opposite side, 26 states have constitutional amendments that prohibit marriage for same-sex couples, and another 17 have similar statutory bans. In addition, the federal Defense of Marriage Act — known as DOMA — prohibits federal recognition for same-sex marriages. The 1996 law also provides that states need not recognize same-sex marriages from other states. (*See map, p. 274.*)

Massachusetts recorded approximately 11,000 same-sex marriages in the three years after the state high court ruling, according to demographer Gary Gates, a senior research fellow at the Williams Institute, UCLA School of Law. He says an exact count is not possible in California because marriage licenses are no longer recording the parties' sex, but a projection based on the increased number of marriages in the months after the state high court ruling indicates more than 5,000 same-sex couples married in the first week after the decision.

All told, Gates and his colleagues at the institute — which studies sexual-orientation policy and law, primarily funded by a gay philanthropist — estimate that 85,000 same-sex couples have taken advantage of recognition provisions in those states permitting that status. But a higher percentage of same-sex couples are opting to marry than are registering for civil union or domestic partnership.[4]

Supporters of marriage equality say the growing number of same-sex couples in legally protected relationships is eroding opposition to gay marriage. "We're seeing a growing public understanding that ending gay couples' exclusion from marriage helps families and harms no one," says Evan Wolfson, executive director of Freedom to Marry, self-described as a gay and non-gay partnership advocating marriage rights for same-sex couples.

Opponents disagree. They point to the gay marriage bans already enacted as the better gauge of public attitudes on the issue. "Supporters of same-sex marriage have a real uphill climb if they hope to undo what has been accomplished in the past 10 years by supporters of traditional marriage," says Peter Sprigg, vice president for policy at the Family Research Council, a Christian organization based in Washington, D.C., promoting traditional marriage.

"one-man, one-woman" definition of marriage into the state constitution. By June 2, they had submitted petitions with approximately 1.1 million signatures — sufficient for the secretary of state to certify the proposed constitutional amendment for the Nov. 4 ballot.

The state Supreme Court added to the urgency of the opposition by declining to stay its decision pending the Nov. 4 vote. Same-sex marriages began in California on June 17. The first marriage license in San Francisco went to two longtime lesbian activists, Del Martin and Phyllis Lyons, who had been together for more than 50 years. San Francisco Mayor Gavin Newsom officiated at the ceremony. Martin died 10 weeks later — at age 87.

An initial poll in California indicated the ballot measure was ahead, but statewide surveys in August and September showed the proposition trailing by at least 14 percentage points.[5] Two other states — Arizona and Florida — will be voting on similar constitutional amendments on Nov. 4. Arizona's measure needs a majority vote; Florida requires a 60 percent vote for a state constitutional amendment (*see p. 291*).

In addition to those three ballot measures, Arkansans will be voting on a statutory initiative to prohibit unmarried couples — whether same-sex or opposite-sex — to adopt or take foster children. The initiative was proposed after a regulation barring adoption or placement with same-sex couples was overturned in court.[6]

As the debates over same-sex marriage continue, here are some of the major questions being discussed:

Should same-sex couples be allowed to marry?

George Gates and Brian Albert met in 1991 when they both worked at the Human Rights Campaign, a gay rights advocacy organization. They held a big commitment ceremony at the posh Jefferson Hotel in Washington, D.C., in 1996 and, five years later, a small wedding on Cape Cod in Massachusetts.

With both of them still in Washington — now working for other nonprofit groups — Gates and Albert get no tangible benefits from their Massachusetts marriage license. But Gates says he and Albert viewed it as a matter of equal rights to take advantage of the Bay State's welcoming attitude toward gay couples. "We did feel that our relationship was no different from an opposite-sex couple," Gates says, "and we felt we were entitled to the same benefits and responsibilities as they are."

Opponents counter that gay marriage amounts to a redefinition of an institution created by God and universally understood in opposite-sex terms until the recent gay marriage movement. "Never before have we had such a serious effort to make such a profound change to the institution of marriage," says Lynn Wardle, a professor at Brigham Young University Law School, which is operated by the Church of Jesus Christ of Latter-day Saints — the Mormons.

The opposing sides disagree more concretely about the effects that legal recognition of same-sex relationships has or would have on heterosexual marriage, on children and on gay men and lesbians themselves. Opponents say gay marriage will harm the institution of

Anti-gay religious protesters picket at the marriage ceremony of Robin Tyler and Diane Olson, in Beverly Hills, Calif., on June 17, 2008. The two women were plaintiffs in one of the lawsuits that led to the overturning of California's gay marriage ban in May.

marriage, hurt children and have no significant effect for same-sex couples. Supporters of gay marriage say legal recognition will promote stable relationships for same-sex couples, benefit children in same-sex families and have no effect whatsoever on opposite-sex marriages.

Liberty Counsel's Staver, who is also dean of the School of Law at Liberty University, the Lynchburg, Va., school founded by the late televangelist Jerry Falwell, calls same-sex marriage "a huge, unknown sociological experiment done . . . with no understanding of the implications on our children and our society." Wardle and other opponents say recognition of same-sex marriages will contribute to a further decrease in the percentage of people who are married.

Wolfson of Freedom to Marry bluntly disagrees. Same-sex marriage "is not going to change anything" for heterosexual marriages, he says. Gay author Jonathan Rauch goes further to argue that recognizing gay marriage would strengthen the institution overall. "America needs more marriages, not fewer," Rauch wrote in a recent op-ed article, "and the best way to encourage marriage is to encourage marriage, which is what society does by bringing gay couples inside the tent."[7]

Opponents also argue that heterosexual marriages are the best environment for raising children. "Same-sex marriage says as a matter of policy moms and dads are irrelevant to the raising of children," Staver says. In like vein, the pro-Proposition 8 Campaign for Families and Children says on its Web site, "From the commitment of a man and woman in marriage comes the best opportunity for children to thrive."

Gay and lesbian advocacy groups cite studies by, among others, the American Academy of Pediatrics to argue that children raised in families with gay or lesbian parents fare as well overall as children raised in opposite-sex households.[8] "All the evidence and common sense arguments indicate that this will help children who are being raised by gay families without hurting other children at all," says Wolfson.

Opponents also say, some more bluntly than others, that same-sex couples are not entitled to marriage because so many couples — particularly gay men — have short-lived, sometimes non-monogamous relationships. "Whether we like it or not, a big part of the gay agenda for decades has been to repudiate what are regarded as overly restrictive expectations of monogamy and sexual fidelity," University of Pennsylvania Law School Professor Amy Wax wrote in an online debate sponsored by the Washington-based Federalist Society, a prominent conservative organization for lawyers.[9]

Gay marriage advocates counter that allowing marriage for same-sex couples would actually help stabilize their relationships. "Marriage advocates argue that marriage provides a mechanism and incentive to form more stable unions," Williams Institute researcher Gates says. "If that's true, then you would expect the same effect among gays and lesbians."

Apart from the individual points of disagreement, Wardle insists that supporters of traditional marriage should not be forced to prove the case against gay marriage. "When you have a proposal to redefine a basic social institution, the burden of proof is on those who advocate a change," Wardle says.

"Both sides agree that marriage is a powerful institution," Gates rejoins. "Opponents make the argument that we have to be so cautious. Proponents say that's exactly why this is important. This is an important social institution, and you're leaving gay people out of it."

Should state constitutions prohibit marriage for same-sex couples?

The anti-gay organization Focus on the Family dispatched its vice president for public affairs, Ron Prentice, to California in 2003 to launch and become executive director of the affiliated California Family Council. Now, as chairman of the Protect Marriage/Yes on Proposition 8 campaign, Prentice is helping lead the effort to overturn the California Supreme Court's gay marriage ruling by amending the state constitution to define marriage as only "the union of one man and one woman." "We are going to change the constitution and say on Nov. 4, 'Judges, you can't touch this,' " Prentice says.[10]

Gay marriage opponents have enjoyed great success with the strategy. Constitutional amendments limiting marriage to opposite-sex couples have been approved by voters in 26 states, which together represent about 43 percent of the U.S. population. Hawaii voters approved an amendment in 1998 authorizing the legislature to limit marriage to opposite-sex couples. Only once — in Arizona in 2006 — have voters rejected an anti-gay marriage amendment.

Supporters say Proposition 22 represents a legitimate political response to the state high court ruling. "A victory in California will not only protect marriage," the Alliance for Marriage, in Merrifield, Va., says on its Web site, "but will send a strong democratic rebuke by voters to radical, activist groups who've used the courts" to try to gain recognition for same-sex couples.

Gay marriage supporters, however, say the tactic is antithetical to American democracy. "The whole idea of amending constitutions to fence out groups of people is yet another debasement of American fundamentals," says Freedom to Marry's Wolfson. "That is a radical idea: the idea that you amend constitutions to carve out a group of people, shove them outside, and say they can't go to the

Census Won't Recognize Same-Sex Marriages

"It really is something out of Orwell," a critic says.

Even though Massachusetts and California recognize same-sex marriages, the U.S. Census Bureau will not count gay or lesbian spouses as married in the 2010 census.

Census Bureau officials say the policy of treating married same-sex couples as unmarried partners is dictated by the federal Defense of Marriage Act, which bars the federal government from recognizing same-sex marriages for any purpose under federal law. The law "requires all federal agencies to recognize only opposite-sex marriages for the purpose of administering federal programs," Census spokesman Stephen Bruckner explained shortly after the policy was disclosed in July.[1]

The policy has drawn criticism from same-sex couples in both states and from gay rights advocacy groups. "To have the federal government disappear your marriage I'm sure will be painful and upsetting," Shannon Minter, legal director for the San Francisco-based National Center for Lesbian Rights, told the *San Jose Mercury News*, which first disclosed the policy. "It really is something out of [*1984* author George] Orwell."[2]

Demographer Gary Gates at the pro-gay marriage Williams Institute, UCLA School of Law, says the decision amounts to deliberately producing inaccurate population data. "Bureau officials should acknowledge the reality that same-sex couples can legally marry in this country," he says, "and stop altering the accurate responses of same-sex couples who describe themselves as married."[3]

Anti-gay marriage groups, however, defend the bureau's decision. "We're dealing with a government entity that is given certain charters and mandates, and they have to subscribe to public law," says Kris Mineau, president of the Massachusetts Family Institute.[4]

The bureau's decision will not affect the overall population count, which the Constitution requires every 10 years in order to apportion seats in the House of Representatives among the 50 states. But detailed information from the household questionnaires is used by the bureau and by independent researchers to provide demographic analyses in such areas as family structure and size, income and education.

The bureau says the questionnaires used in the 2010 census will not be destroyed, so the data will theoretically be available to independent researchers later. But the bureau's decision will slow a count of married same-sex couples in California, where marriage licenses now identify spouses only as "Party A" and "Party B."

---

[1]Quoted in Eric Moskowitz, "Federal rules mean thousands of same-sex marriages in Massachusetts will be ignored in the U.S. 2010 Census," *The Boston Globe*, July 27, 2008, p. B1.

[2]See Mike Swift, "U.S. Census Bureau won't count same-sex marriages," *San Jose Mercury News*, July 12, 2008.

[3]See Gary J. Gates, "Making same-sex marriages count," *Los Angeles Times*, July 18, 2008, p. A25.

[4]Quoted in Moskowitz, *op. cit.*

---

legislature, that they are permanently treated as second class by the constitution where they live."

Overall, state courts have been responsible for the most dramatic gains realized so far by advocates of legal recognition of same-sex relationships. The Vermont Supreme Court in 1999 became the first state high court to require marriage-like rights for same-sex couples; the state legislature enacted a civil union law five months later. The Supreme Judicial Court of Massachusetts effectively required recognition of gay marriage with a November 2003 ruling that took effect six months later. Opponents of the Massachusetts ruling have tried but failed to get the state legislature to

put a constitutional amendment before the voters to overturn the decision.

Gay marriage opponents say the California Supreme Court invited retaliation with a decision that not only nullified the 2000 ballot measure but also used the state constitution's equal-protection clause to require the highest level of scrutiny for any laws discriminating on the basis of sexual orientation. Wardle calls the ruling "a very clear example" of judges "openly using their position to promote their political preference."

Gay marriage supporters had failed to match their victory in Massachusetts until the California ruling — suffering defeats in closely watched cases in New York and Washington. "To their credit, a number of state supreme courts are behaving more judiciously," Wardle says. But gay marriage supporters are hoping the California ruling may influence supreme court justices in two other states — Connecticut and Iowa — with pending marriage cases. "The California Supreme Court is recognized as by far the most influential state high court in the country," says Lambda Legal's Pizer.

In California, opponents of Proposition 8 won a significant tactical victory with the decision by Attorney General Jerry Brown to list the measure's title on the ballot as, "Eliminates Right of Same-sex Couples to Marry." Prop. 8 supporters tried but failed to get a state court judge to order a change in what they called "an inherently argumentative" title.

Prop. 8 opponents are using the title to frame their campaign message. "We think it's always wrong to be voting on taking away people's rights," says Dale Kelly Bankhead, statewide campaign manager for Equality California/No on Proposition 8.

In a later skirmish, Prop. 8 opponents tried but failed to block the initiative from the ballot. In a petition to the state Supreme Court, they argued that the measure amounted to a "revision" of the state constitution that — under the constitution — could not be put on the ballot without a two-thirds vote of the legislature. Prop. 8 supporters called the lawsuit a "desperate" effort to avoid a vote. The court unanimously declined to hear the request, but the issue could be revived if the measure passes in November.

Should states recognize same-sex marriages from other states?

A one-page legal memorandum that New York Gov. David A. Paterson's legal counsel David Nocenti sent to state agency directors on May 14 quietly handed gay marriage supporters a major victory. Following up a ruling by a state appellate court in February, Nocenti directed state agencies to recognize same-sex marriages from other jurisdictions — a list that then included Massachusetts and five countries: Belgium, Canada, the Netherlands, South Africa and Spain.*

---

*The Norwegian Parliament completed approval of a gay marriage law on June 17; the law will take effect on Jan. 1, 2009.

Nocenti made no announcement of the directive — issued, by coincidence one day before the California Supreme Court's ruling. But three days later Paterson disclosed the move in a videotaped message to the annual dinner of the Empire State Pride Agenda, a gay rights advocacy group. Paterson, who had supported unsuccessful bills in the state legislature to legalize same-sex marriage, called the directive "a strong step to marriage equality."[11]

The possibility that states would either choose or be required to recognize same-sex marriages from other states has been a major concern of gay marriage opponents ever since a Hawaii court's preliminary approval of an ultimately unsuccessful gay marriage suit in 1993. Gay marriage opponents included a provision in the federal Defense of Marriage Act (DOMA) in 1996 strengthening states' discretion to refuse to recognize same-sex marriages. At the same time, they began building a firewall against same-sex marriage by pushing for gay marriage bans in individual states.

The United States' federal system leaves marriage laws generally to states — with the inevitable consequence of differences from state to state. For example, some states permit and others prohibit marriages between first cousins.

Northwestern University law Professor Andrew Koppelman, an expert in an area known as "conflict of laws," says state courts over time have developed some general rules for when to recognize out-of-state marriages that would not be valid within their own state. In general, Koppelman says, states recognize marriages for people who travel through or move to a state with laws otherwise precluding legal status for the union. But states will not recognize a marriage for residents who go to another state to circumvent the state's law — especially if the law reflects a strong public policy.

Gay marriage opponents say the gay marriage bans fit that situation. "You don't have to recognize that status," Brigham Young Professor Wardle says, referring to a same-sex marriage from another state. "It's up to the state to choose for itself what domestic status it will recognize."

Koppelman — who supports same-sex marriage — says, however, that the state bans are "badly drafted" and ignore the real-world situations that will inevitably arise as same-sex couples travel or move from the state where their marriage was performed. "A blanket non-recognition rule is absolutely loony," Koppelman says.

Courts in two non-gay marriage states have already bowed to states that grant legal recognition to same-sex couples. In June, the Virginia Supreme Court ruled that Vermont rather than Virginia courts have jurisdiction over a custody dispute between two former lesbian partners following the dissolution of their Vermont civil union. Lisa Miller, who gave birth to a daughter during the civil union and moved to Virginia after the dissolution, had sought to block visitation rights that a Vermont court had granted to her former partner, Janet Jenkins. In an earlier decision, the federal appeals court for Oklahoma invalidated a state law refusing to recognize an out-of-state, court-approved adoption by a same-sex couple.[12]

Both courts said that the Constitution's "Full Faith and Credit Clause" required the state court to recognize court judgments from other states. Koppelman notes that despite widespread misunderstanding, the constitutional provision does not apply to the more common instances that do not involve litigation already in progress.

The California gay marriage ruling heightened the stakes for both sides because the state has no residency requirement to be married. Massachusetts had been enforcing a 1913 law that barred marriages for out-of-state residents if the union would not be recognized in their home states. But the state repealed the law in August. As a result, businesses in Massachusetts and California are now actively encouraging same-sex couples to come to their states to be wed. (*See sidebar, p. 286.*)

Gay marriage opponents still maintain that states can enforce bans against recognizing same-sex unions from other states. "It's contrary to the strong public policy in those states," says the Family Research Council's Sprigg.

Koppelman disagrees. "Same-sex marriage ought to be, as a general matter, recognized," he says. But gay marriage supporters are sufficiently concerned about their prospects that they are urging same-sex couples not to initiate legal challenges to the state bans at this time.

BACKGROUND

Coming Out

The history of same-sex relationships is long, but the issue of legally recognizing those relationships is of recent origin. Up until the mid-20th century, gay and lesbian couples in the United States generally kept a low profile politically and even socially. An outbreak of repressive laws and policies dating from the 1920s helped give rise to a gay rights movement and by the 1970s to a self-identified gay and lesbian community. Marriage, however, was not a priority or even a widely agreed on goal until the AIDS epidemic and the so-called lesbian baby boom of the 1980s prompted many gay men and lesbians to view legal recognition of their relationships as a practical necessity.[13]

Male couples and female couples can be found in history and literature from ancient times to the present. In the United States, same-sex couples formed part of the gay subcultures present but only somewhat visible in many major cities from the turn of the 20th century. Gay and lesbian couples generally drew as little attention to themselves as possible. As one example, the 1993 book *Jeb and Dash* recounts through posthumously published diaries the secret love affair between two government employees in Washington from 1918 to 1945.[14]

The federal government and many state and local governments began cracking down on homosexuals during the period between the two world wars. "Sexual perverts" were barred from entering the country and were made subject to exclusion from the military. Disorderly conduct and anti-sodomy laws were used to break up gay organizations and arrest individuals looking for or engaging in gay sex.

After the repeal of Prohibition in 1933, gay bars could still be shut down through license suspensions or revocations. The repressive atmosphere increased after World War II as homosexuals came to face the same kind of persecution as suspected communists. The historian David K. Johnson suggests that more federal employees lost jobs because of suspected homosexuality during what he terms "the lavender scare" than were dismissed because of suspected communist leanings.[15]

Threatened in their workplaces and gathering places, gay men and lesbians in the 1950s formed the forerunners of the present-day gay rights movement. The gay Mattachine Society and the Daughters of Bilitis both adopted assimilationist stances: no garish costumes, no lavish parades. In 1965, however, a fired government astronomer, Franklin Kameny, staged the first "gay rights" picketing outside the White House, aimed at reversing policies generally barring homosexual from federal

CHRONOLOGY

Before 1970 *Gay rights movement begins to form; same-sex marriage low on agenda.*

1968, 1969 Metropolitan Community Church in Los Angeles performs first public weddings for same-sex couples.

1970s-1980s *Gay rights measures enacted in some states, localities; AIDS epidemic, "lesbian baby boom" spur interest in legal recognition for relationships.*

1971 Marriage rights suits filed by gay Minnesota couple and lesbian couple in Kentucky are rejected; over next six years, 15 states pass laws defining marriage as opposite-sex union.

1984 Berkeley, Calif., becomes first city to provide domestic-partner benefits to employees.

1986 U.S. Supreme Court upholds state anti-sodomy laws.

1990s *Gay marriage rulings spur backlash in Congress, states; Vermont court is first to require state to give legal recognition for same-sex couples.*

1993 Hawaii Supreme Court requires state to justify ban on same-sex marriage; trial court rules ban unconstitutional in 1996, but ruling is nullified by state constitutional amendment approved in 1998.

1996 Congress passes and President Bill Clinton signs Defense of Marriage Act, which bars federal benefits for same-sex couples and buttresses states' authority not to recognize same-sex marriages from other states.

1998 Alaska trial court rules ban on same-sex marriage unconstitutional; ruling nullified by constitutional amendment approved by voters in November.

1999 California passes limited domestic-partnership law for same-sex couples; rights under law expanded in 2001, 2003. . . . Vermont Supreme Court rules state must allow same-sex couples to enjoy legal benefits accorded to heterosexuals; state legislature implements ruling by passing civil-unions law in April 2000.

2000-Present *Massachusetts recognizes marriage for same-sex couples; after setbacks in several states, gay rights supporters win second pro-marriage ruling in California; opponents qualify ballot measure to overturn decision.*

2003 U.S. Supreme Court rules anti-sodomy laws unconstitutional; majority opinion does not address gay marriage. . . . Supreme Judicial Court of Massachusetts rules same-sex couples entitled to same rights as opposite-sex couples; gives legislature 180 days to act.

2004 Voters in 13 states pass gay marriage bans, all by substantial margins. . . . Federal Marriage Amendment fails in Senate (and again in 2006).

2005 Connecticut legislature passes civil-union law — first state to act without court mandate.

2006 State high courts in New York and Washington uphold laws limiting marriage to opposite-sex couples. . . . New Jersey Supreme Court rules same-sex couples entitled to same benefits, protections as opposite-sex couples, with legislature to choose between "marriage" or "civil unions"; legislature approves civil-union bill two months later.

2007 Connecticut Supreme Court hears arguments in gay-marriage case; decision still pending in fall 2008. . . . Judge in Iowa rules gay-marriage ban unconstitutional; same-sex couple weds before decision is stayed pending appeal to state Supreme Court.

2008 California Supreme Court says same-sex couples entitled to marriage, anti-gay laws presumptively unconstitutional (May 15); ruling goes into effect one month later after justices decline request for stay. . . . Gay-marriage opponents qualify Proposition 8 for Nov. 4 ballot; measure would define marriage as union of one man, one woman; bar recognition of same-sex marriages from other states. . . . Same-sex marriage bans also on ballot in Arizona, Florida; Arkansas to vote on banning adoptions, foster-child placements with unmarried couples.

2008 November — Democrat Barack Obama elected president after campaigning on pledge to end military's "don't ask, don't tell" policy on gays, repeal Defense of

Marriage Act (Nov. 4); on same day, California voters approve Proposition 8, banning marriage rights for same-sex couples.

2009 Same-sex couples file federal court suit challenging Proposition 8 (May 22). . . . Maine voters approve referendum to nullify gay marriage law approved by legislature in spring (Nov. 3). . . . District of Columbia Council votes 11-2 to recognize same-sex marriage (Dec. 2).

2010 Winter-Spring — Trial in Proposition 8 case (Jan. 11-27). . . . District of Columbia begins issuing marriage licenses for same-sex couples (March 4). . . . House votes to repeal "don't ask, don't tell" policy (May 27).

Summer — Defense of Marriage Act ruled unconstitutional by federal judge in Boston (July 8). . . . California's Proposition 8 ruled unconstitutional by federal judge in San Francisco; (Aug. 4). . . . "Don't ask,

don't tell" policy ruled unconstitutional by federal judge in Riverside, Calif. (Sept. 9). . . . Republican filibuster on repealing "don't ask, don't tell" thwarts vote in Senate (Sept. 21); advocates vow to renew effort in post-election session.

Fall — Freshman Rutgers student Tyler Clementi commits suicide, days after his roommate streamed his gay sexual encounter live on the Internet (Sept. 22); police charge roommate and an 18-year-old woman in connection with his death. . . . Judge issues nationwide injunction against "don't ask, don't tell" policy (Oct. 12); White House eyes eventual repeal, but Justice Department seeks stay of ruling pending appeal. . . . Pentagon due to complete report on repeal of "don't ask, don't tell" (Dec. 1); meanwhile, on Oct. 15, military recruiters are ordered — for the first time — to accept openly gay and lesbian applicants. . . . Federal appeals court due to hear arguments in Proposition 8 case (Dec. 6).

employment. Then in 1969 the gay patrons of the Stonewall Inn in New York City rose up in protest after a police raid on the Greenwich Village bar. The disturbance attracted little attention in the straight world but quickly became a rallying point for a newly assertive gay and lesbian community.

Marriage was not high on the community's agenda, however.[16] Many other issues were more pressing: pushing for gay rights ordinances, fighting employment bans and seeking to repeal anti-sodomy laws. In any event, many gay and lesbian activists actively opposed marriage, as Yale University historian George Chauncey recounts. Gay liberation celebrated sexual freedom, not committed relationships. And many lesbians viewed marriage as an inherently patriarchal institution to be reformed (or even abolished), but certainly not to be imitated.

The activists' views should not be overemphasized, Chauncey cautions. "Most lesbians and gay men across the country looked for a steady relationship," he writes. Indeed, the Metropolitan Community Church, a gay congregation formed in 1968 in Los Angeles, began blessing same-sex unions at its creation and performed 150 marriages in its first four years. In addition, same-sex couples in Minneapolis and Louisville, Ky., filed lawsuits in 1971 seeking to win the right to marry. Courts in both

cases said marriage was only for opposite-sex couples, even though the state laws did not say so. To fill in the gap, 15 states passed laws from 1973 to 1977 limiting marriage to heterosexual couples.

The AIDS epidemic brought gay men face to face with the consequences of legally unrecognized relationships. The illness or death of a "longtime companion" became even more painful when hospitals, funeral homes or government agencies refused to give any regard to the relationship. Medical costs and medical decision-making were difficult issues as long as the patient lived; at death, many survivors had bitter conflicts with their deceased lover's "real" family over funeral arrangements and disposition of property.[17]

Meanwhile, the growing interest in childrearing also focused attention on the disadvantages of legally unrecognized relationships. Gay men and lesbians who had children from previous opposite-sex marriages typically faced difficulties in winning custody or sometimes even visitation rights. As historian Chauncey explains, the lesbian baby boom of the 1980s "represented something new: a generation of women who . . . no longer felt obliged to marry a man in order to have a child." A biological mother's relationship to her child was not legally difficult, but her partner could gain a legal relationship only through

McCain and Obama Diverge Over Legal Recognition

But both oppose same-sex marriage.

Sen. John McCain voted for the Defense of Marriage Act in 1996.

D emocrat Barack Obama and Republican John McCain both oppose marriage for same-sex couples. But the two presidential nominees diverge significantly on a secondary question about gay and lesbian relationships: Should they receive legal recognition?

Obama favors civil unions that would give same-sex couples all of the legal rights of marriage. The Illinois senator also wants to repeal the federal Defense of Marriage Act (DOMA), which defines marriage as the union of a man and a woman. And he displays both positions along with other gay-rights stances on a full page devoted to GLBT (gay, lesbian, bisexual and transgender) issues on his campaign Web site (www.obama .com).

McCain says same-sex couples should be allowed to establish some rights through "legal agreements," but he appears to oppose civil unions. The Arizona senator voted for DOMA in 1996; the Republican Party platform opposes repealing it. McCain's campaign Web site has no GLBT page; the only tacit references to GLBT issues endorse the one-man, one-woman definition of marriage and oppose "activist" judges (www.mccain .com).

The two candidates also differ on the Nov. 4 ballot proposition in California to overturn the state Supreme Court's decision granting full marriage rights to same-sex couples. McCain favors the measure; Obama opposes it. Both candidates called little attention to statements announcing their positions in late June.[1]

Unsurprisingly, major GLBT advocacy organizations are supporting Obama in the Nov. 4 presidential balloting. "Sen. Obama has consistently shown that he understands, as we do, that, GLBT rights are civil rights and human rights," Human Rights Campaign President Joe Solmonese said in formally endorsing the Democratic ticket on June 6.

But the Log Cabin Republicans, a gay GOP group, is backing McCain — four years after withholding its endorsement from President Bush. In announcing the endorsement on Sept. 2, President Patrick Sammon pointed to McCain's two Senate votes in 2004 and 2006 opposing the proposed constitutional amendment to bar recognition of same-sex marriages by the federal or state governments.

Obama also voted against the amendment and restates his opposition on his Web site. McCain does not mention the amendment on his site.

McCain says on his Web site that only the definition of marriage as the union of one man and one woman "sufficiently recognizes the vital and unique role played by mothers and fathers in the raising of children, and the role of the family in shaping, stabilizing and strengthening communities and our nation." He has been less clear in his position on civil unions.

Campaigning in New Hampshire in March 2007, McCain said he opposed the civil union legislation recently enacted in the state. "Anything that impinges or impacts the sanctity of the marriage between men and women, I'm opposed to it," McCain was quoted as saying in a conference call with several political bloggers.[2] Appearing on the "Ellen de Generes Show" in May 2008, however, McCain said "people should be able to enter into legal agreements" and should be encouraged to do so.[3]

Obama professes strong support for civil unions for same-sex couples. "Barack Obama supports full civil unions that give same-sex couples equal legal rights and privileges as married couples," the campaign Web site states. The entry goes on to call for repealing DOMA and providing federal rights and benefits to same-sex couples in civil unions or other legally recognized unions.

Obama has been somewhat reticent, however, on same-sex marriage. "My religious beliefs say that marriage is something sanctified between a man and a woman," Obama was quoted as saying during his 2004 Senate campaign in Illinois.[4] In the presidential campaign, however, he has generally answered questions about gay marriage only indirectly by explaining his support for civil unions — as can be seen in an undated CNN video clip from a campaign town hall meeting in Durham, N.H.[5]

On his Web site, Obama also calls for adoption rights for "all couples and individuals, regardless of sexual orientation." On his site, McCain — father of an adoptive child — calls for promoting adoption as "a first option" for crisis pregnancies. But the site makes no reference to McCain's statement in a newspaper interview opposing adoption by gay couples or individuals. Under criticism, McCain modified the statement the next day to say that adoption is a state issue.[6]

Longtime gay-rights advocate Winnie Stachelberg says the contrast between the two candidates on GLBT issues "could not be more clear." Stachelberg, a senior vice president at the Center for American Progress, a Democratic think tank, says Obama would promote gay and lesbian equality if elected president. She complains that McCain has "studiously" avoided reaching out to the GLBT community.

From the opposite side, Family Research Council policy Vice President Peter Sprigg voices satisfaction with the

AFP/Getty Images/Emmanuel Dunand

Sen. Barack Obama wants to repeal the Defense of Marriage Act.

Republican platform's support for "traditional marriage," while acknowledging ambivalence about McCain's votes against the Federal Marriage Amendment, a proposed constitutional amendment that would define marriage as a union of one man and one woman. But he complains that Obama "is unwilling to support any kind of actions that would defend the traditional definition of marriage. I kind of think he's playing word games in saying that he does not support same-sex marriage."

[1] See Michael Finnegan and Cathleen Decker, "Quiet stands on gay marriage," *Los Angeles Times*, July 2, 2008, p. A12.

[2] Ryan Sanger, "Exclusive: John McCain Comes Out Against NH Civil Unions," *New York Sun*, April 27, 2007, www.nysun.com/blogs.

[3] Quoted in Jim Brown, "Is McCain for civil unions?" *OneNewsNow*, May 28, 2008, www.onenewsnow.com/elections. OneNewsNow is a service of the American Family News Network, a Christian news service.

[4] Quoted in Eric Zorn, "Change of subject," *Chicago Tribune*, March 25, 2007, p. C2.

[5] CNN, "Election 2008: GLBT Issues," www.cnn.com/ELECTION/2008/issues/issues.samesexmarriage.html.

[6] See Michael Cooper, "Facing Criticism, McCain Clarifies His Statement on Gay Adoption," *The New York Times*, July 16, 2008, p. A15.

Will Gay Weddings Bring Economic Boom?

California and Massachusetts are not cashing in yet.

S ame-sex couples from other states who travel to California and Massachusetts to get marriage licenses may spark a modest economic boom in the two states.

The pro-gay marriage Williams Institute at UCLA School of Law forecasts $64 million in added revenue for state and local governments in California from out-of-state couples coming to wed. A similar study for Massachusetts — prepared this summer as the state was about to repeal a law limiting marriage for out-of-state couples — projects a $5 million revenue gain over three years.[1]

Gay-marriage opponents discount the studies. "Those claims are highly suspect, particularly since the only study was done by a blatantly pro-homosexual think tank," says Kris Menau, president of the Massachusetts Family Institute, the major advocacy group working against gay marriage in the Bay State. "We see no evidence of a great migration by out-of-state homosexual couples to come here to marry."

Anecdotal evidence is ambiguous. A justice of the peace in the gay mecca of Provincetown, Mass., told *The Washington Post* she had to use scheduled vacation days in August to perform weddings for out-of-state couples. "I have a full-time job, and this has become a full-time job," Rachel Peters said.[2]

In California, however, the head of a nationwide trade association for wedding professionals says the predicted boomlet has yet to materialize. "The goal was to pull several hundred thousand from other states to come here and get married," says Richard Markel, president of the Sacramento-based Association for Wedding Professionals International. "I haven't seen it totally yet."

Five months after Massachusetts became the first state to extend marriage to same-sex couples, the respected business magazine *Forbes* forecast that gay weddings could mean an additional $16.8 billion for the nation's $70-billion-a-year wedding industry. A wedding industry newsletter cited in the Williams Institute studies puts the average cost of a wedding in the United States today at $30,000.[3]

For its calculations, the Williams Institute used a more conservative figure of about $3,000 per wedding — assuming that out-of-state couples would be somewhat budget-strapped on their celebrations. But after adding in anticipated tourist spending, the institute predicted $111 million in added spending in Massachusetts from more than 30,000 out-of-state couples over the next three years. In California, the institute predicted that 51,000 California couples and 67,000 out-of-staters would spend $638.6 million.

Whatever the exact figure proves to be, gay marriage has been a definite boon for the lesbian couple who founded the Rainbow Wedding Network in 2002. Co-founder Cindy Sproul says she returned to her home state of North Carolina in August with a good-sized boost for the

a cumbersome second-parent adoption. Moreover, couples who split up had no assurance that courts would respect or enforce agreed-on custody and visitation rights.

Debating Marriage

Marriage gradually moved toward the top of the gay rights agenda in the 1990s as dissenting views within the GLBT (gay, lesbian, bisexual, transgender) community were either transformed or suppressed. An initial victory in Hawaii, however, resulted in a major setback with congressional passage of the federal Defense of Marriage Act in 1996. DOMA limited federal status to opposite-sex couples and buttressed states' prerogatives to refuse to recognize same-sex

marriages from other states. Gay rights advocates' later successes in winning civil unions in Vermont in 1999 and marriage in Massachusetts in 2003 were offset by losses in other state courts and a new flurry of so-called mini-DOMAs approved by voters in the 2004 election cycle.[18]

For gay rights advocates, Hawaii ended as a ballot-box defeat after a potential judicial victory. In 1993, the Hawaii Supreme Court held the state's ban on same-sex marriage presumptively unconstitutional and ordered a trial for the state to try to show a compelling interest to justify the restriction. The trial opened in Honolulu just as the Senate was about to complete action on DOMA in Washington. The judge ruled for the gay couples who

$4.5-million-a-year business after hosting four wedding expos in California in July.

Sproul and Markel both say gay weddings are similar to opposite-sex weddings. Most gay weddings are performed in places of worship and officiated by clergy, Sproul says, though same-sex couples are somewhat more likely to write their own vows than opposite-sex couples. Same-sex couples — typically older than opposite-sex couples — are also more likely to be paying for weddings themselves rather than their parents.

Sproul says most of the companies that advertise through the network are straight-owned, and the owners have no problems with serving gay ceremonies. Markel agrees. "A majority of the people in the business got into the business because they enjoy celebrations, and they enjoy helping people," he says.

Both Sproul and Markel point to some exceptions, however. "We've had some very hostile e-mails and death threats," says Sproul. Markel quotes one photographer as saying he would shoot a lesbian wedding but — using an epithet — questioned whether he would photograph two men getting married.[4]

The Williams Institute predicted that New York would be the major source of out-of-state couples for Massachusetts. For California, the institute forecast influxes from New York, Texas, North Carolina and the nearby Pacific Coast and Southwestern states. But among those who already traveled to California to tie the knot was Sproul and her partner Marianne Puechl, who got married on July 22 on a Malibu beach.

The newlyweds flew home the next day to North Carolina. The state enacted a statutory ban on recognizing

AFP/Getty Images/David McNew

Same-sex wedding cake figurines will be in demand if the gay-wedding business grows as expected in California.

same-sex marriages in 1996. "We hope [the marriage] will be recognized some day," Sproul says.

[1] See Brad Sears and M.V. Lee Badgett, "The Impact of Extending Marriage to Same-Sex Couples on the California Budget," Williams Institute, June 2008, www.law.ucla.edu/WilliamsInstitute/publications/EconImpactCAMarriage.pdf. The Massachusetts study is referenced in Keith B. Richburg, "A Milestone for Gays, A Boon for Massachusetts," *The Washington Post*, Sept. 3, 2008, p. A3. The Charles R. Williams Project on Sexual Orientation and the Law was established at UCLA in 2001 after a $2.5 million contribution from Williams, a gay businessman and philanthropist.

[2] Quoted in Richburg, *op. cit.*

[3] Aude Lagorce, "The Gay-Marriage Windfall: $16.8 Million," *Forbes*, April 5, 2004. See Sears and Badgett, *op. cit.*, p. 7.

[4] See My Thuan Tran, "Gay Weddings Not Quite a Piece of Cake," *Los Angeles Times*, June 21, 2008, p. B1.

brought the suit, but the state high court kept the appeal under advisement long enough for voters to approve a state constitutional amendment in 1998 that authorized the legislature to limit marriage to opposite-sex couples. The next year, the state Supreme Court dismissed the suit.

In Washington, Republican lawmakers cited the Hawaii Supreme Court's 1993 ruling as the motivation for the bills introduced in May 1996 that led to DOMA's enactment four months later. The bills provided that no state was obligated to recognize a same-sex marriage from another state. In a second section, the measures defined "marriage" and "spouse" in opposite-sex terms for federal law, thus precluding same-sex couples from filing joint

tax returns or qualifying for any federal marital or spousal benefits. Opponents said the federal provision was discriminatory, the state law provision either unconstitutional or unnecessary. But the Republican-controlled Congress approved the measure by wide margins: 342-67 in the House, 85-14 in the Senate. President Bill Clinton endorsed the bill as it moved through Congress and then quietly signed it on Sept. 21.[19]

State legislatures followed suit by approving statutes or submitting for voter approval constitutional amendments similarly aimed at precluding legal recognition for same-sex couples. As in Hawaii, a state constitutional amendment approved by Alaska voters in 1998 wiped out a trial court's ruling tentatively backing gay marriage. Gay rights lawyers, however, scored significant victories with cases in two New England states: Vermont and Massachusetts.

The Vermont Supreme Court's ruling in December 1999 held the denial of marital benefits to same-sex couples to violate the state constitution's equal protection provisions and ordered the state legislature to remedy the inequality. The legislature responded in April 2000 with a law creating the marriage-like "civil union" status for same-sex couples. The law took effect July 1, 2000, and by 2008 an estimated 1,485 same-sex civil unions had been registered in the state.

In Massachusetts, lawyers from the Boston-based Gay and Lesbian Advocates and Defenders filed suit in April 2001 on behalf of seven same-sex couples who had been together for periods ranging from three to 30 years. The trial judge rejected the suit the next year, but in November 2003 the Supreme Judicial Court of Massachusetts issued its epochal, 4-3 decision mandating legal recognition for same-sex couples. The ruling gave the state legislature a 180-day deadline to comply. The first marriages were performed on May 17, 2004.

The victory in Massachusetts, however, proved costly for gay rights advocates by re-energizing opponents of gay marriage, who qualified ballot measures in 13 states in 2004 aimed at banning marriage for same-sex couples. Voters approved all 13: two in early voting in September and 11 more in November. With more than 20 million voters casting ballots, the measures triumphed overall by a better than 2-1 margin. Gay rights advocates had looked to Oregon as their only realistic chance of stemming the tide, but the gay marriage ban prevailed there with 57 percent of the vote.

The battles continued. Gay marriage advocates suffered two big disappointments in July 2006 when the highest state courts in New York and Washington both narrowly rejected suits seeking to require marriage equality for same-sex couples. The 4-2 ruling in New York and the 4-3 decision in Washington both said the issue was for state legislatures to decide. In the same month, the Georgia Supreme Court and the federal appeals court for Nebraska reinstated constitutional amendments banning same-sex marriages that lower courts had ruled invalid.

Meanwhile, however, gay rights supporters had scored legislative victories in some states. The California legislature passed a domestic partnership law in 2003 giving same-sex couples virtually all the rights of marriage. Connecticut passed a civil union law in 2005 — the first state to do so without a court mandate. By the end of 2007, same-sex couples had marriage-like status available in three other states: civil unions in New Jersey and New Hampshire and domestic partnerships in Oregon.

California Showdown

Supporters and opponents of legal recognition for same-sex couples have waged virtually nonstop battles against each other in California for nearly a decade. Opponents won the first round in 2000 with the voter-approved Proposition 22 defining marriage in opposite-sex terms. Supporters won the next round in 2003 with enactment of a domestic partnership law granting all marriage rights allowed under state law. Two gay marriage bills were passed by the legislature but vetoed by Republican Gov. Arnold Schwarzenegger, while the landmark gay marriage case moved toward the state Supreme Court. Instead of settling the issue, the court's May 15 ruling only set the stage for another ballot-box showdown.

California voters' approval of the state Defense of Marriage Act in the March 7, 2000, election followed a fractious campaign that cost both sides together more than $16 million. The late state Sen. William "Pete" Knight, a Republican from Los Angeles County's high desert and father of an estranged gay son, drafted the 14-word initiative. Roman Catholic and Mormon churches did much of the legwork supporting the initiative, which carried with 61.4 percent of the vote. "California is not ready for a marriage between a man and a man," Knight told supporters on election night. Gay rights advocates vowed to regroup. "We're stronger and more galvanized than ever before," said Gwen Baldwin, executive director of the Los Angeles Gay & Lesbian Center.[20]

The setback came six months after California had become the first state to provide domestic partner status for same-sex couples without court intervention. The bill that Democratic Gov. Gray Davis signed into law in September 1999 was limited; it provided hospital visitation rights and, for public employees, health insurance coverage for partners. With Davis in office, the Democratic-controlled legislature significantly expanded the rights of domestic partners in 2001 and again two years later. The California Domestic Partner Rights and

Responsibilities Act of 2003 essentially gave state-registered domestic partners all of the rights, benefits and duties of marital spouses recognized by state law. Davis signed the bill on Sept. 22, 2003, before a huge and appreciative crowd at San Francisco's GLBT center in the Castro district. Knight said the law circumvented Proposition 22.

Barely six weeks after signing the bill, Davis was recalled by California voters — who blamed him for a variety of economic problems — and replaced by Republican Schwarzenegger. The change left gay rights groups with a gay-friendly governor from a gay-unfriendly party. Twice — in 2005 and again in 2007 — the Democratic-controlled legislature passed same-sex marriage bills, each time by bare majorities on party-line votes. Schwarzenegger vetoed both bills, saying they amounted to end-runs around the 2000 ballot initiative. "The governor believes the matter should be determined not by legislative action — which would be unconstitutional — but by court decision or another vote of the people of our state," Schwarzenegger's press secretary, Margita Thompson, explained after the first veto in September 2005.[21]

In the meantime, Democratic San Francisco Mayor Newsom had tried to take matters into his own hands in February 2004 by directing the county clerk's office to issue marriage licenses to same-sex couples on request. About 4,000 such licenses were issued over the next month before the California Supreme Court ordered a halt. On Aug. 12, the court voided the same-sex marriages that had been performed. The city-county government then joined with half a dozen same-sex couples in seeking to invalidate Proposition 22 and win a court ruling to permit gay marriage.

The gay marriage plaintiffs won an initial ruling from a San Francisco Superior Court judge in March 2005, but a state appeals court reversed the decision by a split 2-1 vote in July 2006. The seven-justice California Supreme Court scheduled an extraordinary four hours of arguments in the case for March 4, 2008. Attorneys on the plaintiffs' side took some encouragement from some of the questions that Chief Justice George posed.

Still, neither side was completely prepared for the strongly written opinion that George authored for the 4-3 majority on May 15. Shannon Minter, legal director for the National Center for Lesbian Rights, who argued the case for the plaintiffs, called the decision "a powerful affirmation of love, family and commitment."

Liberty Counsel's Staver, one of the lawyers on the other side, said the court had "abandoned the rule of law and common sense."

CURRENT SITUATION

Gay Marriage Ban Trailing

Californians appear to be closely divided on whether to permit gay marriage, but a ballot measure to overturn the state Supreme Court decision granting marriage rights to same-sex couples is trailing in the most recent public opinion surveys. Both sides in the statewide contest, however, expect the election to be close and are planning to spend about $20 million each on advertising and voter mobilization before the Nov. 4 balloting.

The two most recent polls find Proposition 8 trailing by 17 or 14 percentage points: 40 percent to 54 percent in a late August poll by the Public Policy Institute of California (PPIC); 38 percent to 55 percent in a September survey by the long-established Field Poll. The margins approximate the gap for Prop. 8 supporters recorded by the Field Poll in late May, shortly after the California Supreme Court's gay marriage ruling.[22]

A poll by the *Los Angeles Times* and the Los Angeles TV station KTLA one week earlier in May found 54 percent in favor of and 35 percent opposed to the ballot measure. At the time, Prop. 8 campaign officials described the Field Poll as "an outlier" and called the *Times*/KTLA poll a more accurate gauge of public opinion.[23]

After the most recent surveys, Prop. 8 campaign spokeswoman Jennifer Kerns blamed the gap on the ballot title that Attorney General Brown gave to the measure. Still, Kerns is predicting a "close" race that will turn on the level of enthusiasm among voters on both sides.

"There's a great deal of passion in support of this, which bodes well for Election Day," Kerns said. "People who feel most passionate are the people who go to the polls."[24]

The PPIC poll, in fact, found greater interest in the ballot measure among supporters than among opponents. More than half of those in favor of the measure — 57 percent — called the outcome "very important," compared to 44 percent of those opposed.

For their part, gay marriage supporters are also describing the race as close. "It's a dead heat," says Equality California Campaign Director Bankhead.

Should the Defense of Marriage Act (DOMA) be repealed?

YES

Evan Wolfson
Executive Director, Freedom to Marry; author,
Why Marriage Matters: America, Equality,
and Gay People's Right to Marry

Written for *CQ Global Researcher,* September 2008

Congress should repeal the federal anti-marriage law. Couples who are legally married by a state such as Massachusetts or California should not be treated as legal strangers or denied rights by the federal government.

DOMA says that no matter what the need or purpose for any given program, the government will categorically deny all federal protections and responsibilities to married couples it doesn't like, i.e., those who are gay. This is an intrusive departure from more than 200 years in which couples properly married under state law then qualified for the more than 1,138 federal benefits of marriage such as Social Security, tax treatment as a family unit, family unification under immigration law and access to a spouse's health coverage. Through DOMA, Congress for the first time ever gave itself the power to say who is married, a power that under the Constitution belongs to the states.

Even worse, by denying rights such as family leave, child support and survivor benefits to one set of married couples, DOMA penalizes not only the couples themselves but their children. If the government wants to promote strong families, it should treat all married couples, and their children, equally.

There are far better reasons to treat marriages with respect than there are for destabilizing them — for all couples, gay and non-gay alike. And there are many constitutional and legal reasons why DOMA should be repealed: It denies one group of families an important and meaningful safety net; it violates the right of equal protection; it upends the traditional ways in which our country has treated married couples; and it's a power-grab by the federal government at the expense of the states.

Most important, however, Congress should reverse DOMA's radical wrong turn because it leaves no one better off, but it harms some people severely.

When DOMA was stampeded into law back in 1996, no gay couples were married anywhere in the world; Congress was voting on a hypothetical. But today real-life married couples are cruelly affected by DOMA's double standard, and Americans better understand the unfairness of depriving these families of the federal rights and responsibilities that will help them protect their loved ones. Even conservative former Georgia Republican Rep. Bob Barr, the original sponsor, has acknowledged DOMA to be abusive and now calls for its repeal.

In the United States, we don't have second-class citizens, and we shouldn't have second-class marriages. Couples who have made a personal commitment in life deserve an equal commitment under the law.

NO

Peter Sprigg
Vice president for policy, Family Research Council; author, Outrage:
How Gay Activists and Liberal Judges Are
Trashing Democracy to Redefine Marriage

Written for *CQ Global Researcher,* September 2008

Cases asserting a "right" to same-sex marriage were heard in both Hawaii and Alaska in the early 1990s. Both states responded with constitutional amendments to forestall such judicial activism, but the cases triggered a national response as well. Fearing that if even one state legalized homosexual marriages, those marriages might then have to be recognized in every state and by the federal government, a bill was introduced in Congress to accomplish two things. First, it declared that for every purpose under federal law (such as taxation, Social Security, immigration and federal employee benefits), marriage would be defined only as the union of one man and one woman.

Second, it declared that no state would be required to recognize a same-sex marriage or other same-sex union that was legally contracted in another state. The Defense of Marriage Act (DOMA) passed both houses of Congress by large, bipartisan majorities and was signed into law by President Bill Clinton in 1996.

Many states followed with statewide DOMAs declaring homosexual marriage contrary to the public policy of that state. The 45 state DOMAs show a strong national consensus in favor of defining marriage as the union of one man and one woman.

Two state courts (Massachusetts and California) have succeeded in forcing homosexual marriage upon their unwilling populations. But the federal DOMA has been effective in preventing the imposition of this radical social experiment on the rest of the country. Unfortunately, some members of Congress (including Sen. Barack Obama, D-Ill.) are now proposing to repeal DOMA. This would open the door for federal taxpayers to subsidize homosexual relationships through domestic partner benefits and pave the way for lawsuits demanding recognition of same-sex unions from Massachusetts and California in every state.

Family Research Council opposes giving formal recognition or benefits to homosexual relationships under any circumstances, for numerous reasons. Even those who support same-sex marriage, however, should acknowledge that such a radical redefinition of our most fundamental social institution should not be imposed by the federal government in the face of a strong consensus among the states against it. Still less should we allow unelected judges from one or two states to force such a policy upon every other state.

The federal Defense of Marriage Act has served us well in the 12 years since its enactment, and it should not be tampered with.

The PPIC poll found Californians evenly divided — 47 percent to 47 percent — on letting gay and lesbian couples marry. The earlier Field Poll had found a majority in favor: 54 percent to 39 percent. That was the first time in more than a decade of polling that a survey had found a majority in favor of same-sex marriage in the state.

With more than a month before the election, both campaigns are still in low gear. Political observers in the state report few visible signs of the campaign. The Yes on Prop. 8 campaign is reporting having raised around $17.8 million — much of it from religious or socially conservative groups from outside the state. Equality California has raised $12.4 million, also much of it from out of state.[25]

Despite the current edge in fund-raising, Prop. 8 supporters face some daunting obstacles in winning approval for the measure. In a state where Democrats hold an 11-percentage-point edge over Republicans in voter registration, the PPIC poll found Democrats opposing the measure by better than a 2-to-1 margin (66 percent to 29 percent). Republicans favor the measure — 60 percent to 34 percent. But the state's leading Republican, Schwarzenegger, opposes it.

Prop. 8 supporters also cannot rely on the kind of conservative religious constituencies that helped win passage of same-sex marriage bans in other states. "You don't have nearly the same presence of religious conservatives in California as you do in other states," says Jack Pitney, a political science professor at Claremont-McKenna College in Pomona. The Field Poll found Prop. 8 trailing — 44 percent to 48 percent — in inland counties, where religious conservatives are strongest.

To offset the disadvantages, Prop. 8 supporters are making special efforts to target Latino voters — the state's biggest ethnic minority and thought to be socially conservative. But the Public Policy Institute found Latinos opposed to the measure — 54 percent to 41 percent — by only a slightly smaller margin than whites (55 percent to 39 percent). PPIC President Mark Baldassare said the poll did not have a sufficient number of African- or Asian-American respondents for a valid measure of those groups.

Despite the wide margin, Baldassare says the campaign is "early" and the vote "hard to predict." Pitney, however, says Prop. 8 supporters are unlikely to overcome the gap. "It loses," he says. "The pattern in California ballot initiatives is that once a measure starts losing by a large margin in the polls, it almost never passes."

The first marriage license in San Francisco went to lesbian activists Del Martin, left, and Phyllis Lyons, who had been together for more than 50 years. Martin, 87, died 10 weeks after San Francisco Mayor Gavin Newsom performed the ceremony on June 17.

Gay marriage opponents are also lagging in one of the two other states with ballot measures to forestall recognition of same-sex unions. The measures — Amendment 2 in Florida and Proposition 102 in Arizona — would amend the states' constitutions to define marriage as a union of one man and one woman.

In Florida, the most recent poll shows 55 percent in favor of and 41 percent opposed to Amendment 2 — short of the 60 percent majority required for a constitutional amendment.[26]

In Arizona, Proposition 102, a measure submitted by the Republican leaders of the state Senate and House, would fortify a statutory gay marriage ban adopted in 1996. A broader measure that would have blocked any legal recognition for same-sex or unmarried straight couples failed, 48 percent to 52 percent, in 2006.[27]

Marriage Cases Waiting

Gay rights advocates hope — and gay marriage opponents worry — that the California Supreme Court's decision recognizing same-sex marriages could influence justices considering similar suits already pending in two other states: Connecticut and Iowa.

The California ruling is legally significant because it is the only state high court ruling to date holding that gays are a constitutionally protected class and that laws discriminating against gays are subject to "strict scrutiny" — the highest level of constitutional review. "It was just a matter of time before courts would acknowledge that," says Lambda Legal attorney Pizer.

Judges in the Connecticut and Iowa marriage cases had already signaled their interest in reconsidering the legal standard for judging laws adversely affecting gay men and lesbians. Three of the Connecticut Supreme Court's seven justices asked about treating gays as a specially protected class when the gay marriage case was argued in May 2007.[28] In Iowa, Polk County District Court Judge Robert Hanson applied strict scrutiny in striking down the state's gay marriage ban in a 63-page decision in August 2007.[29]

Gay marriage opponents acknowledge the California Supreme Court to be one of the most influential of state tribunals. "What happens in California is noticed not only around the country but around the world," says Brigham Young law Professor Wardle.

Lawyers and advocates on both sides are waiting impatiently for the Connecticut high court to rule on the case, *Kerrigan v. Department of Health*, after deliberating for well over a year. The plaintiffs — eight same-sex couples — filed their suit in state court in New Haven in September 2004. Connecticut enacted a civil union statute the following year.

In July 2006, Superior Court Judge Patty Jenkins Pittman ruled in a 25-page decision that in light of the legislature's "courageous and historic step," the plaintiffs had "failed to prove that they have suffered any legal harm that rises to constitutional magnitude." The couples appealed the ruling, represented by lawyers from the Boston-based Gay & Lesbian Advocates & Defenders.

The Connecticut Supreme Court includes four Republican-appointed justices and three appointed by Gov. Lowell P. Weicker Jr., a one-time Republican elected to the statehouse under auspices of his self-styled Connecticut Party. The Republican-appointed chief justice, Chase Rogers, recused herself from the marriage case because her husband's law firm filed a brief on behalf of a gay rights organization. A retired Democratic-appointed justice, David Borden, sat on the case in her place. Borden was one of the three justices to question lawyers during arguments about applying strict scrutiny to laws discriminating against homosexuals.

The Iowa case, *Varnum v. Brien*, began with a suit filed by six same-sex couples in 2005 after they were denied marriage licenses by the office of the then-Polk County recorder, Tim Brien, in Des Moines. Lawyers from Lambda Legal's regional office in Chicago represented the plaintiffs.

In his decision, Judge Hanson applied strict scrutiny in ruling that the gay marriage ban violated the state constitution's due process and equal-protection clauses. Hanson found that the county attorney's office had failed to prove that the state's ban would "promote procreation," "encourage child rearing by mothers and fathers," "promote stability for opposite-sex marriages," "conserve resources" or "promote heterosexual marriage."

Lawyers completed filing briefs with the Iowa Supreme Court in June; the court has yet to schedule arguments. The seven justices on the court include two Republican and five Democratic appointees.

In a unique twist, one gay couple managed to get married the day after the ruling before Hanson agreed to the county attorney's motion to stay the decision pending appeal. Sean Fritz and Tim McQuillan, both in their early 20s, heard of the ruling on Aug. 30 and drove to Des Moines the next day to be wed. They found a judge who was willing to waive the normal three-day waiting period and got their marriage license at 10:45 a.m. Hanson issued his stay 45 minutes later.[30]

OUTLOOK

'It's About Marriage'

The Massachusetts Supreme Court's decision in 2003 granting marriage rights to same-sex couples produced a strong backlash. Public opinion polls registered a sharp drop in support for same-sex marriage, and gay marriage opponents won enactment of gay marriage bans in 13 states in the 2004 election cycle.

Five years later, no comparable backlash has emerged in the wake of the California Supreme Court's decision in favor of marriage equality — either nationally or in California itself. Nationwide surveys generally indicate a majority of Americans continue to oppose same-sex marriage, but surveys registered only a slight increase in opposition after the May 15 decision. And in August a poll by *Time* magazine actually found an even split between supporters and opponents: 47 percent to 47 percent.[31]

In addition, polls over the past five years indicate a stable majority of between 55 percent and 60 percent in favor of allowing either marriage or civil union status for same-sex couples. As one indication of the popular acceptance of some legal recognition of same-sex couples, supporters of California's Proposition 8 to overturn the state high court decision are arguing that the ruling was unnecessary. The state's domestic partnership law, they say, already gives same-sex couples all the rights of marriage.

With Prop. 8 trailing in the polls, gay marriage opponents are still professing optimism about the outcomes in California and the two other states — Arizona and Florida — with proposed constitutional amendments to ban marriage for same-sex couples. Liberty Counsel's Staver, who is helping to organize support for the measures in Florida and California, envisions three victories to bring the total number of constitutional gay marriage bans to 30. That number, Staver says, is "getting very close to enough to ratify a federal constitutional amendment" to ban same-sex marriages nationwide.

However, the Federal Marriage Amendment, a proposed constitutional amendment that would redefine marriage as a union of one man and one woman, appears to face all but insurmountable obstacles at present. After failing in the Senate twice in 2004 and 2006, the amendment now seems all the more unlikely to win approval in a Democratic-controlled Congress. Public opinion polls over the past several years also show a majority of Americans opposed.

Gay marriage opponents may actually find themselves on the defensive in Congress if Democratic Sen. Barack Obama is elected president. Both Obama and the Democratic Party platform call for repealing the federal Defense of Marriage Act. Repeal would not be a foregone conclusion, however, since Congress passed the law in 1996 with overwhelming bipartisan majorities.

Whether or not DOMA is repealed, states will remain free to decide whether to allow marriage for same-sex couples for their own residents. The existing state constitutional bans mean that for the foreseeable future there will be a patchwork of state laws on the issue — barring the currently remote likelihood of a U.S. Supreme Court decision on the subject.

"We're going to be getting increasingly disparate treatment of same-sex unions," says Mark Strasser, a professor at Capital University Law School in Columbus, Ohio.

Actress Amber Heard and former Army linguist Lt. Dan Choi, who was discharged for violating the "don't ask, don't tell policy," protest a federal appeals court ruling last Aug. 16 supporting California's Proposition 8, which bars gay marriage. Earlier, District Judge Vaughn Walker had ruled against Prop. 8 as unconstitutional.

Getty Images/Kevork Djansezian

Gay marriage proponents think that time is on their side as more Americans come to see or know legally recognized same-sex couples in their communities or workplaces. "Most Americans don't have to fully love the idea of ending discrimination," Freedom to Marry's Wolfson adds. "They just have to realize that they can live with it. And, overall, it benefits the country."

Some opponents also expect eventual recognition for same-sex marriage. "I actually think that it will come within a generation," University of Pennsylvania Professor Wax said in the Federalist Society online debate.

Opponents continue, however, to mount their arguments against recognizing same-sex marriage. In a newly published volume, *What's the Harm?*, Brigham Young's Wardle organizes opposing essays around four perceived harms from legalizing same-sex marriage: to families and child rearing, to responsible sexual behavior and procreation, to the meaning of marriage and to "basic human freedoms," including religious liberty.[32]

"The issue is about marriage," says Wardle. "It's about protecting a basic social institution."

"It's about marriage," echoes Wolfson. "We're not looking to create something new. We're talking about allowing every American to exercise the same freedom to marry, to have the same responsibilities, the same respect as every other American."

UPADATE

Gay rights advocates are celebrating a flurry of court rulings that could spell the end of the U.S. military's "don't ask, don't tell" policy, reinstate gay marriage in California and strike down the law limiting federal rights or benefits for same-sex couples. All three rulings are being appealed, however, with legal experts divided or uncertain as to the likely outcome in higher courts.

In the most dramatic of the court rulings, a federal judge in Riverside, Calif., on Oct. 12, 2010, issued a nationwide injunction against continued enforcement of the "don't ask, don't tell" policy, which calls for the discharge of any openly gay or lesbian service member. The order by U.S. District Judge Virginia Phillips followed her Sept. 9 decision that the policy is unconstitutional because it infringes on gay service members' free-speech and privacy rights while actually undermining the stated goal of enhancing military readiness.

Meanwhile, the U.S. military has begun complying with Phillips' order. In an historic move, the Pentagon on Oct. 15 ordered its recruiters — for the first time — to accept openly gay and lesbian applicants.

Earlier, a federal judge in San Francisco on Aug. 4 struck down California's Proposition 8, a voter-approved state initiative that barred marriage rights for gay or lesbian couples. Chief U.S. District Judge Vaughn Walker said the gay-marriage ban violated federal constitutional rights of due process and equal protection. The measure was approved in November 2008 only six months after a California Supreme Court decision that extended marriage rights to same-sex couples.

In a separate marriage-related case, a federal judge in Boston struck down the federal Defense of Marriage Act, the 1996 law that bars any marriage-based federal benefits or rights to same-sex couples. Ruling in a case

brought by six legally married same-sex couples in Massachusetts, U.S. District Judge Joseph Tauro said the law was unconstitutional because it was based on "irrational prejudice" and served no legitimate government objective.

Even as they cheered the favorable court rulings, gay rights groups were reacting with anguished concern to a string of suicides by gay youths who had been victims of bullying or harassment by classmates or other peers. In the most prominent episode, Tyler Clementi, an 18-year-old freshman at Rutgers University in Newark, N.J., jumped to his death from the George Washington Bridge in late September, a few days after his roommate used a webcam in their room to stream Clementi's sexual encounter with another young man live on the Internet.

"Don't ask, don't tell"

The ruling on the military's policy on gay service members came in a suit filed in 2004 by Log Cabin Republicans, a gay organization. Phillips, appointed to the federal bench by President Bill Clinton in 1999, presided over a seven-day trial in the case in July 2010 that featured testimony from six discharged gay service members and experts opposed to the policy. The government did not present any witnesses but argued any change in the policy was up to Congress, not the courts.

In her 85-page ruling, Phillips said the policy — enacted by Congress in 1993 — violated gay service members' due process rights by limiting their ability to form personal relationships and violated the First Amendment by preventing them from expressing themselves even in private communications. Instead of promoting military readiness and unit cohesion, as the government claimed, Phillips found that the policy actually has a "direct and deleterious effect" on the armed services.[33]

President Obama had called for ending the policy as a candidate in 2008 and after taking office. Congress was moving on efforts to repeal the policy before Phillips' ruling. The House voted 234-194 on May 27 to include a modified repeal provision in the annual authorization for defense spending. The provision called for the Pentagon to end the policy after a study to be completed by Dec. 1 on ramifications of repeal.

The repeal effort stalled in the Senate, however, in the face of a Republican filibuster. A Democratic-led effort to cut off debate failed Sept. 21 on a 56-43 vote, four votes short of the 60 votes needed. Democratic leaders said they would try again in a lame-duck session after the Nov. 2 congressional elections.

Phillips' injunction on Oct. 12 to bar enforcement of the policy drew divided reaction from legal experts about whether she had gone beyond her authority to rule on the case before her. In Washington the next day, Defense Secretary Robert Gates criticized the decision, saying that repeal should come from Congress and only after completion of the Pentagon study. At the White House, press secretary Robert Gibbs reiterated Obama's opposition to the policy. "This is a policy that is going to end," Gibbs said. One day later, the Justice Department filed a motion to stay the injunction pending appeal. In the meantime, however, the Pentagon issued worldwide instructions to halt any suspensions or discharges under the policy.[34]

Earlier, a federal judge in Tacoma, Wash., had dealt the policy another setback by ordering the reinstatement of a lesbian Air Force Reserve nurse discharged under the policy. U.S. District Judge Ronald Leighton ruled on Sept. 24 that evidence showed that Major Margaret Witt's suspension and dismissal in 2006 had "resulted in a diminution of [her] unit's ability to carry out its mission."[35]

Proposition 8

The ruling in the Proposition 8 case came in a suit filed May 22, 2009, on behalf of one gay and one lesbian couple in California to challenge the initiative, which won approval with about 52 percent of the vote on Nov. 4, 2008. Representing the plaintiffs was a seemingly improbable pair of lawyers: Theodore Olson, a conservative Republican, and David Boies, a liberal Democrat, who had been on the opposite sides of the contested 2000 presidential election case in Florida, *Bush v. Gore.*

The plaintiffs challenged the measure on federal constitutional grounds that had not been raised in a state court case that had unsuccessfully sought to invalidate the initiative. In the federal case, Judge Vaughn R. Walker, chief judge of the U.S. District Court in San Francisco, allowed an organization that had helped sponsor the initiative, Project Marriage, to intervene and then presided over a two-and-a-half-week trial, Jan. 11-27, 2010.

Students at Rutgers University view a memorial on campus to freshman Tyler Clementi, who committed suicide on Sept. 22 after he learned that a gay sexual encounter he had in his room was secretly streamed live on the Internet by his roommate. His death was one of at least four gay youth suicides tied to apparent bullying or harassment in September 2010 alone.

AFP/Getty Images/Emmanuel Dunand

Walker, appointed by President George H. W. Bush, ruled on Aug. 4 that Proposition 8 violated the federal Equal Protection Clause because it infringed on same-sex couples' fundamental rights for no legitimate government purpose. The measure, he wrote in a 136-page opinion, "fails to advance any rational basis in singling out gay men and lesbians for denial of a marriage license."[36]

Walker declined to stay his ruling, but the Ninth U.S. Circuit Court of Appeals put a hold on the decision on Aug. 16, pending arguments before a three-judge panel in December. The plaintiffs sought to block the appeal altogether on the grounds that state officials, including Gov. Arnold Schwarzenegger, had declined to defend the initiative and that Project Marriage had no legal standing to file an appeal. The appeals court said it would consider that issue along with the merits of the case.

In the meantime, the District of Columbia in March 2010 had become the sixth U.S. jurisdiction to extend marriage rights to same-sex couples. The District of Columbia Council voted 11-2 to legalize gay marriage on Dec. 2, 2009, but the measure could not take effect until after a period for Congress to review and consider blocking it.[37] Same-sex marriage rights were also recognized in five states: Connecticut, Iowa, Massachusetts, New Hampshire and Vermont. The Maine legislature had approved gay marriage in spring 2009, but the measure was repealed by a voter referendum with about 53 percent of the vote on Nov. 3, 2009.

Defense of Marriage Act (DOMA)

The ruling on the 1996 Defense of Marriage Act came in a suit filed by six legally married gay or lesbian couples in Massachusetts, which in 2004 had become the first state to grant marriage rights to same-sex couples. The act, passed by the Republican-controlled Congress and signed into law by President Clinton, barred any federal marriage-based rights or benefits for same-sex couples by defining marriage in federal law as "one man and one woman." The plaintiffs, represented by lawyers from the Boston-based Gay and Lesbian Advocates and Defenders, argued that the law violated equal protection by denying them benefits, including health or retirement benefits or tax breaks, available to all other legally married couples in the state.

In a 39-page ruling, District Judge Tauro, appointed to the bench in 1972 by President Richard M. Nixon, agreed that the law violated equal protection principles because it served no legitimate government purpose. "Denying marriage-based benefits to same-sex spouses," Tauro wrote in the July 8, 2010, decision, "certainly bears no reasonable relation to any interest the government might have in making heterosexual marriages more secure."[38] In a companion case filed by Massachusetts, Tauro also held that the law intruded on the state's traditional primacy over family-law issues.

The ruling did not immediately affect legally married gay couples in other states. In defending the case, the Justice Department acknowledged that President Obama favored repealing the measure. After the ruling, gay rights groups urged the Obama administration not to appeal the decision. But Justice Department lawyers filed a notice of appeal in October. The appeal was to be heard by the First U.S. Circuit Court of Appeals in Boston.

In another gay-rights victory, a state appeals court in Florida on Sept. 22, 2010, struck down the state law banning adoption by gay men or lesbians. The unanimous ruling by the state's Third District Court of Appeal found no "rational basis" for excluding gay men or lesbians from the pool of potential adoptive parents. Gov. Charlie Crist, elected as a Republican but campaigning

as an independent for the U.S. Senate, said he agreed with the decision and would not appeal. Florida was the only state with a blanket ban on adoptions by gays.[39]

Gay Suicides

The issue of bullying and harassment of gay youths moved to the top of the national agenda in fall 2010 after news emerged about the Rutgers webcam episode that led to Tyler Clementi's suicide on Sept. 22. Clementi, 18, a freshman, leaped to his death from the George Washington Bridge, which spans the Hudson River separating Manhattan from New Jersey, three days after his roommate had used a webcam to broadcast Clementi's gay sex encounter live on the Internet. On the day of his death, Clementi posted on his Facebook page, "jumping off the gw bridge sorry."[40]

Clementi's body was recovered on Sept. 29. On the same day, authorities in Newark charged roommate Dharun Ravi and his friend, Molly Wei, both 18, with two counts of invasion of privacy. According to the police account, Ravi had granted Clementi's request for use of the room alone on Sept. 19, turned on the webcam from another room and streamed Clementi's sexual encounter on the Internet. Ravi was charged with two additional invasion of privacy counts for an unsuccessful attempt to view another encounter two days later. In later statements, lawyers for Ravi and Wei denied any animosity toward gays and depicted the episode as a prank gone bad instead of a hate crime.

Subsequent news stories pointed to at least three other gay youth suicides tied to apparent bullying or harassment in the United States in September 2010 alone.[41] The Gay, Lesbian and Straight Educational Network, a gay advocacy group, noted in its 2009 survey that nine out of 10 gay, lesbian, bisexual or transgender middle- or high school students reported having suffered physical or verbal harassment. In response to the suicides, the gay columnist Dan Savage launched a campaign, "It gets better," with gay adults posting on YouTube accounts of how they overcame difficulties of having grown up gay. U.S. Education Secretary Arne Duncan also issued a strongly worded condemnation of bullying and harassment directed against gay youths.

"It is a time we as a country said 'enough,' " Duncan said on Oct. 1. "No more. This must stop."[42]

NOTES

1. For photo coverage, see "George Takei Beams Up Marriage," *E News*, Sept. 15, 2008; "Ellen & Portia Share the Wedding-Day Love," *ibid.*, Sept. 10, 2008, www.eonline.com.

2. The decision is *Goodridge v. Massachusetts*, 798 N.E.2d 941 (Mass. 2003). For background, see Kenneth Jost, "Gay Marriage," *CQ Researcher*, Sept. 5, 2003, pp. 721-748.

3. The decision is *In re Marriage Cases*, 43 Cal. 4th 757 (2008). For next-day coverage, see Maura Dolan, "Gay Marriage Ban Overturned," *Los Angeles Times*, May 16, 2008, p. A1; Bob Egelko, "California Supreme Court, in 4-3 decision, strikes down law that bans marriage of same-sex couples," *San Francisco Chronicle*, May 16, 2008, p. A1.

4. See Gary J. Gates, M.V. Lee Badgett and Deborah Ho, "Marriage, Recognition and Dissolution by Same-Sex Couples in the U.S.," Williams Institute, July 2008, www.law.ucla. edu/williamsinstitute/ publications/Couples%20 Marr%20Regis%20Diss .pdf.

5. Mark Baldassare, *et al.*, "Californians and Their Government: Statewide Survey," Public Policy Institute of California, August 2008, www.ppic.org/ content/pubs/survey/S_808MBS.pdf; Field Poll, September 2008, www.field.com/ fieldpoll.

6. See Charlie Frago, "Petitions to restrict adoption hit mark," *Arkansas Democrat-Gazette*, Aug. 26, 2008.

7. Jonathan Rauch, "Gay Marriage Is Good for America," *The Wall Street Journal*, June 21, 2008, p. A9. Rauch is a senior writer at *National Journal*, a guest scholar at the Brookings Institution and author of *Gay Marriage: Why It Is Good for Gays, Good for Straights, and Good for America* (2004).

8. See Jost, "Disputed Studies Give Gay Parents Good Marks," *op. cit.*, pp. 732-733.

9. "Same-Sex Marriage," Aug. 6, 2008, www.fed-soc .org/debates/dbtid.24/default.asp.

10. Quoted in Tracie Cone and Lisa Leff, "Gay marriage foes mobilize for ban in California," The Associated Press, Aug. 24, 2008.

11. The memo is posted on the Web site of the New York County Bar Association, www.nycbar.org/pdf/ memo.pdf. For coverage, see Jeremy W. Peters, "New York Backs Same-Sex Unions From Elsewhere," *The New York Times*, May 29, 2008, p. A1.

12. The cases are *Miller-Jenkins v. Miller-Jenkins*, Virginia Supreme Court (June 6, 2008); *Finstuen v. Crutcher*, 496 F.3d 1139 (10th Cir. 2007). For coverage, see Frank Green, "Ruling comes in same-sex custody case," *Richmond Times-Dispatch*, June 7, 2008, p. A1; Robert E. Boczkiewicz, "Victory for gay adoptive parents," *The Oklahoman*, Aug. 8, 2008, p. 1A.

13. Background relies heavily on George Chauncey, *Why Marriage? The History Shaping Today's Debate Over Gay Equality* (paperback ed. 2005). See also William N. Eskridge Jr., *The Case for Same-Sex Marriage: From Sexual Liberty to Civilized Commitment* (1996); Allene Phy-Olsen, *Same-Sex Marriage* (2006), pp. 63-72.

14. Ina Russell (ed.), *Jeb and Dash: A Diary of Gay Life 1918-1945* (1993).

15. See David K. Johnson, *The Lavender Scare: The Cold War Persecution of Gays and Lesbians in the Federal Government* (2004).

16. See Chauncey, *op. cit.*, pp. 89-96.

17. *Ibid.*, pp. 96-104.

18. See *ibid.*, pp. 123-136; Jost, *op. cit.* (2003).

19. See "New Law Discourages Gay Marriages," *CQ Almanac 1996*.

20. See these stories by Jennifer Warren in the *Los Angeles Times*: "Ban on Gay Marriages Wins in All Regions but Bay Area," March 8, 2000, p. A23; "Gays Differ Sharply on Their Next Steps," March 9, 2000, p. A3. The vote on the measure was 4,618,673 yes (61.4 percent) to 2,909,370 no (38.6 percent).

21. Quoted in Nancy Vogel and Jordan Rau, "Gov. Vetoes Same-Sex Marriage Bill," *Los Angeles Times*, Sept. 30, 2005, p. B3. The second veto was on Oct. 12, 2007.

22. See Denis C. Theriault, "Opposition growing to Prop. 8," *San Jose Mercury News*, Sept. 18, 2008; Jessica Garrison, "Bid to ban gay marriage trailing," *Los Angeles Times*, Aug. 28, 2008, p. B1.

23. See "California Poll: Same-Sex Marriage Is OK," The Associated Press, May 28, 2008.

24. Quoted in "Weak support for gay marriage ban," *Monterey County Herald*, Aug. 28, 2008.

25. See Dan Morain and Jessica Garrison, "Backers of California same-sex marriage ban are out-fundraising opponents," *Los Angeles Times*, Sept. 23, 2008; Aurelio Rojas, "Pitt's just another big giver in gay marriage showdown," *Sacramento Bee*, Sept. 23, 2008. Campaign finance filings can be found on the California secretary of state's Web site: http://cal-access.sos.ca.gov/Campaign/Measures/Detail. aspx? id=1302602&session=2007.

26. Mary Ellen Klas, "Same-sex marriage ban falling short," *The Miami Herald*, Sept. 9, 2008, p. B5.

27. See Amanda J. Crawford, "Consistent Message Doomed Prop. 107," *The Arizona Republic,* Nov. 9, 2006, p. 21.

28. The Connecticut case is *Kerrigan v. Department of Health*; for documents, see the Web site of Gay & Lesbian Advocates & Defenders: www.glad.org/marriage/Kerrigan-Mock/kerrigan _documents.html. For coverage, see Lynne Tuohy, "Supreme Court Justices Hear Arguments on Whether State Must Allow Marriage for Same-Sex Couples, Not Just Civil Unions," *Hartford Courant*, May 15, 2007, p. A1; Thomas B. Scheffey, "Following In California's Footsteps?" *Connecticut Law Tribune*, June 30, 2008, p. 1.

29. The Iowa case is *Varnum v. Brien*; for the lower court decision, see Freedom to Marry Web site: www .freedomtomarry.org/pdfs/iowa_ruling.pdf. For coverage, see Jeff Eckhoff and Jason Clayworth, "Judge: ban on gay marriage invalid," *Des Moines Register*, Aug. 31, 2007, p. 1A.

30. See Cara Hall, "Gay couple eyes court rulings," *Des Moines Register*, June 12, 2008, p. 1E.

31. For a compilation, see PollingReport.com, www .pollingreport.com/civil.htm, visited Sept. 19, 2008.

32. Lynn D. Wardle (ed.), *What's the Harm? Does Legalizing Same-Sex Marriage Really Harm, Individuals, Families or Society?* (2008).

33. The decision is *Log Cabin Republicans v. United States*, 2:04-cv-08425-VAP-E, U.S. Dist. Ct., C.D. Cal., www.cacd.uscourts.gov/CACD/RecentPubOp

.nsf/bb61c530eab0911c882567cf005ac6f9/4f03e468 a737002e8825779a00040406/$FILE/CV04-08425-VAP(Ex)-Opinion.pdf. For coverage, see Phil Willon, "Military ban on gays ruled unconstitutional," *Los Angeles Times*, Sept. 10, 2010, p. A1.

34. See Charlie Savage, "Administration Seeks Stay of Ruling That Halted 'Don't Ask,' " *The New York Times*, Oct. 15, 2010, p. A20; David S. Cloud and David Savage, "Legal scholars debate judge's ruling on 'don't ask, don't tell,' " *Los Angeles Times*, Oct. 14, 2010, p. A1.

35. The decision is *Witt v. U.S. Dep't of the Air Force*, 06-5195RBL, U.S. Dist. Ct., W.D. Wash., www.aclu-wa.org/sites/default/files/attachments/Witt-MEMORANDUM%20OPINION.pdf. For coverage, see Robert Barnes, "Judge orders military to reinstate gay nurse," *The Washington Post*, Sept. 25, 2010, p. A2.

36. The decision is *Perry v. Schwarzenegger*, CV 09-2292 VRW, U.S. Dist. Ct., N.D. Calif., Aug. 4, 2010, https://ecf.cand.uscourts.gov/cand/09cv2292/files/09cv2292-ORDER.pdf. For coverage, see Maura Dolan and Carol J. Williams, "Ban on gay marriage overturned," *Los Angeles Times*, Aug. 5, 2010, p. A1.

37. See Keith Alexander, "For gays, a D.C. day to treasure," *The Washington Post*, March 4, 2010, p. A1.

38. The decision is *Gill v. Office of Personnel Management*, 1:09-cv-10309-JLT, U.S. Dist. Ct., Mass., July 8, 2010, http://pacer.mad.uscourts.gov/dc/opinions/tauro/pdf/gill%20et%20al%20v%20opm%20et%20al%20sj%20memo.pdf. For coverage, see Michael Levenson, "Judge rejects gay marriage curb," *The Boston Globe*, July 9, 2010, p. A1.

39. For coverage, see Carol Marbin Miller, "Appeals court: Florida ban on gay adoption unconstitutional," *The Miami Herald*, Sept. 22, 2010.

40. See Kelly Heyboer, " 'jumping off the gw bridge sorry: A grim twist in Rutgers web sex scandal. Freshman's family says he committed suicide," *The Star-Ledger* (Newark, N.J.), Sept. 30, 2010, p. 1. See also Lisa Foderaro, "Private Moment Made Public, Then a Fatal Jump," *The New York Times*, Sept. 30, 2010, p. A1.

41. See Jesse McKinley, "Several Recent Suicides Put Light on Pressures Facing Gay Teenagers," *The New*

York Times, Oct. 4, 2010, p. A9. The survey by the Gay, Lesbian and Straight Educational Network (GLSEN) can be found at www.glsen.org/cgi-bin/iowa/all/news/record/2624.html.

42. www.ed.gov/news/press-releases/statement-us-secretary-education-arne-duncan-recent-deaths-two-young-men.

BIBLIOGRAPHY

Selected Sources

Books

Chauncey, George, *Why Marriage? The History Shaping Today's Debate Over Gay Equality*, Basic Books, 2004.
A Yale University historian compactly links the increased visibility of the gay and lesbian community and changes in the institution of marriage to the gay rights movement's effort to attain marriage equality. Includes chapter notes.

Koppelman, Andrew, *Same Sex, Different States: When Same-Sex Marriages Cross State Lines*, Yale University Press, 2006.
A professor at Northwestern University Law School argues that, based on established legal principles, courts should recognize marriages between same-sex couples that are recognized in their home state. Includes detailed notes.

Phy-Olsen, Allene, *Same-Sex Marriage*, Greenwood Press, 2006.
A professor emeritus of English at Austin Peay State University provides a thorough and balanced account of the background and current debate over same-sex marriage. Includes chapter notes, 24-page annotated bibliography.

Rauch, Jonathan, *Gay Marriage: Why It Is Good for Gays, Good for Straights, and Good for America*, Times Books, 2004.
A writer for *The Atlantic* and *National Journal* and guest scholar at the Brookings Institution argues that gay marriage would be beneficial by establishing marriage as the norm for gay men and lesbians, reversing the trend toward alternatives to marriage and making

the country "better unified and truer to its ideals." The book bears this dedication: "For Michael. Marry me when we can."

Rimmerman, Craig A., and Clyde Wilcox, *The Politics of Same-Sex Marriage*, University of Chicago Press, 2007.
Fourteen essays examine various aspects of the politics of same-sex marriage, including litigation and public opinion on the issue. Notes with each essay. Rimmerman is a professor of public policy studies and political science at Hobart and William Smith Colleges; Wilcox, a professor of government at Georgetown University.

Savage, Dan, *The Commitment: Love, Sex, Marriage, and My Family*, Dutton, 2005.
An author and sex-advice columnist relates with humor and poignancy how his mother goaded him into marrying his boyfriend of 10 years — and how their young son picked out skull rings to symbolize the union.

Stanton, Glenn, and Dr. Bill Maier, *Marriage on Trial: The Case Against Same-Sex Marriage and Parenting*, InterVarsity Press, 2004.
The authors, both with the anti-gay organization Focus on the Family, use a question-and-answer format to argue against recognizing same-sex marriage or encouraging child-rearing in same-sex households.

Wardle, Lynn D. (ed.), *What's the Harm? Does Legalizing Same-Sex Marriage Really Harm Individuals, Families or Society?* University Press of America, 2008.
Twenty contributors on both sides of the issue debate the potential impact of further legalizing same-sex marriage. Each essay includes notes. Wardle is a professor at Brigham Young University School of Law.

Articles

Denizet-Lewis, Benoit, "Young Gay Rites," *The New York Times Magazine*, April 8, 2008.
The writer examines the impact of the Massachusetts ruling legalizing gay marriage through the lives of several same-sex couples in the state.

Reports and Studies

Gates, Gary J., M. V. Lee Badgett and Deborah Ho, "Marriage, Registration and Dissolution by Same-Sex

Couples in the U.S.," **Williams Institute, UCLA School of Law, July 2008, www.law.ucla.edu/Williams Institute/publications/ Couples%20Marr%20Regis %20Diss.pdf.**

The study provides data on same-sex couples who have taken advantage of legal recognition — marriage, civil union or domestic partnership — allowed in 10 states and the District of Columbia. Gates is the co-author with Jason Ost of *The Gay and Lesbian Atlas* (Urban Institute, 2004).

On the Web

Federalist Society, **"Same Sex Marriage," Aug. 6, 2008, www.fed-soc.org/debates/dbtid.24/default.asp.**

Four law professors — two on each side — debate marriage rights for same-sex couples in an online forum sponsored by the conservative lawyers' organization.

Vestal, Christine, "Calif. gay marriage ruling sparks new debate," *Stateline.org*, **June 12, 2008, www.state line.org/ live/printable/story?contentId=310206.**

The online state news service provides an overview of the same-sex marriage debate following the California Supreme Court ruling, along with a national map and state-by-state chart.

Note: For additional earlier titles, see bibliography in Kenneth Jost, "Gay Marriage," CQ Researcher, Sept. 5, 2003, p. 746.

For More Information

Alliance Defense Fund, 5100 N. 90th St., Scottsdale, AZ 85260; (800) 835-5233; www.alliancedefensefund.org. Legal alliance defending the right to speak and hear biblical beliefs.

Alliance for Marriage, P.O. Box 2490, Merrifield, VA 22116; (703) 934-1212; www.allianceformarriage.org. Research and education organization promoting traditional marriage.

Equality California, 2370 Market St., Suite 200, San Francisco, CA 94114; (415) 581-0005; www.eqca.org. Supports GLBT civil rights protections in California.

Family Research Council, 801 G St., N.W., Washington, DC 20001; (202) 393-2100; www.frc.org. Promotes traditional marriage in national policy debates.

Freedom to Marry, 116 W. 23rd St., Suite 500, New York, NY 10011; (212) 851-8418; www.freedomtomarry.org. Gay and non-gay partnership working to win marriage equality.

Gay and Lesbian Advocates and Defenders, 30 Winter St., Suite 800, Boston, MA 02108; (617) 426-1350; www .glad.org. Opposes discrimination based on sexual orientation, gender identity and HIV status.

Human Rights Campaign, 1640 Rhode Island Ave., N.W., Washington, DC 20036; (202) 628-4160; www.hrc.org. America's largest civil rights organization supporting GLBT equality.

Lambda Legal Defense and Education Fund, 3325 Wilshire Blvd., Suite 1300, Los Angeles, CA 90010; (213) 382-7600; www.lambdalegal.org. GLBT civil rights litigation group.

Liberty Counsel, P.O. Box 540774, Orlando, FL 32854; (800) 671-1776; www.lc.org. Nonprofit litigation group supporting traditional family values.

National Gay and Lesbian Task Force, 1325 Massachusetts Ave., N.W., Suite 600, Washington, DC 20005; (202) 393-5177; www.thetaskforce.org. Promotes equality for gays and lesbians.

Protect Marriage; www.protectmarriage.com. California group opposed to gay marriage initiatives in upcoming ballot.

13

Assessing the New Health Care Law

Marcia Clemmitt

Cancer patient Gail O'Brien greets President Obama during a backyard discussion of his administration's proposed health care reform law in Falls Church, Va., on Sept. 22, 2010. The Supreme Court on June 28, 2012, upheld the law's requirement that uninsured people buy medical insurance or pay a penalty. Conservative justices objected to forcing healthy young people to buy insurance they may not need.

From *The CQ Researcher*,
September 21, 2012.

C aleb Medley, a 23-year-old aspiring stand-up comic, was at a midnight showing of "The Dark Knight Rises" in Aurora, Colo., on July 20, when a gunman entered the theater and shot 70 people, killing 12. Shot in the eye, Medley remained in a medically induced coma for more than a month. He has endured multiple brain surgeries, but is slowly improving, according to his family.[1] On Sept. 12, Medley was transferred from the hospital to a long-term-care facility.[2] Meanwhile, his wife, Katie, gave birth to the couple's first child a few days after the shootings.

The Medleys have no health insurance. To help with what doctors said could amount to $2 million in medical bills, Michael West, a longtime family friend, is soliciting donations through a website he set up. "Caleb . . . needs to get better because he needs to be a dad," said West.[3]

Stories of uninsured people who unexpectedly incur high medical bills have figured heavily in debates over the Obama administration's controversial health care law, the 2010 Patient Protection and Affordable Care Act (ACA). Ideological arguments over the legislation came into sharp focus June 28, when the U.S. Supreme Court upheld most of the ACA, whose main provisions take effect in 2014, but said states could opt out of a key provision aimed at expanding Medicaid coverage for the poor.[4]

The court rendered its decision in two parts:

- In a 5-4 ruling dominated by court liberals, with Chief Justice John G. Roberts unexpectedly providing the swing vote, the

Biggest States Have High Rates of Uninsured

The Affordable Care Act and any other attempt to overhaul the health care system to increase insurance coverage will face daunting challenges. Not least is the fact that three of the nation's four most populous states — California, Texas and Florida — have among the highest rates of uninsured residents. Texas leads the pack with one in four residents uninsured.

Percentage of Population Without Health Insurance
(2009-2010)

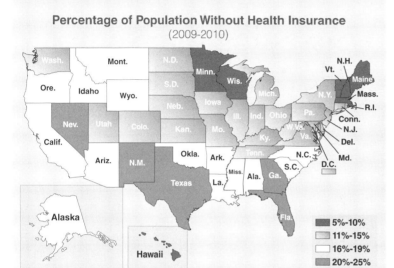

Source: "Health Insurance Coverage of the Total Population, States (2009-2010),U.S. (2010)," Henry J. Kaiser Family Foundation, 2012, www. statehealthfacts.org/comparetable.jsp?ind=125&cat=3&sub=39&yr=252&typ=2&rgnhl=1

over the measure since its enactment in March 2010.

In their dissenting opinion, the court's four conservative justices, who voted to strike down the entire law, asserted that Congress exceeded its constitutional authority by requiring every American to purchase health insurance or pay a penalty. Moreover, they wrote that healthy young people "may decide that purchasing health insurance is not an economically sound decision" — especially, they said, because the ACA allows them to purchase it in later years at the same cost, even if they have developed a pre-existing medical condition by then.[6]

But Justice Ruth Bader Ginsburg, a liberal who voted to uphold the ACA in its entirety, argued that getting everyone — even healthy young people — to buy insurance is the only way to ensure that there is enough money to pay for every American's care. "A victim of an accident or unforeseen illness will consume extensive medical care immediately, though scarcely expecting to do so," Ginsburg wrote. If that person hasn't bought coverage, others have to pick up the tab, she argued.[7]

Ultimately, the ACA's impact on health care costs and insurance coverage remains unclear. With implementation of the law's major provisions more than a year away, much of the debate is still driven by theories rather than data. But the ACA's supporters and detractors have long given voice to the issues raised by the Supreme Court.

President Obama said the court's affirmation of the law is a boon for average Americans. "Insurance companies no longer have unchecked power to cancel your policy, deny you coverage or charge women more than men," he said. Furthermore, "soon, no American will ever again be denied care or charged more due to a pre-existing condition, like cancer or even asthma."[8]

justices upheld the ACA's requirement that uninsured people buy medical insurance or pay a penalty — a stipulation in the law known as an "individual mandate." Conservative justices objected that it is unfair to force healthy young people to buy insurance they may not need.

• In a 7-2 vote dominated by court conservatives, plus two liberal justices, the court greatly narrowed the ACA's requirement that states either accept new federal grants to pay for expanded Medicaid coverage or risk losing all the money they receive from Washington for their Medicaid programs. The court said states can refuse the expansion grants without giving up their existing Medicaid funding.[5]

The Supreme Court's philosophical and legal differences over the health care law reflected a broad national divide

But GOP presidential nominee Mitt Romney, who derides the new law as "Obamacare," has vowed to repeal it if he is elected president in November. He has said he would replace it with another plan that relies more on the private sector to deal with many of the same problems the ACA addresses.[9] "Obamacare puts the federal government between you and your doctor," potentially limiting a physician's options for treating patients, Romney has said.[10] As governor of Massachusetts in 2006, Romney worked with Democrats to enact a plan similar to the ACA, but he has since said health care should be left to the states.[11]

Supporters say the ACA is structured in a way that will make the American health care system more effective and efficient and eventually save hundreds of millions of dollars annually in unnecessary or misdirected care. To keep insurance premiums for older, sicker people from becoming unaffordable, the ACA will subsidize them by raising premiums somewhat for young, healthy people.

And in an attempt to ensure that health coverage is worth its costs, the law also will require that all insurance plans cover a basic but comprehensive slate of benefits, essentially eliminating some bare-bones, low-cost plans available today. Beginning in 2014, four tiers of coverage will be available to individual purchasers, ranging from low-cost plans providing only basic benefits to comprehensive coverage, but at higher premiums.[12]

The ACA represents "tremendous progress towards reshaping our health system into one that saves the lives of at least 44,000 people who die annually simply because they do not have health insurance that could keep them healthy," said Georges Benjamin, executive director of the American Public Health Association.[13]

But many ACA opponents argue that it forces people to buy insurance they don't want and may not need. "Never before has the federal government coerced its citizens to purchase a personal commodity for private use," said Brooks Wicker, a Kentucky Republican running for a

Medical Expenses Worry Younger Adults

The inability to pay medical bills or afford necessary health care services is of greatest concern to adults under age 65, when Medicare eligibility begins. About one in three adults 18-64 has delayed a medical procedure or doctor's visit because of financial concerns.

Health Care Problems and Worries by Age, 2012

Problem or worry	Age 18-29	Age 30-49	Age 50-64	Age 65+
Problems with paying medical bills in past 12 months	29%	30%	26%	17%
Put off or postponed necessary health care	30%	34%	32%	15%
Worried about not being able to afford health care services you think you need	25%	30%	26%	15%

Source: "Health Security Watch," Henry J. Kaiser Family Foundation, June 2012, p. 7, www.kff.org/healthpollreport/CurrentEdition/security/upload/8322.pdf

U.S. House seat. "I'll work to repeal the mandate through legislation and to return [to] the American people the full measure of freedom taken from them."[14]

Meanwhile, some young adults complain that they are being required to buy a minimum level of coverage and, in their view, overpay for it to help hold down premiums for older, sicker people.

The law is biased against young people, who will be forced "to shoulder the burden of the entire health system," complained Ryan Fazio, a columnist for Northwestern University's *Daily Northwestern*, in Evanston, Ill.[15] Richard Cooper, a 26-year-old lawyer in Miami, said requiring all health plans to include basic coverage for such services as mental health treatment and maternity care is "one of the things I'm sort of leery about. I'm going to be paying for things I don't need."[16]

But both young and old will get far more comprehensive coverage from even the cheapest plans than many people find in the insurance they can buy today, said Paul Ginsburg, president of the Center for Studying Health System Change, a nonpartisan research group in Washington. "That's worth something."[17]

While much of the controversy over the ACA has centered on the individual mandate, the law's Medicaid provision has been equally contentious.

Views on the Affordable Care Act

Roughly the same percentages of people oppose the individual mandate requiring Americans to obtain health coverage or pay a penalty whether it is described as a fine or a tax. The act's plan to expand Medicaid is favored by two-thirds of Americans and opposed by fewer than a third. Overall, slightly more Americans have unfavorable views of the act than favorable, and almost the same percentages favor repeal or keeping the law.

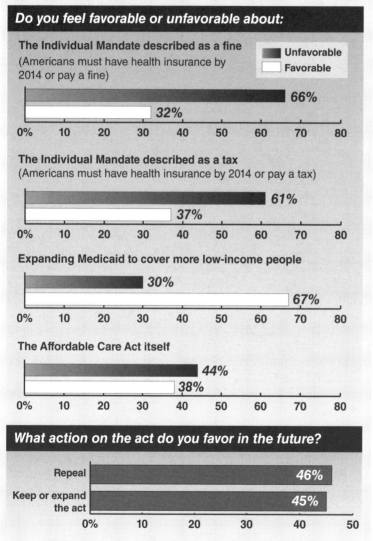

Do you feel favorable or unfavorable about:

The Individual Mandate described as a fine
(Americans must have health insurance by 2014 or pay a fine)

■ Unfavorable
□ Favorable

66%
32%

0% 10 20 30 40 50 60 70 80

The Individual Mandate described as a tax
(Americans must have health insurance by 2014 or pay a tax)

61%
37%

0% 10 20 30 40 50 60 70 80

Expanding Medicaid to cover more low-income people

30%
67%

0% 10 20 30 40 50 60 70 80

The Affordable Care Act itself

44%
38%

0% 10 20 30 40 50 60 70 80

What action on the act do you favor in the future?

Repeal — 46%
Keep or expand the act — 45%

0% 10 20 30 40 50

Source: "Health Reform Source," Henry J. Kaiser Family Foundation, July 31, 2012; "don't know/didn't answer" not shown.

Medicaid is a program financed jointly by the states and the federal government that covers health care, including nursing home care, for some groups of poor people — children, their custodial parents, pregnant women and the blind, disabled and elderly. The ACA expansion provision was designed to broaden coverage to include some 17 million poor, able-bodied, childless adults.

States leery about expanding their Medicaid rolls worry that doing so will bust their budgets, despite the fact that under the law most costs will be covered by federal grants.[18]

But Stan Dorn, a senior fellow at the Urban Institute, a nonpartisan think tank in Washington that studies poverty and health care, says the ACA's Medicaid provision would help states save money and improve health care efficiency. Today states reimburse hospitals for care they provide to uninsured people and for mental-health care provided to low-income adults. The federally funded Medicaid expansion would pay for that care up front, at least as efficiently as today's fragmented programs do, he says.

"It's mind-boggling to see the opposition," given the way the law is structured, says Dorn. "There are lots of ways that states can actually save money on the expansion."

As lawmakers, health care providers and the public ponder the ACA's impact, here are some of the questions being asked:

Should the health care law be repealed?

The ACA's opponents in Washington argue that nothing short of repeal will stop the law from damaging free-market economics and the American health care system. Central to their criticism is the law's individual-mandate provision requiring every American to buy health insurance or pay a financial penalty.[19]

But the law's supporters argue that it is that very mandate that holds the key to the law's success. By requiring universal coverage, they contend, the law prevents insured people from having to shoulder the cost of treating the uninsured, often through costly emergency room visits.

Senate Minority Leader Mitch McConnell, R-Ken., has said that if Republicans gain control of the Senate in November, he will schedule a vote to erase the ACA from the books. Ultimately, that may not work, he acknowledges, unless Republicans also win the White House and control of the House. Still, McConnell says most Americans agree with him that the law should go. "I'm confident they're going to give us the votes to repeal it," he said.[20]

Michael D. Tanner, director of health and welfare studies at the Cato Institute, a think tank in Washington that promotes a philosophy of individual liberty and limited government, said the "individual mandate crosses an important line" because it enshrines in law the principle "that it is the government's responsibility to ensure that every American has health insurance. It opens the door to widespread regulation of the health care industry and political interference in personal health care decisions. The result will be a slow but steady spiral downward toward a government-run national health care system."[21]

Others argue that the ACA usurps responsibilities that rightly belong to the states.

"States shouldn't be forced by the federal government to adopt a one-size-fits-all health care plan," said Sen. Scott Brown, R-Mass., whose home state, under Romney, adopted a health care system similar to the ACA in 2006. "Each state's health care needs are different."[22]

Thomas Miller, a resident fellow at the American Enterprise Institute (AEI), a conservative think tank in Washington that opposes the health care law, instead wants legislation that facilitates development of a nationwide market offering a wide variety of private medical plans for purchase.

Miller says the ACA will undermine the development of free-market dynamics in the health insurance field and force states to accede to federal dictates. At first, he says, states may be able to shape their own insurance exchanges through which people purchase health coverage. But that is simply because Washington made certain "concessions" to the states to induce them to back the law, he says. Once the new health regime is deeply rooted, he predicts, "the long-term dynamics will very much have Washington in control rather than having open markets."

But ACA supporters say the individual mandate — and the fact that the law is national, not limited to some states — ensure that health care will be available to as many people as possible. Furthermore, they say, states will have flexibility to shape their own insurance markets under the law.

Most states aren't willing or able to resolve the problem of the uninsured on their own because states rightly fear bankrupting themselves if they offer universal coverage and other states don't, Justice Ginsburg wrote. She quoted an earlier court ruling that described a universal state coverage program as a potential "bait to the needy and dependent elsewhere, encouraging them to migrate and seek a haven of repose." States that took the lead in offering universal coverage would be "placing themselves in a position of economic disadvantage as compared with neighbors or competitors," she wrote.[23]

The ACA does not create the one-size-fits-all nightmare for states that critics fear, says the Urban Institute's Dorn. The Obama administration's implementation rules for the law permit "a huge amount" of flexibility in the kind of insurance exchanges — markets — states may set up, thus accommodating "hugely different visions," both liberal and conservative, of how the health care market should operate.

"You can have a tightly managed exchange and allow only three health plans to come in and sell only a particular set of benefits" or "simply say that any company can come in" and give consumers a wide choice of health plans, Dorn says.

The ACA's supporters also say that the new law will relieve some of the pressure on workers' compensation and other parts of the health care system that have been strained in recent decades by the lack of universal insurance coverage.

MITTROMNEY.COM

Republican presidential nominee Mitt Romney has vowed to repeal the new health care law if he is elected president in November. He has said he would replace it with a plan that relies more on the private sector to deal with many of the same problems the law addresses. "Obamacare puts the federal government between you and your doctor," potentially limiting a physician's options for treating patients, Romney contends.

Workers' compensation insurance — mostly state-based programs that pay for injuries workers suffer on the job — will function better under the law, according to Joseph Paduda, a Connecticut-based consultant on managed care and workers' compensation insurance. Because so many people lack regular health insurance, workers' comp often ends up paying for care that has nothing to do with on-the-job injuries, he wrote.

In states such as Texas and Florida with high percentages of residents without insurance (*see map, p. 302.*), a person who tears a rotator cuff on the job, for example, may also need treatment for unrelated maladies, such as diabetes or high blood pressure, before having rotator cuff surgery. The ACA's widespread insurance coverage will cut costs and red tape for the workers' comp system, he said.[24]

Will Americans be better off because of the health care law?

With the ACA still in early stages of implementation, researchers have been unable to collect much data that either prove or refute claims of the law's success. Supporters point to millions of additional Americans who will gain insurance coverage. Opponents argue that new taxes and regulations will cripple innovation by medical firms such as health insurers and pharmaceutical companies.

Regardless of the ACA's merits, the changes it brings will cause some problems in the early going, even the law's supporters acknowledge. For example, expanded coverage and the emphasis on preventive care mean "there will (very) likely be an access problem over the near term as primary care providers are inundated with new patients, and over the medium term for specialists as folks who've long avoided care because they could not afford it now get those problems resolved — knee replacements, etc.," wrote insurance consultant Paduda.[25]

Meanwhile, supporters tout an ACA provision requiring insurers to spend a minimum percentage of premium payments on patient care or refund the money to employers and consumers. But many conservatives say this so-called Medical Loss Ratio rule will run insurance companies out of business. Sen. Charles Grassley, R-Iowa, said one insurer, the American Enterprise Group, left the business in Iowa and Nebraska last year, dropping thousands from its rolls and laying off 110 employees, and the "culprit is the new Medical Loss Ratio regulation."[26]

That's because selling health insurance to individuals and very small businesses is an economically tricky enterprise that works much differently than selling insurance to large-employer groups, Grassley said. The medical needs of an individual or employees at a small business are much harder for insurers to estimate than those of workers at a large employer, where the group's health status tends to mirror that of the general population. As a result, individual and small-group insurers must set each year's premiums high enough to ensure coverage of hard-to-predict costs, said Grassley. The Medical Loss Ratio rule, which penalizes insurers in any year the government deems their premiums are too high compared to spending on patient care, simply makes the risks of the insurance business "too great," he said.[27]

Opponents of the ACA point to what they see as other ill effects of the law. To help pay for expanded coverage, the ACA imposes new taxes that threaten research-and-development budgets and medical innovation, said Sally Pipes, president of the San Francisco-based Pacific Research Institute, a think tank that promotes a limited-government philosophy. "Excise taxes on drug-company sales are already in effect," Pipes wrote. "In 2013, there will be a new 2.3 percent excise tax on medical-device companies." As a result, she said, some firms have announced workforce cuts. "These industries are job creators and will no longer be unless the Affordable Care Act is repealed and replaced."[28]

John Goodman, a conservative analyst who heads the National Center for Policy Analysis, in Dallas, has found particular fault with efforts to expand Medicaid, the ACA's main means of insuring the poor. Medicaid, he argued, provides such low-quality care that "the Supreme Court has done a lot of families a big favor" by ruling that states can't be penalized for failing to expand coverage. As an example of what he sees as Medicaid's failings, he said 16 states cap the number of prescriptions Medicaid patients can get, with Mississippi limiting patients to two brand-name drugs and Arkansas limiting adult enrollees to six medications a month.[29]

Supporters of the law are just as vocal as opponents in their views about the ACA's impact on consumers.

Ron Pollack, founding executive director of the national consumer-advocacy group Families USA, says many people will be better off under the law and that some already are. "Right now, a significant but still clear minority of the benefits are already in effect," he says, and "we're hearing from people who've already gotten significant help."

Among those who have benefited are enrollees in Medicare, which provides health insurance for people age 65 and older, Pollack says. Under the ACA, they now receive additional government help with prescription-drug expenses, he says. Young adults also have benefited, Pollack notes. They now can remain on their parents' insurance plans until age 26.

And Pollack cites a host of other benefits: When insurers spend too little premium revenue on health care, they must provide rebates; children with pre-existing illnesses must be offered health coverage; preventive services such as diabetes and cervical-cancer screening are available without deductibles or copayments; and small businesses receive tax credits for providing worker coverage.

Coverage of Young Adults Rises

A provision of the Affordable Care Act that took effect in 2010 allows adult children under age 26 to obtain health care coverage through their parents' policies. Experts credit the provision with increasing the share of young adults covered by medical insurance in 2011.

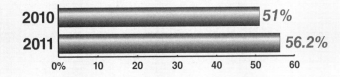

Percentage of Adults Ages 19 Through 25 With Private Insurance Coverage, 2010-2011

Source: Matt Broaddus, "The Census Bureau's Upcoming Report on Health Insurance Coverage in 2011: What to Watch For," Center on Budget and Policy Priorities, September 2012, www.cbpp.org/cms/index.cfm?fa=view&id =3830

A study published in July in the *New England Journal of Medicine* concludes that previous Medicaid expansions similar to what the ACA calls for have resulted in decreased death rates. Researchers from the Harvard School of Public Health examined mortality data from three states — New York, Maine and Arizona — that added low-income, nondisabled adults with no children to their Medicaid programs in the past decade and found that the death rate for people age 20 to 64 decreased in the five years following the expansion.[30]

While the study included all deaths in the states, not just those among low-income people, the mortality rate dropped most for nonwhites and people living in poor counties, suggesting a Medicaid connection. Meanwhile, death rates rose in four neighboring states that didn't expand Medicaid. The coverage expansions are associated with a 6.1 percent decrease in death rates, or about 2,840 fewer deaths per year for each additional 500,000 adults insured.[31]

Some analysts say the ACA will provide economic as well as health benefits. "If basic insurance is made universally available on the individual market," the country could see a substantial drop in so-called job-lock — "people staying in jobs that might not be the best for them" simply because those jobs are the only potential source of health insurance, said Jonathan Kolstad, a professor of health care management at the University of

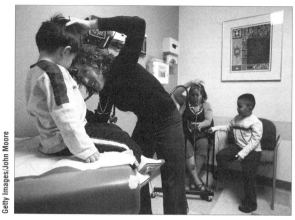

A youngster receives a check-up at a community health center in Lakewood, Colo., for low-income people. Passage of the new health care law will mean additional federal subsidies for such clinics as well as health care insurance coverage for as many as 30 million people.

Pennsylvania's Wharton School. Job-lock not only keeps workers from advancing in their careers but also hurts the economy by inhibiting innovation and productivity, he said.[32]

Will the health care law cost too much?

ACA opponents say both the government and individuals will pay too much for health care under the new law. Supporters say expanded insurance coverage is worth its costs and that provisions aimed at creating a more efficient, prevention-focused system will eventually help to tame soaring medical expenses.

The ACA "virtually ignored the health care cost crisis facing this country and instead imposes billions of dollars in new mandates" — such as requiring insurers to devote a minimum amount of premium dollars to patient care — "and taxes that will increase the costs of coverage," said Robert Zirkelbach, a vice president of America's Health Insurance Plans, the main association representing health insurers in Washington.[33]

"Even accepting the law's assumptions about how the health care system should be reformed, actually putting all the pieces in place is exceptionally expensive," said Joseph Antos, who studies health and retirement policy at the free-market-oriented American Enterprise Institute in Washington. Furthermore, "the Supreme Court decision on Medicaid will . . . drive up federal spending"

even more because in states that decline to participate "the alternative is expanded enrollment in subsidized [private] insurance through the [state insurance] exchanges," and private insurance costs more than Medicaid, Antos said.[34]

Meanwhile, liberal ACA critics argue that by relying on private insurance companies, rather than making the government the single payer for all insured people, the law forgoes most cost savings it might have achieved. Insurance companies "only add cost and complexity" to the system without improving care, said Bill Mahan, a political activist and retiree in Lexington, Ky., who advocates a switch to a single-payer system.[35]

But ACA supporters point to analysis by the Congressional Budget Office, Congress' nonpartisan budget-analysis agency, which has repeatedly found that the law will actually lower government health care spending and pare federal deficits because cost-saving provisions will offset the price of expanded coverage. In 2011, the CBO estimated that the law's coverage expansion would cost the federal government $1.1 trillion between 2012 and 2021, but that the law as a whole would end up saving the government money. That's because the cost of the coverage expansion will be offset by ACA provisions aimed at trimming unnecessary and wasteful health-care spending. As a result, the ACA will lower federal deficits by about $210 billion in that period, CBO said.[36]

The fact that the law saves taxpayers some cash means that a Republican repeal of the ACA "would cause a net increase in federal budget deficits of $109 billion over the 2013-2022 period" — that is, repealing the law would cost money, not save it, as repeal supporters had hoped, the CBO wrote to House Speaker John Boehner, R-Ohio, in July.[37]

The law also invests heavily in studies designed to establish definitively which treatments are most successful. Many analysts believe that, eventually, the federal investment in such "comparative-effectiveness" research will discourage doctors from prescribing costly treatments that don't work. That's "good news indeed for [workers'] comp payers," for example, who are "saddled with back surgeries" that many experts now believe don't help but whose ineffectiveness hasn't yet been established by research, said insurance consultant Paduda.[38]

Few promise that cost savings will come easily, however. Besides comparative-effectiveness research, the law also will launch experiments on potential cost-control measures such as paying health care providers based on whether they keep people from getting sick rather than for rendering individual services. But because neither public nor private health care entities have yet seriously explored such techniques, "it will be at least 10 years" before it's known whether they work, says Robert Laszewski, an Alexandria, Va.-based insurance industry consultant.

BACKGROUND

The Mandate

In their bid to expand coverage to 30 million of the approximately 50 million uninsured Americans, the drafters of the Affordable Care Act (ACA) proposed two strategies:[39]

- Medicaid would be expanded, through a federal-state effort, to cover everyone in households earning less than 138 percent of the federal poverty level (FPL), or $26,344 for a family of three.
- The law would require everyone whose earnings exceed that threshold either to carry employer-sponsored insurance or to buy it from a new, federally subsidized government-regulated insurance market or else pay a financial penalty for not doing so.[40]

Both provisions are controversial. Opponents — largely Republicans — argue that states opting into the Medicaid expansion would be unreasonably burdened financially and that the individual mandate violates Americans' freedom by forcing them to buy a product — insurance — they may not want. Because the U.S. Supreme Court significantly altered the Medicaid provision, the CBO projects that about 3 million fewer people will be covered by the ACA than originally estimated.[41]

The individual mandate is a practical necessity to create a working insurance system, its defenders say. At any given time, only relatively few have high medical costs, and different people experience high costs in different years, wrote David Cole, a professor at Georgetown University Law Center in Washington. Because predicting when and whom serious accident or illness will strike is virtually impossible, it's crucial to bring everyone into the insurance pool so that

Opponents of possible cuts to government entitlement programs, including Medicaid, block a downtown Chicago intersection on Nov. 7, 2011. About 40 of several hundred protesters were arrested. The Affordable Care Act could increase the size of the Medicaid program to cover some 17 million poor, able-bodied, childless adults. But many state officials say they'll reject federal funds to expand health coverage in this way, saying it would strain their already tight budgets.

premiums paid by the currently healthiest can subsidize care for the currently sick and injured, said Cole.[42]

State experience proves that without a mandate, attempts to provide affordable coverage for all will collapse, Cole wrote. In 1994, for example, Kentucky enacted a law similar to the ACA, requiring insurers to cover people with pre-existing health conditions at affordable prices, "but without an individual mandate." Quickly, "costs rose so steeply that they became untenable," insurers left the market and Kentucky had to repeal its law, Cole said.[43]

Ironically, many conservatives have proposed health-system overhauls over the past quarter-century that included a mandate.

"In our scheme, every person would be required to obtain basic coverage, through either an individual or a family insurance plan," Mark Pauly, a professor of health care management at the University of Pennsylvania's Wharton School, wrote in 1991. Pauly, along with other conservative scholars, devised a plan they hoped President George H. W. Bush could use to expand coverage.[44]

"It is reasonable" to impose "a requirement on individuals to enroll themselves and their dependents in at least a basic health plan — one that at a minimum should protect the rest of society from large and unexpected medical costs incurred by the family," Stuart Butler, director of the

CHRONOLOGY

2006-2018 *Congress enacts legislation to expand health insurance coverage; controversies dog the law.*

2006 Massachusetts, under Republican Gov. Mitt Romney, enacts mandatory, universal health coverage with bipartisan support, requiring residents to buy insurance in a state-regulated market.

2007 As of July 1, all Massachusetts residents must purchase health insurance.

2009 To control costs, Massachusetts officials consider paying doctors and hospitals flat, up-front fees to provide care. . . . In December, U.S. Senate passes the Affordable Care Act (ACA) 60-39, but with no Republicans voting in favor; House scheduled to take up the bill in spring 2010.

2010 House passes Affordable Care Act (ACA) 219-212, with no Republican support. . . . President Obama signs the law March 23; it aims to expand coverage to 30 million people and trim costs while maintaining quality. . . . States and private groups challenge the ACA's constitutionality in court. . . . Federal government opens "high-risk" health plan, in which people with pre-existing health conditions can get affordable coverage; sign-up is slow because premiums remain costly. . . . Adults under 26 become eligible for coverage on their parents' health plans. . . . Health insurers must cover children with pre-existing illnesses.

2011 Some Medicare enrollees get ACA rebates for prescription drug expenses. . . . Very small businesses become eligible for tax credits for insuring workers. . . . Newly elected House Republican majority repeatedly votes to repeal or defund the ACA, but Democrat-controlled Senate declines to consider the bills. . . . Federal appeals courts consider challenges to the ACA, upholding some but rejecting others; matter heads to the Supreme Court, which agrees to examine the ACA's "individual mandate" provision requiring people to buy insurance coverage or pay a penalty and the law's Medicaid-expansion provision. . . . Primary-care doctors treating Medicare patients get payment boost. . . . Copayments waived for some preventive-health services under Medicare. . . . High-income Medicare beneficiaries pay higher premiums. . . . States get grants to improve Medicaid care for chronic-disease

patients. . . . Payments cut for private "Medicare Advantage" health plans. . . . Medicare Independent Payment Advisory Board (IPAB) established. Beginning in 2015, Medicare must implement cost-control measures recommended by IPAB, absent a two-thirds "no" vote by Congress.

2012 Supreme Court declares ACA's individual mandate constitutional but makes Medicaid expansion optional for states. . . . Republican governors and state legislatures say they might not expand Medicaid to cover poor adults. . . . Health plans that spend too little on medical care must give cash rebates to enrollees. . . . With bipartisan support, Massachusetts clamps down on health care cost growth and adopts incentives to pay doctors and hospitals for "bundles" of high-quality care, rather than "fees for service." . . . GOP presidential nominee Mitt Romney and many congressional Republicans vow to repeal the ACA if they win November elections. . . . More than 2,000 hospitals lose some Medicare payments because of below-standard patient care. . . . Makers and importers of some brand-name drugs must pay new fees to help finance the law.

2013 Primary-care doctors get Medicaid payment boost. . . . Taxpayers who itemize medical expenses must meet a higher threshold to claim a deduction. . . . Federal sales tax imposed on some medical devices. . . . Payroll tax on Medicare Part A, which pays for hospital services, rises. . . . With the ACA set to extend coverage to more uninsured people, special hospital reimbursements for providing free care to the uninsured are phased out.

2014 ACA's Medicaid expansion and individual mandate slated to begin. . . . Individuals may buy federally subsidized insurance in state- or federally managed markets, called exchanges. . . . Insurers banned from imposing annual dollar limits on individuals' health spending. . . . Fees imposed on large employers who do not offer health coverage. . . . Insurers must sell coverage to people with pre-existing health conditions. . . . New fees imposed on health insurers.

2018 Tax imposed on insurers offering employer-sponsored coverage costing more than $10,200 for individuals or $27,500 for families.

Center for Policy Innovation at the conservative Heritage Foundation, told a congressional panel in 2003.[45]

In 2004, Senate Majority Leader Bill Frist, R-Tenn., a transplant surgeon and heir to the founders of the large for-profit hospital chain Hospital Corp. of America, said "higher-income Americans today have a societal and a personal responsibility to cover in some way themselves and their children."[46]

Recently, though, most conservatives have turned against the mandate, arguing that requiring healthy people to buy insurance to subsidize the sick is an attack on individual freedom.

"The mandate's proponents call it an 'individual responsibility' requirement. But its real aim is to force young people to cover up for irresponsible government policies" — mainly government regulations on health care — "that make insurance too expensive," charged Avik Roy, a senior fellow at the conservative Manhattan Institute in New York.[47]

Mandate supporters, however, insist that buying insurance while healthy is essentially a prepayment plan for the unpredictable but inevitable day when illness or accident strikes. In rejecting mandates — as most Americans do in public-opinion polls — "Americans believe they have a moral right to critically needed health care, whether or not they can pay for it, but also believe that they should be free not to make financial provision for that event beforehand," wrote Princeton University economics professor Uwe Reinhardt.[48]

The Poor

The ACA's other proposed coverage mechanism — Medicaid — also stirs controversy, mainly because many states worry about the program's rising costs and federal rules imposed on it.

Enacted in 1965, Medicaid replaced two federal grant programs that helped states provide medical care to the poor elderly and to people on welfare. Eventually, Medicaid used combined state and federal funds to provide health coverage for very poor families with children, long-term care and other services for low-income elderly and disabled people and, as a state option, coverage for other groups such as poor, childless adults.

States can choose whether or not to participate in Medicaid, and indeed not all states jumped on the Medicaid bandwagon at first. Arizona didn't start a Medicaid program

until the 1980s, for example. Today, every state provides Medicaid, although eligibility rules vary widely.[49] In Alabama and Louisiana, for example, parents with dependent children who make more than 11 percent of the federal poverty level — about $2,100 a year for a family of three — are ineligible for Medicaid, while in Minnesota the same family could earn more than $41,000 and receive benefits.[50]

Before the Supreme Court altered the ACA's Medicaid provision, the law essentially required states to help the federal government expand Medicaid coverage or risk losing the federal Medicaid funds they already received, a penalty intended to ensure that all states would participate.[51]

States provide a hefty share of the funding for traditional Medicaid. In fiscal 2010, for example, they spent a total of $126 billion, supplemented by $263 billion in federal funds.[52] The federal contribution to the ACA's Medicaid expansion is much bigger, with the government picking up 100 percent of costs from 2014 through 2016, then gradually shifting more costs to states until the federal share drops to 90 percent in 2020 and thereafter.[53]

About half of the people who were expected to gain coverage under the ACA were expected to gain it through the Medicaid program, said Alan Weil, executive director of the National Academy for State Health Policy, which helps states improve their health systems. "This is not a small change to Medicaid, and it's also not a small part of the Affordable Care Act."[54]

The Court

As soon as the law was enacted, both the individual mandate and Medicaid-expansion mechanisms came under legal challenge. Twenty-six states eventually joined an anti-ACA lawsuit filed in Florida on March 23, 2010, the same day President Obama signed the act into law. In this and other suits, states and private groups charged that Congress had overstepped its constitutional authority by requiring individuals to buy health insurance or pay a penalty and by requiring states to expand Medicaid or lose federal Medicaid funding altogether.

Some of the first cases reached the U.S. Supreme Court in its 2011-2012 session, and the Court agreed to examine both the mandate and the Medicaid issues.[55]

Caring for the Poorest and Sickest

Expanding Medicaid challenges would-be reformers.

Regardless of what happens to the Affordable Care Act (ACA) — whether it rolls out as planned over the next several years or is repealed under a new Republican administration — American health care still will face perhaps its biggest challenge: caring for the sickest and the poorest. Analysts from across the ideological spectrum agree on the urgency of the challenge, but solutions remain elusive.

Today, Medicaid, which is funded jointly by states and the federal government, provides care for poor families with children as well as many people with severe disabilities; it also provides long-term-care, mostly in nursing homes, for the low-income elderly. But as the costs of care have risen far faster than incomes, more Americans who fall outside these coverage categories continue to lose access to care. In 2010, 49.1 million Americans were uninsured. [1] (As of June 2011, 52.6 million people were covered by Medicaid. [2])

"You can be penniless" and yet receive no assistance in getting health coverage, says Ron Pollack, founding executive director of the national consumer-advocacy group Families USA. "We have 42 states that don't do anything for adults without children," making the Medicaid safety net "more holes than webbing," he says. But the ACA aims to remedy the problem by expanding Medicaid to low-income childless adults.

Some liberals have long predicted that such an expansion would not only provide much-needed access to care but also save money. The savings would come from poor people getting preventive health care rather than ending up seeking expensive emergency room treatment after long-untreated medical conditions worsened. Some conservative commentators, on the other hand, scoff at the ACA expansion, arguing that Medicaid is such a skimpy program and pays doctors and hospitals so little that the new Medicaid enrollees will gain almost nothing of value.

"There's a lot of rhetoric on both sides" of the Medicaid-expansion question, says Katherine Baicker, a professor of health policy at the Harvard School of Public Health. She says new data she and other scholars collected show clearly that the most extreme claims of both proponents and detractors miss the mark.

The scholars, who also include Amy Finkelstein, a Massachusetts Institute of Technology economics professor, conducted the first-ever research on insurance coverage using the most rigorous standards of scientific evidence, says Baicker. In the study, nearly 90,000 very low-income Oregonians, ages 19 to 64, signed up for a lottery that randomly assigned them either to the Oregon Health Plan or left them uninsured. [3] The research, which is ongoing, ultimately will examine and compare the health care usage, health status and financial situations of both the group covered under the state health plan and those in the uninsured control group.

On June 28, the Court issued a mixed ruling that pleased ACA's defenders and left the law's critics with little to do but vow to try to repeal it.

The ACA's supporters and even some conservative legal commentators have argued that Congress has the power to require individuals to buy health insurance because the Constitution's Commerce Clause gives federal lawmakers the right to impose rules on business dealings that cross state boundaries. "The health industry is of course an interstate business; there is a continuous flow of health insurance payments, health insurance reimbursements, drugs, doctors, patients, donations to hospitals, research money, etc., across state boundaries,"

wrote Richard Posner, a conservative judge on the Seventh U.S. Circuit Court of Appeals and a lecturer at the University of Chicago Law School. [56]

But conservative justices, including Chief Justice Roberts, rejected that argument, maintaining that uninsured people to whom the mandate primarily would apply are not actually participants in the health care market and therefore may not be subjected to rules under the Commerce Clause.

Roberts, however, ultimately added his vote to those of the court's four liberal justices to uphold the mandate by a 5-4 majority, despite rejecting the idea that the Commerce Clause authorizes Congress to impose it. He

The data show that, after one year, those who gained Medicaid coverage gave their health status better marks than did their uninsured peers, and they also faced far fewer struggles with medical bills, says Baicker. The newly insured were more likely to describe their health as good and improving and themselves as happier than did the uninsured, she says.

In addition, the newly insured were 25 percent less likely to have had an unpaid medical bill sent to a collection agency and 40 percent less likely to have had to borrow money or leave other bills unpaid to pay their medical bills.

These findings prove that "expanding Medicaid has real benefits," not just for health but for people's financial status as well, says Baicker. The findings should effectively end speculation by Medicaid's critics that the program would be of no help to people if it were expanded, she says.

The data don't "tell you whether it's a good idea to expand Medicaid, but they do give you information about what the effects are," on individuals and on government budgets, Baicker says.

Nevertheless, the same data also dampens expectations by Medicaid-expansion supporters that hospital use might decline, along with expenses, if more people receive Medicaid coverage, says Baicker. Instead, she says, "we found a substantial increase [in hospital use], at least in the first year," she says. Still, she says, the increase came in scheduled hospital care such as non-emergency surgeries, not in pricey emergency-room visits that sometimes result from neglected preventive care.

Meanwhile, conservative economists who hope to see the ACA repealed and replaced with a less-regulated, more market-oriented system also acknowledge the importance — and trickiness — of serving the poorest and sickest people while allowing a free market to flourish in health care for the rest of the population.

"Sometimes there's a tendency to think only in dollar terms, but that's not the be-all and end-all," says Thomas Miller, a resident fellow at the free-market-oriented American Enterprise Institute. Miller says "you need a health care system that works for people" — both the poorest and sickest, who need more assistance than others, and the rest of the population, who are best served by having a health care market that offers them choices.

"You need first to acknowledge that the very poor or the very sick must get more" help to meet costs, Miller says. But at the same time, he adds, "you want to allow a wider variety of choices" for others so that savvy consumers can drive the market toward better quality and lower cost. Subsidies are required for the poor under any system, but the ACA's subsidies are too rich and reach people who earn too much, thereby undercutting the incentives for wiser spending, he says.

— Marcia Clemmitt

---

[1]"The Uninsured: A Primer," Kaiser Commission on Medicaid and the Uninsured, October 2011, p. 1, www.kff.org/uninsured/upload/7451-07.pdf.

[2]"Medicaid Enrollment: June 2011 Data Snapshot," Kaiser Commission on Medicaid and the Uninsured, June 2012, www.kff.org/medicaid/upload/8050-05.pdf.

[3]For background, see Amy Finkelstein, *et al.*, "The Oregon Health Insurance Experiment: Evidence from the First Year," National Bureau of Economic Research, 2011, www.rwjf.org/files/research/72577.5294.oregon.nber.pdf.

concluded instead that the ACA's financial penalty for failing to buy insurance falls under Congress' power to levy taxes.

The penalty raises revenue for the government — the distinguishing mark of a tax — even though it is "plainly designed to expand health insurance coverage," Roberts wrote. "But taxes that seek to influence conduct" — such as by heavily taxing alcoholic beverages or imported goods to dissuade people from buying them —"are nothing new" and are allowable, he said.[57]

But the court struck down the harsh penalty the ACA sought to impose on states unwilling to expand Medicaid, thus effectively transforming the provision from a requirement into a voluntary program. ACA opponents argued that the law's expansion plan as a whole should be struck down because the stiff penalty attached to it violated a basic constitutional principle — that the federal government can't compel states to either enact or administer any federal regulatory program.[58] The Obama administration, on the other hand, contended that the expansion plan falls under a provision in current law that requires states that participate in Medicaid to go along with any future changes Congress may make in the program or cease receiving federal Medicaid funds.

A seven-member court majority, led by Roberts, issued a split decision, allowing the Medicaid coverage proposal

Trying to Trim the Waste From Health Care

Conservatives and liberals both take "big picture" approach.

In this campaign season of extreme political bickering, Democrats and Republicans agree on one thing: the pressing need to slow ever-rising health care costs. In 2010, U.S. spending, public and private, on health care totaled nearly $2.6 trillion, more than 10 times the cost in 1980.[1]

Moreover, conservative and liberal economists take essentially the same big-picture cost-cutting approach — setting annual budgets and giving them teeth by forcing an entity such as an insurance company or hospital-and-physician group to pick up the tab for cost overruns, says Michael Chernew, a professor of health care policy at Harvard Medical School.

In conservatives' preferred model — sometimes called a "voucher" or a "premium-support" system — the annual budget comes in the form of a capped payment that insurers receive in exchange for keeping an individual healthy for a year, says Chernew. (GOP vice presidential candidate Paul Ryan proposes such a plan as a new model for Medicare, for example.)

Under this kind of capped-payment plan, the government — or an employer — calculates what it deems fair for a year's worth of health care and hands each person a check to shop for an insurance plan at that price. Individuals must choose wisely, and insurers must provide adequate care at the set price, since extra spending won't be reimbursed, Chernew explains.

Chernew says left-leaning analysts favor a similar fixed-price approach, but with health-care providers, such as integrated hospital-physician practice groups, rather than insurers getting the cash. The Affordable Care Act (ACA) dubs such groups Accountable Care Organizations (ACOs). In this model, a group of providers, rather than an insurer, gets a "bundled" payment to provide all needed health services. The providers must provide adequate care at that price or else pick up the tab for additional services patients need.

Both models are intended to "change the nature of the good that's being bought" in the health care market from "specific services that are sold at certain fees" to "care overall" — a total package of care to keep people healthy, Chernew says.

The current system of buying one health service at a time encourages consumers to purchase unneeded, or even harmful, medical services, since health-care organizations profit by selling as many services as possible, says Robert Laszewski, an insurance consultant in Alexandria, Va. Both proposed capped-payment systems have promise and pitfalls, though, and which one a policymaker opts for is still largely a matter of ideology, since little evidence exists about either plan's effectiveness.

Chernew says he believes the conservative plan of offering insurers capped payments would encourage competition in the insurance industry. But many questions remain. For example, it is unclear how effective it would be to shape the health care system around consumers' ability to "shop around," Chernew says. Among other issues, such an approach makes it crucial for the government to prevent any insurers from gaining monopoly power, because only with a wide range of buying options can consumers run an overpriced or low-quality health plan out of business.

---

to stand, but only as a voluntary program that states could take or leave without penalty. Roberts concluded that the proposal was outside established Medicaid rules, meaning states' pledges to go along with all legislated changes in the program don't apply.

Medicaid "was designed to cover medical services for . . . particular categories of the needy: the disabled, the blind, the elderly, and needy families with dependent children," and previous Medicaid amendments "merely altered and expanded . . . these categories," Roberts wrote. The coverage expansion, by contrast, is not "a program to care for the neediest among us, but . . . an element of a comprehensive national plan to provide universal health insurance coverage."[59]

CURRENT SITUATION

Uncertain Future

The Supreme Court's June ruling has not ended the legal controversy surrounding the ACA. Church-run institutions are claiming in new lawsuits that a requirement in the

On the ACO side, too, "we know enough to be somewhat optimistic, but not enough to be sure," Chernew says.

Massachusetts, which enacted a universal health-coverage program similar to the ACA in 2006, has been experimenting with a version of ACOs — called Alternative Quality Contracts (AQCs). In an AQC, a hospital or physicians' group negotiates a set price from an insurer to cover the entire cost of care for all the insurer's patients whom the health care providers serve. If the provider group goes over budget, it must pay the difference. That gives it a financial stake in avoiding problems such as untreated chronic conditions that worsen until costly emergency care is needed.[2]

So far, evidence is mixed on AQCs. One study last year found no savings while another reported "modest" savings.[3] A 2012 study, however, concluded that the average AQC spent 1.9 percent less than control groups in the first year of operation and 3.3 percent less in the second year, while providing better chronic-disease and preventive-health care.[4]

Liberal proposals generally set strict rules to prevent an organization receiving a capped payment from skimping on care, while conservatives believe that a robust market will perform that function, says Laszewski. That difference gets to the heart of the debate over the competing models, says Laszewski. "Some people fear big business and prefer to be protected from it by the government, and others fear the government" and its potential to strangle choice and innovation with rules.

Whatever plan economists or lawmakers may propose to slow the growth in medical costs, consumers or the health care industry can undermine the effort. Consumers may balk at cost-cutting, fearing it deprives them of care. And providers, from medical-device manufacturers to individual physicians, have routinely pushed back against such efforts to avoid losing income. In Massachusetts, that dynamic is playing out with AQCs,

said Eric Beyer, president of Boston's Tufts Medical Center, which holds an AQC contract. Contrary to policymakers' hopes, "employers are not signing up for the [AQC] plans in droves — in fact, more of our population is moving toward products that have no requirement for paying providers for quality over quantity," Beyer said.[5]

Meanwhile, fearing they'll lose their clout as the government becomes more aggressive about demanding cost-efficient and high-quality care, doctors and hospitals are linking up into very large medical groups, says Stan Dorn, a senior fellow at the Urban Institute, an independent domestic-issues research group in Washington. Ideally, such arrangements could provide better integrated care, but "big systems can also extract high prices," Dorn says.

— *Marcia Clemmitt*

[1]"U.S. Healthcare Costs," Kaiser Family Foundation, www.kaiseredu.org/Issue-Modules/US-Health-Care-Costs/Background-Brief.aspx; for background, see Marcia Clemmitt, "Rising Health Costs," *CQ Researcher*, April 7, 2006, pp. 289-312.

[2]Dan Diamond, "To Gauge ObamaCare Impact, Ignore CBO and Focus on AQC," *California Healthline*, July 25, 2012, www.californiahealthline.org/road-to-reform/2012/to-gauge-obamacare-impact-ignore-cbo-and-focus-on-aqc.aspx.

[3]*Ibid.*

[4]Zirui Song, *et al.*, "The 'Alternative Quality Contract,' Based on a Global Budget, Lowered Medical Spending and Improved Quality," *Health Affairs*, July 2012, http://content.healthaffairs.org/content/early/2012/07/09/hlthaff.2012.0327.abstract.

[5]Eric Beyer, "State Needs to Take Stock Before Expanding Health Payment Methods Employers Are Rejecting," *The Boston Globe*, July 18, 2012, www.bostonglobe.com/opinion/2012/07/18/state-needs-take-stock-before-expanding-health-payment-methods-employers-methods-rejecting-state-needs-take-stock-before-expanding-health-payment/12nbA6ag2uUOCihzjFk7OI/story.html.

ACA that health plans provide contraception coverage violates the Constitution's guarantee of religious freedom.

The main ACA story of 2012, though, is uncertainty, as most of the law's provisions are a year or more from implementation and the Supreme Court ruling has made Medicaid expansion voluntary for states.

This year, several groups, including colleges run by the Roman Catholic Church and some conservative Protestant churches, as well as at least seven states and some for-profit businesses whose owners strongly oppose contraception out of religious conviction, have filed lawsuits seeking to

exempt employers from the contraception mandate.[60] (Churches, but not employers such as church-run hospitals and schools, already are exempt.)

"We're very clear on the sanctity of life, and this insurance mandate goes against our conscience," said Philip Graham Ryken, president of Wheaton College, an evangelical Protestant institution in Wheaton, Ill.[61]

The Obama administration announced a compromise plan last February. Women who work at nonprofit, church-affiliated entities can go directly to the insurance companies that administer their employer-based health plans

AFP/Getty Images/Timothy A. Clary

Demonstrators in New York City on March 23, 2012, protest a requirement of the health care law that most employers provide health insurance coverage for contraception. Several groups, including colleges run by the Roman Catholic Church, at least seven states and business owners who strongly oppose contraception out of religious conviction, have filed lawsuits seeking to exempt employers from the contraception mandate.

and get contraceptive coverage — free — so that employers can avoid acting as go-betweens. Under the ACA, insurers face stricter government rules than in the past on what coverage they offer and what they charge for it. In this case, the administration argues that insurers may not demand that women pay a higher premium to get contraceptive coverage because contraceptives are a preventive-health measure that reduces overall health spending.[62]

But opponents contend that the compromise still implicates employers in immoral activity.

"We have a president who, for the first time in American history, is directly assaulting the First Amendment and freedom of religion," said former Sen. Rick Santorum, R-Pa., in a campaign speech on behalf of Romney. President Obama, he said, is "forcing business people right now to do things that are against their conscience."[63]

Court Fallout

Since the Supreme Court rendered its decision, numerous Republican governors and state lawmakers have expressed doubt about whether their states will undertake a Medicaid expansion. Officials in states including Mississippi, Nebraska, Missouri, Idaho, Texas, Wisconsin, Florida, Indiana, South Carolina, Iowa, Louisiana and Kansas have suggested they might reject the expansion funds, thus reducing by millions the number of people covered under the law.[64] About 1.8 million uninsured people who were expected to gain Medicaid coverage live in Texas alone, and nearly 1 million reside in Florida.[65]

Some officials have flatly announced that the expansion is a no-go. "I don't see any chance" of Missouri participating, said Ryan Silvey, a budget committee chairman in that state's Republican-dominated legislature.[66]

Opposition, by and large, is not about money, and that's why it will stick, argued Andrew Koppelman, a professor of law and political science at Northwestern University. Because the state funding share is so low — the federal government will pick up 100 percent of costs through 2016, gradually dropping to 90 percent in 2020 — the objections amount to "states refusing to spend federal money to help people that they do not want to help," he contends. "The temptation to trash Obamacare will be irresistible."[67]

However, many analysts expect states eventually to back away from their hardline resistance and adopt the program.

"I'm really excited about the ruling" because by freeing states to turn down the program altogether, it gives them leverage to bargain with the federal government for looser rules about how they structure it, says insurance consultant Laszewski. "I believe that states will implement the law, but [Louisiana's Republican Gov.] Bobby Jindal will do it in a different way than in New York" under Democratic Gov. Andrew Cuomo.

The result will be a variety of natural experiments carried out around the country that will test how different coverage models work, from single-payer systems to the most loosely regulated private markets, he says.

Should the Affordable Care Act be repealed?

YES   Thomas Miller
Resident Fellow, American Enterprise Institute

Written for *CQ Global Researcher*, September 2012

The Affordable Care Act (ACA) — also known as "Obamacare" — was unpopular, unwise and unsustainable when enacted in March 2010. Another two years of stumbling implementation and real-world analysis, amid fierce battles in the courts, on Capitol Hill and throughout the states, provided further evidence of the health law's flaws. The law is too costly to finance, too difficult to administer, too burdensome on health care practitioners and too disruptive of health care arrangements that many Americans prefer.

The ACA is not just too misguided to succeed. It's too dangerous to maintain and far too flawed to fix on a piecemeal basis. The law will jeopardize future economic growth, distort health care delivery and limit access to quality care. It doubles down on our already unsustainable entitlement spending for health care, transferring dedicated funds from one overcommitted program (Medicare) to expand another (Medicaid) and establish a new one — the subsidies the ACA provides consumers to buy insurance in government-run exchanges.

The ACA will further erode meaningful limits on the powers of the federal government. Its maze of current and future mandates, regulatory edicts and arbitrary bureaucracy undermines political accountability and the rule of law.

Obamacare was built on faulty premises, then disguised with accounting fictions and narrowly approved through cynical deal-making. Repealing it in whole is necessary to clear the way for the lasting reforms of health care we so desperately need.

The long overdue journey to health policy that drives sustainable health care improvement must be centered on better incentives, information, choices, competition, personal responsibilities and trust in the decisions of individuals and their families. It should not be guided by top-down mandates, arbitrary budgetary formulas and bureaucratic buck-passing. We won't improve our health until we move personal health care decisions out of politics and back into the hands of patients and physicians.

Repeal of the ACA is not enough by itself. But it opens the door to a more decentralized and market-based alternative that will work and improve the lives of Americans. The country needs a more competitive health care marketplace that encourages more entry and less command-and-control regulation, while retargeting our tax-funded resources on protecting the most vulnerable individuals and their families.

Rebalancing our resources, our values, our hopes and our fears is too important, complex and personal to leave in the hands of the many politicians, experts and entrenched interests that have failed us in the past.

NO   Ron Pollack
Founding Executive Director, Families USA

Written for *CQ Global Researcher*, September 2012

In June, the Supreme Court upheld the constitutionality of the Affordable Care Act. Just last week, however, its theatrical opponents in the House of Representatives staged their 34th loud, divisive and utterly futile vote to repeal it. Afterward, nothing changed; it remains the law of our land. The benefits and protections it grants consumers are real, and many are already in place. Soon, even strident opponents will put aside their showmanship and recognize the positive impact and value of the law.

The law makes sure that insurance companies treat people fairly. Under the law, it will be illegal for insurers to discriminate against women by charging higher premiums simply because of their gender. Nobody — male or female — will be denied coverage or charged higher premiums because of a pre-existing condition, such as asthma or diabetes. No one will live in fear of their insurance being cancelled. People will no longer be subject to arbitrary lifetime or annual caps in what insurers pay out, thereby denying coverage when it is needed the most.

The act also comes with much-needed direct help for middle-class families. They will receive substantial subsidies to make health insurance premiums affordable. Seniors will no longer fall into the huge prescription drug coverage gap in Medicare euphemistically named the "doughnut hole." Comprehensive preventive care will be available at no cost for women, including mammograms and contraception.

A significant number of these benefits, and many others, already are being provided in whole or in part, such as the millions of young adults (under age 26) who are staying on their parents' policies. As more and more people feel the direct protections and benefits of the new law, repealing the Affordable Care Act will increasingly be considered an absurdity.

At its heart, the ACA is about keeping people healthy and giving Americans the peace of mind that health care will always be there when they need it. Irrespective of changes in any person's life circumstances — the desire to switch jobs or start a business, being laid off from work, changes in marital status or the sudden loss of income — the Affordable Care Act ensures the availability of quality, affordable health care.

Instead of playing politics with the act, it's time to fully implement it across the country. In fact, Democrats and Republicans should come together to build on the ACA so that additional steps can be taken to moderate health care costs for America's families and businesses.

Conducting such experiments has always been a good idea, "but the problem is that you need gobs of federal money" for states to do them, which the ACA now offers, he says.

"Virtually every state" will implement the expansion "after the rhetorical season" of the November election is over, says Pollack of Families USA. Some "very influential" health care sectors, such as hospitals, already are urging states to take the funding to help eliminate the unpaid medical bills they struggle with, he says.

"ACA provided a carrot and a stick" for the expansion, and "although the stick is gone, the very big carrot remains," he says.

Only a Beginning

Because many aspects of health care are state responsibilities, such as setting and enforcing rules for health insurance sold to individuals and small businesses, the ACA puts additional burdens on state governments. However, the law allows the federal government to step in if states don't fulfill these responsibilities effectively and on time.

"A few states — including Massachusetts, California and Maryland — appear to be well along in their implementation activities" for the insurance exchanges through which individuals will buy health coverage using ACA subsidies, said Antos of the American Enterprise Institute. Nationwide, however, given the present rate of progress, both the states and the federal government are doomed to fall behind the aggressive schedule the law requires, he said.

For example, 37 states have not yet enacted enabling legislation or issued an executive order to establish an insurance exchange through which citizens can buy coverage, Antos noted. Citizens of those states risk becoming liable for the ACA's mandate-related tax penalty in January 2014 — before their states have managed to set up the exchanges through which affordable coverage is supposed to be available, he wrote. What's more, it's "doubtful that the federal government . . . will be capable of stepping in" to help states get their insurance exchanges up and running, he said. "The task is too large, the time is too short."[68]

But ACA supporter Pollack says the law's opponents are secretly rooting for the law to stumble hard out of the gate. He calls their predictions that lagging ACA implementation will harm citizens "wishful thinking." Even "a lot of governors who actually oppose the law and joined the lawsuit [against it] are still working quietly with folks to get ready" to implement it, he says. That's partly because many Republican governors hope to shape the exchanges according to their own ideas — not the Obama administration's — about how the insurance market should work he says. "It would put a conservative governor in an ironic situation — letting the federal government decide what goes on in the state."

Besides expanding insurance coverage, the ACA also is intended to reshape the way health care is delivered and paid for, with the goal to hold down cost increases while maintaining quality. The law includes a wide range of possible cost-control measures, such as establishment of an independent board empowered to make cost-saving changes to Medicare. It also offers financial incentives to induce physicians and hospitals to provide preventive care. But all these measures "have to be built" before it becomes clear whether they actually work, says insurance consultant Laszewski.

Furthermore, much more must be attempted on the cost-control front, Laszewski says. "This law didn't take a really serious shot at it" — not surprising, given the controversy that surrounds any attempt to reduce medical costs, he says. Massachusetts, which enacted a close-to-universal coverage system similar to the ACA in 2006, "just passed their cost-control bill this year," a full six years into the program's operation, Laszewski says.

OUTLOOK

Voting on Health

Parts of the ACA, if not the law as a whole, undoubtedly will have some impact in the November elections. The ACA provisions intended to trim some wasteful Medicare spending, for example, could undermine President Obama's popularity among older voters. Meanwhile, many congressional Republicans continue to say they'll cut implementation funding for the law and repeal it in January if they have the power.

On July 18, 127 members of the House GOP caucus — more than half its members — wrote House Speaker Boehner and House Majority Leader Eric Cantor, R-Va., expressing "outrage" over the Supreme Court's upholding of the health care law. They pledged to "continue efforts to repeal the law in its entirety this year, next year, and until we are successful."[69] Romney has repeatedly made the same vow in his campaign for the White House.

Still, says Robert Blendon, a professor of health policy and political analysis at the Harvard School of Public Health, the ACA may not be foremost on voters' minds this fall. "The polling is pretty clear," he says. "The economy and jobs are the main issues for voters, but if the election is within three or four points, then other issues matter." Health care counts high among those other issues, but in that category it is mainly Medicare that has voters concerned, Blendon says.

Ryan, the GOP vice presidential nominee, wants to provide future Medicare recipients with a fixed government payment and let them choose among private Medicare plans, Blendon notes. But the idea "has not done well in any poll," he says.

That doesn't mean the Medicare issue is friendly to Obama, however, Blendon says. The Romney campaign "is trying to do something quite politically sophisticated" by taking Medicare and reframing it in campaign ads, speeches and interviews to depict Obama as Medicare's chief foe, he says. Romney charged in an August TV ad and in an interview that in the ACA, Obama "cuts Medicare by $716 billion, takes that money out of the Medicare trust fund and uses it to pay for Obamacare."[70]

But the ACA's defenders argue that the cuts don't trim Medicare benefits but shift the payments in ways aimed at reducing wasteful spending. For example, the law trims payments to so-called Medicare Advantage private health plans that cost more than traditional Medicare. It also lowers payments to hospitals that discharge too many patients too quickly, only to readmit them to treat conditions that could have been prevented with better patient management. If those changes save money, as many expect they will, the savings will fund new Medicare benefits — such as free preventive care — as well as other ACA provisions, PolitiFact Florida, a fact-checking website run by the *Tampa Bay Times*, reported.[71]

Nevertheless, Republican ads and speeches condemning the cuts are successfully harming Obama's standing with senior voters, at least for now, says Blendon. "Just the one big number" — $716 billion — is enough "to make people very nervous," while details that could make the number sound less frightening "are awfully complex to explain to people." In states such as Florida and Ohio, where the presidential vote will be close, the Medicare ads could win the day for Republicans, he says.

In polls, most voters continue to say they dislike the ACA, despite expressing support for some of its provisions, such as its guarantee that people with pre-existing illnesses can buy insurance at a relatively affordable price. Public opposition stems in large part from people's lack of knowledge about what the law does, some analysts argue.

The Urban Institute's Dorn describes a conversation he had with a small-business owner who doesn't provide health insurance for his mainly low-wage workers and buys his personal coverage in the private market. "I said, 'Your own premiums will come down a lot" once the ACA kicks in in 2014, "and your low-wage workers will get subsidies" from the government to help them buy coverage, too. The man responded that he hadn't heard of these ACA features and wasn't sure he believed they existed, Dorn says.

Nevertheless, the ACA has set in motion some changes that will go forward, whatever the election results, says Dorn. For example, states are using ACA funds to automate and streamline their Medicaid administrative procedures, which may trim costs and make it easier for poor people to get access to all the state services they need. And some hospitals and doctors are shifting their focus to preventive care, in anticipation of ACA payment changes that will reward prevention.

"Even if Republicans sweep the table" in November, says Dorn, "they can't take all of those things away."

NOTES

1. "Support Caleb," Facebook, www.facebook.com/supportcalebmedley.

2. Jeremy P. Meyer, "Caleb Medley, Last Shooting Victim at CU Hospital, Released," *Denver Post*, Sept. 13, 2012, www.denverpost.com/breakingnews/ci_21528421/caleb-medley-last-shooting-victim-at-cu-hospital.

3. Quoted in John Blackstone, "Aurora Shooting May Ruin One Victim's Finances," CBS News, July 23, 2012, www.cbsnews.com/8301-18563_162-57478303/aurora-shooting-may-ruin-one-victims-finances.

4. The decision is *National Federation of Independent Business v. Sebelius*, 567 U.S. 2— (June 28, 2012), www.supremecourt.gov/opinions/11pdf/11-393c3a2.pdf; For an account, see Kenneth Jost, "Health Care Law Upheld in Fractured Ruling," *CQ Researcher* Blog, June 28, 2012, http://cqresearcherblog.blogspot.com/2012_06_01_archive.html.

5. Phil Galewitz and Marilyn Werber Serafini, "Ruling Puts Pressure on States to Act," *Kaiser Health News*, June 28, 2012, www.kaiserhealthnews.org/stories/2012/june/28/pressure-on-states-to-act-after-supreme-court-ruling.aspx.

6. *NFIB v. Sebelius, op. cit.* (opinion of Scalia, Kennedy, Thomas, and Alito dissenting), p. 6.

7. *NFIB v. Sebelius, op. cit.*, (opinion of Ginsburg, J.), fn 5, p. 19.

8. Nancy-Ann DeParle, "Supreme Court Upholds President Obama's Health Care Reform," *The White House Blog*, June 28, 2012, www.whitehouse.gov/blog/2012/06/28/supreme-court-upholds-president-obamas-health-care-reform.

9. For background, see Julie Rovner, "Mitt Romney's Shifting Stance on Health Care," *Shots blog*, NPR, Sept. 10, 2012, www.npr.org/blogs/health/2012/09/10/160898409/mitt-romneys-shifting-stance-on-health-care.

10. Robin Abcarian and Maeve Reston, "Romney Uses Healthcare Ruling to Motivate Voters Against Obama," *Los Angeles Times*, June 28, 2012, http://articles.latimes.com/2012/jun/28/news/la-pn-romney-uses-healthcare-ruling-to-motivate-voters-against-obama-20120628.

11. For background, see Mitt Romney, "Romney: As First Act, Out With Obamacare," *USA Today*, May 11, 2011, www.usatoday.com/news/opinion/forum/2011-05-11-Romney-on-fixing-health-care_n.htm.

12. For background, see "Plan Levels/Standardization of Coverage," American Cancer Society, www.acscan.org/pdf/healthcare/implementation/background/PlanLevelsStandardizationofCoverage.pdf.

13. Quoted in Kim Krisberg, "Public Health Reacts to Supreme Court's ACA Ruling: 'Surprised and Then Ecstatic,' " *The Pump Handle blog*, June 28, 2012, http://scienceblogs.com/thepumphandle/2012/06/28/public-health-reacts-to-supreme-courts-aca-ruling-surprised-and-then-ecstatic.

14. "On ObamaCare," Wicker for Congress website, www.brookswicker.com/on-obamacare.

15. Ryan Fazio, "Health Care Reform Biased Against Youth," *The Daily Northwestern*, Feb. 13, 2012, www.dailynorthwestern.com/mobile/forum/fazio-health-care-reform-biased-against-youth-1.2700776.

16. Quoted in Jeffrey Young, "Health Care Reform Will Remake Health Insurance Market for Young Adults," *Huffington Post*, Aug. 1, 2012, www.huffingtonpost.com/2012/08/01/health-care-reform-young-adults_n_1711376.html.

17. Quoted in *ibid.*

18. For background, see Michael Cooper, "Many Governors Are Still Unsure About Medicaid Expansion," *The New York Times*, July 14, 2012, www.nytimes.com/2012/07/15/us/governors-face-hard-choices-over-medicaid-expansion.html?pagewanted=all.

19. For background, see "The Requirement to Buy Coverage Under the Affordable Care Act," *Health Reform Source*, Henry J. Kaiser Family Foundation, http://healthreform.kff.org/the-basics/Requirement-to-buy-coverage-flowchart.aspx.

20. "Mitch McConnell: Odds Are Against Health Law Repeal," The Associated Press/*Huffington Post*, July 2, 2012, www.huffingtonpost.com/2012/07/02/mitch-mcconnell-health-care-law_n_1644466.html.

21. Michael D. Tanner, "Individual Mandates for Health Insurance: Slippery Slope to National Health Care," *Policy Analysis No. 565*, Cato Institute, April 5, 2006, www.cato.org.

22. Quoted in Sarah Kliff, "Scott Brown, Ron Wyden Offering Health Care Revision," *Politico*, Nov. 17, 2010, www.politico.com/news/stories/1110/45316.html.

23. *NFIB v. Sebelius*, (opinion of Ginsburg, J.), *op. cit.*, p. 7.

24. Joseph Paduda, "Update — Health reform, the Supreme Court decision and workers comp," *Managed Care Matters*, June 29, 2012, www.joepaduda.com/archives/002363.html.

25. *Ibid.*

26. Quoted in Steve O'Keefe, "Loss Ratio Means Lost Care for Millions," *Health Care Compact Blog*, Nov. 14, 2011, http://healthcarecompact.org/blog/2011-11-14/loss-ratio-means-lost-care-millions.

27. *Ibid.*

28. Quoted in Kathryn Jean Lopez, "Post-Court Report: Sally Pipes on the Future of Health-Care Reform in America," *National Review Online*, March 29, 2012, www.nationalreview.com/critical-condition/294752/post-court-report-sally-pipes-future-health-care-reform-america-kathryn-je.

29. John Goodman, "The Supreme Court May Have Saved Lives," *The Health Care Blog*, July 30, 2012, http://thehealthcareblog.com/blog/2012/07/30/the-supreme-court-may-have-saved-lives.

30. Pam Belluck, "Medicaid Expansion May Lower Death Rates, Study Says," *The New York Times*, July 25, 2012, www.nytimes.com/2012/07/26/health/policy/medicaid-expansion-may-lower-death-rate-study-says.html?pagewanted=all; Benjamine D. Sommers, *et al.*, "Mortality and Access to Care Among Adults After State Medicaid Expansions," *The New England Journal of Medicine*, July 25, 2012, www.nejm.org/doi/full/10.1056/NEJMsa1202099.

31. Belluck, *op. cit.*

32. Quoted in "The Supreme Court Health Care Ruling: Now What?" *Knowledge at Wharton*, June 28, 2012, http://knowledge.wharton.upenn.edu/article.cfm?articleid=3038.

33. John Rossomando, "ObamaCare Forcing Americans out of Their Health Plans," *Human Events*, July 8, 2011, www.humanevents.com/2011/07/08/obamacare-forcing-americans-out-of-their-health-plans.

34. Joseph Antos, "After the Supreme Court, Higher Cost and Unrealistic Timeline Will Force Major Changes," *Health Affairs blog*, July 2, 2012, http://healthaffairs.org/blog/2012/07/02/after-the-supreme-court-higher-cost-and-unrealistic-timeline-will-force-major-changes.

35. Quoted in Tom Eblen, "Commentary: Medicare for Everyone," McClatchy/*Lexington Herald Leader* [KY], Aug. 7, 2012, www.mcclatchydc.com/2012/08/07/160417/commentary-medicare-for-everyone.html.

36. "Testimony on Last Year's Major Health Care Legislation," Congressional Budget Office, March 30, 2011, www.cbo.gov/publication/25155.

37. Douglas W. Elmendorf, letter to Rep. John Boehner, Congressional Budget Office, July 24, 2012, http://cbo.gov/sites/default/files/cbofiles/attachments/43471-hr6079.pdf.

38. Paduda, *op. cit.*

39. "Overview of the Uninsured in the United States: A Summary of the 2011 Population Survey," Assistant Secretary for Planning and Evaluation, U.S. Dept. of Health and Human Services, September 2011, http://aspe.hhs.gov/health/reports/2011/CPSHealthIns2011/ib.shtml.

40. For background, see Marcia Clemmitt, "Health-Care Reform," *CQ Researcher*, June 11, 2010 (updated May 24, 2011), pp. 505-528, and Marcia Clemmitt, "Health-Care Reform," *CQ Researcher*, Aug. 28, 2009, pp. 693-716.

41. "Estimates for the Insurance Coverage Provisions of the Affordable Care Act Updated for the Recent Supreme Court Decision," Congressional Budget Office, July 2012, p. 3, http://cbo.gov/sites/default/files/cbofiles/attachments/43472-07-24-2012-CoverageEstimates.pdf.

42. David Cole, "Is Health Care Reform Unconstitutional?" *The New York Review of Books*, Feb. 24, 2011, www.nybooks.com/articles/archives/2011/feb/24/health-care-reform-unconstitutional/?pagination=false.

43. *Ibid.*

44. Mark V. Pauly, Patricia Damon, Paul Feldstein and John Hoff, "A Plan for 'Responsible National Health Insurance,' " *Health Affairs*, Spring 1991, p. 10, http://hc.wharton.upenn.edu/danzon/html/CV%20pubs/1991_DanzonPaulyFesteinHoff_APlanForResponsibleNationalHealthInsurance_HA%20Spring%201991.pdf.

45. Stuart Butler, testimony before the Senate Special Committee on Aging, March 10, 2003, www.heritage.org/research/testimony/laying-the-groundwork-for-universal-health-care-coverage.

46. Quoted in Marcia Clemmitt, "Frist: Limit Tax Exclusion for Employer-Based Coverage," *Medicine and Health*, July 19, 2004.

47. Avik Roy, "Opposing View: Individual Mandate Masks and Ugly Deal," *USA Today*, March 28, 2012, www.usatoday.com/news/opinion/story/2012-03-27/supreme-court-individual-mandate/5381 5712/1.

48. Uwe E. Reinhardt, "The Supreme Court and the National Conversation on Health Care Reform," *Economix blogs, The New York Times*, March 30, 2012, http://economix.blogs.nytimes.com/2012/03/30/the-supreme-court-and-the-national-conversation-on-health-care-reform.

49. Galewitz and Serafini, *op. cit.*; for background, see Elicia J. Herz, "Medicaid: A Primer," Congressional Research Service, Jan. 11, 2011, www.ncsl.org/documents/health/MAPrimer.pdf.

50. "Eligibility Levels in Medicaid & CHIP for Children, Pregnant Women, Parents, and Childless Adults," Georgetown University Health Policy Institute, Center for Children and Families, January 2012, http://ccf.georgetown.edu/wp-content/uploads/2012/04/Eligibility-by-State.pdf.

51. "Who Benefits from the ACA Medicaid Expansion," The Kaiser Commission on Medicaid and the Uninsured, June 20, 2012, www.kff.org/medicaid/quicktake_aca_medicaid.cfm.

52. "Federal and State Share of Medicaid Spending FY2010," statehealthfacts.org, Kaiser Family Foundation, www.statehealthfacts.org/comparemaptable.jsp?ind=636&cat=4.

53. "Summary of New Health Reform Law," Kaiser Family Foundation, www.kff.org/healthreform/upload/8061.pdf.

54. Quoted in Julie Rovner, "Medicaid Expansion Goes Overlooked in Supreme Court Anticipation," *Shots blog*, NPR, June 27, 2012, www.npr.org/blogs/health/2012/06/27/155861308/medicaid-expansion-goes-overlooked-in-supreme-court-anticipation.

55. Galewitz and Serafini, *op. cit.*

56. Richard Posner, "Entry 17: The Commerce Clause Was Clearly Enough to Uphold the Affordable Care Act," *Supreme Court Year in Review, Slate*, June 28, 2012, www.slate.com/articles/news_and_politics/the_breakfast_table/features/2012/_supreme_court_year_in_review/affordable_care_act_upheld_why_the_commerce_clause_should_have_been_enough_.html.

57. *NFIB v. Sebelius*, (opinion of Roberts, C. J.), *op. cit.*, p. 36.

58. *Ibid.*, p. 45.

59. *Ibid.*, p. 53.

60. For background, see Robin Marty, "Hobby Lobby Files Suit Opposing Affordable Care Act Birth Control Benefit," *RH Reality Check*, Sept. 13, 2012, www.rhrealitycheck.org/article/2012/09/13/hobby-lobby-lawsuit-opens-new-realm-in-opposing-afforable-care-act.

61. Quoted in "Evangelical College Joins Suit Against ObamaCare Contraception Mandate," FoxNews.com, July 18, 2012, www.foxnews.com/politics/2012/07/18/evangelical-college-joins-suit-against-obamacare-contraception-mandate.

62. David Brown, "U.S. Bishops Blast Obama's Contraception Compromise," *The Washington Post*, Feb. 11, 2012, www.washingtonpost.com/national/health-science/us-bishops-blast-obamas-contraception-compromise/2012/02/11/gIQAlGVO7Q_story.html.

63. Quoted in Andrew Rafferty, "Santorum Says Government Forcing Catholics to Sin," First Read, NBCNews.com, Aug. 15, 2012, http://firstread.nbcnews.com/_news/2012/08/15/13303104-santorum-says-government-forcing-catholics-to-sin?lite.

64. Galewitz and Serafini, *op. cit.*; N.C. Aizenman and Sandhya Somashekhar, "More State Leaders Considering Opting Out of Medicaid Expansion," *The Washington Post*, July 3, www.washingtonpost.com/national/health-science/more-state-leaders-considering-opting-out-of-medicaid-expansion/2012/07/03/gJQADvMsLW_story.html. John Celock, "Health Care Reform Battles Taking Shape at State Level," *Huffington Post*, June 29, 2012, www.huffingtonpost.com/2012/06/28/health-care-reform-battle-states_n_1635545.html.

65. Galewitz and Serafini, *ibid.*

66. Quoted in *ibid.*

67. Andrew Koppelman, "Terrible Arguments Prevail!" *Salon*, June 28, 2012, www.salon.com/2012/06/28/ terrible_arguments_prevail.

68. Antos, *op. cit.*

69. Letter to Reps. John Boehner and Eric Cantor, July 18, 2012, http://rsc.jordan.house.gov/Uploaded Files/Defund_ObamaCare_Letter_July_18.pdf.

70. Quoted in "Romney Says Obama 'Cuts' $716 Billion from Medicare to Pay for Obamacare," *PolitiFact Florida*, Aug. 20, 2012, www.politifact.com/florida/ statements/2012/aug/20/mitt-romney/romney- says-obama-cuts-716-medicare-pay-obamacare.

71. *Ibid.*

BIBLIOGRAPHY

Selected Sources

Books

McDonough, John E., *Inside National Health Reform*, California/Milbank Books on Health and the Public, 2011.
A Harvard professor of public health who supports the 2010 Affordable Care Act explains its background and why he believes it will improve American health.

Starr, Paul, *Remedy and Reaction: The Peculiar American Struggle over Health Care Reform*, Yale University Press, 2011.
A Princeton professor of sociology and public affairs chronicles legislative attempts to overhaul the U.S. health-care system over the past three decades and the vested interests of health-care practitioners, insurers and the public that have made those attempts so difficult.

Turner, Grace-Marie, James C. Capretta, Thomas P. Miller and Robert E. Moffit, *Why ObamaCare Is Wrong for America: How the New Health Care Law Drives Up Costs, Puts Government in Charge of Your Decisions, and Threatens Your Constitutional Rights*, Broadside Books, 2011.
Analysts from the free-market-oriented think tanks Galen Institute (Turner) and American Enterprise Institute argue that the Affordable Care Act (ACA) relies on government regulation rather than market competition to address health-system problems and say alternative approaches would allow consumer choice to determine how the health care market develops.

Articles

Keck, Anthony, "South Carolina's View: The Affordable Care Act's Medicaid Expansion Is the Wrong Approach," *Health Affairs Blog*, Sept. 6, 2012, http://healthaffairs.org/blog/2012/09/06/ south-carolinas-view-the-affordable-care-acts- medicaid-expansion-is-the-wrong-approach.
The director of South Carolina's Medicaid program argues that eliminating waste in the medical system and changing how health care providers are reimbursed can help his state provide care to more poor people than by accepting federal funds under the ACA to expand Medicaid.

Rau, Jordan, "Medicare to Penalize 2,211 Hospitals for Excess Readmissions," *Kaiser Health News*, Aug. 13, 2012, www.kaiserhealthnews.org/Stories/2012/ August/13/medicare-hospitals-readmissions- penalties.aspx.
As ACA provisions aimed at trimming ineffective health care spending and improving care quality take effect, more than 2,000 hospitals will lose some Medicare payments because too many of their elderly patients were readmitted for conditions that could have been prevented during their hospital stay. ACA supporters argue that such penalties prevent hospitals from profiting from readmissions and protect patients from ineffective care. But hospitals that serve low-income neighborhoods contend they're being unfairly penalized because their patient populations tend to need more care than do wealthier people.

Reinhardt, Uwe E., "Health Care: Solidarity vs. Rugged Individualism," *Economix blogs*, *The New York Times*, June 29, 2012, http://economix.blogs .nytimes.com/2012/06/29/health-care-solidarity-vs- rugged-individualism.
A Princeton University professor of economics describes the differences between what he calls the European "social-solidarity" approach to health care and the American "libertarian" approach and why he considers the European view more practical.

Reports and Studies

"The Affordable Care Act: A Brief Summary," *National Conference of State Legislatures*, March 2011, www.ncsl.org/portals/1/documents/health/HRACA.pdf.

A nonpartisan group that provides information to and about state governments offers a plain-language summary of the 2010 health-care law.

Hahn, Jim, and Christopher M. Davis, "The Independent Payment Advisory Board," Congressional Research Service, March 12, 2012, http://assets.opencrs.com/rpts/R41511_20120312.pdf.

Analysts from Congress' nonpartisan research office explain the workings of the ACA's highly controversial expert board that will develop payment and care-delivery changes to trim Medicare costs.

Lunder, Erika K., and Jennifer Staman, "NFIB v. Sebelius: Constitutionality of the Individual Mandate," Congressional Research Service, Sept. 3, 2012, www.fas.org/sgp/crs/misc/R42698.pdf.

Lawyers at Congress' nonpartisan research arm explain the Supreme Court's ruling upholding the 2010 Affordable Care Act's requirement that individuals buy health insurance.

Smith, Mark, Robert Saunders, Leigh Stuckhardt and J. Michael McGinnis, eds., "Best Care at Lower Cost: The Path to Continuously Learning Health Care in America," Institute of Medicine, September 2012, www.nap.edu/catalog.php?record_id=13444.

Experts on improving health care quality say 30 cents of every dollar in health care spending is wasted on useless services. To stem soaring medical costs, the United States should pay medical practitioners based on health outcomes rather than "per service rendered," they contend. Quick adoption of information technology also would help keep doctors up to date on which treatments are supported by science and on patients' medical histories, they also say.

For More Information

ACA Litigation Blog, http://acalitigationblog.blogspot.com. Blog of Bradley Joondeph, a professor of law at the Santa Clara University School of Law in northern California, that chronicles legal challenges to the Affordable Care Act (ACA).

Alliance for Health Reform, 1444 Eye St., N.W., Suite 910, Washington, DC 20005; 202-789-2300; www.allhealth.org. Nonpartisan group that calls on health care experts representing a wide range of opinions to provide information about the ACA and other issues.

American Enterprise Institute, 1150 17th St., N.W., Washington, DC 20036; 202-862-5800; www.aei.org/issue/health/healthcare-reform/beyond-repeal-and-replace-series. Conservative think tank providing information and analysis on developing a more market-oriented health care system.

Center on Budget and Policy Priorities, 820 First St., N.E., Suite 510, Washington, DC 20002; 202-408-1080; www.cbpp.org. Liberal think tank that analyzes how economic policies, including the ACA, affect individuals and state and federal budgets.

Families USA, 1201 New York Ave., N.W., Suite 1100, Washington, DC 20005; 202-628-3030; www.familiesusa.org. Liberal consumer-advocacy group that is tracking the progress and effects of the ACA's rollout.

Health Affairs Blog, http://healthaffairs.org/blog. Blog run by an academic journal covering health policy that presents a range of opinion on the ACA.

Healthcare.gov, U.S. Department of Health and Human Services, 200 Independence Ave., S.W., Washington, DC 20201; www.healthcare.gov/law/index.html. Federal government website providing summaries and information about how the ACA is being implemented.

Henry J. Kaiser Family Foundation, Health Reform Source, http://healthreform.kff.org. Website of a nonpartisan foundation that provides information about U.S. health care and the ACA, including a law summary.

14

Preventing Disease

Nellie Bristol

Mayor Chip Johnson, of Hernando, Miss., supports a wide range of projects designed to make residents healthier while saving taxpayers money. In his six years in office he has developed bike paths and lanes while pushing to require developers to build sidewalks and city engineers to plan roads with walkers and bicyclists in mind. A wellness program he approved for city employees reduced health insurance costs 15 percent. "For us, that's a lot of money," he said.

From *The CQ Researcher*,
January 6, 2012.

S oon after his election as mayor, Chip Johnson began trying to transform Hernando, Miss., into an oasis of healthy living.

In impoverished Mississippi, that was a challenge worthy of the surgeon general. The state ranks highest in the nation in cardiovascular deaths, obesity and infant deaths and second worst in diabetes.[1]

But if residents exercised and ate right, Johnson figured, future illnesses might be prevented, at the same time saving taxpayers money and making the city of 14,000 a more attractive business environment.

Six years later, Johnson has developed bike paths and lanes with $800,000 in federal, state and private grants, while pushing to require developers to build sidewalks and city engineers to plan roads with walkers and bikers in mind. He even started a farmers market that accepts food stamps.[2]

As a Republican, Johnson believes that health and fitness decisions are personal, but he also knows those decisions shape demand for tax-supported health services, influence overall medical costs and help determine the business climate. "We want to recruit corporations to Hernando," he said. "They're not stupid. When they make their decisions, they look at health care costs."[3]

Hernando, a fast-growing bedroom suburb for nearby Memphis, Tenn., is atypical in Mississippi because of its higher rate of affluent and professional residents. Even so, Johnson's efforts are seen as a guide for fostering healthy habits in any community, rich or poor.

Public health experts argue that a locally based, multipronged approach like Hernando's is the only way for communities to reverse

More Than 30 States Have High Obesity Rates

At least one-fourth of adults in 33 states are obese.* In nine states, mainly in the South, 30 percent or more of adults are obese. At least 20 percent are obese in another 16 states. Overall, more than one-third of American adults (more than 72 million people) and 17 percent of children are obese.

Percentage of Adults Who Are Obese, by State, 2009

Percentage of obese adults

☐ 15%-19%
☐ 20%-24%
■ 25%-29%
■ 30%+

* Obesity is defined as a body mass index (BMI) of at least 30, or about 30 lbs. over- weight for a 5'4" person.

** No data available

Source: "Obesity: Halting the Epidemic By Making Health Easier," Centers for Disease Control and Prevention, 2011, p. 2, www.cdc.gov/chronicdisease/resources/publications/aag/pdf/2011/Obesity_AAG_WEB_508.pdf

in obesity, diabetes and childhood poverty. "The country's overall health did not improve between 2010 and 2011," the foundation said.[5]

Negative health trends are taking a toll on the nation's resources. Chronic diseases are responsible for more than three-quarters of U.S. health care costs.[6] The bill is even higher for government health programs, with chronic disease accounting for 96 percent of Medicare spending for the elderly and 83 percent of Medicaid spending for the poor.[7]

Worldwide, chronic, noncommunicable disease is expected to cost the global economy $47 trillion over the next two decades (in today's dollars).[8] The U.N.'s World Health Organization (WHO) estimates that at least 80 percent of heart disease, stroke and Type 2 diabetes cases and more than 40 percent of cancer could be prevented or better managed through smoking cessation, healthy eating and better fitness.[9]

Public health experts say reducing chronic disease requires efforts by a broad range of government and private-sector actors. They advocate government actions such as public health messages, limits on salt, sugar and fat in commercial foods and increased sidewalk construction to encourage exercise. They also are encouraging:

- Packaged-food manufacturers to reduce marketing of sugary breakfast cereals and other unhealthy products to children;
- Restaurants to cut portion sizes and post calories counts;
- Communities to build more playgrounds, and,
- The medical system to offer inexpensive or free preventive services and link patients to local support programs.

Some physicians even call for removing severely obese children from their parents.[10] "It should only be

the major risk factors for chronic disease: poor eating habits, lack of exercise, smoking and alcohol use, which contribute to cardiovascular and lung disease, diabetes and some cancers.

While there is no hard evidence yet that Johnson's initiatives have improved the town's health, a wellness program Johnson approved for the city's 115 employees helped lead to a 15 percent reduction in health insurance costs. "For us, that's a lot of money," he said.[4]

While Johnson is working to get his town on a better health trajectory, the public health picture nationwide doesn't seem to be improving.

The annual health rankings released recently by the United Health Foundation, an advocacy and philanthropy group, showed that positive health trends in 2011, such as reductions in smoking, preventable hospitalizations and cardiovascular deaths, were offset by increases used as a last resort," said David Ludwig, a child obesity expert at Harvard University. "It's also no guarantee of success, but when we have a 400-pound child with life-threatening complications, there may not be any great choices."[11]

While many view that idea as extreme, even modest steps can be highly controversial.

Critics of the preventive health movement say, for example, that the "obesity epidemic" has been overblown by public health officials and is a ruse to allow meddling in personal choices and affairs. "This epidemic has been constructed to the benefit of the medical industry that has in part medicalized the treatment of obesity over the years," said University of Houston sociologist Samantha Kwan.[12]

Julie Guthman, an associate professor of community studies at the University of California, Santa Cruz, agrees. "I'm not convinced obesity is the problem it's made out to be," she says. She argues, for example, that a common tool used to determine obesity — the body mass index (BMI) — doesn't effectively take into account muscle mass. She also says the correlation between body weight and sickness is not fully proven.

"People who are overweight or slightly obese actually seem to have longer life expectancy than people who are of so-called normal weight," she says. "There's a lot of panic without really understanding the dimensions of the problem."

Former Gov. Sarah Palin, R-Alaska, took on the issue by bringing cookies to a school in Pennsylvania in reaction to the news report that the state school board was considering limiting sweets brought to the classroom. "I wanted these kids to bring home the idea to their parents for discussion," she said. "Who should be deciding what I eat? Should it be the government or should it be parents? It should be the parents."[13]

Palin also took on the high-profile Let's Move program developed by first lady Michelle Obama to attack

Smoking Kills Nearly Half a Million Annually

About 443,000 Americans die each year from smoking, including deaths from secondhand smoke. Smoking-induced lung cancer and heart disease each accounts for about 30 percent of the deaths. Tobacco use is the single most preventable cause of disease, disability and death in the United States.

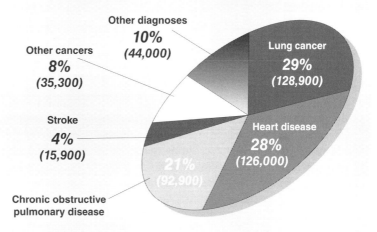

Annual Smoking-Related Deaths, by Disease, Including Secondhand Smoke, 2000-2004

Other diagnoses 10% (44,000)

Other cancers 8% (35,300)

Lung cancer 29% (128,900)

Stroke 4% (15,900)

Heart disease 28% (126,000)

21% (92,900)

Chronic obstructive pulmonary disease

Source: "Tobacco Use: Targeting the Nation's Leading Killer," Centers for Disease Control and Prevention, 2011, p. 2, www.cdc.gov/chronicdisease/ resources/ publications/aag/pdf/2011/Tobacco_AAG_2011_508.pdf

childhood obesity, which has more than tripled since 1980.[14] "Instead of government thinking that they need to take over and make decisions for us according to some politician or politician's wife's priorities, just leave us alone, get off our back and allow us as individuals to exercise our own God-given rights to make our own decisions, and then our country gets back on the right track," Palin said.[15]

The food industry also is pushing back, fighting government requirements to limit certain foods, such as potatoes, in school lunches, reformulate products and curtail some types of advertising to children. Industry officials say they prefer a voluntary approach.

But many people think Americans' increasing weight and sedentary lifestyles call for action. A group of retired generals, admirals and other senior U.S. military leaders declared in 2010 that an "alarming" 75 percent of 17-24-year-olds are unfit for military service, citing obesity as a contributing factor. They urged a ban on junk food in schools, improvement in school lunches and greater access for children to obesity-reduction programs.[16]

"If we don't take steps now to build a strong, healthy foundation for our young people, then it won't just be our military that pays the price — our nation as a whole will suffer also," they wrote.[17]

As lawmakers, employers and individuals struggle to find the best ways to prevent or delay chronic disease, here are some of the issues being discussed:

Does preventing disease save money?

Reducing health care costs is a perennial national priority. Health spending in the United States totaled $2.5 trillion in 2009, or an average of $8,086 per person. Spending on health constitutes 17.6 percent of the U.S. gross domestic product (GDP), more than twice the 7.2 percent of GDP in 1970, according to the Kaiser Family Foundation.[18] And unless changes are made, health care costs are expected to keep growing.

The subject is of special concern to congressional lawmakers, particularly in a time of high budget deficits. Medicare, the federal health care program for the elderly and disabled, accounts for 20 percent of national health expenditures. Medicaid, the joint state/federal program for low-income people, makes up 15 percent of national health expenditures. Altogether, the federal government share of national health spending is 27 percent.[19]

Some lawmakers have zeroed in on disease prevention as a cost-cutting measure, reasoning that preventing people from getting sick would save money on future care. But strictly in economic terms and not improvements in longevity and quality of life, the reality is much more complicated.

"Studies have concluded that preventing illness can in some cases save money but in other cases can add to health costs," wrote Joshua Cohen, deputy director of the Tufts University Center for the Evaluation of Value and Risk in Health, and other researchers. "Whether any preventive measure saves money or is a reasonable investment despite adding to cost depends entirely on the particular intervention and the specific population in question." For example, the authors continued, "drugs used to treat high cholesterol yield much greater value for the money if the target population is at high risk for coronary heart disease,

and the efficiency of cancer screening can depend heavily on the frequency of the screening and the level of cancer risk in the screened population."[20]

To try to quantify the cost effectiveness of certain disease-prevention services, the Robert Wood Johnson Foundation studied preventive services provided in medical settings, including immunizations and screening for a variety of risk factors such as hypertension and high cholesterol. The researchers drew several conclusions, including that preventive services can reduce prevalence of specific diseases and help people live longer and that many preventive services offer good value for scarce health care dollars.

But they also found that most preventive care does not result in cost savings. "Costs to reduce risk factors, screening costs and the cost of treatment when disease is found can offset any savings from preventive care," they wrote. "Additionally, living longer means people may develop other ailments that increase lifetime health care costs."[21]

In fact, the review of 17 medications/immunizations and screening services found only two that reduced costs: childhood immunizations and counseling of adults on the use of low-dose aspirin to prevent cardiovascular disease. However, a number of other services were found to be cost effective. That is, they didn't directly save health care dollars, but the benefits were sufficiently large compared to the costs to make them valuable services for improving health. These included flu shots for adults, counseling on the use of folic acid for pregnant women and a variety of screening tests, including those for colorectal, breast and cervical cancer, hypertension and cholesterol.

The picture is more positive for what are known as community-based prevention efforts. The Trust for America's Health, a disease-prevention advocacy group, evaluated 84 studies of prevention activities targeted at communities rather than individuals. To be included in the review, interventions could not require medical treatment and had to be proven to reduce disease through improving physical activity and nutrition and preventing smoking and other tobacco use. Programs included, for example, establishment of farmers markets, calorie and nutrition labeling, nutrition education for young mothers and raising cigarette and other tobacco taxes.

Overall, the group found that an investment of $10 per person per year in proven community-based disease-prevention programs could save more than $2.8 billion annually in health care costs in one to two years, more than $16 billion annually within five years and nearly $18 billion annually in 10 to 20 years.[22] The group concluded: "a small strategic investment in disease prevention could result in significant savings in U.S. health care costs."

As lawmakers confront rising health care costs, spiraling obesity rates and an aging population, more focus should be placed on evaluating the cost effectiveness of disease intervention, including prevention efforts, some experts say. But such efforts are fraught with controversy. The U.S. Preventive Services Task Force, which makes recommendations about interventions based on a calculation of benefit to risks, has come under fire in recent years for endorsing more limited use of widespread services such as mammography and prostate cancer screening.

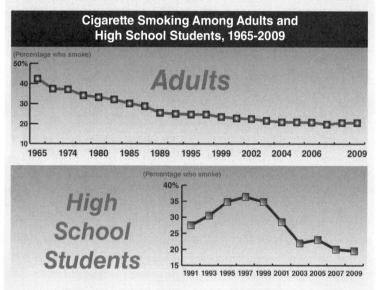

Smoking Declined Among Adults, Students

About 20 percent of adults and high school students smoke cigarettes. The percentage has declined by half for students since the mid-1990s and for adults since 1965.

Cigarette Smoking Among Adults and High School Students, 1965-2009

Source: "Tobacco Use: Targeting the Nation's Leading Killer," Centers for Disease Control and Prevention, February 2011, ww.cdc.gov/chronicdisease/resources/publications/AAG/osh_text.htm#chart2

Putting a dollar value on activities aimed at prolonging life has attracted even more heat. The 2009 economic stimulus legislation, for example, included funding for an Obama administration-supported comparative-effectiveness analysis of medical services, but references to calculating cost effectiveness were dropped following objections in Congress.[23]

But some, including Cohen at Tufts, argue that while costs shouldn't be the only consideration, they should be taken into account. "At any given time, we can only spend so much money as a country on health care, so it's not a question of whether we should be spending money only on those things that save money," he says. "If we do things that are less cost effective — have a smaller benefit per dollar invested — we will be taking away, on some level, from those things that are more cost effective, and we will be decreasing overall population health."

Should government encourage behavior change?

Whose responsibility is it to stop Americans from dying from preventable diseases? The question stirs passions deeply tied to opinions on the role of government in society. Many supporters of government involvement say the most effective approach does not focus necessarily on individuals, but rather on creating environments that "make the healthy choice the easy choice."

But not everyone sees the value of getting the government involved. For example, some argue the obesity "epidemic" is overstated and that the government is overstepping when it tells people what to eat.

Nonetheless, government at all levels is actively trying to improve nutrition and increase access to daily exercise. Specific policies adopted include higher taxes on cigarettes to reduce smoking, trans-fat bans to lower the risk of heart disease and healthier school lunch menus.

Many experts concerned about unhealthy eating say the government should better educate consumers about what is in their food, create more access to fresh fruit and vegetables and ban unhealthy foods in schools. "Where the government comes in is when industry is not acting responsibly," said Margo Wootan, director of nutrition

[handwritten notes: Public health messages, Effection. flu shots. - Regulators, Severely obese children from parents.]

Smoking and Obesity Are Biggest Killers

Some 555,000 people died in the United States in 2000 from smoking or obesity. Alcohol abuse was a distant third in the list of behaviors leading to death.

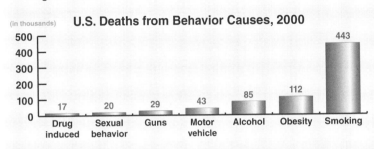

(in thousands)
U.S. Deaths from Behavior Causes, 2000

Drug induced	Sexual behavior	Guns	Motor vehicle	Alcohol	Obesity	Smoking
17	20	29	43	85	112	443

Source: "Preventing Chronic Disease: The New Public Health," Alliance for Health Reform, September 2011, p. 2, www.allhealth.org/publi cations/Public_health/Preventing_Chronic_Disease_New_Public_Health_108.pdf

policy at the Center for Science in the Public Interest, a consumer advocacy group, and that leaves a lot of potential room for government action, she adds. "The food industry has resisted every meaningful policy I've ever worked on — menu labeling, trans fat labeling, getting soda and candy bars out of schools. The industry's job is not to promote American health, it's to make money."

Scott Kahan, associate director of the Johns Hopkins University Weight Management Center, in Baltimore, said government has long had a role in improving health, starting with upgrading sanitation and water quality. It also steps in when the public is faced with infectious disease, including flu outbreaks. "When we look at how we improved the infectious disease problem in America, structural interventions, policy interventions and government interventions were a really important part of that," he says.

Today, he continues, the nation faces a different set of diseases with different causes, but the need for government action is no less. "We live in an environment right now that in many ways could be called toxic, that's not unlike the toxic infectious environment of a hundred years ago," he says. "In this case, it's sort of a toxic environment around the foods that we eat." The unhealthiest, most high-calorie foods tend to be the cheapest and most heavily marketed, he says, often to young children. As a result, "It's going to be extremely important for government and also the private sector to come together to

continue to evolve a set of policies and practices that make the healthier choice just a little bit easier and make the unhealthy choice not so easy."

Former Gov. Parris Glendening, D-Md., now president of the Leadership Institute at Smart Growth America, a coalition of urban advocacy groups, says making changes to the "built environment" to encourage healthier living "is a very legitimate role for state and local governments." Smart growth revolves around the concept that communities should have easy, preferably car-free access to jobs and shopping, and that public policy should encourage sidewalks, bike paths and public transportation to increase daily exercise and reduce air pollution, both of which improve health.

Smart-growth supporters point to a study in Charlotte, N.C., showing that building a light-rail system led users to walk more and lose weight. "The built environment can constrain or facilitate physical activity," said lead investigator John M. MacDonald of the University of Pennsylvania. "Understanding ways to encourage greater use of local environments for physical activity offers some hope for reducing the growth in the prevalence of obesity."[24]

Diane Katz, a research fellow in regulatory policy at the Heritage Foundation, a conservative think tank, says there is nothing wrong with politicians or other leaders encouraging constituents to adopt healthier lifestyles, although she thinks the deficit and other issues should take priority.

But Katz rejects efforts to insert the government into individual food decisions. "Nutrition regulations are commonly justified to defeat an obesity 'epidemic,'" she says, but "both the extent of the problem and the risk it poses are often exaggerated, the product of special-interest propaganda or dubious research." She adds: "Underlying government constraints on food choice is the presumption that individuals are incapable of making dietary decisions and government will do a far better job of it — a conceit that insults the most fundamental principles of limited government and personal freedom."

*ARE people who eat
of many dieras(?)*

Katz turns Kahan's argument on its head, saying that since infectious-disease threats are now reduced, health officials have focused on eating and exercise habits because they need to "concoct new menaces to occupy their time."

Meanwhile, many sectors of the food industry are fighting government involvement. Several battles have erupted recently in the policy realm, including one over serving potatoes and pizza in school cafeterias. The Department of Agriculture recently proposed, based on Institute of Medicine recommendations, to limit the amount of tomato paste that could be considered a serving of vegetables and reduce the starchy vegetables that could be served in schools.[25] Congress altered the tomato paste recommendations spurred by industry groups including, reportedly, the American Frozen Food Institute and Schwan's Food Service, which provides pizzas to schools. Senators from large potato-growing states, Republican Susan Collins of Maine and Democrat Mark Udall of Colorado, worked with the National Potato Council to protest limits on starchy vegetables.[26]

Some companies have begun changing their products to ward off further government action. ConAgra Foods, for example, pledged in 2009 to reduce sodium in about 80 percent of its products by 2015. Kraft Foods said in 2010 it would reduce sodium in its North American products by an average of 10 percent by 2012.[27]

PepsiCo also has been a healthy-products leader. In 2010 it announced 11 goals to improve public health, including product reformulation and changes in marketing.[28] Derek Yach, a former WHO official and now senior vice president of global health policy at PepsiCo, says the government's role is to send the right signals and messages to consumers about healthy eating while industry continues to create healthier products. But that may not be enough to change consumer tastes, he says.

"Even if we put out better products," Yach says, "there's no guarantee they're going to be enjoyed and consumed or whether they're going to displace things

Are You Getting Enough Exercise?

To maintain good health, the federal Centers for Disease Control and Prevention recommends the following guidelines:

Recommended physical activity — Moderate-intensity activities — such as brisk walking, bicycling, vacuuming, gardening or anything that causes small increases in breathing or heart rate — for at least 30 minutes per day, five days a week; or vigorous-intensity activities — such as running, aerobics, heavy yard work or anything that causes large increases in breathing or heart rate — for at least 20 minutes per day, three days a week.

Insufficient physical activity — More than 10 minutes total per week of moderate or vigorous-intensity activities, but less than the recommended levels.

Inactivity — Less than 10 minutes total per week of moderate or vigorous-intensity activities.

Leisure-time inactivity — No reported physical activity or exercise in the previous month.

Source: "Physical Activity Statistics: Definition," Centers for Disease Control and Prevention, May 2007, www.cdc.gov/nccdphp/dnpa/physical/stats/definitionshtm.

with higher salt, sugar and fat, which have been the dietary norm for decades."

Should the health care system focus more on wellness?

The U.S. health care system is designed primarily to treat the sick, not encourage people to stay healthy.

Financial incentives reward health care providers for performing services and procedures, usually after illness has taken hold. But the vast majority of diseases start years and sometimes decades before an affliction drives a patient to a doctor's office. That leaves many experts arguing that caregivers and patients must be given the tools and incentives to stop chronic diseases before they begin.

Several obstacles stand in the way, however:

• An imbalance in the types of services for which physicians are paid;
• A fragmented health system that doesn't give patients comprehensive care;
• A lack of physician training in disease prevention, and;
• An overreliance on technology.

Physicians traditionally have been paid for ordering diagnostic tests, prescribing drugs, performing surgery or conducting other procedures, not for spending time getting to know patients and their potential health risks. As doctors become busier, time with patients has gotten shorter.

"Physicians whom we talk to on a regular basis who truly want to do more health-behavior counseling or coaching with their patients are simply unable to do so because they aren't paid by federal government plans or private insurers to do that kind of preventive medicine work," says Paul Bonta, associate executive director of the American College of Preventive Medicine. Preventive health experts want a system that would pay care providers to delve deeper into lifestyle issues that may be causing disease and to counsel patients on diet modification or smoking cessation.

Other changes also could help, says Georges C. Benjamin, executive director of the American Public Health Association. Insurers should pay for cancer screening without requiring contributions from the patient. In addition, he says, physicians who ensure that patients receive immunizations, blood-pressure screening and other preventive procedures should be financially rewarded.

Preventive health advocates also say physicians need to play matchmaker, linking patients with community programs that offer unique support. "The majority of prevention, especially wellness, probably happens outside the medical system," says Elizabeth Tilson, medical director at Community Care of Wake and Johnston counties in North Carolina. "If you think about it, you may only get into the medical system once or twice a year. The vast majority of the time patients are out in their world."

Medical professionals often aren't aware of community-based support services, such as stop-smoking clinics or nutrition counseling, or don't help patients connect with them, advocates say.

A model of a more comprehensive approach is the "medical home," in which a health care provider tracks a patient's entire care and helps the patient find appropriate programs and specialists. At Martin's Point, a medical center in Portland, Maine, physicians monitor patient care through electronic medical records, and health educators help patients address medication or social issues connected with their disease.[29]

Bonta agrees that physicians need more help in providing ongoing services through their offices or referring patients to community resources. "Often, the patient will go to the physician's office, and the physician will say, 'Start exercising more, we need to get your weight down,' and the patient leaves the office and has no idea how to go about exercising more," he says. "Until we reach the point where we are able to educate or inform physicians about all the work that's going on within their communities, we can't make meaningful inroads in facilitating the behavior change that's needed."

Medical training also needs improvement, says Michael Parkinson, former president of the American College of Preventive Medicine and now a health consultant. He says the centuries-old "false dichotomy" between medical care and "wellness" was made worse in the United States in the early 20th century by the first schools of public health, which Parkinson says split off disease-prevention activities from medical school curricula. As a result, he says, most physicians are not trained in prevention.

Moreover, he adds, the model is outdated in a society in which three-quarters of health care costs could be mitigated through lifestyle changes.

Parkinson says it's unfair to ask doctors who have never been trained in disease prevention and never paid for preventive services to be held responsible for reversing the country's obesity epidemic.

Parkinson also argues that the medical system directs most health spending toward drugs and surgery after disease is present rather than focusing on low-tech strategies of improved diet and exercise. The "medical-industrial complex essentially now consumes nearly 20 percent of the U.S. gross domestic product, and what it lives on is an inherent bias we have for quick fixes with high technology at low or no cost" to consumers, he says.

The payment system also disconnects consumers from the costs of their care, Parkinson says. Patients need to understand, for example, that losing weight could lessen their back pain and risk of arthritis and perhaps help them avoid costly surgery and pharmaceuticals, he says. Those who choose more expensive options should be responsible for some of the extra costs, he adds.

While the increased focus on disease prevention appears to have universal support in the medical field, the shift could create new "winners and losers" in health care reimbursement, Tilson says. "I don't think that conceptually or philosophically anybody is against helping to reimburse for prevention. I just think it's a pure financial argument. There is just not enough money right now," she says.

Investing more in wellness could mean less money for new technologies and could heighten tensions between general practitioners and specialists. Primary-care physicians have argued for years that they aren't afforded the same prestige granted to specialists and can make as little as a fourth of the annual salary of an orthopedist or surgeon.[30] But shifting the advantage to preventive-care practitioners could make today's high earners unhappy.

BACKGROUND

Preventable Diseases

Building on the success of the smallpox vaccine, inoculations have been developed for many diseases, and the number keeps growing. In the 19th century, vaccines were developed for rabies and plague. The 20th century saw a host of new vaccines, including those for diphtheria, pertussis, measles and polio.[31] In 2006, a vaccine was approved that prevents the human papilloma virus, which can cause cervical and other cancers.[32]

While immunizations are considered by many to be the most important public health advance ever, some people are concerned about the safety of vaccines and about the growing number of inoculations children receive, which now cover more than a dozen diseases and can require multiple doses.[33]

As public health and medical advances in the early 20th century began to drastically reduce the prevalence of infectious disease and prolong lives, developed countries began to face a different type of disease burden: noncommunicable disease. The significance of cancer, heart disease and other chronic conditions began to be recognized in the 1930s, but according to James Marks, senior vice president and director of the health group at the Robert Wood Johnson Foundation, people didn't think they could be stopped. "Many people thought for a long time that chronic diseases like heart disease and cancer were inevitable and that there wasn't much we could do about them," he says. Doctors made efforts to control high blood pressure and cholesterol levels, but only in

High school and college-level students struggling to lose weight play soccer during fitness training at Wellspring Academy, in Reedley, Calif. More than one-third of American adults and 17 percent of children are obese.

extreme cases. Slowly, evidence accumulated showing that some diseases were preventable, including lung cancer and heart disease.

A major milestone in preventing chronic disease came in the form of the U.S. surgeon general's 1964 report on tobacco. Cigarette smoking increased dramatically in the first part of the 20th century, bringing with it a precipitous increase in lung cancer. Annual per capita cigarette consumption jumped from 54 cigarettes in 1900 to 4,435 in 1963. In 1930, the lung cancer death rate for men was 4.9 deaths per 100,000, a rate that increased to 75.6 per 100,000 in 1990.[34]

The ill effects of smoking became more apparent during the 1930s, '40s and '50s as more studies suggested smoking was causing the epidemic rise of lung cancer. In 1957 the U.S. Public Health Service officially declared that evidence pointed to a causal relationship between smoking and lung cancer.[35] In 1964, Surgeon General Luther Terry issued a landmark report on smoking and health that cited cigarette smoking as responsible for a 70 percent increase in the mortality rate of smokers compared to nonsmokers.[36]

The report also estimated the average smoker had a nine- to 10-fold risk of developing lung cancer compared to nonsmokers, and heavy smokers had at least a 20-fold risk. It also connected smoking during pregnancy with

CHRONOLOGY

1700s-1800s *Modern vaccine development begins; germ theory attributes diseases to specific organisms and shows they are contagious.*

1789 Smallpox vaccine developed by British physician Edward Jenner.

1854 British physician John Snow traces cholera outbreak in London to a water pump, giving a major boost to the science of epidemiology.

1885 Rabies vaccine developed by French scientist Louis Pasteur.

1897 Plague vaccine developed by Russian microbiologist Waldemar Haffkine.

1900-1950 *U.S. mortality rates plunge with improvements in clean-water technologies, housing, other living standards.*

1917 Cholera vaccine developed by Haffkine, who performs the first human tests of the injection on himself.

1923 Diphtheria vaccine developed by German scientist Emil Adolf Behring.

1924 Tetanus vaccine developed by P. Descombey.

1948 Framingham Heart Study begins; identifies risk factors for chronic disease.

1950-1970 *Risk factors for chronic diseases begin to be identified and addressed.*

1952 Polio vaccine developed by U.S. medical researcher Jonas Salk.

1964 Surgeon General Luther Terry issues landmark report saying cigarette smoking increases mortality rate of smokers by 70 percent compared to nonsmokers.

1965 Congress requires health warnings on cigarette packages.

1967 World Health Organization (WHO) calls for global eradication of smallpox.

1969 Cigarette advertising banned.

1970-1990 *Smallpox eradicated, but new diseases such as HIV/AIDS take hold.*

1973 Airplane cabins divided into "smoking" and "no-smoking" sections.

1975 First indoor clean-air law limits smoking to designated areas in public spaces.

1980 WHO declares smallpox eradicated. . . . First cases of HIV/AIDS appear in the United States.

1989 Congress bans smoking on commercial flights.

1990s-2000s *Cancer rates peak and begin to fall; obesity rates rise.*

1992 Environmental Protection Agency declares secondhand tobacco smoke a Class A carcinogen.

1998 States get a $246 billion windfall after settling a lawsuit against tobacco companies, but little of the money funds smoking-cessation programs.

2000 Government sets goal of reducing childhood obesity rate, estimated at 15 percent, to 5 percent by 2010.

2003 Study links urban and suburban sprawl with weight gain.

March 2010 President Obama signs the Patient Protection and Affordable Care Act, which includes a $15 billion Prevention and Public Health Fund.

May 2010 White House Task Force sets goal of eliminating childhood obesity in a generation; nutrition labeling of chain-restaurant menus becomes law, effective in 2011.

2011 House of Representatives votes to repeal Prevention and Public Health Fund (April); Obama's deficit-reduction proposals include a $3.5 billion cut in the fund (September); House Republicans propose an $8 billion reduction (December).

lower-weight newborns. In 1965, Congress required health warnings on all cigarette packages. In 1969, cigarette advertising was banned on radio and television. Per capita cigarette consumption began to fall, reaching 1,619 in 2006.[37]

As evidence accumulated showing the hazards of secondhand smoke, jurisdictions began imposing smoking bans. The first was in Minnesota in 1975. The state's Clean Indoor Air Act limited smoking to designated areas in public place and at public meetings.[38] More bans followed, and now 3,487 U.S. municipalities restrict smoking.[39] Twenty-five states had comprehensive indoor smoking bans by 2010.[40] Airplanes were divided into smoking and no-smoking sections in 1973; in 1987 Congress began banning smoking on planes.[41]

While lung cancer was the most obviously preventable disease, evidence began to grow in the 1950s and '60s that other conditions could be controlled as well, particularly heart disease. The seminal Framingham Heart Study, launched in 1948 by the National Heart, Lung and Blood Institute, provided the telling data. Researchers recruited 5,209 men and women between the ages of 30 and 62 from Framingham, Mass., to identify risk factors for heart disease and stroke through extensive physical exams and lifestyle interviews.[42]

The study identified high blood pressure, blood triglyceride and cholesterol levels, age, gender, physical inactivity and psychosocial issues as possible drivers of disease. Other studies contributed as well, creating a solid body of evidence that diet, physical activity, smoking and alcohol abuse contribute to chronic diseases including stroke, heart disease, diabetes and cancer.

Focusing on the diseases as well as improvements in medical care began to have an effect. After peaking in the early 1990s, cancer rates have generally fallen since 1998.[43] From 1950 to 1996, deaths from heart disease fell by 56 percent, and deaths from stroke declined 70 percent.[44]

Obesity

As some risk factors for chronic diseases came more under control, including high cholesterol and blood pressure, another major health threat emerged: obesity. In 1960, 13 percent of American adults were obese. By 2008, the figure had risen to 34 percent. During the same period, the percentage of extremely obese adults rose from slightly less than 1 percent of adults to 6 percent.[45]

Excess weight is associated with a variety of diseases, including heart disease, Type 2 diabetes, some types of cancer, hypertension and stroke. In addition to health consequences, obesity is costly. Medical spending is 42 percent higher for obese people than for those of normal weight.[46] Diagnosed diabetes increased 164 percent from 1980 through 2009, according to the Centers for Disease Control and Prevention (CDC).[47] The disease can cause kidney problems and blindness and require lower-limb amputations.[48]

For many years, the afflictions associated with obesity, including diabetes and cardiovascular disease, were attributed to increased wealth and personal choice. But health experts now say a variety of social, policy and commercial factors are fueling the epidemic and must be addressed by policymakers and the private sector. Contributors to the nation's obesity epidemic include high fat, sugar and salt levels in packaged and fast foods, increased portion sizes and a car-based transportation system.

The public-health response focuses on several areas: increased consumption of fruits and vegetables; increased physical activity; breastfeeding; and decreased consumption of sugary drinks and energy-dense foods, such as meat, processed foods and sweets.

But reducing disease risk factors that are so embedded in society, personal in nature and driven by commercial interests from food manufacturers to tobacco companies has proven daunting. Jeffrey Levi, executive director of the Trust for America's Health, a Washington-based health advocacy group, says addressing current health conditions represents a shift for public health experts. (See "At Issue," p. 341.) Prevention traditionally focused on infectious disease, "breaking a chain of infection in some way," he says. Current health efforts, by contrast, focus on more intimate personal behaviors like food choices, "not something public health people traditionally have been terribly comfortable with."

Community Prevention

Federal policies now support the concept of community prevention — developing local efforts to address the

Poor Countries Struggle to Curb Preventable Illnesses

"The world is essentially sleepwalking into a sick future."

Malaria and HIV often get the headlines in stories about global health problems, but the biggest threats in poor countries are the same ones afflicting the wealthy and well-fed: lack of exercise, smoking and diets brimming with fat, salt and sugar.

Chronic, or noncommunicable, disease recently became the world's leading killer, accounting for 63 percent of deaths in 2008, according to the U.N.'s World Health Organization (WHO).[1]

The effects of modern lifestyles — including greater reliance on automobiles, pollution, increases in smoking and unhealthy diets are spreading preventable cancers, diabetes and respiratory and heart disease to every corner of the globe. The illnesses are having the greatest impact, however, where poverty is rampant and health systems are inadequate.

The vast majority of cancers in the developing world, for example, are detected in their late stages, but effective treatments are lacking in general. In Uganda, 96 percent of those who die from cancer never see a health care provider.[2] Moreover, in many developing countries, even pain medications for cancer often are unavailable.

Chronic diseases are killing people at earlier ages in developing countries than in the developed world. Nearly 30 percent of deaths from noncommunicable diseases occur among people under age 60 in low- and middle-income countries, compared to 13 percent in high-income countries.[3]

"In wealthy countries, deaths from heart disease and strokes have declined significantly," said Margaret Chan, WHO's director-general. "But this gives a distorted picture. For some countries, it is no exaggeration to describe the situation as an impending disaster — a disaster for health, for society and most of all for national economies."[4]

In September the United Nations unanimously called chronic diseases "a challenge of epidemic proportions" and set out a plan to develop global and national goals for disease reduction, particularly in low- and middle-income areas.[5]

Included in draft targets are recommendations to reduce smoking and decrease salt levels in food.[6] The WHO also developed a list of low- or no-cost disease-prevention steps that countries could adopt, such as promoting public awareness about diet and physical activity.[7]

In addition, the U.N. is working to accelerate implementation of the WHO Framework Convention on Tobacco Control, an international health treaty developed in 2003 that promotes tobacco regulation.[8]

As in the United States, attacking chronic diseases requires a multiprong approach, including strengthening health systems, changing government policies in areas such as urban planning and school physical education requirements and encouraging the involvement of business.

leading preventable causes of death and disability, obesity and tobacco use. The health reform bill passed by Congress in 2010 included a Prevention and Public Health Fund totaling $15 billion over its first 10 years. In addition to supporting preventive health initiatives, it funds public health infrastructure and workforce improvements, including research and disease tracking.[49] The fund also supports first lady Michelle Obama's Let's Move campaign, which aims to drastically curtail rising rates of childhood obesity through physical activity and improved nutrition.[50]

But not everyone is convinced. Critics said that by providing greater access to preventive services and disease screening, the reform act would in fact increase health costs. In addition, they said there was no guarantee that changes in communities would decrease health costs. Republican senators tried to remove the fund from the Senate version of the bill. Sen. Michael Enzi, R-Wyo., called the prevention fund "new pork barrel spending," adding, "The bill will pave sidewalks, build jungle gyms and open grocery stores, but it won't bring down health care costs or make quality [health] coverage more affordable."[51]

The global food industry has resisted stiffer government regulations, but some companies are participating in voluntary efforts. In 2008, the International Food and Beverage Alliance, which includes such giants as Coca-Cola, Kraft and Kellogg's, committed to five actions over five years to make products healthier: Reformulating food content, providing nutrition information to consumers, advertising responsibly, raising awareness of nutritious diets and promoting physical activity.[9]

But some U.N. officials say such voluntary efforts are too weak to adequately address global health problems.

"World leaders must not bow to industry pressure," said Olivier De Schutter, U.N. Special Rapporteur on the Right to Food, a watchdog role at the international organization. "It is crucial for world leaders to counter food-industry efforts to sell unbalanced processed products and ready-to-serve meals too rich in trans fats and saturated fats, salt and sugars. Food advertising is proven to have a strong impact on children and must be strictly regulated in order to avoid the development of bad eating habits early in life."[10]

Despite the rapid growth in chronic illnesses around the globe, international aid aimed at helping developing countries improve their health systems has been weak. Only an estimated 3 percent of health-related development assistance is devoted to chronic disease.[11] That isn't expected to change any time soon as major donors, including the United States, face their own economic woes and continue to focus on current funding commitments, primarily to fight AIDS, tuberculosis, malaria and afflictions facing children and pregnant women.

Some view the focus as shortsighted. Without a stronger effort to reduce chronic diseases globally, said Ann Keeling, chair of NCD Alliance, an international coalition that focuses on the problem, "the world is essentially sleepwalking into a sick future."[12]

— Nellie Bristol

[1]"Global Status Report on Noncommunicable Diseases 2010," World Health Organization, www.who.int/nmh/publications/ncd_report2010/en/.

[2]"Chronic Disease in Developing Countries: Poor Countries are Developing the Diseases of the Rich, with Lethal Consequences," *The Economist*, Sept. 24, 2011, www.economist.com/node/21530099.

[3]World Health Organization, *op. cit.*

[4]Maddy French, "Why Non-Communicable Diseases Hit the Developing World So Hard," *The Guardian*, June 29, 2011, www.guardian.co.uk/journalismcompetition/why-non-communicable-diseases-hit-the-developing-world-so-hard.

[5]"Political Declaration of the High-level Meeting of the General Assembly on the Prevention and Control of Non-communicable Diseases," U.N. General Assembly, Sept. 16, 2011, www.un.org/ga/search/view_doc.asp?symbol=A%2F66%2FL.1&Lang=E.

[6]Nellie Bristol, "The UN Weighs Solutions to the Plague of Noncommunicable Disease," *Health Affairs*, November 2010.

[7]World Health Organization, *op. cit.*

[8]"Tobacco Control for Global Health and the Development/NCD Summit," Framework Convention Alliance, www.fctc.org/index.php?option=com_content&view=article&id=503:tobacco-control-and-global-health&catid=258:tobacco-control-and-global-health.

[9]"Who We Are," International Food and Beverage Alliance, www.ifballiance.org/about.html.

[10]"World Leaders Must Take Binding Steps to Curb Unhealthy Food Industry-UN Expert," UN News Centre, Sept. 16, 2011, www.un.org/apps/news/story.asp?NewsID=39578&Cr=non+communicable+diseases&Cr1=.

[11]Bristol, *op. cit.*

[12]Kate Kelland, "UN Summit Talks Stalled," Reuters, Aug., 17, 2011, www.idf.org/un-summit-talks-stalled-reuters-interview-ncda-chair-ann-keeling.

Doctors and public health experts increasingly focus on "evidence-based medicine," or scientifically proven medical interventions. They use the same strategies for disease prevention as well. The U.S. Preventive Services Task Force reviews evidence and makes recommendations to physicians about which screening tests, counseling, immunizations and preventive medications should be recommended to patients.[52]

The panel's findings are sometimes controversial. For example, in 2009 it raised the age at which it recommended that women with an average risk for breast cancer should routinely receive mammograms. The change spurred a fierce debate among doctors, women, insurers and politicians. "Their justification: These new guidelines capture 81 percent of mammography's benefits [and] save a lot of resources, with only a 3 percent drop in survivorship from the most common cancer to affect women," said Marisa Weiss, president and founder of BreastCancer.org, a nonprofit cancer awareness and information site.

"But what really is the cost?," Weiss asks. "And who is paying the price? It could be you, your mom, daughter, sister, aunt or grandmother or all of us."[53]

Get Out of Your Car, Urban Planners Urge

"Complete Streets" program promotes bicycling and walking.

State and local lawmakers are trying to accomplish what years of preaching by the President's Council on Physical Fitness and other public health authorities have largely failed to do: Get people moving.

Twenty-five states and 314 city, country or regional jurisdictions have adopted so-called Complete Streets policies, pledging to consider installing bike lanes and sidewalks in future road-construction and major road-rehabilitation projects, according to the National Complete Streets Coalition, a Washington, D.C.-based advocacy group.[1]

The coalition, which encourages people to ditch their cars and build exercise into their daily lives, claims many benefits for the approach beyond disease prevention: improved pedestrian safety, greater use of better-connected commercial centers, fewer traffic jams and better air quality.

"We have this huge infrastructure investment in transportation, and the only thing we do with it is focus on moving cars," says Barbara McCann, the coalition's director.

New Jersey Transportation Commissioner James Simpson is a strong advocate of the approach. The state has its own Complete Streets policy, and 13 municipalities and one county have adopted versions. "A local Complete Streets policy raises awareness among residents, elected officials and the private sector," Simpson wrote. "When projects are proposed, pedestrian, bicycle and transit accommodations are no longer an afterthought — they become an integral feature of the overall investment plan."[2]

But Complete Streets policies don't have universal support. The St. Cloud, Minn., City Council initially rejected a proposal on a tie vote earlier this year because of concerns about redundancy with current policies, effects on new development and costs.[3] The council subsequently approved the proposal, however, when a supportive council member was able to vote a few weeks later.[4]

The New York State Association of Counties recently opposed a Complete Streets proposal in the General Assembly, saying budgets are too tight to give it priority and that the "diversion of effort and funding" mandated by the provision "would further the deterioration of our infrastructure."[5]

In Congress, Complete Streets bills have been introduced in the last three sessions, but none has moved forward.

The Complete Streets approach emerged in the late 1990s, when, McCann says, the President's Council on Physical Fitness was failing in its effort to get more people to exercise. The council brought its concerns to McCann, a writer and transportation expert working on ways to make streets friendlier to walkers and bikers.

"They said, 'OK, we have been trying to get people to go to the gym for years, and it's not working,'" McCann says. "'There's just a totally flat line on the number of people who are willing to make a special time of day to exercise.'"

The movement got a major boost in 2003 when a report by Smart Growth America, a Washington group that supports better urban planning, equated suburban sprawl — and its reliance on driving rather than walking — with weight gain. "The results show that people in more sprawling counties are likely to have a higher body-mass index," a summary of the research says. In addition, the research

CURRENT SITUATION

Public Health Targets

Despite the steady decline in smoking — from 42 percent of adults in 1965 to about 21 percent in 2009 — tobacco remains the primary cause of preventable death in the United States — 443,000 annually.[54] Smoking also is a major focus for public health efforts.[55]

The combination of obesity and inactivity ranks as the nation's second-leading killer, causing 112,000 deaths a year, according to the CDC.[56] While smoking-cessation policies have made progress through increased taxes and smoke-free regulations, public policy to control obesity has proved more difficult.

In order to create environments that support healthier habits, the Obama administration is strongly supporting community prevention efforts. The Prevention and Public Health Fund put $298 million of $750 million doled out in fiscal 2011 toward community efforts. "Prevention is something that can't just happen in a doctor's office," showed a "direct relationship" between sprawl and chronic disease, with the odds of high blood pressure increasing 6 percent for every measured increase in sprawl.[6]

Some criticized the study's methods and conclusions, however. "This is just another attempt by the report's sponsors to spin research showing only trivial weight differences between city and suburban residents into a national crisis requiring land use restrictions," wrote researchers at the Heritage Foundation, a conservative think tank in Washington.[7]

Even McCann concedes that making a direct connection between planning policy and health has been elusive. "Just on the research side, we aren't quite 100 percent there yet on having a direct link between policy and body weight, but there's certainly a chain that's very clear," she says.

Nonetheless, McCann says the connection makes sense on an intuitive level to many planners, and they've started to respond to it. "We're having tremendous success at the state and local level because they really get it," she says.

McCann argues that despite current fiscal constraints, Complete Streets policies are not necessarily more expensive, but simply require engineers to think about a variety of users when planning transportation routes.

"In a way," McCann says, "you're trying to go back to the way communities used to be built."

— *Nellie Bristol*

Bike riders in Brooklyn's Prospect Park West got to keep a controversial bike lane after a judge in August 2011 rejected efforts by local residents to remove the lane. Mayor Michael Bloomberg has sought to make the city more bike and pedestrian friendly.

[1]"Complete Streets Atlas," National Complete Streets Coalition, www.completestreets.org/complete-streets-fundamentals/complete-streets-atlas/.

[2]James Simpson, "Opinion: N.J. Complete Streets Policy Paves Way for Road Safety," *The Times of Trenton*, Nov. 18, 2011, www.nj.com/times-opinion/index.ssf/2011/11/opinion_nj_complete_streets_po.html.

[3]Kari Petrie, "MN: St. Cloud Votes No to Complete Streets Policy," *St. Cloud* [Minn.] *Times*, Sept. 13, 2011, www.masstransitmag.com/news/10356650/mn-st-cloud-votes-no-to-complete-streets-policy.

[4]Kari Petrie, "St. Cloud Leaders OK Complete Streets Policy," *St. Cloud* [Minn.] *Times*, Nov. 7, 2011, www.sctimes.com/article/20111108/NEWS01/111070061/St-Cloud-leaders-OK-complete-streets-policy.

[5]Noah Kazis, "NY Counties Oppose Complete Streets Bill Without Understanding It," Streetsblog.org, Feb. 8, 2011, www.streetsblog.org/2011/02/08/ny-counties-oppose-complete-streets-bill-without-understanding-it/.

[6]Barbara A. McCann and Reid Ewing, "Measuring the Health Effects of Sprawl: A National Analysis of Physical Activity Obesity and Chronic Disease," Smart Growth America, September 2003, www.smartgrowthamerica.org/report/HealthSprawl8.03.pdf.

[7]Wendell Cox and Ronald Utt, "Sprawl and Obesity: A Flawed Connection," Heritage Foundation, Sept. 19, 2003, www.heritage.org/research/reports/2003/09/sprawl-and-obesity-a-flawed-connection.

said Health and Human Services Secretary Kathleen Sebelius. "If we are to address the big health issues of our time, from physical inactivity to poor nutrition to tobacco use, it needs to happen in local communities." Funds were targeted toward reducing tobacco use, improving nutrition and increasing physical activity and coordinating efforts to prevent diabetes, heart disease and cancer.[57] The grants support, for example, a network of national telephone "quit lines" for smokers, and increased HIV testing opportunities.[58]

Food and the Workplace

Employers as well as the federal government are grappling with the right approach to curbing chronic diseases. As the insurance providers for nearly two-thirds of Americans under age 65, employers bear a heavy cost for an unhealthy workforce.[59] The cost to employers for all expenses related to health and lost productivity in 2002 was an average of $18,618 per employee. These costs include health insurance premiums, workers' compensation, short-term disability, long-term disability, sick leave and unpaid leave.

Smoking has declined from 43 percent of U.S. adults in 1965 to about 22 percent in 2009, but tobacco remains the nation's primary cause of preventable deaths — nearly half a million annually. Poor diet, lack of physical activity, smoking and alcohol abuse contribute to deadly chronic diseases including stroke, heart disease, diabetes and some cancers. About 4,000 U.S. communities and at least 25 states restrict smoking.

Expenditures were 228 percent higher for employees with multiple risk factors for heart disease than for employees without the risk factors. Employees who smoke, get inadequate exercise, have high blood pressure and/or poor nutrition cost employers more in health care expenses, absenteeism and overall productivity.[60]

Workplace wellness programs, which try to control costs and improve employees' health, have become popular in recent years. Features include work-site health fairs, screenings and coaching and weight-management programs. Some employers are even developing programs that pay workers to change unhealthy habits.[61] The CDC is conducting a $9 million initiative to encourage workplace wellness programs, which it said could yield an average $3 return for every $1 spent over a two- to five-year period.[62]

Producers of fast food and packaged foods high in fat and sugar also are being targeted in the fight against chronic disease. An earlier Congress and the Obama administration have called on food companies to shift advertising aimed at children to healthier products.[63] Draft guidelines released in April would set voluntary limits on the amount of sodium, sugar and fats in foods advertised to children. Companies spend about $2 billion a year on advertising foods marketed to kids. In 2009, 86 percent of those products were high in calories, sodium, sugar or saturated fat, compared with 94 percent in 2003, when the industry began a self-regulatory program. But experts say the reduction in unhealthy ingredients isn't moving fast enough.[64]

The food and beverage industry is resisting the guidelines, which are now stalled and may be substantially revised. Industry representatives say they are trying gradually to reformulate their products because they worry that quick changes would result in lost customers.[65] "The food industry and the advertising industry have spent billions on reformulating food, changing advertising and putting together public service announcements," said Dan Jaffe, executive vice president for government relations at the Association of National Advertisers. "There is more to be done, but the critics are never going to be satisfied."[66]

Restaurants also are being asked to change. The Food and Drug Administration is drafting regulations to implement calorie count requirements for chain restaurants, a provision included in the health reform act signed into law in 2010.[67] CDC Director Thomas Frieden said the move "empowers people. It gives them information. It also is important because it gets the restaurants to think twice before they put up a 1,500-calorie breakfast. So it both makes the choices healthier and it makes the options healthier by getting some reformulation on the part of the restaurant industry." Nonetheless, Frieden said, calorie labeling remains only a "modestly effective intervention" that can be overrun by things like low prices. He cited a restaurant chain that discounted a high-calorie foot-long sandwich that resulted in an increase in calories consumed per customer.[68]

Unhealthy foods are being attacked in others ways as well. In 2004, restaurants in affluent Tiburon, Calif., voluntarily stopped using cooking oil with trans fats, making it the first "trans fat free" city in the country.[69] Other jurisdictions followed, notably, New York City in 2006.[70]

Other Initiatives

In other federal efforts, the CDC and the Centers for Medicare and Medicaid Services (CMS) recently started the Million Hearts Campaign aimed at reducing heart attacks and strokes over the next five years. The program focuses on improving access to effective, quality care, increasing

Should Americans be penalized for unhealthy behaviors?

YES

Michael Parkinson
Past President, American College of Preventive Medicine

Wendy Lynch
Co-Director, Center for Consumer Choice in Health Care, Altarum Institute

Written for *CQ Global Researcher,* December 2011

Should they be penalized? They already are — and dramatically so. The health and pocketbooks of all Americans already have been hurt by our collective failure to clearly align financial and other incentives — both "carrots" and "sticks" — to help individuals improve health and reduce preventable disease. In truth, those who do not take an active role in their health and health care already are penalized by poor health and higher costs. When we shield consumers from the consequences of their own inaction — by shifting the entire excess cost to their fellow plan members — we compromise their safety and health while costs continue to escalate.

So, let's pose the same question from a reverse perspective: Should we give consumers an opportunity to save money by doing things that are known to improve health and lower costs? We would say yes.

Unsustainable cost trends not only place an unbearable burden on our national debt but also strain the budgets of each family. Some of the overarching drivers of cost are preventable chronic illnesses, medical errors and use of unnecessary or ineffective treatments. All of these cost drivers can be reduced when consumers take an active role in their own care. We can support that active involvement by creating an "environment" (culture, physical spaces, policies and programs) that promotes and sustains better individual choices and actions.

Over a lifetime, one's own behaviors contribute more to health and health care needs than medical treatments will. Individuals who are engaged in their care are less likely to experience errors such as incorrect medications and are more likely to choose appropriate care. Thus, anything that encourages prevention and rewards wise health care choices not only saves money but also averts harm.

Our preferred method of giving people an opportunity to save money is through a funded Health Savings Account. That money serves as a pool of funds to cover expenses before a deductible is reached. If the consumer does not need health care, or can find less expensive alternatives, it accumulates. But consumers can choose to spend it if they want or need to. In this way, each family can choose whether it is worth protecting money (and health) by preventing disease and making wise care choices. That is not punishment, it is personal choice.

NO

Jeffrey Levi
xecutive Director, Trust for America's Health; Chair, Advisory Group on Prevention, Health Promotion, and Integrative and Public Health

Written for *CQ Global Researcher,* December 2011

It is not government's place to ensure that citizens do every last push-up or sit-up. Each of us is personally responsible for making healthy choices for ourselves and our children to prevent illness and promote well-being in our own lives.

However, local, state and federal policymakers can help kids and everyone else, too, by making healthy choices easy choices by providing accessible, safe places to walk, jog, bike, swim, take an exercise class or play sports. In addition, government can improve nutrition and physical-education programs in schools and launch initiatives to reduce tobacco use, especially among children and adolescents.

Ensuring a healthy citizenry isn't about taking punitive measures but, rather, encouraging people to be what they want to be: healthy, productive and happy.

Thankfully, with the creation of the Prevention and Public Health Fund, included in the Affordable Care Act, government has sent the message that it is going to do its best to help people stay healthy in the first place, rather than wait for them to get sick. This is the best, most commonsense way to reduce health care costs and spur economic growth.

A hallmark program of the prevention fund is the Community Transformation Grants (CTGs), which provide communities with the resources needed to work together at the local level to create health initiatives tailored to their specific needs. This can involve small-business owners, faith leaders, youth leaders, employers, community groups, parents, law enforcement officials, schools, and health care providers. Through the CTGs, communities are empowered to create the programs and initiatives that they know will help make the healthy choices easier for all.

You catch more flies with honey than vinegar, as the saying goes. It is government's role to support individuals and communities as they choose to stay active and fit, not penalize them if they fail to do so.

Through support and encouragement, we can spare millions of Americans from developing serious, preventable diseases and, in so doing, shift the paradigm from a sick-care system that focuses on treating disease after it happens to a health care system, where we keep people healthy in the first place.

The road to healthier living — and a more business-friendly community — leads to the farmers market in Hernando, Miss. "We want to recruit corporations to Hernando," said Mayor Chip Johnson. "They're not stupid. When they make their decisions, they look at health care costs."

clinical attention to heart attack and stroke prevention, promoting heart-healthy lifestyles and consistent use of high-blood-pressure and cholesterol medications.[71]

Medicare also is focusing more on prevention. CMS announced in November that the program would begin covering obesity screening and counseling in a primary-care setting for beneficiaries whose body mass index (BMI) is 30 or more. Under the change, beneficiaries are entitled to a face-to-face counseling session with a health care provider each week for a month followed by sessions every other week for an additional five months. Participants who lose at least 6.6 pounds during the first six months of counseling are entitled to additional visits every month for six months.[72]

Earlier in the month, CMS announced Medicare coverage of intensive behavioral therapy for cardiovascular disease. The program includes promotion of aspirin use, screening for high blood pressure and intensive behavioral counseling to promote a healthy diet to fight known risk factors for cardiovascular and diet-related chronic disease.[73]

Preventive medicine expert Parkinson is concerned that the level of payment is too low and that many physicians may not have the skills necessary to adequately perform the task. "Beyond wagging their finger at you and saying, 'you really need to lose weight,' most doctors really don't have the cognitive therapy, the motivational skills to do that." Nonetheless, he says, "the physician

initiating and asking about how you're doing on weight and saying how important it is to reverse your diabetes is very, very pivotal."

Getting the imprimatur of a health care payer as large as Medicare is an important step in better engaging the health care system to address lifestyle issues, he adds. The coverage changes, he says, "are important landmarks to progress because what Medicare has finally said is the physician and the delivery system have an important role, not a sole role, but a very important role to both initiate and sustain behavior change, which is the only way we're going to get out of this crisis."

OUTLOOK

Two Steps Forward . . .

The importance of chronic disease prevention is gaining attention as more people realize both its health and fiscal costs.

Employers are developing new ways to help employees change unhealthy behaviors. Meanwhile, policymakers are paying more attention to the way social environments and commercial forces affect lifestyle choices.

In the policy realm, the Patient Protection and Affordable Care Act — the Obama administration's signature health care law — has given unprecedented attention and funding to prevention activities. "In addition to establishing the Prevention and Public Health Fund, the act also requires Medicare and some private insurers to cover certain preventive services, such as cancer screening, without patient co-pays.

However, the fund is threatened by federal budget cuts, and the health care law's legality is being challenged in the Supreme Court, which will decide that issue this year.

Jud Richland, president and CEO of Partnership for Prevention, a coalition of business, nonprofit and government groups, says even if the health care law is repealed or struck down, insurers are likely to continue to support clinical preventive services but that many community intervention programs are likely to lose funding if the prevention fund is raided or killed.

On the state and local levels, lawmakers could continue to enact policies limiting trans fats, requiring menu labeling and mandating other health-related measures.

Richland notes that indoor clean-air laws took years to be passed but became popular once implemented. "The momentum's going in the right direction" for other preventive health laws, he says.

New technologies may encourage prevention as well. Smart-phone applications are coming on line that will help people keep track of their blood pressure, count calories or get fitness coaching.[74] A recent report by ABI Research said the market for health and fitness apps will reach $400 million by 2016.[75]

Nonetheless, despite years of messages about good diet and exercise, experts worry Americans could continue to fall short in those areas.

After dropping consistently for several decades, the proportion of Americans who smoke has stayed relatively steady since 2004.[76] Fewer than 20 percent of adults participate in adequate leisure-time aerobic and muscle-building activity.[77] Only 26 percent eat vegetables three or more times a day.[78]

Overall, the United Health Foundation found that reductions in smoking, preventable hospitalizations and cardiovascular deaths were offset last year by increases in obesity, diabetes and childhood poverty.[79]

A massive culture shift is needed, says North Carolina preventive medicine physician Tilson. "It's hard to get people to change behaviors, especially when their entire environment and culture is against them every step of the way," she says. "It's really hard to be healthy in our society right now."

Tilson says her own office reflects that difficulty. Despite having a workplace wellness plan that promotes a healthy diet and adequate exercise, she says, staff members frequently bring in baked goods, and product sales representatives bring cookies and candy for the staff.

"Even our closest friends undermine us," she says. Love and support is "equated with giving sugar."

NOTES

1. "America's Health Rankings," United Health Foundation, November 2011, http://statehealthstats .americashealthrankings.org/#/state/US/MS/2011.

2. "Healthy Americas for A Healthier Economy," Trust for America's Health, October 2011, http://healthy americans.org/report/90/.

3. *Ibid.*

4. *Ibid.*

5. "United Health Foundation's America's Health Rankings Finds Preventable Chronic Disease on the Rise; Obesity, Diabetes Undermining Country's Overall Health," United Health Foundation, Dec. 6, 2011, www.americashealthrankings.org/mediacenter/ mediacenter1.aspx.

6. "Chronic Diseases: The Power to Prevent, The Call to Control: At a Glance 2009," Centers for Disease Control and Prevention, Dec. 17, 2009, www.cdc .gov/chronicdisease/resources/publications/AAG/ chronic.htm.

7. "An Unhealthy Truth: Rising Rates of Chronic Disease and the Future of Health in America," Partnership to Fight Chronic Disease, www.fightchronicdisease .org/. . ./UnhealthyTruths_UPDATED.pptx.

8. "Non-Communicable Diseases to Cost $47 Trillion by 2030, New Study Released Today," World Economic Forum, Sept. 18, 2011, www.weforum .org/news/non-communicable-diseases-cost-47-tril lion-2030-new-study-released-today.

9. "Preventing Chronic Diseases: A Vital Investment," 2005, World Health Organization, p. 9, www.who .int/chp/chronic_disease_report/full_report.pdf.

10. Dan Harris and Mikaela Conley, "Childhood Obesity: A Call for Parents to Lose Custody," ABC News, July 14, 2011, http://abcnews.go.com/ Health/childhood-obesity-call-parents-lose-custody/ story?id=14068280.

11. *Ibid.*

12. "Obesity 'Epidemic' May Be Overstated," UPI.com, March 27, 2009, www.upi.com/Health_News/ 2009/03/17/Obesity-epidemic-may-be-over stated/UPI-50681237311372/.

13. Andy Barr, "Sarah Palin Brings Cookies, Hits 'Nanny State,' " *Politico*, Nov. 10, 2010, www.polit ico.com/news/stories/1110/44936.html.

14. "Childhood Obesity Facts," Centers for Disease Control and Prevention, www.cdc.gov/healthyy outh/obesity/facts.htm.

15. Nell Katz, "Sarah Palin: Americans Have 'God-Given Right' to be Fat?" CBS, Nov. 30, 2010, www

.cbsnews.com/8301-504763_162-20024104-10391704.html.

16. "Too Fat to Fight: Retired Military Leaders Want Junk Food Out of America's Schools," Mission: Readiness: Military Leaders for Kids, 2010, http://cdn.mission readiness.org/MR_Too_Fat_to_Fight-1.pdf.

17. *Ibid.*

18. "Fast Facts," Kaiser Family Foundation, http://facts .kff.org/.

19. "National Health Expenditure Data," Centers for Medicare and Medicaid Services, www.cms.gov/ NationalHealthExpendData/25_NHE_Fact_sheet .asp.

20. Joshua T. Cohen, *et al.*, "Does Preventive Care Save Money? Health Economics and the Presidential Candidates," *The New England Journal of Medicine*, Feb. 14, 2008.

21. Sarah Goodell, *et al.*, "Cost Savings and Cost-Effectiveness of Clinical Preventive Care," Robert Wood Johnson Foundation, September 2009, www .rwjf.org/files/research/48508.costsavings.preven tivecare.brief.pdf.

22. "Prevention for a Healthier America: Investments in Disease Prevention Yield Significant Savings, Stronger Communities," Trust for America's Health, July 2008, http://healthyamericans.org/reports/pre vention08/Prevention08.pdf.

23. Uwe E. Reinhardt, "Cost Effectiveness Analysis and US Health Care," Economix, *The New York Times*, http://economix.blogs.nytimes.com/2009/03/13/ cost-effectiveness-analysis-and-us-health-care.

24. "Public Transit Systems Contribute to Weight Los and Improved Health, Study Finds," *ScienceDaily*, June 28, 2010, www.sciencedaily.com/releases/ 2010/06/100628203756.htm.

25. Jill U. Adams, "'Pizza Vegetable' Controversy is a Hot Potato: A Law Blocking New Regulations of Tomato Paste, Spuds and Salt in School Meals Causes a Stir," *Los Angeles Times*, Nov. 28, 2011, www.lat imes.com/health/la-he-school-lunch-nutrition-201 11128,0,4859084,print.story.

26. *Ibid.*

27. Derek Yach, *et al.*, "The Role and Challenges of the Food Industry in Addressing Chronic Disease,"

Globalization and Health, 2010, 6:10, www.global izationandhealth.com/content/6/1/10.

28. *Ibid.*

29. Julie Rovner, "Future of Primary Care? Some Say 'Medical Home,'" NPR, Aug. 26, 2010, www.npr .org/templates/story/story.php?storyId=129432707.

30. Parija B. Kavilanz, "Family Doctors: An Endangered Breed," CNNMoney, July 18, 2009, http://money .cnn.com/2009/07/16/news/economy/healthcare_ doctors_shortage/index.htm.

31. "Immunization Timeline," Keepkidshealthy.com, www.keepkidshealthy.com/welcome/immuniza tions/immunization_timeline.html.

32. Rita Rubin, "First-ever Cancer Vaccine Approved," *USA Today*, June 8 2006, www.usatoday.com/news/ health/2006-06-08-cervical-cancer-vaccine_x.htm.

33. Shari Roan, "Despite Concerns, Most Parents Get Their Kids Vaccinated," *Los Angeles Times*, June 9, 2011, http://articles.latimes.com/2011/jun/09/news/ la-heb-child-vaccines-20110609. For background see the following *CQ Researcher* reports: Nellie Bristol, "HPV Vaccine," May 11, 2007, pp. 409-432; Kathy Koch, "Vaccine Controversies," Aug. 25, 2000, pp. 641-672 and Sarah Glazer, "Increase in Autism," June 13, 2003, pp. 545-568 (updated July 22, 2010).

34. "Achievements in Public Health, 1900-1999: Tobacco Use-United States, 1900-1999," *MMWR*, Centers for Disease Control and Prevention, Nov. 5, 1999, 48(43); 986-993, www.cdc.gov/mmwr/preview/ mmwrhtml/mm4843a2.htm#fig1.

35. "The Reports of the Surgeon General: the 1964 Report on Smoking and Health," National Library of Medicine, http://profiles.nlm.nih.gov/ps/retrieve/ Narrative/NN/p-nid/60.

36. *Ibid.*

37. "Smoking and Tobacco Use, Consumption Data," Centers for Disease Control and Prevention, www .cdc.gov/tobacco/data_statistics/tables/economics/ consumption.

38. Martiga Lohn, "Minnesota Lawmakers Approve Smoking Ban," The Associated Press, May 13, 2007, http://articles.boston.com/2007-05-13/ news/29226864_1_bars-and-restaurants-public health experts smoking-ban-limited-smoking.

39. "Overview List-How Many Smoke Free Laws?" American Nonsmokers' Rights Foundation, www.no-smoke.org/pdf/mediaordlist.pdf.

40. Mike Stobbe, "Will Every U.S. State Have a Smoking Ban by 2010?" *The Huffington Post*, April 21, 2011, www.huffingtonpost.com/2011/04/21/cdc-predicts-every-us-wil_n_852125.html.

41. Glenn Kramon, "Smoking Ban Near on Flights in the US," *The New York Times*, April 17, 1988, www.nytimes.com/1988/04/17/us/smoking-ban-near-on-flights-in-us.html.

42. "History of the Framingham Heart Study," Framingham Heart Study, www.framinghamheartstudy.org/about/history.html.

43. "Trends Progress Report," National Cancer Institute, http://progressreport.cancer.gov/doc_detail.asp?pid=1&did=2009&chid=93&coid=920&mid=#trends.

44. "Achievements in Public Health 1900-1999: Decline in Deaths from Heart Disease and Stroke, United States 1900 to 1999," Centers for Disease Control and Prevention, www.cdc.gov/mmwr/preview/mmwrhtml/mm4830a1.htm.

45. Cynthia Ogden, *et al.*, "Prevalence of Overweight, Obesity and Extreme Obesity Among Adults: United States, Trends 1960-1962 through 2007-2008," Centers for Disease Control and Prevention, June 2010, www.cdc.gov/NCHS/data/hestat/obesity_adult_07_08/obesity_adult_07_08.pdf.

46. Nellie Bristol, "US Target Disease Prevention in Health Reforms," *The Lancet*, Dec. 12, 2009, http://download.thelancet.com/pdfs/journals/lancet/PIIS0140673609621073.pdf.

47. "Crude and Age Adjusted Percentage of Civilian, Noninstitutionalized Population with Diagnosed Diabetes, United States 1980-2009," Centers for Disease Control and Prevention, www.cdc.gov/diabetes/statistics/prev/national/figage.htm.

48. For background, see the following *CQ Researcher* reports: Barbara Mantel, "Preventing Obesity," Oct. 1, 2010, pp. 797-820; Alan Greenblatt, "Obesity Epidemic," Jan. 31, 2003, pp. 73-104; and Adriel Bettelheim, "Obesity and Health," Jan. 15, 1999, pp. 25-48.

49. "Affordable Care Act: Laying the Foundation for Prevention," HealthReform.gov, www.healthreform.gov/newsroom/acaprevention.html.

50. Let's Move, www.letsmove.gov.

51. *Ibid.*, http://articles.chicagotribune.com/2009-08-05/news/0908050021_1_health-care-bike-paths-additional-pork-barrel-projects.

52. "Recommendations for Adults," U.S. Preventive Services Task Force, www.uspreventiveservicestaskforce.org/adultrec.htm.

53. Lauren Cox, "Stop Annual Mammograms, Govt. Panel Tells Women Under 50," ABC News, Nov. 16, 2009, http://abcnews.go.com/Health/OnCallPlusBreastCancerNews/mammogram-guidelines-spur-debate-early-detection/story?id=9099145.

54. "Trends in Tobacco Use," American Lung Cancer Association, July 2011, www.lungusa.org/finding-cures/our-research/trend-reports/Tobacco-Trend-Report.pdf.

55. "Tobacco Use: Targeting the Nation's Leading Killer At a Glance 2011," Centers for Disease Control and Prevention, www.cdc.gov/chronicdisease/resources/publications/AAG/osh.htm.

56. "Frequently Asked Questions about Calculating Obesity-Related Risk," Centers for Disease Control and Prevention, undated, accessed Jan. 2, 2012, www.cdc.gov/PDF/Frequently_Asked_Questions_About_Calculating_Obesity-Related_risk.pdf.

57. "HHS Announces $750 million Investment in Prevention," Department of Health and Human Services, www.hhs.gov/news/press/2011pres/02/20110209b.html.

58. "The Affordable Care Act's Prevention and Public Health Fund in Your State," Department of Health and Human Services, www.healthcare.gov/news/factsheets/2011/02/prevention02092011a.html.

59. "Employer-Sponsored Health Insurance: Trends in Cost and Access," Agency for Healthcare Research and Quality, www.ahrq.gov/research/empspria/empspria.htm.

60. "Promoting Workplace Health," The Healthy States Initiative, January 2008, www.healthystates.csg.org/

NR/rdonlyres/B6FC0AB2-A14A-4321-AAF8-778E57AA9752/0/LPBWorkplaceHealth_screen.pdf.

61. Lenny Bernstein, "Do Programs that Pay People to Lose Weight Really Work?," *The Washington Post*, Oct. 10, 2011, www.washingtonpost.com/lifestyle/wellness/do-programs-that-pay-people-to-lose-weight-really-work/2011/10/06/gIQAiIABbL_story.html.

62. "Affordable Care Act Helps Improve the Health of the American Workforce, Increase Workplace Health Programs," Centers for Disease Control and Prevention, press release, Sept. 30, 2011, www.cdc.gov/media/releases/2011/p0930_improve_healthcare.html.

63. William Neuman, "Ad Rules Stall, Keeping Cereal a Cartoon Staple," *The New York Times*, July 23, 2010, www.nytimes.com/2010/07/24/business/media/24food.html.

64. Gretchen Goetz, "Obama Urged to Push Kids' Food Marketing Regs," *Food Safety News*, Sept. 29, 2011, www.foodsafetynews.com/2011/09/academics-urge-obama-to-push-child-food-marketing-regulations.

65. Barbara Mantel, "Preventing Obesity," *CQ Researcher*, Oct. 1, 2010, pp. 977-1000.

66. *Ibid.*

67. Jonathan Berman, "Proposed FDA Regulations to Require 'Chain Restaurants' to Post Nutrition Information," Sept. 27, 2011, www.mondaq.com/unitedstates/x/146784/Healthcare+Food+Drugs+Law/Proposed+FDA+Regulations+To+Require+Chain+Restaurants+To+Post+Nutrition+Information.

68. Eli Y. Adashi, "CDC Director Talks About the Nation's Biggest (and Winnable?) Health Battles," *Medscape Internal Medicine*, Nov. 5, 2010, www.medscape.com/viewarticle/731362.

69. Jim Staats, "Tiburon's Trans Fat Ban Started National Movement," *The Marin Independent Journal*, Feb. 3, 2007, www.marinij.com/fastsearchresults/ci_5155266.

70. Thomas J. Lueck and Kim Severson, "New York Bans Most Trans Fats in Restaurants," *The New York Times*, Dec. 6, 2006, www.nytimes.com/2006/12/06/nyregion/06fat.html.

71. "Million Hearts: About the Campaign," Department of Health and Human Services, http://millionhearts.hhs.gov/about-mh.shtml.

72. Robert Lowes, "Medicare Decision to Cover Obesity Counseling Mostly Praised," *Medscape News*, Nov. 30, 2011, www.medscape.com/viewarticle/754531.

73. "Decision Memo for Intensive Behavioral Therapy for Cardiovascular Disease," Centers for Medicare and Medicaid Services, Nov. 8, 2011, www.cms.gov/medicare-coverage-database/details/nca-decision-memo.aspx?NCAId=248.

74. Carla Carter, "Smartphone Apps Keep Health at Your Fingertips, From Fitness to First Aid," *USA Today*, Feb. 2011, http://yourlife.usatoday.com/health/story/2011/02/Smartphone-apps-keep-health-at-your-fingertips-from-fitness-to-first-aid/44130448/1.

75. Chris Gullo, "By 2016: $400M Market for Health, Fitness Apps," *Mobihealthnews*, Nov. 28, 2011, http://mobihealthnews.com/14884/by-2016-400m-market-for-health-fitness-apps/.

76. "Trends in Current Cigarette Smoking Among High School Students and Adults, United States, 1965-2010, Centers for Disease Control and Prevention, www.cdc.gov/tobacco/data_statistics/tables/trends/cig_smoking/index.htm.

77. "Exercise or Physical Activity," Centers for Disease Control and Prevention, www.cdc.gov/nchs/fastats/exercise.htm.

78. Kim Severson, "Told to Eat Its Vegetables, America Orders French Fries," *The New York Times*, Sept. 24, 2010, www.nytimes.com/2010/09/25/health/policy/25vegetables.html?pagewanted=all.

79. "America's Health Rankings Finds Preventable Chronic Disease on the Rise; Obesity, Diabetes Undermining Country's Overall Health," United Health Foundation, Dec. 6, 2011, www.americashealthrankings.org/mediacenter/mediacenter1.aspx.

BIBLIOGRAPHY

Selected Sources
Books

Duffy, John, *The Sanitarians: A History of American Public Health*, University of Illinois Press, 1990.
A preeminent historian of medicine examines public health in the United States.

Faust, Halley, and Paul Menzel, eds., *Prevention vs. Treatment: What's the Right Balance?*, Oxford Press, 2012.

A preventive medicine physician (Faust) and a philosophy professor (Menzel) review a range of issues on preventive care, including spending on prevention and preventive care's apparent lack of emphasis in the medical field.

Guthman, Julie, *Weighing In: Obesity, Food Justice and the Limits of Capitalism*, University of California Press, 2011.

An associate professor in the Community Studies Department at the University of California, Santa Cruz, takes on the "obesity epidemic," challenging many widely held assumptions about its causes and consequences.

Articles

Kliff, Sarah, "What if Prevention Doesn't Save Money?" *The Washington Post*, Dec. 12, 2011, www .washingtonpost.com/blogs/ezra-klein/post/what-if-prevention-doesnt-save-money/2011/12/11/gIQA M60OnO_blog.html.

A health care reporter considers whether preventive services reduce medical costs.

Konrad, Walecia, "Preventing Sickness, With Plenty of Red Tape," *The New York Times*, Sept. 20, 2011, p. D5, www.nytimes.com/2011/09/20/health/policy/20consumer.html.

Ambiguity persists among consumers and insurers as to what qualifies as preventive care.

Landro, Laura, "Improving Global Health: Focus on Chronic Disease," *The Wall Street Journal*, Nov. 21, 2011, http://online.wsj.com/article/SB10001424052 970203699404577042540087339770.html.

Health care experts discuss medical challenges in developing countries.

Lazar, Kay, "Employers Seeing Pluses in Keeping Workers Healthy," *The Boston Globe*, May 31, 2011, p. 1, articles. boston.com/2011-05-31/bostonworks/29604741_1_ wellness-programs-health-promotion-programs-profes sor-of-health-economics.

More employers are embracing wellness programs to foster healthier lifestyles.

Stewart, Kirsten, "Mixed Messages on Health Prevention Baffle Consumers," *The Salt Lake Tribune* (Utah), May 26, 2011, www.sltrib.com/sltrib/home2/51876215-183/cancer-health-prevention-burt.html.csp.

Medicare beneficiaries are taking advantage of new federal regulations that give them free wellness checkups, but few are lining up for high-cost procedures.

Williams, Misty, "Costs Inspire Wellness Plans, Higher Deductibles," *The Atlanta Journal-Constitution*, Nov. 24, 2011, p. A1.

Rising out-of-pocket health care costs are encouraging more and more Atlanta-area workers to join wellness programs.

Reports

"F as in Fat: How Obesity Threatens America's Future," Trust for America's Health, 2011, Robert Wood Johnson Foundation, http://healthyamericans .org/report/88/.

Adult obesity rates increased in 16 states in the past year and did not decline in any state. Twelve states now have obesity rates above 30 percent.

"Global Status Report on Noncommunicable Diseases, 2010," World Health Organization, 2011, www.who .int/nmh/publications/ncd_report2010/en/.

WHO presents the latest global figures on noncommunicable diseases and recommendations for addressing them.

"Healthier Americans for a Healthier Economy," Trust for America's Health, November 2011, http:// healthyamericans.org/report/90/.

Six case studies examine how health affects the ability of states and cities to attract and retain employers and how wellness programs can improve productivity and reduce health spending.

"Measuring the Health Effects of Sprawl: A National Analysis of Physical Activity, Obesity and Chronic Disease," Smart Growth America, September 2003, www.smartgrowthamerica.org/report/HealthSprawl8.03.pdf.

An advocacy group discusses research showing connections among urban sprawl, weight gain and high blood pressure.

"Preventing Childhood Obesity: Health in the Balance," Institute of Medicine, Sept. 29, 2004, www .iom.edu/Reports/2004/Preventing-Childhood-Obesity-Health-in-the-Balance.aspx.
A leading medical advisory group offers a comprehensive national strategy that recommends specific actions for families, schools, industry, communities and the government.

"Preventing Chronic Disease: The New Public Health," Alliance for Health Reform, September 2001, www.all health.org/publications/Public_health/Preventing_ Chronic_Disease_New_Public_Health_108.pdf.
The United States faces "an epidemic of chronic disease," and preventive steps at the community level are an important antidote, says the nonpartisan organization.

For More Information

Centers for Disease Control and Prevention, 1600 Clifton Rd., Atlanta, GA 30333; 800-232-4636; www.cdc.gov. U.S. agency tasked with protecting public health and safety primarily through disease control and prevention.

National Complete Streets Coalition, 1707 L St., N.W., Suite 250, Washington, DC 20036; 202-207-3355; www.complet-estreets.org. Advocates for the development of state, local and national policies to encourage making streets safe and accessible to all types of transportation, including walking and biking.

Partnership for Prevention, 1015 18th St., N.W., Suite 300, Washington, DC 20036; 202-833-0009; www.prevent .org. A group of business, nonprofit and government leaders advocating evidence-based disease prevention and health promotion.

Robert Wood Johnson Foundation, Route 1 and College Road East, PO Box 2316, Princeton, NJ 08543; 877-843-7953; www.rwjf.org. Provides research and grants for health-improvement activities.

Smart Growth America, 1707 L St., N.W., Suite 1050, Washington, DC 20036; 202-207-3355; www.smart growthamerica.org. Advocates neighborhood planning that allows for sidewalks, bike paths and easy access to public transportation.

Trust for America's Health, 1730 M St., N.W., Suite 900, Washington, DC 20036; 202-223-9870; http:// healthyamericans.org. Promotes public health and disease prevention.

United Health Foundation, Mail Stop: W150, 9900 Bren Road East, Minnetonka, MN 55343; www.unitedhealth-foundation.org/Main/Default.aspx. Provides funding and resources for programs that lead to better health outcomes and healthier communities.

World Health Organization, Avenue Appia 20m 1211, Geneva, 27, Switzerland; +41 22 791 21 11; www.who.int/ en/. United Nations agency that coordinates international public health efforts.

15

Unrest in the Arab World

Kenneth Jost

Holding a copy of the Koran, a supporter of Egyptian President Mohammed Morsi rallies with members of the Islamist Muslim Brotherhood in Cairo on Dec. 14, 2012, in support of the country's draft constitution. The controversial document, which was approved later in December, guarantees freedom of worship to Jews, Christians and Muslims — but not to others — and reaffirms Islam as the state religion.

From *The CQ Researcher*, February 1, 2013

With a brutal civil war raging, Syrian President Bashar Assad emerged into public view for the first time in several months on Jan. 6 to deliver a defiant speech blaming the conflict on criminals, terrorists and foreign influences. Assad, whose strongman father ruled Syria for 30 years before the son's succession in 2000, outlined a plan for a negotiated political solution but rejected any notion of stepping aside.

"This is a fight between the country and its enemies, between the people and the criminals," Assad said in a 50-minute oration before a cheering audience assembled in the Opera House in Damascus, Syria's capital city. "I would like to reassure everyone we will not stop the fight against terrorism as long as there is one single terrorist left in the land of Syria," he added.[1]

Assad spoke only four days after a United Nations-commissioned study said nearly 60,000 people had been killed in the conflict, which began with peaceful protests against the Assad regime in March 2011 as the so-called Arab Spring movement was hitting its stride elsewhere in the Arab World.[2] Three days earlier, Lakhdar Brahimi, the Algerian diplomat designated as a mediator by the U.N. and the 22-member League of Arab States, had warned that the conflict could claim another 100,000 lives over the next year. Without a peace agreement, Brahimi said at the league's headquarters in Cairo, Syria could be "transformed into hell."[3] (*See chart, p. 352; sidebar, p. 358.*)

The grim news from Syria contrasts sharply with the ebullient reaction to the Arab Spring, a succession of anti-government protests and demonstrations in North Africa and the Middle East that

Freedom Continues to Elude Arab World

Revolutions and popular unrest across much of the Arab world have yet to lead to full democracy and individual rights in any of the region's countries. No country is rated as "free," and only six are rated "partly free," by the international human-rights group Freedom House. Furthermore, only Bahrain, Qatar and the United Arab Emirates have achieved even a middling score on political corruption by Transparency International, a Berlin-based anti-corruption advocacy group.

Arab Countries With Recent Pro-Democracy Protests

Country *Type; head of government*	Population	GDP per capita	Freedom House freedom rating, 2013	Transparency International corruption score, 2012 (0 to 100, with 0 being the most corrupt)
Algeria	37.4 million	$7,300	Not free	34
Republic; independent from France since 1962. Prime Minister Abdelmalek Sellal in power since September 2012.				
Bahrain	1.2 million	$27,700	Not free	51
Constitutional monarchy; independent from U.K. since 1971. King Hamad bin Isa Al Khalifa in power since 1999.				
Egypt	83.7 million	$6,500	Partly free	32
Republic; British protectorate until 1922. Mohammed Morsi elected president in June 2012, more than a year after former President Hosni Mubarak was deposed in a revolution.				
Iraq	31.1 million	$4,200	Not free	18
Parliamentary democracy; independent from British administration since 1932 as part of a League of Nations mandate. Prime Minister: Nouri al-Maliki, elected in 2006.				
Jordan	6.5 million	$5,900	Not free	48
Constitutional monarchy; independent from British mandate since 1946. King Abdullah II in power since 1999.				

began in Tunisia in December 2010. Within a two-month span, the "Arab street" — the oft-used metaphor for disaffected Arabs shut out of the political process — forced Tunisia's longtime president Zine El Abidine Ben Ali to flee the country and Egyptian leader Hosni Mubarak to step down after 30 years as president. By August 2011, a popular uprising in Libya, aided by military support from the United States and some NATO allies, had toppled the longtime dictator Moammar Gadhafi.

Country Type; head of government	Population	GDP per capita	Freedom House freedom rating, 2013	Transparency International corruption score, 2012 (0 to 100, with 0 being the most corrupt)
Kuwait	2.6 million	$41,700	Partly free	44
Constitutional emirate; independent from U.K. since 1961. The emir, Sheik Sabah Al Ahmed Al Sabah, has been in power since 2006.				
Lebanon	4.1 million	$15,500	Partly free	30
Republic; independent from French administration since 1943 as part of a League of Nations mandate. President Michel Suleiman, in power since 2008.				
Libya	5.6 million	$6,000	Partly free	21
Operates under a transitional government following the deposition and death of ruler Moammar Gadhafi. Prime Minister Ali Zaidan took office in October 2012.				
Morocco	32.3 million	$5,100	Partly free	37
Constitutional monarchy; independent from France since 1956. King Mohammed VI in power since 1999.				
Oman	3.1 million	$27,600	Not free	47
Monarchy; independent since mid-1700s following Portuguese and Persian rule. Sultan Qaboos bin Said al-Said in power since 1970.				
Qatar	2 million	$98,900	Not free	68
Emirate; independent from U.K. since 1971. Sheik Hamad bin Khalifa al Thani in power since 1995.				
Saudi Arabia	26.5 million	$24,400	Not free	44
Monarchy; founded in 1932 after several attempts to unify the Arabian Peninsula. King Abdullah bin Abdul Aziz Al-Saud in power since 2005.				
Syria	22.5 million	$5,100	Not free	26
Authoritarian regime; French mandate until 1946. President Bashar Assad's family has been in power for 42 years.				
Tunisia	10.7 million	$9,400	Partly free	41
Republic; independent from France since 1956. Moncef Marzouki elected in December 2001 as president of interim government, which will remain in power until a new constitution is drafted.				
United Arab Emirates	5.3 million	$47,700	Not free	68
Federation with some powers reserved for member emirates; independent from U.K. since 1971. President: Sheik Khalifa bin Zayed Al Nahyan, in power since 2004.				
Yemen	24.8 million	$2,300	Not free	23
Republic; independent from Ottoman Empire since 1918. South Yemen unified with North Yemen in 1990. President Abed Rabbo Mansour Hadi took power on Feb. 27, 2012 after Ali Abdullah Saleh stepped down after 22 years as president.				

Sources: "Corruption Perceptions Index 2012," Transparency International, 2012, cpi.transparency.org/cpi2012/results; "Freedom in the World 2013," Freedom House, January 2013, pp. 14-18, www.freedomhouse.org/sites/default/files/FIW%202013%20 Booklet.pdf; The World Factbook, Central Intelligence Agency, January 2013, https://www.cia.gov/library/publications/the-world-factbook.

The protests spread to other countries, from monarchical Morocco in the west to the Gulf state monarchies and emirates in the east. Two years later, the political atmosphere has shifted in much of the Arab world, but the pace of change has slowed. "Things aren't as exciting as they were two years ago, but there are changes that are taking place," says James Gelvin, a professor of history at UCLA and author of a compact overview, *The Arab Uprisings*.[4]

Paul Salem, director of the Carnegie Middle East Center in Beirut, Lebanon, part of the Carnegie Endowment for International Peace, acknowledges the country-by-country variations in the degree of political

Timeline: The Syrian Civil War

2011

March 15-16	Demonstrators demand release of political prisoners; at least 20 protesters die as demonstrations widen in following weeks.
April 21	President Bashar Assad lifts state of emergency, releases political prisoners; security forces kill 72 protesters.
July 29	Some security forces refuse to fire on protesters; defectors form Free Syrian Army.
Aug. 3	Syrian tanks move into Hama, killing at least 45 protesters.
Aug. 23	U.N. Human Rights Council condemns Syrian government's response to protests; opposition forms National Council of Syria, demands Assad's removal from office.
Nov. 12	Arab League suspends Syria's membership.
Dec. 19-20	Security forces execute 110 protesters in Jabal al-Zawiya region; two suicide bombings in Damascus kill 44 people.

2012

February-March	Syrian forces begin shelling of Homs; hundreds killed.
March 21	Peace plan presented to U.N. Security Council by Arab League is championed by special envoy Kofi Annan and accepted by Russia, China; Assad accepts plan, then reneges.
April	U.N. observers enter Syria to monitor progress of Annan plan; U.N. suspends monitoring after deaths of women, children.
May 10	Two car bombs kill 55 people outside military intelligence building in Damascus; ceasefire nullified as government continues shelling cities; death toll reaches 9,000.
June 22	Syrian forces shoot down Turkish fighter jet; fighting later crosses Turkish border.
Aug. 2	Annan resigns as special envoy amid escalating violence.
Oct. 2	U.N. reports that 300,000 refugees have fled Syria.
Nov. 29	Syrian government shuts down Internet, telephone service; launches major offensive surrounding Damascus; U.S. delivers 2,000 communication kits to rebel forces.
Dec. 11	Obama says U.S. will recognize Syrian rebels as legitimate government; U.S. designates Jabhat al-Nusra, an Islamist militia backing Syrian rebels, as terrorist organization.
Dec. 22	Syrian military forces begin using Scud missiles against rebels.

2013

Jan. 1	U.N. puts death toll at 60,000; says it could reach 100,000 in coming year.
Jan. 6	Assad, in Damascus, vows to remain in office, continue fight against "criminals," "terrorists" and "foreign influences."
Jan. 17	Homs massacre kills 106 people; U.K.-based Syrian Observatory for Human Rights blames pro-Assad forces.
Jan. 21	Syrian National Coalition (SNC) fails to agree on transitional government; new plan promised for governing rebel-held areas.

Source: Compiled by Ethan McLeod from various news sources

reform. "It's spring in many places, winter in many places," he says. Even so, he says events will have a lasting impact on the political climate throughout the Arab world.*

"What has happened is a transformation of public consciousness and public political values," says Salem, a Harvard-educated dual citizen of Lebanon and the United States. Arabs throughout the region are now disavowing dictatorships and committing to political accountability and competitive elections, Salem says. "This paradigm shift is throughout the region," he adds, "and will be with us for the next generation."

Other experts are less convinced that the Arab world, long resistant to democratization and human rights, is now firmly on a different path. "We have seen a little bit of movement in a few countries," says Seth Jones, associate director for the RAND Corp.'s International Security and Defense Policy Center in Washington. "But for the most part we are not seeing the broad democratization that most people had hoped for."

For now, none of the 16 Arab countries stretching from Morocco to Iraq are rated as free, according to the annual survey "Freedom in the World 2013" by the international human rights group Freedom House. The report, released on Jan. 16, raises

---

* This report does not detail events and conditions in Iraq, which will be covered in a forthcoming report in March. It also does not encompass these six members of the League of Arab States: Comoros, Djibouti, Mauritania, Palestinian National Authority, Somalia and Sudan.

Egypt's and Libya's rating to "partly free," bringing the total in that category to six along with Kuwait, Lebanon, Morocco and Tunisia. The 10 other countries are all listed as "not free." In seven countries, according to the survey, the status of political rights or civil liberties worsened over the past year.[5] (*See map, p. 350.*)

The uprisings caught most analysts by surprise, U.S. scholars Mark Haas and David Lesch write in *The Arab Spring*, published in November. The waves of democratization that swept across Latin America, Eastern Europe and Central Asia during the late 20th century were unfelt in the Arab world except for a short-lived and largely abortive "Arab spring" of 2005.[6] Yet Haas, a political scientist at Duquesne University in Pittsburgh, and Lesch, a historian at Trinity University in San Antonio, say conditions were ripe for revolutionary uprisings in the Middle East. They note in particular the anger and frustration felt by the Arab world's disproportionately young populations as the global economic crisis of 2008 raised prices and drove up unemployment in much of the region.[7]

The 2010-2011 uprisings have resulted in "some grudging but nonetheless impressive gains," according to the Freedom House report, despite widespread predictions that the push for political reform would fall victim to what it calls the region's "perennial antidemocratic currents." The report sees "generally positive" gains in Libya and Tunisia, but it voiced concern about events in Egypt.

The Freedom House report lightly faults the "flawed but competitive" presidential campaign that resulted in the election of Mohammed Morsi, a leader of the once-banned Muslim Brotherhood, the Islamist group behind the now-dominant Freedom and Justice Party. It then criticizes a number of Morsi's actions in office, including what it calls the hasty process to draft a new constitution and hold a referendum that resulted in its approval with 64 percent of the low-turnout vote in December. (*See sidebar, p. 362.*)

Freedom House says political rights had diminished in several other Arab countries, including Lebanon, Jordan and four Gulf states: Bahrain, Kuwait, Oman and the United Arab Emirates. Saudi Arabia retained its status in the survey as one of the "worst of the worst" countries in terms of political and civil rights. But Syria is singled out as having suffered "by far" the worst of the repercussions from the Arab Spring.

Assad responded to the popular uprisings in 2011, the report says, "by waging war against his own people." Over the next year, "amid inaction by the international community," the conflict developed what the report calls "starker sectarian overtones" as it drew in fighters affiliated with al Qaeda and other terrorist groups. Today, many experts foresee only more bloodshed in Syria's future. "By every measure, it's getting worse," says Andrew Tabler, a senior fellow with the Washington Institute for Near East Policy.

The Freedom House report stresses the importance of the stance that Islamist groups such as the Muslim Brotherhood take as they gain power or influence. Fears of the Islamists' influence led Christian and liberal secularists to boycott the drafting of Egypt's new constitution. In other countries, political reforms are complicated by sectarian conflicts within Islam's two major branches: Sunnis, the worldwide majority, and Shiites, who comprise about one-third of the Muslim population in the Middle East. Syria's ostensibly secularist regime is tightly linked to the country's Alawites, a small minority branch of Islam viewed as heretical by both Sunnis and Shiites.[8]

The U.S. role in the events has been limited. "I don't think these events have been driven by the United States," says Jeremy Pressman, an associate professor of political science at the University of Connecticut in Storrs. "I don't think the way they turn out will be primarily driven by what the United States does."

President Obama called for Mubarak to step aside in Egypt but only after the longtime U.S. ally's fate had been sealed by weeks of demonstrations in Cairo's Tahrir Square and the military's decision to side with the revolt. In Libya, the United States helped doom Gadhafi's rule, but only after Britain and France took the lead in establishing a no-fly zone to help protect the popular uprising. And in Syria, despite calls for stronger action, the administration has limited the U.S. role to economic sanctions, covert assistance, humanitarian aid and public calls for Assad to step down. (*See "At Issue," p. 367.*)

With the unrest now in its third year, many experts caution that the situation will not be resolved quickly. "We're at the beginning of a long process," says UCLA's Gelvin.

Gawdat Bahgat, an Egyptian-born professor of political science at the National Defense University in Washington, agrees. "The process of moving away from authoritarianism to democracy is very unsettled," he says. As the events play out, here are some of the questions being debated:

Has the Arab Spring stalled?

New York Times op-ed columnist Nicholas Kristof was in Bahrain in February 2011 as government troops fired for several days on unarmed protesters, killing seven and wounding at least 200 others. Two years and at least 50 deaths later, Bahrain's Sunni monarchy still holds tight power over the country's Shiite majority, thanks in part to military help from its Sunni-ruled neighbor Saudi Arabia. And when Kristof tried to return late in 2012, he found that he had been blacklisted and was not allowed back in to report on the continuing repression in the Gulf state, home to the U.S. Navy's 5th Fleet.[9]

Despite U.S. ties, Bahraini authorities have spurned the Obama administration's urgings to negotiate a political solution with the simmering opposition. And in January Bahrain's highest courts upheld prison terms ranging from five years to life for 20 leaders of the revolt, following their convictions by a military tribunal. "The uprising was basically snuffed out," says the Carnegie Endowment's Salem.[10]

Bahrain provides the most dramatic example of what the Freedom House report labels the "intransigence" exhibited by many Arab nations toward popular uprisings. The report tags neighboring Oman and the United Arab Emirates with downward arrows based on increased arrests of activists calling for political reform and a crackdown on online activism. In other countries, including Jordan and Kuwait, governments have successfully tamped down discontent with modest political reforms that have left the underlying power structures unchanged. And in Egypt, the report cites continuing controversies over Morsi's actions, including his dismissal of the lower house of parliament in June and his claim of broad executive powers in November, to warn that the fate of democracy in the Arab world's most populous nation "remains very much an open question."

The moves to repress or stifle popular movements lead some experts to predict little democratization for the foreseeable future. "That's likely to be the case for the next couple of years," says Jones, the RAND expert. Jones' colleagues, writing in a book-length study, say the

government security apparatuses in the region pose formidable obstacles to popular political movements. In addition, oil-endowed countries have used their economic wealth to buy off potential opposition with what Jones calls "staggering benefits" in the form of government jobs and subsidies for food and other necessities.[11]

In Egypt, Jones says, the early signs pointed to a model of democratization, but Morsi's power-grabs now temper the early optimism. "There's serious reason to be concerned about the use of his position to establish broad executive, legislative and, to some degree, judicial power," Jones says.

Other experts, however, say it is too early to write off the Arab Spring as spent. "There have been continuous protests and uprisings" since the initial months in 2010 and 2011, according to Gelvin, the UCLA professor. "We see them taking place all the time. They just don't get covered."

Bahgat, at the National Defense University, agrees that the first few months of the uprisings resulted in unrealistic expectations about the future pace of change. "It makes sense that there will be ups and downs," says Bahgat. "It is not one straight line. The setbacks make sense. People should expect them."

As for his native Egypt, Bahgat finds the controversial moves by Morsi and the Muslim Brotherhood unsurprising and less than alarming. "It makes sense to me that they are trying to grab as much power as they can," Bahgat says. "That reflects the balance of power that is in Egypt now. But maybe in 10 years or so, it may be different."

"I don't think things have stalled," says the University of Connecticut's Pressman. "We should not come to these summary judgments after two years." Still, Pressman cautions that further democratization is not assured. "I'm in no way saying things are guaranteed."

Economics, more than politics, may determine the future course of events, according to many of the experts. "The Middle East is not doing well," says Gelvin. "That's the elephant in the room that no one's talking about." The initial wave of uprisings, he notes, "was not only social-networking youth. It was also workers."

The uprisings have hurt tourism in Egypt and elsewhere and slowed foreign investment, according to Joshua Landis, director of the Center for Middle

Syria at a Glance

Government

President Bashar Assad — Leader of Syria and regional secretary of the Arab Socialist Ba'ath Party. Elected in 2000 in unopposed referendum and initially seen as a potential reformer. Heavily criticized for human-rights violations and political corruption.

Minister of Defense General Fahd Jassem al-Freij — Appointed in July 2012 after assassination of predecessor; Assad has divided al-Freij's power among various commanders.

Syrian army — Estimated 280,000-member land force, responsible for suppressing rebels. Suffered up to 60,000 defections to the opposition in the past year.

Opposition

Free Syrian Army (FSA) — Formed in July 2011 by Syrian Army defectors. Estimated force of 100,000 soldiers with basic military training; has grown from a select group of defectors along the Turkish border to a broader group of insurgent civilians and military groups. Many rebels have adopted the FSA name.

Colonel Riad al-Asaad — Former commander of the FSA. Established the FSA in late July 2011 after defecting from the Syrian army earlier that month.

Brigadier General Salim Idris — Syrian Army defector appointed to replace Riad al-Asaad as chief of staff of the FSA in December 2012.

National Coalition for Syrian Revolutionary and Opposition Forces (Syrian National Coalition) — Formed in November 2012 as an inclusive leadership council of 63 (now 70) members. Aims to replace Assad's regime and become the international representative for Syria, but internal divisions have presented problems in forming a government. Supports the FSA. Recognized by more than 140 countries as representative of Syrian people.

Coalition President Moaz al-Khatib — Former Sunni imam of the Ummayad Mosque in Damascus; imprisoned several times for speaking out against Assad and forced to flee Syria in July 2012.

Syrian National Council (SNC) — Coalition of several opposition groups dominated by Sunni Muslim majority. Military bureau coordinates activity for the Damascus Declaration for Democratic Change, the Muslim Brotherhood, Syrian Revolution General Commission and Kurdish and tribal factions.

President George Sabra — Elected chairman of the left-wing Syrian Democratic People's Party, banned by the country's government, in November 2012.

National Coordination Committee for Democratic Change — Comprises 13 leftist and three additional Kurdish political parties, plus an assortment of independent and youth activists. Calls for a withdrawal of military from streets, an end to military attacks against nonviolent protests and the release of all political prisoners. Favors economic sanctions on Assad as a means of applying international pressure. Rejects foreign military intervention.

Jabhat al-Nusra — Salafi Jihadist rebel group with links to al Qaeda; has gained popular support in recent months. Worked with FSA factions to carry out attacks and large-scale bombings in the past year. The United States designated it a terrorist organization in December.

Ahrar al-Sham battalion — Rebel group composed of conservative Salafist and Islamist groups; has close ties to Jabhat al-Nusra. Has drawn attention from other, more radical rebel groups in Syrian rebel front.

Sources: "Guide to the Syrian opposition," BBC, Nov. 12, 2012, www.bbc.co.uk/news/world-middle-east-15798218; "Structure of SNC," Syrian National Council, www.syriancouncil.org/en/structure/structure.html; Elizabeth O'Bagy, "Middle East Security Report 6: Jihad in Syria," Institute for the Study of War, September 2012, www.understandingwar.org/report/jihad-syria; Khaled Yacoub Oweis, "Syria's army weakened by growing desertions," Reuters, Jan. 13, 2012, www.reuters.com/article/2012/01/13/us-syria-defections-idUSTRE80C2IV20120113; Samia Nakhoul and Khaled Yacoub Oweis, "World Powers Recognise Syrian Opposition Coalition," Reuters, December 2012, www.reuters.com/article/2012/12/12/us-syria-crisis-draft-idUSBRE8BB0DC2012 1212; Yelena Suponina, "Free Syrian Army's Riad al-Asaad: Political resolution of the crisis in Syria is impossible," Voice of Russia, Aug. 9, 2012, english.ruvr.ru/2012_08_09/Political-resolution-on-the-crisis-in-Syria-is-impossible/.

— Compiled by Ethan McLeod and Darrell Dela Rosa

East Studies at the University of Oklahoma in Norman. "We're caught in this race of whether the new governments can see their countries through these very dangerous and difficult times," says Landis.

The RAND researchers say economic failures do not necessarily doom efforts at democratization, but they warn that transitions in the Arab world may be "especially fragile" and "more vulnerable to economic strains than many past cases."[12]

Do Islamic groups pose a threat to political reform in the Arab world?

Egyptians were getting ready to vote on a new constitution that promises freedom of religion when an Egyptian court on Dec. 12 sentenced Alber Saber, an avowed atheist, to three years in prison for blasphemy.

Saber, 27, born into a Christian family, had been arrested in September based on never-confirmed reports that he had posted the controversial anti-Islam film "The Innocence of Muslims" on his blog. Authorities found enough evidence, however, to charge him with blasphemy for insulting both Islam and Christianity. "Egypt is a religious state," Saber said after appealing the sentence. "If you disobey the norms, you get judged and sentenced."[13]

The new constitution, approved in two rounds of balloting on Dec. 15 and Dec. 22, guarantees freedom of worship to believers in the three "monotheist" religions — Judaism, Christianity and Islam — but not to others. It also carries over a provision from the 1971 constitution designating Islam as the state religion and Islamic law, known as Sharia, as the source of legislation.

Under Mubarak, the government had banned the Muslim Brotherhood but protected the country's Christians, who comprise only 1 percent of the population. With the Muslim Brotherhood's Freedom and Justice Party dominating the new government, Christians and non-believers worry about possible repression. "Expect to see many more blasphemy prosecutions in the future," says Heba Morayef, a Cairo-based researcher with Human Rights Watch, the New York City-headquartered advocacy and monitoring organization.[14]

Whatever happens in Egypt, experts agree that Islamic parties will play an increasingly important role in Arab countries. Political Islam "is the one ideology that has roots with the people," says University of Oklahoma professor Landis. "Secularists are a distinct

minority. We're going to see Islamic governments from one end of the Middle East to another."

For much of the 20th century, Islamist organizations such as the Muslim Brotherhood — which was founded in Egypt in 1928 and later spawned branches in other countries — advocated violence as a political tactic, leading to bans and crackdowns from established regimes. UCLA's Gelvin now sees "a paradigm shift" as the groups, well organized despite a history of government repression, see opportunities in the new political openings. "It doesn't mean that Islamist organizations are going to be completely pro-democracy and human rights," Gelvin says. "But opportunities have opened for them to participate in democratic government."

With their superior political organization, Islamist parties are bound to be "the most powerful actors in the new regimes, at least in the short run," scholars Lesch and Haas write in their overview.[15]

Bahgat, the National Defense University professor, agrees. "It makes sense that they are winning many elections," he says, citing the voting in Tunisia and his native Egypt as examples. "They are winning because they are better organized than all other political groups."

Salem, the Carnegie expert in Beirut, acknowledges the disagreements in Egypt and Tunisia between Islamists and what he calls "non-Islamists" and "old regime forces." But he professes to be unconcerned. "Issues are being contested," he says, "but the good thing is they're being contested through political processes."

The sectarian division within Islam between Sunnis and Shiites is also an important factor in the ongoing political developments, according to Toby Jones, an associate professor of history at Rutgers University in New Brunswick, N.J. "Religious and ethnic differences have crept into politics in ways that we haven't seen before," says Jones, who specializes in the modern Middle East. "It's relatively new. It's very dangerous."

Sunni rulers in the Gulf states as well as Assad in Syria depict the popular protests as sectarian-motivated as a stratagem to stay in power, Jones says. "They all have an interest in claiming that sectarianism is the force that is at work," Jones explains. "It gives them legitimacy."

The Freedom House report gives Tunisia good marks on political reforms so far but takes a wait-and-see attitude toward Egypt. "The moderate Islamists in Tunisia who constitute the government have said mostly the

CHRONOLOGY

2010-2011 *Arab Spring begins; autocrats ousted in Tunisia, Egypt, Libya; Syria in civil war.*

December 2010 Tunisian fruit vendor Mohamed Bouazizi sets fire to himself to protest treatment by police (Dec. 17); incident sparks nationwide riots; President Zine El Abidine Ben Ali vows to punish protesters; Bouazizi dies on Jan. 4.

January 2011 Protests break out in Algeria, Egypt, Jordan, Yemen. . . . Ben Ali flees Tunisia (Jan. 14). . . . Demonstrations in Cairo's Tahrir Square call for Egyptian President Hosni Mubarak to resign (Jan. 25).

February 2011 Mubarak resigns; military council forms interim government (Feb. 11). . . . Libyans protest arrest of activist in Benghazi (Feb. 15); protests spread; leader Moammar Gadhafi vows to stay in office. . . . Protests erupt in Bahrain (Feb. 14), Morocco (Feb. 20).

March 2011 Protests banned nationwide in Saudi Arabia (March 5). . . . U.N. Security Council authorizes no-fly zone over Libya (March 17); rebels begin to capture territory, form transitional government. . . . Syrian security forces kill several people in provincial city of Daraa protesting arrest of political prisoners (March 18); protests spread to Damascus, other cities; tanks used to quell protests. . . . President Bashar Assad orders release of political prisoners (March 25-26).

April-June 2011 Protests in Egypt demand quick transfer of power by military. . . . Assad lifts state of emergency in Syria (April 21); security forces continue crackdowns. . . . Death toll in Egypt uprising: at least 846, according to judicial panel (April 19). . . . Four protesters sentenced to death in Bahrain (April 28). . . . Death toll in Tunisia uprising: at least 300, according to U.N. investigator (May 21). . . . Yemeni President Ali Abdullah Saleh injured in rocket attack, flown to Saudi Arabia (June 4).

July-September 2011 Free Syrian Army formed by defectors (July 29). . . . Battle of Tripoli: rebels capture city; Gadhafi overthrown (Aug. 20-28). . . . Saudi King Abdullah grants women right to vote, run in municipal elections (Sept. 25).

October-December 2011 Gadhafi captured, killed (Oct. 20). . . . Moderate Islamist party Ennhada leads in

elections for Tunisian parliament (Oct. 23). . . . Sunni groups form National Salvation Council in Syria; Islamist groups refuse to join (November). . . . Saleh agrees to yield power in Yemen (Nov. 23). . . . Parliamentary elections begin in Egypt (Nov. 28); Muslim Brotherhood's Freedom and Justice Party leads after balloting concludes (Jan. 3).

2012-Present *Protests ebb; new governments take shape; Syrian civil war continues.*

January-March 2012 Syrian conflict intensifies; Russia, China block U.N. Security Council action (Feb. 4). . . . Abed Rabo Mansour Hadi elected Yemeni president in single-candidate vote (Feb. 21). . . . Egyptian parliament creates Islamist-dominated Constituent Assembly to draft new constitution; liberal lawmakers protest (March 24).

April-June 2012 Egyptian Constituent Assembly dissolved by court order (April 10). . . . Mubarak receives life sentence for role in killings of protesters (June 2); wins retrial (Jan. 13, 2013). . . . New Constituent Assembly created; critics still dissatisfied (June 12). . . . Ben Ali convicted in absentia for role in killings of protesters in Tunisia; sentenced to life (June 19). . . . Muslim Brotherhood's Mohammed Morsi elected president in Egypt (June 24).

July-September 2012 Liberal National Front Alliance leads in Libyan parliamentary elections; Islamists distant second (July 7). . . . U.S. ambassador, three others killed in attack on consulate in Benghazi (Sept. 11).

October-December 2012 Egyptian court skirts challenge to Constituent Assembly (Oct. 23). . . . Bahrain bans all protests (Oct. 30). . . . Morsi curbs judiciary's powers (Nov. 22); withdraws move under pressure (Dec. 8). . . . Draft constitution approved by Constituent Assembly (Nov. 29-30); approved by voters (Dec. 15, 22).

January 2013 Death toll in Syria put at 60,000 (Jan. 2); Assad vows to remain in office (Jan. 6). . . . Libyan government sharply reduces death toll estimate in civil war: 4,700 rebels killed, 2,100 missing; government losses thought comparable (Jan. 8). . . . Women named to Saudi advisory council for first time (Jan. 11). . . . New violence in Egypt marks second anniversary of revolution; military chief fears "collapse" of state (Jan. 25-29).

Syrian Civil War Has Region's Highest Death Toll

More than 60,000 are dead and millions homeless.

Students at Aleppo University in Syria were busy with exams on Jan. 15 when at least two massive bomb blasts shattered the campus. Dozens were killed and scores were wounded in carnage remarkable even for a country devastated by nearly two years of civil war.

"The most painful scene was a chopped hand with a pen and notebook right next to it," one student told *The New York Times* over Skype. "I saw blood [and] flesh littered all around."[1]

Tens of thousands of Syrians have witnessed similar scenes as strongman Bashar Assad tries to retain his presidency in the face of potent resistance by a confederation of rebel groups, some controlled by Western-oriented reformers and others by Islamist extremists.

Syria's civil war has killed more than 60,000, according to a United Nations-commissioned estimate released Jan. 2. The conflict has also laid waste to vast portions of the country stretching along the western border from Aleppo to Damascus. At the same time, the war has led to a humanitarian crisis, with more than 2 million refugees displaced inside Syria and possibly 1 million requiring humanitarian aid within the next six months in Jordan, Lebanon, Turkey and elsewhere.[2]

Without a quick resolution to the conflict — a scenario widely viewed by international observers as unlikely — "thousands more will die or suffer terrible injuries as a result of those who harbor the obstinate belief that something can

be achieved by more bloodshed, more torture and more mindless destruction," according to Navi Pillay, the U.N. High Commissioner for Human Rights.[3]

The Syrian conflict is by far the deadliest of a string of uprisings that have rocked the Arab world in the past two years, but the death count is in the thousands in at least two other countries. Libya's new government released new, sharply reduced estimates on Jan. 8 that the civil war there claimed at least 4,700 lives on the rebels' side, with 2,100 missing; government losses were thought to be similar. The Yemeni government estimated in March 2012 that more than 2,000 had died in the political unrest there.

The death toll was in the hundreds in two other countries: Egypt and Tunisia. A judicial panel in Egypt in April 2011 said 846 people died in the revolution there. An investigative panel in Tunisia reported in May 2011 that 300 people had died in the Tunisian uprising. In Bahrain, a reform group counts 91 deaths, but news organizations put the death toll less exactly at more than 50.[4]

The International Rescue Committee's Commission on Syrian Refugees has been responsible for supplying medical aid and humanitarian assistance to women affected by sexual violence and to refugees displaced by the conflict. The IRC commission says sexual violence and child kidnappings by Syrian army troops have been primary causes for many families' decisions to flee the country.

rights things and have done mostly things that advance democracy," says Arch Puddington, vice president for research and editor of the annual volume. But he calls Egypt "another case." Morsi's tendency "is to address his message to his fellow brothers," Puddington says, referring to Muslim Brotherhood members, "and to the entire population second."

Other experts are also cautious about prospects in Egypt. "We're going to have to see how it plays out," says Landis. But Bahgat expects the Muslim Brotherhood to face more serious political competition as time goes on.

"The Islamists will not be able to solve the economic problems," Bahgat explains. "In the next round of elections, other groups, most likely liberals, will get better organized, and the people will have less confidence in the Islamists."

Can a stable political solution be found in Syria?

The capture of a key Syrian military air base by rebels on Jan. 11 further weakens the Assad regime's hold on the country, but the victory is a mixed blessing for the United States and others hoping for democratic change

Aleppo, Syria's largest city with more than 2 million people, bristles with military checkpoints. Vast tracts of homes and businesses have been damaged or destroyed. Pedestrians risk being shot in crossfires on bombed-out streets.[5]

Aleppo became a prime target in late July 2012 as Syrian army forces began shelling the city in a thus-far unsuccessful attempt to drive out the rebels. The attack on the public university, the country's flagship educational institution, was unprecedented.

The responsibility for the Aleppo University bomb blasts is disputed. Pro-rebel factions contend that Assad directed the Syrian air force to bomb the university; Syria's state-run news service said an unnamed terrorist organization was responsible. The Syrian Observatory for Human Rights said the explosions could have resulted from government airstrikes or from car bombs, which have been used by rebel groups.

What students saw, however, remains undeniable and clear: "Two big holes, caused by two missiles," in what had been the campus square, student Abu Tayem said. "I could not see it any more, it's vanished."[6]

— Ethan McLeod

AFP/Getty Images/STR

Bombs devastated Aleppo University on Jan. 15, 2013, killing at least 87 people. More than 60,000 people have died in Syria's civil war, and some experts say the toll could reach 100,000 or more.

[1]Hwaida Saad and Rick Gladstone, "Dozens Killed as Explosions Hit Syrian University," *The New York Times*, Jan. 15, 2013, www.nytimes.com/2013/01/16/world/middleeast/syria-violence.html?pagewanted=2&_r=0.

[2]See "Syria: A Regional Crisis: The IRC Commission on Syrian Refugees," International Rescue Committee, January 2013, www.rescue.org/sites/default/files/resource-file/IRCReportMidEast20130114.pdf. For coverage, see Ashish Kumar Sen, "Refugees flood Syria's neighbors," *The Washington Times*, Jan. 17, 2013, www.washingtontimes.com/news/2013/jan/17/syrian-war-creating-historic-refugee-crisis/.

[3]"Data Suggests Syria Death Toll Could be More than 60,000, Says UN Human Rights Office," United Nations News Centre, Jan. 2, 2013, www.un.org/apps/news/story.asp?NewsID=43866.

[4]Information drawn from, Ian Black, "Libyan revolution casualties lower than expected, says new government," *The Guardian*, Jan. 8, 2013, www.guardian.co.uk/world/2013/jan/08/libyan-revolution-casualties-lower-expected-government; Ahmed al-Haj, "Yemen Death Toll: Over 2,000 Killed In Uprising," The Associated Press, March 18, 2012, www.huffingtonpost.com/2012/03/19/yemen-death-toll_n_1361840.html; Almasry Ahmed, "At least 846 killed in Egypt's revolution," *Egypt Independent*, April 19, 2011, www.egyptindependent.com/news/least-846-killed-egypt%E2%80%99s-revolution; "Tunisia: High death toll challenges claims of smooth transition," *Los Angeles Times*, May 22, 2011, latimesblogs.latimes.com/babylonbeyond/2011/05/tunisia-uprising-violence-repression-human-rights-torture-.html; "91 Killed Since 14th February 2011," Bahrain Justice and Development Movement, www.bahrainjdm.org/78-killed-since-14th-february-2011/.

[5]See C. J. Chivers, "Rubble and Despair Redefine Syria Jewel," *The New York Times*, Dec. 18, 2012, www.nytimes.com/2012/12/19/world/middleeast/aleppo-residents-battered-by-war-struggle-to-survive.html?pagewanted=all.

[6]Saad and Gladstone, *op. cit.*

in post-Assad Syria. The rebels who seized the Taftanaz military base in the northwestern province of Idlib were primarily from Jabhat al-Nusra, a jihadist group designated by the United States as a terrorist organization and thought to have ties to al Qaeda in Iraq. By gaining weapons and credit from the victory, analysts said, the jihadists strengthened their position and stoked fears among Syria's minority Alawite community of a sectarian bloodbath if Assad falls.[16]

At the outset, the uprising in Syria caught outside observers, not to mention the Assad regime itself, totally

by surprise.[17] Assad, a Western-educated ophthalmologist, had been viewed as a reformer when elected president at age 37 in 2000 after his father's death. He remained well-liked in Syria despite the regime's crackdown on protests before 2011, according to Lesch, the Trinity University professor who came to know Assad well while writing a biography.[18] The regime seemed to satisfy the country's Sunni majority while also protecting the interests of the Shia minority and the Alawite community that was the elder Assad's home and the regime's political base. In addition, the initial protests in Damascus and elsewhere in early 2011 drew small numbers and were easily put down.

The unrest became more serious and the crackdown turned deadly when security forces killed at least five people in the southern provincial town of Daraa on March 18, 2011, as they were protesting the arrest of schoolchildren for anti-government graffiti. In the nearly two years since, the unrest has turned into a bloody civil war. Rebel forces now control parts of the country, but the government counters with lethal force, including missile attacks in civilian neighborhoods.

Tabler is one of many experts who believes Assad must either step aside or resign himself eventually to being deposed. RAND expert Jones agrees. "The prognosis for the Assad regime is bleak," Jones says. "It's likely to fall, but it's hard to put a time frame on that." Some Syria-watchers think Assad could fall from power any day, but many others expect him to hold on for a while.

"Syria is looking forward to a long, hard-fought struggle that's going to devastate the country," says University of Oklahoma professor Landis, who hosts an up-to-date blog, *Syria Comment.*[19]

The experts are equally bleak in their predictions for a post-Assad Syria. The Syrian opposition is loosely organized — "fragmented," as University of Connecticut professor Pressman puts it. "There is no clear leadership," says Bahgat, at the National Defense University. Gelvin at UCLA says Muslim Brotherhood groups "claim to be for democracy and human rights," but "we don't know much about them." The jihadist groups, he says, are better known. "They are very sectarian," Gelvin says. "For the most part, they are not interested in ruling Syria. They want to use Syria as a jumping-off point for a larger uprising in the Islamic world."

The opposition's support among the Syrian people is difficult to gauge but at the least subject to doubt. The nationalist Free Syrian Army, formed in summer 2011 by defectors from Assad's security forces, is said to be losing support as individual commanders turn into local warlords. Jihadist groups are gaining good will, in part because they are helping to provide food and supplies to beleaguered towns such as Aleppo in the northwest. Peter Harling, an analyst with the International Crisis Group, says the opposition has failed to woo Alawites within the regime or to reach out to other disaffected communities.[20]

Many Alawites fear a bloodbath if the rebels force Assad from power. "If I were Alawi, I would fight to the end," says Bahgat. "If Assad falls, the Alawi will pay a price."

Salem, with the Carnegie Endowment, agrees. "There's a lot of people who want to take revenge," he says.

The government is responding to its weakened position with "a scorched-earth policy," according to Salem. "Rather than cede power to another party, it prefers to destroy what is left and leave nothing standing to whoever comes after," he says. The remnants of Assad's government can continue the fight by retiring to the Alawite community's northwest coastal home, he notes.

"I see no signs that this conflict will do anything but worsen," Tabler concludes.

Landis is just as pessimistic about the political dynamic. Syria "is not going to be a democracy for a long time," he says.

BACKGROUND

Strangers to Democracy

The Arab world knew little of freedom or democracy before or during most of the 20th century. The defeat of the Ottoman Empire in World War I left Arab lands from Morocco to Iraq under European rule as colonies or protectorates. As Arab nations gained independence after World War II, they emerged not as democracies but as autocracies ruled by long-serving monarchs or by strongmen from the ranks of the military. The leaders used nationalist and pan-Arabist rhetoric to hold popular support even as social and economic problems festered.[21]

An Arab empire once stretched from Spain in the west to the Asian subcontinent in the east, but the Ottoman Empire displaced it by conquest in the 15th century. European colonial powers gained footholds in North Africa in the 1800s. Britain and France took over parts of the Ottoman Empire in the Middle East after their victory in World War I. Britain controlled Palestine, Transjordan and Iraq and exercised strong influence over Egypt after unilaterally granting it nominal independence in 1922. France got the territory that became Syria and Lebanon and maintained colonial rule over Morocco, Algeria and Tunisia. Italy controlled what was to become Libya. The Ottoman Empire had been decentralized and religiously tolerant but with no tradition of political rights. Britain and France were granted mandates by the League of Nations in order to guide the Arab nations to self-governance, but they instituted only limited reforms and installed compliant rulers who protected the Europeans' interests even as nationalism was emerging as a force. Meanwhile, Saudi Arabia was formed in 1932 as an Islamic kingdom on the Arabian peninsula, an area viewed as worthless desert until the discovery of oil later in the decade. The end of World War II brought independence for Jordan and Syria and, in 1948, the creation of the Jewish state of Israel — with unsettling consequences for the politics of the region.

The defeat of the then-seven member Arab League in the first Arab-Israeli War (1948-49) stoked nationalist and pan-Arabist sentiment in many of the now-independent Arab nations. In Egypt, a military coup ousted the pro-British monarchy in 1952 and created a republic that was transformed over the next four years into a one-party state led by Gamal Abdel Nasser. Nasser translated his pan-Arabist views into an agreement with Syria in 1958 to form the United Arab Republic, but the union lasted only until 1961 as Syria chafed under the domination of its larger partner. Nasser ruled Egypt until his death in 1970; his successor, Anwar Sadat, reinstituted a multiparty system and moved away from Nasser's Arab socialism during 11 years in office until his 1981 assassination by opponents of Sadat's landmark 1979 peace agreement with Israel.

Syria, meanwhile, experienced two decades of extreme political instability after gaining independence from the French after World War II. Politics came to be dominated by the Arab Ba'ath Party (translation: "resurrection" or "renaissance"), founded by pan-Arabist Syrians in 1947. Power lay, however, not with political institutions but with the military and security establishment. Baathists divided in the 1960s into civilian- and military-oriented wings, with Air Force officer Hafez Assad — the father of Bashar — emerging as a major figure in successive coups in 1963 and 1966. As minister of defense after 1966, Assad maneuvered against the de facto leader, Salah Jadid, and then gained unchallenged power after mounting successive military coups in 1969 and 1970.

Strongman rulers came to the fore in several other countries, generally stifling any significant moves toward democracy. In Tunisia, the anti-colonialist leader Habib

AFP/Getty Images/STR

Refugees fleeing Syria's civil war face harsh conditions, including supply shortages, freezing temperatures and snow, in a camp in Turkey on Jan. 9, 2013. The war has created what Human Rights Watch calls "a dire humanitarian situation." More than 2 million Syrians have been displaced internally, and possibly 1 million more may require humanitarian aid within the next six months in Jordan, Lebanon, Turkey and elsewhere.

Bourguiba became president in 1957 of what would become a single-party state; he held office until 1987 when Ben Ali engineered his removal on grounds of mental incompetency. In neighboring Libya, Gadhafi led a bloodless military coup in 1969, ousting a corruption-tainted monarchy while espousing reformist and nationalist views; he wielded power, often ruthlessly, until his death in the Libyan Revolution of 2011. In Iraq, Saddam Hussein rose through the ranks of the Ba'ath Party to become president in 1979, the beginning of a sometimes brutal, 24-year rule that ended with his ouster in the U.S.-led invasion of 2003. In Yemen, Ali Abdullah Saleh began a 33-year tenure as president in 1978 — first as president of North Yemen and after 1990 as president of the Yemeni Arab Republic following the unification with formerly Marxist South Yemen.

Saudi Arabia gained influence in the region through its oil wealth, but political power remained consolidated in the royal family through a succession of long-serving successors to the kingdom's founder, Ibn Saud (1932-1953).

Among the Gulf states, the island sheikhdom of Bahrain took a stab at parliamentary democracy after declaring independence from Britain in 1971, but Sheikh Isa bin Salman Al Khalifa clamped down on dissent after

Egypt's New Constitution Gets Mixed Reviews

Some say the document creates "prospects of a religious state."

Egypt's new constitution includes a host of provisions that appear to strengthen protections for individual rights. But human rights advocates in Egypt and in the United States say it is deeply flawed because it vests too much power in the president, creates significant exceptions for some rights and opens the door to instituting Islamic law at the potential expense of religious freedom.

"From a liberal democratic perspective, there is much to like in the document," writes Nathan Brown, a professor of political science and international affairs at George Washington University in Washington, D.C. But, Brown adds, "the document includes just as much that causes concern."[1]

Egyptian voters approved the new, 234-article constitution with about 64 percent of the vote in a low-turnout, two-stage referendum on Dec. 15 and 22 that drew only one-third of the electorate to the polls. Opponents complained the referendum was hastily called after a drafting process by the Islamist-dominated Constituent Assembly that was itself too rushed and too contentious. President Mohammed Morsi made a nationally televised address on Dec. 26, the day after the results were announced, to acknowledge unspecified "mistakes" in the process while promising "to respect the law and constitution."[2]

The new constitution, replacing one that was adopted in 1971, shortens the president's term from six years to four and imposes a two-term limit instead of allowing unlimited terms. But Brown says the constitution "is more presidential than might have been expected." And Hafez Abu Saeda, head of the Egyptian Organization for Human Rights, complained in advance of the referendum about provisions allowing the president to appoint the prime minister, dissolve parliament and name members of the Supreme Constitutional Court.[3]

In another analysis before the referendum, the U.S.-headquartered Human Rights Watch praised the charter for its "strong protection" against arbitrary detention, torture and inhumane treatment and for freedom of movement, privacy of communication and freedom of assembly and association. But it noted that other provisions imposed significant qualifications on those rights — such as provisions against "insulting" individuals or "the prophets." The group noted that criminal prosecutions for insulting the president or the judiciary have increased since Morsi took office.[4]

The new constitution carries over a provision from the 1971 charter — Article 2 in both documents — that declares Islam to be the state religion and Islamic law, or Sharia, the principal source of legislation. The new constitution adds a new provision, Article 219, that defines Sharia broadly to include what is translated into English as "general evidence and foundations, rules and jurisprudence as well as sources accepted by doctrines of Sunni Islam and the majority of Muslim scholars." In a separate provision, the constitution specifies that scholars at the Islamic Al-Azhar University shall be consulted on all matters of Sharia law.

Magdi Khalil, an Egyptian who serves as executive director of the Belin-based Mideast Freedom Forum, calls the provisions "catastrophic" because they "create prospects of a religious state."[5] But Brown and coauthor Clark Lombardi, an associate professor at the University of Washington School of Law in Seattle, say the meaning of the new provisions remains to be seen. "There will continue to be fierce argument," they write, "about what types of law are permissible in a self-styled Islamic state and, of course, about which are wise."[6]

— *Kenneth Jost*

[1] Nathan J. Brown, "Egypt's Constitution Conundrum," *Foreign Affairs*, Dec. 9, 2012, www.foreignaffairs.com/articles/138495/nathan-j-brown/egypts-constitution-conundrum.

[2] See David D. Kirkpatrick, "Despite 'Mistakes,' Morsi Says Constitution Fight Was Democracy in Action," *The New York Times*, Dec. 27, 2012, p. A8. See also Sarah el Deeb, "Egypt's Morsi: constitution dawn of new republic," The Associated Press, Dec. 26, 2012. A video of the speech, delivered in Arabic, is posted on an Egyptian news site: http://nilesports.com/news/2012/12/26/video-president-mohamed-morsi-speech-december-26-2012/. For other background, see Ingy Hassieb and Abigal Hauslohner, "Egyptian voters adopt faith-based constitution," *The Washington Post*, Dec. 24, 2012, p. A8; David D. Kirkpatrick and Mayy el Sheikh, "As Constitution Nears Approval, Egypt's Factions Face New Fights," *The New York Times*, Dec. 23, 2012, p. A1.

[3] "Egyptian Human Rights Experts Analyze Draft Constitution," Washington Institute for Near East Policy, Nov. 15, 2012, www.washingtoninstitute.org/policy-analysis/view/egyptian-human-rights-experts-analyze-the-draft-constitution.

[4] "Egypt: New Constitution Mixed on Support of Rights," Human Rights Watch, www.hrw.org/news/2012/11/29/egypt-new-constitution-mixed-support-rights.

[5] See "Egyptian Human Rights Experts," *op. cit.*

[6] Clark Lombardi and Nathan J. Brown, "Islam in Egypt's New Constitution," *Foreign Policy*, Dec. 13, 2012, http://mideast.foreignpolicy.com/posts/2012/12/13/islam_in_egypts_new_constitution.

leftists and Shiites won nearly half the seats in parliamentary elections in 1973. Elsewhere, constitutional monarchs — Jordan's King Hussein (1953-1999) and Morocco's King Hassan II (1961-1999) — dominated the political scene while instituting reforms: modest in Morocco, more extensive in Jordan.

Overall, Freedom House's survey of the 16 Arab lands from Morocco to Iraq in 1979 rated none of them as free, nine as partly free and seven as not free.[22]

'Freedom Deficit'

A rab and Muslim countries remained impervious to the advances for political rights and civil liberties in much of the world as the 20th century ended. Repression was the order of the day in many countries — with Egypt and Syria among the worst. In Egypt, an emergency decree ordered by Mubarak after Sadat's 1981 assassination by Muslim fundamentalists remained in effect until Mubarak was forced out of office in February 2011. In Syria, Assad put down Sunni opposition to his regime with a ruthlessness best exemplified by the 1982 massacre in the city of Hama that claimed at least 10,000 lives. By 2001, Mali in West Africa was alone among the 47 majority-Muslim countries to be rated by Freedom House as free.[23]

Mubarak rose from Air Force ranks to become Sadat's vice president and then to succeed to the presidency unopposed in a referendum held a week after the slaying. He won three additional six-year terms in successive referendums, also unopposed. Mubarak called the assassination part of a plot to overthrow the government.

The emergency decree adopted after Sadat's slaying sharply limited political activity and allowed detention and imprisonment of political dissidents. As many as 30,000 people may have been held as political prisoners during the period. Parliamentary elections were held under rules favoring Mubarak's governing National Democratic Party. The Muslim Brotherhood, the largest opposition group, remained under a ban imposed in 1954. Throughout the period, Mubarak remained an important U.S. ally, even as political conditions failed to improve and evidence of personal and government-wide corruption grew.

Assad ruled Syria through a combination of guile and ruthlessness for nearly 30 years until his death in June 2000. His secularist policies — including equal rights

for women — drew opposition from the Muslim Brotherhood beginning in the mid-1970s. Assad responded to the Brotherhood's attempt to take control of the west central city of Hama in February 1982 by ordering the city shelled and having its civilian population pay the price in lives lost.

Assad's military-security apparatus crushed any incipient opposition with similar ruthlessness, including torture. But Assad also won loyalty through financial ties with Syria's business community, patronage in a bloated state sector and tough anti-Israeli rhetoric. The United States designated Syria a state sponsor of terrorism from 1979 on but also worked to win Assad's support for, or at least acquiescence in, Arab-Israeli peace negotiations.

Hussein in Iraq and Gadhafi in Libya earned reputations as the region's other two worst dictators and biggest problems for U.S. policy. Both countries were designated as state sponsors of terrorism, though Iraq was removed from the list during the 1980s when the United States supported Baghdad in its war with Iran. Both men ruled through a combination of cult-of-personality adulation and coldblooded repression of political dissent. Hussein survived Iraq's defeat by a U.S.-led coalition in the Gulf War in 1991, his stature within Iraq seemingly enhanced; he won show elections in 1995 and 2002 with 99.9 percent and 100 percent, respectively, of the vote. Gadhafi survived a retaliatory U.S. air strike on his home in April 1986 and, like Hussein later, appeared only to gain political stature at home from his successful defiance of Washington.

The rise of Islamist parties unsettled politics in several countries, resulting in repressive crackdowns — most notably, in Algeria. The Algerian government's decision to cancel parliamentary elections in 1991 to thwart a potential victory by the newly formed Islamic Salvation Front touched off a decade-long civil war that may have claimed as many as 200,000 lives. In neighboring Tunisia, Ben Ali followed suit by cracking down on Islamist groups, abandoning the political liberalization of his first years in office. In Bahrain, the Shiite majority, chafing under Sunni rule and adverse economic conditions, clamored for restoration of the post-independence constitution, but the government responded by jailing dissidents. Meanwhile, Yemeni president Saleh held on to power despite secessionist sentiment in the south that continued after the north's victory in a brief civil war in 1994.

Freedom House contrasted political developments in the Muslim world with changes in other regions in its 2001 annual report. Despite "significant gains for democracy and freedom" in Latin America, Africa, Eastern and Central Europe and South and East Asia, the report stated, the Muslim world "experienced a significant increase in repression."[24]

A year later, a group of Arab intellectuals convened by a United Nations agency cited what they called the Arab world's "freedom deficit" as a major factor in the region's lagging social and economic indicators.[25] The 180-page report, sponsored by the U.N. Development Programme's regional bureau for Arab states, concluded that despite supposed acceptance of democracy and human rights in constitutions and legal codes, representative democracy was "not always genuine and sometimes absent."

Freedoms of expression and association were "frequently curtailed," the report continued, and political participation was "less advanced" than in other developing regions. The report tied political conditions to "deep and complex economic and social problems," including "high illiteracy rates," "rampant poverty" and "mounting unemployment rates." But it closed on the hopeful note that the problems could be eased with political reforms.

Warming Trends?

The Arab world felt stirrings of political change during the early years of the 21st century, but only in 2011 did popular discontent succeed in toppling regimes. Political developments unfolded against the backdrop of increased global attention on the Muslim world as the United States waged war first against the anti-American Islamist terrorist group al Qaeda in Afghanistan and then against Saddam Hussein in Iraq. Sectarian politics complicated democratization in Iraq and figured in unfolding events elsewhere, including Syria. The ouster of leaders in Tunisia, Egypt and Libya in 2011 encouraged democratization advocates, but Syria's civil war defied resolution, and only limited reforms were instituted elsewhere.

Midway through the century's first decade, Freedom House in 2006 reported a "positive regional trajectory" for political and civil rights in the Middle East and North Africa. Among the gains cited was Lebanon's popular "Cedar Revolution," which set the stage for free elections after forcing the withdrawal of Syria's occupying troops.

The report also noted competitive elections in Egypt, Iraq and Palestine. The gains were easy to exaggerate, however. In Egypt, Mubarak won his first competitive presidential election in September 2005 with 89 percent of the vote, and the ruling National Democratic Party still commanded a two-thirds majority in parliament after December balloting despite 87 seats won by Muslim Brotherhood candidates running as independents. Parliamentary elections in Iraq the same month resulted in a fragile coalition government still riven by sectarian disputes. And in balloting a month later, the hard-line organization Hamas won a majority in the Palestinian parliament.

Five years later, the Arab street wrought more significant changes, starting in Tunisia.[26] The uprising — dubbed the Jasmine Revolution in the West but not in Tunisia itself — began with the Dec. 17, 2010, self-immolation of unlicensed street vendor Mohamed Bouazizi to protest his alleged mistreatment by police. Protests driven by unemployment and inflation as well as political repression spread through the country quickly and picked up more steam after Bouazizi's death on Jan. 4. With a nationwide strike called and the military backing the revolution, Ben Ali fled on Jan. 14 for exile in Saudi Arabia. After false starts, a transitional government with no holdovers from Ben Ali's regime scheduled elections in October. The once-banned Islamist party Ennahda won a 41 percent plurality of the vote, but the party's leader, the once exiled Rachid Gannouchi, pledged to support democracy and human rights. Meanwhile, Ben Ali was convicted in absentia in June of embezzlement and sentenced along with his wife to 35 years' imprisonment; the next summer, a military court convicted him, again in absentia, of his role in the deaths of protesters and sentenced him to life in prison. Saudi Arabia has refused to extradite him.

Events in Egypt proceeded even more rapidly than in Tunisia, especially after "Day of Revolt" protests in Cairo and several other cities on Jan. 25, 2011. Six days later, hundreds of thousands massed in Cairo's Tahrir Square — al Jazeera estimated the crowd at 2 million — to protest Mubarak's continued rule. Mubarak tried to quiet the unrest the next day by promising reforms and pledging not to seek re-election in September, but the protests continued with military leaders significantly pledging neutrality.

Mubarak tried again on Feb. 10 by delegating powers to his vice president, but the next day — prodded by a phone call from U.S. President Obama — Mubarak formally resigned. In parliamentary elections held between November 2011 and January 2012, the Muslim Brotherhood's Freedom and Justice Party won 47 percent of the seats; Morsi's election as president in June made him the first Islamist elected leader of an Arab state. Meanwhile, Mubarak had been convicted in June of failing to stop the killing of protesters and sentenced to life imprisonment.

The ouster of Gadhafi in the Libyan civil war took longer and required outside military assistance. Gadhafi's intelligence chief responded to information about a planned anti-government demonstration in February 2011 by arresting one of the leaders, Fathi Tarbel. Despite Tarbel's release shortly afterwards, the Feb. 15 arrest ignited protests that spread from the eastern city of Benghazi through much of the country. Gadhafi responded with brute force, calling in foreign mercenaries to aid his own troops and air force. In March, the U.N. Security Council authorized a no-fly zone to protect civilians; NATO set up the protective zone with U.S. help. Gadhafi's fate was sealed when rebels took over the capital city of Tripoli in late August; the fallen dictator was found on Oct. 20 hiding in a culvert west of the central coastal city of Sirte and killed on the spot. The liberal National Front Alliance won 48 percent of the seats in parliamentary elections in July 2012, with the Islamic Justice and Construction Party a distant second with 10 percent of the seats.

The uprising in Syria grew from protests over the March 2011 arrest of graffiti-writing school boys in Daraa into full-fledged civil war. Assad responded on March 30 with promises of political reform and some economic concessions, but then with force as the unrest continued. By summer, the death toll had exceeded 1,000. Military defectors formed the Syrian Free Army in July; the next month, opponents established the National Council of Syria, which demands Assad's resignation and democratic elections. The fighting continued even as former U.N. Secretary-General Kofi Annan attempted mediation; he abandoned the effort by August 2012 in the face of mounting casualties and a flood of refugees. With high-level defections from the regime, more and more observers concluded that Assad's days were numbered, but he defied opponents by pledging on Jan. 6 to stay in office.

Protests in the two lesser conflict zones —Yemen and Bahrain — achieved no substantial change. In Yemen,

AFP/Getty Images/Khaled Desouki

AP Photo/SANA

On the Hot Seat

Egyptian President Mohammed Morsi (top) has been criticized by Freedom House for his dismissal of the lower house of parliament in June and his claim of broad executive powers in November. The democracy advocacy group warns that the survival of democracy in the Arab world's most populous nation "remains very much an open question." President Bashar Assad of Syria (bottom) blames the country's ongoing civil war on criminals, terrorists and foreign influences. Assad, whose strongman father ruled Syria for nearly 30 years before his succession in June 2000, responded to the popular uprisings in 2011 "by waging war against his own people," says Freedom House.

Saleh replied to protests beginning in January 2011 with a pledge not to seek re-election in 2013. With the protests continuing, Saleh was injured in a rocket attack in June and flown to Saudi Arabia for treatment. He returned in September and two months later handed over power to his deputy, Abed Rabbo Mansour Hadi, who won an uncontested presidential election in February 2012. In Bahrain, the government responded quickly to protests that began in the capital city of Manama in February 2011 by calling in help from Saudi troops the next month. The government clamped down by destroying the Pearl Monument, the focal point of the demonstrations; banning political parties; and arresting and prosecuting leading dissidents. New protests in October 2012 prompted an indefinite ban on all political gatherings.

CURRENT SITUATION

Transition Troubles

Egypt's Muslim Brotherhood-dominated government is working to consolidate power while grappling with economic difficulties and continuing opposition from liberal and secularist groups, many of whom protested in Cairo and elsewhere on Jan. 25 to mark the second anniversary of the beginning of the Egyptian revolution.[27]

Tens of thousands joined the opposition-organized protests in Cairo's Tahrir Square, Alexandria and Suez on Jan. 25, two years to the day after the first of the 2011 protests that culminated in Mubarak's resignation. Protesters complain that the new government, led by Morsi and dominated by the Muslim Brotherhood-founded Freedom and Justice Party, has betrayed the revolution's democratic aspirations and failed to reverse an economic slide blamed largely on declining foreign investment and tourism.

To avoid confrontations with the opposition, Islamist parties — which have prevailed so far in six elections for president, parliament and a new constitution — marked the anniversary in public gatherings elsewhere. Protesters clashed with police, however, resulting in more than 200 injuries to demonstrators or security forces. More than 40 deaths were reported in Suez.[28]

The disorder widened over the weekend of Jan. 26-27 after a court in Port Said sentenced 21 local soccer fans to death for their role in a brawl at a match between Port Said and Cairo teams on Feb. 1, 2012, that resulted in 74 deaths. Protests over the verdicts in several cities led Morsi to impose martial law. By Jan. 28, more than 50

people had been killed in demonstrations that fused anger over the verdicts with disapproval of Morsi's leadership.

"The government is trying to assure everybody that we are on the right track," says Bahgat, the Egyptian-born professor at National Defense University in Washington. "On the other side, the opposition and a good number of people are not happy."

Despite the protests, the Islamist parties have the advantages of better organization and greater unity than the opposition groups in the run-up to elections in April for the lower house of parliament. The opposition groups reportedly are divided over previously announced plans to run as a single ticket in April.[29]

The governing Freedom and Justice Party has officially designated itself as a "civil" party to counteract Christian and secularist fears that it intends to establish a theocracy. But the constitution that Morsi pushed toward voter approval in December reaffirms Islam as the state religion. Other Islamist parties now form the Islamist Alliance, which differs with the Freedom and Justice Party in taking a stricter approach on some issues of Islamic law and a harder line toward Israel.

Opposition groups formed the umbrella National Salvation Front in December in an unsuccessful effort to reject the proposed constitution. The groups range from the Wafd Party, successor to an elite-dominated party banned by Nasser in the 1950s, to the April 6 Youth Movement, the social media-based grouping that figured prominently in the January 25 Revolution.

Apart from election-related maneuverings, Morsi is working to put his stamp on the machinery of government even as his government faces two high-profile challenges: negotiations with the International Monetary Fund (IMF) over a $4.8 billion loan and the court-ordered retrial of Mubarak for failing to prevent bloodshed during the 2011 uprising.

The IMF loan is needed to offset the loss of foreign currency from investment and tourism and the resulting sharp decline in the value of the Egyptian pound. To approve the loan, the IMF is likely to require politically difficult reductions in subsidies for food and fuel. Bahgat expects an eventual agreement. "The IMF recognizes that Egypt is too big to fail," he says.

Meanwhile, Mubarak, 84 and in ill health, remains in a military hospital after his arrest and his conviction and life sentence in June 2012 for failing to stop the killings of protesters. An Egyptian appeals court reversed the conviction

AT ISSUE

Should the U.S. and its allies intervene militarily in Syria?

YES   Andrew Tabler

Senior Fellow, Program on Arab Politics, Washington Institute for Near East Policy; Author, In the Lion's Den: An Eyewitness Account of Washington's Battle with Syria

Written for *CQ Global Researcher*, February 2013

"You break it, you buy it" may have proven true for the United States in Iraq, but great powers are often forced to help clean up conflicts they did not cause but that threaten their interests. If Washington continues its "light footprint" policy of non-intervention in Syria, the American people will likely have to foot the bill for a more expensive cleanup of the spillover of the Syria conflict into neighboring states and the overall battle against international terrorism.

Every indicator of the conflict between the Alawite-dominated Assad regime and the largely Sunni opposition has taken a dramatic turn for the worse, with upwards of 65,000 killed, 30,000 missing and up to 3 million Syrians internally displaced during one of the worst Syrian winters in two decades. The Assad regime shows no sign of ending the slaughter anytime soon, increasingly deploying artillery, combat aircraft and most recently surface-to-surface missiles against the opposition. Reports quoting high-ranking U.S. government officials say the Assad regime has already loaded chemical weapons into bombs near or on regime airfields for possible deployment.

Signs are growing of a sectarian proxy war as well, with the Islamic Republic of Iran and Lebanese Hezbollah backing their fellow Shia at the Assad regime's core and Qatar, Saudi Arabia and Turkey backing their Sunni brethren in the opposition. Al Qaeda affiliates, as well as jihadists, are now among the opposition's best-armed factions.

The Obama administration has refrained from directly intervening or supporting Syria's increasingly armed opposition, based on an argument that neither would make the situation better. But allowing the conflict to continue and simply offering humanitarian and project assistance treats merely the symptoms while failing to shape a political settlement that would help cure the disease: a brutal Assad regime that was unable to reform trying to shoot one of the youngest populations in the Middle East into submission.

The Obama administration spent its first two years encouraging a treaty between the Assad regime and Israel that would take Damascus out of Iran's orbit and isolate its ally Hezbollah. While the method proved wrong, the strategic goals of containing Iranian influence in the region and keeping it from obtaining a nuclear weapon remain as valid as ever. Helping the Syrian opposition push Assad and his regime aside more quickly would help the United States and its allies achieve those objectives.

NO   Brian Fishman

Counterterrorism Research Fellow, New America Foundation

Written for *CQ Global Researcher*, February 2013

If we learn nothing else from more than a decade of war in Iraq and Afghanistan, it must be that high hopes and good intentions help begin wars but do not help end them. Limited war in Syria is a recipe for mission creep and another long-term U.S. commitment to war in the Middle East.

That is why proposals for increased American military intervention in Syria are unconvincing. Broad-based American military action could tip the scales against the dictatorial Syrian regime but would not resolve the deep political conflicts in Syria. And more constrained proposals for military intervention would be unlikely to resolve the conflict.

The United States has many laudable goals in Syria that could plausibly justify military force: undermining an Iranian ally, eliminating a dictator, safeguarding civilians. Indeed, the United States should never hesitate to use military force when it is necessary to protect U.S. interests, but it must use military force only when the killing and dying that it implies are likely to achieve American political goals. That is not the case in Syria.

Public discussions about Syria were hyper-optimistic after the outbreak of peaceful protests against Bashar al-Assad in early 2011. Bolstered by the successes of the Arab Spring, many hoped the protests would not turn violent; they did. Observers ignored the presence of jihadis in the insurgency for months after it became clear that groups linked to al Qaeda were a major force driving the fighting. Still, today the clear split between Arab and Kurdish elements of the rebel coalition is poorly reported in the American press. And many observers have underestimated the cohesion of the Syrian regime, even as the country collapsed around it.

The situation in Syria is undoubtedly terrible. Assad's regime limps on with backing from Iran, and al Qaeda has emerged as one of the most powerful militant networks in the country. But the idea that limited military action — a no-fly zone coupled with increased military aid to rebels — will resolve these challenges is more hyper-optimism from well-intentioned people. One example: The threat will increase that Syria's chemical weapons will be used or proliferate as the regime's hold on power weakens.

Limited military force will redefine but not end the civil war in Syria and it will commit the United States to "solving" Syria politically. During the 1990s in Iraq, no-fly zones failed to destroy Saddam Hussein's regime, and military action to depose him in 2003 heralded chaos that empowered al Qaeda and Iran. Advocates of force in Syria have not offered a plausible argument for why we would do better this time.

Shiite Muslims in Malikiya, Bahrain, demonstrate against the government and in support of political prisoners on Dec. 4, 2012. Government action against protesters in Bahrain has led to an estimated 50-100 deaths. Besides Syria, Bahrain provides the most dramatic example of what Freedom House labels the "intransigence" exhibited by many Arab nations toward popular uprisings.

and sentence on Jan. 13, sending the case back to a lower court for a new trial and possibly further investigation. Mubarak and his security chief, Habib el-Adly, whose conviction also was reversed, were the only security officials found guilty in trials stemming from the more than 800 deaths in the uprisings.

Post-revolutionary transitions in neighboring countries to Egypt's west are proceeding on significantly different paths, with generally successful democratization in Tunisia but violence- and abuse-riddled chaos in Libya.

Tunisia conducted "relatively free and fair elections" for the National Constituent Assembly in October 2011, according to Human Rights Watch, resulting in an interim coalition headed by the moderate Islamist party Ennahda in partnership with two secularist parties.[30] The government has now scheduled voting for parliament and direct election of president for June 23, with a runoff for the presidency if needed on July 7. A draft constitution, as revised by the Constituent Assembly in December, includes some favorable rights-protecting provisions but needs additional measures to safeguard the judiciary's independence, according to Human Rights Watch.

The country, accustomed to relative internal peace before the revolution, is experiencing sporadic violence

attributed to radical religious groups viewed as aligned with the government. The groups are trying to "impose their political and ideological model on society through a variety of means," Slahhedine Jourchi, an analyst of Islamist movements in Tunisia, told The Associated Press.[31]

Libya also held a relatively successful parliamentary election in July 2012, eight months after the end of the civil war, according to Freedom House's report, but violence by regional militias, Islamist groups and others delayed the balloting and remains a major problem. The leading party in the voting was the National Forces Alliance, a coalition headed by the relatively liberal politician Mahmoud Jibril, with 39 seats, followed by the Muslim Brotherhood's Justice and Construction Party with 17 seats. Plans and timeline for drafting a new constitution were uncertain as 2012 ended.[32]

In the most serious episode of violence, an armed assault on the U.S. consulate in Benghazi killed U.S. Ambassador Christopher Stevens and three other Americans. The attack became a major political issue in the United States as Republicans criticized the Obama administration for initially terming as spontaneous an attack that later intelligence indicated was planned by a branch of al Qaeda.

Meanwhile, Jordanians voted in higher-than-expected numbers in parliamentary elections on Jan. 23, despite calls for a boycott by a protest group that views the parliament as weak, unrepresentative and corrupt. Loyalists to King Abdullah II appear to dominate the new, 150-member body, but leftists and Islamists increased the number of seats won. Under reforms announced by Abdullah, the new parliament is to choose the prime minister, but the king still has the power to dismiss governments and dissolve parliament.[33]

Battle Fatigue

Syrians are continuing to suffer under a brutal civil war as rebels consolidate territorial gains, the government steps up attacks in civilian areas and neither side nears a decisive victory.

Human-rights groups say the Assad regime is countering rebel forces' gains on the ground by increasing what they call indiscriminate aerial assaults in civilian areas, including deliberate targeting of bakeries and bread lines and, in at least one instance, a hospital. Government forces also frequently detain humanitarian workers and human-rights monitors, according to Lama Fakih, a researcher with the U.S.-based Human Rights Watch who regularly crosses into Syria from her native Lebanon.[34]

Rebel forces have also been linked to such abuses as kidnapping, torture and extrajudicial executions as well as use of child soldiers and destruction of Christian and Shiite religious sites, Fakih says.[35] The government also has used "numerous torture techniques" on prisoners, she says. With its superior firepower and more extensive security apparatus, the government's abuses are far greater than those of the rebels, Fakih adds.

The civil war, now near the end of its second year, has created what Human Rights Watch calls "a dire humanitarian situation." More than 2 million Syrians have been displaced internally, and another 600,000 have registered as refugees in neighboring countries — chiefly Turkey and Jordan.

In conflict zones, "Syria does not resemble anything like normalcy," Fakih says. In opposition-controlled territory, entire villages may be emptied as residents seek safe havens. There is less disruption elsewhere, including in Damascus, according to Fakih. But throughout the country the mood is "one of fatigue," she says.

Neither side shows any interest, however, in the recurrent calls for a ceasefire, such as the most recent appeal by the Arab League's general secretary, Nabil El-Araby, at the league's Jan. 21 meeting in Riyadh, Saudi Arabia. Militarily, Fakih agrees with the many experts who say that neither side can achieve a decisive victory over the other for the foreseeable future.

Assad, out of public sight since his Jan. 6 speech in Damascus, is widely reported to be determined not to step aside. "I can win the war even if Damascus is destroyed," Assad is reported to have told U.N. and Arab League envoy Brahimi when they met in December.[36]

The anti-government forces remain far from unified, however. Meeting in Istanbul, Turkey, the Syrian National Coalition failed on Jan. 21 in its second attempt to agree on a transitional government. The 70-member coalition had been formed in Qatar in November with Gulf and Western backing. The coalition said in a statement that a five-person committee would try again to come forward with a proposal within 10 days, according to Reuters' account.[37]

The disunity among seemingly mainstream Sunni Muslims in the anti-government camp appears to be

benefiting Jabhat al-Nusra, the avowedly jihadist group designated by the United States as a terrorist offshoot of al Qaeda. Some Free Syrian Army commanders have been criticized for warlordism, according to news accounts, while al-Nusra forces have built up good will by helping to deliver food and supplies to opposition-controlled areas cut off by government forces.[38]

Among other countries in the region to confront popular pro-democracy unrest in the past two years, Bahrain appears to be taking the toughest line. After declaring martial law early in 2012, the Sunni-led government clamped down further on the Shiite opposition movement Oct. 30 by banning all protest gatherings.[39] In Washington, a State Department spokesman condemned the action. Two people were killed in bomb blasts in the capital of Manama the next week (Nov. 5). Protests have continued in the tiny Gulf kingdom. Security forces used tear gas and stun grenades in Manama on Jan. 18 to disperse protesters who numbered in the hundreds.

Other Gulf countries are also resisting political change. In Kuwait, police used tear gas and stun grenades on Jan. 6 to disperse a crowd estimated at 1,000 or more who had defied a ban on public demonstrations and continued protesting changes in voting laws. The United Arab Emirates has drawn fire from Egypt's Muslim Brotherhood-dominated government by arresting 11 Egyptian nationals accused of trying to form a Brotherhood cell despite the emirate's ban on political parties.

All of the Gulf countries have moved to limit political dissent, including on social media.[40] Human Rights Watch blasted a Qatari court for its decision on Dec. 4 to sentence poet Muhammad Ibn al-Dheeb al-Ajami to life imprisonment, apparently for poems criticizing the ruling family and one in January 2011 praising the Tunisian revolution. In July 2012 the group had urged Oman to drop cases against online activists for postings the government viewed as critical of the sultan.[41]

Meanwhile, al Qaeda continues to pose a threat to security in some countries in the region. The assassination of a deputy police chief in a city near the Yemeni capital of Sanaa on Jan. 16 marked the third slaying of a security official in Yemen since October. The killing was apparently in retaliation for the government's moves against al Qaeda. And in Algeria, the West Africa branch of al Qaeda seized a natural gas plant on Jan. 16 in retaliation for France's decision, with Algeria's support, to send troops to Mali to combat Islamists there. At least 29 militants were killed when Algerian troops retook the plant after a four-day siege; at least 38 of the plant's personnel were killed, including three Americans.

OUTLOOK

Unfinished Spring

"I t's not easy being Arab these days," the Lebanese journalist and historian Samir Kassir wrote in an evocative dissection of the Arab peoples and their political and cultural plight in 2004. He found "a deep sense of malaise" throughout the Arab world that he said would persist unless Arabs freed themselves from "a sense of powerlessness" in order to create an Arab "renaissance."[42]

Kassir lived long enough to see Syria end its occupation of his country during the earlier Arab Spring of 2005 but not long enough to enjoy his country's freedom from Syrian suzerainty. He was killed by a car bomb on June 2, 2005, a still unsolved assassination that was surely carried out by Syrian agents or Lebanese surrogates.

Some five-and-a-half years later, a Tunisian fruit peddler frustrated by the petty arbitrariness of a local police woman threw off his sense of powerlessness in a fashion so dramatic — he set himself on fire — as to inspire fellow Arabs throughout North Africa and the Middle East. This time, the Arab Spring toppled three dictators, helped ease a fourth out of office, shook strongman rulers in other countries and helped prompt modest reforms even in countries with only minimal agitation in the Arab street. In Saudi Arabia, King Abdullah granted women the right to vote and run in municipal elections in September 2011; he followed up on Jan. 11 by naming 30 women to serve on the advisory Shura Council for the first time in the kingdom's history.[43]

After two years, however, the Arab Spring must be seen as unfinished business, as Robert Malley, regional director for North Africa and the Middle East for the conflict-mediating International Crisis Group, put it in a presentation midway through the unrest's second year. Even in countries with changes of government — Tunisia, Egypt, Libya and Yemen — Malley saw "the same fights, the same unfinished, unconcluded fights, between military and civilian, between Islamist and secular, among Islamists, among tribes, between regions." Elsewhere, Malley saw

"uprisings that have not begun" and the likelihood of an "ever descending" civil war in Syria.[44]

Today, as the Arab unrest continues, experts agree that the course of future events remains uncertain. "We still don't know what the final political outcome of the Arab Spring will be," says Toby Jones, the Rutgers professor. Gelvin, at UCLA, agrees. "We shouldn't make predictions," he says. "Nobody foresaw any of this happening, and nobody saw the paths that these rebellions were going to take."

The United States has multiple and sometimes conflicting interests in the events, including continuing counterterrorism initiatives and maintaining oil supplies. "It's mixed for the United States," says Pressman, the University of Connecticut professor. Moves toward democracy undermine what he calls the "narrative" of U.S. adversaries, such as Iran and al Qaeda, but changes in leadership can be "unsettling" for relations. RAND expert Seth Jones notes that the United States inevitably has to work with both democratic and nondemocratic countries in the region.

Egypt looms as the most important test of the political openings in the Arab world, but two years after Mubarak's fall, many Egyptians are disappointed. "The expectations were very high," says the National Defense University's Bahgat. "Progress, if any, is very slow. This is why there is frustration."

Bahgat sees frustration in the West as well. The new constitution "falls short of what we in the West would like to see," he says.

Syria's civil war is widely expected to lead eventually to the fall of a fifth Arab dictator, Assad, but the path for a post-Assad Syria is hard to predict. "It's like looking into a crystal ball," says Tabler, the Washington Institute expert, "but it's increasingly cloudy." No one predicts an easy transition for a country riven by conflict with no experience in self-rule.

The chance of successful democratization in Syria is "very slight," says the University of Oklahoma's Landis.

For many experts, the Arab glass is not even close to half full. The Arab Spring has produced only "a slight increase" in democratization — "far short of a fourth wave," says Seth Jones, the RAND expert. "The vast majority of countries remain authoritarian."

From his Beirut watching post, however, Salem, the Carnegie expert, sees more reason for democracy advocates to cheer. "If you look at the arc of history," Salem says, "in 24 months we've seen an amazing leap forward in the Arab world in the direction of democratization."

NOTES

1. For coverage, see Anne Barnard, "Syria President's Defiant Words Are Another Roadblock to Peace," *The New York Times*, Jan.7, 2013, p. A1; Liz Sly, "In Syria, a Defiant Speech by Assad," *The Washington Post*, Jan. 7, 2013, p. A1. For the full text, see "President al-Assad: Out of Womb of Pain, Hope Should Be Begotten, From Suffering Important Solutions Rise," SANA (Syrian Arab News Agency), Jan. 6, 2013, http://sana-syria.com/eng/21/2013/01/06/460536.htm. Assad had not spoken in public since June 3, 2012. See Neil MacFarquhar, "Assad Denies Government Role in Massacre, Blaming Terrorism," *The New York Times*, June 4, 2012, p. A4.

2. For background, see Roland Flamini, "Turmoil in the Arab World," *CQ Global Researcher*, May 3, 2011, pp. 209-236.

3. See Megan Price, Jeff Klingner, and Patrick Ball, "Preliminary Statistical Analysis of Documentation of Killings in the Syrian Arab Republic," 2 January 2013, www.un.org/apps/news/story.asp?NewsID=43866. The analysis was commissioned by the United Nations Office of the High Commissioner for Human Rights. For coverage, see Ben Hubbard and Frank Jordans, "UN says more than 60,000 dead in Syrian civil war," The Associated Press, Jan. 2, 2013, http://bigstory.ap.org/article/syrian-rebels-attack-air-base-north. Brahimi spoke in a news conference at the headquarters of the Arab League in Cairo, Egypt. For coverage, see Kareem Fahim and Hwaida Saad, "Envoy to Syria Warns of Slide to Hellish Fiefs With Huge Toll," *The New York Times*, Dec. 31, 2012, p. A9, www.aina.org/news/20121231004313.htm; Carol Morello, "Surge in Syrian death toll predicted," *The Washington Post*, Dec. 31, 2012, p. A7.

4. James L. Gelvin, *The Arab Uprisings: What Everyone Needs to Know* (2012).

5. "Freedom in the World 2013: Democratic Breakthroughs in the Balance," Freedom House, Jan. 16, 2013, www.freedomhouse.org/sites/default/files/FIW%202013%20Booklet.pdf.

6. For background, see these *CQ Global Researcher* reports: Brian Beary, "The Troubled Balkans," Aug. 21, 2012, pp. 377-400; Brian Beary, "Emerging Central Asia," Jan. 17, 2012, pp. 29-56; and Roland Flamini, "The New Latin America," March 2008, pp. 57-84, 29-56. See also these *CQ Researcher* reports by Kenneth Jost: "Russia and the Former Soviet Republics," June 17, 2005, pp. 541-564; "Democracy in Latin America," Nov. 3, 2000, pp. 881-904; "Democracy in Eastern Europe," Oct. 8, 1999; pp. 865-888; and "Democracy in Asia," July 24, 1998, pp. 625-648.

7. See Mark L. Haas and David W. Lesch (eds.), *The Arab Spring: Change and Resistance in the Middle East* (2012), pp. 3-4. For previous coverage, see Flamini, "Turmoil," *op. cit.*, pp. 209-236; Kenneth Jost and Benton Ives-Halperin, "Democracy in the Arab World," *CQ Researcher*, Jan. 30, 2004, pp. 73-100.

8. For background, see Leda Hartman, "Islamic Sectarianism," *CQ Global Researcher*, Aug. 7, 2012, pp. 353-376.

9. See Nicholas D. Kristof, "When Bahrain Said: Get Lost," *The New York Times*, Dec. 23, 2012, p. A11, www.nytimes.com/2012/12/23/opinion/sunday/kristof-when-bahrain-said-get-lost.html.

10. Reem Khalifa, "Bahrain court upholds life sentences on opposition," The Associated Press, Jan. 7, 2013, http://bigstory.ap.org/article/bahrain-court-upholds-life-sentences-opposition; Kareen Fahim, "Court in Bahrain Confirms Jail Terms for 13 Dissidents," Jan. 8, 2013, p. A4. Seven of the dissidents were tried in absentia.

11. See Laurel E. Miller, *et al.*, *Democratization in the Arab World: Prospects and Lessons From Around the Globe* (2012), pp. 35-53, www.rand.org/content/dam/rand/pubs/monographs/2012/RAND_MG1192.pdf.

12. *Ibid.*, p. 325.

13. Quoted in Maggie Fick, "AP interview: Egypt atheist blasts Islamist regime," The Associated Press, Dec. 19, 2012, http://news.yahoo.com/ap-interview-egypt-atheist-blasts-islamist-regime-173344116.html. Other background drawn from article.

14. Quoted in David D. Kirkpatrick, "Cairo Court Sentences Man to 3 Years for Insulting Religion," *The New York Times on the Web*, Dec. 12, 2012, www.nytimes.com/2012/12/13/world/middleeast/cairo-court-orders-3-year-term-for-insulting-religion.html.

15. Lesch and Haas, *op. cit.*, pp. 5-6.

16. See Babak Dehghanpisheh, "Syrian rebels, led by Islamists, capture key military air base," *The Washington Post*, Jan. 12, 2013, p. A7, http://articles.washingtonpost.com/2013-01-11/world/36272269_1_base-in-idlib-province-air-base-taftanaz-airport; Anne Barnard, "Syrian Rebels Say They Seized Helicopter Base in North," *The New York Times*, p. A5, www.nytimes.com/2012/11/26/world/middleeast/syrian-rebels-said-to-have-seized-military-airport.html?gwh=2F79954EB2025D2A5374630DBD41370E.

17. See David W. Lesch, "The Uprising That Wasn't Supposed to Happen: Syria and the Arab Spring," in Haas and Lesch (eds.), *op. cit.*, pp. 79-96; Gelvin, *op. cit.*, pp. 100-118.

18. David W. Lesch, *The New Lion of Damascus: Bashar al-Assad and the Modern Syria* (2005).

19. Syria Comment, http://joshualandis.com. In an unscientific poll on the blog, 39 percent of respondents predict Assad will have lost Damascus by June 1, 61 percent disagree.

20. Harling quoted in Anne Barnard, "Rebels Find Hearts and Minds Elusive," *The New York Times*, Jan. 16, 2013, p. A4. See also David Ignatius, "Anarchy in Syria," *The Washington Post*, Jan. 13, 2013, p. A21.

21. Background on the six nations most affected by the recent unrest in the Arab world (Bahrain, Egypt, Libya, Syria, Tunisia and Yemen) drawn in part from individual chapters in Lin Noueihed and Alex Warren, *The Battle for the Arab Spring: Revolution, Counter-Revolution and the Making of a New Era* (2012). See also Gelvin, *op. cit.*; Haas and Lesch (eds.), *op. cit.*

22. Raymond D. Gastil, *Freedom in the World 1980: Political Rights and Civil Liberties* (1980), p. 26, http://books.google.com/books?id=LIvHFydpgBg

C&printsec=frontcover&source=gbs_ge_summary_r&cad=0#v=onepage&q&f=false.

23. Adrian Karatnycky (ed.), *Freedom in the World 2000-2001*, www.freedomhouse.org/article/new-study-details-islamic-worlds-democracy-deficit. For coverage, see Verena Dobnik, "Annual study shows freedom gap between Islamic countries and rest of world," The Associated Press, Dec. 18, 2001.

24. Quoted in Dobnik, *op. cit.*

25. "Arab Human Development Report 2002: Creating Opportunities for Future Generations," United Nations Development Programme/Arab Fund for Social and Economic Development, www.arab-hdr.org/publications/other/ahdr/ahdr2002e.pdf. For coverage, see Barbara Crossette, "Study Warns of Stagnation in Arab Societies," *The New York Times*, July 2, 2002, p. A11; Karen DeYoung, "Arab Report Cites Development Obstacles," *The Washington Post*, July 2, 2002, p. A10.

26. For timelines in the following summaries, see www.washingtonpost.com/wp-srv/special/world/egypt-protest-timeline/index.html. See also individual chapters in Noueihed and Warren, *op. cit.*

27. For a well-organized, updated guide to events and issues in Egypt, see Carnegie Endowment for International Peace, "Guide to Egypt's Transition, http://egyptelections.carnegieendowment.org/. Background on political parties drawn from this source.

28. See David D. Kirkpatrick, "Deadly Riots Erupt on Anniversary of Egypt Revolt," *The New York Times*, Jan. 26, 2013, p. A1, www.nytimes.com/2013/01/26/world/middleeast/tens-of-thousands-fill-tahrir-square-on-anniversary-of-egyptian-revolt.html.

29. See Abigail Hauslohner, "Egypt's anti-Islamists lack cohesion," *The Washington Post*, Jan. 22, 2013, p. A4, http://articles.washingtonpost.com/2013-01-21/world/36472981_1_islamists-parliamentary-elections-liberal-al-wafd-party.

30. "Human Rights Watch: Tunisia," www.hrw.org/middle-eastn-africa/tunisia (visited Jan. 25, 2013). See also Tarek Amara, "Tunisia's ruling coalition agrees to hold elections next June," Reuters, Oct. 14, 2012, www.itv.com/news/update/2012-10-14/tunisias-ruling-coalition-agrees-to-hold-elections-next-june/.

31. Bouazza Ben Bouazza and Paul Schemm, "Violence plagues Tunisia's politics 2 years later," The Associated Press, Jan. 14, 2013, http://bigstory.ap.org/article/violence-plagues-tunisias-politics-2-years-later.

32. "Libya," www.freedomhouse.org/report/freedom-world/2013/libya. See also "Human Rights in Libya," Human Rights Watch, www.hrw.org/middle-eastn-africa/libya.

33. See two articles by Kareem Fahim in *The New York Times*: "Loyalist to Dominate Jordan's New Parliament," Jan. 25, 2013, p. A11; "Despite Boycott, More Than Half of Voters Are Said to Turn Out in Jordan Election," Jan. 24, 2013, p. A6; and Taylor Luck, "Jordanian officials claim vote turnout as a victory," *The Washington Post*, Jan. 24, 2013, p. A6.

34. For ongoing coverage, see these sites: Human Rights Watch, www.hrw.org/middle-eastn-africa/syria; Syrian Observatory for Human Rights, http://syriahr.com/en/.

35. For background, see John Felton, "Child Soldiers," *CQ Global Researcher*, July 2008, pp. 183-211.

36. "Assad will stay in power 'even if Damascus is destroyed,'" *Middle East Monitor*, Jan. 23, 2013, www.middleeastmonitor.com/news/middle-east/5060-assad-says-he-will-stay-in-power-qeven-if-damascus-is-destroyedq.

37. See "Syrian opposition fails to form transitional government," Reuters, Jan. 21, 2013, www.reuters.com/article/2013/01/21/us-syria-crisis-opposition-idUSBRE90J0EW20130121.

38. See, e.g., Kelly McEvers, "Jihadi Fighters Win Hearts and Mind by Easing Bread Crisis," NPR, Jan. 16, 2013, www.npr.org/blogs/thesalt/2013/01/18/169516308/as-syrian-rebels-reopen-bakeries-bread-crisis-starts-to-ease.

39. See Reem Khalifa, "Bahrain bans all protest gatherings amid violence," The Associated Press, Oct. 30, 2012, http://bigstory.ap.org/article/bahrain-bans-all-protest-gatherings-amid-violence; and subsequent AP dispatches.

40. See Brian Murphy, "Gulf rulers take sharper aim at Web dissent," The Associated Press, Jan. 9, 2013, http://bigstory.ap.org/article/gulf-rulers-take-sharper-aim-web-dissent. For background, see

41. Jennifer Koons, "Future of the Gulf States," *CQ Global Researcher*, Nov. 1, 2011, pp. 525-548.

41. www.hrw.org/news/2012/12/04/qatar-poet-s-conviction-violates-free-expression; www.hrw.org/news/2012/07/21/oman-drop-cases-against-online-activists.

42. Samir Kassir, *Being Arab* (English translation, 2004), published same year in French as *Considerations sur le malheur arabe*. The opening sentence, quoted in text, uses the French word facile (easy); the translator substituted the English word "pleasant."

43. See Rashid Abul-Samh, "Saudi women on Shura Council," *Al-Ahram Weekly*, Jan. 16, 2013; Neil MacFarquhar, "Saudi Monarch Grants Women Right to Vote," *The New York Times*, Sept. 26, 2011, p. A1. For background, see Sarah Glazer, "Women's Rights," *CQ Global Researcher*, April 3, 2012, pp. 153-180.

44. "The Arab Spring: Unfinished Business," Carnegie Council on International Ethics, June 27, 2012, www.carnegiecouncil.org/studio/multimedia/20120627/index.html.

BIBLIOGRAPHY

Selected Sources
Books

Ajami, Fouad, *The Syrian Rebellion*, **Hoover Institution Press, 2012.**
A senior fellow at the Hoover Institution traces Syria's history from the rise of the Assad family through the current civil war. Includes source notes.

Cook, Steven A., *The Struggle for Egypt: From Nasser to Tahrir Square*, **Council on Foreign Relations/Oxford University Press, 2011.**
A senior fellow at the Council on Foreign Relations chronicles modern Egypt's major historical episodes, from the decline of British rule and Nasser's rise as a pan-Arab leader to the Sadat and Mubarak eras and the demonstrations at Tahrir Square that overthrew an entrenched regime. Includes detailed notes, 40-page bibliography.

Gelvin, James L., *The Arab Uprising:* **What Everyone Needs to Know, Oxford University Press, 2012.**

A professor of Middle East history uses a convenient question-and-answer format to explain the origins of and prospects for the current uprisings in Arab countries. Includes source notes, further readings, websites. Gelvin is also author of *The Modern Middle East: A History* (3d. ed., Oxford University Press, 2011).

Haas, Mark L., and David W. Lesch (eds.), *The Arab Spring: Change and Resistance in the Middle East*, Westview Press, 2012.

A collection of 12 essays explores the course of events in major countries affected or unaffected by the Arab uprisings and the regional and international implications of the events. Haas is an associate professor of political science at Duquesne University, Lesch a professor of Middle East history at Trinity University in Texas.

Lesch, David W., *Syria: The Fall of the House of Assad*, Yale University Press, 2012.

A professor of Middle East history at Trinity University in Texas details the gradual shift in the popular view of President Bashar Assad from hopeful reformer at the start of his tenure to repressive tyrant. Includes detailed notes.

Miller, Laurel E., *et al.*, *Democratization in the Arab World: Prospects and Lessons from Around the Globe*, RAND Corp., 2012.

Researchers from RAND Corp., a global policy think tank, compare the most recent uprisings in the Arab world with past revolutions in Europe and the Americas. Includes notes, detailed list of references.

Noueihed, Lin, and Alex Warren, *The Battle for the Arab Spring: Revolution, Counter-Revolution and the Making of a New Era*, Yale University Press, 2012.

The book explores the origins of the current Arab uprisings; the course of events in Tunisia, Egypt, Libya, Bahrain, Yemen and Syria; and the likely nature of future Arab politics. Includes detailed notes, brief bibliography and source list. Noueihed is a Reuters editor

based in London; Warren is a director of Frontier, a Middle East and North Africa consultancy, also based in London.

Osman, Tarek, *Egypt on the Brink: From Nasser to Mubarak*, Yale University Press, 2011.

An analysis of the past five decades of Egyptian politics explains the growth of Arab nationalism in the country amid deep religious and economic divisions in the Egyptian population. Osman, whose work has appeared in numerous international news outlets, attended American University in Cairo and Bocconi University in Italy.

Articles

Berman, Sheri, "The Promise of the Arab Spring," *Foreign Affairs*, 2013, www.foreignaffairs.com/print/135730.

An associate professor of political science at Columbia University's Barnard College compares Western countries' past responses to transitioning from autocracy to democracy to the current problems faced by Arab countries with authoritarian regimes.

Jones, Seth, "The Mirage of the Arab Spring," *Foreign Affairs*, 2013, www.foreignaffairs.com/print/135731.

A senior political scientist at the RAND Corp. warns that it remains difficult for Arab countries overthrowing unpopular governments to establish political stability and therefore should not be burdened by Western pressure to form democracies.

Reports and Studies

"Freedom in the World 2013," Freedom House, Jan. 16, 2013, www.freedomhouse.org/event/upcoming-event-freedom-world-2013-launch.

This annual report by a non-government organization that advocates for democracy, political freedom and human rights ranks the status of political freedom in countries in the Middle East and North Africa.

For More Information

Carnegie Endowment for International Peace, 1779 Massachusetts Ave., N.W., Washington, DC 20036; 202-483-7600; www.ceip.org. Foreign-policy think tank promoting active international engagement by the United States and increased cooperation among nations.

Council on Foreign Relations, 58 E. 68th St., New York, NY 10065; 212-434-9400; www.cfr.org. Nonprofit think tank specializing in U.S. foreign policy and international affairs.

Freedom House, 1301 Connecticut Ave., N.W., Suite 400, Washington, DC 20036; 202-296-5101; www.freedom house.org. Publishes annual report on the status of freedom, political rights and civil liberties worldwide.

Human Rights Watch, 350 Fifth Ave., 34th Floor, New York, NY 10118; 212-290-4700; www.hrw.org. Conducts research and advocates for human rights in the Middle East and other regions.

International Crisis Group, 149 Avenue Louise, Level 24, B-1050 Brussels, Belgium; +32-2-502-90-38; www.crisis group.org. Non-governmental organization committed to preventing and resolving conflict worldwide.

Middle East Institute, 1761 N St., N.W., Washington, DC 20036; 202-785-1141; www.mei.edu. Promotes a greater understanding of Middle East issues among the American public.

Project on Middle East Democracy, 1611 Connecticut Ave., N.W., Suite 300, Washington, DC 20009; 202-828-9660; www.pomed.org. Examines how democracies can develop in the Middle East and how the United States can best support the democratic process.

Washington Institute for Near East Policy, 1828 L St., N.W., Suite 1050, Washington, DC 20036; 202-452-0650; www.washingtoninstitute.org. Promotes policies that advance American interests in the Middle East.

16

Privatizing the Military

Marcia Clemmitt

Kristal Batalona, the daughter of an American security guard who was killed in Iraq, testifies on Feb. 7, 2007, before a congressional committee investigating the use of private military contractors. As the United States increasingly turns to so-called guns for hire, critics argue that private contractors are not fully accountable for human rights violations and that they allow the government to take military action without citizens' or lawmakers' consent.

From *The CQ Researcher*, July 13, 2012.

The surveillance operation might never have come to light if the small plane hadn't developed mechanical trouble over the Central African Republic in the summer of 2010. After an emergency landing, the American civilians aboard, along with two military observers from neighboring African countries, were detained by suspicious local officials.

"We felt like we were going to prison," one of the Americans told *The Washington Post*.[1]

As private security contractors working under contract to the Pentagon, the Americans had been hired to watch suspected terrorists. Using contractors, rather than military or CIA personnel, helps the Pentagon keep its expanding African counterterrorism campaign low-profile and provides the government with "deniability" if mishaps occur, explained Peter W. Singer, director of the 21st Century Defense Initiative at the Brookings Institution, a think tank in Washington.[2]

Indeed, when the detained Americans called the State Department and United Nations for help, both agencies — wanting to avoid being linked to the surveillance effort — declined to intervene. "Eventually," one of the contractors said, "we were able to talk our way out of it."[3]

The episode helps underscore the rapidly expanding role that private security contractors are playing for the Pentagon, CIA, State Department and other agencies in hot spots across the globe.

The government has increasingly turned to security companies over the past two decades to assist in armed and unarmed military

Most Contractors Are Non-U.S. Citizens

Most private contractors employed by the Pentagon in Afghanistan and Iraq in March 2011 were non-Americans. In Afghanistan, more than half were Afghan nationals, and more than one-fourth were citizens of other countries. In Iraq, 14 percent were Iraqis, and nearly 60 percent came from other countries.

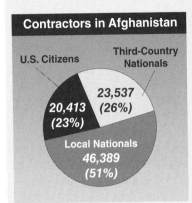

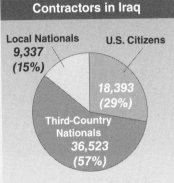

Percentages may not add to 100 because of rounding.

Source: Moshe Schwartz and Joyprada Swain, "Department of Defense Contractors in Afghanistan and Iraq: Background and Analysis," Congressional Research Service, May 13, 2011, pp. 10-11, www.fas.org/sgp/crs/natsec/R40764.pdf

such as surveillance, prisoner interrogation and intelligence gathering to help the military accurately target drones — plus jobs in which the contractors bear arms. In 2011, for example, 10,448 contractors working in Iraq — 16 percent of the total — provided armed security, including in armored vehicles and helicopters.[5]

The rise of armed contractors in the past decade has marked a new era in the long history of military privatization, according to an analysis by RAND, a think tank in Santa Monica, Calif., that studies military issues. While the military hired an increasing number of contractors during the 1990s, including as armed guards in conflict zones and disaster-relief situations, for example, there remained a long-held reluctance to send armed private citizens into actual war zones, RAND noted. Until the 2003 U.S.-led invasion of Iraq, such mercenaries had been rarely used in American history, it said.[6]

operations and help other government agencies working abroad. The trend, originally driven by military downsizing in the wake of the Soviet Union's collapse in the early 1990s, has accelerated sharply in recent years. The wars in Iraq and Afghanistan have fueled it, as has increased public acceptance of privatization as a way to increase quality and efficiency while reducing the number of jobs handled by government.

As of March 2011, approximately 155,000 Department of Defense (DOD) contractors were in Afghanistan and Iraq, comprising more than half of the DOD workforce in the two countries.[4]

The overwhelming majority of private American contractors around the world perform unarmed support duties, such as running food-service operations on military bases or constructing temporary buildings. "Most of the time they don't do sexy stuff," says Joanna Spear, an associate professor of international affairs at George Washington University. "Much of it's boring."

A growing number of contractors, however, over the past decade have taken on delicate, mission-critical jobs,

The State Department points out that, unlike troops, contractors are under orders to use force only in defense, never in attack mode, and to back off from armed clashes whenever possible. "We run. We go. We do not stand and fight," said Undersecretary for Management Patrick Kennedy, who oversees security for the U.S. Embassy in Baghdad.[7]

But many analysts say that an increasing number of contractor activities skate perilously close to duties that should be performed only by military personnel.

In Iraq and Afghanistan, for example, tens of thousands of armed contractors have defended sensitive military installations, yet they are not part of the tight military chain of command. "They don't get the same intelligence information," said Steven Schooner, a professor of government procurement at the George Washington University Law School. "So when things begin to develop quickly, there's an awful lot of people around with weapons" who will not receive the same commands and information as troops receive, he said.[8]

Most armed private contractors were formerly in the U.S. or another national military. That raises questions about how easily they will obey the far more restrictive rules of force that apply in their private-sector role, said Dov Zahkeim, who worked in the Defense Department under President Ronald Reagan and as a foreign policy adviser to President George W. Bush. "If you're coming under fire and you happen to have a gun in your hand, you're a former military person — are you really going to cut and run?"[9]

Military personnel pledge to uphold the public trust, support the national military mission and respect international law. But military contractors are not bound by that same pledge. Some analysts worry that the widespread use of contractors could erode the commitment of service members to adhere strictly to the military code. Laura Dickinson, a research professor of law at George Washington University, pointed, for example, to the 2004 scandal at U.S.-run Abu Ghraib prison near Baghdad, in which detainees had

Comparing Contractor and Troop Casualties

At least 2,300 private military contractors died and more than 50,000 were injured in the Iraq and Afghanistan wars from 2001 through March 2011. U.S. troop fatalities stood at nearly 6,000 for the same period. Because private companies are not required to report contractor deaths or injuries, some experts believe the number of contractor casualties is higher than those reflected here.

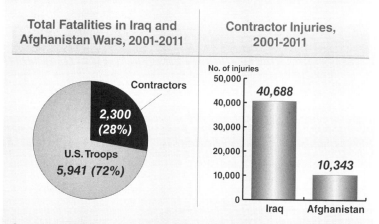

Total Fatalities in Iraq and Afghanistan Wars, 2001-2011

Contractors 2,300 (28%)
U.S. Troops 5,941 (72%)

Contractor Injuries, 2001-2011

No. of injuries
Iraq 40,688
Afghanistan 10,343

Source: Steven L. Schooner and Collin D. Swan, "Dead Contractors: The Un-Examined Effect of Surrogates on the Public's Casualty Sensitivity," Journal of National Security Law and Policy, *2011, p. 46,* www.wartimecontracting.gov/docs/forum2011-05-02_statement-Schooner.pdf

been severely abused by contractors and service members. The military's own internal report concluded that heavy reliance on contracting had watered down the culture of respect for law and order, contributing to "an environment of lawlessness that resulted in torture," Dickinson wrote.[10]

Contractors fall into a legal gray area that makes them more difficult to prosecute than military personnel for illegal or improper actions. For example, a contractor may be a citizen of one country, work in a second, be employed by a company based in a third and work under contract to the government of a fourth. No international rules stipulate where, how or even if a person in that situation can be tried for a crime, RAND analysts note.[11]

If service members are accused of a crime, they are generally apprehended and subject to court-martial. "But if a contractor shoots someone, he may be out of the country by nightfall," says T. X. Hammes, a retired Marine colonel who served in Iraq and now is a senior

research fellow at the Department of Defense's National Defense University in Washington.

Some prosecutions of contractors have gone forward, but progress is slow. In June, for example, the U.S. Supreme Court agreed with an appeals court that four former contractors should be subject to criminal charges in connection with the allegedly unprovoked shooting deaths of 17 Iraqi civilians in Nisour Square, near Baghdad, in 2007. The four were employed by Blackwater Worldwide, a major military contractor now known as Academi.[12]

Military contractors have many defenders, however. Fears that contractors may be more likely than military personnel to commit crimes and human-rights abuses are greatly overblown, wrote independent military-affairs analyst David Isenberg, author of *Shadow Force: Private Security Contractors in Iraq.* Violence is an integral part of war, and "even the worst of classical mercenaries from ancient times or the Middle Ages would have a hard time rivaling the record of human and physical destruction

Private Contractors vs. Military Personnel

Cost comparisons can be hard to calculate.

Do private contractors save taxpayers money? The answer is something of a toss-up. Some analysts argue that contractors' wages are so much higher than military wages for similar jobs that contracting does not save money and might actually be more expensive than using military personnel.

"In 2007, private security guards working for companies such as Blackwater and DynCorp were earning up to $1,222 a day," wrote Nobel Prize-winning economist Joseph Stiglitz, a professor at Columbia University, and Linda Bilmes, a Harvard University lecturer on budget and public administration. "By contrast, an Army sergeant was earning $140 to $190 a day in pay and benefits."[1]

Such comparisons are flawed, however, according to the nonpartisan Congressional Budget Office (CBO), which provides economic analysis to Congress. The $1,222 a day that Bilmes and Stiglitz cite as a salary is actually a salary plus additional money that goes not to the individual workers but to the company they work for, to cover costs such as overhead, the CBO said.[2]

Hiring a private contractor costs roughly the same as using a comparable military unit, the CBO found. And over the long run, using contractors might actually be cheaper because military units continue to cost the government money during peacetime, while contractors do not, the budget analysts said.[3]

Hiring private security companies to guard embassies in Iraq costs the State Department less in four out of five cases reviewed by the Government Accountability Office (GAO), Congress' nonpartisan auditing agency, than it would have cost to use State Department personnel. The cost difference stems mainly from the fact that State Department guards would serve in Iraq for only a year at a time before rotating to posts in the United States. That means the government would have to hire additional guards to cover the Iraq duties while simultaneously paying the State Department personnel for their stateside posts. By contrast, the government does not have to pay any individual contractors unless they're actually on the job.[4]

GAO said it was unable to come up with a similar cost comparison for Department of Defense (DOD) contractors because the DOD couldn't provide enough information about its own costs. DOD said it didn't have information readily available about the number and rank of military personnel that would be required to fulfill a security contractor's duties or about how much it would cost to train service members to do the jobs.[5]

The fact that private contractors are temporary employees whom the government does not have to retain or train achieved by regular military forces," he said. "Mercenaries did not invent concentration camps, firebomb cities from the air, use chemical or biological weapons or use nuclear weapons on civilian cities."[13]

Contractors can make it possible to carry out some valuable foreign missions that could not be done otherwise, wrote Anna Leander, a professor at Denmark's Copenhagen Business School who studies so-called "non-state actors" in world politics. For example, she said, private security contractors have been "used to break cycles of violence" in countries that experience devastating civil wars or potential ethnic genocides. In North Africa, contractors have assisted international organizations and human-rights groups trying to end a prolonged genocidal conflict in Sudan's Darfur region. When a country torn apart by such violence lacks strategic importance, a powerful nation such as the United States may not want to intervene with military force; however, it might hire contractors to do humanitarian work, avoiding the need for legislative approval or public support to deploy armed troops, she wrote.[14]

Since the end of the Cold War in the early 1990s, "a lot of what [the U.S. government] would like to see done in the world doesn't tie simply to a clear national interest," as it more clearly did when the United States faced off against the Soviet Union, says Deborah Avant, a professor of international security and diplomacy at the University of Denver. That makes contractors a valued option when the White House or Congress believes that an international mission is necessary but fears the public won't support armed intervention.

certainly makes them a lower-cost option, said Doug Brooks, president of the International Stability Operations Association, a security-contractor industry group. "As soon as the job's over, you stop paying them," he said. Yet the government continues to pay for service members even after they leave the military, providing education benefits through the GI Bill and veterans' health care, for example, he said.[6]

While some analysts say private contractors are cheaper than government or military personnel, however, others say they can wind up costing more. "Warfare is usually characterized by secrecy, heavy time constraints and the imperative of victory," so the government spends little effort on rigorous competitive bidding or cost oversight of contractors, wrote independent military analyst David Isenberg. Between 1998 and 2003, for example, only 40 percent of government contracts were awarded through competitive bidding, and that number has risen only marginally more recently, Isenberg said.

Furthermore, more than half of the contracts aren't monitored to assure that companies fulfill their contractual obligations, he said. "Thus, the market for private security services is only partially competitive," and in some cases it's a near monopoly — hardly the recipe for cost efficiency, Isenberg wrote.[7]

— *Marcia Clemmitt*

Military service members earn far less than many private security guards, according to scholars Joseph Stiglitz and Linda Bilmes.

[2]*Ibid.*

[3]*Ibid.*

[4]"Warfighter Support: A Cost Comparison of Using State Department Employees versus Contractors for Security Services in Iraq," Government Accountability Office, March 4, 2010, p. 5, www.gao.gov/assets/100/96571.pdf.

[5]*Ibid.*, p. 2.

[6]Quoted in "Private Warriors," PBS Frontline, www.pbs.org/wgbh/pages/frontline/shows/warriors/interviews/brooks.html.

[7]David Isenberg, "Private Military Contractors and U.S. Grand Strategy," International Peace Research Institute, 2009, p. 23, www.cato.org/pubs/articles/isenberg-private%20military-contractors-2009.pdf.

[1]Quoted in "Contractors' Support of U.S. Operations in Iraq," Congressional Budget Office, August 2008, p. 14, www.cbo.gov/sites/default/files/cbofiles/ftpdocs/96xx/doc9688/08-12-iraqcontractors.pdf.

"If people don't want to use private contractors, the choices are simple: Either scale back U.S. geopolitical commitments or enlarge the military, something that will entail more gargantuan expenditures and even, some argue, a return to the draft down the road," wrote Isenberg.[15]

As private contractors become a standard feature of military and other international operations, here are some of the questions being asked:

Does the United States over-rely on private contractors to conduct missions abroad?

When a group of retired military officers assessed the nature of future military operations back in 2007, they predicted an expanding role for private contractors.

"Whatever threats the Army next faces will be different from the last, but they are likely to be expeditionary" — carried out entirely in foreign countries —"and likely to involve high numbers of contractor personnel," the officers declared.[16]

So far, history has borne out their conclusion. Not only is the U.S. military hiring more and more contractors, but so too are civilian agencies active in foreign countries, including the State Department and the U.S. Agency for International Development (USAID).

Many analysts point out that contractors provide technical expertise that the military may lack and give government the flexibility to expand its forces on short notice. But others warn that the increased use of private contracting makes it easier for presidents to launch foreign missions without robust public discussion or congressional oversight.

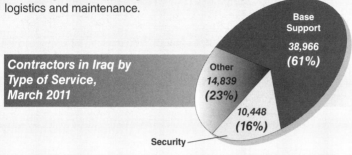

Iraq Contractors Used Mainly for Base Support

Contractors working in Iraq in March 2011 performed mainly base-support duties, such as ground maintenance, laundry operations and food services. Security duties were composed primarily of training police and other local security forces. Other functions included translating and interpreting, construction, transportation, logistics and maintenance.

Contractors in Iraq by Type of Service, March 2011

Base Support
38,966
(61%)

Other
14,839
(23%)

10,448
(16%)

Security

Source: Moshe Schwartz and Joyprada Swain, "Department of Defense Contractors in Afghanistan and Iraq: Background and Analysis," Congressional Research Service, May 13, 2011, www.fas.org/sgp/crs/natsec/R40764.pdf

Things that go wrong among armed troops can turn lawmakers and the public against a valuable international mission, says Spear of George Washington University. For example, if the military is training troops abroad and a foreign trainee shoots a trainer who is a U.S. service member, even accidentally, the event can destroy legislative support for the mission. But a similar shooting would cause little uproar if the trainer were a private contractor, she maintains.

Because governments often don't anticipate dangerous international situations, contractors give officials the "ability to quickly mobilize and deploy large numbers of personnel," wrote Hammes, the retired Marine colonel. Contractors also offer the possibility of more continuity of staff, since many are willing to stay in a conflict zone longer than the six- to 12-month rotation period that the Pentagon maintains for service members. What's more, private security companies often hire local people, potentially boosting the local economy and enhancing U.S. "nation-building" efforts in countries such as Iraq and Afghanistan, Hammes noted.[17]

Nevertheless, many analysts cite serious potential downsides to contracting. Some argue that contractors' higher salaries and more flexible working schedules not only damage the morale of lower-paid troops but also encourage service members to abandon the military in favor of a private-sector security job.*

"Private military contractors can be a morale deflator for our military guys," said a staff member in the Office of the Secretary of Defense. "They create disincentives for staying with the military."[18] (RAND analysts note, however, that, while many service members express this view, data don't show that hiring contractors has significantly harmed military retention.)[19]

By using contractors the government can avoid having to justify its foreign policy persuasively enough to make the case for recruiting troops from among the citizenry, says Avant of the University of Denver. As a result, "leaders can become less accountable to the populace. Everything that makes it easier to mobilize armed force means you can have a more aggressive foreign policy."

Accordingly, the use of contractors allows presidents to mislead the public about how serious a military commitment the government is making, says Hammes. Contractors aren't listed in government reports on the number of troops involved in a mission, he notes. In late 2011, for example, when President Obama announced a temporary "surge" of 30,000 troops to Afghanistan, a more accurate number — including contractors — was likely around 130,000, he says. "That might have changed the equation. People might have said, 'No.' So the fundamental question is, 'Is this good for democracy?' "

Contractors help governments escape international scrutiny as well, says Hammes. "There are rumors of a large contingent of Chinese contractors in Africa," for example, but because contractors are involved, the details are unknown. "If they'd moved an infantry division" to

---

* In 2005, some individual security contractors in Iraq earned $33,000 per month, compared to the $12,000 to $13,000 monthly salaries for Special Operations Forces. Private contractors also had much more liberal leave options, according to the Government Accountability Office.

Africa, the details would be much more likely to come out and there would be international debate, he says.

Many security companies and other contractors are founded and staffed by high-ranking military officers. That raises the question of how objective Pentagon decision-making involving contractors can be when former staff members submit bids for contracting jobs, and current members mull jobs they might take after retirement.

"Using a previous relationship as an entrée to selling something" creates at least the perception of conflict of interest, suggested William "Buck" Kernan, a retired four-star Army general who once worked for the large Alexandria, Va.-based contractor MPRI. Often, he said, a contractor is a "previous superior" to the contracting officers at the Pentagon to whom he or she is pitching services. That can raise "all kinds of questions" about the objectivity of contracting decisions, he said.[20]

Has using private contractors worked well in Iraq and Afghanistan?

Private contractors have played a large role in the Iraq and Afghanistan wars, doing jobs that would have been difficult without their help, such as keeping supply lines open through the Hindu Kush — the treacherous mountain range between central Afghanistan and northern Pakistan whose name translates to "Hindu killer." However, contractors also have perpetrated high-profile violence against local people that likely harmed U.S. interests — such as the abuse of prisoners at Abu Ghraib prison that came to light in 2004 and the 2007 shooting deaths of 17 Iraqi civilians in Nisour Square by State Department contractors.

In 2007 Gen. David Petraeus, then commanding general of the multinational forces in Iraq, defended the heavy use of armed contractors in Iraq and Afghanistan. Because they guarded bases and performed other routine jobs, he told Congress, service members were available to carry out military missions. "Tens of thousands of contract security forces . . . guard facilities . . . that our forces . . . would otherwise have to guard and secure," said Petraeus, who is now director of the Central Intelligence Agency (CIA).[21]

RAND, the California-based think tank, said it found little evidence that private contractors working for the U.S. government in Iraq had behaved in a reckless fashion. "It does not appear that a majority of either the military or State Department personnel perceive private security contractors to be 'running wild' in Iraq," as some critics charge, said RAND, basing its conclusions on a survey of about 1,000 service members and 1,700 State Department personnel.[22]

While contractors have participated in abuse of civilians, such as at Abu Ghraib, service members have been equally if not more culpable in many incidents, wrote military analyst Isenberg. At Abu Ghraib, for example, while contractors abused prisoners, most abuse was "carried out by regular military forces," he noted. Furthermore, one of the most serious human-rights breaches was the attempt to avoid oversight of activities at the prison, an action in which no contractors were involved, he said. It was government agencies such as the CIA that tried to hide prisoners' records, Isenberg said.[23]

Eleven service members were convicted of abuses at Abu Ghraib; no contractors were criminally charged. Federal courts are still determining whether a civil suit against contractors brought by former Abu Ghraib prisoners can proceed.[24]

Some service members and other government workers surveyed by RAND praised contractors they'd worked with.

"We hired Kroll" bodyguards, and the company did a good job of avoiding negative interactions with Iraqis, a USAID staffer said. "They were former [Special Air Service] guys" from the British army, and "overall they did a pretty good — an excellent job. . . . They learned how to keep a low profile" to help USAID maintain good relations with local people.[25]

New York City-based Kroll ended its bodyguard work in Iraq and Afghanistan in late 2006, after several employees were killed by suicide bombers.[26]

But while private companies may perform well on specific jobs, they are less likely than the military to behave in ways consistent with a larger U.S. mission, some analysts say. For example, contractors have not been as effective as military personnel at winning over the "hearts and minds" of local people in so-called counterinsurgency efforts in Iraq and Afghanistan, they say.[27]

In the RAND survey, 20 percent of service members who said they'd interacted with private contractors in Iraq said they had observed contractors behaving in a "threatening, arrogant or belligerent way" toward Iraqis.

Private guards for the Blackwater security firm (now Academi) take positions near the Iranian Embassy in Baghdad, Iraq, following a roadside-bomb attack in July 2005. In 2007, four Blackwater guards working for the State Department were charged with manslaughter in connection with the shooting of 17 Iraqi civilians in Baghdad's Nisour Square. In June 2012, the U.S. Supreme Court held that the former contractors should be subject to criminal charges for the deaths.

Fourteen percent said they'd observed armed contractors taking offensive action, even though private companies are banned from anything but the defensive use of force.[28]

About one-fifth of State Department officials reported having seen armed contractors "often" or "sometimes" mistreating Iraqi civilians, according to RAND analysts. In a mission heavily dependent on winning over Iraqi loyalty to the United States, the number of incidents "does not need to be very high for it to be significant," they said. Furthermore, about half the surveyed State Department officials who'd dealt with contractors told the analysts that they'd had to spend time managing disputes between Iraqis and contractors.[29]

In some instances, contractors have flouted international principles of how civilians should be treated, said Mary Picard, senior disaster law officer at the International Federation of Red Cross and Red Crescent Societies, in Geneva, Switzerland. Because local people generally don't distinguish between private-sector and public-sector American workers, such events make it "much more difficult for the military to maintain law and order and to be perceived as doing the right thing."[30]

Military missions require a high degree of coordination between commanders and commanded, but the spread of contracting makes such coordination tougher, some analysts say.

"I didn't even have authority to speak to the contractors" onsite to request changes in procedure, said Hammes, the retired Marine colonel, of his Iraq experience. "I had to call the [company's] home office" in the United States.

Technical barriers also inhibit coordination, said Ian Wing, an associate professor of policing at Charles Sturt University, in Australia, who served with the Coalition Forces' Combined Operations Intelligence Center in Iraq. Troops and contractors "don't have the same radios, they don't have the same procedures," he says. Furthermore, contractors "do what their contract requires, and they won't do anything else."[31]

Being able to rely on contractors makes it easier for governments to say "yes" to some military missions when they should not, and the Afghanistan invasion may be an example, says Hammes. "Foreign militaries have never succeeded in pushing supplies through the Hindu Kush," he says. The United States "has used local contractors to accomplish it. But when you're in a position to absolutely need contractors to do something, you should probably ask yourself, 'Is doing this a good idea?' "

Are nations doing enough to hold contractors accountable for fraud or abuse?

Over the past several years, the United States and other nations have stepped up their efforts to monitor the work of private contractors. (*See sidebar, p. 380.*) However, many analysts argue that both the capacity and the political will to significantly increase oversight may be lacking.

By the late 1990s, Congress recognized that the rapidly growing sector of private security businesses based in the United States but operating abroad fell into a legal gray area. No court — military or civilian — had clear jurisdiction to prosecute criminal activity.

In response, Congress enacted the Military Extraterritorial Jurisdiction Act in 2000 to place contractors working abroad with the military under the jurisdiction of federal criminal law for any offense punishable by more than one year in prison. In 2004, Congress expanded the law to include contractors working abroad with other U.S. agencies during periods of armed conflict.[32]

In 2007, the Uniform Code of Military Justice was amended to allow wider latitude to prosecute contractors in military courts. Previously, only contractors employed during wars declared by Congress could face court-martial, but the amended law includes contractors who work in so-called "contingency operations" — military activity undertaken without a formal congressional declaration of war, such as the wars in Iraq and Afghanistan.[33]

The government has made heroic efforts to pursue cases despite the high price of investigating and prosecuting incidents that happen abroad, says Gary D. Solis, a former Marine prosecutor who is an adjunct professor at Georgetown University Law Center and author of the 2010 book, *The Law of Armed Conflict.* For example, after the 2007 shooting deaths of Iraqi civilians by Blackwater (Academi) contractors at Nisour Square, the government spent millions of dollars to collect and preserve evidence, even "boxing up the vehicles [involved in the case] and shipping them to the United States."

Nevertheless, many analysts say it's still far too easy for contractors to avoid oversight and accountability.

The government's "whole regulatory infrastructure for contracting is sparse," says the University of Denver's Avant. Oversight offices don't have the resources, experience or authority to investigate potential problems before they worsen, she says.

Several years ago, the Pentagon outsourced some contractor oversight to a private company, and the move spurred charges that the company would inevitably have conflicts of interest that would interfere with its work. But the arrangement worked better than the Pentagon's internal oversight system, says Doug Brooks, president of the International Stability Operations Association, a membership group for contractors in the security and disaster-relief fields. The company's contract stipulated that it would take on only a manageable workload, whereas the military's own contract auditors are "often trying to deal with a workload 20 times the reasonable size," Brooks says.

Because "the military is hesitant to apply" its expanded authority under the Uniform Code of Military Justice, the amendment to the code has done little to increase contractor accountability, as evidenced by the fact that hardly any cases have been brought, Solis says. The Pentagon is hesitant to pursue cases under the code for fear that the Supreme Court will strike down the

law's expansion, he says. In the 1950s and '60s, the court declared that the military did not have authority to court-martial civilians.

When it comes to Americans charged with crimes abroad, "the United States has always said, 'We will prosecute our own,' partly to assure people a fair trial. But now we seem to have gone further with that approach: We don't prosecute at all," Solis says. What's lacking is "political will," he argues. "The attorney general has to say, 'I don't care how difficult it is. I want somebody in court in 30 days.' "

"Looked at through the lens of partisan politics," however, it's hard to aggressively prosecute Americans who work in dangerous situations abroad, Solis says. "Anyone who started prosecuting civilians would probably be a one-term president."

The issue is not whether contractors are ultimately found innocent or guilty of offenses with which they're charged but whether cases are pursued to conclusion, says Solis. If the government continues its apparent reluctance to see cases through, the result will be an "erosion in the confidence people have in America's ability and willingness to achieve justice."

BACKGROUND

Private Enterprise

Armed forces for hire — either individual mercenaries or groups of salaried soldiers working as an army for hire — are nothing new. From ancient times until about 200 years ago, hired guns traveled the world to work for different governments. They were the most common kind of armed force, and, while the trend waned for a time, it never went out of existence.[34]

Before about 1800, few rulers had the ability, or even the inclination, to assemble large armed forces of their own citizens.

Waging war effectively required specialized skills, such as shooting a crossbow or wielding a sword, that were best honed over decades. But few governments needed a standing army or could afford to pay soldiers to keep their skills sharp in peacetime. As late as the 19th century, most governments were either weak or despotic, and most people were poor, making it difficult for rulers to assemble a force of any size from among their citizenry.

Furthermore, until the 19th century there were few nation-states of the kind that we know today, with firm boundaries and stable populations, that citizen armies defended in war. Instead, kings presided over territories with shifting boundaries that they fought to expand into far-ranging empires, employing foreign soldiers-for-hire who were better suited for the task than local farmers or knights.

As a result, "the foreign soldier hired for pay, the mercenary, is an almost ubiquitous type in the entire . . . history of organized warfare," wrote Singer, the Brookings Institution scholar. "Even the Bible tells their tales. The Pharaoh chased the Israelites out of Egypt with an army that included hired foreigners, while [the Israelite King] David and his men . . . were employed in the Philistine army."[35]

But employing freelance warriors had its downside, especially between wars, when the soldiers weren't paid. Mercenary groups lived "off the land," forcing local people to hand over food and money, "leaving the countryside devastated in their wake," wrote Singer.[36]

On the high seas, from the 13th through 19th centuries, armed sailors for hire — known as privateers — served governments in wartime but often terrorized other vessels as pirates in peacetime. At least some rulers "turned a blind eye," probably because piracy honed the skills sailors needed "when serving as the king's wartime privateers," wrote Janice E. Thomson, a retired professor of political science at the University of Washington.[37]

Warfare as business grew steadily larger and by the 17th century had become the "biggest industry in Europe," according to Singer. "European armies of the period often were simple amalgamations of hired mercenary companies, all with their own specialties." Eastern Europeans and Greeks were cavalry specialists, and the Swiss wielded pikes. "'Patriotism' was a meaningless concept to the average soldier," in stark contrast to the strong nationalistic commitment that is a hallmark of modern armies, Singer noted.[38]

During that period, a "new class of military entrepreneurs . . . recruited and equipped military units at their own cost" and leased them to rulers.[39] In addition, countries such as Britain and the Netherlands granted monopolies in international trade to shareholder-owned "mercantile companies" such as the English East India Company. Empowered to develop and manage foreign trade — between India and Europe, for example — the companies received royal permission to conquer territories, make treaties and engage in combat to ensure that the country to which they were bound by contract dominated trade along a designated route.

Rise of States

Some thinkers doubted the wisdom of relying on private armies. In Florence, Italy, political philosopher Niccolò Machiavelli (1469-1527) — author of the influential political treatise *The Prince* — warned that private armies, by definition, are disloyal. "Mercenary commanders are either skilled in warfare or they are not," Machiavelli wrote. "If they are, you cannot trust them because they are anxious to advance their own greatness by coercing you, their employer. If, however, the commander is lacking in prowess, as often as not, he brings about your ruin."[40]

While mercenary warfare persisted — and even expanded — during the 17th century, the era also saw technological and political trends that decreased mercenaries' dominance.

The Thirty Years War (1618-1648) destroyed towns across Europe, caused famines and drove rulers into bankruptcy as two powerful imperial families — the Hapsburgs and the Bourbons — fought each other and numerous regional opponents, such as the Germans, to control huge swaths of the continent. So damaging was the war that, in the end, "the only conceivable resolution" was to abandon the struggle for imperial power that had dominated European politics to that point and "let each nation decide its own internal matters," wrote Singer.

This principle was enshrined in the Peace of Westphalia treaties that ended the fighting. Afterward, freelancing mercenary armies "began to be replaced by standing state armies made up of citizens" who defended their own borders, he wrote. "The wars of kings finally evolve[d] into the wars of people."[41]

As guns and cannons replaced swords and pikes, combat skills mattered less than sheer numbers of soldiers, another trend that favored temporary conscription of citizens over hiring mercenaries. Furthermore, during the Enlightenment of the 17th and 18th centuries the idea arose that a "social contract" bound rulers and their people in a relationship of mutual responsibilities, rights and duties. As citizens, people were more willing to fight for their countries than when most were mere subjects of all-powerful emperors. In addition, citizens were increasingly viewed as representatives of their home state, leading governments to bar their

C H R O N O L O G Y

1980s-1990s *Cold War's end increases supply of soldiers for hire.*

1989 U.N. circulates treaty pledging signatories to ban mercenary activity.

1990 South Africa begins dismantling apartheid, its brutal segregation system; some ex-government security officers form mercenary companies.

1991 Cold War ends; shrinking defense budgets leave thousands of former military personnel looking for work.

1993 The deaths of 18 elite U.S. forces in Mogadishu, Somalia, in a raid to capture violent rebel leaders, helps turn Americans against foreign military missions.

1995 South Africa-based Executive Outcomes helps Sierra Leone put down a years-long violent uprising.

1999 Contractors working in Bosnia for Virginia-based DynCorp International allegedly buy young girls from organized criminals for prostitution; accused workers are relocated but never charged.

2000s-Present *Security contracting expands into major industry.*

2000 Military Extraterritorial Jurisdiction Act (MEJA) extends federal courts' jurisdiction to contractors charged with serious crimes.

2001 The film "Black Hawk Down" is a fictionalized account of the 1993 Mogadishu raid. . . . Pentagon report states that any military job a private company can perform should be outsourced to industry. . . . U.N. anti-mercenary treaty takes effect, ratified by 20 nations; the United States and other highly industrialized nations do not sign.

2002 British government issues regulatory options for security companies; to date, none has been implemented.

2003 U.S. invasion and occupation of Iraq relies heavily on contractors.

2004 Contractors and military personnel accused of abusing detainees at Baghdad's Abu Ghraib prison. . . . Iraqi insurgents in Fallujah kill four

Blackwater employees, hang two bodies from bridge; Marines attack the city in response.

2007 Congress expands situations in which contractors may face military court-martial to times when war is not officially declared. . . . Army-commissioned report says all future missions will demand heavy use of private contractors. . . . Blackwater guards charged with manslaughter in connection with deaths of 17 Iraqi civilians in Baghdad's Nisour Square. . . . Responding to congressional inquiries, Pentagon collects and releases data on contractor totals and costs.

2008 United States and 16 other countries sign nonbinding Montreux Document affirming their obligation to protect human rights when using armed contractors.

2010 Contractor deaths in Iraq and Afghanistan in 2010 exceed service-member deaths for first time. . . . Security contractors provide disaster assistance after Haitian earthquake. . . . Pentagon conducts 7,390 contract audits, down from 26,623 in 2004, but says the audits are much more thorough. . . . Afghan President Hamid Karzai declares that a government-controlled Afghan Public Protection Force will replace most armed contractors; shift delayed until 2012.

2011 Congressionally chartered Commission on Wartime Contracting concludes that the government over-relies on contractors. . . . Contractors make up at least 45 percent of Pentagon's Iraq/Afghanistan workforce. . . . U.S. military leaves Iraq, replaced by 15,000 U.S. embassy staff members and 5,000 private security contractors. . . . New government database on contractors includes lawsuit and contract-suspension data.

2012 Supreme Court rules that 2007 Nisour Square shooting case must proceed to trial. . . . Pentagon disburses more than $3 billion in drug war-related contracts. . . . Congressional bills introduced to further expand civilian criminal courts' authority over contractors working abroad, stiffen contract oversight and crack down on contractors' abuse of workers. . . . More than 400 security contractors have signed an International Code of Conduct based on the Montreux Document, but companies, governments and groups representing the public struggle to agree on enforcement procedures.

Setting Standards for Security Contractors

New code of conduct sparks many disagreements.

Differences among nations make it difficult to devise international rules on the use of private security forces. And countries that, until recently, were subjugated colonies are especially fearful that stronger nations can use hired force to make it even easier to impose their wills.

Not surprisingly, George Washington viewed "hired guns" with suspicion, having fought against mercenaries in the Revolutionary War. "Mercenary armies . . . have at one time or another subverted the liberties of almost all the countries they have been raised to defend," the first president said.[1] By the mid-20th century, though, American leaders' views had changed.

The United Nations has always worried that armed contractors could threaten "people's right to self-determination," said José L. Gomez del Prado, former chairman of the U.N. Working Group on the Use of Mercenaries.[2]

Beginning in 1989, the U.N. circulated a treaty to ban mercenary activity. It took effect in 2001 with 20 nations ratifying. The United States and other highly industrialized countries did not sign, however.[3] The United States believed that "we could regulate the companies ourselves, in our own interests," says Deborah Avant, a professor of international security and diplomacy at the University of Denver.

By the mid-2000s, many security contractors were large businesses interested in winning clients by demonstrating professionalism. "The more corporate a company is, the bigger stake they have in showing they're legitimate," says Molly Dunigan, an associate political scientist at RAND, a think tank with offices around the world.

At the same time, the Iraq and Afghanistan wars had led to high-profile reports of alleged human rights abuses by contractors, including unprovoked shootings of civilians. To many, the time seemed ripe to go beyond the traditional

U.N. treaty process — in which governments agree to abide by and enforce certain rules — and create a regulatory system devised by security companies themselves in concert with governments, other potential clients such as multinational corporations, and representatives of the public.

Contracting is "a market," says Avant, "so you can accomplish things by changing the way people buy" and "changing the profit equation for companies" so that the most responsible get the most business.

To start, the Swiss government and International Committee of the Red Cross led development of the Montreux Document — a non-legally binding pledge by governments that contractors they hire or that are based in or work in their countries comply with human-rights standards. In September 2008, 17 countries including the United States, the United Kingdom and China announced that they had signed. (Forty-one governments are signatories today.)[4]

Then governments, security companies and so-called civil-society participants representing the interests of the public — such as universities and human-rights organizations — developed an International Code of Conduct (ICOC) for security contractors.

"We're proud of the code" and its "very detailed" statement of companies' responsibilities for fulfilling Montreux Document principles, says Meg Roggensack, senior adviser for the Business and Human Rights Initiative at Human Rights First, a Washington-based nonpartisan advocacy group, and a member of the committee drafting an implementation mechanism for the code. "It represents a real breakthrough."

The toughest job is now under way — creating a credible system to monitor compliance and help people who allege violations by a company to have their complaints resolved through that company's formal grievance mechanism.

citizens from fighting abroad, since rulers might be held responsible for harms they inflicted.[42]

Thus, a new norm arose in which governments were considered to hold a "monopoly" on violence, and mercenary fighting became less common.

Weak governments and governments fighting abroad continued to hire some contract soldiers, however. Great

Britain famously employed Hessians — troops hailing mainly from the German state of Hesse — to fight against the colonists during the American Revolution.

And while the United States relied mainly on a citizen army during its foreign wars of the 19th and 20th centuries, it gradually expanded the tasks assigned to private companies, from maintaining weaponry to training foreign

Unless an "independent, credible oversight mechanism" is created, the ICOC would remain "just a fig leaf" that unscrupulous contractors and those who hire them could hide behind, knowing that violations would have no real consequences, says James Cockayne, co-director of the Center on Global Counterterrorism Cooperation, a New York-based policy group.

Early this year, a draft plan was released for comment. Responses revealed numerous disagreements over issues such as the balance of power between contractors and other stakeholders, the degree of confidentiality provided for allegations of wrongdoing and the procedures for dealing with companies that don't quickly remedy their violations. In June, negotiators said they aim for a revised version by year's end.[5]

Such disagreements are no surprise, says Sylvia White, general counsel and board director of the London-based security company Aegis and a member of the drafting panel. A similar process occurred as the code was written, she says. "First, there was lots of interest, then people couldn't necessarily agree on everything, then finally we got a great weight of people agreeing," she says. "I'm hopeful we'll get to that tipping point in the next few months."

White says that the industry is committed to fully implementing the code, partly to end what she calls the widespread misconception "that there are no rules" for how security companies behave.

The enforcement mechanism's feasibility raises questions, however. For example, it's not clear how an industry-funded office to handle grievances could be truly independent, wrote an ex-Marine and security contractor who blogs about security issues under the name "Matt" at his *Feral Jundi* blog. "Isn't it a conflict of interest if a mediator is getting payment by one group in the form of dues/membership fees, and then claiming to help out the other side (the aggrieved) who does not pay dues?"[6]

Strong government commitment is also crucial but not assured, says Laura Dickinson, a research professor of law at George Washington University. "I think the U.S. government

should mandate membership [in the ICOC mechanism] before it awards contracts."

Meanwhile, at the Pentagon's request, ASIS International, a membership group for security professionals in Alexandria, Va., has developed business-management standards to help companies conform to the ICOC, says Marc Siegel, commissioner of ASIS's Global Standards Initiative. Companies that sign on will undergo periodic audits to ensure they follow the standards, which stipulate best practices for business functions vital to security contractors, such as accurately evaluating the risks at a job site and hiring staff for jobs that require bearing arms.

"If you're a client hiring a firm for a high-risk environment where people can be hurt and rights violated, it behooves you to look for companies that are well managed," Siegel says.

— Marcia Clemmitt

[1] Quoted in Jackson Nyamuya Magogot and Benedict Sheey, "Private Military Companies and International Law: Building New Ladders of Legal Responsibility," *Cardozo Journal of Conflict Resolution*, 2009, Vol. 11, Issue 1, p. 99, http://cojcr.org/vol11no1/index111.html.

[2] José L. Gomez del Prado, "Mercenaries, Private Military and Security Companies and International Law," lecture, University of Wisconsin Law School, Jan. 31, 2008, www.law.wisc.edu/gls/lawwarhuman security.html.

[3] *Ibid.*

[4] For background, see Anthony H. Cordesman, "Private Security Forces in Afghanistan and Iraq: The Potential Impact of the Montreux Document," Center for Strategic and International Studies, Nov. 17, 2010, http://csis.org/files/publication/10115_Private_Security_Forces_Afghanistan_Iraq.pdf, and "Participating States of the Montreux Document," Federal Department of Foreign Affairs, web site of the government of Switzerland, www.eda.admin.ch/eda/en/home/topics/intla/humlaw/pse/parsta.html.

[5] Minutes, TSC Meeting, June 5-7, 2012 in Washington, U.S., International Code of Conduct web site, www.icoc-psp.org/uploads/Minutes_TSC_Meeting_5-7_June_2012_Washington_DC.pdf.

[6] Industry Talk: So What IS Going on With the ICoC, *Feral Jundi* blog, Oct. 4, 2011, http://feraljundi.com/3643/industry-talk-so-what-is-going-on-with-the-icoc.

militaries, such as occurred during the Vietnam War in the 1960s.

Turning Points

In the late 1980s, when the Soviet Union collapsed and the half-century Cold War ended, both the supply of and demand for private military contractors increased.

Many long-simmering power struggles began boiling over in regions once controlled by the Soviets, as independence movements grew and small nations once allied with either the United States or Soviet Union fended off threats. Such conflicts provided new markets for mercenaries. At the same time, mining companies and other international corporations and nonprofit organizations

Contracting Takes Unacknowledged Human Toll

"Everyone believes we're underreporting contractor deaths."

As the number of private security companies swells, the death and injury toll for contractors continues to rise, and other contracting-associated problems also are coming to the fore, such as mistreatment of contract workers by the companies who hire them or by labor recruiters.

At least 430 employees of American contractors were killed in Afghanistan in 2011, versus 418 U.S. service members.[1] And the contractor death toll is likely much higher. Until about four years ago, the Department of Defense collected little data of any kind on security companies, including information on contractor deaths. The most reliable mortality data come from the Labor Department, which tallies contractors for whom insurance claims are submitted under a compensation program for federal workers.[2]

"No one believes we're underreporting military deaths. Everyone believes we're underreporting contractor deaths," said Steven L. Schooner, a law professor at George Washington University, in Washington.[3]

The silence surrounding the deaths is disrespectful to the dead and harmful to democracy, argues Schooner. "An honest, accurate tally is important for the public and the nation's elected leaders to understand the true human toll"

of wars, in order to reckon their true costs and benefits, he wrote.[4]

The high potential for death is not the only threat facing contractors. Many suffer from traumatic brain injury, post-traumatic stress disorder and other post-service conditions that also plague military personnel. But unlike service members, contractors are ineligible for veterans' care, so their conditions are even more likely to go untreated than those of service personnel.

In addition, contractors have virtually no job security. In hiring private companies, government can quickly staff up for an emergency mission and just as quickly lay off workers when the mission is over. Thus contractors must cope with short-term, unpredictable employment.

Furthermore, while some contractors are covered by health and life insurance while on a job, "coverage usually lapses when they change jobs or return home," says the U.S. Institute of Peace, a congressionally authorized, nonpartisan federal institution that studies and seeks to end armed conflicts.[5]

"There's a moral obligation that's being overlooked. Can the government really send people to a war zone and neglect [its] responsibility to attend to their emotional

such as environmental groups hired private security personnel to protect staff members working in the unstable states.

In 1995, the government of Sierra Leone, in West Africa, hired several hundred troops from a South Africa-based mercenary company — Executive Outcomes — to put down a four-year-long civil war that government forces were too weak to stop. Executive Outcomes hit rebel forces with precision air and ground attacks, driving them away from the capital and the diamond fields that provided the government with its funding.

During the Cold War, the U.S. government could generally count on public support for military operations abroad, on the grounds that the Soviet Union posed a

serious national threat. When that threat vanished, however, making the case for sending troops into armed conflicts or on humanitarian missions grew more difficult. Private contractors increasingly enabled the U.S. government to conduct such operations, however, especially as the supply of potential contractors grew during the past two decades.

In recent years, contractors have come from many countries, but in the 1990s most came from three sources: South Africa, Russia and the other countries that had made up the Soviet Union, and the United States and its allies, such as Australia.

As the United States and the former Soviet Union countries downsized their militaries after the Cold War, needs after the fact?" asked Paul Brand, CEO of Mission Critical Psychological Services, a Chicago company that counsels civilians who work in war zones.[6]

Also facing potential hazards are foreign nationals recruited by private companies under contract with the U.S. government to work in Iraq and Afghanistan. Many companies have been caught running bait-and-switch schemes in which workers are promised good salaries, only to face much lower pay, bad living conditions, disrespect, mistreatment and sometimes virtual imprisonment.

In one incident, 35 former Colombian soldiers were flown to Baghdad on the promise of being paid $4,000 a month to work for Virginia-based Blackwater (now Academi). The men were recruited by Colombia-based ID Systems S.A., a Blackwater subcontractor, and by the time they arrived, ID Systems allegedly had cut the wage to $1,000 per month. When the men protested, their tickets home were taken away, and they were told they'd have to find their own way back.[7]

In December 2008, a group of South Asian workers staged protests of their treatment by Kuwait-based Najlaa International Catering Services, a subcontractor to Houston-based KBR, one of the largest Pentagon contractors. After promising jobs to about 1,000 workers, Najlaa held the workers upon their arrival and denied them work or pay for months.[8]

The U.S. government already had a "zero tolerance" policy on such abuses at the time of the 2008 protests by the Najlaa workers, but its commitment to that policy is suspect, charges the Project on Government Oversight (POGO), a Washington-based government-watchdog group. "The U.S. has directly awarded contracts to Najlaa

after the . . . protests, including one contract that lasts through 2012," POGO analysts said.[9]

— *Marcia Clemmitt*

[1]Rod Nordland, "Risks of Afghan War Shift from Soldiers to Contractors," *The New York Times*, Feb. 11, 2012, www.nytimes.com/2012/02/12/world/asia/afghan-war-risks-are-shifting-to-contractors.html.

[2]Steven L. Schooner and Collin D. Swan, "Contractors and the Ultimate Sacrifice," *Service Contractor*, September 2010, p. 16, http://papers.ssrn.com/sol3/papers.cfm?abstract_id=1677506.

[3]Quoted in Nordland, *op. cit.*

[4]Schooner and Swan, *op. cit.*, p. 18.

[5]Robert Perito, "The Private Sector in Security Sector Reform," U.S. Institute of Peace, January 2009, www.usip.org/files/resources/USIP_0109.PDF.

[6]T. Christian Miller, "The Other Victims of Battlefield Stress; Defense Contractors' Mental Health Neglected," *ProPublica*, Feb. 26, 2010, www.propublica.org/article/injured-contractors-the-other-victims-of-battlefield-stress-224.

[7]Emily Speers Mears, "Security Privatisation in the Middle East," Global Consortium on Security Transformation," November 2010, p. 7; Peter Krupa, "Vote Tallying Company Also Hired Blackwater Mercenaries," *Lat/Am Daily* blog, March 21, 2010, www.latamdaily.com/2010/03/21/olombian-vote-tallying-company-also-hired-blackwater-mercenaries; "Atrapados en Bagdad," *Semana.com*, Aug. 19, 2006, www.semana.com/nacion/atrapados-bagdad/96550-3.aspx.

[8]David Isenberg and Nick Schwellenbach, "Documents Reveal Details of Alleged Labor Trafficking by KBR Subcontractor," Project on Government Oversight blog, June 14, 2011, http://pogoblog.typepad.com/pogo/2011/06/documents-reveal-details-of-alleged-labor-trafficking-by-kbr-subcontractor.html.

[9]*Ibid.*

thousands of service members searched for jobs, helping to fuel the growth of security-contracting firms. At the same time, South Africa ended apartheid, its brutal racial segregation policy. From the country's large, newly unemployed army of white government security forces arose powerful armed private contractors, such as Executive Outcomes.

With this workforce available, the U.S. government could contract with private security companies to conduct missions abroad — or simply introduce foreign leaders to companies that they might hire. The Clinton administration likely did both as it engineered a series of arms-length interventions in civil and ethnic violence that raged in the Balkan states in the 1990s.

In the mid-1990s, Virginia-based MPRI — Military Professional Resources Inc., (now L-3 MPRI) — provided consulting services under contract to the fledgling state of Croatia that may have included military training and possibly military strategizing. Croatia had declared independence from the former Soviet-allied Yugoslavia at the end of the Cold War. But it faced armed resistance from a Serbian ethnic minority hoping to push Croatia to rejoin Serb-dominated Yugoslavia.

As Croatia's military foundered, ethnic strife left hundreds of thousands dead and millions homeless. But in 1995, the Croats suddenly launched a highly professional strike that quickly ended that phase of the fighting. Many observers argue that there's no way to explain the Croat army's quick transformation without ascribing it to military training from L-3 MPRI. The U.S. government did not hire L-3 MPRI but reportedly brought Croat leaders together with the company, whose founders and staff have included scores of retired top military officers, including a former U.S. Army chief of staff.[43]

"According to European military officers who witnessed the attack, the initial Croatian river crossing into Serb-held territory was a 'textbook U.S. field manual river crossing. The only difference was the troops were Croats,'" wrote Brookings' Singer.[44]

L-3 MPRI, however, says it provided only business-management training. "We don't teach . . . battlefield skills . . . We didn't teach that in Croatia," said Lt. Gen. Ed Soyster, an L-3 MPRI vice president and retired chief of the Defense Intelligence Agency. "We teach general management, . . . planning, programming, . . . budgeting."[45]

Over the past 20 years, a new philosophy of government that advocates privatizing as many jobs as possible has bolstered contracting. A congressionally mandated periodic review of Pentagon priorities declared in 2001 that "only those functions that must be performed by [the Department of Defense] should be kept by DOD. Any function that can be provided by the private sector is not a core government function."[46]

Furthermore, armed security contractors do not work only for governments. As the supply of contractors has grown, multinational corporations have increasingly hired the companies to act as militarily trained, sometimes heavily armed private police forces, protecting mines and other such operations. In some cases, severe human-rights abuses by contractors are alleged. In July 2011, for example, the London- and Hong Kong-based mining company Monterrico Metals paid damages but did not admit liability to settle a lawsuit brought by Peruvian environmental protesters, who alleged that contractors tortured and sexually assaulted them.[47]

New Era

While private security contracting grew during the 1990s, the 2003 Iraq invasion marked a new era, according to analysts at RAND. Before that, while the military hired contractors aplenty, "*armed* contractors had rarely been used in a [U.S.] war zone," they said.[48]

Since the Iraq invasion, the use of contractors has burgeoned, though the Pentagon did not begin gathering and releasing contractor data until the second half of 2007. It says that because of the difficulty of counting subcontractors, all its tallies are estimates.[49]

As of March 2011, DOD counted approximately 155,000 contractors in Afghanistan and Iraq combined, making up slightly more than half of the Defense Department's workforce.[50] In Iraq, 10,448 contractors — 16 percent of the total contracting force — were armed security personnel.[51] Out of the 90,000 contractors Defense counted in Afghanistan, about 20,000 were U.S. citizens, 46,000 were Afghans and 24,000 came from other countries.[52]

While contractors were once hired mainly for support services, such as running food service operations for the military, they have taken on duties closer to core military missions in the Middle East. When a 2010 drone strike killed 15 civilians and injured a dozen more in central Afghanistan, for example, Air Force investigators found that although military personnel operated the drone and made the decision to fire, that "decision was largely based upon intelligence analysis . . . conducted and reported by a civilian contractor," wrote Capt. Keric Clanahan, an Air Force lawyer.[53]

Public awareness of contractors has come mostly from periodic high-profile incidents of alleged misbehavior.

In 1999, the Army asked Falls Church, Va.-based DynCorp International to oust five employees from Bosnia, in the Balkans, after the men were accused of purchasing female sex slaves, some as young as 12, from an organized-crime group and employing them in a prostitution ring. Ultimately, however, neither the U.S. military nor Bosnian police claimed jurisdiction to prosecute, and none of the accused was charged. One worker admitted guilt and left the company. DynCorp fired two whistleblowers who had reported the behavior and moved most of the accused to jobs in other countries.[54]

The incidents demonstrated that DynCorp didn't effectively screen, monitor or discipline employees and may have turned a blind eye to human-rights violations, said independent military analyst Isenberg. But the company "was not particularly hurt by the scandal" and continued to receive security contracts from the United States, Great Britain and others, he said.[55]

In 2009, workers from Arlington, Va.-based ArmorGroup North America — under contract to guard the American Embassy in Kabul — reported misbehavior by coworkers that included illegal brothel visits and sexual hazing of other guards. In one incident, guards hid in abandoned buildings at night, dressed as Afghans and carried illicitly borrowed embassy equipment such as night goggles, apparently acting out a fantasy "reconnaissance mission."[56]

In 2009, the State Department announced it would not renew ArmorGroup's embassy contract, but allegations of wrongdoing by another contractor picked for the job caused repeated delays in the handover. In 2011 ArmorGroup paid the government $7.5 million to settle some charges arising from the incidents.[57] The contract was eventually awarded to London- and Virginia-based Aegis.[58]

In August 2011, the congressionally chartered Commission on Wartime Contracting reported that heavy use of contractors has dangerously diminished the knowledge base within federal agencies and overwhelmed inadequately staffed oversight offices. The government "has come to over-rely" on private companies and should restrict the use of armed contractors, the panel concluded.[59]

CURRENT SITUATION

New Jobs

As military contracting continues, Congress and a range of international groups, as well as security companies themselves, are mulling new regulatory mechanisms. But whether rules will be tightened remains unclear. (*See sidebar, p. 388.*)

The U.S. military left Iraq in 2011, and a U.S. Embassy staff of about 15,000 is taking its place in efforts to rebuild the war-ravaged nation. Up to 5,000 armed contractors are assisting the diplomats, driving armored transports and providing protective air cover from armed helicopters.[60]

Afghan President Hamid Karzai announced in 2010 that all armed contractors except those protecting diplomats would be replaced by the central-government-controlled bodyguard group called the Afghan Public Protection Force (APPF). Karzai charged that private contractors cost too much and encourage bribery, nepotism and other corruption. The changeover date has repeatedly slipped as the APPF proved hard to assemble,

train and fund. But a gradual phase-in of the public force finally began this spring.[61]

That doesn't necessarily mean that the number of security contractors is on the wane, however. New clients and new kinds of work are emerging.

The Pentagon is rapidly expanding the use of contractors to combat drug trafficking, which it increasingly calls a national-security threat equivalent to terrorism. This year, the Counter Narco-Terrorism Program Office will hand out more than $3 billion in contracts for jobs such as providing helicopter training for Mexico's public-security forces, operating drones and helping governments with surveillance tasks such as analyzing media to spot hidden trends.[62]

In the past, nonprofit groups that act as human-rights watchdogs have not hired armed contractors, saying they wanted to avoid compromising their neutrality. Recently, however, violent incidents reportedly have led even staunchly anti-mercenary organizations, including the International Red Cross and Doctors Without Borders, to hire armed guards.[63]

Congressional Action

Even as security contractors proliferate, their legal status remains "opaque," wrote analysts at RAND. "A number of both international and domestic U.S. laws are arguably applicable to private contractors in war zones," but all are difficult to apply with confidence, they wrote. Among other problems, "There is currently no standard formula for prosecuting contractors who come from one country, operate in another country, and work for a firm based in a third country."[64]

Up for consideration in 2012 are congressional proposals first introduced five years ago to expand civilian courts' jurisdiction over contractors working abroad for federal agencies, even when no military mission is occurring there. Current versions of the bills — sponsored by Rep. David Price, D-N.C., and Sen. Patrick Leahy, D-Vt. — would apply to contractors who work abroad for any federal agency, as well as to their dependents, and include federal offenses such as assault, murder, drug or human trafficking, corruption-related crimes such as bribery and treason-related crimes such as providing support to terrorists.[65]

In March, bipartisan bills were introduced in both houses of Congress to crack down on abusive labor practices by contractors, such as seizing workers' passports

Should Congress increase oversight of private contractors?

YES — Lawrence J. Korb
Senior Fellow, Center for American Progress Action Fund

From a statement for the record, Senate Homeland Security and Governmental Affairs Committee, Contracting Oversight Subcommittee, April 17, 2012

If the U.S. is to protect its vital national interests in a cost-effective manner, the Congress must pass and the president should sign S 2139, the Comprehensive Contingency Contracting Reform Act of 2012, as soon as possible. [The law would increase contract oversight at the Defense and State departments and the U.S. Agency for International Development and require automatic suspension of contractors charged with contracting fraud.] If we do not act expeditiously, we will continue to needlessly squander blood and treasure and undermine our image in current and future conflicts. . . .

S 2139 addresses most of the . . . problems identified by the Commission on Wartime Contracting in Iraq and Afghanistan.

This legislation is necessary because officials in the executive branch have shown that they are unable or unwilling to implement most of the commission's recommendations. If S 2139 is not passed, large amounts of appropriated money will continue to be wasted: In Iraq and Afghanistan at least $31 billion and possibly as much as $61 billion of $200 billion appropriated to contracts has been lost to contractor fraud and waste. Additionally, if S 2139 does not pass, contractors will continue to perform activities that are inherently governmental, thus frequently undermining the mission.

Title I deals with the organization and management of the federal government for contracting for overseas contingency operations. The first title mandates the president [to] include information and the director of the Office of Management and Budget [to] provide the Congress with details of why Overseas Contingency Operations (OCO) funds are needed and subsequently report in detail on how those funds were spent. Hopefully these provisions will limit the various agencies' tendency, exploited in particularly egregious fashion by the Department of Defense, to transfer items more appropriately included in the core budgets into the OCO accounts to hide budget growth and cost overruns. . . .

Title II focuses on transparency, sustainability and accountability. It demands that, unless there is a waiver granted, contracts should be limited to three years for competitively bid contracts and one year for noncompetitive contracts; that contracts have only a single tier of subcontractors; and that the secretaries of State and Defense perform an annual review to determine for which functions it is appropriate to use contractors.

NO — Stan Soloway
President and CEO, Professional Services Council

From a statement for the record, Senate Homeland Security and Governmental Affairs Committee, Contracting Oversight Subcommittee, April 17, 2012

The Comprehensive Contingency Contracting Reform Act of 2012, S 2139, contains some valuable and thoughtful proposals that can enhance future operations. At the same time, we also feel strongly that several provisions in the bill would have precisely the opposite effect.

As various reports have indicated, despite well-documented instances of malfeasance, the vast majority of the challenges and problems in both Iraq and Afghanistan have not been driven by fraud and abuse. Rather, the "waste" that has occurred has been predominantly driven by poor planning, a lack of coordination, and workforce gaps.

What is also clear is that contracting varies significantly based on the nature of the operation. What worked in Iraq and Afghanistan may not be appropriate for operations in East Timor or Haiti. Congress should be careful to avoid legislating for the last contingency and limiting agencies' or contractors' flexibility to respond rapidly to the U.S. government's mission needs.

[The Professional Services Council] strongly opposes Section 113 as currently written. In effect, the provision amounts to a "suspend first, ask questions later" policy that tramples on the due-process rights that all citizens and companies are entitled to. The current Federal Acquisition Regulation (FAR) already allows government suspension and debarment officials (SDO) to take appropriate and immediate actions to suspend a contractor for a broad array of inappropriate behaviors. . . .

The Professional Services Council (PSC) supports initiatives to prevent trafficking in persons, and Section 222 may be helpful. Unfortunately, Section 222 also places excessive requirements on contractors. While contractors may be able to implement prevention and monitoring procedures, it is impossible for them to "certify" with absolute certainty that none of their employees, subcontractors, or recruiters or brokers have engaged in any such activity.

PSC is a strong supporter of the current structure for evaluating contractor past performance. One critical element of the current process is that contractors shall be provided with completed evaluations as soon as practicable; given an opportunity to submit comments or provide additional information; and entitled to an evaluation review at one level above the contracting officer. Section 224 would universally do away with these important protections. Contractors would be left with little recourse for actions taken by an individual contracting officer that posted an unsupported or improper negative past performance evaluation.

to trap them in a low-paying or abusive job. The bills would require companies with contracts worth $1 million or more to implement plans to prevent worker abuse and authorize the government to suspend contracts for violations.[66]

The Comprehensive Contingency Contractors Reform Act of 2012, introduced by Democratic Sens. Claire McCaskill of Missouri and Jim Webb of Virginia, would increase contract oversight at DOD, the State Department and USAID and require automatic suspension of contractors charged with contracting fraud.[67]

Meanwhile, the federal Court of Appeals for the Armed Forces is reviewing the constitutionality of the military's expanded authority to prosecute under the Uniform Code of Military Justice (UCMJ), amended by Congress in 2007.

Military courts give the accused fewer rights than do civilian courts — no juries or bail exist, for example — because warfare requires a strictly disciplined force that carries out a mission without deviation. Critics say subjecting civilians to military court jurisdiction is troublesome. It could unduly blur "the line between military and civilian authority — a very real concern of the [country's] Founders" that is evident in both the Declaration of Independence and the Constitution, wrote Stephen Vladeck, a professor at American University's Washington College of Law.[68]

The key question is whether the UCMJ's expansion might subject civilians to harsh military discipline even in nonwar situations that the president or Congress might designate a "national emergency," he said.[69]

But while academics and some courts debate big-picture questions, few officials in the upper hierarchies of government are doing so, argues Hammes, the retired Marine colonel. "I don't think there is a serious discussion at the power centers" such as Congress or the White House, he says.

The law that created the Commission on Wartime Contracting, for example, explicitly limited what the panel could investigate to issues of contract oversight. Congress thereby effectively banned the panel from exploring such questions as whether contractor use might make it too easy for presidents to start wars without public consent or make it harder for officers in the field to command and control a mixed public-private force, he says.

Former Blackwater guard Paul Slough leaves federal court in Salt Lake City, Utah, with his wife on Dec. 8, 2008. He is among four of the security firm's guards charged with manslaughter in connection with the shooting of 17 unarmed Iraqi civilians in Baghdad in 2007. The guards used machine guns and grenade launchers against the civilians, some with their hands up, federal prosecutors alleged. Blackwater (now Academi) said the guards returned fire after they were ambushed by insurgents while responding to a car bombing.

OUTLOOK

Regulated or Unregulated?

As the market for armed security expands, the debate over how effectively contractors can be regulated is likely to grow. More than 360 contractors have signed onto the International Code of Conduct for Private Security Service Providers (ICOC), which was completed in late 2010, says Brooks of the International Stability Operations Association. Now representatives of several of the largest companies, governments including those of the United States and the United Kingdom, and other groups, such as nonprofit human-rights watchdog organizations, are working to create an enforcement mechanism. Public comments on a first draft revealed widely varying views of how the mechanism should work, however.

Completion must not be long delayed, warns James Cockayne, co-director of the Center on Global Counterterrorism Cooperation, a New York-based policy group. Otherwise, he argues, public-interest groups will grow "skeptical over whether governments and companies are truly committed to effective international oversight," and contractors may decide that, if governments aren't fully committed, it's not imperative for the industry either.

Failure to fully implement the ICOC would have serious consequences for the U.S. government, which has been a leading participant, Cockayne says. For one thing, he says, "it will give ammunition to countries — especially Cuba — who have long argued that the ICOC will not work and that an international treaty" — rather than a public-private partnership —"is needed to regulate this industry." A collapse of the ICOC would also cast doubt on the future of other U.S.-backed public-private efforts to commit international businesses to human-rights protections, such as worldwide fair labor practices, Cockayne says.

Despite missing an initial, ambitious deadline, however, the ICOC process has strong momentum, says Mark DeWitt, vice president and deputy general counsel of Triple Canopy, a Reston, Va.-based security company, and chair of the enforcement-mechanism drafting panel.

"Now that we've homed in on the main issues" that must be addressed to get buy-in from the stakeholding groups, "it's better to be careful and do it right" than to rush, says DeWitt. "We've gotten to the point of having to talk about and build bridges on the really hard issues. I'd say we're going in the opposite direction from losing credibility."

The ICOC may provide a basis for additional oversight, DeWitt says. For example, he says, a U.N. treaty "could be built on top of multi-stakeholder efforts like this." The U.N.'s working group on mercenaries seems to be seriously considering such an effort, DeWitt says.

Eventually, hiring security companies that fully embrace the code will become the norm, not just for governments but for nongovernmental buyers, such as international corporations that hire contractors to protect mining operations, for example, predicts Sylvia White, general counsel and board director of Aegis, a London-based security company. When the code is fully operational, hiring companies that operate outside it "would be embarrassing for them," she says.

Others are leery about how privatization of government services will affect the military itself. Joining the service has long been viewed as a commitment to professionalism and the upholding of public values, says Jon Michaels, an acting professor of law at the University of California, Los Angeles. As more positions become jobs-for-hire — and pay more than government service itself — "there's a danger that people will stop thinking of [service

positions] as careers and start thinking of them as just the credential you need before you can become a contractor."

NOTES

1. Quoted in Craig Whitlock, "Contractors Run U.S. Spying Missions in Africa," *The Washington Post*, June 14, 2012, www.washingtonpost.com/world/national-security/contractors-run-us-spying-missions-in-africa/2012/06/14/gJQAvC4RdV_story.html.

2. Quoted in *ibid.*

3. Quoted in *ibid.*

4. Moshe Schwartz and Joyprada Swain, "Department of Defense Contractors in Afghanistan and Iraq: Background and Analysis," Congressional Research Service, May 13, 2011, p. 6, www.fas.org/sgp/crs/natsec/R40764.pdf.

5. *Ibid.*, p. 16.

6. Sarah K. Cotton, *et al.*, "Hired Guns: Views About Armed Contractors in Operation Iraqi Freedom," RAND, 2010, p. 11, www.rand.org/pubs/monographs/MG987.html.

7. Quoted in Tom Bowman, "No U.S. Troops, But an Army of Contractors in Iraq," NPR, Dec. 27, 2011, www.npr.org/2011/12/27/144198497/no-u-s-troops-but-an-army-of-contractors-in-iraq.

8. Quoted in "Private Warriors," Frontline, PBS, July 2005, www.pbs.org/wgbh/pages/frontline/shows/warriors/interviews/schooner.html.

9. *Ibid.*

10. Laura A. Dickinson, *Outsourcing War and Peace: Preserving Public Values in a World of Privatized Foreign Affairs* (2011), p. 19.

11. Cotton, *op. cit.*, p. 15.

12. James Vicini, "Supreme Court Rejects Blackwater Iraq Shooting Appeal," Reuters, June 4, 2012, www.reuters.com/article/2012/06/04/us-usa-iraq-blackwater-idUSBRE8530KB20120604.

13. David Isenberg, "Shadow Force: Private Security Contractors in Iraq," Feb. 16, 2009, www.cato.org/publications/speeches/shadow-force-private-security-contractors-iraq.

14. Anna Leander, "The Market for Force and Public Security: The Destabilizing Consequences of Private Military Companies," *Journal of Peace Research*, September 2005, p. 605, http://jpr.sagepub.com/content/42/5/605.abstract; Anna Leander and Rens van Muster, "Private Security Contractors in the Debate About Darfur: Reflecting and Reinforcing Neo-Liberal Governmentality," *International Relations*, May 23, 2007, http://ire.sagepub.com/content/21/2/201.short.

15. Isenberg, *op. cit.*

16. "Urgent Reform Required: Army Expeditionary Contracting, Commission on Army Acquisition and Program Management and Expeditionary Operations," U.S. Commission on Army Acquisition and Program Management in Expeditionary Operations, 2007, p. 3, www.army.mil/docs/Gansler_Commission_Report_Final_071031.pdf.

17. T.X. Hammes, testimony before the House Oversight and Government Reform Subcommittee on National Security and Foreign Affairs, June 22, 2010, http://oversight.house.gov/wp-content/uploads/2012/01/20100622Hammes.pdf.

18. Quoted in. Cotton, *op. cit.*, p. 19.

19. *Ibid.*, p. 20.

20. Quoted in Bryan Bender, "From the Pentagon to the Private Sector," *Boston Globe*, Dec. 26, 2010, www.boston.com/news/nation/washington/articles/2010/12/26/defense_firms_lure_retired_generals.

21. Nominations Before the Senate Armed Services Committee, 110th Congress, First Session, transcript, 2007, www.gpo.gov/fdsys/pkg/CHRG-110shrg42309/html/CHRG-110shrg42309.htm.

22. Cotton, *op. cit.*, p. 33.

23. Isenberg, *op. cit.*

24. "Army Tosses Abu Ghraib Conviction," *USA Today*, Jan. 10, 2008, www.usatoday.com/news/world/2008-01-10-AbuGhraib-me_N.htm; Keith Herting, "Federal Appeals Court Revives Lawsuit Against Abu Ghraib Contractors," *Jurist*, May 13, 2012, http://jurist.org/paperchase/2012/05/federal-appeals-court-revives-lawsuits-against-abu-ghraib-contractors.php.

25. Cotton, *op. cit.*, p. 28.

26. For background, see Guy Dinmore and Rebecca Knight, "Kroll to Sell Iraq and Afghan Security Unit," *Financial Times*, Nov. 2, 2006, www.ft.com/intl/cms/s/0/24fa237c-6a13-11db-952e-0000779e2340.html#axzz1xWHZLznq; "Iraq Bomb Blast Killed UK Workers," BBC, Feb. 26, 2007, news.bbc.co.uk/2/hi/uk_news/6397759.stm.

27. For background, see Thomas J. Billitteri, "Afghanistan Dilemma," *CQ Researcher*, Aug. 7, 2009, updated May 25, 2011.

28. Cotton, *op. cit.*, p. xiv.

29. Cotton, *op. cit.*, p. xv.

30. Quoted in "Private Military Contractors," transcript, "Law Report," ABC Radio National (Australia), Sept. 9, 2008, www.abc.net.au/radionational/programs/lawreport/private-military-contractors/3182656.

31. Quoted in *ibid.*

32. For background, see Missye Brickell, "Filling the Criminal Liability Gap for Private Military Contractors Abroad: U.S. v. Slough and the Civilian Extraterritorial Jurisdiction Act of 2010," Legislation and Policy Brief, Spring 2010, http://digitalcommons.wcl.american.edu/cgi/viewcontent.cgi?article=1014&context=lpb.

33. For background, see Peter W. Singer, Frequently Asked Questions on the UCMJ Change and its Applicability to Private Military Contractors, Brookings Institution website, Jan. 12, 2007, www.brookings.edu/research/opinions/2007/01/12defenseindustry-singer.

34. For background, see Peter W. Singer, *Corporate Warriors: The Rise of the Privatized Military Industry* (updated edition, 2007).

35. *Ibid.*, p. 20.

36. *Ibid.*, p. 29.

37. Janice E. Thomson, *Pirates, Mercenaries and Sovereigns* (1996), p. 23.

38. Singer, *op. cit.*, p. 28.

39. *Ibid.*, p. 29.

40. Quoted in Singer, *op. cit.*, p. 164.

41. *Ibid.*, p. 29.

42. *Ibid.*, pp. 30-31.

43. Leadership, L-3 MPRI website, www.mpri.com/web/index.php/content/our_company/leadership.

44. Singer, *op. cit.*, p. 5.

45. Quoted in David Isenberg, "MPRI Couldn't Read Minds: Let's Sue Them," *Huffington Post*, Aug. 19, 2010, www.huffingtonpost.com/david-isenberg/mpri-couldnt-read-minds-l_b_688000.html.

46. Quadrennial Defense Review Report, Department of Defense, Sept. 30, 2001, www.defense.gov/pubs/qdr2001.pdf, p. 53.

47. *PSMC Bulletin*, Business & Human Rights Resource Centre, Sept. 16, 2011, www.business-humanrights.org/media/documents/pmsc-bulletin-issue-1-16-sep-2011.pdf.

48. Cotton, *op. cit.*, p. 11.

49. Schwartz and Swain, *op. cit.*, p. 4.

50. *Ibid.*, p. 6.

51. *Ibid.*, p. 16.

52. *Ibid.*, p. 10.

53. Keric D. Clanahan, "Drone-Sourcing? United State Air Force Unmanned Aircraft Systems, Inherently Governmental Functions, and the Role of Contractors," *Federal Circuit Bar Journal*, May 4, 2012, http://papers.ssrn.com/sol3/papers.cfm?abstract_id=2051154.

54. David Isenberg, "Sex and Security in Afghanistan," *Asia Times*, Oct. 6, 2009, http://atimes.com/atimes/South_Asia/KJ06Df03.html.

55. *Ibid.*

56. For background, see "POGO Letter to Secretary of State Hillary Clinton Regarding U.S. Embassy in Kabul," Project on Government Oversight website, Sept. 1, 2009, www.pogo.org/pogo-files/letters/contract-oversight/co-gp-20090901.html#clintlett; David Beatson, "Kiwi Connections in Kabul Embassy Scandal," *Pundit* [New Zealand], Dec. 14, 2009, www.pundit.co.nz/content/kiwi-connections-in-kabul-embassy-scandal; and State Department Oversight and Contractor-Employee Conduct, transcript, Commission on Wartime Contracting in Iraq and Afghanistan, Sept. 14, 2009, www.wartimecontracting.gov/images/download/documents/hearings/20090914/CWC_State_Dept_Contractor_Oversight_Transcript_2009-09-14.pdf, p. 29.

57. "ArmorGroup North American and Its Affiliates Pay $7.5 Million to Remove False Claims Act Allegations," press release, U.S. Department of Justice, July 7, 2011, www.justice.gov/opa/pr/2011/July/11-civ-889.html.

58. "Audit of the Department of State Process to Award the Worldwide Protective Services Contract and Kabul Embassy Security Force Task Order," Office of Inspector General, U.S. Department of State, December 2011, http://oig.state.gov/documents/organization/180395.pdf.

59. "Transforming Wartime Contracting: Controlling Costs, Reducing Risks, Commission on Wartime Contracting in Iraq and Afghanistan," Commission on Wartime Contracting in Iraq and Afghanistan, August 2011, www.wartimecontracting.gov.

60. Tom Bowman, "No U.S. Troops, But an Army of Contractors in Iraq," NPR, Dec. 27, 2011, www.npr.org/2011/12/27/144198497/no-u-s-troops-but-an-army-of-contractors-in-iraq.

61. Quil Lawrence, "Afghan Public Protection Force Replaces Contractors," NPR, May 23, 2012, www.npr.org/2012/05/23/153354514/afghan-public-protection-force-profile.

62. Spencer Ackerman, "Pentagon's War on Drugs Goes Mercenary," Danger Room blog, *Wired*, Nov. 22, 2011, www.wired.com/dangerroom/2011/11/drug-war-mercenary.

63. Benjamin Perrin, ed., "Private Security Organizations and Humanitarian Organizations: Implications for International Humanitarian Law," *Modern Warfare: Armed Groups, Private Militaries, Humanitarian Organizations* (2012), p. 134.

64. Cotton, *op. cit.*, p. 15.

65. Charles Doyle, "Civilian Extraterritorial Jurisdiction Act: Federal Contractor Criminal Liability Overseas," Congressional Research Service, Feb. 15, 2012, www.fas.org/sgp/crs/misc/R42358.pdf. The bills are HR 2136 and S 1145.

66. Pete Kasperowicz, "GOP, Dems Come Together to Fight Human Trafficking by Contractors in Iraq, Afghanistan," *The Hill*, March 27, 2012, http://thehill.com/blogs/floor-action/house/218353-gop-dems-come-together-to-fight-human-trafficking

-by-contractors-in-iraq-afghanistan. The bills are HR 4259 and S 2234.

67. Neil Gordon and Jake Wiens, "McCaskill, Webb Introduce Wartime Contracting Legislation that Could Save Taxpayers Billions," POGO blog, March 1, 2012, http://pogoblog.typepad.com/pogo/2012/03/mccaskill-webb-introduce-wartime-contracting-legislation-that-could-save-taxpayers-billions.html. The bill is S 2139.

68. Steve Vladeck, "Can the Military Court-Martial Civilian Contractors?: Reflections on the Oral Argument in the United States v. Ali," *Lawfare blog*, April 12, 2012, www.lawfareblog.com/2012/04/can-the-military-court-martial-civilian-contractors-reflections-on-the-oral-argument-in-united-states-v-ali.

69. Steve Vladeck, "United States v. Ali and Military Jurisdiction Over Civilians," *Lawfare blog*, Dec. 8, 2011, www.lawfareblog.com/2011/12/united-states-v-ali-and-military-jurisdiction-over-civilians.

BIBLIOGRAPHY

Selected Sources

Books

Dickinson, Laura A., *Outsourcing War and Peace: Preserving Public Values in a World of Privatized Foreign Affairs*, Yale University Press, 2011.
A George Washington University law professor contends that increased privatization threatens government accountability and respect for human rights.

Singer, Peter W., *Corporate Warriors: The Rise of the Privatized Military Industry*, Updated Edition, Cornell Studies in Security Affairs, 2007.
A scholar at the centrist Brookings Institution describes the long history of private armed forces.

Articles

"Rise in Mercenary Activities Warrants Urgent Attention, Says UN Expert Group," UN News Centre, UN News Service, Nov. 1, 2011, www.un.org/apps/news/story.asp?NewsID=40270&Cr=mercenar&Cr1.
The U.N. working group on mercenaries says contractors are helping governments subvert peaceful protest.

Ackerman, Spencer, "Pentagon's War on Drugs Goes Mercenary," Danger Room blog, *Wired*, Nov. 22, 2011, www.wired.com/dangerroom/2011/11/drug-war-mercenary.
The Pentagon is handing out more than $3 billion this year to hire contractors to fight illegal narcotics around the world.

Bender, Brian, "From the Pentagon to the Private Sector," *Boston Globe*, Dec. 26, 2010, www.boston.com/news/nation/washington/articles/2010/12/26/defense_firms_lure_retired_generals.
As more military officers join private security companies after retiring, questions arise about whether the prospect of lucrative employment sways Pentagon decision-making.

Cockayne, James, and Emily Speers Mears, "Private Military and Security Companies: A Framework for Regulation," International Peace Institute, March 2009, www.ipacademy.org/publication/policy-papers/detail/81-private-military-and-security-companies-a-framework-for-regulation.html.
Current national and international regulation of security companies is flawed.

Isenberg, David, "The Rise of Private Maritime Security Companies," *Huffington Post*, May 29, 2012, www.huffingtonpost.com/david-isenberg/private-military-contractors_b_1548523.html.
An increase in piracy provides opportunities for private security companies and new legal challenges.

Reports and Studies

"Hired Guns: Views About Armed Contractors in Operation Iraqi Freedom," RAND National Security Research Division, 2010, www.rand.org/pubs/monographs/2010/RAND_MG987.pdf.
A survey of service members finds both support for and concern about contractors' impact in conflict zones.

Gomez del Prado, Jose L., "Why Private Military and Security Companies Should Be Regulated," September 2010, http://198.170.85.29/Gomez-del-Prado-article-on-regulation-of-private-and-military-firms-3-Sep-2010.pdf.
A member of the United Nations working group on mercenaries argues for strong oversight of security companies.

Isenberg, David, "Private Military Contractors and U.S. Grand Strategy," International Peace Research *Institute, Oslo*, 2009, www.cato.org/pubs/articles/isenberg-private%20military-contractors-2009.pdf. An independent analyst argues that heavy U.S. reliance on contractors encourages a unilateral approach to international crises.

Mears, Emily Speers, *Security Privatisation in the Middle East, Working Paper No. 10, Global Consortium on Security Transformation*, November 2010, **www.securitytransformation.org/images/publicaciones/190_Working_Paper_10_-_Security_privatisation_in_the_Middle_East.pdf.** An analyst for a British nonprofit research and advocacy group on international development describes the range of private security operations in the Middle East.

Schooner, Steven L., and Collin D. Swan, "Dead Contractors: The Un-examined Effect of Surrogates on the Public's Casualty Sensitivity," *Journal of National Security Law & Policy*, April 16, 2012, www.jnslp.com/2012/04/16/dead-contractors-the-unexamined-effect-of-surrogates-on-the-publics-casualty-sensitivity. Analysts from George Washington University Law School argue that by failing to publicize contractor deaths, the U.S. government misleads the public about the costs of war.

Schwartz, Moshe, and Joyprada Swain, "Department of Defense Contractors in Afghanistan and Iraq: Background and Analysis," Congressional Research Service, May 13, 2011, www.fas.org/sgp/crs/natsec/R40764.pdf. Analysts for Congress' nonpartisan research office describe contractor use in two wars.

Spear, Joanna, "Market Forces: The Political Economy of Private Military Companies," *Fafo*, 2006, www.fafo.no/pub/rapp/531/531.pdf. A George Washington University professor discusses the history of security contractors as corporate entities.

For More Information

ASIS, 1625 Prince St., Alexandria, VA 22314-2818; 703-519-6200; www.asisonline.org. International membership group for security professionals.

Civilian Contractors in Iraq and Afghanistan, www.americancontractorsiniraq.org. Website run by injured contractors and their families; includes information and commentary on contractor deaths and job-related issues.

Feral Jundi blog, http://feraljundi.com. Provides news and commentary by an ex-Marine and wilderness firefighter who works as a security contractor.

International Code of Conduct for Private Security Service Providers, www.icoc-psp. Website of an international government/security-company/civil-society consortium to create an international regulatory system for activities involving hired security.

International Stability Operations Association, 1634 I St., N.W., Suite 800, Washington, DC 20006; 202-464-7021; http://stability-operations.org. Trade association for companies working in disaster-relief and conflict zones; publishes the *Journal of International Peace Organizations*.

PrivateMilitary.org. Independent website that lists military and security contractors and provides links to academic research and other information.

Private Warriors, "Frontline," PBS website, www.pbs.org/wgbh/pages/frontline/shows/warriors. Website of 2005 television documentary that includes interviews with a range of experts.

Project on Government Oversight/Contract Oversight, 1100 G St., N.W., Suite 500, Washington, DC 20005; 202-347-1122; www.pogo.org/investigations/contract-oversight. Independent government watchdog group.

U.N. Working Group on the Use of Mercenaries, Office of the United Nations High Commissioner for Human Rights (OHCHR), Palais des Nations, CH-1211 Geneva 10, Switzerland; 41-22-917-9220; www.ohchr.org. Monitors mercenary activity and recommends actions to protect human rights in situations involving hired force.